D1520835

THE CITIZENSHIP REVOLUTION

{ JEFFERSONIAN AMERICA }

Jan Ellen Lewis, Peter S. Onuf, and Andrew O'Shaughnessy

EDITORS

The Citizenship Revolution

POLITICS AND THE CREATION OF THE AMERICAN UNION 1774–1804

Douglas Bradburn

UNIVERSITY OF VIRGINIA PRESS
CHARLOTTESVILLE AND LONDON

University of Virginia Press

Printed in the United States of America on acid-free paper

First published 2009

9 8 7 6 5 4 3 2 1

LIBRARY OF CONGRESS CATALOGING-IN-PUBLICATION DATA

Bradburn, Douglas., 1972–
The citizenship revolution : politics and the creation of the American union, 1774–1804 / Douglas Bradburn.
p. cm. — (Jeffersonian America)
Includes bibliographical references and index.
ISBN 978-0-8139-2801-2 (alk. paper)
1. United States—Politics and government—1775–1783. 2. United States—Politics and government—1783–1809. 3. Citizenship—United States—History—18th century. 4. Citizenship—United States—History—19th century. 5. Political culture—United States—History—18th century. 6. Political culture—United States—History—19th century. 7. Constitutional history—United States. 8. Federal government—United States—History—18th century. 9. Federal government—United States—History—19th century. 10. United States—History—Revolution, 1775–1783—Influence. I. Title.
E302.1.B73 2009
973.3—dc22 2008039884

For Nadene

This country had but lately gone through a great Revolution; in all nations and countries where a revolution has taken place, it generally affects the whole age in which it has happened, and often much more. They who undertake to judge of characters and events, must judge of them as standing in relation to those events and as to be explained on principles in some measure peculiar to themselves, or they will be led into error. . . . The events of our times had not yet got beyond the reach and influence of causes peculiar to that revolution; probably they who came after us may discover relations in characters and events, which form the real picture of nature and of life, and which are overlooked by man at the present time.—Abraham Baldwin, 1799

CONTENTS

ACKNOWLEDGMENTS

I COULD NOT HAVE WRITTEN THIS BOOK WITHOUT MUCH SUPPORT, financial and intellectual, and I take great pleasure remembering the people and places that helped. Numerous institutions have provided research assistance, including the Virginia Historical Society, the Library Company of Philadelphia, the American Philosophical Society, and the University of Chicago. Two year-long fellowships, the first at the Newberry Library and the second as the Gilder Lehman Junior Research Fellow at the Robert H. Smith International Center for Jefferson Studies at Monticello, made my transition from graduate school to full-time employment productive and bearable. The State University of New York, Binghamton University has provided generous leave time and money to aid in the completion of this book.

At the University of Chicago I was extremely fortunate to work with Edward M. Cook Jr., who took my ridiculous bombast and helped me become a historian. Ever supportive and frank, he allowed me to pursue my own interests yet never let me go off the deep end, giving my arguments whatever true moderation they contain. Steven Pincus, the second reader on my dissertation, provided inspiration and crucial guidance, and Kathleen Neils Conzen, in whose seminar class I devised the project, always helped me find the significant points.

Good friends from graduate school, including A. J. Aiseirithe, Brooke Coleman, R. Scott Hanson, Scott Lien, James Lothian, Ajay Mehrotra, Rebekah Mergenthal, Ben Stone, and Mark Schmeller, provided help and encouragement at a very difficult, very exciting time. Intellectual support, readings, and critiques came freely from people I had no right to expect them from (and who got little in return), including Bernard Bailyn, Rob Cox, Jordanna Dym, Max Edling, Victor Enthoven, David Gerber, Jon Gjerde, Chris Grasso, Sally Hadden, Ron Hoffman, Dick Holway, Steven Innes, David Konig, Brian Murphy, Johann Neem, Greg Nobles, Andrew O'Shaughnessy, Kara Pierce, Emma Rothschild, Eric Slauter, Rogers Smith, Jan Lewis, Rob Parkinson, Erica Pani, Kristofer Ray, and, most recently, Rosemarie Zagarri. All of these people have made this book better, and if I had actually followed their advice properly, it would no doubt be better still.

Of the many people who selflessly read my work, I must mention in particular Alfred F. Young, whose words at a crucial moment gave me the steam to carry on. Peter Onuf, who has proven to be a steadfast supporter and constant guide to my thinking on the early Republic, saved me from many a blunder. The late James Kettner, whose work on citizenship is still the place to start, offered generous aid. And John Coombs, my comrade, has repeatedly refreshed my enthusiasm about a project that I have lived with for far too long.

I benefited from the support of my family, who bore with me as only a family is required to do. My sons, Charles and Samuel, did little to help with this book, but their arrival did give me more excuses as to why it wasn't yet complete. Finally, I thank Nadene, from whom all good things come. Without her strength, this book would not exist.

Some portions of this book have been previously published in articles and reappear now with permission of the journals. Parts of chapters 5 and 7 appeared in "'True Americans' and 'Hordes of Foreigners': Nationalism, Ethnicity, and the Problem of Citizenship in the United States, 1789–1800," *Historical Reflections/Reflexions Historiques* 28 (Spring 2003): 19–41. Chapter 6 borrows heavily from "A Clamor in the Public Mind: Opposition to the Alien and Sedition Acts," *William and Mary Quarterly*, 3rd ser., 65 (July 2008): 565–600.

THE CITIZENSHIP REVOLUTION

Introduction

It is an age of Revolutions in which everything may be looked for.
—Thomas Paine, *The Rights of Man*

IN 1812 THE UNITED STATES OF AMERICA DECLARED WAR against Great Britain with an alarming nonchalance. With a tiny national army and the war hawks rejecting any attempt to expand the navy on the eve of the fighting, the country exhibited a reckless and even comic disregard for nearly all the assumptions of modern war making. Inevitable taxes were postponed, and the individual state militias were expected to rise to the occasion. Throughout the war, many states continued to trade openly with the enemy, supplying thousands of tons of grain to the British armies in Europe. Some states refused to mobilize their militias in the service of a national strategy, or threatened to withhold taxes and troops.[1] The results were disastrous, epitomized by the plundering and burning of Washington, D.C., by an expeditionary force of only five thousand men. By 1814, the governor of Massachusetts was hinting at the possibility of a separate peace.[2] Disunion seemed imminent. Reflecting on the chaos, John Adams despaired, in capital letters, "ARE WE ONE NATION OR 18?"[3]

Adams was right to understand the failure of the U.S. war effort as a problem of nationhood. He knew that the states were the preeminent force in the lives of the American citizenry, and this fact assured that the national state did not possess the will, purpose, energy, or resources to fight a modern war. In 1811 the national government was only willing to spend $1 per capita on public expenditures, at a time when Great Britain spent twenty-five times as much.[4] In the words of Thomas Jefferson, the states controlled the "principal care of our persons, our property, and our reputation, constituting the great field of human concerns"—a jurisdiction which assured that American nationhood remained a highly ambiguous affair in the nineteenth century.[5]

In 1812 the meaning of American citizenship reflected the diverse municipal regulations of the states. While in the best of times all citizens considered themselves fellow nationals, in law there was very little national uniformity to American citizenship: states controlled the extent or limit of the franchise; some states possessed religious establishments; states followed different derivations of the English common law; one state (Louisiana) possessed a completely alien legal code; some states supported slavery, some disallowed it, and some were gradually ending it; and numerous minor differences complicated the civil and political rights of citizens and non-citizens throughout the United States. This confusion reflected the lack of national purpose that annoyed Adams, but even he had to admit that this patchwork decentralization was precisely what the American citizenry wanted and had in fact demanded, and was the only arrangement that assured the persistence of the American Union. Supporters of the decentralized nature of American nationhood considered the arrangement a fulfillment of the promises of the Revolution of '76—as the best protection of the natural rights of man, the purpose of all government. And anyone who called for a strong national state or encouraged a national standard for American citizenship dissented from the common view.

To those prone to believe that the ratification of the Constitution assured the importance of national authority and law in the lives of the American people, the emphasis on the significance and power of the states as the arbiters of American rights and the character of nationhood may seem strange. But the local control of the ultimate meaning of American citizenship under the Constitution represented the fruits of a political settlement that ended a crisis of authority, allegiance, and sovereignty that had exploded in the American Revolution—a crisis only delicately resolved in the first years of the nineteenth century. Such a consensus, about the nature and limits of the Union, ended the first great phase of the American "citizenship revolution": the transformation in the status of persons, the potential of rights, and the meaning of sovereignty that opened when a miscellaneous collection of colonials rejected their British subjecthood and began calling themselves American citizens.

The abjuration of allegiance to George III, the rejection of the authority of British-made law, and the Declaration of Independence broke the old colonial system and created a new and untested status—"American citizens"—complicated by the indistinct meaning and revolutionary potential of both "American" and "citizen." Fighting the war was one problem, but sharing power in republican governments presented a multiplicity of concerns. Who was an American? What did it really mean to be a "citizen" and not a subject? By what authority did some citizens claim to dictate to others? As these questions related directly to the problems of representation, rights, sovereignty, and identity that had ignited the imperial conflict, a lack of easy consensus promised a crisis of grave proportions. The birth and settlement of this crisis—the problem of American citizenship in the Age of Revolution—is the subject of this book.

The Problem of American Citizenship

"Citizenship," in its most generic application, refers to membership in a community. Broadly considered, such a community can be any locality, municipality, or state, but citizenship has come to apply most particularly to belonging in a nation-state. Citizens, in this sense, are the individuals that comprise the nation, and these individuals have a relationship to other citizens defined by commonly understood sets of duties and rights. Outsiders are foreigners, or "aliens," and citizens of communities are recognized as such by other communities.[6] Legally, at least, "Americans" did not exist as a people independent of the British Empire before 1776, or perhaps 1778 when they were officially recognized by France, or perhaps 1783 when King George acknowledged American independence. So the problem of "American" citizenship reflects two intertwined and historically contingent questions: Who can be considered to be a member of an American nation—a nation first imagined and born in the process of asserting and fighting the War of Independence? And what were (and are) the accepted set of duties, privileges, immunities, and rights attendant to American citizenship? This book describes the first lasting resolution of these two interrelated (and ongoing) problems.

During the War for American Independence, the "nation-state" was not the representative ideal in the minds of many Americans—be they Loyalists, Trimmers, or Patriots.[7] Hindsight encourages historians to search for precocious references to an American nation, and to assume that the only modern form is the nation complete with a centralized state, but the leaders of the American war were as likely to search for analogies to their present and future state with reference to city-states, empires, composite kingdoms, and federative republics, as much as they did to nation-states, imagined and real, ancient and modern. While some precocious nationalists among the Patriots attempted to invoke and encourage national solidarity, such thinking was more the consequence than the cause of the colonial resistance movement, which only gradually became an independence movement, then a civil, and ultimately a revolutionary war. This does not make them any less "modern." In fact, the political community of the United States—"the Union"—remodeled older examples of federal and composite states into a Revolutionary regime intended not only to represent nationhood but also to ensure a broad protection for individual rights, while at the same time attempting to recast the international order as a realm of law more than power, using justifications distinct from the operation of the colonial world.

The political and legal construction of the Union, and its relationship to a national American people, only gradually took shape in the years following Independence. The potential for continuing revolution in America only ended when a majority of citizens were satisfied with the meaning and operation of the Union. Properly understood, the citizenship revolution, and the politics that ultimately created the American Union, began with a rejection of one model of centralized nationhood—the British national state. But this rejection came only after a decade of vigorous calls for inclusion.

Britons and Americans

The initial protests of "No taxation without representation" that greeted the early efforts of Parliament to raise revenue in the colonies were not attempts at secession but pleas for better incorporation into the British polity. James Otis, in *The Rights of the British Colonists Asserted and Proved* (1764), set the tone. Otis wrote, "There is not one man in a hundred (except in Canada) who does not think himself under the best national civil constitution in the world." The British Constitution was the best because it was the product of the settlement of the "Glorious" Revolution of 1689, when the British Convention Parliament—"assembled in a full and free representative of this nation"—offered the crown to William and Mary, after Parliament had declared "their undoubted rights and liberties." The settlement affirmed two fundamental principles, the bedrock of British freedom: that "the great end of government" must be to "provide for the best good of all the people," and that sovereignty—supreme permanent authority—rests "*originally* and *ultimately* in the people." But, as the Parliament must legislate for the nation, it should have representatives of the *entire* nation. The colonies were not, "as the common people of *England* foolishly imagine," populated by "a compound mongrel mixture of *English, Indian* and *Negro,*" but with "freeborn *British white* subjects, whose loyalty has never been suspected." Ultimately, conflating "English" with "British," Otis believed that these "true Britons" must have their fair representation in "the grand legislation of the nation." Otis spoke in the language of nationalism—not American but British nationalism. He argued that the colonials had a right to the power of the British state because they were connected by race to the British people.[8]

Yet, for a variety of reasons, the idea of an all-powerful Parliament governing an extended British nation possessed limited serious appeal in the North American colonies. Otis's vision of a *national* British Constitution, with the sovereign authority of the British people controlled and represented by the King-in-Parliament, was a relatively recent orthodoxy, having only gradually emerged as the dominant understanding of the legal organization of the British state by the middle of the eighteenth century.[9] And while Otis and the best-informed North Americans understood this mainstream orthodoxy of the sovereign authority of the King-in-Parliament, and struggled to defend North American property and interests within it, few other colonials did—or were willing to—accept such a vision of the British Empire.

From the perspective of many North Americans who continued to rely upon their charters and peculiar histories to understand their place in the empire, the idea of a unitary national sovereignty represented a threat to their understanding of "English liberties"—the rights and privileges of subjects which were protected and defined by established institutions: jury trials, assemblies, chartered governments, time-honored traditions, and customary law. "English liberties," although the heritage of a particular people and a particular historical process—with important touchstones like the Magna Charta and the Bill of Rights of 1689—were understood to be much more than a legacy of Englishness; for "English liberties" ultimately protected and embodied the natural rights of individuals—rights which could not be taken away or legislated out of existence.[10] Granting absolute authority to Parliament, which claimed the ability to revoke charters, prorogue assemblies, recall justices, tax without consent, annul traditional land policies, expand admiralty jurisdictions to enforce customs regulations, and change religious establishments, endangered the very existence of "English liberties," and ultimately the fundamental rights and interests of many colonists. Such authority was a threat, and the rejection of an absolutely sovereign national Parliament gradually became the goal of colonial resistance.

As long as leading Americans claimed to be true Britons, the lawyers and polemicists had a difficult time explaining exactly when and where Parliament could be limited in its ability to legislate for the entire empire. But by the early 1770s, after nearly a decade of debate and conflict over the proper jurisdiction of Parliament, leading and eventually strong supporters of American independence began to argue that Americans were not the same, but *separate* people from the British. Samuel Adams, and by default all the town meetings of Massachusetts in their approval of his circular, made such an argument as early as 1772. He agreed with the common Anglo-American assumption that in every government sovereignty ultimately rested in the people, and that legislatures were established by the people to create binding law. But the people of Massachusetts already had a supreme "sovereign" legislature—their own General Court—and each colony should submit only "to the authority of our Provincial Legislatures," just as the people of Great Britain "acknowledge the power of parliament over them." Separate peoples required separate supreme legislatures.[11] By the mid-1770s, numerous politicians and polemicists in the cause of defending British America—including John Adams, James Wilson, and Thomas Jefferson—articulated a similar view, arguing that each of the colonies were separate "peoples," or "societies," connected to Great Britain only by their shared allegiance to the king, with their own supreme legislatures independent of the presumptive authority of a grand National Parliament. They came to understand their place in the empire as like that of Scotland's before the Act of Union of 1707—as free states that could only be governed unlawfully by an English Parliament.

These assertions of the distinctiveness of the people (or peoples) of America were not full-throated expressions of American nationalism by any means, but they did reflect a fundamental shift necessary for eventual independence. Such a rejection of British identity was difficult, shocking, and never universal, but also not entirely surprising. Historians have rightly emphasized the broad ties of identity, affection, culture, and interest between Britons throughout the extended dominions of the British Empire by the 1770s; in some ways, North American society became "Anglicized" over the course of the eighteenth century. But it was always a complicated affair, and easy to overstate. Local identities, particular histories, massive migratory trends, regional cultures, and competing religious persuasions throughout the colonies promised numerous possible affiliations to compete with the relatively new and occasional enthusiasm for "British" nationality.

Certainly many leading British Americans never did abandon their belief that Britons and Americans were the same people, and they came to rue the American Revolution as a bloody and unnatural civil war. As the Loyalist Charles Inglis lamented, "The Americans are properly Britons": they share "manners, habits, and ideas with Britons." As resistance turned to war, he hoped for a time when "those who are connected by the endearing ties of religion, kindred, and country, should resume their former friendship."[12] Some others, who would eventually become Patriots, would only renounce their British heritage grudgingly, or petulantly, as a response to the sting of rejection. We can see this anxiety in some reluctant rebels, like Benjamin Franklin, who had built careers by embracing a pan-Atlantic British identity. The Briton Franklin celebrated and invoked a vision of a grand Anglo-Saxon nation overspreading North America, designed a Union intended to secure those ends, and tied his family fortunes and interests to the powerful patronage of the British state. Ultimately, his own son, Royal Governor of New Jersey William Franklin, would not abandon British subjecthood.[13]

But for many more—like the swarming backcountry Presbyterian Irish, or the entrenched Creole gentry in numerous colonies, or the growing populations of dissenting Protestants, among others—the experience of the empire had often been bittersweet, or outright antagonistic, and imperial Britain could easily represent an alien nuisance to their own plans and assertions of autonomy and their own distinctive understandings of the imperial Constitution.[14] Even during the celebrations of British victories in the French and Indian War, New England newspapers complained of the insults and abuse of the supposed "mother country." "We call *Britain* the *mother* country," one author noted, "but what good mother besides would introduce thieves and criminals into the company of her children to corrupt and disgrace them?"[15] For a generation of men in Connecticut and Massachusetts, and for many others throughout the colonies, the experience of campaigning with the British during that war provided ample opportunity for disillusionment, horror, indifference, and contempt toward their "countrymen" in Great Britain.[16] By 1775, after years of perceived and real insults by the British government, a precocious American nationalist like the West Indian–born Alexander Hamilton asserted enthusiastically that it was impossible "to transmute the people of America into those of Great-Britain." Only "in imitation of that celebrated sophist Spinoza" could one ever prove "'Britons' and 'Americans' the same."[17]

Still, the colonists' ties to Great Britain were at least as strong as their ties to each other, which exhibited an extreme diversity. In fact, the differences among and within the colonial societies of British North America attracted the regular comment of visitors and locals alike. Andrew Burnaby, a young English clergyman who toured the American colonies in the 1750s, noted that "the difference of character, of manners, of religion, of interest of the different colonies" would never allow the Americans to create a "permanent union." If the colonials "were left to themselves," he argued, "there would soon be civil war, from one end of the continent to the other; while the Indians and Negroes would, with better reason, impatiently watch the opportunity of exterminating them all together."[18] John Adams famously remembered late in life that the colonies on the eve of Independence exhibited different "constitutions of government" and a "great variety of religions," and were "composed of so many different nations," with "customes, manners, and habits" with "so little resemblance," that uniting them seemed nearly impossible and success ultimately proof of the hand of Divine Providence.[19] For some of the most astute observers, especially those not expecting Providence to aid the rebels, the idea that the Americans could ever act as one people seemed absurd. Joseph Galloway, when the Continental Congress rejected his attempts to promote reconciliation with Great Britain, abandoned the cause of the Patriots and predicted chaos and civil war. As he wrote of the colonies:

> Their different forms of Government—Productions of the Soil—and Views of Commerce, their different Religions—Tempers and private Interest—their Prejudices against, and Jealousies of, each other—all have, and ever will, from the Nature and Reason of things, conspire to create such a Diversity of Interests, Inclinations, and Decisions, that they never can unite together even for their own Protection. In this Situation controversies founded in Interest, Religion or Ambition, will soon embrue their Hands in the blood of each other.[20]

That America was nothing but a jangled collection of strange peoples who would cut each other's throats without the guiding tie to Britain was a commonplace assumption—and a challenge to any notion of independent nationhood. As Americans actually moved toward war and independence, Unity became a matter of pressing importance of the highest nature.

In time of war, the effort to encourage national uniformity was left in the hands of the propagandists—asserted by oath taking, shaped by local pressures and ad hoc Revolutionary committees, and enforced at the point of a gun, with striking effectiveness. Americans were inventing traditions out of necessity and adapting their English patriotic ways to American needs. Through the course of events they found their first national heroes (Washington) and archtraitors (Benedict Arnold); their first demonized enemies; their first days of national celebration and mourning.[21] On the ground, loyalties changed with the progress of the war, and many people remained indifferent and silently hostile to the new allegiance demanded by untested Revolutionary regimes. The more recalcitrant could be imprisoned or exiled, their property confiscated, their reputations destroyed. Tens of thousands of the disaffected, of all ranks of society, fled the colonies during and after the rebellion, a stunning exodus which allowed many old Patriots to believe that by the end of the war "everybody was true," for the "Tories we'd either killed or driven to Canada."[22]

Even the powerful myths of unanimity could do little about the real weakness of nationhood. The Continental Congress encouraged the creation of fictive national symbols—like the motto on the first Seal of the United States, "E Pluribus Unum," that acknowledged difference but emphasized unity. The master polemicist, Thomas Paine, who understood the transformative power of reimagining the world, could do little more than urge people to think of themselves as fellow nationals, despite their obvious local differences. "Our citizenship in the United States is our national character, our citizenship in any particular state is only our local distinction," he repeated in some of his final pamphlets of the American Revolution. "Our great title" he continued, "is American," while "our inferior one varies with the place."[23]

But without a "Cause" there was very little to hold the states together. The great variety of interests in the new country, and the sense of deeper, more permanent divisions throughout the states, assured that unitary nationhood remained in doubt after Independence. Eventual "disunion" was assumed by the British government as it crafted its post-Independence foreign policy, and many members of Congress anticipated the worst in 1783.[24] As Charles Thomson wrote to his wife, Hannah, "The temper, disposition and views of the inhabitants are so discordant, that I have serious apprehension they will not be long kept together."[25] During the movement to form a more national government the advocates for the Constitution could often be found waxing poetic on the oneness of the American people, but as many voices emphasized the differences throughout the country. The New England anti-federalist, James Winthrop, writing as "Agrippa," argued that it was impossible for "one code of laws to suit Georgia and Massachusetts," as "the inhabitants of the warmer climates are more dissolute in their manners, and less industrious, than in the colder climates."[26] By the 1790s, foreign observers could not explain the nature of American society without referring to its diversity. As the Englishman Edward Thornton wondered, "What will be the language, or what the national character of a people composed of such heterogeneous particles collected and huddled together from all parts of the world, it is impossible to say."[27]

The citizenship revolution had created this problem of American identity and nationhood. What *would* be, as Thornton asked, "the national character" of such a heterogeneous people? How would the different peoples that made up the United States be able to live together if they could not live within the expansive British Empire? Yet the problem of American citizenship in the Age of Revolution related to more than the complexity of American nationality, for in the course of winning independence the new American people not only rejected British allegiance and identity, they also rejected the idea of subjecthood itself. They had fashioned "citizens" out of "subjects"—a change in status that implied a new attitude about the legitimacy of organized power, and which opened possibilities for the transformation of the political world that were only vaguely glimpsed in the early years of resistance.

Subjects and Citizens

Although technically we could speak of the "citizenship" of individual members of the British Empire before American independence as a standard for membership, it is an anachronistic and ultimately misleading usage of the term. Being a "citizen" in the English-speaking world before the creation of the United States of America still remained most commonly associated with having the "freedom of a city"—a local, corporate distinction applying only to a select few. While certain members of the eighteenth-century British political world might invoke a status of "citizen" in a broader sense—to emphasize the popular aspects of the British Constitution, or to pose as public-spirited men in the classical tradition for political effect—being a "citizen" remained limited in legal meaning, completely subsumed by the fundamental status of all members of the British Empire as "subjects."

Every slave and slaveholder, every servant and master, every governor or tenant farmer, every Indian and courtier, every man, woman, and child throughout the British realms was considered a subject of the Crown and Parliament. It was the fundamental status of membership in the British Empire, and it did not imply any tangible relationship to the instruments of state policy—save for a presumption of dependency and filial, indeed perpetual, allegiance. The British system institutionalized distinct inequalities of power among and between subjects, overlapping hierarchies that required gradations of duties and privileges that were based upon differing levels of dependency controlled and ascribed by tradition, statute, and common law. Thus, in the Parliament—the governing body of Great Britain—the King, Lords, and Commons theoretically balanced the interests of widely unequal subjects, some with hereditary claims to participate in the governance of the state, some with propertied claims, some with confessional claims, and others with ancient, legal, or corporate claims to share in the active governance of the British state.[28]

When the American revolutionaries asserted a new republican status, denying the legitimacy of hereditary monarchy and aristocracy and investing all fundamental members of the republic with an equal portion of the sovereignty of the whole, they gave to "citizen" a crucial and heady status, one distinct from the inequality required and expected of subjecthood. Citizens, as the early historian of the American Revolution, David Ramsay, asserted, are "a unit of a mass of free people who collectively, possess sovereignty,"[29] while subjects, "from the latin words, *sub* and *jacio*," implies "one who is under the power of another."[30] When dressed in the language of Revolution, subjecthood and citizenship were understood to be polar opposites, with subjecthood representing a feudal status of perpetual allegiance and inferiority, and citizenship representing a "modern" status of equality and freedom, a mark of "a new order." As one particularly vigorous advocate of this Revolutionary view argued:

> Citizenship, which has arisen from the dissolution of the feudal system; and is a substitute for allegiance, corresponding with the new order of things. Allegiance and citizenship, differ, indeed, in almost every characteristic. Citizenship is the effect of compact; allegiance is the offspring of power and necessity. Citizenship is a political tie; allegiance is a territorial tenure. Citizenship is the character of equality; allegiance is a badge of inferiority. Citizenship is constitutional; allegiance is personal. Citizenship is freedom; allegiance is servitude. Citizenship is communicable; allegiance is repulsive. Citizenship may be relinquished; allegiance is perpetual. With such essential differences, the doctrine of allegiance is inapplicable to a system of citizenship; which it can neither serve to control, nor to elucidate.[31]

For such enthusiasts, citizenship and subjecthood were founded upon completely different systems of thought. In the moment of Independence, some Americans constructed a vision of citizenship that reflected these most forward principles of their Revolution—and many more would go on to understand citizenship in these terms within the first two decades of American independence. As an ideal, the notion of an equal American citizenship would be a powerful status that implied a potent rearticulation of the fundamental relationship between the governed and the government. In theory, no citizen would have more power than any other to control the other's destiny, there would be no institutionalized ranks or artificial distinctions within the citizenry, and citizens would not be bound but by their own consent.

But it never was, and never would be, that simple. At first the colonists in rebellion only fitfully called themselves "citizens." In their oaths of allegiance and abjuration—crafted more to deal with the problems of loyalty in the midst of rebellion than to create a new political world—the inhabitants often promised to behave as "good and faithful subject[s]" of the state.[32] Although the newly independent polities understood their new status of "citizen" to be characterized by equality under the law, and some of the first new states created statements of rights which helped to refashion the meaning of citizenship, American laws and institutions still reflected some traditional concepts of governance which allowed and even required hierarchical and paternalistic status relationships. English common law, which was partially retained in the different states, defined the relationships between masters and servants, between owners and tenants, between men and women, between established clergy and dissenters, in ways that could seamlessly reinforce the hierarchical nature of colonial society. Not simply this—the persistence of numerous colonial institutions, including county courts, town churches and vestries, slavery, and the increasingly patriarchal family, could still reinforce the idea and purpose of the old regime. Such legal structures, and the ingrained habits that sustained them, assured that society would not immediately abandon the cultural trappings of hierarchy; there would be many small, few great leaps forward. In many places and for a long time, great men were still expected to rule. The former monarchical world could cast long cultural shadows. Americans could not immediately destroy, even if they had all wanted to, a world of privilege and deference, of responsibility and submission—a world in which inequalities were not hidden, but expected, demanded, and accepted.[33]

There were limits, then, to the amount of social transformation that a new "citizenship" could immediately produce. Despite the universality that claims of "equality" implied, many of the actual privileges of individual citizens were still bound by custom, property, and place, not defined as "rights" attached to individuals. The most obvious example of the limitations of equal citizenship from a presentist view may perhaps be the franchise, "the right to vote." Best understood not as a civil but a political right of citizenship, the franchise remained limited among citizens by property and residency requirements—racial and gender distinctions often not dissimilar from the restrictions that defined colonial voting rights. Limited access to suffrage could produce particular antagonism because the ideal equal share of sovereignty that each citizen supposedly controlled could be readily imagined in tangible form as a vote—"one person, one vote."[34]

Women, whose legal status in society remained defined by their relationships to men—fathers and husbands within households—possessed an ambiguous relationship to the political character of the new citizenship, especially as the ideal of the equal citizen became more and more rarified. Ambiguity could provide opportunity, but as we'll see, the nature of that opportunity depended upon political pressure.

Republican citizenship would be firmly gendered masculine, just as it would retain many aspects more reflective of a hierarchical past than of a hopeful, equal future. White male Americans were much more comfortable justifying ranks within the citizenry and among citizens if those distinctions were considered to be "natural," and not some "artificial" arrangement that sprang from the mind of man. As the logical and unexpected potential of "equality" became clear, the need to clarify both the gender and racial limits of "citizenship" spoke to the power of the citizenship revolution to shake the deep-rooted assumptions of the colonial world. Increasing clarity that white men were the only proper political citizens of America—evident everywhere by the early nineteenth century—helped define the limits of Revolution.[35]

So as the colonies redefined themselves as independent states, the legal rights and privileges of citizens often remained unequal and uncertain. Like the ambiguity of nationality in the new United States, the stresses between the ideal and the reality of equal citizenship in America remained complex and potentially destabilizing. In these years of the founding, no theoretical tract, no court of justice, no constitution alone resolved these conflicts, because many of the assumed meanings, forms, and metaphors of the colonial world had been abandoned in the assertions of independence and the compromises of the war. The fundamental boundaries of the polity, like the unmapped territorial boundaries of the new nation in the world, were open to deep contestation. How much relative equality should exist in the new governments? What jurisdictions would ultimately control justice: state or nation? How could ethnic and racial difference be accommodated to a national people? Who represented "American" interests? How could Union be maintained, Independence secured, and rights still protected? These are the problems initially opened in the American citizenship revolution, and the solutions were decided in political struggles, traced in this book, which plot the course of the American Revolutionary experience.

Causes Peculiar

At the end of the 1790s, during a typically strident debate in the House of Representatives, Georgia Congressman Abraham Baldwin took a moment to reflect on his times. "This country had but lately gone through a great Revolution," he noted, and "in all nations and countries where a revolution has taken place, it generally affects the whole age in which it has happened, and often much more." The "characters and events" of his moment had to be considered "as standing in relation" to "causes peculiar to that revolution." His moment must be "explained on principles" related to the great event. He noted wistfully that future historians ("they who came after us") would "discover relations in characters and events, which form the real picture of nature and of life, and which are overlooked by man at the present time."[36]

Many historians have given meaning to Baldwin's instincts, relating the characters and events of his time to "causes peculiar" to the American Revolution, clarifying "the real picture and nature of life" in dramatic focus. Concerned as it is with traditional problems of the Revolutionary Era—rights and constitutionalism, power and liberty, the nature of the Union and the First Party System—this book builds upon a rich and extensive literature. General studies on American citizenship still can rely on the path-breaking work of James Kettner's *Development of American Citizenship,* and the more recent expansive study of American notions of citizenship in Rogers Smith's *Civic Ideals.*[37] Crucial arguments about the nature of rights, representation, and sovereignty in the ideology of the Revolutionary Era have been suggested in the now classic works by Bernard Bailyn and Gordon Wood, and expanded upon by many others.[38] A series of challenging studies by John Philip Reid, the reigning master of a pure legalistic/constitutional approach to the Revolution, continue to help drive the interpretation of the era.[39] More recently, interesting studies examining the nature of American nationalism have contributed a new perspective on a long-neglected topic.[40] And currently, in the works of Peter Onuf, David Hendricksen, and Daniel Hulsebosch, studies on the ratification and the meaning of the Union are undergoing a paradigmic shift—away from an obsession with the relative reactionary or progressive nature of the Constitution and toward a more historically satisfying context concerned with problems drawn from the history of early modern federalism, international law, and empire.[41]

While indebted to this substantial literature, both old and new, this book provides a grand revision of a basic premise of much of the received wisdom about the pace and meaning of the American Revolution. As this book shows, the Union, rather than the Nation, is the most important product of Independence. Revolution and war spread from a fatal breakdown of politics, and accompanied a broad rejection of the fundamental philosophies which maintained the status quo. Only when a majority of the political community in the newly independent states agreed to the rules that would govern their relationships with each other did a functioning political consensus reemerge. This consensus, although fragile, gained ascendancy in the early nineteenth century as a vision of Union intended to guarantee the fundamental rights of white citizens and govern the status of all others. The ending of the Revolution was contingent upon political struggles over the shape of the newly independent polity, and was a process of co-option, incorporation, and compromise that created the character and significance of "the Revolution" for the people who lived through it. By providing an analytical narrative structured around political fights over the meaning of citizenship, this book illuminates the stakes, contingencies, and meaning of the paths both taken and rejected during the founding years of the United States. Simply put, through a study of political fights over the meaning of American citizenship, this study clarifies the political settlement of the American Revolution.

When politics is emphasized, transformations that can seem consensual, automatic, and reasonable with the gift of hindsight often appear haphazard and temporary. Many historians of the era have explored deeply the meaning of ideas and ideologies, but they have sometimes downplayed the decisive importance of the political fights over the instruments of the state that gave effect to ideas and institutionalized ideologies. As John Adams remarked bitterly late in life, "All the great affairs of the world, temporal and spiritual, as far as men are concerned in the discussion and decision of them, are determined by small majorities"—often of only a few votes—that shape the resultant meaning of policy and the historical memory of the possible.[42] At times, historians of ideas and ideologies too easily summon grand metaphors to describe the process of Revolution in post-Independence America: great "contagions of liberty," or Revolutionary flood tides "overspreading" the land.[43] While the metaphors evoke the grand significance of Revolution in the era, and are a potent rhetorical device necessary for historians to make sense of complicated stories, metaphors can hide as much as they reveal. Sometimes they serve to personify "the Revolution" itself and not the agents of Revolution: the numerous groups, interests, and individuals who fought over the meaning and extent of transformation. A reaction to this perceived weakness in the history has been to stress "forgotten" narratives: microhistories, the history of the exploited, and the peculiar experiences of some exceptional figures. Although provocative and exciting ways to explore the diversity of human experience in the Revolutionary Era, such studies can weaken the clarity of the more typical experiences and ultimately the stakes, significance, and broader contours of the founding of the United States.[44] In fact, to completely understand why particular people become marginalized, we need to clarify the various political forces and unseen processes setting the pace of change and continuity in the era.

To find a common ground in the story of the Revolution, this book emphasizes the political fights over citizenship and nationhood that brought ideas and interests viscerally together.[45] "Citizenship" provides an excellent point of departure for the politics of the era because it embraces both the problems of political thought and the mobilization of people and groups—often with distinct ethnic, religious, racial, or socioeconomic solidarities—fighting for rights, representation, and power.[46] The extent of change was often decided by close political contests: votes, ratifications, committee meetings—the monuments of the politically possible. The meaning of American citizenship was limited not only by what could be imagined but also at times by the vagaries of a jury trial. Individual "Founders"—the Greek gods of America's mythic birth—are crucial,[47] but their relative influence as political players often defined, or greatly reduced, their particular influence as thinkers and philosophers. Law does not simply march logically forward. It is manipulated, used, and made by groups and individuals as they fight for access to power and true justice. During the Revolutionary Era, lawyers and politicians were desperate advocates who interpreted the past to make arguments about their present and future hopes, always responding and sometimes chastising other voices they considered illegitimate—which nevertheless continued to speak. Ideas can be used to both describe and mask other tangible interests and prejudices.

The failure of consensus that precipitated the War for Independence caused a scramble for stable justifications of the fundamental institutions of political society, a scramble that only ended when a new political consensus was born that could accommodate continued stresses to American unity—and when voices of deep dissent and alternative visions were marginalized, co-opted, or excluded. Until the political community could agree (and, crucially, agree to disagree) about fundamentals, the possibilities of Revolution still charged the potential of political struggle. As Abraham Baldwin understood viscerally but only vaguely in the late 1790s, political contests were still deeply reflective of "causes peculiar" to the American Revolutionary experience. A study of politics necessarily foregrounds conflicts, but it also helps clarify the real range of possibilities: not all things were imagined and some were simply unattainable—because of the powerful interests, personalities, or alternatives of the moment.

To properly explain the political settlement of the American Revolution, it is necessary to expand beyond the traditional chronological boundaries marked by the end of the war in 1783 or the ratification of the U.S. Constitution in 1788. Following Baldwin's instincts, this study situates the 1790s decisively and intentionally into "a whole age" of Revolution, tied not only to the shock waves of American independence, but also to the French Revolution, and to the sympathetic revolutions throughout Europe and the Caribbean that readily produced ideas and migrants for the American stage. The many peoples of the United States were still fighting over fundamentals when the French Revolution erupted, and so the American Revolutionary settlement was shaped in the midst of world war and revolution. The Americans experienced the French Revolution not as a strange phenomenon happening in a distant foreign country, but as dangerously close, familiar, and tangible. No political history of the first generation of the United States can ignore the overwhelming presence of the French Revolution in America—brought by emigrants (both royal and radical), trumpeted in newspapers, fought on the high seas, re-created in civic festivals, worshipped and damned in countless official, informal, and personal papers.

Such a scope is crucial to a meaningful contextualization of a decade which has always appeared rather strange—a time when all the Founders are suddenly at odds, with Thomas Jefferson and John Adams, or James Madison and Alexander Hamilton, old comrades in Revolution and Ratification, arraigned against each other. The leading historian of the era, Gordon Wood, describes "the decade of the 1790s—the Federalist era," as "the most awkward in American history." "It seems," he argues, "unrelated to what preceded or followed it, a fleeting moment of heroic neoclassical dreams that were unsupported by American reality."[48] But the 1790s are not unconnected from the preceding decade. In fact, the conflicts of the first decade after the ratification of the U.S Constitution continued the fundamental battles over the jurisdictions of representation, sovereignty, and rights that had ignited the imperial conflict with Great Britain—conflicts that deeply complicated the meanings of American citizenship that had first emerged with Independence. Indeed, when understood as a continuation of a particular dynamic—especially when one emphasizes the international context of Atlantic revolution and migration—the continuing American conflicts in the 1790s over the legitimacy of national power, the contingency of Union, the boundaries of individual liberty, and the "sovereignty" of the state governments help explain the decades that followed. As this work shows, the outcomes of the conflicts of the 1790s created the political settlement of the American Revolution and fashioned the assumptions, compromises, and political alliances that defined the potential of American citizenship and the character of national politics in the antebellum United States.

From the perspective of citizenship, the ratification of the U.S. Constitution cannot represent either a culmination or a beginning. Nowhere does the Constitution define who or what a citizen might be; nowhere does it explicitly assign the privileges and duties of a citizen;

nowhere does it clearly delineate the relationship of state citizenship to national citizenship; nowhere does it clarify who should settle fights between the states and the nation. And despite what many American historians have powerfully argued, the Constitution—and the debate about it—did not resolve the fundamental problem of ultimate sovereign power in the Union, or the character of democracy in that Union.[49] No overwhelming political consensus existed about the fundamentals of American nationhood at the time of its ratification. An emphasis on political fights over citizenship in a transatlantic Revolutionary world requires us to rethink the traditional chronologies of the American Revolutionary experience. It would take *twelve* amendments, numerous national, state, and local elections, countless polemics and histrionics, and at least one fatal duel, before the country would settle on a type of nationhood and character of citizenship that a majority of the political community could stomach. This fragile consensus of a Revolutionary regime—the Union—lasted for six decades, until it was rejected by people who denied the ideals of the Revolution itself, which led ultimately to a massive civil war, initially waged to "preserve the Union," and to a new chance at nationhood.

The citizenship revolution began in the radical turn of the independence movement as protest slipped into outright rebellion. And so we begin our analysis, in September of 1774, as delegates from twelve of the British colonies along the North American Atlantic Coast collected themselves in Philadelphia to organize a response to the closing of the port of Boston. They would debate the contours of continuing resistance to the authority of Parliament, and create a political strategy to address their shared grievances—real, imagined, and inevitable.

{ 1 }

The Revolutionary Moment

NATURAL RIGHTS, THE PEOPLE, AND THE CREATION OF AMERICAN CITIZENSHIP

There will be no End of it. New Claims will arise. Women will demand a Vote. Lads from 12 to 21 will think their Rights not enough attended to, and every Man, who has not a Farthing, will demand an equal Voice with any other in all Acts of State. It tends to confound and destroy all Distinctions, and prostrate all Ranks, to one common Levell.—John Adams, May 1776

We expect from the representatives of a free people, that all partiality and prejudice, on any account whatever, will be laid aside, and that the happiness of the Citizens at large will be secured upon the broad basis of perfect political equality. This will engage confidence in Government, and unsuspicious affection toward our fellow Citizens. . . . Strangers will be encouraged to share our freedom & felicity, & when civil and religious liberty go hand in hand, our late posterity will bless the wisdom & virtue of their fathers.—Presbytery of Hanover, Virginia, 1784

When the first Continental Congress began to organize itself in the fall of 1774, early rumors of Boston being bombarded by the British navy heightened the sense of crisis. The orators took the initiative, and Patrick Henry, the firebrand from the Virginia Piedmont, struck a radical pose:

> Government is dissolved. Fleets and Armies and the present State of Things shew that Government is dissolved. Where are your Land Marks? Your Boundaries of Colonies. We are in a State of Nature, Sir.

As he famously proclaimed, "The Distinctions between Virginians, Pensylvanians, New Yorkers and New Englanders, are no more." He denied that there remained "any such distinctions as Colonies." He was "not a Virginian, but an American." A bit later in the debate, lest delegates forget his position, he thundered again: "Government is at an End. All Distinctions are thrown down. All America is thrown into one Mass."[1]

Such braggadocio had been heard in the colonies by 1774, but few such speeches had this potential to create havoc. This was not a gathering of tavern politicians or a speech at a liberty tree, but an assembly of colonial leaders who could in fact lead a revolt against Great Britain. For over ten years American provincials had been challenging the authority of the British Parliament in a variety of ways, but this group of men found themselves at the head of a widely articulated popular outrage, expressed through numerous petitions and remonstrances "of the people," by various types of extralegal meetings, committees, and rump assemblies throughout the British North American colonies. The petitioning began in response to the first news of Parliament's punishments for the destruction of the tea in Boston—the closing of the port of Boston, the revocation of the Massachusetts charter, the establishment of military rule in Massachusetts—and it served as a call for action, both a mandate and a threat, to the men assembling as a Continental Congress. In Massachusetts, royal government had ceased to exist outside of the military reach of General Gage in Boston. Courts were closed, militias organized, and an ad hoc and illegal convention and committee system began to take on the powers of government. Henry's claims, if taken seriously, would be tantamount to a declaration of independence. But very few were ready to take Henry seriously, especially on those terms.[2]

Two facets of Henry's opening salvo are notable, for their revolutionary implications. First, by claiming the mantle of "American" and assuring his surprised audience that "all distinctions"—that is, British colonial distinctions—were "thrown down," Henry embarked on a bold imagining of a new nationhood, of a type that would eventually inspire colonized peoples throughout the age. Here would be something, if not entirely unprecedented, then completely revolutionary in the world, a new nation to take its place among European nations. A real, civilized national people "beyond the line," that would change forever the way Americans and Europeans throughout the hemisphere thought of themselves and of the world.

But just as powerful and revolutionary in Henry's speech was his invocation of the mythic "state of nature." A "state of nature" was a philosophical abstraction—a time and place imagined by jurists, divines, and moral philosophers—the kind of thing for books and speculation, not something to willfully invoke in what was still a transatlantic constitutional debate. Unless, of course, one was interested in more than debates about jurisdiction, more than simple resistance, and wished to use the powerful notion of men with "natural rights" that existed before and without the sanction of government—in a state of nature—to justify a dramatic change, a Revolutionary change, in political allegiance and circumstance. Change Henry relished.

But Henry's arguments landed heavily on his audience. Many delegates still desired reconciliation with Great Britain and disputed Henry's analysis of "the Present State of things." John Jay, of New York, called for restraint and patience, denying that the colonies had entered a state of nature, and noting, "I cant yet think that all Government is at an End." Jay insisted, "The Measure of arbitrary Power is not full, and I think it must run over, before We undertake to frame a new Constitution."[3] Other voices echoed Jay's, and it soon became clear that Henry, despite his celebrated oratorical talents, would represent but an extreme position in a spectrum of complaints, arguments, and suppositions about the real character of the imperial conflict and the best route to true justice. But no parties existed in this unusual Congress, few participants were familiar with one another, and set speeches among men trying to outdo one another threatened both demagoguery and inaction. To find common ground and coordinate a sober plan of action, these men relied upon their shared experience with the art and politics of legislative maneuvering, and for the meantime, the principles of resistance could be settled in parliamentary style—in committee.

It was not the last time that Revolutionary talk would be channeled in safer directions by a congressional committee, but it did mark the beginning of the end of the transformation of British colonial resisters into American revolutionaries—from subjects of Britain to citizens of the United States. The early historian David Ramsay portrayed the change as immediate and clear-cut—"A nation was born in a day"—and many subsequent historians have followed his cue. Gordon Wood, for instance, rightly emphasizes the strange, vertiginous sensations that accompanied the break with Britain; to many contemporaries, the world seemed to have changed almost "overnight."[4]

Yet the break with Britain was much less clean—and much less clear. The citizenship revolution emerges as a process fueled by political struggle—occurring in the committees of the Continental Congress, in the conventions of the new states, in the local committees, in the ranks of the militia, and at the bar of the courts. What is telling is the fitful, violent, and contested politics that created an ideal of citizenship in the midst of war and state formation, as reformers, old colonial leaders, and rising new figures who gained strength from the mobilization of new constituencies fought over the shape of the new order. The unprecedented political mobilization necessary to secure the Revolutionary governments, to root out traitors and Tories, to fight the British armies and their Native allies in the West, assured that citizenship would not be a mere replica of subjecthood under a new flag. In the militias, in the statehouses, and at the county courts, the rejection or attempted rejection of mainstream British methods and models of authority refashioned the limits of political possibility and changed the fundamentals of the political world. Groups and individuals traditionally excluded from controlling and distributing power in the colonial order clamored for natural rights and access to power, while some others strove to hold the line on legal and political transformation, all the time fighting an increasingly unpopular war. These originating conflicts created new justifications and meanings for the authority of governments, transformed legitimating assumptions about the rights of subjects and citizens, defined the first communities of "the people," and created a new system of politics.

Pandora's Box

The initial contours of a new political world can be seen in that first important congressional committee, established to deal with the problem of rights in the empire—of states' and of individuals'—and to create a plan for redress and resistance. Here the colonial leadership of the resistance to Great Britain, a group of men who knew very little of each other, began to make final arguments about their future relationship to the mother country. The committee quickened the earlier debate, and the choices available to the colonials both narrowed and polarized, between those who wanted to revolutionize their standing in the world, and those others who sought to guarantee traditional English liberties under a clarified British Constitution and a chastised Parliament. In fact, as the committee on states' "Rights, Grievances and Means of Redress" first met to decide upon the language and justifications that the colonists should use to challenge Parliament, the contest came down to fundamental questions: Should the colonists employ "natural rights" as found in "the Law of Nature" as the basis for their grievances against Parliament? Or should they restrain themselves to their liberties within the British Constitution, which included the common law, parliamentary statute, royal patents, and the sundry colonial charters?

On the cautious side of the argument stood some of the leading Patriots of the 1760s, yet men who could not tolerate ambitious and abstract claims of rights, including John Rutledge of South Carolina, Joseph Galloway of Pennsylvania, and James Duane of New York. A formidable group. While the record is fragmentary, the positions are clearly drawn. John Rutledge, trained in the law at Middle Temple and considered one of the greatest members of the Charleston bar, was succinct and to the point: "Our Claims I think are well founded on the British Constitution, and not on the Law of Nature."[5] James Duane, who practiced English law in New York, thought that recurrence to "the Law of Nature" would be nothing but "a feeble support." The proper basis "for grounding our Rights" was "on the Laws and Constitution of the Country from whence We sprung." Duane argued vigorously that "England was government by a limited Monarchy and free Constitution," and that the colonists enjoyed the "Privileges of Englishmen" as a "Birthright and Inheritance," of which they could not be deprived.[6] Defending the British Constitution while drawing on a vision of the "ancient constitution" was the only solid ground of resistance. Joseph Galloway, who spent the month of September in a failed bid to receive congressional endorsement for a bold attempt to reform the imperial Constitution, delivered the most extensive attack upon the enthusiasm for natural rights:

> I never could find the Rights of Americans, in the Distinctions between Taxation and Legislation, nor in the Distinction between Laws for Revenue and for the Regulation of Trade. I have looked for our Rights in the Laws of Nature—but could not find them in a State of Nature, but always in a State of political Society. I have looked for them in the Constitution of the English Government, and there found them. We may draw them from this Source securely.[7]

English liberties guaranteed by law and practice, not visionary rights, were the true inheritance of our "ancestors."[8] Unable to embrace the rights of nature, or the people who increasingly talked about such vagaries, Galloway eventually abandoned the Patriots and fled to London—with disastrous consequences for the British perception of the independence movement.

On the other extreme was Richard Henry Lee, like Patrick Henry a Virginian, and the man who would eventually follow the instruction of the Virginia House of Delegates and move for a "Declaration of Independence," in June of 1776. Lee supported Henry's audacious stance, and asserted that "Life and Liberty," both of which "is necessary for the Security of Life," could not be relinquished "when We enter into Society." He could not "see why We should not lay our Rights upon the broadest Bottom, the Ground of Nature."[9]

In the middle could be found the pragmatic center: delegates interested in defending charter rights and their liberties as Englishmen and who preferred to base their grievances on "accepted" meanings of the British Constitution, but who believed that further action and, if necessary, complete independence might be justified only with recourse to fundamental "natural rights." There was no "right of revolution" in traditional English liberties, and even if there were, what foreign power would help the colonists in a quixotic quest for "the liberties of Englishmen"? John Adams represented this middle position. He argued that "Natural Law," with attendant rights of man, should not be idly asserted in the place of charter and constitutional claims but should be retained "as a Resource to which we might be driven, by Parliament much sooner than we are aware."[10] Ultimately, the list of grievances was the first of many compromises in which the members agreed "to found our Rights upon the Laws of Nature, the Principles of the English Constitution, & Charters & Compacts."[11]

As he noted at a later period, Adams understood the problem of pushing a claim of natural rights as a political tactic. Similar abstract claims of rights could threaten all government and social order, and he famously acknowledged with trepidation the "new claims" which would inevitably come with Independence. Not only would "women . . . demand the vote," but "lads from twelve to twenty-one will think their Rights not enough attended to," and also "every Man, who has not a Farthing"—leading only to confusion and the reduction "of all Ranks to one common Levell."[12] Natural law was certainly the "broadest Bottom," but perhaps it was much too broad and threatened to swallow everything artificially contrived to assure order and society.

Adams was not alone in imagining an appeal to "natural rights" as both a blessing and a curse, and a political movement that had celebrated the greatness and balance of the British Constitution would not easily reject such known territory for the vastness of a darling state of nature. The leaders in the Continental Congress were too obsessed with history to forget that many movements that began as well-intentioned resistance to tyrants had devolved into anarchy, bloodshed, and cruel dictatorship. Just as much as they ever feared ministerial conspiracy, they feared a potential Cromwell or a Masaniello, they feared the many-headed hydra of the mob and the rapacious hunger of the army, and they feared that without civil government and the protection of ordered liberty they would end their costly gamble in a worse condition under themselves than they had been under Parliament. By 1774, some of the earlier radicalism of the resistance movement to Great Britain had already been effectively channeled in safer directions.[13] Chastising Parliament and containing Revolution were one and the same. Members of Congress moved in response to pressure from "out of doors," but they would move deliberately.

In the end, events forced the Continental Congress, as Adams suspected they must, to support war and ultimately Independence—with an appeal to natural law and the rights of man. The efforts of the Continental Congress to restrain and influence the hand of British policy—first in the Non-Importation Association, then in the assumption and creation of the Continental Army—broke the old systems of colonial politics, both imperial and local. The association, introduced into every town and county in the thirteen colonies over the course of 1775, mobilized new constituencies in the name of "the people" to enforce the will of Congress, and it created the first lists of the "enemies of American liberties." New militia movements, both state-sponsored and ad hoc, emerged rapidly as open war broke out in the spring of 1775. In some colonial governments, royal authority collapsed entirely, and Congress began authorizing, always with an eye toward ensuring order, the formation of new provisional state governments. First in Massachusetts, then New Hampshire, where the royal governor fled, and soon after in South Carolina, where civil war emerged in the backcountry—new governments without royal mandate were organized over the summer of 1775 in the name of expediency, supposedly based upon popular sovereignty and intended to best serve and protect "the happiness of the people."[14] In the spring of 1776, anticipating a formal declaration of independence and reflecting the critical breakdown of the old colonial system, Congress encouraged all the colonial governments to frame new constitutions as a way to check the trends toward licentiousness and bolster the grip of law.[15]

So the architects of rebellion in Congress tried to limit the impact of the radical break in allegiance and law by encouraging the colonies to form new governments before they declared independence. Law and (hopefully) order could be maintained even as the most crucial bonds of allegiance were severed. But neither Congress nor many of the states were as careful as they might have been, for when they finally declared independence, they based their claims on abstract natural rights—invoking a right to cast off allegiance and form new governments, declaring "that all men are created equal," and justifying legitimate government in the name of popular sovereignty. They philosophized in the midst of fighting, and by doing so, the rebels empowered and reinforced numerous challenges to the status quo, and catalyzed the citizenship revolution. They did *not* have to emphasize these particular arguments.

Months before Congress moved to declare independence, William Henry Drayton issued a precocious assertion of the independence of

America from the bench of a South Carolina court. Arguing that King George, by his many crimes, had abdicated the throne, Drayton recreated an argument made during and about the Glorious Revolution; in fact, he included documents from 1689 in his instructions to the grand jury. The abdication of the king did not mean that the colonists indulged in their "natural right" to resist tyranny; rather, they achieved independence by being abandoned by their liege lord. Allegiance and obedience required reciprocal duties of king and people, and the king had broken his side of the bargain. Drayton did not emphasize a right of men to resist, but a right to persist: by his logic, Americans were not forming *new* governments but protecting traditional ones. Nowhere did Drayton bring up the equality of all men—something he thought visionary, untrue, and entirely unnecessary. If Drayton had drafted the Declaration of Independence, the long list of King George's crimes would probably have looked the same, but it would have been a very different Declaration indeed.[16]

A recent trend in the literature of the law and rights in the American Revolution has rejected the importance of "natural rights" to the imperial crisis. John Phillip Reid has repeatedly asserted that "natural law principles played a relatively minor role" in the contest, which depended upon traditional legal and constitutional defenses of the privileges of the colonies in the empire.[17] Such an argument reflects an old trend—as old as the Revolution itself—and has enough truth in it to be occasionally convincing. After all, just as we can find Judge Drayton crafting a legal defense of American independence based upon received principles of Whig constitutionalism, we can find judges and lawyers in British America in 1774 rejecting appeals to natural rights as nothing but "a feeble support" and urging reliance on more positive expressions of accepted, limited, and defined privileges. During and after the French Revolution certain groups in the United States encouraged such a limited model of resistance, and in 1800 John Quincy Adams enthusiastically translated Friedrich von Gentz's comparative history of the "Origins and Principles" of the American and French revolutions to argue that the American Revolution was essentially defensive (and therefore conservative) in nature. Gentz asserted that the "idle *declarations of rights*" which proceeded the American state constitutions, and the many assertions of "popular sovereignty" at the height of American resistance, represented nothing more than an "empty pomp of words, which had no effect on the course, legitimacy, or progress of American independence."[18] Such an argument, about the insignificance of the language of natural rights to the meaning of the American Revolution, also supports the way natural rights would come to be most commonly defined in the jurisprudence of the United States long after the Revolutionary uproar had passed. The British skeptic, Jeremy Bentham, voiced the opinion of many American nineteenth-century jurists when he argued famously that the natural rights of man—"natural and imprescriptible rights (an American phrase)"—was mere "rhetorical nonsense, nonsense upon stilts."[19]

But nonsense or not, the notion of natural rights connected to individuals, defined in only vague terms (the most vague being life, liberty, and the pursuit of happiness), and discoverable by human reason—rights which governments could not touch or infringe upon—was absolutely fundamental to the meaning and experience of the American Revolution, as it was to American understandings of the British Constitution. It is one thing to argue that "natural law" was not *necessary* in the constitutional debates over the nature of the empire in the 1760s and early 1770s, or to say that the Continental Congress could legitimately argue that the American colonies had no relation to the English people or Parliament without a reliance on natural rights (despite the fact that some of them did).[20] But this is the difference between a mere constitutional debate and a revolution, and between what could have happened and what did happen. It is a wholly different argument—and absolutely untenable—to suggest that natural law was not important to the making of the American Revolution. In fact, it was precisely the limited availability of "natural rights" as an accepted constitutional argument, and the danger of vague claims of rights, that made the rhetoric of "rights" so important—so revolutionary. Natural rights language, employed by people to seize a piece of power, or to elucidate the true nature of a grievance, or to rethink the assumptions of the colonial world, drove the *revolutionary* aspects of the American Revolution. Such language was ubiquitous and transformative, especially after the Declarations of Rights engrafted into many of the early state constitutions. Natural and unalienable rights were, after all, as Bentham noted, "an American phrase." "Inherent natural rights," as the Virginia Convention of 1776 argued, were the alpha and the omega, "the basis and foundation of government." Governments existed to protect natural rights, and if they did not, they could be overthrown and refashioned.

There were numerous intellectual strains that emphasized the importance of natural rights in one shape or another available in Anglo-America, which stemmed from both distinct and overlapping sources: the polemical Whigs, John Trenchard and Thomas Gordon, channeling the moral philosophy of John Locke and Algernon Sydney, who were themselves widely read and celebrated and who had incorporated natural law thinking into their work; the English Civil War Leveller tradition; certain contractual aspects of the New England mind; common law constitutionalism (especially as interpreted in colonial British America); the law of nature and nations' jurisprudence available in Hugo Grotius, Samuel Puffendorf, Emmerich de Vattel, and Jean Jacques Burlemaqui; and the political literature of the classical world, among others. In short, there were any number of authorities and traditions which justified the employment of the rhetoric of natural rights to spur civil, and occasionally violent, resistance, all of which were cited (often quite selectively) at some time or another in the midst of the Independence struggle.[21]

So we see even William Blackstone's *Commentaries on the Laws of England,* which tended to downplay the importance of natural law in favor of the absolute authority of the positive statutes of Parliament, and which denied John Locke's right of revolution, cited as an authority on the importance of natural rights. And why not?—Blackstone spent the first chapter of his second volume on the "absolute rights of individuals," which properly understood are the "absolute rights of man," granted by God and the law of nature. "English liberties" are merely "the *residuum* of natural liberty" and "other civil privileges, which society has engaged to provide" in lieu of natural liberties: they are rights ultimately "founded on nature and reason." But only in England, and a few other places, were these rights still celebrated, since "most other countries are now more or less debased or destroyed." While these rights were certainly the birthright of all Englishmen, properly understood, they were the "rights of all mankind." These rights could be reduced to three: "the right of personal security, the right of personal liberty, and the rights of private property"—life, liberty, and property.[22]

And so we find a young Alexander Hamilton—citing Blackstone, not yet trained in the law—writing enthusiastically in 1775 in terms that presaged language Thomas Paine would later use to shout down Edmund Burke. As Hamilton wrote, "The sacred rights of mankind are not to be rummaged for among old parchment or musty records." The rights of man "are written, as with a sunbeam, in the whole volume of human nature, by the hand of divinity itself, and can never be erased or obscured by moral power."[23] Rights written by God and nature with sunbeams in the book of humanity: not exactly overly legalistic constitutionalism. Natural rights were used to justify all sorts of deeds and misdeeds by a wide array of types: the Deist, slaveholding Thomas Jefferson; the common lawyer, John Adams; the New Light Congregationalist minister, Joseph Lyman; the charismatic mystic, Herman Husbands; the English radical, Thomas Paine; the Great Man, George Mason; the rebel, Daniel Shays; the squatter, Abraham Clark; the

Green Mountain Boy, Ethan Allen; the dramatist and historian, Mercy Otis Warren; the freed slave, Caesar Sarter—a motley and eclectic crew of philosophers.[24]

Historians of ideas too often assert an overly strict genealogy to the influence of particular strains of ideas through time, with a teleological trajectory that distorts the way ideas evolve, are misused, and are manipulated in the chaotic blur of historical change—especially in political fights. In this fashion, usage of natural rights language should not quickly be described as a kind of "liberalism," because it does not mean that all those who employed such rhetoric had the same understandings of political economy. We should be careful about employing "liberal," in a nineteenth-century sense, to describe the political use of natural rights in the eighteenth century.[25] An obsession with rights may imply a certain individualism, but not always, and it can often be found as a powerful rhetoric of group solidarity, specifically when combined with notions of popular sovereignty—"the rights of the people." Natural and common law bound people together with natural *duties* as well as rights, and so rights rhetoric could be employed for many anti-individualistic, communal purposes. While some Americans described the language of the Declaration of Independence as "copied from Locke's treatise on government,"[26] and while the notion that some Americans in 1776 possessed a "Lockean" perspective of the proper relationship between the governed and the government is certainly important,[27] the language of abstract natural rights in the American Revolution should be recognized first as containing *universal* and *revolutionary* principles, because such rhetoric can be described in the context in which it was *used*—to challenge, to transform, to revolutionize some established norms of the colonial ancien régime. Such an understanding does not diminish all politics to a grubby contest of interest, for powerful ideas shaped the dynamic in ways that earlier formulations of the problem could not encompass. When the notion of the natural equality of man was freed from the confines of theoretical jurisprudence and brought into popular imagination as a truth that society should emulate, the potential for revolution in the status of people in the United States was abounded. When ideas were combined with interest and serendipity, Revolution could result.

In America, natural rights rhetoric in the midst of war and state-formation became the ultimate political weapon—something it had long possessed the potential to be: a Revolutionary language, a complaint and justification of people asserting an original authority based in nature and reason to restructure the assumptions of their world. When we understand as well that the common law was widely thought to be the product and equivalent of *natural law,* it is impossible to deny the crucial importance of natural law and "inalienable natural rights" to the ultimate meaning of American citizenship in this Founding Era. It was the "broadest bottom"; and appeals to rights from 1774 to 1783, in the midst of political fights over the pace of Revolutionary change, created a modern vision of citizenship.

From "Subject" to "Citizen": The Appeal to Natural Rights

When John Adams reflected on the nature of the new governments being erected in 1776, he was struck by a shocking realization. They were, he admitted to Abigail, "remarkably popular, more so than ever I could have imagined, even more popular than the 'Thoughts on Government'"—referring to his brief on constitutional design that was being circulated among leading men throughout the country. He was particularly surprised by the new governments and ruling coalitions of North Carolina, Virginia, and Pennsylvania, which he considered remarkable for their choice of leaders with "Capacity, Spirit and Zeal in the cause," over those with "Fortune, Family, and every other Consideration which used to have Weight with Mankind." In Philadelphia, he observed the transformation in the governing class with interest and growing alarm, noting that all the "old Members" had been left out, cut down "like grass before the scythe."[28]

What was happening? Why were the new governments so much more "popular" than Adams had expected? As leading Americans began forming their new governments to ensure that American citizenship would possess the numerous protections of English liberties, it quickly became clear that they would not make American citizenship the simple equivalence of British subjecthood under a new name. A political process characterized by two dominant trends—one born of general consensus, the other catalyzed through conflict—created a new vision of American citizenship.

First, Americans would be citizens of republics, not subjects of monarchies. Throughout the new states there would be no kings or princes to govern. But more significant, the new states also rejected all legal hierarchies based upon birth alone, and even the notion that someone could become titled through meritorious service was considered suspicious. Not only would they have no King George, they would have no *Sir* George. As the draft of the Virginia Declaration of Rights—a document destined to be copied and studied in the enthusiastic Age of Revolutions—argued: "No Man, or Set of Men are entitled to exclusive or separate Emoluments or Privileges from the Community," and "the Idea of a Man born a Magistrate, a Legislator, or a Judge is unnatural and absurd."[29] This fact has seemed somewhat mundane, even unsurprising (there were only a few titled aristocrats living in the North American colonies in 1776), but the rejection of legally protected hereditary privilege anticipated a much larger leveling of political authority, and became an important component of the broader meaning of the new status of "citizen." There was no precedent in English law for such an assertion; this was new, and revolutionary.[30]

The rejection of hereditary entitlements reflected the powerful appeal of the notions of original equality that undergirded an obsession with natural rights in the moment of Independence, a radical result of the leveling hopes of the new polities being constructed in 1775–77. It was a completely unnecessary theoretical requirement, considering the common understanding of "republican" government in the eighteenth century and the contemporary and historical examples of republics available for Americans to emulate: the Dutch Republic was soaked through with titles and nobility; the Venetian Republic was governed by aristocrats and old nobles, clogged by ancient rules of various hereditary privileges; the senate of the Roman Republic was a collection of noble houses. Even more conspicuous, leading American thinkers on republics, as abstract governments, did not believe that a free republican government and a king (either elected or hereditary) were incompatible.[31]

But something more than a simple rejection of hereditary power was at stake in the initial organization of the American republics, something that would press American citizenship farther from the meanings, assumptions, and hierarchies of British subjecthood. Adams, after all, saw many colonies erecting "remarkably popular plans," with governments led by a new type of leader. What was happening? He gives us a tantalizing clue for Pennsylvania: "I wish I were at Perfect Liberty, to pourtray before you, all those Characters, in their genuine Lights, and to explain to you the Course of political Changes in this Province. It would give you a great Idea of the Spirit and Resolution of the People, and shew you, in a striking point of View, the deep Roots of American Independence in all the Colonies. But it is not prudent, to commit to Writing such Free Speculations, in the present State of Things." He hoped that time would lift the veil and lay open "the secret Springs of this surprising Revolution."[32] For Pennsylvania, at least, it has.

If Adams had been at "perfect liberty" to explain the "deep roots" of the Independence movement in Pennsylvania, he would have no doubt related a remarkable overthrow of the "powers-that-be" by individuals and groups that had been traditionally excluded from political power. Up to 1774, the leaders of the resistance to the innovations of

Parliament in Pennsylvania were drawn from the ranks of the ruling ascendancy of Quakers and Anglicans. But with the official colonial government delaying and opposing every hot measure in the Continental Congress, a coalition of traditionally marginalized individuals and communities seized control of the resistance movement and shoved the colony toward leveling democracy—all the time clamoring for their natural rights. With the creation of the committee system to enforce the Non-Importation Agreements of 1774, numerous Philadelphia artisans representing the "mechanic" interest, in alliance with the largely Presbyterian Irish and the German Reformed communities in the backcountry, easily excluded the peaceful Quakers and cautious Whig leadership of the Pennsylvania assembly. Clearly worried about their failure to control the pace of events in Philadelphia, Robert Morris, Andrew Allen, Thomas Willing, Charles Humphreys, and John Dickinson—the majority of the official Pennsylvania delegates to the Continental Congress—continued to press for reconciliation as late as July 2, 1776.[33]

Meanwhile, the new popular leaders in Philadelphia—an alliance between artisans like James Cannon, Thomas Young, Timothy Matlack, and Thomas Paine, and "men of reason" like the mathematician and astronomer David Rittenhouse—systematically ignored the old rump assembly and led the Revolutionary construction of the Pennsylvania constitution along the principles of the rights of man. Drawing support from a widespread popular militia movement, nearly all the leaders of the pro-Independence faction in Pennsylvania were political unknowns before April of 1775.[34] At a rainy outdoor town meeting on May 20, 1776, orchestrated by the Philadelphia Committee of Inspection, an estimated crowd of seven thousand resolved that the colonial assembly had ignored the "will of the citizens" and therefore forfeited its right to govern.[35] As the movement to call a convention and draft a new constitution in Pennsylvania accelerated, constituencies that had been excluded from active power—constituencies for which Englishness and English liberties had meant little or nothing—called for an expansive and nearly universal franchise. The German associators of the city of Philadelphia, for instance, called for all taxables to have the right to vote.[36]

Their arguments were supported by the radical and visionary "Committee of Privates for the City and Liberties of the City of Philadelphia," an elected group of privates and noncommissioned officers of the Pennsylvania Military Association that helped organize the drive for Independence in the spring of 1776.[37] The political awakening of the militia had a permanent impact on expectations for the power wielded by the new citizenry: this was not an army of an ancien régime, not even a provincial army of the British colonial world, but a militia composed of a citizenry which governed themselves. Everywhere, militias demanded control over the choice of their officers, and often the choice over when they appeared in arms. The backcountry Presbyterian Irish, who had been marginalized on both sides of the Atlantic—consistently denied, by their own telling of the story, the liberties of Englishmen—seized much of the control of the new state. As General Charles Lee observed in 1780, the democratic political order in Pennsylvania resembled a "Macocracy."[38] The constitution created by these outsiders—who were outside of the traditional religious, ethnic, regional, educational, and often socioeconomic patterns of the leadership of colonial Pennsylvania—endowed American citizenship with one of its most equal manifestations in the 1780s: an expansive declaration of "natural, inherent and unalienable" rights, nearly universal male suffrage, a unicameral legislature, and an elective judiciary.[39] Pennsylvania's political revolution was an extreme case, but one with power to shape an American notion of citizenship and to inspire and disgust various political groups throughout the continent.

The success of traditional outsiders in the crafting of North Carolina's Revolutionary settlement is best evidenced by the dramatic rejection of Samuel Johnston, a member of the Tidewater elite, as a member of North Carolina's Fifth Provincial Congress.[40] This congress was called specifically to craft a new state constitution, and an alliance of western farmers and urban artisans succeeded in transforming the character of the new assembly. James Iredell, Johnston's son-in-law and a future Supreme Court justice, considered the exclusion of Johnston repulsive. Reflecting on the violent politics that had characterized the Chowan County election—which had been capped by Johnston being burned in effigy—Iredell drafted the satirical "Creed of a Rioter," which lampooned Johnston's opponents. The "Creed" consisted of eleven principles, such as "I am a sworn enemy to all gentlemen, I believe none in that station of life can possibly possess either virtue or honor," and "I believe the best way to have a good understanding, is never to cultivate the mental powers, and that the most ignorant in appearance, are in fact the most knowing."[41] Iredell was one of those Americans who dropped their British identity reluctantly, as he attested in his open letter to King George: "Sir, I am an Englishman myself, and am deeply affected with this Prospect." He had "in that kingdom many near and respectable connections, whose fate will be involved with the multitude." And he still had "a strong attachment to my native Country." Although he "was once your Subject, but is now your enemy," he wished "to be as little so as the indispensable Safety of America (which it is his duty to support) will suffer him to be." The letter was signed "A British American."[42] Johnston himself downplayed the sting of his rejection, believing that the forces that had defeated him were outsiders—nobodies, who had invoked Revolutionary principles—and that the subsequent Congress exhibited a pathetic leveling fervor. As he noted, "Every one who has the least pretensions to be Gentlemen is suspected and born down *Per ignoble Vulus* [by an insignificant rabble]," by a "set of men without reading experience or principle to govern them."[43]

William Hooper, concerned about the tenor of politics in Pennsylvania, hoped North Carolina's constitution would not reflect the dangerous trends evidenced by Johnston's defeat. Writing to Johnston in September 1776, Hooper called Pennsylvania's constitution a "motley mixture of limited monarchy, and an execrable democracy—a Beast without a Head." Added to this, "the Mob made a second branch of Legislation—Law subjected to their revisal in order to refine them, a Washing in ordure by way of purification." It seemed in Pennsylvania that the "taverns and dram shops are the councils" that would ultimately govern the state.[44] Concerned enough about the potential of similar trends in his own home state, Hooper sent a long letter to the North Carolina Congress at Halifax ("my mite to raising the glorious structure") advising the assembly to imitate the intended "balance of power" of the British Constitution, which in uncorrupt form promised leadership by "a select few" whom "heaven had given talents" to be the "choice of the people." Stay away from the example of Pennsylvania, he warned, which now was received by the people (or at least the people Hooper cared to deal with) "with horror."[45]

The ultimate constitution developed by North Carolina represented less transformation than Iredell, Hooper, and Johnston feared, and can best be thought of as a political compromise between the new popular forces of western North Carolina and the established Tidewater political leadership.[46] Even so, the Congress that framed the constitution expanded the franchise to taxables, not simply property owners—a crucial step in the gradual development of a notion of suffrage that rejected traditional models of representation in favor of one tied to personhood. Notably, in Orange County, in one of the contested elections to this Congress, numerous angry residents who were unable to vote complained that they could not exercise their "Right of Electing," a "Right Essential to and inseparable from freedom."[47] Many of these settlers in the western part of the state were Presbyterian Irish. Some of them had participated in the Regulation riots, but many others were simply new settlers in the rapidly growing, nearly unrepresented, and poorly governed western counties. In the new constitution they narrowly lost a fight to have the power to elect their county court justices. Nevertheless, the leaders of these new western forces would dominate the politics of the state into the 1780s, controlling the appointment of judges through the new legislature. Disliking the men who dominated the new state, many of the moderates, like Hooper, declined to serve under the new government.[48] There would not be another Regulation in North Carolina, because the disenfranchised westerners had achieved access to political and legal power.

In Virginia, in the refashioning of the body politic in rebellion we can see a striking example of the dynamic relationship between interests, transformative ideas, and opportunity as a new politics of citizenship emerged. Despite retaining many of the old rules for suffrage and keeping the strength of representation solidly in the long-settled Tidewater, the first elections under the new state constitution rejected numerous scions of the old guard—who were thought to be too cautious, haughty, and aristocratic.[49] The new constitution also contained the first extensive American declaration of natural rights, which began and ended in abstraction: "That all men are by nature equally free and independent, and have certain inherent rights, of which, when they enter into a state of society, they cannot, by any compact, deprive or divest their posterity; namely, the enjoyment of life and liberty, with the means of acquiring and possessing property, and pursuing and obtaining happiness and safety." The draft of this Virginia Declaration of Rights, first published in June 1776, would eventually influence, directly and indirectly, the Declaration of Independence; the Declarations of Rights fashioned by the states of Pennsylvania, North Carolina, Maryland, Delaware, Massachusetts, and Vermont; and the French Declaration of the Rights of Man and Citizen (1789)—and subsequently all declarations of human rights in the modern age.[50] While its author was no social leveler—George Mason was one of the largest and wealthiest slave owners in North America—the Declaration of Rights was more manifesto than legal argument. The draft contained the following bit of reasoning, for instance—a philosophy for the Age of Revolutions:

> That Government is, or ought to be, instituted for the common Benefit and Security of the People, Nation, or Community. Of all the various Modes and Forms of Government, that is best, which is capable of producing the greatest Degree of Happiness and Safety, and is most effectually secured against the Danger of mal-administration. And that whenever any Government shall be found inadequate, or contrary to these Purposes, a Majority of

> the Community had an indubitable, inalianable and indefeasible Right to reform, alter or abolish it, in such Manner as shall be judged most conducive to the Public Weal.[51]

This marriage of popular sovereignty with "indubitable, inalianable and indefeasible" rights would convulse the world. Containing the implications of such enthusiasm would prove extremely difficult.

The impact of such a celebration of fundamental principles on the meaning of American citizenship was felt immediately. Religious dissenters in Virginia had been complaining—occasionally, sporadically, and impotently before 1776—of their lack of access to power and of the burdens of taxation imposed by a state-established church. But after the state moved to draft its constitution, they began to find their voice. Within weeks of the appearance of the draft Declaration of Rights in the newspapers, fifty men from a Baptist church in Prince William County argued that since the country was fighting for "the liberties of mankind," they should be given freedom of worship, exclusion from the requirement of supporting any ministers but their own, and the right to marry without clergy. It was as much extortion as anything. The petitioners implied that only when these privileges were "granted" would they "gladly unite with our Brethren of other denominations" and "promote the common Cause of Freedom."[52]

By the fall, the trickle of complaints became a flood, all of which invoked natural rights or the Declaration of Rights itself. At the first meeting of the House of Delegates held under the new constitution of the Commonwealth, the assembly had to deal with no fewer than ten petitions, with signatures from between 10 percent and 15 percent of the adult white male population, calling for disestablishment.[53] One petition, running to 250 pages in manuscript and signed by 10,000 men from across the state—"dissenters from the Ecclesiastical Establishment"—noted that their "hopes" had been "raised and confirmed" by the "declaration of the Honourable House with regard to equal liberty." "Equal Liberty!" they continued, "which though it be the Birth right of every good man," had been denied by unfair taxation for the support of Anglican ministers.[54] The most elaborate petition came from the presbytery of Hanover County, which "flattered itself" that the legislature, based upon the new "equitable and liberal foundation" of the Commonwealth, would remove "every species of religious, as well as civil bondage." The petitioners believed that the "Declaration of Rights" which had been "so universally applauded" for the "precision with which it delineates, and asserts the privileges of society, and the prerogatives of human nature," should never be "violated without endangering the grand superstructure it was destined to sustain."[55]

The pressure of these particular petitions was not definitive in 1776, for by the end of the session two petitions, representing the clergy of the established church and the Methodists, argued against disestablishment. The session of 1777 would see even more petitions, on both sides. Nevertheless, tax funding of the clergy ceased, and the momentum of the dissenters was inexorable, and ultimately not to be denied. This was a demand of right, by people—citizens—increasingly confident that their natural rights were more expansive than the privileges attendant to their colonial subjecthood. As the petitioners from Albemarle, Amherst, and Buckingham counties asserted, "Your memorialists have never been on an equal footing with the other good people of this colony." But considering that the conflict with Great Britain required that "the form of government should be new modeled," they hoped to "secure equal right" to all citizens.[56]

Finally passed in 1786 after a long political fight, Thomas Jefferson's "Act for Establishing Religious Freedom," which would ultimately justify and legitimate these early claims, was (and remains) a Revolutionary program. The act destroyed the prerogatives of the county vestries, transferred responsibility for poor relief from the Church of England to the State of Virginia, exempted all inhabitants from the requirement of supporting religious institutions, and declared "that the rights hereby asserted are of the natural rights of mankind, and that if any act shall be hereafter passed to repeal the present or to narrow its operation, such an act will be an infringement of natural right."[57] Such a sentiment embodied the most aggressive triumph of a new citizenship over an old subjecthood.

That dissenters in Virginia called upon natural rights to justify their claims and explain their grievances would not have surprised the leaders of rebellion in New England, who experienced a similar phenomenon. Despite the fact that many British subjects in Massachusetts already possessed many of the main markers of active citizenship—such as the vote—we can clearly see many people in the midst of rebellion who wished to ensure that American citizenship represented a more active, equal, and powerful status than their experience of British subjecthood. Some historians have emphasized the "democratic" nature of Massachusetts society in the years before the American Revolution, and have even described it as a "middle-class democracy"—as a way to downplay the importance of real social and economic conflicts to the meaning and course of Revolution in that prominent and leading state. Scholars have emphasized the broad franchise and the participatory structures of town governance as evidence of a society offering democratic promise, especially by the standards of the day, to the property-holding rural farming people who comprised the bulk of New England society.[58] One would expect, in such a society, that the free men of Massachusetts would be more than content with a kingless version of the status quo—with their new citizenship a simple copy of their old subjecthood.

But emphasizing the broad franchise overplays the usefulness of the vote for rural people, especially in western Massachusetts, by obscuring some of the most important fonts of real power: the county court system, family connections, and the prerogative power of the governor (and king). From 1774 to 1780, in the movement to close the courts and call for a constitutional convention in Massachusetts, we can see the extent to which some new Americans wished to make citizenship mean something much more powerful than the existing conditions of their subjecthood, and justified their claims with an appeal to the natural equality of men in a state of nature.

In 1774, as the counties set up provisional county "conventions" to organize and protest against the Intolerable Acts and the Massachusetts Government Act, the farmers in western Massachusetts closed the courts. Denying the legitimacy of the existing forms of government, they demanded that "the Courts of justice immediately seace, and the People of this Province fall into a State of nature." This extraordinary demand called for the courts to stay closed until "our grievances are fully redressed."[59] Within weeks, crowd action, mobbing, and massive public demonstrations closed the courts throughout the colony.

As resistance continued and open war began at Lexington and Concord in the spring of 1775, the courts remained closed. Any justices who did not submit were attacked as Tories and subjected to numerous abuses of violent crowd action.[60] The courts in Berkshire County would remain closed until 1780. In Hampshire and Worcester, county courts were closed until 1778, with power effectively in the hands of ad hoc Committees of Public Safety, county conventions, and crowds. It was in this posture that western Massachusetts fought the War for Independence. The committees regulated their own internal governance, and, when called upon, the local committees and conventions would dispense militias and supplies. Who were these people, and why did they overthrow the courts? Why were they not content to rely on traditional "English liberties" to solve their political problems? Did they wish to join the Revolutionary movement because they felt alienated from English identity or because they saw an opportunity to fashion a new order?

The most prominent social fact, in describing the characteristics of the population in western Massachusetts in 1775, is its *newness*. In the years following the end of the French and Indian War, western Massachusetts (like many areas along the frontier of the British colonies) experienced rapid population growth, the establishment of many new towns, and a growing religious and ethnic diversity among the population. In Hampshire County, straddling the Connecticut River, in just over one hundred years, from 1636 to 1741, only nine towns had been incorporated. This trend changed dramatically in the second half of the century, as thirty-five towns, and one unincorporated town, were established from 1741 to 1770—a mere third of the time it took to settle the first nine. From 1765 to 1776, the population of Hampshire County doubled, from 17,298 to 34,947; in the new towns established since 1741, the population tripled, from 8,617 to 25,543. In Berkshire County, which had been barely settled before the 1760s, the population increased five hundred percent.[61]

The men who closed the courts in western Massachusetts justified their defiance with an appeal to first principles. When forced to explain the continued closure of the courts despite the resumption of the charter, the resisters expressed a strong contempt for both the individuals and the institutions that had controlled their lives up to 1774. As a Pittsfield petitioner to the General Court complained, "We have been ruled in this County for many years past with a rod of Iron."[62] Since the charter still gave the power to appoint local officers to a distant authority, the Pittsfield men would not allow the courts to open or function until changes in the fundamental structures of government had been made. The local justices that the General Court had "appointed to rule us" were considered "greatly obnoxious to the people in general." The status quo would not do; they desired a reconfiguration of power entirely, based upon the natural equality of man and the original sovereignty of the people. They demanded a new government, modern in its design and effects, one that would create such "a Broad base of Civil and religious Liberty as no length of time will corrupt and which will endure as long as the Sun and Moon shall endure."[63]

Over the next year, sometime after the leader of the resisters—the Reverend Thomas Allen—read Thomas Paine's *Common Sense* from his pulpit in lieu of a sermon, the movement to stop the courts developed a more cohesive plan of action. As the resisters still believed that the colonies had "fallen into a State of Nature," they reconceptualized their demand for a new government as a new originating "Compact."[64] Since "the people are the fountain of power," no government could be legitimate in Massachusetts without a convention of all the people and a new constitution formed in compact. These "Berkshire Constitutionalists," as they would become known, refused to open the courts until a constitutional convention was called.

In many petitions from western Massachusetts, and in the critique of the two constitutions that the General Court circulated for approval, towns and committees called for an overthrow of the traditional government of the Bay, and for the creation of a new social and legal order based upon the equality of man in nature. The privileges they desired struck at the very power of the early modern state: the law, the church, and the military. Government, and all its officers, would need to be controlled as immediately as possible by the direct choice of the people. As the Berkshire petitioners argued, they wanted to see "the Rights of Mankind united in the Bands of Society."[65] Officers of the state needed to be directly elected, since "mankind being in a state of nature equal, the larger Number (Caeteris Paribus) is of more worth than the lesser," and they would not submit, lest "we shall sink down into a dead Calm and never transmit to posterity a single Right."[66] They could hardly be more emphatic. The "natural and inherent and unalienable Rights" of man needed to be *directly* and *practically* fused into the institutions of the new order. The character of American citizenship needed to reflect the natural equality of man, not the variegated hierarchy of colonial subjecthood.[67]

While the Berkshire Constitutionalists and their sympathetic allies throughout western Massachusetts eventually acquiesced in a form of government they had consistently opposed, Berkshire, Hampshire, and Worcester counties would not remain quiet.[68] In 1782 the courts were forcibly closed in Berkshire again, and in Hampshire and Worcester, county conventions and court closings would continue apace into the 1780s.[69] In 1782, demands by the Hampshire Convention for an end to the administrative powers of the Courts of Quarter Session erupted into a two-month war, with state militia fighting against self-styled "Regulators," exchanging prisoners, seizing ground, and supporting opposing governmental institutions. In 1786, when Daniel Shays and fifteen hundred men closed the Courts of Common Pleas in Worcester, they began a general rebellion that spread to Berkshire, Hampshire, Worcester, Middlesex, and Bristol counties. The dynamics of the resistance in each of the counties was somewhat different, but the Revolution was clearly still being waged. They justified their appearance in arms as a defense of the "real rights of the people."[70] When the armies were crushed and support evaporated, rebel leader Eli Parsons called upon his neighbors in familiar terms: "Will you now tamely suffer your arms to be taken from you, your estates to be confiscated, and even support a constitution and form of government, and likewise a code of laws, which common sense and your consciences declare to be iniquitous and cruel?" He continued, lamenting his lack of skill as a "ready writer," to remind his audience, "as citizens of a republican government," of their duty to "support those rights and privileges that the God of nature hath entitled to you." He concluded by urging his friends and followers to turn out to "assert your rights" and to do what they had done so decisively in the War for Independence, to "*Burgoyne* Lincoln."[71] "Natural rights" again was being employed to challenge the supporters of law and order, in favor of a more meaningful citizenship.

While the rural people of western Massachusetts failed to transform their status as completely as they wanted, their brethren who flooded into the New Hampshire Grants and the northeast corner of New York succeeded in founding a new state employing similar ideas. Rejecting the efforts of the New Yorkers to restrain them in renter relationships, and defying the authority of the traditional powers to the east, the people of this recently settled area declared themselves in a "state of nature" and founded the "republic of Vermont." Their leaders, Ethan Allen and his brother, Ira Allen, were nephews of the leader of the Berkshire Constitutionalists, the Reverend Thomas Allen of Pittsfield. Their democratic constitution—which allowed for the local election of county officers and universal male suffrage, separated church and state, and provided for a constitutional prohibition against slavery—reflected the sincere desire to institutionalize the principles of equality attendant to a state of nature and the natural rights of man.[72] They were aided in the drafting of their constitution by a timely gift of a copy of the Pennsylvania Constitution of 1776, sent in defiance of New York authorities by the radical artisan leader and Albany native, Thomas Young. As an example of the potential of the new American citizenship, Vermont would go as far as any new state, if it was American at all.[73]

Between the experiences of Pennsylvania and Massachusetts was the process of Revolution in numerous other states, all of which exhibited the tendencies of both. Groups that had been excluded, unincorporated, and marginalized in the colonial system—groups that could find little succor in "English liberties" or that were poorly governed in the overburdened, baroque British imperial order—pressed the new states to expand the meaning of political belonging to reflect the promise of natural equality and popular sovereignty, and together they helped fashion a Revolutionary model for American citizenship. Just as John Adams did not want a "nabob" to rule over him, many people did not want an Adams to rule over them; behind every Congregationalist who did not wish to support an Anglican bishop was a Baptist who did not wish to support a Congregationalist preacher; for every planter who revolted against political slavery were multitudes of blacks who revolted against actual slavery. Adams anticipated all of this, as had many Loyalists, who knew that the vague logic of natural rights opened a Pandora's box. The logic of equality possessed an inexorably leveling aspect, because the notion of equality always carried with it a claim of right. Natural rights preceded government, and many Americans, as they looked to remake their societies, intended to ensure that as much natural equality as possible was fused into the new institutions of the state. They would have an equal citizenship, not a subjecthood wrapped in a new flag.

So out of the consensus that American citizens would not be legally unequal by birth—a consensus that the American republics would not create a legal establishment of hereditary privileges—emerged the conflicts that pressed American citizenship to be even more distinct from British subjecthood. The rejection of the legal establishment of hereditary power immediately transformed the meaning of American citizenship, from a status that expected and even required legal inequalities, as the British Constitution demanded, to a status that *expected equality.* Any legal distinction in the fundamental relationship between those who controlled the state and the average citizen was not seen as a privilege *granted* to a deserving group so much as equality *denied:* the insulted group, the marginalized citizen, the outsider, the opposition, began to demand equal access to power as a "natural right."[74]

Common Law, Natural Law: A Jurisprudence of American Citizenship

Much of the specific meaning of the different duties, privileges, immunities, freedoms, and rights of the citizens of the new states would continue to be adjudicated by common law procedures and principles. The relationship of the common law to the meaning of American citizenship in the Revolution needs to be clarified. By 1775, there were numerous reasons why the common law was generally understood not only as a necessary, but as an *essential* tool to shape and define the meaning of citizenship and membership in these new republics. There was not one "common law" in the colonies; each colony possessed its own version of common law, which had evolved over the years from an eclectic mixture of local rules and regulations, statutes of Parliament that existed before the founding of the particular colony, and accepted practices that fit the distinct circumstances of the colony. But provincial Americans shared broad assumptions about the grander meaning of the common law, which assured that the new American republics would "retain" it as the basis for their citizenship.

The common law had evolved in the colonies as a jurisprudence of fundamental law that protected free people from arbitrary power. This "common law constitutionalism" had many antecedents in seventeenth-century England but was counter to certain trends in the eighteenth-century English legal system, which was gradually moving toward a consensus that Parliament could pass any law without regard to any other "fundamental" law. In the American colonies, the common law remained crucial to the meaning and defense of "English liberties." Refined and clarified in the Revolutionary mind, this meant rights attached to individuals—rights many Patriots believed (like Blackstone) were ultimately derived from the "natural rights of mankind." The common law was customary law, but customs that had changed by experience, nature, and reason. Thus, Roger Sherman argued that the colonies claimed the "common Law, not as Law, but as the Highest Reason," as a way to protect their rights against Parliament.[75] American revolutionaries often conflated "custom with reason, and reason with natural law."[76] As Judge Alexander Addison noted, "The *common law* is founded on the law of nature and the revelation of God."[77] Indeed, for American jurists, the common law, broadly considered, was synonymous with natural law. Although some lawyers might distinguish between the "artificial reason," or "right reason," of the common law and the "intuitive reason" of man's natural capacities, most generally understood "reason" and "common sense" as the natural capacity of adult men.

As a system of natural law, the different common laws of the states therefore were loaded with the fundamental rights, responsibilities, duties, and obligations of citizens to citizens and to the community, which were entirely compatible with a notion of citizenship rooted in natural rights. The common law protected people against murder and thieves; it encompassed the law of contracts, the "rights of property," the obligations and processes related to conflicts over debts and obligations. The purview of the common law included the relationships of women to men, of children to adults, of individuals to the community. In other words, as Judge Addison noted, the common law set the broad parameters to the ultimate meaning of "natural rights, the rules of common justice, of debts, contracts and property, and of the redress of wrongs"—issues relating to life, liberty, and the pursuit of happiness.[78] The common law clarified the accepted terms of the natural relations of mankind in society, and the widely held sense that the common law simply confirmed the manifold rights and duties of nature, in procedures both practical and accepted, assured that American revolutionaries would make it the fundamental jurisprudence of their new citizenship.

Yet there were many things in colonial common law practices that were not suitable to a system of equal citizenship. The establishment of the English church, for instance, was part of the common law. So was "the right of primogeniture," and many of the prerogatives and rights of the king relating to both his office and his person. If the Americans had just accepted the common law as it was, they would have imported, as James Madison noted, "a monarchical code."[79] So the makers of the new American states would keep the common law, but they would "improve" it—with the principles of reason, the statutes of popularly elected legislatures, and the power of written constitutions. Thus, Delaware's Constitution of 1776, in language typical to early statutes and declarations of rights of nearly all the states, noted "that the common law of England, as well as so much of the statute law, as had theretofore been adopted in practice in that state, shall remain in force," except those parts "as are repugnant to the rights and privileges contained in the constitution," and those altered by a "future act of the legislature."[80] The leaders of the states were fundamentally aware of many anti-republican aspects of accepted common law practices. This is why the first American declarations of rights often contained numerous statements that are not only what modern jargon considers "constitutional rights," but that also contain procedural concerns and general statements of principle, intended to influence interpretation of the law. For instance, the state constitutions often contain (1) disavowals of specific types of laws: "ex post facto laws," laws establishing "perpetuities and monopolies," and "sanguinary laws";[81] (2) clarifications of particular *procedures:* "in all criminal prosecutions, every man hath a right to be informed of the accusation against him; to have a copy of the indictment or charge in due time (if required) to prepare for his defense"; and (3) general statements of principle: "that the doctrine of non-resistance, against arbitrary power and oppression, is absurd, slavish, and destructive of the good and happiness of mankind."[82]

In the early constitutions, one institution was crucial in this *re-publicanization* of the common law: the jury trial—at once a right, a procedure, and a principle. The jury trial was not new, but it was indispensable in assuring that the common law was excised of monarchical tendencies.[83] Twelve impartial citizens interpreting the law, granting justice, and deciding cases was popular sovereignty in action. The jury trial held sacred power for the American revolutionaries. It was in juries that much of the common law would be expounded and heard. And in the late eighteenth century juries had extensive power to decide on both the law and the facts of the cases within their purview. Nearly every new state constitution explicitly demanded the jury trial for citizens accused of crimes or engaged in civil disputes, most in enthusiastic language.

As the Pennsylvania constitution declared concerning simple lawsuits: "In controversies respecting property, and in suits between man and man, the ancient trial by jury is preferable to any other, and ought to be held sacred."[84] Or, as North Carolina noted: "The ancient mode trial by jury is one of the best securities of the rights of the people, and ought to remain sacred and inviolable."[85] Here, the ancient jury would serve Revolutionary purposes. As a proven "security of the rights of the people," it would remain necessary to continue to protect the rights and duties of citizens. John Adams understood the jury trial not only as the true inheritance of Englishmen but as one of the crucial "rights of nature." Along with representative assemblies, the jury trial assured that governments did not become arbitrary.

Finally, although the common law was "unwritten law," it was of course often written *about* by numerous learned scholars, whose treatises were used by lawyers and students to understand the mysteries, practices, and usages of the common law. So the common law had been reshaped by numerous authors over time, for various purposes—for clarity of procedure and efficiency of language, for political and religious imperatives—and always in service of "Reason." These treatise writers had never been mere compilers of precedents, even though the treatises were often used as such by lawyers. By the eve of the Revolution, common law treatises available and in use in the colonies incorporated many of the assumptions of republican citizenship—namely, that society is based in compact; that reasoned consent is crucial to the legitimacy of contracts; that children are exempt from certain rights, responsibilities, and crimes until they reach an ability to "reason" and consent; and that natural rights exist which can not be legislated away. William Blackstone's *Commentaries* were infused with principles of the Enlightenment, and he seamlessly incorporated much of John Locke and European natural law jurisprudence into his improved vision of the common law.[86] So the principles of the common law in America in 1775 did not look like some arcane collection of random ancient precedents, but as natural law that had been improving with age and would continue to improve.

Generalizing about the changes to the common law, which he lived through and later taught as professor of law and police at the College of William and Mary, St. George Tucker described nothing less than a revolution in the common law. As he argued, "every rule of the common law, and every statute of England founded on the nature of regal government" that were seen to be "in derogation of the natural and unalienable rights of mankind," or "inconsistent with the nature and principles of democratic governments," were "absolutely abrogated, repealed, and annulled" by the establishment of the states. The transformation was a "natural and necessary consequence of the revolution."[87]

This is why the American revolutionaries, unlike actors in many other modern revolutions, did not attempt (or see the need) to create a *specific* code of citizenship, defining in minute detail the rights and duties of various people, citizens, inhabitants, aliens, minors, and others. Instead, Americans established a vision of a *republicanized* common law—one restrained by written declarations of rights and procedures, refined by the statutes of popularly elected legislatures, protected and clarified by juries—a republican common law that would gradually improve as a jurisprudence of citizenship. Since most lawyers in the Revolutionary Era thought of the common law as both the epitome and the consequence of a process of natural evolution—as natural law—they anticipated that it would gradually be perfected. The law would evolve to fit society, within institutions defined by republican conceptions of right and justice, and would become a true code of modern freedom. As James Kent argued in introducing his lectures in the law at Columbia University in 1794, students must understand that the "principles" of the "British Constitution and Code of Laws," which possessed many axioms of jurisprudence "utterly subversive of an Equality of Rights," were "totally incompatible with the liberal spirit of our American Establishments." Those "American Establishments" could be reduced to two: "the admirable Fabrics of our Constitutions, and the all pervading Freedom of our Common Law."[88] These two "establishments" created the fundamental double helix of American citizenship—which together protected and defined the rights, responsibilities, and duties of everyone.

So American citizenship was founded upon natural law, with its attendant rights *and* duties ultimately elaborated in a republicanized common law. Countless statutes passed between 1773 and 1783 in the individual states—statutes relating to naturalization; to treason; to crime and punishment; to land sales, jurisdiction, and titles; to the structure and competence of various courts of law—transformed numerous colonial common law usages, all impacting the differences between British subjecthood and American citizenship.

The new states, created in the Revolution, represented the institutional manifestation of popular sovereignty and completed the process of inventing American citizenship. Institutions formerly intended to serve the interests of the Crown—appointed by prerogative power, responsible to the whims of imperial oversight—became servants of the citizenry, often paid, and subject to regular election and instruction, in many cases, annually. Colonial governors (with the exception of those in Rhode Island and Connecticut) had been appointed by a politics based in the byzantine world of family interest, corruption, and patronage that characterized late Hanoverian Britain, while the new governors depended upon the representative processes of the states, with governors in Georgia and New York elected by the people at large. The upper houses of the new states became law-making, representative Senates, greatly expanded to represent geographic diversity, unlike the mere Councils serving the Crown and governor before Independence. The new legislatures became much larger, more popularly elected, more geographically representative, and substantially more powerful. The making of law was entirely in the hands of the electorate, with the actual lawmakers responsible to their constituents.[89]

The new states were loaded with latent power. They were modern states, Leviathans, which claimed and asserted jurisdiction over all their internal police and policy; controlled the ultimate legal sanction of life and death (with no higher appeal); destroyed the old jurisdictions held by individual proprietors as well as the overlapping claims of the English church and state; annihilated the ancient prerogatives, communal land ownership, and protections of numerous Native American groups within their borders; and redefined the immunities and duties of the inhabitants of their territory. They could and would issue their own charters of incorporation; reform their fundamental law; establish educational institutions, penal systems, and military establishments; and mobilize resources and raise taxes to serve their own interests. They would create cities and counties, define the process of internal development, and regulate and shackle markets as trends and politics demanded. And the justifications for what they did and were had been transformed by the Revolution. They existed in the name and at the service of new sovereign peoples. Authority and power in independent America flowed and would be distributed by an entirely different calculus—which created a new political system.

The conversation and contestation which created these new states and provided the leaven for a new political order were symbiotic. Old ideas, traditional assumptions, accepted justifications were pushed, prodded, and shaped in the creation of the new polities. Rational principles were liberally applied. A few fundamentals emerged, which even if they were not supported by everyone, were quickly becoming the catechism of the American Revolution. Inherent natural rights existed, attached to individuals, which governments could not change and were intended to secure. The people were the font of all sovereign power, and magistrates ought to be considered as their servants, subject to election and dismissal. Representatives were intended to be directly responsible to their particular constituents, open to instruction. The vote was being claimed as a right attached more to personhood than to property, and at the very least was seized as a right to provide taxpayers with a chance to consent to all taxes. Allegiance was not based solely upon natural obligations (where someone was born) but also upon individual consent, and a stake in political society was granted to a much broader slice of the population. Fundamental law differed from law created by mere legislative power, and the people alone, as sovereign, could change the fundamental law. The social organization of American life was defined and protected by the common law of nature, just as the independence, freedom, and responsibilities of the states were governed by the common law of nations. American citizens were emerging as the polar opposite of British subjects.[90]

But the significance of this transformation for the character of politics and the meaning of the American Revolution is much more than a sum of the parts. An ideal of citizenship emerged clearly by the end of Independence and transformed the nature of politics in the new United States. The greatest of the contemporary historians of the American Revolution recognized this achievement explicitly. As David Ramsay observed, "The principle of government" had been "radically changed by the revolution," and the "political character of the people was also changed from subjects to citizens." And, he wrote, "the difference is immense":

> Subjects look up to a master, but citizens are so far equal, that none have hereditary rights superior to others. Each citizen of a free state contains, within himself, by nature and the constitution, as much of the common sovereignty as another. In the eye of reason and philosophy, the political condition of citizens is morc cxulted than that of noblemen. Dukes and earls are the creatures of kings, and may be made by them at pleasure: but citizens possess in their own right original sovereignty.

In addition to possessing an "individual's proportion of the common sovereignty," individual citizens choose their allegiance, either by tacit or direct consent, while subjects merely reciprocate protection with natural allegiance. "These original citizens," Ramsay noted, are properly considered "the founders of the United States."[91]

The Limits and Possibilities of Revolutionary Citizenship

The fundamental break between a world organized by the presumptions of subjecthood and one increasingly emphasizing the power of citizenship opened horizons only vaguely perceived by the end of the

War for Independence. With hindsight (a testament to the transformative power of this new ideal of citizenship), we instinctively lament some of the lack of transformation in these first years. We consider the limits of the Revolution to be fantastically evident flaws, even gross hypocrisy. Ramsay himself uses the gendered pronoun "he" to describe his ideal citizen, and it is clear that he (and almost all other theorists) thought of women as outside the new "political character of citizenship" that he celebrated. He also asserted simply that "Negroes are inhabitants, not citizens." As mere inhabitants, blacks have "no farther connection with the state" in which they live, and possess security and protection "agreeably to the fixed laws, without any participation in government."[92] To Ramsay's assumptions we could add other categories of men and women, black, white, and red—slaves, minors, paupers, vagrants, indentured servants and felons, even sometimes apprentices and tenants—who were presumptively or legally excluded from the new political character of American citizenship in various ways. Catholics and Jews, although they often could vote, could rarely hold office.

But the continued hierarchies in the first manifestations of American citizenship, and the limitations which persisted in many of the states on who could vote or participate in governance should not be surprising. Even where certain groups were mobilized and aided in their assertions by sympathetic and influential people, the amount of transformation could be limited by the power of their opponents—coalitions that considered such new claims to be dangerous, absurd, or simply unimportant. Just because groups and individuals could articulate a "natural right" to participate as equal citizens does not mean that their complaints would be simply accepted. Many Americans, particularly those protecting strong positions and interests in colonial society, often wanted citizenship to retain numerous characteristics of British subjecthood, characteristics that they believed had guaranteed ordered liberty: traditional interpretations of law, hierarchically arranged power structures, two legislative chambers, coercive church establishments, and ascriptive limits on the franchise and office-holding.[93]

In addition, many of the groups who called upon natural rights to justify their own representation in government did not persist as political factions. In some cases their grievances were addressed and answered, and thus their common interest disappeared—such as with frontier peoples who were barely governed in the late colonial order. More importantly, many constituencies reveling in the aggressive justification of natural rights would not recognize every other claim of right to be a legitimate complaint. Simply because they shared a similar language of resistance did not ensure that they shared similar goals or compatible interests. Such a dynamic is evident in John Adams's fear that "new claims" would be made. The most obvious example, of course, are the claims of "natural right" being made by slaves and free blacks during the resistance to Britain. Certainly the slaveholding planters who celebrated natural rights and the equality of the state of nature were not part of the same political constituencies.

But that is the trouble with using universal principles to refashion the political order: the implications and effects of such politics are difficult to restrain. In 1774, former slave Caesar Sarter represented an emerging trend among some Americans, black and white, by directly connecting the American struggle against the British to the slave's struggle against bondage:

> As this is a time of great anxiety and distress among you, on account of the infringement not only of your Charter rights; but of the *natural rights and privileges of freeborn men;* permit a poor, though freeborn African, who, in his youth, was trepanned into Slavery and who has born the galling yoke of bondage for more than twenty years; though at last, by the blessing of God, has shaken it off, to tell you, and that from experience, that Slavery is the greatest, and consequently most to be dreaded of all temporal calamities.[94]

Sarter shows precisely the contours of the continuing debate of the Patriot resistance, by recognizing that many Americans had been complaining about both English liberties ("your Charter rights") and the "natural rights and privileges of freeborn men" in the climactic moments of the resistance. But complaints about charter rights could do little for Sarter's particular grievances because the charter had nothing to do with slavery. He could appeal to the charter for a thousand years and never find an argument that would free enslaved people from bondage. Colonial common law in Massachusetts recognized slavery. But in the "natural rights and privileges of freeborn men" he had an opportunity to claim *universal* rights—principles that transcended the jurisdiction of men and nation, that implied a mysterious original equality and therefore delegitimized the subsequent fact of dependence. As early as 1774, such pressure was having effect. The town meeting of Providence, Rhode Island, passed a resolution calling for the gradual emancipation of slaves, because "the inhabitants of America are engaged in the preservation of their rights and liberties," and "personal liberty is an essential part of the natural rights of mankind."[95]

But simply because some people *could* appeal to natural rights did not mean that they would achieve their ends. When the framers of the

Virginia constitution approved their declaration "that all men are born equally free and independent," Robert Carter Nicholas openly worried that such an assertion would be the "forerunner or pretext of civil convulsion." But he was voted down by delegates who assured him that slaves "could never pretend to any benefit from such a maxim."[96] Some pro-slavery planters in Virginia had little difficulty using the defense of property based upon natural rights to defend the legitimacy of slavery in the midst of the Revolution.[97] And yet various Quakers in Virginia, "who never ceased to ply the Assembly with the bill of rights and topics arising from human nature," created momentum for the passage of the first real manumission bill in Virginia in over a century—a bill later called a "partial emancipation of slavery."[98] So the boundaries of American citizenship, and the eventual fate of that law (which would be immediately vilified by many and ultimately repealed in 1806), would only be settled by the political realties of the next quarter-century. The important point is that the differences between the new ideals of citizenship and the realities of actual citizenship were always defined through political struggles rooted in the social, cultural, and economic substance of the late colonial world. Without a political dynamic, it was all just talk.

The continued importance of the common law to the ultimate meaning of American citizenship in the Founding Era also limited the possibilities of transformation. Even when checked and "improved" by juries and declarations of rights, the common law was still a jurisprudence that was intimately concerned with status relationships rooted in a hierarchical past. People, in common law, were understood by a series of social markers, which ultimately meant not an "equal" status as citizens, with the same specific rights, but a variegated one, defined by "office, property, household position, race, gender, infirmity, and age." For white men, many of these status markers would become less important over time (with the rapid decline in servant/apprenticeship, for instance), but for many others the fundamental status boundaries remained restraining. So even a republicanized common law, with its "all pervading Freedom," was not an *agent* of social change but a system of organic law which evolved to fit changing social conditions.[99]

The retention of such a common law assured that women would remain "unequal" citizens—understood at common law to have no individual "will" outside of their status relations with men. Women and men had different rights and duties in common law, based theoretically on their different natural attributes. Yet the continued restrictions on women in this first citizenship reflects not only the continuation of colonial precedents, practices, and the widespread prejudices and assumptions of paternalistic society, but also the important *lack* of political pressure from women (or sympathetic men) claiming new and outlandish rights during the formative years of Independence. There are significant exceptions, of course, but the power of whimsy was never enough.

Individual women made a few scattered appeals to fundamental political rights during the years following American independence, but these efforts never captured the imagination of a significant proportion of women, and convinced even fewer men to attempt to level the differences between male and female citizens. Abigail Adams famously asked her husband to "remember the ladies" when revising the laws, and often chided him about women's lack of representation, but she did so in terms reflecting patriarchal assumptions—imploring the new lawmakers to "regard us then as Beings placed by providence under your protection and in imitation of the Supreem Being make use of that power only for our happiness."[100] A more aggressive example of an assertion of rights (with a more sympathetic correspondent) was made by Hannah Corbin, the sister of Virginia's Richard Henry Lee, who complained that widows holding property "ought not to be liable to tax" without direct representation. Lee agreed, arguing that propertied women had "as legal a right to vote as any other person" and he thought the doctrine of representation "ought to be extended as far as wisdom and policy can allow."[101] But these thoughts were mere speculations between family members, not a political program.

In New Jersey, propertied women actually were enfranchised—although scholars continue to argue whether this was intentional or not. Some New Jersey election laws referred to voters as "he," but the original New Jersey Constitution of 1776 mentioned "all inhabitants" worth fifty pounds. Evidence that it was intentional rests upon more assertion than proof, but it is clear that debates over representation in the Middle States touched upon the problem of women's voting rights. The author of "Essex," for instance, who drafted an ideal constitution which promised that "widows paying taxes" would have an "equal right to a vote as men of the same property," may have been New Jersey framer William DeHart.[102] Nevertheless, women voted in earnest in the 1790s, and they certainly were *disenfranchised* intentionally in 1807 when New Jersey opened the vote to most adult white men. The enfranchisement of New Jersey women from 1776 to 1807 is no mean part of the Revolutionary epoch, but it stands more as an illusive exception than a real trend in the making of republican citizenship after the Revolution. It would have a lasting legacy, however, among a generation of women who grew up after the ambiguities had been strained from the system.[103]

The gendered nature of natural rights rhetoric itself worked against the imagination in the eighteenth century—such rights were, after all, "the rights of men." Of all the truths sought in a rational investigation of the intentions of nature in the Revolutionary Era, the idea that women were "designed," as John Adams put it, "for domestic concerns," remained one of the most widely held—among men and women alike. Political rights for women would have been "unnatural." Mercy Otis Warren, although defending her own role as a student and historian of politics, agreed that "there are certain important duties assigned to each sex" by Providence and nature. In addition to these widely held prejudices, the political realms opened by men in the midst of Revolution—in the militias, in the statehouses, and in the courts—were male domains. In the courts, women could appear as plaintiffs, defendants, and witnesses, but never as jury members or justices, bailiffs, or clerks: the court was a man's world. Assemblies themselves had traditionally little to do with women's place in society, which was legally defined by common law and Chancery courts. Under the presumptions of coverture, women possessed no legal will, no capacity to make political choices, necessary for the newly modeled citizenship—a status which was being reinforced in the 1760s by trends in English law stemming from William Blackstone's attempts to clarify paternalistic authority. Militias did not even possess the camp followers of regular armies—another male domain, and one which became particularly important in reinforcing the masculine character of political citizens. Women might enthusiastically make cartridges for the militia, but they were not expected to "man a post."[104]

And yet, unlike black men (as will be shown), white women were imagined as *essential* in the attempts to perfect a republican citizenry and a national community, and although women's public status as citizens was curtailed by their gender, their status as *Americans* was never denied, and often eagerly extolled. As American women were refashioned as republican mothers, sisters, and daughters, they simultaneously became more active, as popular participants in American politics and as agents in the civic life of their communities in voluntary associations and charitable institutions.[105] Most publicly, women were present in the informal politics of the dinner table and in the emerging politics of the street—as enthusiasts, participants, and critics of American political society—throughout the 1790s.[106]

But it is foolish to assume and insist that men and women had inherently divergent interests during the Revolution—there is almost no significant evidence that women, considered as a group, were deeply disappointed by the fruits of Independence. Women were crucial to the success of Independence, from the very first boycotts to the final battles, as individual heroines and as the essential glue of community. It is clear that some of the legal changes that resulted from Independence, namely, the attempts to make property and capital more susceptible to market forces, sometimes worked against the traditional common law protections of women's dower rights. Yet when we look through the eyes of one of the most articulate women of the era, the historian Mercy Otis Warren, her vision of the meaning of the Revolution is little different from that of many white men, especially those of her rank. Like a good Whig, she considered it as a fight for liberty against tyranny, an example of true patriotism always under threat from internal corruption and the disruptions of the Revolutionary politics. And she hoped that future generations of Americans "would never forget the energetic struggles of their fathers, to secure the natural rights of men."[107]

From Subjects to Citizenry: Creating "the People"

Just as Patrick Henry's exclamation that British America had fallen into a "state of nature" was politically aggressive, portentous, and not entirely correct—or universally approved—his celebration of a potential "American" identity remained more rhetorical than real. There was an emerging "Cause" of "American liberty," and there quickly became "enemies to America," but the first two Continental Congresses organized more as surrogates of British imperial authority, or as international-style congresses of states, than as a unifying government of a self-aware American people. "Union" became the watchword of resistance at all levels. Unanimity and cooperation were understood as both essential and fragile. Symbols of Union quickly came to characterize the enthusiasm for the cause, and the desire to find a more effective link, or "some bond of union, in writing," as Benjamin Franklin noted in his proposed Confederation of 1775, rapidly shaped the contours of the debate over confederation, Union, and nationhood.[108]

Even so, the most contentious problems of the alliance, including numerous fundamentals, like who the American people actually were, always yielded to "the main business, that of subdueing our common enemy."[109] As far as Congress was concerned, potential Americans could be found in Canada, Bermuda, the West Indies, even in Ireland—all of whom they invited to join in the struggle in 1775. Yet there was one group excluded from the "American" people from the start. An early suggestion for the first seal of the "confederated States" called for a design which incorporated the coats of arms of the various "nations from whence America has been peopled, as English, Scotch, Irish, Dutch,

German," flanked by Liberty and a rifleman.[110] Notably, Indians were not one of these originating peoples.

One of the most immediate consequences of the citizenship revolution was the bright line drawn between American citizens and American Indians. By the early 1770s, most Native tribes in British North America acknowledged themselves, like the thirteen colonies, to be subjects of Great Britain. Although Congress reached out to the other British provinces in the Atlantic, from the beginning there existed a widely held presumption that Indians were not Americans, despite the fact that the rebels often reveled in the symbolic power of Native tropes, and regardless of the fact that some Indians were fighting for the American "Cause" as early as 1775. The official efforts of many states and Congress implored the Natives to remain neutral and promised eternal war upon the Indians who dared to breach the peace.

But as the war evolved and all neutrals, Indian or not, were forced to choose, the fact that many Native peoples chose the cause of their British king shaped and reinforced the widely held prejudice against Indians, which helped assure their eventual exclusion and marginalization. The process of exclusion was accelerated both by the political shifts of the Independence struggle and by the experience of the long war. For instance, long-standing cultural and growing racial antagonism to nearly all Indians animated much of the *new* ruling interests of Revolutionary Pennsylvania—the Irish Presbyterians, and the Reformed and Lutheran German churches—in contradistinction to the more friendly policies of the Quakers, Anglicans, and pietistic sects. During the Paxton Riots in the 1760s, backcountry Pennsylvanians complained, in constitutional terms, about the autonomy of the Native groups within their midst. According to them, the Indians always "asserted and exercised the right of making war and peace as independent nations." They "never came under our laws, nor acknowledged subjection to our king and government," but instead "have governed themselves by their own customs, and exercised the power of life and death over their own people." It was, they complained, an "imperium en imperio."[111] Rejecting the idea of Native autonomy within the boundaries of the new Revolutionary states was implicit in the claims of sole control over the "internal policy and police" of their own territory. Westerners engaged in the bloody war demanded the exclusion of Indians and began the first great racial bounding of the American nation, even as they extended the boundaries of the American Union. Native groups would not be autonomous parts of the new-modeled institutions of the American Union, as they had been within the British Empire. They would be outside of the

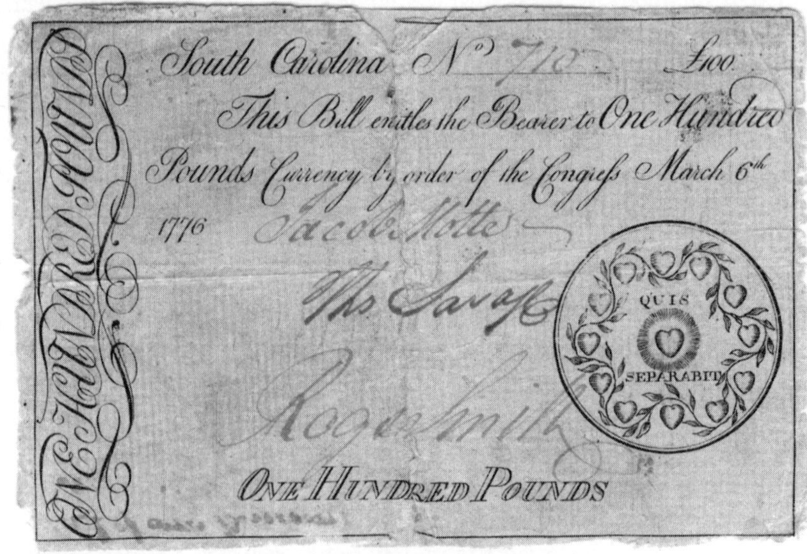

FIGURE 1. Samples of the currencies of South Carolina (*top*) and the Continental Congress (*bottom*). These representations of Union exemplify the earliest symbolic motifs of the Confederation. Like the Seal of the United States itself, with the motto "E Pluribus Unum," these interlinking chains and circles of stars and hearts were graphic representations of the promise of a Confederation that would finally approve its fundamental Articles in 1782. (Courtesy of the American Antiquarian Society)

American empire, to be treated with, bargained with, and bribed, and when these means failed, to be removed by force.[112]

Even those Native Americans fighting alongside the new American states, like the Presbyterian Oneida, the Catawba in South Carolina, or the Massachusetts Stockbridge Indians, were not considered as part of the citizenry, but as allies or, more correctly, tribute peoples and ultimately subjects of the states. It is unclear whether Indians *as groups* wished to be incorporated as citizens during or immediately after the war—most merely asked for compensation for losses during the war and hoped for protection of their ancestral claims to independence on their own terms. But autonomy could not exist within the proud states. In time, individual Native Americans within the states would fall under laws related to all people of color, like "free negroes and mullottoes."[113]

As for who else could claim to be part of the "American" people, the first tentative clarifications of the body politic emerged from the enforcement of the Non-Importation Agreements. In the first committees of the Non-Importation Association, the twin practices of surveillance and intimidation helped set the process of Revolution in motion. To local intimidation and social ostracism would eventually be added fines and penal taxes, treason laws, test acts, confiscation acts, and the continuing pressures of war: more laws that "perfected" the common law in favor of consent and contract.[114] Loyalty to the community became the crucial arbiter of membership in the people. Old ties did not bind, and without affirmative oaths or other signs of overt adherence to the cause, no amount of property or colonial rank could secure American citizenship. Connections to patronage stemming from royal authority, which had once conveyed power and legitimacy, became the markers of traitors. In some areas of the theater of war—throughout North Carolina, South Carolina, and Georgia, and in certain areas of New York and New Jersey—a violent maelstrom of family vendetta, civil war, religious war, and brigandry was justified by cries of "treason" on all sides. And "the people," when they could be said to exist, were set upon little more than "cutting one another's throats."[115]

The enforcement of loyalty and, in many ways, the construction of the legitimate "people" occurred at the local level from the very beginning, coordinated by the mandates of the states and ultimately given sanction by Congress, which had instigated the process by defining treason and calling on the states to enforce these laws in 1776.[116] Property was confiscated on a grand scale. Thousands of people—on evidence provided by their neighbors—were brought before local councils and committees of safety, "committees for the detection of conspiracy," and courts of oyer and terminer, and made to promise obedience, take oaths, post bail, or surrender themselves for punishment. Expectations of male militia service, both legal and otherwise, became both an important arbiter and agent of loyalty. From the beginning, the new states tended to choose fines, brief imprisonment, and forced exile over execution, and for every hanging for treason there were scores of pardons. The contractual model of the people did not require the continued presence of intestine enemies, and "Loyalists" tended not to control assets or authority beyond the reach of the new states. This process of forcing the most recalcitrant out of the country contributed to a myth of unanimity which began to emerge quickly after the war ended, despite the fact that many areas remained in the hands of people loyal to the Crown for most of the war. The myth of consensus was strengthened by numbers—current estimates suggest that between sixty thousand and eighty thousand people chose exile over American citizenship.[117]

The coercive and often violent process which excluded the "Loyalists," or "Tories," from membership in "the People" actually reinforced the volitional model of citizenship and the contractual origins of the political world. By the end of the war, anyone left in the new states had either directly or implicitly consented to the Revolution. Although women could be held responsible for committing a crime against the new states and the Revolution, for the most part, women were not expected, or required, to have a political will. Even so, many women still were forced to take oaths for good behavior, especially if their husbands and sons were known Loyalists.[118] Test Acts, oath-taking, and enforcement had a transformative effect. As David Ramsay noted, during the war, those people who refused to take oaths "were ordered to depart." But as the war drew to its close, oaths became less and less necessary, and so citizenship became available by "tacit consent or acquiescence," because at "twenty-one years of age, every freeman is at liberty to chuse his country, his religion, and his allegiance."[119] In Virginia, Thomas Jefferson drafted an extraordinary new law of citizenship intended to "to preserve to the citizens of this commonwealth, that natural right which all men have of relinquishing the country, in which birth or other accident may have thrown them."[120] So all citizens either choose to join the people or choose to stay: love it or leave it.

Before the peace had officially been declared, the debate began in earnest over whether former Loyalists could be brought into the new peoples. The first state naturalization laws were crafted with a heady awareness of the possibility for former Loyalists to return to their former place in society, while still encouraging immigration. All the early naturalization policies required strident oaths and affirmations, not only of loyalty to the new state but also of renunciation of all other ties of allegiance. In many states, former Loyalists were restricted in their civil rights, no matter what oath they took. In its early naturalization laws, the State of Georgia explicitly forbade Scots from naturalizing, since people of Scottish descent were widely thought to have been universally "Tories" during the bloody, chaotic, and anarchic civil war in the Deep South. In all the states, strong resistance to the easy naturalization of former Loyalists clashed with the spirit of the Treaty of Paris of 1783, which asked but did not compel the states to remove all restrictions on former Loyalists.

In Charleston, South Carolina, the evacuation of the British army in 1783 led immediately to a "flood" of British merchants, banished native South Carolinians, and former Loyalists clamoring for citizenship. One opponent to their admission called them "a standing army of merchants, factors, clerks, agents and emissaries" who posed a long-term threat, "greater than any posed by Clinton or Cornwallis."[121] Even so, some wealthy members of Charleston society, like Francis Kinloch, welcomed this influx as a sure protection against inevitable "civil dissentions" which will "end in blood." In the South Carolina legislature, in February and March of 1784, most of the restrictions on Loyalists were lifted, against the vocal and occasionally violent (but ultimately uncoordinated) protests of numerous Carolina citizens.[122]

Similar contests, of varying degrees, emerged in all the states. In New York, the volume of cases dealing with the attempts of former Loyalists to seek restitution or challenge the restrictions on their full citizenship simultaneously helped Alexander Hamilton learn the practice of law and leap to the front of serious political influence—if not popularity—in New York City. Between 1784 and 1785 he tried over sixty cases challenging the various New York State laws which penalized and threatened the property of former Loyalists. In New York, more than any other state, some former Loyalists—like Josiah Hoffman; Samuel Jones, Sr. and Jr.; Cadwallader Colden; William Rutherford; and Richard Harison—returned to positions of considerable influence in politics and law.[123]

One of the most contentious politics concerning the process by which former Loyalists could be brought into the people occurred in Pennsylvania, the only state in which the problem became a "party" issue. The political coalition which swept Pennsylvania into Independence and swept out all the "old members" of the colonial assembly, had been strained and cracked through the long war. Pennsylvania's democratic constitution became the focus of the discontent of many increasingly organized interests, including the old governing coalition, led by John Dickinson. Finally, in 1785, former Loyalists, Quakers, Neutrals, and

Trimmers of all sorts were brought into "the people" of Pennsylvania, a victory for opponents of the democratic constitution of Pennsylvania, and a necessary step in that document's ultimate revision in 1790.[124]

The re-incorporation of former Loyalists into American citizenship represents the end of the Revolutionary invention of citizenship and the beginning of the politics of citizenship—which would animate some of the most important political conflicts in the next decade. The assumptions of what citizenship was, and could be, of its difference from subjecthood, of its relationship to the state and the people, was ossifying into a series of procedures and rules to be increasingly clarified and protected by a republicanized common law. With certain assumptions in place, the citizenry would aggressively fight over the policy of the new states, of how to use the new sovereignty gained in Independence. One of the racial boundaries of "the people," the exclusion of Native Americans, was clear by the end of the war. But the place of newly freed blacks—a population which would grow rapidly in the 1780s and 1790s—remained unsettled.[125]

But who, ultimately, ruled in America? "The people," to be sure. But which people? The new nation of Americans, or the separate peoples collected together in the states? These were questions that had threatened to break the Union from the very first, and they re-created, in their own way, the constitutional crisis of the British Empire of the 1760s. The articulation of the place of the states within the Union, and the relationship of a nascent national American people to the Confederation, can properly be understood as part of a continuation of the problematic debates over the nature of the British Empire and the relative autonomy of the colonies—"causes peculiar to that revolution." The problem of governing an extended polity required flexibility in the details, as it had in the British Empire. And the movement to create "a more perfect Union" was partially an effort to clarify the chaos. But this was not a conservative moment; it was a generative, creative one—as it always had been—as fights over the nature of the Union became arguments over possible modern states.

{2}

State v. Nation

FEDERALISM AND THE PROBLEM OF NATIONHOOD

Whoever considers, in a combined and comprehensive view, the general texture of the Constitution, will be satisfied, that the people of the United States intended to form themselves into a nation for national purposes. They instituted, for such purposes, a national Government, complete in all its parts, with powers Legislative, Executive and Judiciary; and, in all those powers, extending over the whole nation. Is it congruous, that, with regard to such purposes, any man or body of men, any person natural or artificial, should be permitted to claim successfully an entire exemption from the jurisdiction of the national Government? Would not such claims, crowned with success, be repugnant to our very existence as a nation?—*CHISHOLM V. GEORGIA*, 1793

If you accede to the claim of the federal judiciary, you will be accessory in overturning the federal government and establishing in its stead an *Imperial* one. If you do not oppose it you will surrender the sovereignty of the people of Massachusetts . . . to a *foreign* power. . . . If you submit to the demand, you will authorize a foreign jurisdiction, to exercise a power, which can never be exercised by it, but to the destruction of your own power; to the overthrow of the state governments; to the consolidation of the Union; for the purposes of arbitrary power; to the destruction of liberty, and the subversion of the *Rights of the People*. —"BRUTUS," 1793

WHEN U.S. SUPREME COURT JUSTICE JAMES WILSON delivered his opinion on the fundamental and "radical" question, "Do the people of the United States form a NATION?" he answered with a resounding "Yes." He had arrived at his question by considering the claims of Alexander Chisholm, who sued the State of Georgia for nonpayment of a contract that dated to the war. Georgia claimed the debt had been paid, and refused to acknowledge a summons to appear in federal court to resolve the matter. Wilson was not yet concerned with the merits of Chisholm's case; rather, he was disturbed by the recalcitrance of Georgia. Georgia did not recognize the jurisdiction of the Court in this matter, and was, as Wilson noted, "claiming to be Sovereign."

Georgia did not appear in court, arguing that its sovereignty predated the Constitution. After all, the Constitution had only been ratified in 1788, while Georgia had been an independent state since 1776. Even with ratification, Georgia argued that the Constitution represented a limited grant of power, not a prescription for dependence, and the "more perfect" Union was not an all-powerful national government with cognizance over the internal affairs of Georgia. Certainly the state could not be forced to receive instructions from the bar of the Supreme Court to do the bidding of a handful of justices. Georgia was independent and *sovereign.*

But the justices agreed with Wilson 4 to 1, rejecting Georgia's assertion of sovereignty.[1] Chief Justice John Jay even went so far as to say that Georgia was like any other corporate municipality in the United States—the city of Philadelphia or a mutual aid society, for example—with no more right to claim sovereign immunity than any other incorporated body of citizens. The United States was a nation of equal citizens, Jay noted, not an aristocracy of blended privileges and immunities. In a nation, one judicial authority *had* to be supreme, and the highest U.S. federal court had the name to back up its claims. But the states were so outraged by the implications of this decision, they amended the Constitution, specifically denying the Supreme Court the ability to hold states accountable in any suits, "either in law or equity." So what of Wilson's "radical" question? *Did* the people of the United States form a nation? Not yet.

The problem of getting the thirteen independent states to recognize themselves as beholden to a national people, and thereby allow their own authority to diminish in the face of new and untested national institutions, represented the most enduring problem of American citizenship in the early republic. Indeed, the conflicts over the relative equality of citizens that characterized the fights of the early war years came to depend on who, *ultimately,* controlled the lives and laws of the citizenry, and that question fell upon the problem of how authority and power were distributed among diverse peoples collected in separate states, all part of the American nation. The problem of citizenship in the United States therefore became directly intertwined with the problem of the national state: Did the American nation have a national government? To what extent would national institutions impact the daily lives, liberties, and properties of the American citizenry? To whom could individual citizens finally appeal their grievances, or their sense of inequality? Who ultimately interpreted the law?

There had been no resolution to this problem from the very beginning; in fact, there had been deep ambiguity. The ambivalence speaks to the fluid meaning of the many forms of government under consideration by the Americans. In the eighteenth century, "Empires," "Nations," "Confederacies," "States," and "Unions" could reflect distinct *types* of governments—but not always. "Britain" could be at once a Union, a Confederacy of kingdoms, an Empire of peoples, a National fiscal-military state, or simply "England" writ large. When Americans began debating the character of their own Union, they had in mind a variety of forms, all pointing to some kind of federal solution, in the eighteenth-century understanding of the term—they sought not a particular type of government but a Union of equal partners sharing a mutual interest and therefore a sympathetic connection. Within this broad compass, the early debates over the nature of the American Confederacy in the 1770s, which occurred over a long period of time ("from day to day, & time to time for two years"), were often burdened with references to numerous types of federal Unions, ancient and modern, permanent and temporary. John Witherspoon called upon the examples of the United Kingdom, ancient Sparta, the Roman Empire, the East India Company (which behaved as sovereign as any state in the eighteenth century), and the Dutch Republic to draw out the distinctions between an "incorporating Union & a federal Union." He wished for a Union wholly federal, by which he meant that the states "ought to be thought of as individuals."[2]

In these debates over the Articles of Confederation, the federal origins—as opposed to the national origins—of the alliance of the United States comes into close focus. The first definitive statement in the Articles of Confederation about the location of ultimate sovereignty came in April of 1777. Here, Thomas Burke from North Carolina successfully amended a guiding provision of the draft Articles that originally reserved to the states only "the power of regulating internal police," a limit that Burke believed "reigned in every other power." Noting that "it appeared to me this is not what the States expected," Burke insisted upon a provision in the Articles which "held up the principle, that all sovereign Power was in the States, separately," and that, with the exception of "carefully enumerated powers," each state would "exercise all the rights and powers of sovereignty uncontrolled." Burke was happy to give Congress "power enough to call out and apply the common strength for the common defense," but he was loath to allow an amalgamation of power in the Congress, "for the partial purpose of ambition."[3] Burke's clause was only opposed by James Wilson of Pennsylvania and Richard Henry Lee of Virginia, and eventually it became the second article of the Articles of Confederation—the first U.S. Constitution. So the states would retain "sovereignty," except for "carefully enumerated powers"—a fact only reinforced by the long problem of ratifying the Articles, which was not completed until the spring of 1781, when Maryland had to be pressured by the French to finally join the Union.

Even so, throughout these many debates over the nature of the Confederacy—bound up as they were with the practical problems of fighting the war, raising revenue, and coordinating a novel diplomacy—a small but vocal minority of continental leaders began advocating for a more centralized, consolidated government. They sought a national state that possessed an ultimate sovereign power, one that escaped the problem of *imperium in imperio*—of a government within a government. John Adams early on suggested that the Congress represented "the people" as a whole, and that the individuality of the colonies was "a mere sound." The question was not, Adams noted, "what we are now," but what the alliance should become: "one common mass." James Wilson showed his inclinations as well. He rejected the notion that Congress was little more than the diplomatic body of the states, arguing that it should be a truly national institution, as "the objects of its care are all the individuals of the states." He thought it absurd that "annexing the name of 'State' to ten thousand men, should give them an equal right with forty thousand." Such a phenomenon was the "effect of magic, not of reason." According to Wilson, "If any government could speak the will of all, it would be perfect; and that so far as it departs from this it becomes imperfect." He wanted one ultimate power to decide the needs and policy of the nation.[4] But the British Parliament had asserted just such supremacy in the Declaratory Act of 1766, and very few colonies were ready to re-create the British Supreme Parliament in America. As Burke noted, "This is not what the States expected" from their Congress.

The litany of problems that followed the Peace of 1783, all of which played some role in the growing desire to strengthen the Union, is well known. Absence of an effective trade policy, either to protect American crafts or to promote American produce abroad, left commerce weak and unstable, fluctuating and depressed. An inability to raise revenue—a result of the dislocation of trade, a new absence of specie, and the increasing recalcitrance of the states—made the pleas of Congress as foolish as they were weak. A centrifugal tendency toward disunion tugged at the boundaries of the country, as settlers split off into their own republics (like Vermont, or the "State of Franklin" in far western North Carolina); began taking oaths to the king of Spain so they could trade at New Orleans; fought with Indians; or simply squatted on their own terms—a trend that was not yet checked by the successful passage of the Northwest Ordinance. Diplomacy rapidly deteriorated into a series of pleas for short-term loans to pay interest on war debt. Meanwhile, British forts in American territory remained British, and the Spanish continued to refuse to open the Mississippi to American commerce. Persistent disagreement and confusion over the jurisdictions of the states led to title conflicts, land disputes, and even border feuds, which all fed a growing concern that the American republics were on the brink of dissolution and war. Within the states themselves, there was a perception of simple majoritarianism running wild over decency, property, and, as James Madison put it, "the rights and interests of the minority, or of individuals."[5] And then came Shays's Rebellion, which only heightened the immediate stakes of portentous anarchy.[6]

These endemic problems—of trade, of taxation, of Western disorder, of the authority of law at all levels, and of the fragility of the economic system—were both old and new. Similar pressures had exacerbated the conflicts between the British ministry and the colonies in the 1760s. The men who met in Philadelphia in 1787 were hoping to diminish the potential for continuing revolution, conflict, and inevitable disunion, and they were continuing to participate in the longer-range problem of Anglo-America in the second half of the eighteenth century: how to govern an extended and rapidly growing polity.

A small minority of men who had always hoped for a truly national government saw in the momentum to reform the Articles of Confederation a chance to diminish the pretensions of the states. Henry Knox, a leading advocate for a stronger national state, understood implicitly the conflicts fomented by the citizenship revolution, over the meaning of equality and the problem of nationhood. As he noted, the problem of nationhood looked like the more difficult dimension of the two: "The State systems are the accursed thing which might prevent our being a nation. The democracy might be managed, nay, it would remedy itself after being sufficiently fermented; but the vile State governments are sources of pollution, which will contaminate the American name for ages—machines that must produce ill, but cannot produce good; smite them in the name of God and all the people."[7] "Democracy" might be managed, but the states, as "sovereign" governments, needed to be annihilated. The "American name"—the existence of the nation—was at stake.

Some of the advocates for a more perfect Union took this stark position, that the nation would only survive by crushing the states, "in the name of God and all the people"—but not many. Most who desired to reform the Union, like George Washington, considered the problem in less clear terms. Complaining of the aggressive autonomy of the states, the imbecility of Congress, the potential for continuing revolution, anarchy, civil war, and, ultimately, despotism, Washington did not believe that America "can exist long as a nation without having lodged some where a power, which will pervade the whole Union in as energetic a manner, as the authority of the State Governments extends over the several States." Failure to do so meant certain disaster and "a triumph for the advocates of despotism," who argued that "we are incapable of governing ourselves, and that systems based upon the basis of equal liberty are merely ideal and fallacious!"[8] Thomas Jefferson thought even differently, as he counseled his friends on the coming Constitutional Convention. Writing to Madison before the convention, Jefferson argued that any reform of the Articles of Confederation should attempt to "make us one nation as to foreign concerns, & to keep us distinct in Domestic ones." Such a formula "gives the outline of the proper division of power between the general and particular governments."[9] Annihilating the states was not, necessarily, the only way to reform the Union.

But, although many of the men who gathered in Philadelphia in 1787 hoped, like Washington, to establish one power "some where" which would "pervade the whole," the Constitution as written and ratified left the matter strangely ambiguous. The series of compromises necessary to reform the Union, and to satisfy all the interests of the states at the Constitutional Convention of 1787, had assured the continued importance of the states in the Union, even designing them as a check on centralized national power. After the convention disbanded, as the fight over ratification was about to begin in earnest, James Madison admitted that they had failed to solve this fundamental problem, despite the clear evidence that confederacies, historically, had continually suffered by the inability to find an ultimate arbiter of sovereign authority, or at least a "controuling power" which could keep the parts in balance. A lack of such a power had destroyed numerous confederacies, and had driven others into constant confusion and war, from the Amphyction Confederacy in ancient Greece to that of the Holy Roman Empire. Madison admitted that the new Constitution, although providing more power in the central government, and attempting to draw out clear limits on those powers, still presented the "evil of imperia in imperio," which, unless remedied, would assure instability in the Union. In fact,

Madison noted that his theory of "extending the sphere" of republican government—to counteract the inevitable disruptions of faction and simple majoritarian rule—would only work with a neutral arbiter somewhere at the top. He would excise these doubts from his Federalist No. 10, putting on the best case he could.[10]

So, far from resolving the issue, the Constitution exacerbated the problem. While the states certainly held ultimate control under the Articles, the Constitution created new institutions with national reach: a national legislature, executive, and judiciary—powerful new agents that could compete with state and local governments for the legitimacy to govern America. Within these institutions existed the latent power to resolve the question of ultimate authority in the Union—power feared by the anti-federalists. Only in the political contests over control of these new institutions, in the fights to limit and expand the nature of the new American state, would the character of American citizenship and nationhood be drawn for succeeding generations.

The case of *Chisholm v. Georgia,* and the subsequent rapid passage of the Eleventh Amendment to the Constitution, occurred in the midst of this increasingly bitter politics over the future direction of the new national state. It was a crucial continuation of the Founding moment, greatly underplayed in the standard histories of the politics of the 1790s. The decision in *Chisholm* and the passage of the Eleventh Amendment—as important as *any* amendment to the Constitution before the Civil War—were inextricably linked to fights over the meaning of the American Revolution itself, and they created a lasting legacy.

The simplest way to understand the emerging contest over the direction of the new national state created by the Constitution, and its impact on the future meaning of American nationhood and citizenship, is through the breakdown in the consensus of the authors of the Federalist Papers—Alexander Hamilton, James Madison, and John Jay, together writing as "Publius." As these few true propagandists for the ratification of the Constitution stopped being promoters and began being leading politicians within the country's new national institutions—the executive, legislative, and judiciary branches, respectively—it rapidly became clear that they possessed distinct notions of the relationship of these institutions of the national state to the Constitution, to the state governments, to the rights of individual citizens, and, finally, to the purpose and meaning of the American Revolution. Publius had a multiple personality disorder. The problems of governing America shattered the federalist coalition that had supported ratification, and created the contours of American political debate for the next decade:

a fight over conflicting visions of the type of national state which best suited the people of America and which best realized the ongoing purpose of the Revolution.

The Minister and the Virginians: The National State against the Constitution

Alexander Hamilton and James Madison, the two leading minds behind Publius, who together wrote eighty of the eighty-five Federalist essays, possessed starkly different visions about the type of state the United States should become. Hamilton wished to re-create a British-inspired fiscal-military state, and to extinguish the importance and influence of the state governments gradually—with the general government eventually dominating, guiding, and controlling all aspects of American governance. Madison rejected such a vision, believing the new Constitution provided a good blueprint for an extended republican system—a "compound republic": a government "partly national and partly federal," a "feudal system of republics" in which the states retained "a residual and inviolable sovereignty" in the face of a *limited* national government. Under the Constitution, Madison noted, "the powers delegated by the proposed Constitution to the federal government are few and defined," while the powers held by the "state governments" were "numerous and indefinite," extending to "all the objects" which "concern the lives, liberties, and properties of the people, and the internal order, improvement, and prosperity of the States."[11]

Hamilton detested the Constitution for precisely these reasons. By 1787, he believed that the only solution for America was an energetic national government and the effectual destruction of state sovereignty and state power. From Hamilton's perspective, the power of the states weakened the potential strength of the whole country, distorted the common good of the whole people in the service of particular interests, and inhibited the growth of truly national feelings among the citizenry—emotional attachments necessary for stability and order. As things stood under the Articles of Confederation, all of the passions and interests that bound the citizenry into willing obedience fell "into the current of the States," and did not "flow in the stream of the Genl. Govt."[12] As Hamilton argued at the beginning of the convention: "We must establish a general and national government, completely sovereign, and annihilate the state distinctions and state operations; and unless we do this, no good purpose can be answered."[13] While the states might be retained as "distinct tribunals" for "local purposes," they should nevertheless be "reduced to corporations, and with very limited powers."[14] Although he supported ratification of the Constitution as a final "chance of good" against inevitable "anarchy and Convulsion," he admitted at the end of the Constitutional Convention that "no man's ideas were more remote from the plan than his [own] were known to be."[15] He would carry his distain for the Constitution throughout the next decade, noting in 1802, out of power, that it was but a "frail and worthless document."[16]

But all was not lost. The potential for a truly powerful national state existed in embryo in the design of the executive branch of the new government. Hamilton recognized that the "administration of government"—understood to be the conduct of foreign affairs, the design and execution of fiscal policy, "the application and disbursement of the public monies in conformity of the general approbation of the legislature," the management of the army and navy, and the direction of "operations of war"—was nicely centralized in the executive branch.[17] Effective execution of a properly designed policy could serve to "extinguish State Governments gradually."[18] So Hamilton did not run for any elective office under the Constitution, because he wanted to administer the government from the Department of Treasury.[19] In the Treasury he could implement his plan for the financial stability and prosperity of the country, the essential purpose of statecraft that he believed, if managed properly, would attach the interest of individuals throughout the country to the national state and help assure the growth of national loyalties, patriotism, and solidarity. "Imagining a nation" was never enough—the interests of the people needed to be bound together with the power of the state.

To achieve his ends, Hamilton designed a system of public finance centered on the creation of a permanent national debt, which would serve to transfer creditor interest from the states to the national government. The debt would be managed and augmented by a National Bank, as a "necessary auxiliary" to serve as "an indispensable engine in the administration of the finances," and the whole system would be accompanied by an aggressive plan for government investment in commercial agriculture, internal and external trade, transportation, and mixed-scale manufacturing, which Hamilton believed would blend the different sentiments of the country into "one great common cause" that would result in "the perfect harmony of all the parts." Sectional differences and rivalries would melt away in the face of an abiding national concern.[20] The plans reflected his vision of how the citizenry could be taught to love their new government, how the power of the states could be effectively destroyed, and how the "frail and worthless" Constitution could be vigorously interpreted into the fundamental law of a strong, wealthy, and powerful national state. At root, his policies were based upon an enthusiasm to establish a system of finance and administration that emulated the success and stability of the British fiscal state of the eighteenth century; only then did he believe that American nationhood could ever achieve stability and diminish the potential problems of local diversity and antagonism he lamented in 1787.

Along with his plans came the centralization of political influence in his own hands, and an aggressive influence on policy in all departments. By 1792, his patronage extended across the Union, and included the comptroller, the auditor, numerous clerks, all the customs officials, surveyors and inspectors of the revenue, port inspectors, commissioners of loans, officers of the revenue cutters, and even the numerous employees of the post office—commanding a total compensation from the national state amounting to nearly $300,000.[21] Within a year, Hamilton gained control of the patronage of the Excise Department, which he carefully designed and with which he intended to extend his influence into the backcountry.[22] To fight for his agenda, Hamilton cultivated and mobilized a group of supporters in Congress, most of whom were rewarded and connected to the Hamiltonian state.[23] Notable among friends and allies of Hamilton in Congress were the initial directors of the National Bank, including South Carolinian William Loughton Smith, who championed Hamiltonianism in the House of Representatives; New Yorker Rufus King, who led Hamilton's program in the Senate; and the scions of New England Federalism, Congressman Fisher Ames and Senator George Cabot.[24] Writing speeches, drafting legislation, participating on congressional committees, assembling majorities, by 1792 Hamilton was behaving as prime minister. He considered the emerging opposition to the government as an assault upon "my administration." When defending his system, he spoke of himself in the third person, as "the Minister."[25]

Hamilton needed to marshal his political support, because the opposition to his plans, centered around James Madison and Madison's Virginia allies, quickly gained organizational force. In the states and in Congress, erstwhile anti-federalists and many federalists viewed Hamilton's schemes as the dread realization of their fears of the consolidating tendencies of the U.S. Constitution. Hamilton anticipated this opposition, worried constantly about the motives and intentions of those who rejected his vision of the country, and worried about the large states, whose size, population, and power threatened to dominate the whole with their particular interests. In 1790, the biggest of the states by a large margin was Virginia, which possessed one-fifth of the entire population of the Union and participated in one-third of the commerce of the United States. In accordance with Hamilton's prophetic concerns, leading Virginians—in the state, in the federal legislature, and in the executive department—led the attack on his authority.

The antagonism of some Virginians to Hamilton's vision of the national state drew upon several tendencies of thought and interest—economic, political, and ideological. First, Virginians did not invest in the national debt at the same rate as those in other parts of the Union. As the planter George Lee Turberville noted, "The example set by Great Britain," of providing for the debt with a permanent loan to bondholders, "will never answer in America." Not, at least, until the country "becomes as thickly populated—as commercial and as highly Cultivated as G. Britain." Indeed, why would a man in Virginia, where money was so dear, settle for 6 percent or 4 percent interest on "ready money"? Turberville believed that unimproved land bought in the Tidewater would be a more profitable investment for any man with money to spare.[26] In fact, in 1795, Virginians received only $62,000 annually from the interest on government securities, while the citizens of Massachusetts received over $300,000.[27] So Virginians' taxes went to other parts of the Union.

But the funding system was not only seen as "unjust in Principle," it also was "baneful in its Effects." As the governor of Virginia, Beverly Randolph, warned James Madison, the people of the state considered Hamilton's plan as "intending in Effect to produce a perfectly consolidated Government."[28] When Virginia legislators decried the assumption of state debts by Congress, calling the act "unconstitutional," they complained of the effect it would have on their ability to manage their own finances. The House of Delegates resolved that the assumption of the state's debts was needless interference, and was "dangerous to the rights and subversive to the interest of the people."[29] Hamilton's funding plan would assure the eventual "prostration of agriculture at the foot of commerce," and it would lead to "a change in the present form of federal government" into one much more *national*—a change they considered "fatal to the existence of American liberty."[30] Despite their paper resistance, the Virginians quickly lowered state taxes, providing no resources for the state's creditors. As the auditor of the Treasury Department, Oliver Wolcott Jr., noted derisively, without a rival system of funding the "opinion of the [Virginia] legislature is not of much importance."[31] He was right. The initial state resistance remained rhetorical.

James Madison had been unable to stop Congress from interfering with the Virginians because his fellow Virginian, Thomas Jefferson, secretary of the Department of State, had used the controversial bill to broker a deal to place the new federal capital on the Potomac. It was a deal Jefferson came to rue. He later claimed that he "was duped

[by] the Secretary of the treasury, and made a tool for forwarding his schemes"—schemes that were, as Jefferson admitted, "not then sufficiently understood by me."[32] The scales fell from Jefferson's eyes as Hamilton presented his future plans for the maintenance of public credit: the establishment of an excise tax to supplement the imposts already being collected, and the creation of a National Bank. This program was unveiled in the fall and winter of 1790–91, a period that coincided with Jefferson's first reading of Madison's notes of the debates of the Constitutional Convention. In these extensive notes, Jefferson certainly saw the character of Hamilton's speech and plan to the convention: his lusty celebrations of the British Constitution, his proposals for a lifetime Executive and Senate, his desire to diminish the significance of the states, and his eager endorsement of the use of "influence" to secure prominent individuals to the government.[33] From the introduction of the Bank Bill, Jefferson consistently worked in concert with Madison to stop Hamilton.

Jefferson and Madison informed their opposition by drawing upon shared understandings of the peculiar demands of a republican citizenry, the unique promise of a land-rich America to realize that republican citizenry, the role of the Constitution in securing that republican promise, and the ongoing potential of Revolutionary rights of individuals for the betterment of society. The fierceness of their opposition to Hamilton was based upon a generally correct—if exaggerated—understanding of Hamilton's intention to re-create the British fiscal and administrative national state in the United States, and on a fundamental belief that Hamilton's strong national state was a rejection of the federal balance of the Constitution, a balance intended to secure the blessings of republican government and individual rights for which, they believed, Independence had been fought. Hamilton's plan upset the balance of the Union and betrayed the whole purpose of the American Revolution.[34]

Outraged by the probable effects of Hamilton's system on the economic equality of the American citizenry, and disgusted by Hamilton's seeming infatuation with large-scale manufacturing, the Virginians were most immediately concerned with the effect of the new fiscal state on the delicate balance of power and liberty intended by the Constitution, as they understood it. The gist of the problem was Hamilton's aggressive creation of a permanent national funded debt, which inevitably created an interested group of politicians tied to the policy of the bank and the executive branch. The fact that the debt connected interested people to the government was precisely the problem. Madison subscribed to the belief that "a Public Debt is a Public curse," and a "greater" curse in a republican or representative government "than in any other."[35] By Jefferson's reasoning, Hamilton's plan increased the national debt by a needless one-third by assuming the state debts, and further increased the debt by unfavorable purchases on the market.[36] Jefferson believed that Hamilton desired the debt to remain unpaid, so that it could be used as "a thing wherewith to corrupt and manage the legislature."[37] Madison, for his part, saw the moneyed interest as "the pretorian band of the government—at once its tools and its tyrants; bribed by its largesse, and overawing it by clamors and combinations."[38] In his battles against the Treasury Department in the legislature, Madison began to believe that "he could at all times discover a sympathy between the speeches and the pockets of all those members of Congress who held certificates."[39] With a corrupt party in the legislature, extensive influence throughout the executive branch, and massive patronage throughout the country, Jefferson warned Washington that "the department of the treasury possessed already such an influence as to swallow up the whole of the Executive powers."[40] Jefferson and Madison saw what Hamilton was doing and imagined in his power the gradual destruction of republican government. Protecting their vision of the Constitution—and the Union that it created—became their driving ambition.[41]

Jefferson and Madison accused Hamilton of attempting to subvert the states through his expansive and flexible constructions of the Constitution, an accusation that Hamilton did not deny. As he wrote to Edward Carrington in defense of his constructions of the Constitution, "If the States were all the size of Connecticut, Maryland or New Jersey, I should decidedly regard the local Governments as both safe & useful." Unfortunately, "as the thing now is the Government of the U States will not be able to maintain itself against" state influence. Already, the influence of the large states was "penetrating the National Councils & perverting their direction." "Hence," he concluded, "a disposition on my part towards a liberal construction of the powers of the National Government."[42] So Hamilton admitted what Jefferson and Madison charged: Hamilton's liberal construction of the Constitution was fundamentally connected to his belief that the states needed to be reduced to mere local tribunals.

Why was the balance of the Union so important to Jefferson and Madison? Consider Jefferson's recommendations for the proper route to resist the Bank Bill, which he and Madison both believed to be an unconstitutional assertion of powers not granted to the federal government. Although he initially thought highly of a plan to establish a rival "agricultural" bank in Richmond, he rejected such action by the state of

Virginia in favor of more dramatic measures. He considered a rival state bank to be a mere "milk and water measure," which was highly "objectionable" and "unworthy of the Virginia assembly." What would he recommend? In an extraordinary note, charged with a bitter feeling of a recent, unsatisfying meeting with George Washington, he suggested to Madison that "the assembly should reason thus":

> The power of erecting banks and corporations was not given to the general government it remains then within the state itself. For any person to recognize a foreign legislature in a case belonging to the state itself, is an act of *treason* against the state, and whosoever shall do any act under the colour of the authority of a foreign legislature whether by signing notes, issuing or passing them, acting as a director, cashier or any office relating to it shall be judged guilty of high treason and suffer death accordingly, by the judgment of the state courts. This is the only opposition worthy of our state, and the only kind which can be effectual.

Here the "foreign legislature" is, of course, the U.S. Congress. Such a striking assertion of the limited nature of the powers of the general government, and of the proper consequences of federal usurpation of powers—by the U.S. secretary of state, no less—implied a highly decentralized notion of the Union, with a federal state strictly controlled in its legitimate sphere: a mere shadow of a national state.

Such opinions, uttered in haste and anger, are not wonderful constitutional guides, to be sure, but they nevertheless speak to the importance that the Virginian agrarians put to the state governments, in their conception of the true nature of the American republic, and ultimately in the local control of the boundaries of American citizenship. Jefferson wanted the "counter-rights of the states" to be protected at all cost—even to the tranquillity of the Union.[43] Madison never indulged in the extremes of such talk of resistance, but he shared with Jefferson a commitment to an extremely limited national state under the Constitution, and to a citizenship largely defined by relationships to state authority. Madison's "compound republic" highlighted the continuing role of the states in the meaning of American nationhood, as the states were meant to control all the power that extends to "the lives, liberties, and properties of the people." Both Madison and Jefferson believed a federal Union instituted to protect the principles of the Revolution—the natural rights of man—was much more important than the relative wealth and national strength of the central government: they believed America should be a Revolutionary federal republic.

There were other voices of assent and dissent in the formative years of state creation after the ratification of the Constitution—not surprisingly, since a large portion, perhaps even a majority, of the political community did not support ratification of the Constitution as drafted in convention. John Adams possessed his own unique view of his place in the government as vice president and never really approved of the direction that Hamilton attempted to take the new national state. Adams possessed political allies who felt the same way. Other voices, both popular and elite, from all regions of the country, criticized Hamilton's policies and administration.[44] Yet the mainspring of political combat in the new institutions initially emerged from the clash of Hamilton's vision and administration of a powerful national fiscal state with the fears and beliefs of Madison in the House and Jefferson in the executive branch. But what of the "non-political" branch of government? Perhaps the jurists of the nation could resolve the fundamental conflicts over the direction of the national state.

The Premier: John Jay and the National Citizen

Like Madison and Hamilton, John Jay participated in the drafting of the Federalist Papers. As originally conceived, Jay expected to write many more than the five essays (Nos. 2, 3, 4, 5, and 64) that he produced, and he was well qualified to do so. In 1787 he was more accomplished than Madison and Hamilton combined. He had served as a leader of the moderates during the Continental Congress of 1774–76, and as president of the Congress of 1777–78, and with John Adams and Benjamin Franklin had helped negotiate the Treaty of Paris that ended the war in 1783. He had drafted the constitution of the state of New York, which served as one important guide for the framers in Philadelphia, and at the time of the convention he served as the secretary of foreign affairs. Yet Jay was too sick to work in the winter and spring of 1787.[45] So with the exception of his few essays as Publius and a moderately interesting tract, *An Address to the People of the State of New York,* the main work of pamphlet advocacy for the Constitution fell to others.[46] Given his extensive experience, however, Washington offered Jay his choice of offices in his administration. While rumors placed Jay in both the Treasury Department and the Department of State, Jay had his eye on the Supreme Court. As chief justice, presiding in a gown of black silk with white and salmon-hued facings, Jay stood apart from the other men on the bench, projecting so much authority that Attorney General Edmund Randolph disparagingly nicknamed him "the Premier."[47]

After his appointment as chief justice, Jay continued to serve as an informal counselor to Washington and Hamilton in the initial organization of the new government, and he led support for the new government in New York. He possessed better political instincts than Hamilton, took insults less personally, and interpreted national political conflicts with more patience. When the Virginia General Assembly passed its resolutions declaring the funding and assumption programs "unconstitutional" and "dangerous to the rights and subversive to the interest of the people," it was Jay who counseled Hamilton to ignore them. Hamilton pressed for swift action by the national state, arguing that the resolutions were "the first symptom of a spirit which must either be killed or will kill the constitution of the United States." Hamilton thought that the "collective weight of the different parts of the Government" should be mobilized to defeat the principles of the resolutions.[48] But Jay, sensing the impotency of the threats of the assembly, argued that "the national Govt has only to do what is right and if possible be silent." The "indecent" actions of the state governments would "diminish their Influence" without an improvident display of national authority.[49] Hamilton continued to rely on Jay's advice and acumen.

As the first chief justice of the Supreme Court, Jay sought to assert the jurisdiction of the national court over the states, and to maintain the independence of the judiciary against the encroachments of both Congress and the executive branch. Unlike Hamilton, who had little desire to maintain a strict separation of the powerful departments in his new administrative fiscal state, Jay possessed a strong inclination to separate the powers of the branches. As he wrote to Washington before the Constitutional Convention, he would not support a new government that did not "divide the sovereignty into its proper departments." Any new system must, at a minimum, "let Congress legislate—let others execute—let others judge."[50] In fact, at a circuit court, in April of 1792, Jay presided over the first rejection of a congressional law that specifically involved the division of powers. The offending law, passed by Congress on March 23, 1792, required the justices to sit in judgment of the claims of invalid pensions and allowed the secretary of war and the Congress to revise their findings. Arguing that "neither the Legislative nor the Executive branch can constitutionally assign to the Judicial any duties but such as are properly judicial, and to be performed in a judicial manner," Jay and his court refused to uphold the law.[51]

The Jay Court similarly strove to maintain the authority of the national judiciary over the states. In a series of circuit court cases beginning in Connecticut as early as May of 1791, Jay and his court struck down state laws that breached the contract clause of the Constitution or violated the treaty obligations of the United States. But no case was more important in Jay's brief tenure on the Court than the case of *Chisholm v. Georgia*, and no opinion promised such a swift transformation in the relationship between the states and the Court than Jay's opinion in that case.

The case involved the suit of the executors of the estate of Robert Farquhar, a merchant from Charleston, South Carolina, against the State of Georgia for payment of a debt that dated to 1777.[52] In that year, Georgia had authorized two commissioners of the state, Thomas Stone and Edward Davies, of Savannah, to find supplies for a large American army, under the command of General James Jackson, encamped near Savannah. Stone and Davies contracted with Farquhar for a vast array of goods—cloth, thread, silk, handkerchiefs, nankeen, blankets, coats, jackets—for the large sum of $169,613.33. Farquhar fulfilled his end of the bargain and delivered the goods on November 3, 1777. At that point, things went astray. The state legislature provided Stone and Davies with Continental Loan Office certificates in the necessary amount to pay Farquhar, but Farquhar never received the money. What happened to the money—whether it was missing because of confusion, error, deceit, incompetence, or greed on the part of Stone and Davies—is unknown. In 1784, Robert Farquhar died without having received the funds, and his cause was taken up by his executors—John Farquhar, Peter Dean, and Alexander Chisholm—on behalf of Elizabeth Farquhar.

The group of executors, aided in 1789 by Elizabeth's new husband, Peter Trezevant, tried numerous avenues to receive payment for the old debt. Finally, after the state legislature refused again to pay the claim of Robert Farquhar, the executors (led now by Alexander Chisholm) brought suit against the state in the U.S. circuit court for the District of Georgia. Georgia defied a summons to appear in court and denounced the intended suit. Governor Edward Telfair argued that Georgia was "a free, sovereign and independent State," which could not be "compelled" to answer "before any Justices of the federal Circuit Court," or before "any Justices of any Court of Law or Equity whatsoever."[53] When the case was heard, both Supreme Court Justice James Iredell and District Judge Nathaniel Pendleton agreed with the state. Chisholm and his friends were not to be denied, however, and they immediately appealed the decision to the Supreme Court. Summons on Georgia were issued from Philadelphia on February 8, 1792, for an appearance on August 11, 1792. Georgia failed to respond to the summons, and the Court postponed the case until the following winter term.[54]

The case began on February 5, 1793, with the presentation of the "written remonstrance and protestation" on behalf of Georgia, delivered by Alexander Dallas and Jared Ingersoll.[55] Asked to make a case, they declined. Georgia did not recognize the jurisdiction of the Supreme Court and had given Dallas and Ingersol "positive instructions" that prescribed their role to that of mere presenters of Georgia's protest. With Georgia offering no defense, Attorney General Edmund Randolph developed a long argument pursuing the question at hand: "whether a state could be sued by one or more individuals of another state." Basing his answer on largely technical issues of construction and interpretation, he answered the question in the affirmative with a two-and-a-half-hour speech. Nonetheless, as he closed, he noted that he hoped the question would not become the fodder of politics, declaring that "no degradation of sovereignty" in the states would result from their submission to the Supreme Court. In fact, he was emphatic that he did not wish to challenge any of the rights of the states. As he noted, "Some may call this an attempt to consolidate." He wanted to assure the skeptics that "the prostration of State-rights is no object with me." He had no "covered stratagem" to destroy the states.[56]

The justices generally agreed with his concern for the feeling of the public, and they authorized an extraordinary debate. Seeing the "importance of the subject now before them" and "the necessity of obtaining every possible light on it," they opened up the Court to any "gentleman of the bar" who might wish to "take up the gauntlet in opposition to the attorney general." But no man rose to the challenge, and the Court began its deliberations. Fourteen days later, "in the presence of a numerous and respectable audience," each justice delivered a separate decision from the bench, and supported the attorney general's position 4 to 1.[57]

In accordance with the argument made by Edmund Randolph, Justices William Cushing and John Blair believed the problem could be resolved by sticking to technical issues. Did the language of the Constitution and the Judiciary Act give the Supreme Court the power to adjudicate a conflict between a state and a citizen of another state? They both answered in the affirmative, suggesting that the language of the Constitution was really quite clear. As they each noted, the second section of the third article of the Constitution expressly extended the judiciary power to controversies "between a State and citizens of another state."[58] Arguing that the mere order of words had nothing to do with whether a state was defendant or plaintiff in a hypothetical case, they held that the Constitution clearly gave the Supreme Court the power to sit in judgment.

The lone dissenter in the case, and the first to speak, was Justice James Iredell of North Carolina. Iredell argued that the problem involved more than the mere question of whether a state could be sued or not, and he specifically worried about the ability of the Court to *compel* a state to pay damages. As he pointed out, a state may be a plaintiff quite happily, but if citizens of any state could sue a state as a defendant in the Supreme Court, and the state lost, a mechanism would need to be specified that would compel the state to abide by the decision of the Court. Since the legislature had provided no guidelines, it was dangerous to attempt to press a decision that might embarrass the Union by exposing the weakness of the Court. He could find no guide in statute, in common law, or in the law of nations that would clarify the issue, so he was disposed to argue against the exercise of the power without a specific policy assertion by the Congress. In addition, Iredell gave the states the benefit of an original sovereignty. As he noted, "A State does not owe its origin to the government of the United States, in the highest or in any of its branches," for the states were "in existence before it."[59] This fact complicated the issue even more, because the states retained powers separate from the jurisdiction of the general government; in many respects the states were "independent" of the general government. The Court needed to tread lightly into this confusing territory and wait for the legislature to act, so that the courts would not become the "makers of a new law" but rather the "expositors of an existing one."[60]

Iredell's concerns were significant, and they could not be satisfactorily answered by a mere technical assertion of constitutional sanction. But James Wilson and John Jay approached the problem from a much broader perspective, one that both challenged Iredell's notion of the sovereignty of states and confidently asserted the national authority of the Court. Justice James Wilson began his opinion with vigor, expanding the fundamental question before the Court into a basic question about the nature of the American constitutional order. As he stated:

> This is a case of uncommon magnitude. One of the parties to it is a STATE; certainly respectable, claiming to be Sovereign. The question to be determined is, whether this State, so respectable, and whose claims soar so high, is amenable to the jurisdiction of the Supreme Court of the United States? This question, important in itself, will depend on others, more important still; and, may, perhaps be ultimately resolved into one, no less radical than this—"do the people of the United States form a NATION?"[61]

Unfortunately, Wilson's clarity dissipated rapidly after this initial frame of the question. Wilson, in addition to being a justice of the Supreme Court, taught law at the College of Philadelphia, and the attorney general referred to him disparagingly as "the Professor." Like an academic dissertation, Wilson's decision ranged wildly across time and space—from ancient Troy and the "Ephori of Sparta," to Christopher Columbus and the kings of England, both Saxon and modern—and indulged in questions often beside and beyond the point.[62] As he noted after one particularly long passage in which he described the constituent parts of the British Parliament and decided that the "PEOPLE" are "No where!" to be found in that estimable institution, he admitted that "whether this description is or is not a just one, is a question of very different import."[63] His decision was, as one ally wrote, "more like an epic poem than a Judge's argument."[64]

Nevertheless, Wilson's decision did assert a broader foundation for the authority of the national judiciary than a mere technical construction of the Constitution. His argument was based upon the ultimate sovereignty of the people of the nation. State claims of "sovereignty," he considered extravagant and dangerous. "Is it congruous," he wondered, that any body of citizens or corporation, "any person natural or artificial," could claim a complete "exemption from the jurisdiction of the national government?" If such a claim were respected, it would be "repugnant to our very existence as a nation," and with the ratification of the Constitution, founded upon the broad sovereignty of the American people, all parties in the country were accountable to the jurisdiction of the national court.[65]

While Wilson's decision could answer the theoretical concerns of Iredell (if not the practical ones), the opinion that most people outside of the Court discussed was the opinion of Chief Justice Jay. Free of the academic fireworks of Wilson, yet broader and more comprehensive than the opinions of Blair and Cushing, Jay's opinion galvanized both supporters and opponents of the Court's decision. Like Wilson, Jay saw the question of nationhood implicit in the challenge of the State of Georgia, and he also approximated some of Wilson's reasoning, although toward a more coherent and forceful conclusion. Jay divided his decision into roughly two parts: first he examined the difference in the meaning of sovereignty in England and America after the Revolution, and second he examined the justice of the claims of a state to sovereign immunity under the Constitution, which he understood to be a wholly national compact.

Noting that Georgia claimed immunity from prosecution because "she is a Sovereign State," Jay began by tackling the meaning of sovereignty. Before Independence, the people of the colonies were subjects of the king of Great Britain, and "all the civil authority then existing or exercised here, flowed from the head of the British Empire."[66] To each other, the colonists were little more than fellow subjects, "in a strict sense," but "in a variety of respects," the Americans were "one people." Recognizing their nascent nationality, the American people united in common defense against the encroachments of Parliament, and by the time of the Declaration the people were already "united for general purposes," so the sovereignty of the king of Britain passed to the people of America. In this national history, therefore, the nation came before the states—a direct refutation of Justice Iredell and the remonstrance of Georgia. From the Declaration of Independence, Jay asserted, the American people continued to act and think "in a national point of view, as one people." This unity culminated in the ratification of the Constitution, which Jay—pointing to the Preamble—noted was established in the name of "the people of the United States." The sovereignty of the nation was therefore "in the people of the nation."[67]

The basis of Jay's decision rested on his belief that the American Revolution had transformed the meaning of sovereignty, at least as it applied to the new American nation. The meaning of popular sovereignty throughout the United States differed substantially from the principles of "princely sovereignty" in practice throughout most of Europe, including England. In the Old World, Jay asserted, sovereignty sprang from feudal principles that considered the "Prince as the Sovereign" and the people as his subjects. The Prince's person was the object of allegiance, and the Sovereign Prince was the "fountain of honor and authority," and "from his grace and grant derives all franchises, immunities and privileges." In Europe, the Sovereign and his regents possessed the right to rule and administered the state as an extension of that power. The Princely Sovereign therefore remained immune from suit in any "Court of Justice," for both the court and the execution of the court's decision could not exist without the mandate of the Sovereign.[68]

In America, the people, as citizens, were "joint-tenants in the sovereignty" of the whole nation, and the administrators of government were the mere agents of the people, with no powers or exemptions other than the authority of their offices. In regard to sovereignty, they were no different "than as private citizens."[69] There were no subjects in America (save, perhaps, as Jay noted, for "African slaves"), and "the citizens of America are equal as fellow citizens."[70] So where did that leave the states? For Jay, it left them no different from any large or incorporated group of citizens under the national umbrella. In fact, as he noted, he could see no reason why states possessed any more right of sovereign immunity than any other municipality in the country. As he continued:

> In this city [Philadelphia] there are forty odd thousand free citizens, all of whom may be collectively sued by any individual citizen. In the State of Delaware, there are fifty odd thousand free

> citizens, and what reason can be assigned why a free citizen who has demands against them should not prosecute them? Can the difference between forty odd thousand, and fifty odd thousand make any distinction as to right? . . . In this land of equal liberty, shall forty odd thousand in one place be compelled to do justice, and yet fifty odd thousand in another place be privileged to do justice only as they may think proper? Such objections would not correspond with the equal rights we claim; with the equality we profess to admire and maintain, and with that popular sovereignty in which every citizen partakes.[71]

Since sovereignty was held equally in the people of the nation, the citizenry must be equal across and regardless of state boundaries in their ability to secure justice in the highest court in the nation. Jay therefore utterly rejected the separate authority of the states, placing them in no higher regard than any local tribunal or municipal jurisdiction.

Jay's association of the Revolutionary meaning of popular sovereignty and equal citizenship under a national law promised a monumental precedent in American nation-building. His decision represented the most dramatic assertion of national power over the pretenses of state sovereignty that the Supreme Court would issue before the Civil War. Jay's claim reached beyond all of Marshall's most national-minded decisions. It was free of any ambiguity or the commitment to state power that Marshall would occasionally endorse.[72] Jay couched his belief that the states could be sued and forced to pay a settlement against a citizen to a strongly articulated nationalist history of the American Revolution and Constitution, one that provided very little space for state pretensions to sovereignty. In Jay's mind, the people had been united as a nation before Independence, so the independent states that followed came after the sovereignty of the British king had already devolved upon the united people of America. Jay's ruling pressed the implications of equal national citizenship under the law to limits that would not be reached until the passage of the Fourteenth Amendment.

For those who knew John Jay well, his decision did not come as much of a surprise. For one thing, Jay was comfortable insisting that the American people were truly a national people, distinct from any other on earth, with a divine sanction to govern themselves under a government of their own creation. In Federalist No. 2 he argued that "Providence has been pleased to give this one connected Country" to one nation—"a people" with "the same ancestors, speaking the same language, professing the same religion, attached to the same principles of government, very similar in their manners and customs." The country and people were "made for each other," and "as a nation we have made peace and war; as a nation we have vanquished our common enemies."[73] To realize the promise of self-governing nationhood, he had very little desire to emphasize sectional and local differences in a rigid (or even flexible) federal separation of powers. In 1785, as he considered the defects of the Articles of Confederation, Jay looked toward a national government that reduced the states to the status of mere municipalities. As he wrote to James Lowell, "It is my first Wish to see the United States assume and merit the Character of one Great Nation," in which the states remained as jurisdictions "merely for more convenient Government and the more easy and prompt administration of Justice," just as states were themselves subdivided into counties and townships.[74]

But for those who worried about these opinions of Jay's, and who wished to maintain the balance of the Union—realized in their own vision of the Constitution's purpose—Jay's decision outlined an ominous future for the states. In less than two years after he issued his argument from the bench, twelve states ratified an amendment to the Constitution that effectively overturned the decision of *Chisholm v. Georgia* and stripped the Supreme Court of any power to compel a state to respond to the suit of an individual.

Defending the States: The Passage of the Eleventh Amendment

The government did not possess any formal scheme to disseminate the opinions of the Court, and the first reports to appear in the newspapers were sketchy. Recognizing that the decision of the Court "may give umbrage to the Advocates of 'State sovereignty,'" the clerk of the court, Samuel Bayard, attempted to correct "erroneous" reports circulating in the papers by sending a summary of the case to the local newspapers.[75] The opinions themselves were published in a pamphlet under copyright and at a rather high cost (50¢), so the distribution of the opinions in the newspapers was much more limited than the normal proclamations, reports, resolutions, speeches, and laws of the other branches of the U.S. government, which routinely comprised the bulk of the newspaper content.[76] Nevertheless, the significance of the case did not go unnoticed.

The Hamiltonian and pro-government *Connecticut Courant* eagerly celebrated the decision, happy that the Court had fixed "a most material and rational feature in the judiciary of the United States."[77] It was John Jay's opinion that attracted attention. Jay's argument was in fact the only opinion published *in full* in the newspapers. As one paper asserted, the chief justice's opinion should be considered "one of the most clear, profound, and elegant arguments perhaps ever given in a court of judicature."[78] The *Salem Gazette,* one of the few newspapers to print Jay's complete opinion, congratulated the chief justice on "the great coolness, candor and regard to the rights of citizens" that characterized his decision, and it celebrated Jay for deciding the case on both constitutional and "national grounds."[79] The supporters of the decision of the Court generally followed Jay's line, emphasizing the weakness of the states in the face of national popular sovereignty and asserting the importance of holding the states accountable to justice. "Crito" expanded upon Jay's decision by pointing to the Preamble of the Constitution to emphasize the national nature of the new government ("We, the people"), placing the states in the role of corporations. Given the demands of equal citizenship, "Crito" thought that no "man or body of men ought to have an exclusive legal privilege of defrauding with impunity," and he could see no room for the claim of the states.[80] Rejecting complaints that the decision had stripped the states of their independence, another paper noted, "If by losing independence is meant losing the power of doing wrong, if setting justice and common sense at defiance, if oppressing the individual with the insulting reply that the State is above the law, lawless, then God be praised that such independence exists no longer." After all, the states were merely a collection of citizens, not divinely ordained institutions from whence all power flowed, and republican equality demanded that they could be held accountable before the national court.[81] Indeed, supporters of the Court's decision believed that complaints of "State Sovereignty and Independence" were "a mere political battering ram" intended to "beat down the walls" of the national state.[82]

But despite the enthusiasm of some partisans, a movement to overturn the decision began almost immediately, and was pursued throughout the country. The supporters of the Court's decision faced an immediate challenge because of the compelling memory of the recent "intent" expressed during the ratification debates. During the fight over ratification, numerous anti-federalists had specifically charged that the national judiciary would bring the states to trial and thereby destroy their sovereignty and independence. The proponents of the Constitution almost universally asserted that such a jurisdiction could never be implied in the new Constitution.[83] At the Virginia ratifying convention, for instance, when George Mason declared that the extent of the judiciary department would create "one great, national, consolidated government," James Madison quickly assured the delegates that it was "not in the power of individuals to call any state into court." A young John Marshall also replied to Mason, noting that "no gentleman will think that a state will be called before the bar of a Federal court."[84] Hamilton himself, in Federalist No. 81, had addressed this particular concern of the anti-federalists, and noted that even if the federal courts possessed jurisdiction, they could not enforce a suit by an individual against a state "without waging war against the contracting State." Therefore, to ascribe such a power to the federal courts "would be altogether forced and unwarrantable."[85] Now, with the decision of the Court in *Chisholm*, such a power had been positively asserted.

For opposition voices already concerned about the centralizing tendencies of the Hamiltonian fiscal state, the Court's decision offered new evidence that state sovereignty would be ultimately destroyed. One newspaper recognized that the decision "must excite serious ideas in those who have from the beginning been inclined to suspect that the absorption of the State governments has long been" the dark motive of many characters in the national government. Federal jurisprudence had often "aimed a blow at the sovereignty of individual States," and now the Supreme Court had "placed a ridgepole on the wide extended fabrick of consolidation."[86] Other newspapers complained that the decision "fritters away States to corporations."[87] An author writing as "Brutus" saw in the scheme of the Court "more danger to the liberties of America than the claims of the British Parliament to tax us without our consent." Brutus warned that if Americans "submit" to the Court, they would authorize a precedent that could "never be exercised [but] to the destruction of your own power," a precedent that would overthrow the state governments, lead "to the consolidation of the Union for the purpose of arbitrary power," and eventually overthrow the federal balance of the Constitution. The federal relationship must remain as a check on central power.[88] Finally, the newspapers hoped that the "free citizens of the independent States" and their representatives would oppose and overturn the decision of the Court.[89]

The official opposition to the Court's decision began immediately. On February 19, the day after the opinions of the justices were read from the bench, a resolution was introduced into the House of Representatives to amend the Constitution to protect states from any suit "in law or equity" in the federal courts. A similar resolution was introduced into the Senate the next day. With the session ending—Congress adjourned on March 3—no action was taken on the amendment resolutions, but the states did not wait for Congress to protect themselves against suit in federal court.

The most adamant defense of the interest of the states, predictably perhaps, came from Georgia. For Georgia, the *Chisholm* decision represented an infuriating defeat. Georgia had repeatedly denied the Court's jurisdiction, had refused to answer numerous summons and writs, yet the Court had claimed authority. The Georgia House moved quickly to give its defiance the sanction of law and passed "An Act declaratory of certain parts of the retained Sovereignty of the State of Georgia." The House rejected the "pretended claims" of Alexander Chisholm and declared that any person attempting to levy property from Georgia or the ministers of the state of Georgia would be "declared to be guilty of a FELONY, and shall suffer DEATH, without the benefit of clergy, by being HANGED."[90] But the Georgia Senate held up passage of such a dramatic law because, although Georgia had been told it must be amenable to the decision of the Supreme Court, the Court had not actually decided on the merits of Chisholm's claim. Georgia was not yet liable for anything. Besides, other states had already suggested amendments to the Constitution—a more constructive solution, and one that did not require the employment of the gallows.[91]

The first legislature to suggest amendments was that of Massachusetts, a state that moved swiftly to assert its rights. One month after the decision in *Chisholm*, the General Court of Massachusetts organized a committee to consider the consequences and recommend any measures that the "honour and interest" of the Commonwealth of Massachusetts "may demand."[92] Before the committee could reach any conclusion, however, events overtook its investigation, when the federal marshal of the district court served a writ on Governor John Hancock and Massachusetts attorney general James Sullivan, calling the Commonwealth to trial as a defendant in a suit in equity for property confiscated during the Revolutionary War. Considering the summons as "a matter in which the inhabitants of this FREE Commonwealth are deeply interested," Hancock immediately (the same day) called for a special session of the General Court to craft a response. Set to meet in September, the anticipation of the session excited a large newspaper debate in Massachusetts, with the majority of writers decrying the effects of the Jay Court's decision on state sovereignty and calling for an amendment to the Constitution.[93]

One problem for Massachusetts, and for many states, was the potential exposure to financial liability that the Court's ruling presented. Massachusetts had confiscated the property and estates of numerous British sympathizers and outright Loyalists throughout the war. Considering the amount of treasure and blood the people of Massachusetts had lost during the war, they believed any lawsuit by a former Loyalist to be unjust. As one newspaper noted, "Nothing remains but to give the key of our treasury to the agents of the Refugees, Tories, and men who were inimical to our Revolution."[94] But the concern of the opponents of the decision never merely referred to the potential costs of lawsuits, for the very structure of the federal system seemed to be overturned in the decision of the Jay Court. One author, writing as "Uncle Toby," noted, "We have not yet arrived in that slumbering era, when we may be yoked with impunity." Governor Hancock had acted as the "watchful guardian of our rights and liberties" by calling for the special session of the General Court, and "our political existence as a State depends on the result of it." Acquiescence in the decision of the Jay Court would be to "tamely give up all the ideas of the sovereignty of our State."[95] One New England legislator wondered how the judiciary could have been so bold as to "reduce the States to a situation too humiliating to have been tolerated or conceived, even under our former Provincial vassalage."[96]

On September 18, the special session of the General Court convened. In a speech to the assembled members, Governor Hancock asked the legislature to decide upon the means to combat the suit of William Vassall, a former Loyalist assentee whose property was confiscated during the war. Although Hancock claimed he did not wish to assert an opinion on "whether the Commonwealth may be sued," he made clear his own feelings from numerous suggestive statements peppered throughout the speech. For instance, he asserted, "I cannot conceive that the people of this Commonwealth," at the ratification of the Constitution, "expected that each State should be held liable to answer on *compulsory civil process,* to every individual resident in another State or in a foreign kingdom." He continued, "A consolidation of all the States into one Government, would at once endanger [the] Republic, and eventually divide the States united, or eradicate the principles which we have contended for."[97] He concluded his speech with an apology for his weakened condition, saying, "I feel the *seeds of mortality* growing fast within me," but that he thought he had "done no more than my duty."[98] Hancock died within a month; it was his last public speech. After his death, the newspapers noted that he had called the special session just in time. It was "as if it was the intention of Heaven, that the man who has ever been foremost in vindicating the liberties of the states, should be the first to check any infringements on their sovereignty and independence."[99]

After the governor's speech, the Massachusetts House of Representatives created a committee that condemned the decision of the Jay Court, reporting simply that "it is not expedient that a State should be sued." Shortly thereafter, a joint committee of both houses of the General Court convened to draft resolutions outlining their response to the suit. After an initial resolution that some delegates believed "did not go far enough," a vigorous debate ensued in the lower chamber. A long speech by Dr. Charles Jarvis assured that a more radical resolution would be passed. Jarvis claimed to be stunned by the "amazing accumulation of power" that the judiciary "now claimed." He emphasized the importance of state sovereignty to the existence of republican government in America by noting that the problem before them was not—as Chief Justice Wilson had suggested—"whether the people of the United States form a nation," but "WHETHER WE ARE TO BE A STATE." Rejecting the belief that "the Sovereignty of the Commonwealth was absorbed and extinguished in the Federal Government," as some delegates had argued, Jarvis insisted that "the Independence and Sovereignty of the State is its vital and essential principle." "It is," he noted, the "soul of the body politic." Without independence, "there will be nothing left but to drop a tear to its memory, and to consign its remains to that necessary repose, from which it cannot be recovered." He completed his exhortation with a vivid burst of rhetoric, warning: "What shall we think and feel, when the public business is exposed to interruption—when the Federal Eagle shall darken the State with the shadow of his wide-spread pinions; and shall seize, and bear away in his talons, your most important and necessary officers, from the discharge of their Constitutional functions?"[100] In the face of this oratory, the initial resolutions were rejected and Massachusetts established a scheme for opposition.

First, the legislature noted, "no answer" would be made to the suit of Vassall in court. Second, the legislature resolved to agree with the governor that "at the time of the adoption of the Constitution, it was not in the contemplation of the people to grant a power to the Federal Judiciary, by which a State should be compellable to answer to the suits of individuals." This assertion of the need to interpret the Constitution based upon the original intent, or "contemplation" of the framers, seemed a simple matter of common sense—after all, the Constitution was only a few years old. Next, the Massachusetts legislators called any attempt to enforce the ruling of the Jay Court "unnecessary and vexatious," claiming it "might be productive of danger to the freedom and independence of the States."[101] Finally, they instructed their federal representatives to immediately move for "the adoption of such Amendments to the Constitution as will resolve any clause or Article of the said Constitution which can be construed to imply or justify a decision that a State is compellable to answer in any suit by an individual or individuals in any Court of the United States."[102] Its work done, the General Court adjourned until January. The total bill for the session was 963 pounds, 9 shillings—much cheaper than a lawsuit.[103]

Such a strident rejection of national authority by Massachusetts reflected, in part, a continuing conflict between the allies of Governor

Hancock and the national government. Like many in the Southern states, many people in Massachusetts resented the importance of the financial centers of Philadelphia and New York in the policy of the nation, and they fought to maintain their own local influence against the rapid spread of Hamiltonianism in the Connecticut River Valley, Boston, and Salem, and in the rising commercial hub of Newburyport in Essex County. To combat the interest of the National Bank, the Commonwealth of Massachusetts chartered a rival "Union Bank" (the name's the thing) that would directly compete with the branch of the National Bank in Boston.[104] The Commonwealth and its new bank resisted Hamilton's efforts to assume the remaining portion of the state's war debt and provided its own program to fund the debt. Unfortunately for creditors, in the winter of 1794 the General Court passed a new "Act for the Provision of the Debt of Massachusetts," which required creditors to redeem old certificates "at the rate of four dollars [for] one dollar in specie"—a stark devaluation of certificates.[105] The purchase of the debt was to be under the supervision of the president of the Senate, the speaker of the House of Representatives, and the president of the Union Bank. Angry creditors complained that this type of action by the state was precisely the reason the decision of John Jay in *Chisholm* needed to be upheld. As a "friend" wrote:

> The Funding bill just passed will serve to convince ye of your error. Now ye see the Court is going to pay FOUR dollars with one! Don't you see that if the State was suable, ye must pay the whole sum according to the former act of the Court, and the promise on the bills! This is liberty and State SOVEREIGNTY—ye would have lost this JEWEL, if some *wiseacres* had not pulled hard against ye SOVEREIGNTY is the soul of State liberty—With this POWER the General Court can quarter the new Bills again, whenever they please—and kick the Funding bill into no-entity—and, I had almost said, kick Congress after it. And if any one dares to lift up his tongue for justice, *guillotine* him and *burn* him.[106]

With such a brisk denunciation of the action of the General Court directly connected with the question of suability and associating the organizers of the plan with motives as dangerous as the worst revolutionaries in the world, one might assume that many of the New England Hamiltonian supporters in Congress would react similarly to any attempt to overturn the decision in *Chisholm*. The evidence, however, is to the contrary. In fact, nearly all the New England allies of Hamiltonian policy voted for the amendment.[107]

Despite their enthusiasm for many of Hamilton's nationalizing schemes, historians have generally not emphasized that the complete consolidation and loss of independence of local institutions would have greatly disturbed these New England Hamiltonians. For one thing, some of the small states of New England had led the effort at the Constitutional Convention to secure the representation of the states in the Senate, a compromise that Hamilton considered a nearly insurmountable blow to the creation of a powerful national state. In the Constitutional Convention, Oliver Ellsworth of Connecticut (later a strong supporter of Hamiltonian finance in the Senate) argued for the "necessity of maintaining the existence & agency of the States."[108] Using language similar to that used by Madison, he hoped that the general government would not meddle in the internal affairs of state citizens. As he argued, "the Natl. Govt. could not descend to the local objects" on which "domestic happiness depended." He would look therefore "to the State Govts." for the "preservation of his rights," for "his happiness depended on their existence, as much as a newborn infant on its mother for nourishment."[109] He was a son of New England, and he had no desire to bind his happiness to a new set of foster parents.

In the post-Constitution years, many leading New Englanders experienced a reawakening of the distinctiveness of their regional character and a growing sense of the importance of their local institutions to the preservation of American strength and stability. Part of this arose from a more active engagement with representatives of the rest of the country in the national government. Oliver Wolcott's experience reflects this sectionalism nicely. As comptroller and auditor of the Treasury Department, Wolcott actively supported Hamilton's financial schemes. But he did not share an enthusiasm to destroy state institutions, and from his experience working in New York and Pennsylvania and in observing the machinations of national politics, he became increasingly enamored of New England's distinctive culture. It was his "sober opinion," he wrote to Noah Webster, "that the hopes of mankind as they respect the eventual success of the republican system, depend chiefly on the conduct of the people of New England." Since he had "left that country" (meaning New England), he had become "an enthusiast, if not a fanatic, with respect to the customes of the northern States." Wolcott wanted Webster to write a "philosophical, historical and political view of the manners, customs and institutions of New England," including the "civil and religious corporations."[110] Similar sentiments encouraged the creation of local institutions specifically intended to promote and protect New Englanders' sense of their history and uniqueness, epitomized in the organization of the Society for the Propagation of the Gospel and the Massachusetts Historical Society.[111]

National politics animated such regional identities. Tired of the Virginians' attempts to escape their pre-war British debts, Wolcott wanted the issue to be settled once and for all. As he noted, "The experiment of a union with the southern states ought to be now made conclusively," and "if it shall prove unsuccessful we ought to part like good friends, but the separation ought to be eternal."[112] His correspondents responded in kind. Reflecting on reports of wild elections in Pennsylvania, and on the dangers of such an example to the people in Connecticut, Chauncy Goodrich assured Wolcott that no person could "gull people in New England by their noisy clamor." As he noted, "Our common folks know their true character," and "a Yankee won't be bullied by anybody."[113] Goodrich, for his part, did not think Virginia would ever really support the federal government "till [the government] accommodates itself to a state of Negro-hood, debt luxury and gambling."[114] Lemuel Hopkins felt assured that New England would continue to maintain the proper standard for the country, "as long as our schools, presses and town corporations last."[115] Much of this sentiment came as a natural reaction to the dangers implicit in the French Revolution. As Wolcott wrote, "On this, as on all trying occasions, the friends of true liberty look to New England for protection."[116] The solution was the maintenance of their traditional institutions from any threatened destruction, whether from Jacobins or even from well-intentioned centralizing power. In moments of crisis and conflict, this strain of New England Federalism could decisively animate the politics of the region.

The Virginians did not need the example of the New Englanders to form a resistance to the ruling of the Court in *Chisholm,* and when the decision became known in the South, their assembly responded with predictable defiance. At the time of the decision, the Virginia assembly was already in a peevish mood toward the national judiciary, and its legislators often complained of the federal court's willingness to rule on cases involving pre–Revolutionary War debts that Americans owed to British merchants. The peace treaty of 1783 had promised that Americans would faithfully pay their pre-war debts to British creditors, but before the Constitution, no force outside of the state governments existed to compel the debtors—many of whom dominated the planter class of the South—to redeem their old responsibilities. Now the federal courts recognized the treaty as the fundamental law of the land and were ruling favorably for British creditors seeking to regain long overdue debts. By the fall of 1793, federal courts had struck down laws of Georgia, South Carolina, Connecticut, and Rhode Island that provided impediments to foreign creditors for the collection of pre-war debts, and British merchants were rapidly settling old accounts in courts throughout the Union.[117] As Rufus King noted, "The national judiciary without having been much employed, has been the means of settling a large proportion of our foreign Debts," and "from the Potomac east nothing remains to be settled." While King celebrated the payment of foreign debts in South Carolina, "where immense sums were due," he could only lament the recalcitrance of Virginia, the state that King thought "will be the last" to deal with old obligations.[118]

The Virginia assembly intended to be the last. When it opened its session in early November, news that the federal courts had begun ruling in favor of British creditors in Virginia charged the atmosphere in both houses. The delegates took to the floor and in speech after speech condemned the "injustice" of the rulings. The Virginians complained that the treaty of peace should be enforced in both directions, and they immediately crafted an angry statement, asserting that "the treaty of peace between Great-Britain and the United States of America" had been "in every instance" complied with by the Americans and "violated" by the British. After all, the British still fortified the frontier, and had continuously refused to return "stolen" slaves who had run off during the British forays into Virginia. The Virginia House ordered its congressional representatives to immediately ask the executive of the United States to "endeavor to effect such measures" to bring the British into compliance.[119]

As members of the Virginia assembly approached the topic of the Court decision in *Chisholm*, they were not only in a mood for passing angry resolves, they were in a mood for amending the U.S. Constitution. A few days before the assembly took up the question of state suability, a House of Delegates committee that had been assigned to compare the amended U.S. Constitution with the amendments that had been proposed by the Virginia ratifying convention issued a sobering report. While the committee found that some of the proposed amendments had been incorporated and added to the Constitution—not surprising, since Madison worked with the proposed Virginia amendments in hand—*twenty-seven* of the proposed measures for amendments and a bill of rights had apparently been ignored and one proposal for the bill of rights that called for strictures against a standing army had only partially been adopted.[120] Another proposed amendment concerning decisions on the salaries of senators had only been adopted by six states.[121] The assembly narrowly defeated a motion to require their U.S. senators—John Taylor and James Monroe, both former anti-federalists—to resubmit all of the original amendments at the next session of Congress and transfer them all to the other states.

While advocates for more amendments could not find support for such a dramatic challenge to the Constitution—which one opponent considered as an attempt "to destroy the constitution"—they did succeed in proposing an amendment that they hoped would help to exorcise Hamiltonianism from the U.S. Congress.[122] Complaining of "influence," the Virginia assembly instructed its federal representatives to support an amendment to the Constitution that would "prohibit any director or stockholder of the Bank of the United States, from being a member of either House of Congress."[123] A slightly weaker version of the amendment did make it to the floor of the Senate, in early January 1795, but it could not garner the necessary two-thirds majority.[124]

With the decision of the Jay Court in *Chisholm,* the Virginia assembly felt itself on the defensive against an inexorably encroaching federal power. Like Massachusetts, Virginia also had much to fear from former Loyalists and others intent on compensation, and like Massachusetts, the state was immediately sued after the decision in *Chisholm.* The Indiana Company, a land corporation that claimed title to lands in the western extremities of Virginia's ancient boundaries—titles rejected by Virginia in 1779—was now pressing its claim in the federal courts.[125] As its first salvo against the *Chisholm* decision, the Virginia assembly resolved "that the decision of the legislature of this commonwealth in the year 1779, upon the claims of the Indiana company was definitive, and that this commonwealth is not bound, and ought not to appear before the Supreme Federal Court to any suit whatever, relative to that subject."[126] The House of Delegates also began crafting other resolutions to challenge *Chisholm,* since members believed the Court's decision was "unnecessary and inexpedient," and, even worse, "dangerous to the peace, safety and independence of the several states." Upon this basis, they designed their plan of attack. First, they passed a resolution in both the House and Senate of the General Assembly that derided the decision of the Court:

> Resolved, that a state cannot, under the constitution of the United States, be made a defendant at the suit of any individual or individuals, and that the decision of the Supreme federal Court, that a state may be placed in that situation, is incompatible with, and dangerous to the sovereignty and independence of the individual states, as the same tends towards a consolidation of these confederated republics.

Not surprisingly, the Virginia assembly reacted with a strong assertion of state sovereignty, as it had done in the past against Hamilton's funding and assumption plan. But this time the Virginia assembly echoed Massachusetts in calling for direct action. The second resolution instructed Virginia's U.S. senators to seek and support an amendment to the Constitution that would relieve the Constitution from any ambiguity—states could not be made a defendant in the Supreme Court—and, like Massachusetts, Virginia invited each of the other states of the Union to work with it to pass an amendment. The assembly published its final resolutions as a broadside and circulated the sheet throughout Richmond.[127] There were a few voices that dissented from the tone and hasty attack on the *motives* of the Supreme Court. After all, Virginia had not even received any official record of the opinions and decision in the case, but the instruction to their representatives was passed unanimously.[128]

With both Virginia and Massachusetts instructing their representatives to pass an amendment to the Constitution, the rapid assent of the U.S. Congress was all but assured. A draft amendment was admitted into the Senate on January 2, 1794, and passed two weeks later by a vote of 23 to 2. It was a simple assertion with large implications: "The judicial Power of the United States shall not be construed to extend to any Suit in Law or Equity, commenced or prosecuted against one of the United States by Citizens of another State, or by Citizens or Subjects of any foreign State."[129]

The amendment passed more slowly through the House, which was distracted by a long series of debates over trade with France and Britain between Madison and Hamilton's proxy, William Loughton Smith of South Carolina. After being originally read in the third week of January, the House finally voted on the amendment in early March—prompted perhaps by the appearance of a petition for the payment of the Georgia debt from the executors of Robert Farquhar's estate.[130] Despite the logistical delay, the amendment passed by an overwhelming vote of 81 to 9.[131] On March 12, 1794, the Senate of the United States together with the House of Representatives asked the executive to transmit the proposed amendment to the states.[132]

At this point, the record of ratification becomes rather chaotic, and even comical. After the House of Representatives passed the Joint Resolution on March 12, 1794, the president transmitted the amendment to the states for ratification—most of which were already prepared to act because of the resolutions passed by Massachusetts and Virginia in 1793. The first state to ratify was the home state of John Jay, which had also been sued. New York passed the amendment on March 27, 1794. Jay's great rival, Governor George Clinton, opened the session of the legislature by denouncing Jay's national interpretation of the United States, pressing the legislature to pursue measures "corresponding with our own sovereignty."[133] Rhode Island and Connecticut followed shortly thereafter, then New Hampshire, Massachusetts, Vermont, and, by the end of the year, Virginia, Georgia, Kentucky, and Maryland. Delaware passed the amendment on January 23, 1795, and North Carolina, less than a year after the amendment had passed out of Congress, became the necessary twelfth state to ratify the amendment, on February 7, 1795.[134]

But nothing happened. There were no announcements, no insertion into the Constitution. In an age of poor transportation, poor communication, and a lack of rules governing the process, no one person anywhere knew which states had or had not passed the amendment. Some of the states informed the executive branch of their decision, others either forgot or assumed someone else already had. With a rapid turnover in officials, including the election of a new president of the United States, continuity of administration at all levels was dearly lacking.

In light of the confusion, and reflecting uncertainty about the status of all the amendments proposed by the Congress, the Senate in December 1796 ordered a committee to investigate the matter. At the end of January 1797, the committee recognized that only New York, Massachusetts, Vermont, New Hampshire, Georgia, Delaware, Rhode Island, and North Carolina had returned "authentic documents" to Congress verifying ratification.[135] Congress finally requested the Adams administration to find out the status of the amendment. Over the course of the year, with passage of the amendment reported by South Carolina and with proof finally deposited from numerous states with secretary of state Timothy Pickering, the amendment officially became part of the U.S. Constitution on January 8, 1798.[136] On February 4, 1798, the Supreme Court recognized the Eleventh Amendment and dismissed all pending cases between an individual and a state.[137]

Despite the slow realization of passage, the rapid agreement of the states deserves special attention. Why did the Eleventh Amendment pass so quickly? Any historian who has mentioned the matter has generally followed Charles Warren in his classic *The Supreme Court in United States History* by asserting that the reaction against the decision of the Jay Court was "due in large measure to the filing of suits against other states."[138] While it is true that the states could have been subject to great liability over the decision of the Jay Court, a belief that the Eleventh Amendment reflected only a crass material motive is a much too thin explanation and ignores the bulk of the evidence of the public debate. It is equivalent to arguing that the independence movement was brought about because the Americans did not wish to pay taxes—true at one level, but missing the larger significance of the political struggle at hand. Indeed, as "Brutus" had argued, the scheme of the Court presented "more danger to the liberties of America than the claims of the British Parliament to tax us without our consent."[139] The crucial concern is "without our consent." It was a matter of *who* controlled the obligations of justice.

In fact, there was an attempt in both the House and the Senate to amend the amendment so that it would allow the Supreme Court to adjudge the states, but only in cases arising from behavior *after* the ratification of the amendment. Such an amendment would have effectively absolved the states from any liability for confiscation of Loyalist property or any confiscations of the 1780s. If the states were *solely* concerned about the financial liability of the war, one would expect this amendment to receive fairly broad support in the House and Senate, particularly among those members who often supported the centralization of fiscal policy in the national state. But the attempt to change the federal meaning of the amendment was strongly defeated in the Senate and garnered only eight votes in the House of Representatives, one less than the number that actually voted against the Eleventh Amendment.[140] The passage of the Eleventh Amendment was driven by a fear of the loss of independence, not by a fear of financial liability.

Both Massachusetts and Virginia recognized the financial concerns of the decision, but they based their defiance on a much broader belief: the idea of the "independence and sovereignty" of the states. The majority of the citizenry believed the states played a vital role in the maintenance of American society and citizenship. In fact, the rapid approval of the Eleventh Amendment represented a stark rejection of the nationalist interpretation of the Constitution that Jay and Wilson described in their decision. The bulk of the country emphatically endorsed a vision of Union that retained the sovereignty of states and ensured that the American state would be a compound and not a consolidated government. The country reflected the opinion of Madison and Jefferson much more than that of Jay. In fact, Jay's and Hamilton's interpretation of the extent of the national government's authority, and the interpretation that the majority of historians have tended to emphasize, was supported by only a small minority of Hamiltonian enthusiasts. In both New England and the South, strong prejudices against the surrender of local autonomy to national structures of power remained extremely important to many people, and a vision of "independence" animated their reaction to overt displays and assumptions of national power. The boundaries of American citizenship remained shaded by at least two, if not more, sovereign authorities.

In actual impact, the Eleventh Amendment is perhaps the most important amendment to the Constitution before the American Civil War.

By protecting the states from lawsuits in federal courts, and therefore providing no judicial mechanism for the national government to intervene between the states and the citizenry, the amendment assured that states would set the parameters of citizenship. The case at hand was a property case, which has hidden the crucial citizenship implications of the arguments made by James Wilson and John Jay, in favor of state suability. Any legal decisions that argued that the American people were a national people—thereby making all citizens necessarily equal, without reference to the states—would have given the Court a tremendous power, one it currently holds, to immediately impact the character of the particular civil rights, duties, and privileges of all Americans. Such a powerful Court could indeed have made a mockery of the claims of the "sovereignty" of the states, and the fear of such a Court explains the rapid passage of the Eleventh Amendment.

We the People of the States

During the final drafting of the U.S. Constitution, Gouverneur Morris in the Committee on Style performed the single greatest sleight of hand in American history: he redefined the "people" who properly held the reigns of sovereignty under the "more perfect" Union. The committee was merely intended to ensure the regularity and clarity of the prose in the Constitution, which all the framers knew would be manipulated and studied by subsequent politicians, judges, and demagogues alike. In redrafting the Preamble, Morris made some seemingly innocent changes, which contained the seeds of transformation that would eventually, and almost immediately, be used as the perfect justification for the expansion of the power of the new government. The draft Constitution, which was printed internally for the members to use in their final debates, began: "We the people of the States of New-Hampshire, Massachusetts, Rhode-Island and Providence Plantations, Connecticut, New-York, New-Jersey, Pennsylvania, Maryland, Virginia, North-Carolina, South-Carolina, and Georgia, do ordain, and establish the following Constitution for the Government of Ourselves and our Posterity."[141] Here the "people" are the people of the individual states, not a national sovereign people acting in their collective capacity, but as contracting peoples. The language can be read in other ways, but at the very least it is ambiguous. The "government" agreed upon was clearly defined by the Constitution that followed—as one with limited powers—and there was no expansive rhetoric about the "general welfare."

The version which emerged from the Committee on Style is, of course, much more elegant. But it possessed, and has proven to contain, many different implications: "We, the People of the United States, in order to form a more perfect union, establish justice, ensure domestic tranquility, provide for the common defense, promote the general welfare, and secure the blessings of liberty to ourselves and our posterity, do ordain and establish this constitution for the United States of America." The portentous comma after "We" sets the guide for later interpretation.[142] The "People of the United States," in their collective capacity, suggests an undivided national sovereignty. The implied intentions of the revised Preamble, especially the enthusiasm for the promotion of "the general welfare," would in time come to justify an extraordinary expansion of the actually enumerated powers. During the ratification debates, anti-federalists attacked the phrase as the sign that the new government would sprint toward the consolidation of all power in a national government.[143] Jay used the Preamble to help make his case that the national people were sovereign. As we have seen, it was used by "Crito" in support of the ruling of John Jay in *Chisholm.* It was also used by Hamilton in his defense of the constitutionality of his unsuccessful legislative program outlined in his "Report on Manufactures." By the end of the decade, it would be used to justify the Alien Act, the Sedition Act, and the existence of a national common law.[144]

Historians, as well, have tended to be charmed by the Preamble. Yet in spite of the successes of Hamilton's initial programs and the ambitious ruling of the Supreme Court, the bulk of the citizenry clearly desired to retain the federal nature of their constitutional alliance, with "sovereign" states. In this environment, citizenship would itself necessarily reflect a compound nature, and no national citizenship jurisprudence would emerge until after the Fourteenth Amendment was passed in 1865. In the early 1790s, Hamilton and Jay were the odd men out. Both Hamilton and Jay possessed striking national visions for government created by the Constitution, hoping for a united national people, of equal citizens. They anticipated a national authority that would become the ascendant interpretation of the Constitution, not in the late eighteenth century but in the mid-twentieth. In the 1790s, their interpretations of the Constitution were minority opinions.

After *Chisholm* was rejected, Jay did not stay long on the bench. Taking an assignment to negotiate a treaty with Great Britain, he eventually left the Court for a seat of *real* power—the governorship of New York. He had no desire to return to the bench; as he noted to John Adams at the end the decade, "I left the bench perfectly convinced that under a system so defective it would not retain the energy, weight, and dignity which are essential to its affording due support to the national government, nor acquire the public confidence and respect which, as the last resort of the justice of the nation, it should possess."[145] Jay's refusal of Adams's offer of the vacant chief justiceship opened the place for John Marshall to be appointed in the last moments of Adams's administration. Hamilton remained powerful as long as his great patron, Washington, survived. After Washington's death, in 1799, Hamilton's ego could not sustain his ambitions. He retained a following among the creditors of the nation, but he refused to hold a secondary place in the leadership of the Federalist Party. Out of favor and out of power in 1802, Hamilton lamented his "odd destiny." He believed that "no man has sacrificed or done more for the present Constitution than myself," and despite the fact that he suffered from "the murmurs of its friends no less than the curses of my foes," he still worked to "prop the frail and worthless fragment."[146] In two years, spurred by the "curses of his foes," Hamilton would die on the dueling ground.

But if Hamilton and Jay were forward-looking, and ultimately defeated, visionaries of a strong and centralized national state, were Jefferson and Madison backward-looking reactionaries merely regurgitating arguments common to the Tory opposition to Walpole in the eighteenth century?

Historians have been too quick to judge one or the other of these positions as either backward-looking or modern and forward-looking. Either Hamilton is the forward-looking nation-builder, or he becomes the retrenching monarchist. Jefferson must be either a voice for liberal democracy, or he is the reactionary planter-oligarch. In fact, both of their visions represented contesting modern states made up of citizens with rights: Hamilton's, the modern centralized national state-capitalist system, and Jefferson's, the liberal federal Union. There were "Conservatives" in American politics of the 1790s (like some of the "old Tories," such as Connecticut's senator John Allen), but neither the Hamiltonians nor the Virginia agrarians can rightly be considered as such.

The problem of creating a state from the Constitution remained stuck in the ambiguity of Revolutionary politics. Even among the supporters of the Constitution, no broad consensus existed across the country that agreed on how the new institutions should operate. Most people simply knew what they did not want. As we will see, the new national state would not only need to abide by the interests and independence of the states, but it also could be challenged by the desires and claims of individuals. In the face of international war and revolution, the corporate will of the nation, represented by the policy of the government, came to be repeatedly flouted by individuals claiming to follow the "rights of man" as their only polestar. The conflicts that began as a reaction against Hamilton's plan merged with popular movements that celebrated the French Revolution, and the ad hoc coalitions of early national politics quickly entrenched themselves as two national parties, responding to the challenges and possibilities created in the upheavals of European politics. The parties quickly delegitimized their opponents by denying their ability to speak for the American citizenry. The next chapter will help describe the birth of these two parties—Federalists and Republicans—and their emerging struggle over the meaning of American citizenship.

{3}

The Politics of Citizenship

EXPATRIATION, NATURALIZATION, AND THE RISE OF PARTY

I hold the right of expatriation to be inherent in every man by the laws of nature, and incapable of being rightfully taken from him even by the united will of every other person in the nation. If the laws have provided no particular mode by which the right may be exercised, the individual may do it by any effectual and unequivocal act or declaration. —THOMAS JEFFERSON, 1806

Under this unhappy prospect, the national character and existence of America are lost; and instead of being members of a great nation, we become a band of miserable Algerines.—WILLIAM RAWLE

WHEN GIDEON HENFIELD, A "SEA-FARING MAN" FROM Salem, Massachusetts, joined the crew of the privateer *Citizen Genet,* he was assured that the first prize would be his to command. The vessel had been armed in Charleston, with the enthusiastic support of Governor William Moultrie and with funds provided by the first ambassador from the new French Republic, Edmond Charles Genet—"Citizen Genet" himself—in April of 1793. With six guns and fifty hands, most of them American citizens, the privateer set out to strike a blow in the great new war of the French Revolution, or in the terms of Genet: "the common glorious cause of liberty."[1] Within weeks of her departure, the *Citizen Genet* seized the British merchantman *William* in Delaware Bay. As promised, Henfield was given command of the *William* as prize-master, and he set sail for Philadelphia to dispose of the ship and its goods in a French prize court, to the highest bidder.

But when Henfield arrived in Philadelphia, he was arrested for committing "depredations on the commerce of nations currently at peace with the United States." Much had changed since Henfield had left Charleston. The Washington administration had issued an executive proclamation stating that the United States remained at peace with Great Britain and the numerous European powers allied against France—a proclamation against the opinion of many Americans who believed that treaty obligations required the United States to aid the French in their desperate hour. The British pressed Washington to live up to his pledges of neutrality. Having learned of the capture of the *William*, George Hammond, the British minister to the United States, warned that Great Britain would not abide "breaches of that neutrality which the United States profess to observe." Washington demanded the prosecution of American citizens engaged in privateering, and U.S. district attorney for Pennsylvania, William Rawle, had Henfield and his fellow American, John Singletary, arrested when they arrived in Philadelphia.[2]

When Henfield was first brought before the magistrates, he pled ignorance. He assured the mayor that he was in fact an American citizen, and "that as such he would die." He loved his country and would never "intend anything to her prejudice." He had no knowledge of Washington's proclamation. He "had the greatest respect" for Washington. If he had only known of the wishes of the president, he would never have accepted a position on the *Citizen Genet*.[3]

But one month later, at the grand inquest prepared to indict him, Henfield changed his tune. To the inquest he declared that he "espoused the cause of France" and "considered himself as a Frenchman." In time, he intended to "move his family"—still in Salem, Massachusetts—"within [French] dominions."[4] He claimed to have relinquished his American citizenship. He had exercised his "natural right of expatriation," one of the inalienable and universal rights of man. It was a novel defense.

Henfield's trial became the kind of show trial that mobilizes and clarifies fierce partisan sentiments. It was at once a contest between those who denied Washington's legitimate authority to issue a "Proclamation of Neutrality" and those who did not, between those who believed Americans should be fighting with France and those who did not, between those who celebrated the principles of the "rights of man" as the same as the principles of '76 and those who did not, and between strong supporters of Hamilton and the growing opposition to his plans and policies. The trial, and its surrounding drama, catalyzed and completed the trends toward the formation of national party politics. By mingling deep differences over fundamental political principles with local, national, and international politics, the prosecution of Henfield exposed real divisions in the American political landscape. Ultimately, the zeal which surrounded the Henfield case revealed the extent to which the American people disagreed over the fundamental character of the American Revolution, the importance of the national state in their lives, the sanctity of traditional legal notions and institutions, and, ultimately, the meaning of American citizenship.

The shocking realization that the fundamentals of the American political order were still ambiguous and fraught with the extravagant potentialities of an age of revolution took hold rapidly over 1793 and 1794 and polarized the political rhetoric of the country. In the face of international war and revolution, the emerging parties developed two opposing worldviews which understood the other with reference to the debates and examples of international politics. In particular, supporters of the policies of the Washington administration, calling themselves "Federalists," viewed the growing opposition and the forms of their political mobilization—which resembled the radical committees of the American Revolution and the Revolutionary clubs of France—as evidence of the dangerous spread of "French" principles alien to a society whose own Revolution they now liked to remember as a legal and defensive restoration. The opposition, who called themselves "Republicans," viewed the administration's lack of support for the French Revolution, the strong fiscal state of Hamilton, and the reactionary language of the Federalist judiciary as powerful evidence that their own Revolutionary republic had been usurped by men too much enamored with the forms, hierarchies, and corruption of the British state. These were startling facts which represented a danger to the survival of what *they* considered as the fruits of the American Revolution: republican government and the Revolutionary principles of the "rights of man."

The problem of American citizenship stands at the center of this moment of polarization. American conflicts over the right and legitimacy of expatriation—as a theoretical problem of citizenship, as a constitutional problem related to the potential existence of a national common law unchecked by the states, and as a practical dilemma in a touchy international diplomacy—clarified divisions and tendencies in an increasingly organized fight for control of the institutions of government, and defined the ruts in which the two parties would travel in the 1790s. In the end, we find Congress divided by fundamental differences, driven by party discipline, aware of public scrutiny, and bound into ideologically charged anxieties over the future character of the American citizenry. These differences are immediately manifest in the party politics behind the Naturalization Bill of 1795—one of the most important and influential naturalization bills in American history.

Making and Unmaking the Body Politic: Naturalization and Expatriation

Membership in the American nation was expanded by natural increase and naturalization. In the twelve years after the ratification of the Constitution, the Congress of the new national government debated and devised four general bills of naturalization to create a process for the creation of American citizens from aliens. With the passage of an 1802 bill that repealed the Naturalization Act of 1798 and largely restored the naturalization law of 1795, the U.S. Congress did not pass another general bill of naturalization of major importance until the twentieth century.[5] Why so many in these formative years under the Constitution—and then so few over the nineteenth century, which saw the largest immigration streams in American history?

After an initially optimistic and extremely progressive naturalization law was crafted in 1790, American legislators grew increasingly worried over the potential damage that immigrants could create in American society. Notably, within four years of the passage of the first bill, the two rival political parties emerged, and as they acknowledged distinct concerns over the dangers posed by immigrants, their fears reflected their different ideological commitments to the American nation, and American citizenship in general. The general rules devised by the Congress of 1794–95 for creating citizens out of aliens would stand for over a century and define the route to citizenship for millions of immigrants to the United States.

The debates over the place of immigrants in American society first articulated in the 1790s have been echoed time and again as Americans define and redefine their status as a "nation of immigrants." But despite such timeless application, and even the continuing resonance of the arguments of the debates, the Naturalization Act of 1795 was very much a product of a historical moment enveloped by a Revolutionary politics characteristic of the Age of Revolutions. The two parties exhibited deep differences over the meaning of American citizenship and the character of American nationhood, and thus completely disagreed over the "types" of immigrants that would make the best citizens. To understand the gulf in their perspectives, we must recognize the politics in the 1790s surrounding expatriation, the antithesis of naturalization—the way citizens became aliens.

Expatriation represented an act of renunciation of one's allegiance, an abandonment of citizenship or subjecthood which stripped an individual of all original responsibility to the home country. Such an act had no place in English common law principles. British subjecthood depended upon feudal conceptions of perpetual natural allegiance, enshrined by such standards as Coke's interpretation of *Calvin's Case* of 1603. English practice at the end of the eighteenth century continued to assume that subjects could never relinquish their filial responsibilities, and the doctrine of "once a subject, always a subject" still dominated the English common law understanding of allegiance. Lockeian ideas stressing the contractual relationships of commonwealths and their members challenged such pronouncements, but these remained abstract considerations. Blackstone confirmed the English understanding of expatriation and emigration (terms interchangeable in eighteenth-century legal practice), noting that "the natural-born subject of one prince cannot by act of his own, no, not by swearing allegiance to another, put off or discharge his natural allegiance to the former."[6] Yet, recognizing the eighteenth-century conceit of allegiance founded upon consent, Blackstone provided for the *theoretical* possibility of expatriation, but only under the direction of specific legislation designed for that purpose by a properly authorized sovereign. No such law existed. In fact, in the 1790s, the British operated a policy of naval impressments that denied subjects of the British Empire the ability to free themselves of the responsibilities of their natural subjecthood, even if they were naturalized as citizens or subjects of another state—a policy that helped lead to the American embargo of 1808 and the War of 1812.[7]

In rejecting subjecthood for citizenship, many Americans rejected the very logic of filial allegiance, opening the way for a challenge to British models of expatriation. Here Thomas Jefferson is implicated again, as he early refashioned the laws of Virginia to support reason. Among his efforts to create a new body of Virginia laws—including the laws abolishing quitrents, primogeniture, and entail—and in addition to his work on the Virginian Statute for Religious Freedom, Jefferson aided in the creation of a "citizenship bill." The new law provided procedures for naturalization, but it also described a process for citizens to "relinquish that character" and become aliens. Unknown throughout the world, the statute called expatriation a "natural right which all men have of relinquishing the country in which birth or other accident may have thrown them."[8] While Jefferson and the Virginia assembly drafted a legal process for expatriation, there is no reason to believe that he thought such a law was needed before any individual could take advantage of the natural right of expatriation. As he noted in 1806, the "right of expatriation" was "inherent in every man by the laws of nature, and incapable of being rightfully taken from him even by the united will of every other person in the nation." If the law "provided no particular mode by which the right may be exercised, the individual may do it by any effectual and unequivocal act or declaration."[9]

Other states pressed the issue. In addition to the Virginia statute, the Pennsylvania Constitution of 1776 asserted "that all men have a natural inherent right to emigrate from one state to another that will receive them, or to form a new state in vacant countries, or in such countries as they can purchase, whenever they think that thereby they may promote their own happiness."[10] The Vermonters seized upon this language and reproduced it in their own Declaration of Rights. Here, "emigration" and "expatriation" are synonymous. In a British tradition where no subject could escape from allegiance, a subject could not in theory "emigrate" to escape the laws of the realm or the long arm of allegiance. The assertion of the Pennsylvania Bill of Rights was a direct rejection of the British practice.[11]

But American opinion was far from settled about the right of expatriation. This was the problem with "natural rights"—one person's undeniable right could be another's absurd presumption. A telling difference from Jefferson's stance on this matter exists in the example of Alexander Hamilton defending Tories in the 1780s against damages sought by the New York legislature. He argued that British Loyalists could not simply have become "aliens" by adhering to the cause of the British—as Jefferson asserted explicitly[12]—because this would be the same as admitting the right of expatriation, which Hamilton considered "an altogether new invention unknown and inadmissible in law."[13] Writing as "Phocion" in 1783 against a number of harsh laws passed by New York against former Loyalists, Hamilton similarly argued that no one could "at pleasure renounce their allegiance to the state of which they are members," and "devote themselves to a foreign jurisdiction." Such a principle would be "contrary to law and subversive of government."[14]

The difference between Jefferson and Hamilton in their understanding of the place of the natural right of expatriation in settled society represents a significant conceptual distance between their specific understanding of the nature of American citizenship after the Revolution. Jefferson, in drafting the Virginia statute, was not merely acting as a rather enthusiastic reformer (which he was), and Hamilton was not merely acting in the interest of his clients (as he was). In fact, the difference in their opinions on the meaning of expatriation goes to the heart of one of the perspectives on the meaning of the American Revolution that represented a fundamental break between the Republican and Federalist parties—a difference over citizenship that played an important political and ideological role in the initial organization of the two national parties. And yet these differences between Hamilton and Jefferson over the meaning of expatriation may have largely remained theoretical concerns, mere "speculations of the closet," had it not been for the dramatic events surrounding the arrival of the French ambassador, "Citizen Genet," and the curious claims of American citizens like Gideon Henfield.

Revolutionary Politics and the Problem of Expatriation

The story of Citizen Genet and his remarkable year as an unruly, opinionated, and ambitious French minister has been a staple of histories of the 1790s since the visit itself. From his initial, celebrated landing at Charleston and his popular tour north to Philadelphia; to his openly "secret" preparations for an invasion of Spanish Florida and Louisiana with the complicit assistance of American citizens and officials; to the wary stance of the Washington administration, his arrogant denial of Washington's Proclamation of Neutrality, and his rumored threat to appeal directly to the American people; to the resulting break and ultimate recall of Genet—all have rightly received the attention of close and careful study.[15] For our purposes, because of what he represented to each party, the visit of Genet helps highlight problems of American citizenship, allegiance, and nationhood that so often characterized the politics of the United States in the 1790s. Indeed, the controversies created directly in his wake help us discern the nature of the different attitudes toward individual rights and national citizenship that helped to define the different parties at the moment of their emergence.

To many Americans, Genet embodied the truest principles and promises of the American Revolution. They interpreted the cause of the French Revolution as they interpreted their own—as a universal cause to free mankind from the oppression and degradation of feudal institutions, whose ultimate goal was a progressive and even millennial future of peace and prosperity for mankind. Throughout the fall of 1792, popular celebrations of the French victory at Valmy and the enthusiastic embrace of the French anthems "Ça Ira" and "La Marseilles" became tangible expressions of the popular associations many Americans were making between the American and French revolutions. Despite the extremes of revolution in France, in the United States the emerging opposition to the government, which by the congressional elections of 1792 was showing signs of cross-state communication if not quite organization, continued to embrace the French cause. Genet's grand arrival in Charleston and his triumphal march overland to Philadelphia were characterized by numerous popular extensions of solidarity and support. Since many Americans believed Genet embodied the ideals of the American and French revolutions, he was actively courted, and even encouraged in his efforts to raise an army to assault Spanish Florida and Louisiana. In Charleston he was supported by Governor Moultrie, who would become the president of the highly sympathetic Democratic-Republican Society of that city.

With the spread of "Democratic clubs" across the United States in the spring and summer of 1793 and 1794, the nascent Republican Party gained ideological and organizational focus as older state-party alliances, personal interests, and occasional factions merged into a national opposition party.[16] These societies formed throughout the United States to spread information encouraging the principles of the French Revolution, but they never existed entirely outside a framework of electoral politics. The Democratic-Republican Societies and the rapidly spreading opposition newspapers around the country connected the cause of the French with the cause of the American Revolution and the inevitable expansion of freedom in the "modern" world, aligning themselves with universal principles that revolved around a celebration of the "rights of man." It was a universalism that celebrated America itself as a revolutionary society, where citizenship could be gained and affirmed by men sharing the principles of the rights of man. With their proper command of the true principles of the American Revolution, the societies set themselves up as representatives of the voice of "the people"—an assertion which was seen as a bold challenge to the actual representative government.[17]

The charter and constitution of the Democratic Society of Philadelphia, a charter that many Democratic Societies copied for their own guidance, celebrated this sense of the newness of the age and the importance of the rights of man. As the document's preamble proclaimed:

> The RIGHTS OF MAN, the genuine objects of Society, and the legitimate principles of Government, have been clearly developed by the successive Revolutions of America and France. Those events have withdrawn the veil which concealed the dignity and the happiness of the human race and have taught us, no longer dazzled with aristocratic splendor, or awed by antiquated usurpation, to erect the Temple of Liberty on the ruins of Palaces and Thrones.

Notably, these Republicans connected themselves to a distinctly universalist orientation. They argued they were "unfettered by religious or national distinctions" in their cause for the "Freedom and Equality" of all humanity.[18] This leading society was made up of opposition leaders in Philadelphia, and they feted and fawned on "the Citizen," and connected the French and American revolutions explicitly. On May 17, 1793, for instance, Ambassador Genet was one of the guests of honor along with the governor of Pennsylvania at a feast aboard the French frigate *L'Embuscade.* Notable among the toasts was one offered to "the Rights of Man—may they become universal law!"[19]

To the strong supporters of the Washington administration, and to the numerous people who loathed the idea of war with Great Britain for reasons of interest, policy, and affection, Genet's arrogance and popularity took on a dangerous character. By the time he arrived, numerous Americans already considered the republican turn of the French Revolution as a typical example of licentiousness overcoming reform. With the flight of Lafayette, in the fall of 1792, and the imprisonment and eventual execution of Louis XVI—news of which arrived with the same gale winds that brought Genet, in April 1793—many Americans, like Washington himself, saw in the French Revolution something altogether foreign from their own independence movement. Some Americans began to view Genet as a tangible example of the insidious and ambitious foreigner attempting to usurp the power of the nation for a foreign purpose. And anyone who supported Genet clearly wished to deliver the power of the United States into the hands of a foreign purse. "True Americans" did not, and could not, have anything to do with the devious wiles of a French diplomat. When combined with the increasing ubiquity of radical émigrés in American political and cultural life and the spread of the Democratic-Republican Societies, Genet represented all those who wished to deny to Americans any sense of "their national character" and to disrupt America's "advancement as a nation."[20] One pro-administration author wrote, "Perish the American! Whose soul is capable of submitting to such a degrading servitude!" How could an "American" forsake "the genuine purity of our national worship, and offer at a foreign shrine the tribute of his slavish adoration!"[21] The popularity of Genet seemed unnatural, un-American.

As the privateers sponsored in Charleston and Philadelphia made their effects known, capturing and selling British prizes in American ports, the minister began to openly clash with Washington's administration—the beginning of the end for Genet. These events put Jefferson in a particularly vulnerable political spot. As the secretary of state and the official voice of the U.S. government to foreign powers, Jefferson was wary of associating himself too publicly with the activities of the growing opposition to the Washington administration (although he continued to patronize the leading opposition newspaper, the *National*

Gazette), despite the fact that he found himself increasingly alienated from the dominant position of Washington's cabinet.[22] He was particularly displeased at having to show outward support for Washington's Proclamation of Neutrality—which he considered impolitic, unconstitutional, and needlessly pro-British in its language—and when Washington condemned the growing western Pennsylvania resistance to the whiskey excise, he privately retracted his public support for the administration. As he noted to James Madison, it represented "another instance of my being forced to approve what I have condemned uniformly from its first conception."[23]

His own feelings in favor of the French Revolution were initially extended enthusiastically to Citizen Genet, who upon first meeting seemed prudent enough to ensure that moderate supporters of the French Revolution would not be offended by any arrogant French act. Jefferson went so far as to give Genet's efforts in the western states his unofficial support, providing a letter of introduction for the French botanist, André Michaux, to the governor of Kentucky on Michaux's secret trip to raise support for an invasion of Louisiana—perhaps a treasonable violation of the administration's official neutrality.[24] In addition, Jefferson assisted the French cause by giving a formal imprimatur to those who wished to accept commissions as privateers from the French Republic. Under the auspices of the U.S. State Department, numerous newspapers printed an English translation of the "official" stock form of the letters of marque of the French Republic, with no other form being "valid."[25]

But when the aptly named privateer *Citizen Genet,* with a crew of numerous American citizens—including Gideon Henfield—captured the British merchantman *William* in American waters and attempted to sell the ship in Philadelphia, Jefferson quickly found himself stuck between ideology and politics. The *Citizen Genet* was but one of the eventual twelve privateers that Genet supported and outfitted. Largely financed and manned by American citizens, this fleet of privateers succeeded in capturing more than eighty British prizes in a little over two years. Washington pledged himself to protect American neutrality, and pressed Jefferson to provide the proper information to arrest the privateers. So when the ship docked in Philadelphia to dispose of its prize, Henfield was arrested for violating the official neutrality of the United States.[26] The issue concerned the nature of American citizenship directly. Henfield claimed the protection of French citizenship, denied that he still possessed any allegiance to America, and argued that he had exercised his "natural right of expatriation."

When he initially heard of the arrest of Gideon Henfield and Henfield's shipmate, John Singletary, Genet expressed his shock and dismay to Jefferson. Genet wrote that he believed the crime laid at the feet of "citizen Gideon Henfield and John Singletary" was "the crime which my mind cannot conceive, and which my pen almost refuses to state." The crime apparently was "the serving of France, and defending with her children the common and glorious cause of liberty."[27] He did not know of "any positive law, or treaty" which stopped American citizens from serving the noble cause of liberty. He finished with a flourish, calling upon Jefferson and the president to order the "immediate releasment" of the officers in question, and he assured that these men should be considered as having gained "the right of French citizens, if they have lost that of American citizens."[28]

Jefferson attempted to reply with ambiguity and delay, even implying that American citizens could in fact serve on French vessels, but Hamilton and Knox urged Washington to demand much stronger language. Jefferson complied, and issued a rather dogmatic denial of the claims of Genet. Although Genet had asserted that there was "no positive law" which stopped American citizens from engaging in missions under the commission of the French Republic, Jefferson noted that the law of nations required neutral nations to control the activities of their citizens. Genet was not impressed. He was a revolutionary, and he did not have time for the niceties of the "law of nations." His answer to Jefferson's denial was true to form. "Discussions are short," he noted, "when matters are taken on their true principles." "Let us explain ourselves as republicans," he went on. The law of nations, inasmuch as it affirmed the rights of man, was fine, but the positive law of nations, derived from the treaties of kings and princes, was nothing but a history "of ancient politicks by diplomatic subtleties." How could the United States "punish the brave individuals of your nation, who arrange themselves under our banner," while knowing "perfectly well, that no law of the United States gives to the government the sad power of arresting their zeal by acts of rigour." He finished with another flourish: "The Americans are free; they are not attached to the glebe like the slaves of Russia; they may change their situation when they please, and by accepting, at this moment, the succour of their arms in the habit of trampling on tyrants, we do not commit the plegiat of which you speak."[29]

Genet's argument had changed emphasis. He still considered any appeal to "ancient politicks" to be meaningless in this enlightened age, but he was now asserting that Henfield and his compatriots *had* changed "their situation." Unlike "the slaves of Russia," Americans had the right, he noted, to "arrange themselves under our banner." Henfield, Genet asserted, had in fact expatriated himself; he was a citizen of France.[30]

Here Genet expressed many of the elements that the most forward critics of the administration would later employ in sympathy with Henfield and the hapless crew of the *Citizen Genet.* Jefferson actually found himself needing to justify his official correspondence privately against the bitter attacks of the opposition press, and it is clear that his own position on expatriation and Washington's Proclamation of Neutrality was closer to Genet's than to the administration's, but he doubted whether Henfield actually had intended to expatriate himself. Using the same logic Jefferson had used to attack would-be aristocrats in America, one writer challenged Jefferson with charges of apostasy and sophistry, ridiculing Jefferson's efforts to play the Republican while using the language of polite diplomacy—the language of subtle tyranny.[31] The Democratic Society of Grenville, in South Carolina, changed its name to the Madisonian Society as a way to place Madison ahead of Jefferson in its ranking of Republican heroes.[32] Jefferson would not forgive Genet for placing him in an uncomfortable alliance with those he considered to be striving for aristocracy, and by late July he was urging Republicans to abandon Genet. They did not.[33] By the time of Gideon Henfield's trial in the federal circuit court in Philadelphia at the end of July, the case had taken on national celebrity. The official ambassadors of both Britain and France had been engaged from the first. Genet actually paid Henfield's legal fees, and the case engendered a contentious debate over the usefulness, policy, constitutionality, and honor of Washington's Proclamation of Neutrality.

Representing the United States was the U.S. district attorney for Pennsylvania, William Rawle, and the U.S. attorney general, Edmund Randolph. Rawle had learned his law at Middle Temple, was a Loyalist during the American Revolution, and a strong Federalist in the 1790s; he later prosecuted Thomas Cooper, at the behest of John Adams and Timothy Pickering, under the Sedition Act.[34] Rawle and Randolph were aided in their case by the strong opinion of Justice James Wilson in his message to the grand inquest that had indicted Henfield, the finer points of which he repeated as his instructions to the jury. Alexander Hamilton also added his mite to Rawle's arguments, sending him books, forwarding him legal citations, and providing marginalia on Rawle's preliminary opinions.[35]

The prosecution made a few simple points. First, the United States was a neutral nation, by the proclamation of the executive and by the treaty of peace with Great Britain. Second, Gideon Henfield was still a citizen of the United States and was bound by his duty as a citizen to obey the policy of the nation. While Rawle agreed that American citizenship was not held to "the slavish doctrine of unalienable allegiance," he could never admit that American citizens could escape the duties of citizenship without the consent of the nation as a whole. Ultimately, the "common welfare" of the nation must control the imagined rights of citizens to do as they wished; otherwise, "a few individuals, for avaricious purposes, might involve the nation in war, taking opposite sides, might destroy the nation in detail." If the brazen claims of Henfield were to be countenanced, "the national character and existence of America are lost; and instead of being members of a great nation, we become a band of miserable Algerines."[36] The question was not one to be based upon "the speculations of the closet," but upon the authority of "national common law," of which the "law of nations" is a part. It was true, Rawle noted, that a man in a state of nature possessed the "right of expatriation" as well as the right of making war, but the United States was not in a state of nature, but rather in a state of "civil society." He continued, "It is prostrating the right of civil society to support the right of man in a state of nature" for citizens of a constituted nation.[37] The collective survival of the nation would be risked if the law allowed all the whims of individual claims of rights against the policy of the whole. Indeed, this is why people leave a state of nature for civil society: the nation "is instituted to prevent the pernicious effects of those rights."[38]

The attorneys for the defense were Peter Stephen Du Ponceau, Jared Ingersoll, and Jonathan Dickinson Sargent, three of the most prominent Pennsylvania Republicans. Each of them had participated in the celebration of Genet's arrival in Philadelphia, and all were charter members of the formidable Democratic-Republican Society of Pennsylvania. Their argument, although little explicit language survives, followed much of the reasoning of Genet. There was no "positive law" that forbade what Henfield had done; the treaties, or positive law, of nations was a mere history of "ancient politics"; the Constitution did not provide for a national common law—the states controlled the regulations of citizenship; the Proclamation of Neutrality should be considered as an ex post facto law; and in any case, Henfield had the inalienable "natural right of expatriation," which he surely exercised by receiving a commission and the protection of the French Republic, and this was a natural right explicitly recognized by the Virginia statute and by the Pennsylvania constitution.[39] The opposition newspapers considered the argument to be "efficient and unanswerable."[40]

Justice James Wilson had an answer, however—which he made clear in his instructions to the jury. Wilson considered the question "a case of first importance." The jury's verdict would decide the fate of "four millions of your fellow citizens." "As a citizen of the United

States," Wilson argued, "the defendant was bound to keep the peace in regard to all nations with whom we are at peace."[41] Informing the jury that "two principal questions of fact have arisen, and require your determination," he went on to explain how they should resolve them. The first question, as to whether Gideon Henfield "has committed an act of hostility against the subjects of a power with whom the United States are at peace," Wilson considered "clearly established in the testimony." The second question, "whether Gideon Henfield was at that time a citizen of the United States," was something Wilson believed had been "explicitly acknowledged."[42] Since the importance of how these facts related to the law needed to be fully comprehended by the jury, he proceeded to "explain the law to the jury." The arguments of the defense were simply wrong, he asserted. Wilson continued, "It has been asked by his [Henfield's] counsel, in their address to you, against what [positive] law has he offended?" "The answer," Wilson explained, "is against many and binding laws." Not only had Henfield trampled over the treaty obligations of the United States, but he had broken "not an ex post facto law" but "the law of nations," a part of the natural common law that "was in existence long before Gideon Henfield existed."[43] Wilson went on to add that although "much had been said on this occasion, by the defendant's counsel, in support of the natural right of emigration," it did not make any difference, because "little of it is truly applicable to the present question."[44]

Despite Wilson's commanding instruction to the jury, they ignored him and returned a verdict of "not guilty." George Washington was mortified. Considering the verdict an insult to the dignity of his administration and to the honor of the nation generally, Washington asked his cabinet if he should call a special session of Congress to clarify the policy of American neutrality. While not taking such extreme action, the government published Justice Wilson's instructions to the grand inquest as a way to clarify the government's position. Hamilton issued a circular to the collectors of the customs the day after the verdict, which contained a set of "Rules adopted by the President" that explicitly made the arming and support of privateers illegal and subjected those engaging in such acts to arrest and heavy penalty.[45] Hamilton mobilized his customs agents and revenue cutters to frustrate any Americans attempting to serve the French. Within days, the administration officially asked the French for the removal of Genet from his post. Furthermore, at the opening of the next session of Congress, in December, Washington informed the House of Representatives of his great discontent with Genet, whose actions could "involve us in war abroad, and discord and anarchy at home." He made it clear that he would not allow the policy of the nation to be controlled by independent juries, and he would take action to honor the "stipulations of our treaties according to what *I judge* their true sense." If juries failed to act, the United States would compensate the injured parties and provide restitution for property seized illegally by American citizens.[46] Jefferson, conflicted as to the significance of the acquittal, was pressed to write a personal letter of explanation to Gouverneur Morris, the American ambassador to Great Britain.[47]

The growing opposition to the Washington administration, however, considered the verdict a startling affirmation of "the rights of man." Philip Freneau's *National Gazette* attacked the judge and prosecution for opening the "sluices" of "aristocratic torrent" against the better judgment of an honest jury. The author derided the spirit of the prosecution, and could scarcely believe that the prosecution had attempted to perfect the "infamous doctrine, that American *citizens* (like some European *subjects*) are *slaves,* attached to the soil; and cannot, without the leave of their 'masters,' enter into the service of France, or any other foreign power."[48] With great optimism, the paper noted that the jury had ruled on both the law and the facts, and that therefore a great precedent had been set: "that a citizen of the United States may lawfully enter on board a French vessel." Even more important, however, was the example provided by the "virtue and independence of our juries," who would be venerated through the ages "for adding to the security of the rights and liberties of mankind."[49]

Citizen Genet immediately began advertising for all "FRIENDS to LIBERTY" to serve upon French ships of war, and he also held a celebratory feast for supporters in Philadelphia, to "meet Citizen Henfield" and officially welcome Henfield into the French fold.[50] He published a handbill, meant for the docks of New York and Philadelphia, which implored "all able bodied seamen willing to engage in the cause of liberty" to make their applications at his residence. In recognition of the trends of Revolutionary immigration, he noted that "particular attention will be paid to the generous and intrepid natives of Ireland."[51] Within days of the acquittal, Genet was toasted and received in New York by leading Republicans. Although they were ready to honor Washington's proclamation, the committee receiving Genet promised that, "as the sentiment relates to question and principle there is no neutrality," and that they were loath to "shrink from the common cause of human nature."[52] In Boston, "the toast of the day in all republican circles" celebrated "the virtuous and independent jury of Pennsylvania who acquitted Henfield."[53] The Democratic-Republican Society of Charleston upon hearing of Henfield's acquittal offered toasts recognizing the "right of expatriation" as a "natural right." One such toast, which received three cheers, celebrated "the patriotic jury of Philadelphia who acquitted Gideon Henfield, and supported the rights of man."[54]

The next major legal and political battle over emigration reached its climax in the fall 1795 term of the Supreme Court. The case at hand, *Talbot v. Janson,* featured a showdown between a leading opposition lawyer and pro-government lawyers from numerous states over another privateering episode. The issue concerned the seizure, on May 16, 1794, of a Dutch vessel carrying goods from Curaçao to Amsterdam.[55] The Dutch brigantine *Magdalena* had been taken off the Cuban coast by Captain Edward Ballard, an "expatriated" Virginian. Ballard was formerly a branch pilot of the Chesapeake Bay, but now he flew a French standard on his ship, *L'Ame de la Liberte.* After a brief rendezvous with his partner, Captain William Talbot—another expatriate American citizen—aboard Talbot's privateer, *L'Ami de la Point a Petre,* the two escorted the *Magdelena* to Charleston, and proceeded to claim the ship as a prize. The Dutch owners immediately filed a grievance and a libel against the two men, and Captain Ballard was arrested and held on charges of piracy by the Charleston authorities. Captain Talbot, holder of a commission from the French authorities of Guadalupe as well as papers showing his naturalization as a French citizen, was not arrested. He filed a countersuit, asserting his rights under the rules of war to dispose of the prize ship. He also attempted, briefly, to claim he had no relationship with Ballard.[56]

Over the next year and a half, the case moved through the courts. Ballard was eventually indicted but acquitted by a friendly Charleston jury of the charge of piracy, which required rather stringent proofs of criminal intent. But the libel, to provide restitution to the Dutch owners of the ship and cargo, was a case in admiralty, which meant judges, not juries, would decide the outcome. Talbot lost in the federal district court at Charleston. The decision was appealed to the circuit court, which upheld the district court's decision, and the U.S. Supreme Court heard a final appeal in August of 1795.

The lead counsel for the appellant (Ballard and Talbot) was Alexander J. Dallas, secretary of the State of Pennsylvania and, like his co-counsel, Peter Stephen Du Ponceau, a co-founder and officer of the Democratic-Republican Society of Pennsylvania. He had been an intimate of Genet's, and he defended his friend against the aspersions of allies and enemies alike. It was in a conversation with Dallas that Genet had supposedly voiced his intention to appeal directly to the American people if Washington persisted in his doctrine of neutrality, and although Dallas was used by the pro-government forces to attack the motives of the French minister, he continued to defend the minister's real intentions.

The crux of Dallas's arguments surrounded the "right of expatriation." He needed to prove first that such a right existed and that both Ballard and Talbot had availed themselves of said right before becoming citizens of the French Republic. If such could be proven, his clients could be declared to have legally served the French and lawfully disposed of their prize in an American port, which, at the time, no positive law—either treaty or statute—forbade them from doing. Proving the right of expatriation Dallas considered self-evident: "The right of expatriation is antecedent and superior to the law of society."[57] It was one of the "rights of man." Since governments were formed of a compact intended to "shield the weakness, and supply the wants of individuals," when the government failed, "suffering individuals are permitted to withdraw" from the compact. It was a right in the abstract that Dallas claimed had been recognized "by every writer, ancient and modern, by the civilian, as well as by the common-law lawyer; by the philosopher, as well as the poet."[58] Despite this supposedly universally recognized right of expatriation, Dallas admitted that some "human institutions," especially those of "the feudal system," had created a "law of allegiance," from which "arose the doctrine of perpetual and universal allegiance" which Blackstone, English common law, and the British Admiralty asserted.[59] But so what? What were these authorities to the American citizenry? The slavish allegiance of subjects had been replaced through the Revolution with the free compact of citizens, as he asserted, laying out the most articulate creed of the citizenship revolution:

> . . . citizenship, which has arisen from the dissolution of the feudal system; and is a substitute for allegiance, corresponding with the new order of things. Allegiance and citizenship, differ, indeed, in almost every characteristic. Citizenship is the effect of compact; allegiance is the offspring of power and necessity. Citizenship is a political tie; allegiance is a territorial tenure. Citizenship is the character of equality; allegiance is a badge of inferiority. Citizenship is constitutional; allegiance is personal. Citizenship is freedom; allegiance is servitude. Citizenship is communicable; allegiance is repulsive. Citizenship may be relinquished; allegiance is perpetual. With such essential differences, the doctrine of allegiance is inapplicable to a system of citizenship; which it can neither serve to control, nor to elucidate.[60]

Since a "system of allegiance" could neither control nor elucidate a "system of citizenship," traditional authorities that limited, defined, or outlawed the right of expatriation should carry no weight. Law needed a flexibility that a *modern* notion of allegiance demanded. Was not the common law perfected in the Revolution? Here Dallas explicated most clearly an argument for the extension of Revolutionary principles to the very structures of citizenship, law, and government. In English legal practice by the middle of the eighteenth century, jurists used "subjects" and "citizens" as roughly interchangeable terms, simply referring to the fundamental constituent members of commonwealths. Dallas, however, emphasized that "citizenship" was part of a modern perspective, while "subjecthood" relied upon concepts of allegiance that descended directly from feudal relationships—relationships abandoned by the Americans in 1776. In Dallas's articulation of citizenship, individual intentions deserved great deference, while the interests of the institutions of power, and the arguments that maintained their authority—inasmuch as they were products of a feudal way of thinking—warranted slight regard.

Dallas had little chance of winning the argument. Since an enthusiastic jury would not decide *this* case, such novel ideas could have little effect. The counsels for the Dutch, which included future Federalist Senator Joseph Reed, were arguing to a pro-administration-dominated Court, which again included James Wilson, one of the judges whose decision in the circuit court was being appealed. On the question of expatriation, counsel made three points. First, although Ballard had availed himself of a Virginia statute allowing expatriation, he possessed no proof of naturalization by the French Republic that the Court was willing to recognize. For Talbot, even though Ballard had proof of naturalization from the officials in Guadalupe and a commission as a French privateer, he had not been released from the duties of American citizenship by any responsible national authority. Second, national citizenship and allegiance trumped state citizenship, so even if Virginia law allowed its citizens to expatriate themselves, they could only give up their status of Virginian citizenship, still holding citizenship under the national authority of the United States. It was a question of nationhood. If a mere state could dictate the terms of American citizenship, then the national government remained nothing more than a cipher, a more contemptible institution than the one created by the Articles of Confederation. Finally, although Dallas had asserted that a man could expatriate himself at any time, and that his acceptance of a general call for privateers by a minister of the French Republic might be enough to assume naturalization as a French citizen, such an argument was too visionary to be permitted. Counsel for the Dutch ship owners were not willing to deny expatriation entirely, which English common law and practice demanded, but they argued that expatriation could only be accomplished "under the regulations prescribed by law."[61] If society followed the arguments of Dallas, wherein citizens could easily and quickly relinquish their citizenship and act on their individual interests, the world "might behold a political monster, all the citizens of a country at war, though the country itself at peace."[62] Natural rights, however sacred, needed to be regulated by the legally constituted authorities. "The power of regulating emigration," like its counterpart, the power of naturalization, was "vested exclusively in Congress" by the Constitution.[63] Since neither Ballard nor Talbot had followed the proper rules for expatriation (and apparently no one could, until Congress crafted an expatriation law), they must both be considered bound, as American citizens, by the policy of the national state and the law of nations.

The justices unanimously upheld the circuit court decision, and expanded the retribution due from Ballard and Talbot to include interest and court costs. With the cost of the ship, interest, and fines for delay and demurrage, Ballard and Talbot were responsible for nearly $7,000.[64] The lead decision was crafted by William Paterson, who expressed very little patience for Dallas's expansive view of the right of expatriation.[65] Since the United States possessed no statute on expatriation generally, he did not believe that Revolutionary principles such as those Dallas advocated should be the guide, but rather the law of nations. He also agreed with the counsel for the Dutch that there was a question of national citizenship. Virginia was but a state of the Union, and even if citizens could legally expatriate themselves from Virginia, this did not imply that they had escaped their responsibilities to the United States. Such a situation would not only be a denial of the supremacy of the national allegiance, but would create a "citizen of the world," an absurdity unknown in the law of nature and nations. To allow states to control the powers of expatriation was to deny the existence of an American nation entirely. In short, Ballard and Talbot had failed to be properly expatriated by the laws of their country and must be accountable to the American treaties with the Dutch.

Of the other justices, including James Wilson, William Cushing, and Edward Rutledge, only Justice Iredell commented on the question of expatriation in the abstract.[66] He believed the question deserved "more deference," since the constitution of the state of Pennsylvania explicitly recognized the right.[67] It was the "law of nations," however, and all the highly esteemed authors on those laws, that needed to guide the justices on the question, and not the opinions of the present day. The problem to Iredell was a difference in opinion in America as to "the proper manner of executing this right." Dallas had "ingeniously argued at the bar" for an expansive execution of the right, as Iredell acknowledged. "Some hold," he began, "that it is the natural unalienable right in each individual; that it is a right upon which no act of legislation can lawfully be exercised." If this were true, "it must be left to every man's will and pleasure, to go off, when, and in what manner he pleases."[68] Iredell thought such arguments put the "mere inclinations" of individuals in higher regard than the "principles of patriotism and public good" which in all governments must "predominate."[69] While he also did not wish to deny absolutely the possibility of emigration and expatriation, he argued that the laws of the country must provide the legal arrangements, for if Dallas had his way, "no rights are secured, but those of the *expatriator* himself."[70]

In a different case, in 1796, Iredell's opinion on the place of individual rights in society was even more fully articulated. "All governments depend more or less upon the confidence and support of the people for whose benefit they do or ought, to subsist," he began. This applied particularly to a "free government." So, in the United States "every citizen" owes "to his country, by all possible and honorable means, to promote its prosperity, and to do nothing either negligently or with design to counteracting it." "Considering himself as a member of a single community, which is itself a member of another in a larger sphere," the citizen "should reflect that he is only one individual connected with a great number of others, whose authority separately is equal, and each of whose sentiments are entitled to equal deference with his own." Ultimately, "individual interest, when it comes into competition, must yield to that of the State."[71] The Federalist desire to check the enthusiasm for the absolute invocations of individual rights in society is quite clear. Although Iredell and Paterson were willing to grant a possibility for expatriation, it certainly could not exist without the direct regulation of the written laws of society. Citizens had rights, but these individual claims could not trump the common good and the policy of the nation.

The Federalist chief justice Oliver Ellsworth went further than Iredell and Paterson in denying the right of expatriation. In district court, Ellsworth ruled on the evidence of Isaac Williams, a citizen of the United States who had accepted a commission as third lieutenant on a French 72-gun frigate in the fall of 1792. Upon arriving in France, Williams had taken oaths to the French Republic and had renounced his allegiance to all other countries, "particularly to America." Continuing his service in the French navy, over the next five years Williams moved his family to Guadeloupe and established his residency there, only returning to the United States for a brief time to visit friends and extended family.[72] His intention was clearly to remain a French citizen in perpetuity. But on one brief trip to Connecticut he was arrested and indicted as an American citizen for committing acts of war against Great Britain. On the question of whether the jury should be moved by Williams's claims to have expatriated himself by renouncing his allegiance to America, taking a commission in the French navy, and moving his family and property to the French colony of Guadeloupe, Ellsworth articulated an extreme position. Noting that "the common law of this country remains the same as it was before the Revolution," Ellsworth took a position which denied any right of expatriation without the explicit consent of the community, a situation which he denied the policy or the interest of the nation allowed. In addition, he contended that even "the most visionary writers on this subject do not contend for the principle in the unlimited extent, that a citizen may at any and at all times, renounce his own, and join himself to a foreign country"—the attitude which claims of a "natural right of expatriation" seemed to assert. He argued that the facts of the prisoner's naturalization as a citizen of France, his commission, and his emigration to Guadeloupe were "totally irrelevant; they can have no operation in law; and the jury ought not to be embarrassed or troubled with them." The Connecticut jury was not, indeed, troubled by them, and Williams received two $1,000 fines and eight months in jail.[73]

In the reactions to the trial of Henfield and in the continuing controversies over whether a "natural right to expatriation" existed, we can discern the deep differences in the political thought of the two emerging American national parties. Federalists, who supported the national administration, and Republicans, who opposed the Federalists, came to understand the rights attendant to American citizens in very different ways—perspectives deeply rooted in hardening opinions as to what the American Revolution had been about. Federalists tended to see the American Revolution as an independence movement that merely attempted to restore a society based upon the great institutions which had provided security and liberty: a constitutionally defined government, a principled common law, and a strong sense of national commonwealth. Intimately bound onto these tendencies was the Federalist assumption that the national courts could draw upon a "national common law," and that state citizenship was merely a subsidiary membership of national citizenship. Republicans tended to see the American Revolution as an overthrow of feudal institutions, the birth of a modern republican system based upon inalienable natural rights attached to individuals, and the dawn of a new era in which reason could purify the contemptible corruption that ancient politics had heaped upon the interactions of citizens in society. The states protected these principles with their constitutions, declarations of rights, and republicanized common law, each bound into a Union which carefully proscribed the powers of the general government. There was no national common law. These divergent perspectives, which had antecedents in the moment of Independence itself, were sharpened and clarified by the explosive potential of the French Revolution.

Republicans were not daunted by the arguments that Federalists used to deny expatriation. The assertion of a natural and inalienable right of expatriation was a challenge to the authority of the national government and the principles of allegiance which defined subjecthood. As all the Federalist justices recognized, it put great stock on the interests of the individual and placed little emphasis on the place of national institutions in controlling the citizenry. For the Republicans who wished to press the "rights of man" to reform social and political relationships, the fact that the common law failed to recognize the right of expatriation was a reason to reform the common law, not the idea of expatriation, which they continued to affirm throughout the 1790s.

The adoption of Jay's Treaty with Great Britain brought out more such sentiments. One of the complaints against Jay's Treaty by the Democratic Society of the Washington District of South Carolina was an article in the treaty that restricted the citizens or subjects of either party from accepting commissions in an army hostile to either of the parties to the treaty—a regulation considered by the Democratic club to be "a gross violation of the natural rights of man" and a clause that should have been "indignantly spurned at!"[74] A voluntary toast offered by the crowd at a similar event called for "the right of expatriation to all those who wish to quit our country."[75]

The most explicit popular affirmation of the natural right of expatriation was a message to Citizen Genet about the dangers of counter-revolution sent by a group of mechanics in Charleston, South Carolina, and written after Genet had fallen from grace with Washington's administration. Its authors explicitly connected themselves with the "true Republicans" of America, and they claimed to be writing to warn Genet's countrymen against groups who would attempt to hand away the fruits of their Revolution. Beware that "after your army has bestowed peace, and perhaps liberty to the world," you may see arise among you a "Junto," who "under cover of law" would "rob the French Soldier of the price of his blood shed for the liberty of his country." Or perhaps this "Junto" would strip "the honest citizen of the fruits of his labour." It might also come to pass that your "Judges will so far disgrace the Sacred Bench of Justice as to pronounce from thence in a solemn mood" that a man "has no right to expatriate himself," and "and the Liberty of your country will be lost, if there is no jury" to say otherwise. For good measure, the group closed with a long attack on banks and the funding system.[76]

The insistence on the "natural right of expatriation," against the principles of English allegiance and against the subtle experts of the treaties of nations, represented a strong desire to bring "common sense" and "reason" to the rules that governed the interactions of free people. The emerging opposition to the Washington administration, which increasingly saw itself excluded from a government it feared was captured by foreign interests and British ideas, was replaying the initial struggles of the 1770s and 1780s (now informed by the experience of the 1790s), when numerous groups and people fought to inject the institutions that governed citizenship with as much natural equality as possible. "Citizenship" required whole new sets of laws that did not use the same logic that defined English "subjecthood," and in the coalescence of a national party opposed to Federalists, these local battles over citizenship took on national, and international, significance. Combined with complaints about taxes, banks, and the funding system, these idealistic perspectives gained powerful force in people's lives. It was a continuing effort to endow American citizenship with Revolutionary principles. It was indicative of their understanding of the difference between subjects and citizens. Subjecthood was perpetual and based upon blood; citizenship was flexible and based upon principles. It was radical, and to the Federalists it promised anarchy of a French style, especially since they considered themselves the properly elected representatives of the people and the policy of the nation.[77]

International Revolutionary Politics and the Rise of Party

Although we must stress the unbending nature of the polarities through which Federalists and Republicans defined each other—their increasing tunnel vision—we should not be daunted from recognizing the actual diversity of the constituent components of these party coalitions. First and foremost, the "Federalists" and the "Republicans" are not synonymous, in any real way, with the "federalists" and "anti-federalists" who fought over the ratification of the Constitution. Historians continue to make this mistake. The old "federalist" coalition was never a fully articulated party—it was a one-issue coalition, which ended in different parts of the country at different times. The anti-federalists, where they existed in strength, were always a complex mingling of different individuals, tendencies, and interests. Once Madison started moving in coordination with Jefferson and the Virginia anti-federalists John Taylor and James Monroe against Hamilton's ambitious plans, the old federalist alliance shattered at the top, where it had been most fully organized.[78] In each of the states, the alliances in favor of or against the Constitution realigned based upon internal state dynamics, personality struggles, and the increasingly organized opposition to the Hamiltonian system. In general, former anti-federalists began to remember the fight over the Constitution as largely a fight over how to get the proposed Constitution amended—which it was. So both parties defended the Constitution—they just had different visions of how to interpret the powers enumerated in the Constitution.

The administration, especially after the retirement of Thomas Jefferson at the beginning of 1794, became entirely controlled by the Hamiltonian tendency, and those who supported them and their policies united as the national Federalist Party. There were divisions among the Federalists, mostly oscillating between friends and allies of John Adams and supporters of Alexander Hamilton. And there were powerful sectional differences among the Federalists—reflected whenever slavery became an issue. As a whole, however, Federalists consistently emphasized the importance of national sovereignty, the legitimacy of the government as the only true arbiter of the opinion of "the people," and law and order as the best way to secure the affections of the American people to the national state and navigate the troubling waters of international war and revolution.

The Republicans were more actively organizing throughout the 1790s, both during elections and in Congress, but they were also less unified, and they did not control the national government. The Republicans shared many things but most powerfully came together against specific policies of the government that were seen to enlarge the power of the national state, at the expense of the balance of the Constitution and the rights of the states, and to align the country with Britain. They were quick to argue natural rights against law. But as an opposition movement they did not really have to create anything, except momentum to throw the Federalists out of office. In this they did not succeed on a national scale until after 1800. As an opposition party, Republicans embraced a diversity of economic and political thought to articulate their separate political strategies, but the very nature of opposition allowed them to be much less rigid in their plans and platforms. Historians have lately reemphasized the diversity of Republican political thought.[79] "Parties" are always coalitions of numerous elements, interests, and groups, and as such we can note that the constituencies of the parties were being increasingly clarified over the course of the 1790s. Yet even by the end of the decade, not every political action can be completely subsumed by the alliances of the parties or by people who would have called themselves "Federalists" or "Republicans." The Whiskey Rebellion and, later,

Fries's Rebellion, for instance, drew upon strains of popular protest in western Pennsylvania which had never been effectively channeled into party purposes, except as fodder for mutual recriminations.[80]

Yet the parties came to determine the meaning of every event in the 1790s, filtered through their particular worldview. The striking truth of the national politics of the 1790s remains the quickness by which Americans divided their political debates into neat polarities. From the halls of Congress to the local struggles in the smallest hamlet, observers defined their opponents as "French" or "British" parties, respectively, and subtlety in contemporary analysis is difficult to find. Even James Madison, who wrote a series of eighteen articles examining the nature of parties in the United States, ultimately assured his readers that the parties were merely the recrudescence of the Revolutionary fights between Tories and Whigs, now remade as Monarchists and Republicans—or, as he argued, those in favor of "usurpation and monarchy" against the real "friends of the Union," who still adored the principles of "true republicanism."[81] You can guess which side he was on. As war unfolded in Europe and Americans increasingly saw the gulf between "French" principles of revolution and "British" conceptions of law, order, and national community, Americans fashioned their own party attachments accordingly. So we can generalize, because *they* generalized.

The polarization of American political rhetoric in the 1790s fed upon itself, reinforcing polemical views of political history. As Thomas Jefferson wrote later in life, "The same political parties which now agitate the U.S. have existed thro' all time." One party sought to exult "the power of the people," while the other fought for the prerogatives of the αριστοι—the "aristocrats."[82] Since Jefferson became the leader of the opposition against the Federalist government, and as he obviously saw himself as one of those serving the interests of the people, the Federalists could easily be fused into proponents of aristocracy and monarchy, enemies to the "principles of '76." Jefferson, like most of the Republicans, believed the "principles of '76," or "the standard of Common Sense," *were* the principles of equality and independence that had pressed provincial British colonials to declare themselves independent Americans. A telling moment in this regard is Jefferson's rapid dismissal of John Adams's "Discourses on Davila." Published as a series of essays in the *Gazette of the United States* from February to April 1791, Adams's dense arguments, filled with numerous references to obscure political tracts, challenged the loose and idealistic thinking of the French revolutionaries with an argument recognizing the importance of the "natural aristocracy" in the stability of societies and constituted governments.[83] Jefferson quickly lumped Adams's essays in with those of other authors and politicians—like Edmund Burke—who, in their condemnation of the French Revolution and their avowed regard for the British Constitution, he considered to be apostates "from the true faith." As he put it to the publisher of the first American edition of Thomas Paine's *The Rights of Man,* he was "extremely pleased to find [the book] will be reprinted here, and that something is at length to be publickly said against the political heresies which have sprung up among us. I have no doubt our citizens will rally a second time round the standard of Common Sense."[84]

The swipe at recent "political heresies" was seen as an attack on John Adams, who Jefferson believed had become an advocate of "hereditary monarchy & nobility."[85] While *we* can separate Adams's thoughts on natural aristocracy in these essays as distinct from a "Burkean" political philosophy, it is clear that Jefferson, like all good revolutionaries, had little time for splitting hairs. Adams apparently was on the wrong side of the question—and there were only two sides. For Jefferson, his old friend John Adams, the great New England republican, somehow had joined the enemies of America. Jefferson interpreted Adams in light of what he considered Burke's own transformation. As he noted pithily, after reading Burke's *Reflections on the Revolution in France,* "The Revolution in France does not astonish me so much as the revolution in Mr. Burke."[86] In a few years, even the façade of friendship between Adams and Jefferson would disappear. By the end of the decade, Jefferson could recognize and lament party politics, but his own worldview helped to create the problem, and he could not escape himself.

Just as Henfield and his compatriots were engaging in an international war, the American political parties formed in the midst of an international debate about rights, nations, the sanctity of tradition, and the legitimacy of revolutionary violence. Americans fought over the principles of citizenship, not as a mere rhetorical cipher of the great debates over the justice of the French Revolution, or even as a reactionary reflex to the turn of events in Europe, but as active participants in an international political contest. For many, American citizenship embodied the principles of independence which man possessed in a state of natural equality, not the constraints of traditional forms of legalism. What the Americans had called natural and inalienable rights, the French and Tom Paine were now calling the "[natural] Rights of Man." These were the universalisms of the Revolutionary Age, principles which the Republican Party believed were infused in the very meaning of American citizenship.

And yet the heavy emphasis placed upon "natural rights" and the "rights of man" promised, as it had during the 1770s, to transform

American politics and society. Federalists objected to the opposition rhetoric and tactics as unsettled, philosophic, universal, and visionary. Federalists were all for "liberties," but liberties were defined in the institutions of civil society; they were not something plucked from the ether of an imagined state of nature whenever individual whim or interest called for it. And the ultimate civil authority was the national state, not the state governments, which the opposition claimed to be the sole arbiter of American citizenship, with a few carefully defined exceptions. So the polarities that informed the national political alliances in America of the 1790s were deeply involved in the struggles of the American Revolution, and the Revolutionary Age in general. Americans found themselves as part of an international conversation, one in which their own Revolution played an important part, and one that in its broadest outlines can be discerned in the attitudes of Edmund Burke and Thomas Paine toward the French Revolution—the friends of order against the rights of man.[87]

Historians have too often underplayed the international context of American political and constitutional thought in the first decades after Independence. But it was only because the French Revolution opened problems related to both national policy *and* the political thought of citizenship and nationhood that it exerted such important pressure upon American party development in the 1790s. If it had just been Genet, or even an executed king, the French Revolution would not have been such a powerful marker in the rise of the two national parties. The trials over expatriation revealed deep disagreement among Americans. Each party seemed to the other to be willfully misinterpreting the Constitution—and the meaning of the American Revolution. These men, who took their party affiliations seriously, were not simply deluded and paranoid. They saw in each other *real* differences of political thought, and they worried that their own conceptions of the American republic were being challenged by foreign ideas.

Only by recognizing that the two parties were divided both by policy *and* political thought can we understand the vicious language and high stakes of the political debate. As the parties coalesced throughout the 1790s, Republicans and Federalists perceived their "enemies" as proponents of either monarchy or anarchy, respectively, embodied in two warring foreign nations—the forces that had traditionally destroyed free republics. The Federalists regarded the French Revolution—with its *sans-cullotes,* Jacobins, atheists, and guillotines—as a daunting example of the chaos that had too often undermined well-intentioned reform. The Englishman D. M. Erskine observed, "The Federalists accuse the other party of being democrats" who "wish to introduce Anarchy & plunder & the French."[88] Republicans could be defined by any number of terms: "a Democrat, a Jacobin, a San-culot, a Frenchman, an Anarchist, a Revolutionist, a Leveller, a Disorganizer, a Regicide, a Liberticide." Similarly, Federalist John Quincy Adams saw in the opposition only "anti-federalism and servile devotion to a foreign power," which reflected tendencies "that *true* Americans deplore."[89] Southerner Charles Lee characterized opponents of the administration as "anti-Americans."[90] One Federalist newspaper noted that the two parties seemed to have different meanings for common words. To remedy the confusion, the editor published a list of "Federal definitions" adjacent to "Jacobin Definitions." The Federal definition of "American" was a person who "prefers the honour and felicity of his native country to every other," and who "believes that *America* to be free and happy, must have national opinions, sentiments and fashions of her own." The Jacobin definition of "American" was as person who "sings the *'Ca ira'* because a French sailor sings it; who dances the *'Carmagnole'* because it is danced at Paris, and who toasts the 'French Republic' in preference to his native land." "In short," a Jacobin is "one who has no opinion of his own, but is apt enough to follow any leash that any *foreigners* may give him."[91] The opposition were not "true" Americans in their thoughts, words, and actions.

The Republicans denied the Federalist authority to speak for the American people just as fiercely. The Democratic-Republican Societies argued that the elected government was corrupt, dominated by the elite moneyed interests of the country, and that the clubs were formed to speak for "the People of America."[92] So Republican Thomas Law wrote to James Madison of "an enemy to America" who differed with Law's belief that French immigrants were desirable.[93] Republicans believed the Federalists were the friends of "British emissaries, British pensioners, British merchants, old Tories, Refugees, Traitors, aristocrats," and "monarchists." At the very least, the Federalists were "landjobbers & stockjobbers," who were "contending for Monarchy, Aristocracy & British influence."[94] Thomas Jefferson called the Federalists an "Anglo Monachico, aristocratic party" that wanted to impose "the *substance* as they have already given us the forms of the British government."[95]

Between the acquittal of Gideon Henfield in 1793 and the conviction of Isaac Williams in 1799, the lines between the first American national parties were drawn. Much of the conflict was played out in the streets,[96] through popular and political songs, festivals, rituals and parades, and the newspapers—all of which combined local, national, international, and personal politics into a savage and partisan interpretation of events.[97] Party politics sharpened the problems of the Union,

FIGURE 2. "A Peep in the Anti-federal Club." This famous engraving attacks the legitimacy of the emerging opposition to the government in 1793. The people associated with the anti-federalists were considered to be foreigners, fanatics, desperate men, and power-hungry hypocrites. (Courtesy of the American Antiquarian Society)

as theoretical debates turned into party fights over the future of the country. Plenty of wags decried party politics, but few could do much to stop the polarization. As one author noted, "Party spirit is as great a curse to society as can befall it," since party "rends a government into two distinct peoples" and "makes fellow citizens greater strangers and more adverse to each other, than if they were two different nations."[98] As both parties denied the legitimacy of the other to speak for the American people, both developed competing visions of the American citizenry and nation. Indeed, each party eventually "ethnicized" the other: in the eyes of party, Republicans seemed more French and Federalists more British than any American should. And so we can see the effect of party—born in the midst of fights over expatriation, mobilizing to make a new law of naturalization to protect the Union from the types of immigrants which they believed strengthened the hand of the other party and threatened the independence of America.

The Politics of Naturalization

Antagonistic party relationships were exacerbated by substantial increases in the numbers of immigrants seeking safety in America. The revolution in France and the European wars that it spawned; the inspired plots and rebellion in Ireland; the Haitian uprising; and the British proclivity for banishing troublemakers—all inflicted thousands of political refugees upon an unwilling American public. Between 1783 and 1810, an estimated 275,000 Europeans and Euro-Caribbeans migrated to the United States.[99] Although historians of immigration have been slow to acknowledge this important pressure in the early and mid-1790s, discussion of the stress of immigration can be found throughout the popular press of the 1790s. One newspaper, for instance, reported in 1794 that "the emigrations from every part" of Europe "are becoming general." And, most significantly, ships from Bristol, Liverpool, Cork, and Portsmouth, "for these twelve months past have been crowded with families."[100] In New York, Boston, and Philadelphia, new charitable societies organized themselves, arguing that "the great increase of emigration from Europe" made such organizations "highly expedient." The New York Society for the Information and Assistance of Persons Emigrating from Foreign Countries noted that "persons of various descriptions are emigrating to the United States for protection and safety" from "the oppressions of many of the governments of Europe."[101] In one highly public landing, over three thousand refugees from the revolution on St. Domingue landed unexpectedly and without provisions in Baltimore, became the subject of an extended debate, and eventually received financial aid from the government.[102]

The combination of rabid party politics and the increased visibility of immigrants in America focused attention on the possible effect parties could have on foreigners, and foreigners could have on the American nation. When the very-high-profile emigrant, Dr. Joseph Priestly, arrived in America from England in the summer of 1794, he was met by a collection of groups and individuals that can only be described as the greeting committee of the New York Republican coalition: Governor George Clinton, members of the Democratic Society, Tammany, the Associated Teachers, the Medical Society of the State of New York, and "the republican natives of great Britain and Ireland." Tammany and the Democratic Society invited him to join their ranks.[103] He also received numerous warnings of the dangers of American party politics. "A citizen of New York" warned Dr. Priestly that party leaders often make themselves "efficaciously attentive" to emigrants "on [their] first arrival," and that "foreigners were frequently drawn into parties in this manner, to the prejudice of their own interest."[104] Priestly stayed out of politics, but very many immigrants did not.[105]

Republicans noted with concern the great number of "aristocrats" who every day seemed to be finding asylum in America, and worried of the effect such aliens would have on the manners of republican America. In addition, as the British navy began confiscating American merchant vessels and pressing American citizens into the service of the British fleet, Republicans began to view the British merchant interests in the cities with increased hostility, especially their easy access to the privileges of American citizenship.[106]

Federalists interpreted three events of the early 1790s as representative of the subversion of the nation by foreigners, and of the dangerous effect that a certain type of immigration played in these disruptions. First, the arrival of the French consul, "Citizen Genet," gave fresh evidence that foreign powers would attempt to corrupt and undermine the new American national government. Federalists lamented Genet's influence, arguing that the rise of the Democratic Societies directly reflected Genet's desire to "connect himself with a particular party" to "separate from the whole body" those American citizens who would then lose themselves in the bosom of foreign promises.[107]

Federalists also saw the birth of the Democratic-Republican clubs as emblematic of the danger radical immigrants were inflicting on American character. Arguing that the clubs were "composed of a few unworthy sons of America and the scum of Europe," Federalists believed the clubs would impede America's "advancement as a nation." The clubs, by "joining themselves to all the discontented emigrants from Europe," meant to deny to Americans any sense of "their national character."[108] For another writer lamenting the effect of the Democratic clubs on America, the problem remained not so much the presence of foreigners in the clubs, but foreigners' susceptibility to believe what the clubs asserted. As he noted, "Our democratic societies" prey on "the minds of the ignorant and jealous, especially foreigners and those who are sore from suffering in foreign countries," to secure a "dismemberment of the union."[109] Another author concurred, noting that the Democratic clubs, which had played such a diabolical role in stirring up the Whiskey rebels, created a system "whereby strangers and foreigners are liable to be deceived, and induced to entertain an opinion derogatory to the American character, and disgraceful to true Republicanism."[110]

In fact, such assertions became the consensus among Federalists on the role the Democratic Societies and emigrants played in encouraging the Whiskey Rebellion. One author noted that "many" of the rebels "are deceived, being strangers in our country," by the inflammatory rhetoric of those who wish to alarm "emigrants from one state of disorder to another."[111] The rebels themselves were not Americans, but "the wild Irish," who "threatened to shoot every man who may not choose to oppose the old in the hopes of establishing a new government."[112] The ultimate insult emerged during the congressional elections of November 1794. Federalist newspapers in New York, Boston, and Charleston reported with disgust the large number of aliens participating in the elections. In Boston, the paper was poised to bring forward many persons "who can testify that a number of Frenchmen," wearing the tricolor cockade in their hats and singing French national songs, "refused compliance with the laws," marched "*en masse*" to the hustings, and "did actually vote."[113]

In the end, the increased immigration, or at least the increased visibility of immigrants, encouraged both parties to reconsider their liberal naturalization policies. Debates on the 1790 naturalization bill, although certainly contentious, were based largely on theoretical concerns over the possible trouble that aliens could exert on the American scene. But as real threats now emerged to taint the innocence of the American character and deceive Americans from the true path of nationhood, action seemed necessary to secure the American experiment. By the end of 1794 Congress expressed a general "disapprobation of the facility by which, under the existing law, aliens may acquire citizenship," and a new bill was debated at the beginning of the second session of the Third Congress.[114]

The bill that the Congress of 1794–95 strove to replace had been created in an optimistic moment after the ratification of the Constitution. Passed in March of 1790, it offered extremely generous terms. It provided that "all free white persons" migrating to the United States could achieve all the rights of citizenship after taking an oath of allegiance and "residing" within the United States for one year. The actual character of their belonging would afterward be regulated by their state of residence. After two years, the alien would be able to hold office in the "state or general government."[115] Many voices had criticized the liberality of the first bill, but the hot rhetoric simply dissipated into the air, for the Congress that debated the first bill on naturalization was a rare specimen in American politics—a legislature without party.[116] This was a debate characterized by the amorphous and competing interests of legislation without program, without a caucus to establish a plan, or a leader securing a set of votes. Sandwiched between the vigorous contentions surrounding Hamilton's proposals for funding and assumption, the naturalization bill received little notice, and certainly did not spawn the pamphlet literature that both articulated and moved public opinion.[117] The debate was largely concerned with the theoretical legal dilemmas and potential problems which immigration might create, and did not reflect any immediate conflicts between immigrants and citizens. For Michael Jenifer Stone of Maryland, the real danger of making immigrants into citizens still lay in the future. "The present inhabitants," he argued, "have been engaged in a long, hazardous, and expensive war," and as such, they possess "a laudable vanity in having affected what the most sanguine hardly dared to contemplate." For such reasons, difficulties with immigrants "may allude to the next generation more than this."[118] Stone's intuition proved prophetic, although the first conflicts came much sooner than he predicted.

The Congress that assembled in 1794 contained many of the same people, now arrayed against each other as bitter party enemies. In the first draft of a new naturalization bill, introduced a few days before Christmas in 1794, the amount of time immigrants were required to reside in America before gaining access to citizenship was left blank, "to be filled up after more mature consideration." Before considering the residency requirement, both Federalists and Republicans advocated amendments to encourage particular types of immigrants.[119] Federalist Samuel Dexter of Massachusetts suggested that each alien present at least two credible witnesses who would give oaths that the alien "was of good moral character and attached to the welfare of the country."[120] His colleague, Theodore Sedgwick, not only seconded the motion, but spoke at some length of the need to protect the "character of Americans" from "the discontented, the ambitious, and the avaricious of every country." He noted that republican governments had struggled through the ages to keep themselves from "adulteration by foreign mixture." No example could be named "in the history of man" which justified "the experiment which had been made by the United States," of allowing foreigners such easy access to citizenship.[121]

Sedgwick specifically worried about the existence of ethnic groups within a nation-state, arguing that "whenever inhabitants of one country should be permitted to settle in another," they would form unions based on "national affections," which prove "unfriendly" to "the ancient inhabitants" and "also to the social order." He finished by pointing out the danger posed by immigrants infected with the passions of the French Revolution having easy access to power in the United States. "The present," he argued, was "the most inauspicious time" to open the gates to foreigners. "Emigrants were to be expected" from those European states where "fierce and unrelenting passions" shook "to their foundations" all the "ancient political structures in Europe."[122] William Vans Murray of Maryland agreed, and declared that he was "quite indifferent if not fifty emigrants came into this continent in a year's time, since they would inevitably come from a quarter of the world so full of disorder and corruption, they might contaminate the purity and simplicity of the American character." He noted that "it would be unjust to hinder them, but impolitic to encourage them."[123]

Republicans believed the amendment to require two witnesses revealed a Federalist ploy to introduce only wealthy immigrants to citizenship. New Jersey's Jonathan Dayton foresaw "many difficulties arising to poor men in attempting to get two such witnesses." He noted that some members believed "merchants and men of large capital" to be the only "meritorious emigrants," and that, for them, such requirement would work "extremely well." For his part, he wished America to be filled up with "useful laboring people."[124] James Madison agreed that "it would be very difficult for many citizens" to secure two reputable witnesses. Poorer immigrants tended to move often, and "in three years time, a person may have shifted his residence from one end of the Continent to the other." Madison noted that "greater mischief was to be feared" from "those who should obtain property in shipping," and these "mercantile" people were the only "class of emigrant" he wanted to regulate strictly.[125] After lengthy debate, the amendment passed the House, but it failed, under Republican pressure, to survive the Senate revision.

Republicans added their own amendment to the bill, to ensure that the displaced aristocracy of Europe did not set themselves up in America. William Giles of Virginia acknowledged that he believed the two-witness requirement was intended to "guard the Government against any disturbance from the people called Jacobins," should their passion run "to a dangerous and seditious extreme." But he believed more danger was to be expected from the "prejudices of the aristocrats." Their beliefs, he noted, exhibited a quality "more hostile to the spirit of the American Constitution" than those of the revolutionaries of Europe. He argued that America could expect upward of "twenty thousand" French aristocrats seeking asylum, and he was determined to strip them of their titles before they could expect to exercise the rights of American citizens. He therefore introduced another oath into the naturalization process, whereby immigrants "must renounce all pretensions" to any titles or ranks they possessed in any other kingdom, nation, or state.[126]

Giles's motion excited a long and nasty debate. Samuel Dexter immediately scorned the usefulness of the amendment, believing it to be a waste of time, and dangerous, because it tended to institutionalize "Democratical principles." Large portions of his remarks were spent ridiculing the Roman Catholic religion, and he concluded that "priestcraft had done more mischief than aristocracy."[127] James Madison jumped to the defense of both Giles's motion and Catholics around the globe. "Americans had no right to ridicule Catholics," he noted, reminding Dexter that they had "proved good citizens during the Revolution." He pointed out that Catholics were fully qualified to make good republicans, as evidenced by the number of cantons in Switzerland that were "of the Roman Catholic" persuasion. As for the motion, Madison agreed with Giles that numbers of "titled characters" were daily being "thrown out" of Europe, and he did not welcome any man to citizenship who would not relinquish his titles.[128] John Page castigated New England members for their opposition to the measure, lecturing that "equality is the basis of good order and society, whereas titles turn everything wrong." He continued, with the palpable condescension of a Virginian elite who had seen very little of cities: "A scavenger was as necessary to the health of a city as any one of the magistrates."[129]

As the debate evolved, it increasingly reflected sectional tensions that always simmered between the parties and within the Congress. The high-minded tone taken by Page and others concerning the dangers of aristocrats was mocked by the New England Federalists, who attacked the pretensions of slaveholders to be such zealous democrats. Giles responded by calling for the "yeas and nays," a roll call vote intended to mark the specific votes of each member for the record—and for the newspapers. Although Virginia's Richard Bland Lee tried to cool the passions of the debate by noting that Southerners could not "assume a superiority of political-virtue, over their fellow citizens in the East," the motion for the roll call vote had ended any chance at peaceful compromise. Uriah Tracy of Connecticut immediately attacked Giles, noting that he "feared that the taking of the yeas and nays would look like party, as if intended to cast an odium on gentlemen who should vote against the motion."[130] Fisher Ames wondered too what could be the intent of Giles's motion and his need for a roll call vote. Referring to the recent trouble with the Whiskey Rebellion, he wondered if Giles's intention was to "rouse again the sleeping apparitions which have disturbed the backcountry." Such arguments, he concluded, must come from "diseases of the brain," and could not be cured by reason.[131] Massachusetts's Sedgwick rose in anger and accused Giles of using the call for "the yeas and nays" to "fix a stigma upon gentlemen in that House as friends to a nobility" and to raise a "popular opprobrium against them."[132] Referring to the charges of the Republican newspapers, Sedgwick reminded the members that it had been repeatedly alleged "that there was a party in the United States, not only for Aristocracy, but even for Monarchy." If the roll was taken on this vote, "it might be said that the Eastern States were represented by aristocrats."[133]

In a desperate attempt to dampen the enthusiasm of some members for a roll call vote, Samuel Dexter attached an unfriendly amendment to Giles's bill, which would have required any alien to "renounce all possession of slaves" and declare "that he holds all men free and equal" before he would be allowed access to citizenship. Seconded by his fellow New Englander, George Thatcher, the proposal elicited vigorous protest from Republicans.[134] Giles immediately responded that he was "sorry to see slavery made a jest of in the House," and that he understood Dexter's ploy to be but "a hint against Southern members." James Madison argued that Dexter obviously possessed no real knowledge, that "the operation of reducing the number of slaves was going on as quickly as possible" in Virginia, and that to speak of such things in the House "had a very bad effect" on the slaves themselves.[135] North Carolina's Joseph McDowell considered Dexter's motion to reveal "monarchical or despotic principles" he had never before heard uttered. He wondered what right the House had to make such strictures on the type of property a man could hold. With one eye on St. Domingue, he also agreed with Madison about the incorrectness of discussing slavery at the present time:

> [He] wished the gentleman to consider what might be the consequence of his motion, at this time when the West Indies are transformed into an immense scene of slaughter. When thousands of people had been massacred, and thousands had fled for refuge to this country, when the proprietors of slaves in this country could only keep them in peace with the utmost difficulty, was this a time for such inflammatory motions? He was amazed that a gentleman of whom he had so high an opinion, could for a moment, embrace an idea, which was, in all points of view, so extremely improper and dangerous.

Although McDowell's directness caused Dexter to withdraw his amendment temporarily, he activated it again as the House moved to take the roll on Giles's amendment. In a highly party-driven and sectional vote, Giles's motion passed, while Dexter's was defeated.[136]

By mid-January 1795, members were ready to take up the question of residency requirements and to fill the blank in the original bill. Ironically, settling on a length of time for achieving citizenship proved relatively easy. Since Republicans wished to exclude would-be aristocrats from easy access to citizenship and Federalists expressed concerns over the possible ease with which European revolutionaries achieved citizenship, a compromise figure of five years was achieved, which more than doubled the existing requirement. Some hard-liners remonstrated for a requirement of ten or seven years, but "the mere waste of time" that had dogged the bill from the beginning pressed many weary congressmen into compliance.[137]

The acrimony that characterized the debates on naturalization reflected the fever pitch which party rhetoric had reached by the mid-1790s. At the root of this concern remained the general fear that America would be subverted by enemies to its true interests, and the growing reality of a national politics that revealed different partisan alignments. Of particular note is the awareness of the debaters that their speeches were being reported across the country and the posturing they engaged in to set themselves and their arguments in the best possible light. The debates in the House (and later the Senate) were staples of the American newspapers, and as such they are an extremely important part of early national political culture and the rise of a party culture. The first celebrities of American political life emerged from the vigorous debates within Congress, and depending on one's appeal, a vociferous congressman might be exalted and publicly toasted or burned in effigy and mocked by local partisans and partiers alike. Federalist concerns about the political consequences of a mere appearance of support for "titles" or "aristocracy," and the reluctance of Southern members to even discuss slavery in the aftermath of the Haitian Revolution, belie the extent to which congressional debates influenced the topics of discussion and mobilization in the streets.[138]

Despite the clear antagonism between the parties, the reconsideration of the easy naturalization policy of the First Congress reflected a clear consensus that quick and easy access to citizenship threatened the stability of the body politic. Whether haughty aristocrats or propertyless revolutionaries, the new visibility of recent immigrants represented a dangerous influence on a still fledgling national character and government. No specific ethnic groups had been mentioned—although Roman Catholics had excited some controversy—but congressmen clearly worried that American character and political institutions were being dangerously fatigued by the assaults of partisan politics, and they needed to be saved from imminent failure by a more diligent regulation of citizenship.

For the rest of the decade the character of the American nation could not be separated from the character of American citizens, and the rights and duties of American citizens would animate the most divisive politics of the decade. From this moment until the election of Jefferson, the opposition to the government consistently mobilized around the Revolutionary and universal principles of the rights of man protected by a Union of republican states, while the Federalists emphasized national unanimity and traditional authority as a challenge to abstract and visionary notions of individual rights. When the Federalists found themselves in the ascendancy in the spring of 1798, they moved decisively to create in law their idealized vision for the American nation—and at the same time created one of the most dramatic battles in the history of American citizenship.

As for "Citizen" Henfield, the protections of his presumed French citizenship proved somewhat less sure at sea than in an American jury court. He is last found in the mid-1790s languishing in a British prison, having been captured in a failed raid on a British merchantman.[139] Genet, for his part, found the independent national power of the United States a safer guarantee of his life and property than French citizenship. In 1794, the Washington administration refused to arrest him on behalf of the French Republic and thus probably saved him from the fate of Louis Capet. Genet married the daughter of the longtime governor of New York, George Clinton, and became the American "Citizen Genet," by a process of naturalization in 1804 that he had so inadvertently helped fashion. He is last seen on the Atlantic stage talking to a young French visitor to America, Alexis de Tocqueville, about the nature of the revolutions in France and the United States.

{4}

"True Americans"

THE FEDERALIST IDEAL AND THE LEGISLATION OF NATIONAL CITIZENSHIP

Few nations have arrived at any great degree of eminence, without indicating a pride of character . . . this passion, like all others, is an essential spring of the human machine; and cannot strictly speaking, be denominated a virtue or a vice. Its application may produce actions, that participate of either. If it is directed toward improper objects, or carried to an extreme, in a right direction, it may become detrimental, or vicious.—JOHN FENNO, 1789

With the greatest pleasure, I reciprocate your congratulations "On the prospect of unanimity" that now presents itself to the hopes of every American, and on that spirit of Patriotism and Independence that is rising into active exertion in opposition to seduction, domination and rapine, I offer a sincere prayer that the citizens of Philadelphia may persevere in the virtuous course and maintain the honorable character of their ancestors, and be protected from every calamity physical, moral and political.—PRESIDENT JOHN ADAMS, 1798

ON MAY 7, 1798, PRESIDENT JOHN ADAMS STOOD IN FULL military regalia on the steps of the Executive Residence in Philadelphia. Despite his lack of military experience, he struck a martial pose on this day—one he had designated as a day of "national fasting"—to receive the compliments of the patriotic youth of Philadelphia. Upset with the recent evidence of French contempt toward American ministers, nearly twelve hundred "Young Citizens" had marched through the streets to present their petition praising the Adams administration and pledging their lives and honor in support of "Liberty and Independence." Cheered on by martial music and a "concourse of Spectators" with patriotic cockades in their bonnets, and surrounded by "the America standard," Adams exhorted the assembly to exert all efforts to secure "the immemorial Liberties of our Ancestors."[1] There was no talk of the "rights of man." Within weeks, buoyed by such public events and a mobilization of Federalist support throughout the country, the Federalist-controlled Congress pressed through a legislative package of extraordinary scale. Mingled between bills establishing a new army and navy—and the loans, taxes, and tax collectors to pay for them—was a new naturalization law, the third in eight years, and a number of laws controlling aliens and sedition.

When historians have considered the Alien and Sedition Acts in the history of American attitudes toward citizenship, they have generally asserted that the Federalists were interested in little more than attacking their political enemies and a few radical polemicists. But this reading presents a much too superficial comprehension of a crucial moment in the history of American citizenship and nationhood.[2] The Federalists wanted America to be a true national community, where the citizens shared rights and duties consistent with their national character and toward a common national interest. But to become that ideal American nation, the barriers to entry needed to be high, and the laws needed to be expanded to control, regulate, and constrain all foreign and seditious elements. National character, which was assured by national citizenship, needed to be protected and nourished by the authority of national power. This all became an immediate problem of the moment when the Federalists found themselves threatened by an expansionary French Republic that would seemingly use any means necessary to delude, cajole, and threaten the American people into submission—tactics the French were successfully using to undermine numerous ancient European states. So, in the midst of a popular enthusiasm in the long spring of 1798, Federalists passed a series of laws intended to deny those deemed un-American—by birth or politics—access to the rights of citizens. Since the laws of the national state were the true support for liberty, people who looked outside the state—to the idealism of Paine and other "visionary theorists of government"—could not be guaranteed the liberty of the Constitution. The laws attempted to re-create the America being described in memorials like the one offered by the "youth" of Philadelphia—a citizenry of clear national character cast in the *cultural* terms of the eighteenth century: ancestry, manners, character, habits, language, and support for the government. Only with a unified citizenry and a strengthened national government could Federalists imagine a way to confront the raging strength of Revolutionary rhetoric in the United States and throughout the Atlantic.

The Character of Nations: European National Difference in the Eighteenth Century

To comprehend the completeness of the Federalist vision, we must first explore some components of eighteenth-century notions of nationality. The designation "ethnic" did not become a part of the English language until the middle of the nineteenth century, and "ethnicity" did not see general use until well into the twentieth.[3] In early modern and Enlightenment Western thought, European peoples were generally divided into "nations," whose collective "national character," or "national spirit," could be surmised from the influences of such variables as religion, manners, customs, language, law, government, and climate.[4] In the terms of Montesquieu, "Many things govern men: climate, religion, laws, the maxims of government, examples of past things, mores, manners," and these create "the general spirit of a nation." For Montesquieu, true morality and "justice" required legislators to "follow the spirit of the nation."[5] David Hume generally downplayed the importance of climate and geography to national distinctions, emphasizing instead "moral causes" which were created by "the nature of government, the revolutions of public affairs," and structures of wealth—"the plenty or penury of the people."[6] But even though thinkers like Montesquieu and Hume would argue that the differences among national peoples could be explained by different causes, both believed in the notion of European peoples with distinct national characters.

Thus, the elements (if not always the cause) of the different character of European nations in the eighteenth century are explicit in George Berkley's famous query, intended to defend the Irish: "whether the upper part of this people are not truly English, by blood, language, religion, manners, in character and interest."[7] When George Washington feared the possible influence of the French army in Canada in 1778, he noted astutely that the Canadians shared "all the ties of blood, habits, manners, religion, and former connexions of government" with the troops—a fact that might encourage the French to remain in North America after their immediate usefulness disappeared.[8]

Assuming distinct national characters among the nations of the world is essential to understanding eighteenth-century conceptions of the proper action of sovereign states. As Emerich de Vattel noted in his famous treatise on the Law of Nations, as beings at law, a "nation" must act "in its national character" as is determined by its "essential attributes," just as a man in a state of nature would act "in a manner conformable to his nature."[9] These "essential attributes" correspond to the variables of "blood, language, religion, manners," etc.—what we can define broadly as "cultural" characteristics. For those not prone to philosophizing national difference, the distinct cultures of the European peoples were caricatured and stereotyped for the use and amusement of the masses in countless plays, popular literature, prints, and satires.[10]

European intellectuals of the eighteenth century, with their penchant for scientific lists, often explored the elements and causes of national difference and attempted to index the characteristics of distinct peoples. Geographies, which became increasingly popular throughout the eighteenth century, encompassed the various concerns of ethnography, philology, government, history, and natural history. A popular geography would not only exhibit the latest maps, or "discoveries," but also would promise to articulate the "genius, manners, customes, and habits" of "the Nations of the World."[11] Magazines and newspapers were filled with cultivated essays and pseudo-scientific pieces sketching "National Characters," which described the different natural attributes or cultures of European peoples in authoritative prose.[12] Thus, a typical essay might declare that a German tended to be "ever studious in the secrets of nature, indefatigable in his pursuits after chemistry, and as indefatigable in drinking," and a representative Spaniard would be "jealous of his honor" and "romantic in his projects."[13]

Among the "enlightened" in the eighteenth century, the prejudices created by "national pride" were thoroughly deplored.[14] In his lengthy treatise *Von dem Nationalstolze* (*Essay on National Pride,* 1758), the German scholar Johann Georg Zimmerman attempted to dissect the causes of national prejudices and cataloged the character and conceits of the world's nations.[15] Zimmerman located the source of national prejudice within the proud breast of human nature: "Every nation contemplates itself through the medium of self-conceit, and draws conclusions to its own advantage, which individuals adopt to themselves with complacency, because they confound and interweave their private with their national character." So that "every nation is exceedingly pleased with itself, and considers all other societies of men, more or less, as beings of an inferior nature." For the Romans and Greeks, "a foreigner and a barbarian were synonymous terms" and "are still so with the majority of the French nation."[16]

Zimmerman spared no nation from his critique, and noted with particular disdain the role histories played as "memorials of the partiality of nations for themselves."[17] He also ridiculed the Europeans' tendency to date "their antiquity to the remotest ages," which "pleases them as much as a genealogical parchment does a country gentlemen, who, filled with ham and pease, plumes himself on his long line of ancestors."[18] Certain Americans reviewing the book in the 1790s were enthusiastic of Zimmerman's efforts. "Zimmerman on National Pride," opined an eager critic, "is one of the best books that ever was written." "It lays before men their *real* characters," the reviewer continued, and helps "all nations" realize that along with their "valuable traits of character—all have their follies and vices."[19]

Zimmerman could not, of course, praise or criticize *American* national character, because none existed in 1758—a situation that leading American revolutionaries consistently lamented. After all, most observers of America in the 1760s agreed with John Adams's assessments of British America as a disjointed group of peoples "composed of so many different nations," with "customes, manners, and habits" with "so little resemblance."[20] The perceived necessity of creating an American character out of the multiple characters of the colonial establishments became one of the most eagerly encouraged efforts of the Revolutionary Era, and the danger of foreign influence on a precocious but still immature American character influenced all sides of debate. The character of different nations—and the implicit understanding of a *cultural* basis for national belonging—therefore remained quite visible for eighteenth-century Americans, and Americans' attempts to separate themselves from European influence attracted much public comment in the years after the war.

American National Character before the Constitution

During the war with Britain, the English expatriate Thomas Paine served as one of the leading advocates of a national vision of American character. As a recent immigrant, with no local commitment to colonial identities, he became the perfect propagandist for American solidarity. As he emphasized throughout his *Crisis* essays, "Our citizenship In the United States is our national character," while "our citizenship in any particular state is only our local distinction." The "great title" of the people is "American," while "our inferior one varies with the place."[21] For the education and language reformer Noah Webster, the biggest problem Americans faced in the aftermath of Independence related to their fragile nationality. He argued that "every engine should be employed to render the people of this country national, to call their attachments home to their own country, and to inspire them with pride and national character."[22] Webster anticipated the great German Romantics by wanting to start the process in the classroom, noting, "As soon as [the student] opens his lips he should rehearse the history of his own country."[23] In the political realm as well, Americans were pressing for the development of an American distinctiveness. Alexander Hamilton observed, "We are laboring hard to establish in this country principles more and more national, and free from all foreign ingredients."[24]

In the face of strong state power and regional identities—not to mention an unruly West and popular debtor revolt—the movement to ratify the Constitution often emphasized the need for a truly national state to complement a unique and culturally homogeneous American nation. Some leading federalists brought their Constitution to the people with a vision of a truly homogeneous nation-state. As we have seen, John Jay in Federalist No. 2 contended that "Providence" had given "this one connected Country to one united people." This was "a people descended from the same ancestors, speaking the same language, professing the same religion, attached to the same principles of government, very similar in their manners and customs."[25] In other words, a people with a real national character. Hamilton as well, invoking the common interests of the American people, warned, "A NATION without a national government, is, in my view an awful spectacle."[26]

To the extent that Americans worried about "ethnic" groups in their midst, they worried about immigrants who retained their foreign national character and attempted to press their foreign ideas, manners, and habits on an unsuspecting American people. The danger, of course, was to the existence of the republican government, a fragile form which history had repeatedly shown depended on the character of the people to survive and thrive. Occasionally and episodically in the 1780s, the possible negative effect of the "follies and vices" and peculiar habits, manners, and customs of people from various European nations competed with a vision of America as an "asylum" for the oppressed of the world. Even in an expansive mood over the prospect of American independence, John Adams took time to recognize that New Englanders exhibited superiority in the American scene largely because they were "purer English Blood, less mixed with Scotch, Irish, Dutch, French, Danish, Sweedish &c. than any other; descended from Englishmen too who left Europe, in purer Times than the present."[27] In his *Notes on the State of Virginia,* Thomas Jefferson questioned the "present desire of America," which seemed intent "to produce rapid population [growth] by as great importations as possible." Since such foreigners would inevitably come with absolutist "principles of government," accepting too many too quickly could transfigure American society into "a heterogeneous, incoherent, distracted mass."[28] And a common complaint of New England anti-federalists worried about sharing national power with the unworthy of other states is reflected in James Winthrop's "Agrippa" essay. "Pennsylvania has chosen to receive all that would come there," he warned. Such liberality created a character that could not "equal" any of "the eastern states," in "morals, education," and "energy." He hoped anxiously that other states would try to keep "separate from foreign mixtures," to emulate New England, and to "keep their blood pure."[29]

But unlike later, nineteenth-century thought, which divided the world into racial stocks with immutable (biological) qualities, the variables of language, religion, government, manners, and climate which defined the "essential attributes" of the character of eighteenth-century European nations were alterable—hence the disparity in opinions about the *origins* of national difference. A substantive change in any one of the eclectic list of attributes could potentially alter, for better or worse, the character of the nation. Thus, readers of the *Pennsylvania Magazine* in 1775 read of the different facial features of Europeans, so that "the face of a Spaniard is not like that of an Englishman; the French differs from both, the Dutch from all three and so on." All "nations have originally a face peculiar to themselves." Even so, the faces of national people were constantly undergoing revolutions, as "manners have a powerful effect in forming, transforming, and reforming the fashion of our faces." So "when a whole nation is influenced by any particular set of manners, their countenances will undergo a general change." In addition to "manners and habits," the history of the changing "national character in faces" would "revolve by intermarriages."[30] In an essay from the end of the 1780s, another author confidently asserted that "a change of principles precedes a change of manners," and so "when a nation is beginning its political existence," it should be careful to frame not only good laws but "good habits," so that eventually societies, "by their natural progress, create that additional tie, that is imposed by a sense of duty, and a regard to character."[31]

The decisive effect of "habits" and "manners" in the character of the nation is a crucial reason that "virtue" exhibited such power in the American lexicon of the Revolutionary Age. "Virtue" as an individual moral quality (the opposite of "vice") not only served to establish moral practices, but it also protected against the "debasement" of personal and national character. As "Pro Republica" argued in "Thoughts on the present Situation of the Foedral Government of the United States," Americans needed "to spurn those trifling gratifications, which tend to enervate our bodies, vitiate our morals; and dissipate our substance," which would serve "to debase the national character, and impoverish the country."[32] At the same time, "virtue"—as representative of the classical selflessness that defined the soul of patriotism—could help Americans transcend provincial characters and to act, as Governor James Bowdoin of Massachusetts argued in his annual address in 1786, in regard to their "new and important character—a national character."[33] So both private *and* public virtue were crucial to the development and protection of national character.

The potential for both corruption and improvement in national character deeply impacted American attitudes toward immigrants. Ideally, time and education could produce lasting changes, foreign mores could be replaced by American habits, and European immigrants could become assets and not dangers to the new republic. The most famous description of the process by which Europeans became Americans was articulated by the Loyalist French expatriate J. Hector St. John de Crèvecoeur, who described an ideal transformation whereby European peasants "melted" into American farmers in "this great American asylum." Crèvecoeur understood the influences that created the different national characters of eighteenth-century European peoples. As he noted, "We are nothing but what we derive from the air we breathe, the climate we inhabit, the government we obey, the system of religion we profess, and the nature of our employment."[34] In America, all of these elements, especially the availability of land, the gentle nature of the law and government, and the eager intermarriage of diverse European peoples, create "a new race of men" from people "once scattered all over Europe."[35] Notably, this argument does not allow a place for those who refused to give up their foreign nature.

This vision of a melting away of difference to describe a process of assimilation has resonated throughout American history, and it remains a popular metaphor for the symbolic adoption of immigrant groups into the American nation. But the key is not the mechanism but the final result—one national character. For Jedidiah Morse, a Yale-educated minister whose geography texts, first written in the 1780s, dominated the American school and popular markets until the 1840s, assimilation was the preferred solution to the ethnic diversity in the United States. Describing the plurality of European peoples that inhabited America in the late eighteenth century, Morse longed for the day when ethnic distinctions would disappear:

> Intermingled with the Anglo-Americans are the Dutch, Scotch, Irish, French, Germans, Swedes and Jews; all these . . . retain, in a greater or lesser degree, their native language, in which they perform their public worship, converse, and transact their business with each other. The time however is anticipated . . . when the language, manners, customs, political and religious sentiments of the mixed mass of people who inhabit the United States, shall have become so assimilated, as that all nominal distinctions shall be lost in the general and honorable name of AMERICANS.[36]

The hope for such a transformation assumed that America could best thrive as a true nation, one homogeneous in its population and sharing a common good that reflected the character of a nation with a collective national identity and pride. Assimilation assured that all migrants must eventually become Americans, "all nominal distinctions shall be lost," and everyone would share *American* "language, manners, customs, political and religious sentiments."

But before the Constitution there was no broad consensus that Americans had a true national character. Taking stock of the state of American national character on the eve of the ratification of the American Constitution, John Fenno, printer of the *United States Gazette,* thought "the united states" had not yet shown "very partial displays of national pride." And why should they? "Are we independent in our laws, opinions, manners, and fashions?" Fenno asked. "The fact is," he lamented, "in none of those respects, have we formed a distinct national character." Without "a peculiar national character," Americans "cannot efficiently feel national pride," and "without such pride, we must not expect to realize all the benefits." After urging Americans to reform their laws, manners, habits, and fashions, Fenno argued that "the establishment of a new constitution" could, "with proper management, form a national character." The new institutions promised to "remove evils" created by the "clashing views and prejudices of the different parts of the union." A new "common centre," or national "court," would set the standard for American fashion; would give "one tone" to American civil discourse; would focus the genius of America around *one* standard for elegance, taste, etiquette, and refinement. Fenno believed the lack of national pride in the 1780s related to a discordant, unconnected, and "unproductive public opinion," not to "any extreme violence of party spirit," which did not yet exist on a continental scale. The new government promised to focus the mind of the nation by both creating and sustaining a "national pride of character." And yet Fenno acknowledged the potential for the abuse of such pride. "If it is directed toward improper objects, or carried to an extreme," the mobilization of national pride of character "may become detrimental, or vicious."[37]

Five years after Fenno wrote this essay, American politics, as we have seen, had fundamentally changed. The ratification of the Constitution had created new centralizing entities along with a new national citizenship. This national citizenship became the embodiment in law of the American character, and the instruments of national power—the Congress, the presidency, and the courts—became the means by which the manners of the American people could be secured or indefinitely corrupted. While the American mind had been focused, it had also been polarized by differences over the power and policy of the national state and the pressures of international war and revolution. A strong expansion of party spirit had replaced the jangling distractions of the 1780s, and these polarities had exhibited themselves in fundamental debates over the future of the American citizenry. The rejection of caricatured "types" of immigrants—Jacobins and aristocrats—temporarily united the fractious parties of the country in the creation of the new naturalization law of 1795. But in an increasingly dangerous world at war, that small change did not end the threat of international intrigue and foreign influence.

The depredations on American shipping that followed the ratification of the Jay Treaty increased tensions between the French Republic and the Federalist governments. The resulting conflict, a "Quasi-War" with France at the end of the 1790s, in combination with deeply felt concerns over American national character, encouraged the creation of a program intended to purify the American citizenry from all foreign elements. It included another new national naturalization law, strong national laws regulating aliens and seditious speech, and the establishment of a national common law, and represented a concerted effort to assure that American citizenship would be available only to those deemed culturally acceptable. This was a "national pride of character" carried "to an extreme."

The Federalist Ideal: A National Character

With loud partisan wrangling so much a part of the national political scene, appeals to unity and expressions of patriotism became common by the mid-1790s, especially from the party in control of the national state, the Federalists.[38] Contending with the constant Republican invocation of the "rights of man" and the rapid expansion of an increasingly well-organized formal opposition party, Federalists appealed to the American "nation," stressing the "duties of citizens" to support the nation's legitimate government. George Washington's Farewell Address is representative of an emerging transition in Federalist arguments. From arguing that America *should* develop a distinct national character, Federalists began insisting that Americans *had* a distinct national character, one that needed to be defended and protected at all costs. It was, in fact, considered essential for the survival of the United States.

Noting that the "unity of government which constitutes you one people" was threatened by "batteries of internal and external enemies," Washington encouraged the American people to always "cherish a cordial, habitual, and immovable attachment" to the government. He urged the citizenry to "concentrate their affections" on the "common country." "The name of AMERICAN," he noted, "belongs to you in your national capacity" and "must always exalt the just pride of patriotism," *since each citizen* has "the same religion, manners, habits and political principles."[39] Americans had a national character.

The two chief dangers that Washington believed had the potential of destroying the American republic were the hazard of sectionalism and the threat of foreign entanglements, both of which could clearly be perceived by the time of his retirement. He worried about the efforts of "designing men," who would inevitably attempt to convince good Americans that their localities, "*Northern* and *Southern—Atlantic* and *Western,*" possessed unique and not common national interests.[40] Such intrigues served to "render alien to each other those who ought to be bound together by fraternal affection." Even worse, Washington asserted that the ambitious men encouraging such fratricide would often be foreigners, and wondered if each section of the country could be "deaf to those advisers" who attempted "to sever them from their brethren, and connect them with aliens."[41] Repeating the classical mantra again and again, Washington noted the "slavery" that undue affection for a foreign nation caused. At times, the tone of his argument reached the level of pleading: "Against the insidious wiles of foreign influence (I conjure you to believe me, my fellow citizens) the jealousy of a free people ought to be *constantly* awake; since history and experience prove, that foreign influence is one of the baneful foes of Republican government."[42] Thus, Washington's famous articulation of American neutrality was an effort to encourage Americans to revel only in those natural ties of affection that the nation needed to cultivate to survive and prosper. By appealing directly to the patriotism and loyalty of an American people defined as a unique people, a people with the same "religion, manners, habits, and political principles," Washington denied the ability of opposition voices to speak for the American nation. Since the American people had elected the government freely, the government alone could speak for the nation.

This fact implied that "true Americans" would support their government at all costs, and Federalists emphasized the "duty of citizens" to do so. As Washington argued, the government was "the offspring of your own choice uninfluenced and unawed." As such, "respect for its authority, compliance with its laws, acquiescence in its measures, are duties enjoyed by the fundamental maxims of true liberty." Acknowledging that the loud advocates of the Revolutionary message had raised the power of the people to the heights of sovereignty, Washington tempered such power with responsibility, noting, "The very idea of the power and the right of all the people to establish government, presupposes the duty of every individual to obey the established government."[43] For Washington, as for all Federalists, "liberty" was something secured by the power and authority of national law and government, not some licentious grant from the imaginations of men, or discovered in Revolutionary chaos.

Federalists would have frequent opportunity in the years following Washington's retirement to exalt the national character of the American people while appealing to their duty as citizens to support the government. French depredations on American shipping became more common, the Spanish Crown refused to evacuate its forts in disputed West Florida, and Western intrigues again highlighted the weak attachment of the Western states to the national government. Republicans, despite their failure in the national elections, had succeeded in lodging the archenemy Thomas Jefferson in the vice presidency, and they continued to exert their unnatural influence through a growing opposition press. By 1797, leading Federalists commonly worried about the commitment of the people to the national state. As John Jay wrote in the fall of that year, "We are in a better state than we were: but we are not yet in a sound state." Americans still seemed to be too divided, and "that nation is not in a sound state whose parties are excited by objects interesting only to a foreign power." Jay concluded, "I wish to see our own people more *Americanized,* if I may use the expression; until we feel and act as an independent nation, we shall always suffer from foreign intrigue."[44] As events placed the country in imminent threat, Federalists would move to "Americanize" the people.

With the war in Europe continuing to escalate, and the French continuing to prey on neutral American shipping, in 1797 Adams sent John Marshall, Elbridge Gerry, and Charles Cotesworth Pinckney as ministers extraordinary to treat with the French. In March of 1798 the three ministers revealed that the French government had refused to officially recognize them, thus denying the most common diplomatic courtesy given to sovereign nations. Instead, through their unofficial agents—X, Y, and Z—the French threatened to destroy American shipping and invade the United States if the Adams administration failed to provide substantial "loans." This was a ploy they had used with effect throughout Europe. The French agents also arrogantly insinuated that the American people were divided from their government, and that French agents already in America could be mobilized to undermine the political and social order of the United States.

The threats of France were real, as was its power in the world—this was not an American "paranoid" mind running amok. Thus, in February of 1798, for example, Americans could read in the "Historical Chronicle," published in a variety of newspapers and magazines, a running description of the exploits of the French Republic in Europe: of the new Batavian Republic, built on the ruins of the old and dear United Netherlands; or of the new "Cisalpine" and "Ligurian" republics, cobbled together from bits of old states and cities in Italy (the name of "Genoa" gone forever)—all of them new Revolutionary regimes in the pocket of France. They could read of the fall of the ancient Venetian Republic, which had lasted from the fourth century to the spring of 1797, "undisturbed in its laws and civil immunities," now broken and subjugated. They could read of the French Republic's planned invasion of England; or of the 12 million livres paid by the pope at Rome to "Citizen Buonaparte, the new Ambassador from the French Republic." The tribute was a symbol of the pontiff's submission "to the hard impositions of a republican general." Finally, Americans could read of the impending fall of Switzerland, which looked like it would follow the fate of Genoa and Venice: "In many parts of the Cantons, the revolutionary machines are in motion." Discontent, disorder, and political differences at Zurich, St. Gall, Appengell, and Berne were being voiced "in loud and menacing terms," so that "we may very soon expect to hear of the whole of the Cantons being in [French] possession."[45] So when the French threats to the American diplomats were made public, in early April 1798, it is not surprising that many Americans throughout the country exploded with indignation and nationalist fervor—the French *could* attempt what they had threatened.

Through the spring and early summer, both in rhetoric and in law, Federalists most clearly articulated their vision for American citizenship. They would settle once and for all the true national character of America by restricting access to the rights of citizenship to only "true Americans." As we will see, they explicitly rejected the Revolutionary formulations of citizenship that the Republicans espoused, and the anti-nationalism the French universalism symbolized. They hoped to secure national citizenship to only those with the proper religion, manners, habits, customs, language, and political principles: the eighteenth-century understanding of "nationality." As Rev. John Thorton Kirkland remarked to the Phi Beta Kappa Society at Harvard College, American "nationality of sentiment" came from the *principles, manners,* and *institutions* they had been bequeathed from their fathers, and they were not "the ephemeral production of the day," nor "the nostroms of upstart political quackery" or "the vagaries of brains; distempered with revolutionary fervor."[46] Both in the streets and in law, Federalists moved quickly to ratify a homogeneous vision of the American citizenry, to secure the United States from the threats of war, foreigners, and sedition.

From the revelation of French audacity in April through the summer of 1798, Federalists throughout the United States organized petitions in support of the Adams administration and the efforts of his government to defend the American nation. The numerous petitions to the president, representing tens of thousands of voices, provide a unique and powerful tool to identify the vision of Federalist citizenship being constructed in the spring and summer of 1798. Beginning in early April, Federalist polemicists exhorted all "true Americans" to support the government and express the "sense of the people."[47] As one author calling himself "Patriotism" argued, "Never since America has been a nation has she known so eventful, so alarming a crisis."[48] One Federalist asserted that the threats to the country should be "sufficient to induce all true Americans firmly to unite in defense of their common country."[49] From London, Rufus King presented leading Federalists with a similar plan of action. As he wrote to Hamilton, "You will be at no loss to understand this state of things." "Nothing but vigour and energy will save our country," for "moderation and forbearance" have been "faithfully employed and without success." Americans could see throughout Europe "the wretched Pictures exhibited by the Countries where France has introduced her detestable Principles," and the example of France in Europe "should admonish us to give up half-way measures with half-way men; they do not belong to the Times in which we live." King argued that "the people of America will support their Government" only "if that Government acts with decision, if it appeals to the Pride, Patriotism, and Honour of the Nation!"[50] Federalists mobilized throughout the spring and summer, both in response to and in imitation of such patriotic appeals. As petitions were prepared, Federalist newspapers confidently noted that "No true American can or will hesitate to add his name to this patriotic list."[51] One author exhorted petitioners to "support, at every hazard, the rights, the honour and the independence of the United States." Americans must "remember that it is not the establishment of an abstract theoretical point of Government for which we are to contend, but for the real and substantial enjoyment of our liberty and existence as a nation."[52]

From Wilkes County, Georgia, to the town of Arundell in the District of Maine, petitions streamed into Philadelphia supporting the Adams administration.[53] Petitions to the president were unanimous in recognizing "this present crisis" which gripped the nation. With "a view of the present alarming and critical situation of the United States," their signatories expressed their anxiety and defiance.[54] The nearly 250 extant petitions present a representative slice of the leading forces of the early republican political world.

The signers of the petitions were all male, and probably all white, although this is unknowable. They represented militia groups, grand juries, students, incorporated societies, and, most importantly, "the respectable inhabitants and citizens" of numerous towns and counties.[55] Of the extant petitions, as table 1 shows, the Middle States contributed 119 petitions, or 49 percent of the total; New England and the South were roughly equal, with 26 percent (64 petitions) and 22 percent (55 petitions), respectively; and the Northwest Territory and the states south of the Ohio River (Kentucky and Tennessee) each contributed 3 petitions. The numerical dominance of the Middle States most likely reflects their proximity to the national seat of government and the clear expectation of Federalist petitions. Philadelphia and its suburbs contributed 9 petitions alone, with over eleven thousand signatures combined.[56]

Also, the Middle States were much more evenly divided in their politics than either New England (except parts of Vermont, solidly Federalist) and the South (solidly Republican—except for Charleston, eastern North Carolina, and various sections of Virginia). This may have led to more localized partisan conflicts, with the petitioning ritual providing local Federalists with an unprecedented opportunity to temporarily control the street politics of their area. But petitions did not only come from the regions of Federalist dominance. Lexington, Kentucky, for instance, managed a petition in favor of the Adams administration—although it only had about fifteen signatures, whereas petitions against the Alien and Sedition Acts had thousands of signatures. By August 1798, a broadsheet published in Lexington ("There is a Snake in the Grass!!") warned Kentuckians not to put their signatures on any "address to the President, approving the conduct of our government." "Citizens of Kentucky," it warned, "be upon your guard, if applications should be made to you to sign addresses."[57]

In any case, the high number of petitions from the South, relative to New England, does not reflect the politics of Southern representation in the Congress. This is due to the many petitions from the states south of the Potomac that came from port cities or large market towns, military groups, and marginal or frontier counties that had traditionally been outside the mainstream of state politics. For instance, four of the six petitions from South Carolina were from Charleston, where the Federalist merchant/planter alliance remained extremely strong. A full 22 percent of the petitions from the South came from militia organizations and volunteer cavalry.

Of all the petitions, 61 percent came from groups claiming to represent the "inhabitants" or "citizens" or "freeholders" or "young citizens"

Table 1. Number of Petitioners in Support of the Adams Administration, by Type and Geographic Distribution

		Type of Petitioner					
Geographic Region	*Total no. of petitions*	*"Citizens"*	*Government*	*Students*	*Military*	*Religious*	*Incorporated societies*
States south of the Potomac (Va., N.C., S.C., Ga.)	56 (22%)	36 (65%)	6 (11%)	—	13 (22%)	—	1 (2%)
New England states (R.I., N,H., Conn., Mass., Vt., Me.)	64 (26%)	34 (53%)	12 (19%)	4 (6%)	7 (11%)	2 (3%)	5 (8%)
Middle States (Md., Pa., Del., N.Y.)	119 (49%)	74 (62%)	19 (16%)	2 (2%)	18 (15%)	—	6 (5%)
Western states south of the Ohio River (Ky., Tenn.)	3 (1%)	3 (100%)	—	—	—	—	—
Western states north of the Ohio River (Northwest Territory)	3 (1%)	2 (67%)	—	—	1 (33%)	—	—
Unsure	1 (—)	1 (100%)	—	—	—	—	—
Totals	246	150 (61%)	37 (15%)	6 (2%)	39 (16%)	2 (1%)	12 (5%)

of a particular town or county. While 16 percent of the total number of petitions came from military organizations, both volunteer and professional, 15 percent came from governmental institutions, including members of grand juries or inquests, city officials (i.e., mayors, aldermen, etc.), and state legislatures. Nearly 6 percent of the total number of petitions came from religious organizations, philanthropic associations, fraternal societies (Masons), and other incorporated bodies, and another 2 percent came from university students. But despite these varied geographic and professional differences, the petitioners spoke in a common language.

They agreed that the greatest danger to the country was the French nation's grasping ambition. Here, Federalists relied upon a classic argument against tyranny (and France) that they had inherited from *English* political culture. As Steven Pincus and others have argued, an important vein in English nationalist ideology of the seventeenth century relied upon the belief that English liberty and independence were constantly threatened by the desires of various of the Continental nations for "universal dominion." Depending on the crisis, this could be the Spanish, the French, or the Dutch.[58] The Federalists drew on this particular heritage of English political culture to drive their point home. The "inhabitants of Arlington and Sandgate," in Vermont, for example, noted that the French were "following in the steps of ambitious tyrants in the road to universal empire."[59] The "Inhabitants of Concord" noted that France "was grasping at universal dominion."[60] "Inhabitants of Quincy," in Massachusetts, noted that the "heart of every true American exults" with support of their country as the French desire for "universal empire" becomes known.[61] Congregational ministers in Massachusetts asserted that the "boundless avarice and ambition" of the French combined their schemes of "universal plunder and domination" with a crass attempt to "divide the American people from their rulers."[62] The "Young Men of Richmond" noted that the French exhibited "an ambition which grasps at the dominion of the world."[63] John Adams, who replied assiduously to each petition he received, enthusiastically reinforced this aspect of Federalist ideology. To the "Inhabitants of Kent County," Adams noted with approval their condemnation of the French "lust for dominion."[64] At one point in his reply to the towns of Arlington and Sandgate, Adams referred directly to the English tradition, noting that the French were displaying "a repetition of their character . . . under Louis the fourteenth."[65]

The difference for Adams and others between the specific activities of Louis XIV and the then current French appetites was the dangerous ideas embedded within the larger concepts of their Revolution—

new and "visionary" ideas that subverted national institutions, national religion, national character, and national rights.[66] French nonchalance about the rights of nations—guaranteed by reason and treaty in the Law of Nations—struck at the very independence of America. The students of Williams College perceived clearly the French efforts to "stretch her colossean empire across the Atlantic" to challenge "our national rights" with principles which "undermine the vast fabrics of religion and government."[67] At Harvard College, petitioners insisted that the French trampled "the laws of God and nations" by "scattering principles which subvert social order."[68] The grand jurors of the County of Hampshire assured Adams that they would not let "this new species of philosophy," or any "new system of opinions," obstruct their duty to the nation.[69] The dangers were potent, because "the minds of men are so intoxicated with ideas of reform, and visionary schemes for ameliorating the condition of humanity."[70] The officers of the militia of Guilford, North Carolina, asserted that "We abhor the modern innovations, and that word 'reform,'" which, aiming at fantastic plans "for the amelioration of the situation of men," were striving like "a monster ready to engulph all social order, annihilate civil government, and subvert the heretofore approved course of things."[71] John Adams agreed, noting that French ambition was now "intermixed" with "the wildest philosophy."[72] It was a "rage for innovation" that threatened American national character. It was "absurdities, the most monstrous" that had been "carried to such a pitch of madness" in "this latter end of the boasted eighteenth century."[73]

As a universal tyranny indulging in the "madness" of new ideas, the French were seen as an "anti-nation," subverting the rights of national peoples to govern themselves with their own traditions. As the "Mayor, Alderman, Common Council and Freemen of the city of Vergennes" declared, the French would find that "We are not that degraded, nationless people" who would "tamely lay our well-worn glory and national happiness" at the mercy of French ambition.[74] New York Federalists gathered at Hunter's Hotel to assert that "the American republic would not be erased from the list of nations."[75] Federalists recognized the importance of cultivating a national spirit: "There can never be a time when it will be more necessary for the nation to express the sentiments by which it is motivated, than when it is deeply injured." It was surely time to "draw our affections home, and concentrate them upon their proper object—our own country." John Adams expressed the need for an independent nationalism well: "The present period of universal effervescence through the world, is indeed pregnant with events highly important to the safety of all nations: *nation* must be unconnected with the rest of mankind, which can depend upon a total exemption from its feelings, and sympathies."[76] The "nation" remained the proper arbiter of justice for citizens of America, not "the rest of mankind" or so-called new ideas. Another group of petitioners knew that "every true American" would revolt at the "cruel attack made upon our national rights."[77]

In the face of such danger to American national rights and American national character, the petitioners urged the celebration of both. Many spoke of "love" of country. "Inhabitants of the County of Otsego," in New York, claimed they were "attached to every tie that can bind us to the most ardent love of our country."[78] "Officers of the Brigade of the City and County of New York and County of Richmond" noted they were "attached to our country by every tie of nature and affection."[79] The "Youth of Portsmouth" possessed an "ardent attachment to the constitution and laws" of the nation, as "blessings we have received as our birth-right."[80] The memorialists wished to secure their "birth-rights," and often romanticized earnestly about their "ancestors" and "forefathers." Federalists in Carlisle, Pennsylvania, were "inspired" by their own "love of country" to celebrate "liberty as a birthright." They toasted that their "birth-rights may never be ignobly bartered or surrendered."[81] In Westmoreland, Virginia, citizens presented a vision of American history that any good New Englander would endorse: "When our forefathers exchanged their native country for the wilderness of America, devotion to their God, obedience to the principles of morality, love of liberty guided by love of order, were their governing principles: This precious inheritance our fathers cherished with sincere affection."[82] The vision of an America with a common history and a common ancestry, upholding traditional principles and religion against the grasping and visionary universalisms of the French Revolution, was fundamental to Federalist constructions of national citizenship.

American citizens, specifically all "true Americans," were said to be united and speaking with "one voice" in their support of the government. Indeed, it was the duty of all citizens to do so. Citizens of Caroline County expressed their "sentiments of duty and love to our county," which they thought must "impress the heart of every citizen."[83] Citizens in Philadelphia congratulated Adams on what seemed to be "the spirit of patriotism" that assured "the prospect of unanimity that now presents itself."[84] From upstate New York, petitioners noted that "one sentiment appears to pervade the land."[85] The "Soldier Citizens" of New Jersey assured Adams that in the "feelings of every American bosom" there was "but one voice."[86] One newspaper noted that the addresses "created an enthusiastic Americanism that will prove her salvation."[87]

Adams agreed. Seeing the numerous petitions, he could only conclude that "all America appears to declare, with one heart and one voice," the determination to vindicate "the honor of our nation."[88] Adams thanked the officers of the Thirty-third Regiment of Militia in Richmond, Virginia, for their sentiments, which "breathes the genuine spirit and expresses the soundest sentiments of 'TRUE BORN AMERICANS.'"[89] John Marshall returned home in the midst of the Federalist enthusiasm and experienced "infinite pleasure" to behold "the unconquerable spirit of Americans rising into action." He, "like all true Americans," felt an elevated pride for "the dignity and grandeur of the American character."[90] "All America"—one people, "one voice," unanimous, one nation.

The claims of unanimity in the petitions were repeated in newspapers, orations, sermons, essays, and countless Federalist private letters, even in the face of what would prove to be massive evidence to the contrary. On May 7, 1798—the day John Adams had reserved for national contemplation, prayer, and fasting; the day twelve hundred "Youth of Philadelphia" marched to the president's house to present their petition; and the day countless orations and sermons celebrated the unanimity of the American people—a "fray" ensued during which the capital "was so filled with confusion from about 6. to 10. oclock . . . that it was dangerous going out."[91] Republican newspapers had kept up their pressure on the Federalists, and had even challenged the legitimacy of the petitioners. In New York, the Republican *Argus* ridiculed the supposed "youth" of the young petitioners from New York, noting that "another *boy,* not quite *sixty,* graced the assembly with his presence." The charges ended in a fatal duel.[92] In North-Stamford, Connecticut, deep in the heartland of Federalism, Adams was hung and burned in effigy in front of the meetinghouse, on the very day everyone was supposed to be praying and fasting. The perpetrators, although unknown, were considered to be "two or three obscure illiterate and deluded individuals."[93] In Portsmouth, Virginia, Republicans crafted a petition of their own, assailing the hostile posture of the Adams administration. A Federalist response attacked the leader of the petitioners as "a Frenchman," and possibly un-naturalized.[94]

Federalists were able to accept their pretensions to speak for all American citizens because their nationalism dismissed the voices of opposition as illegitimate by birth, class, and virtue. As Abigail Adams affirmed, "No Native American is willing" to oppose the measures of the government.[95] As far as she was concerned, the only "real Americans" who had ever been deceived by French politics were "the mass of the lower class of people," and even they, she maintained, "are uniting & united" in the current crisis.[96] The petitioners from Dedham believed "that all Americans *by birth,* except perhaps a few abandoned characters, have always preserved a superior affection to their own country."[97] In Maryland, Federalists in Calvert County decried with "abhorrence" the efforts of "foreigners and others, to alienate our fellow-citizens from the government of their choice."[98] Anyone in opposition was either a foreigner or among a small handful of other "designing men."[99] An anonymous author asserted that he "would blush for my country could I believe that there existed even a weak party of *native Americans* who would oppose" the government.[100] For William Cobbett, perhaps the most rabid of Federalist polemicists (and himself, ironically, a foreigner), a large portion of the opposition were "the sans-cullottes, the poor ignorant ragamuffins, who hung idly about the great towns, and who are in great part, composed of foreigners."[101]

The leading Federalist essay circulating in the spring of 1798 was a production by Joseph Hopkinson, son of the famous jurist and poet, Francis Hopkinson, and himself the author of the lyrics for the first "national song"—"Hail Columbia." Hopkinson presented "Hail Columbia" at a Philadelphia benefit on April 25, 1798. Federalist newspapers were extremely excited by the patriotic song, and they quickly published copies of it throughout the country. As the Philadelphia papers noted, "The Introduction of a patriotic song upon the stage being a novelty interesting and welcome to Americans, was received with an applause at once unanimous and enthusiastic." It was a song written by "A NATIVE AMERICAN, and glowing with the true love of OUR OWN Country—It is hoped that this first attempt to introduce a NATIONAL SONG on the stage will be encouraged."[102] Hopkinson's pamphlet, *What is our situation? And what our prospects? A few pages for Americans, by an American,* sought to expose the treachery of "those among us who are stirring up sedition and strife, who pant after confusion, tumult and national ruin."[103] True Americans needed to focus on their enemies already in the country, who allied themselves with French ambition that "would strip and desolate every nation on earth" in service of visionary "Rights of Man."[104] Hopkinson considered the pamphlet and song as one piece, doing the same work on the American mind. So he sent a copy of both to George Washington, noting:

> The theatres here and at New York have resounded with it night after night and the men and boys in the Streets sing as they go. I mention these things as pleasing and convincing testimonies of the great change that has taken place in the *american* mind, when american tunes and american sentiments have driven off those execrable french murder shouts—which not long since tortured

> our ears in all places of public amusement, and in every lane and alley in the United States.[105]

Hopkinson imagined the song and his pamphlet transforming the "American mind," and he could hear the effects of his effort in the streets.

Hopkinson's pamphlet had one clear point. "The great source of all our political evils and misfortunes," he argued, stemmed from "the facility with which foreigners acquire the full and perfect rights of citizenship."[106] For the most part, the emigrants who had taken advantage of American citizenship had imbibed the delusions of the French Revolution and believed "any government, and all laws are now too tyrannical." These people considered "the bolts and bars that secure their neighbour's property" as "encroachments upon their *natural rights.*"[107] The emigrants represented "none but the vile and worthless, none but the idle and discontented, the disorderly and the wicked," who have "inundated upon us from Europe."[108] Since "our antagonists meet with few proselytes in this county," the opposition "depend for recruits on the annual supplies of imported patriots," and "watch eagerly from the wharves for the gangs of discontented and factious emigrants that flock in from all parts of the world." The time had come, he pleaded, for "the AMERICAN SPIRIT" to "stand forth in its native dignity and strength" to rewrite the laws of national citizenship.[109]

Abigail Adams sent the pamphlet to many of her correspondents, noting to her son, John Quincy Adams, in Germany, that Hopkinson's arguments required "the serious consideration of every American."[110] William Shaw, the nephew of John Adams and one of the Harvard students who had composed their own patriotic address to the president, believed Hopkinson's pamphlet to be full of sage advice. "His observations on imigration were to me particularly pleasing and interesting," he wrote, and he hoped that Americans would "no longer pray, that America may become an asylum to all nations." In fact, he believed new laws were necessary to restrict immigrant access to citizenship, as "the grand cause of all our present difficulties may be traced to this source—to so many hordes of *foreigners* imigrating to America."[111]

Other voices lamenting the effect of easy immigrant access to citizenship were evident throughout the Federalist newspapers. As one essayist noted, "Every *native American* must observe with pleasure the great change in the public mind relative to the admission of aliens to the rights of citizenship." It was time to reform "the mistaken policy that citizenship could not be too easily acquired here."[112] Another author admitted that in the past, America had attempted to serve as an asylum for all oppressed peoples, "but even granting that by prohibiting foreign emigration we should expose many individuals to misery and death," the nation must "look at the effects which [immigration] produces in our own country." While in theory the idea of an asylum of liberty was laudable, in point of fact immigration threatened the very existence of the United States, because it "has a tendency to render the manners and principles of the people of this country dissimilar, and thereby to destroy all hope of permanent union—that it has a tendency to corrupt the public morals, to prevent the establishment of a national character." One Federalist stripped his language of all overt polemics and described the situation succinctly, describing the problem in the language of eighteenth-century notions of national difference:

> Emigrants arrive from Ireland, from Holland, from Germany, and from other parts of Europe. These all differ from us, and they differ from one another. They bring with them their peculiar habits, and their peculiar prejudices. They have been accustomed to different forms of intercourse, and to different modes of doing business. Thus a national character can never be established, and the sentiment of national honor can never be strongly felt.

Nations possessed uniform habits, manners, and cultures, and the United States would never become a truly national people and community with a constant influx of foreigners—"a national character can never be established" with an open immigration policy. Since it was widely recognized that men "who differ in their habits and manners must have different systems of governments," a steady stream of foreigners would "prevent the assimilation of manners on which the permanency of our union depends." Americans needed to protect their national character from the evils of immigration.[113]

Taken together, the memorials of the petitioners, which supported and extolled a fragile national character, and the pamphlets and opinions, which emphasized that foreigners were behind the difficulties faced by the American nation at that crucial moment, created a clear path for an articulation in law of a national citizenship that supported America's status as a distinct national people in a world of distinct nations. The Federalists wanted and declared America to be a true national community where the citizens shared duties consistent with their national character and toward a common national interest. But to become (and maintain) that national community, foreign elements needed to be excluded and unsavory elements already enjoying the rights of citizens needed to be controlled by the national state. National citizenship would have to be purified from seditious (foreign) elements, and national authority needed to be certified. So in the midst of this popular enthusiasm in the long spring of 1798, with the "pride of national character" in ascendancy, Federalists crafted and pressed through Congress a series of laws intended to purify the American citizenry and ensure the survival of a distinct American nation. The laws attempted to re-create the America being presented in the memorials: a citizenry of clear national homogeneity—in ancestry, manners, habits, language, and support for the government.

The Legislation of National Citizenship

The legislative history of the second session of the Fifth Congress is well known but still misinterpreted. By April and May of 1798, the congressmen who had begun this session's work, at the beginning of November 1797, were growing tired and agitated. Numerous members were returning home for the summer. The uproar created by the publication of the XYZ letters injected life into the sleepy members, who created a torrent of legislation between May and July of 1798. In addition to laws directly related to the defense of the country—including the creation of the Department of the Navy; the creation of an additional regiment of artillerists and engineers; an act authorizing the president to raise a provisional army; an act allowing the president to borrow $5 million from the National Bank at his discretion; and a direct tax to pay for anticipated costs—Federalists created a series of laws to exorcise all foreign elements from the American citizenry. The new Naturalization Act of 1798, the Alien Friends and Enemies Acts, and the Sedition Act represented a break with past efforts to deal with immigrants and political dissidents in the United States. No longer sure that the American character could remain inviolate against the dangers of foreign influence—despite the numerous memorials of loyalty—the Federalists in Congress strove to regulate immigrants and aliens, and to legally deny all legitimacy to any opposition to the Federalist government.

Many of these laws emerged out of the debates over the new naturalization act. This is not surprising, since the law was the brainchild of the Committee for the Protection of Commerce and Defense of the Country, organized in the midst of the XYZ Crisis in the spring of 1798. Arguing that the naturalization law of 1795 failed to ensure that aliens wishing to naturalize provide "evidence of their attachment to the laws and welfare of this country," the committee recommended three substantial changes.[114] First, it resolved that the term of residence required by prospective citizens be lengthened substantially. Second, the committee recommended the establishment of a permanent registry of all resident aliens, including information regarding their place of birth, citizenship, and residence. Finally, it asked for a law providing for the removal of alien enemies, that is, aliens who were citizens of a nation at war with the United States.[115]

As Congress considered the resolutions of the committee in early May, a few outspoken Federalists began pressing for more extreme restrictions. Robert Goodloe Harper, South Carolina's leading Federalist representative, opened debate on the naturalization law by urging the House to take decisive action. It was "high time," he began, that America should "recover from the mistake which this country fell into when it first began to form its constitutions"—the mistake "of admitting foreigners to citizenship." It was time to declare "that nothing but birth should entitle a man to citizenship in this country."[116] Although his motion was deemed out of order, Harper and his Massachusetts colleague, Harrison Gray Otis, continued to press for unprecedented restrictions on immigrants and on the rights of naturalized citizens. Otis introduced a bill that would have denied persons born outside of the United States the ability—even if naturalized—to hold "any office of honor, trust, or profit, under the United States." Harper attached a friendly amendment to Otis's bill, which would additionally deny naturalized citizens the right of voting for any popular representative at *all* levels of government—local, state, or national. In explaining himself, Harper noted that he wished foreigners to have the rights of property and was "willing that they should *form* citizens for us," but that he believed "the rights of citizenship" should not be enjoyed by any but "persons born in this country." In effect, Harper would create ranks within the citizenry by granting native-born citizens full rights and naturalized citizens only the basics.[117] Although both Otis's proposition and Harper's amendment were eventually cast off because they were determined to require amendments to the Constitution, the mood of the Federalists was clear.[118] Foreigners and immigrants were no longer seen as an asset to the republic; they should not be considered part of the national community; and the rights of national citizenship needed to be carefully guarded. Without immediate correction of the laws of naturalization, Federalist congressmen believed America would never sustain the uniformity of character required to sustain the national Union.

The new naturalization act anchored the efforts of the Federalists in the House of Representatives to purify the character of the American citizenry. The law of 1795 was thrown out, and the requirement of five years residency before aliens could acquire the rights of citizenship was replaced by a requirement of fourteen years residency. It was an extreme requirement, and considering that some in the Congress of 1790 had thought *two* years to be "illiberal and void of philanthropy," the 1798 requirements were clearly intended to deny all but the most persistent of citizenship. Federalists did not try to hide the true nature of the new bill. As Samuel Sitgreaves noted approvingly, a long residency requirement was a way to escape "Constitutional embarrassment" and still deny aliens the rights of citizens.[119] In addition to the long residency requirement, the new law created an ambitious system of national surveillance of all aliens within the country. It provided for a centralized registry of aliens, under the Department of State, and with the addition of "An Act respecting Alien Enemies" (which began as a section of the new naturalization law but was split into its own bill), aliens from a country at war with the United States were also denied the ability to become citizens. This was an assertion of federal power into the states that was unprecedented.

Efforts in the House to inhibit immigrant access to citizenship were aided by the controversial Act Concerning Aliens, passed by the Federalist Senate in early June. Popularly called the Alien Friends Act, or the Alien Act, the bill gave the president extraordinary power to seize, detain, and deport any alien "he shall judge dangerous to the peace and safety of the United States." Alien rights of due process and habeas corpus were left to the president's personal discretion.[120] The act also required "every master or commander of any ship or vessel" who brought immigrants to the United States to provide their names, ages, place of nativity, the place from which they had emigrated, the "nation to which they belong or owe allegiance," and even "a description of their person." Ship owners who failed to provide such information could be fined $300 or have their ship confiscated. While Republicans attacked the law as unconstitutional and full of "principles which would have disgraced the age of Gothic barbarity," Federalists pushed it through.[121]

The final bill in the group was "An act, in addition to the act entitled, 'An act for the punishment of certain crimes against the United States,'" or, as it was popularly known, the "Sedition Act." The Sedition Act was intended to stop people in America from conspiring to overthrow the government of the United States. To do so, the act provided the federal government with broad powers to prosecute "any person" who "shall write, print, utter, or publish" any attack on the government of the United States.[122] In debate over the bill, Republicans attacked its broad powers as a violation of the constitutional amendment protecting the liberty of the press. Federalists saw it as a clarification of (supposedly) preexisting national common law libel principles, which governed an individual's relationship to the community.

The Federalists took direct aim at the country's opposition press, quoting liberally from the arch-Republican rags, the Philadelphia *Aurora General Advertiser* and the New York *Time Piece,* as they sought to emphasize that only foreigners and a few—a small few—of confused, factious individuals would even be affected by the law. Holding up a Republican newspaper in triumph, one Federalist congressmen declared that the attacks of the opposition press exulted in "the wild visionary" theories that were "calculated to destroy all confidence between man and man," which lead "to the dissolution of every bond of union," and which cut "asunder every ligament that united man to his family, man to his neighbor, man to society, and to Government."[123] This was not simply an attack on political opponents, but on *ideas*—the very foreign ideas which threatened American national character. Connecticut legislator John Allen felt relatively confident that the law would not touch the "*citizens* and *natives*" of this country, because the calumny of the opposition press was obviously generated to disrupt "the peace of our Zion." As for those in opposition, he continued, "I hope, for the honor of human nature, and of our country, they are foreigners."[124] Passed by the Senate in early July and the House on July 10, the bill was the capstone of Federalist efforts to purify the American citizenry. With the new naturalization laws and the two Alien bills, dangerous foreigners could be expelled from America; with the Sedition Act, those dangerous foreign ideas—the visionary schemes of reform—could be expunged from American public debate as well.

Voting on the acts clearly shows the partisan nature of the support for the measures and the sectional nature of the political parties.[125] The Middle States were almost evenly split, while the Southern and Southwestern states were predominately Republican, and the New England states solidly Federalist. Like their assumption that the country unanimously called for war with France in the spring of 1798, historians, by conflating Republican attacks against "aristocratic" immigrants during the debates over the 1795 Naturalization Act with the concerns of 1798, have sometimes missed the clearly partisan nature of the support for the 1798 legislation. Many general histories of the period, when discussing these acts, casually suggest that Republicans supported these acts, and actually quote from the debates over the 1795 Naturalization Bill. This trend seems to have begun with John C. Miller's *Crisis in Freedom,* which notes, "Republicans too, feared immigration—but from a different quarter," and then goes on to quote James Madison's speech from 1795.[126] In fact, an analysis of the voting on these bills (where it can be discovered) clearly shows a strict party split, with Federalists pushing the legislation through. The Alien Enemies Bill did indeed garner little *opposition* from Republicans, but it was passed after the

Alien Friends Act, and Republicans considered the Enemies Bill both redundant and constitutional. If the government could deport and imprison aliens without due process at any time, certainly the government could deport and imprison "alien enemies" in time of war. Despite the claims of the Federalists to speak for all the American people, the deep divisions among the population, even evident at the height of Federalist ascendancy, did not bode well for that party's national political future or the success of its attempt to legislate a national citizenship in defense of national character.[127]

Nevertheless, as the second session of the Fifth Congress drew to a close, Federalists returned to their home districts confident that they had taken the steps necessary to secure the American government to the American people—and that they had done the people's bidding. They had greatly increased the power of the national government. They had provided for a professional army, a marine corps, and a navy; greatly expanded the federal funding available for state militias; and commissioned numerous lighthouses, armaments, cannons, and transport vessels. They had created a national stamp tax and a one-time property tax; and had enlarged the offices of the federal tax collectors. They had given the executive branch the power to borrow up to $5 million from the Bank of the United States. They had extended the power and jurisdiction of the federal judiciary. And, of course, they had secured in law a properly "national" American citizenship, with an improving national common law—a citizenship and a nation that would be purified of all contentious elements, one that reflected the shared character of true Americans while being protected from the heterogeneity that immigration promoted. This was not a purely *jus sanguinis* approach to American nationhood and citizenship, because Federalists still operated with eighteenth-century notions of the mutability of national character. But they were clearly moving toward an organic definition of the American people: a national people exhibiting all the unique qualities of language, manners, habits, and principles that approximated the cultural differences among European nations.[128]

With their songs, their orations, their militias, their memorials—and finally with their legislative agenda—Federalists across the country displayed their patriotism, voiced their approval of the Adams administration, and pronounced that all true Americans were now eager to fight the French. They presented America as a homogeneous nation with one voice—one that celebrated a common language, religion, history, habits, manners, and ancestry, and one whose citizens properly controlled the national government. "True Americans" rallied to the cause, while "hordes of foreigners" and a few other sinister souls continually stirred discontent and treason or simply diluted the American national character. As the only "true" citizens, Federalists embodied their "duty" to the nation in their addresses in support of the president and by volunteering themselves for the struggle to come. With their parallel celebration of and concern for American national character, Federalists attempted to secure in law the America their petitioners created in rhetoric. Federalists had attempted to delegitimize the purpose and threat of revolution itself, by dissolving its potency in a solution of nationalism. America needed to be guided by a homogeneous citizenry speaking with one voice and led by an energetic central government—a true nation-state—and by the summer of 1798 they had taken the steps deemed necessary to secure that future.

But the lie to their vision existed even as they celebrated. They did not and could not speak for all Americans, and the opposition fiercely challenged the legitimacy of their program. Even as the bills passed under heavy opposition through Congress, evidence of an unruly and headstrong resistance in Kentucky began to excite the imaginations of Federalists in Philadelphia. As resistance to the acts spread to the important states of Virginia, Pennsylvania, New York, and even Massachusetts, Federalists began to realize that they had united the political interests and ideological tendencies of the opposition into a daunting combination. As the next chapter shows, a wide opposition united their voices against the Federalists as a fight for the "rights of man" protected by the sovereignty of the states, and presented a very different vision of American nationhood and citizenship.

{ 5 }

States' Rights & the Rights of Man

THE OPPOSITION TO THE ALIEN AND SEDITION ACTS

He asked if those laws were correspondent with human rights? Those rights he said, were, freedom of speech, freedom of person, a right to justice, and to a fair trial. If any alien possessed those rights, he asked, could he avail himself of them under the present law? Could a citizen under the sedition law, exercise the freedom of speech, or of religion, which last, a few days before, he had heard called a social right? It was not so. . . . What would be the effect of those laws? They would establish executive influence, and executive influence would produce a revolution.—JOHN TAYLOR OF CAROLINE, INTRODUCING THE VIRGINIA RESOLUTIONS OF 1798

Then freeman assemble at "liberty's call,"
Resolve—and to congress petition,
That the law called alien to nothing may fall,
And also the bill of sedition.
—"A NEEDY WAR-WORN SOLDIER," 1798

IN THE MIDDLE OF AUGUST 1798, IN FAYETTE COUNTY, KENtucky, thousands of people massed in the small town of Lexington to protest the Alien and Sedition Acts. Unable to fit inside any public building, the crowd sprawled across the square at the center of town to listen to the local leadership of the Republican Party, led by the distinguished Colonel George Nicholas. Like most of the leading figures in Kentucky, Nicholas was a transplant from Virginia. He had served in the Virginia House of Delegates during the Revolution, as a delegate to the Virginia ratifying convention for the U.S. Constitution, and he was the brother of Wilson Cary Nicholas, friend and confidant of Thomas Jefferson. Perched atop a wagon that served as a makeshift stage, Nicholas lectured for four hours about the dangers of the recent Federalist legislation—to peace in the West, to the federal nature of the

Constitution, and to the preservation of the rights of man. One loving biographer called his oration "a speech of eloquence and power, scarcely ever equaled, and certainly never surpassed."[1] But when he finished, despite the Homeric length of his harangue (or perhaps because of it), the crowd wanted more. Seizing the moment, twenty-one-year-old lawyer Henry Clay mounted the wagon and earned his reputation as "another Patrick Henry" by assailing the pretenses of aristocrats.[2] Clay, himself recently arrived from Virginia, where he had trained in the law with Jefferson's mentor, George Wythe, was a strong Republican and as yet uninterested in compromise. After Clay, a few daring Federalists attempted to seize the stage, but they were pulled away, shouted down, and jeered. The assembled crowd then passed a set of ten angry resolutions, which pronounced the Alien and Sedition Acts "void" and characterized the Federalist agenda as "unconstitutional, impolitic, unjust, and a disgrace to the American name." Noting an impending crisis of the Union, the resolutions also asked each man to "furnish himself without delay" and "at his own expense" with arms for the defense of republican government. Nicholas and Clay were carried away in triumph.[3]

The meeting in Lexington was one of many similar mass meetings with participants in the thousands that were held across the state in the summer of 1798. The uproar in Kentucky, or what the Easterners came to call "the Kentucky frenzy," marked the beginning of the unmaking of the Federalists' national dominance. Frontier Lexington was about as far from Newburyport, Massachusetts, as one could get in the United States, with dice, whiskey, and the *code duello* more evident to critics of the society than law and order. The Lexington resolutions exemplified the emerging character of the American West—confident, democratic, and defiant—and provided the early hints that the Federalist policies of the spring of 1798 had overreached.

But it would take more than a few boisterous complaints from the backwoods to shake the Federalists from their triumphalism. Kentucky, that "new fledged State," merely proved its own immaturity and "the height of insolence" by attacking the government and flying "in the face of a benevolent foster parent."[4] As one Federalist noted, "It is probable Kentucky is yet semi-barbarian in its legislature, as in its morals, manners, and literature."[5] Celebratory petitions lauding Adams and his administration continued to pour into Philadelphia from across the Union, and the friends of government lavished in the "glow of patriotism" which they continued to believe "pervades all our citizens."[6] Grand juries throughout the country began presenting indictments under the Sedition Act, and Secretary of State Timothy Pickering pressed Adams to find a suitable test for the Alien Act.[7] Federalist Massachusetts, in an effort to complete the work begun by Congress, approved a new amendment to the Constitution that would have allowed only "natural born citizens" the right to hold *any* elected office in the federal government.[8] And as Hamilton and Washington began organizing their paper army, American ships began open warfare with French commerce. By mid-summer, the Federalist press was urging their representatives to formalize the "Quasi-War" into a *real* war. As the next session of Congress approached, the calls in the Federalist newspapers became general. As one editor noted, the "Grand Council of the Nation" would have the opportunity to either "fix the fortune or seal the ruin of this great Empire." The moment had come to "fix the country in a settled and positive state by immediately declaring war."[9]

But as the summer wore on and the popular attacks on the Federalist agenda spread from Kentucky to the crucial states of Virginia, Pennsylvania, New Jersey, New York, and Vermont—and with evidence of discontent and symbolic protests emerging in nearly all states—the ominous proof of an organized and obstinate opposition to war could not be denied. By the fall of 1798, even as they pursued convictions under the Sedition Act with vigor, Federalists acknowledged a creeping realization not only that they had failed to mobilize a unified movement toward war with France—a movement intended to help ensure the ascendancy of a strong national character, an energetic national government, and a homogeneous national citizenry—but that they had created an issue which wed opposition politics and ideology in a powerful combination across sectional and class interests. By the opening of the next congressional session, in December of 1798, leading Federalists realized the political danger of the concerted and sustained opposition to the acts. As one Federalist reported to Rufus King, serving as American ambassador in London, "Much Clamor has been made about the Alien and Sedition Bill, & a Vigorous Attack in the course of the Session, supported by all the Virginia faction, will be made on it, in order to alarm the Public Mind, & prepare the way for their success, in the Ensuing election in April next."[10] The "clamor" about the Alien and Sedition Acts proved overwhelming, ultimately bringing the conflicts of the citizenship revolution to a climax.

As clamors go, this one has not received its due. The extent, character, and meaning of the extensive petitioning and mobilization against the Alien and Sedition Acts is simply unknown.[11] Most studies of the moment have focused on the famous Virginia and Kentucky Resolutions (the resolutions against the Alien and Sedition Acts passed by the state legislatures of those two states) as a way to explore the history of states' rights,[12] or as a window into the constitutional beliefs of Thomas Jefferson and James Madison,[13] or as part of the history of embattled civil liberties.[14] Recent work on the cultural politics of the early republic has essentially ceded 1798 to the Federalists; it was the reign of the witches, and the "public sphere" was, for all important purposes, successfully captured by pro-war enthusiasts.[15]

And yet it is widely assumed that the Alien and Sedition Acts were deeply unpopular. It is an easy refrain: the Federalists overreached during the war hysteria of the spring of 1798, and their arrogance ultimately led to their downfall. Somehow we know that the opposition to the Alien and Sedition Acts played a part in the "Revolution of 1800"[16]—many scholars have considered the Virginia and Kentucky Resolutions as "the opening guns of the election of 1800."[17] Recent scholarship has also begun to reemphasize the election of 1800 as a watershed transformation in participatory democracy in the United States—with an expansion of the active electorate, the growth of sophisticated forms of mobilization and party organization, and the arrival of a new "type" of democratic activist.[18] How can we integrate what we know of the vague unpopularity of the Alien and Sedition Acts with the process of political transformation under way in the United States at the end of the 1790s? Where does the opposition to the acts—both as a political moment and as an alternative vision of nationhood, as voiced in the Virginia and Kentucky Resolutions in their broadest context—fit with the eventual defeat of the Federalists, and what is the meaning of that defeat?

The "clamor" against the Alien and Sedition Acts is the missing link. The protestation, mobilization, petitioning, and remonstrance against the Federalists in the summer, fall, and winter of 1798–99 provided the original momentum, organization, and ideology that would strip Adams of the presidency, overturn the Federalist majorities in Congress and in numerous state legislatures, and move the United States off a trajectory of consolidation and centralization inaugurated and designed by the Federalists in power. The sights and sounds of politics—the songs, liberty poles, and cockades—extended the effect of the formal mechanisms of political activity: the petitioning of local towns and counties, the resolutions of grand juries and states, and the elections. The clamor is crucial both for what it can show us about political practices in the early republic—how distinct, local *publics* came to be seen as one, *national* movement—and as a clear articulation of the political and constitutional thought that motivated the people who rejected the policy choices of the Federalists and that assured the party's eventual defeat. A vision of Union that assumed local diversity and the importance of the states in defining and defending the rights of citizens would mock the Federalist nationalism. And having forced the Federalists into obscurity, it was that vision which would set the course and dynamics of U.S. politics into and throughout the nineteenth century.

The Mobilization of Dissent

Organized resistance to the Federalist program of the spring of 1798 began almost simultaneously in local communities in Kentucky and Virginia. In Lexington, on the Fourth of July, the *Kentucky Gazette* put forth a plan for resistance even before the acts were actually passed, calling for a set of meetings, committees of correspondence, and a general mobilization to oppose Federalist policy and the rush to war.[19] Within a week, polemics against war with France and assertions of the right of states and individuals to disobey unconstitutional laws were being published regularly in both the *Kentucky Gazette* and the Frankfort *Palladium of Liberty,* the leading Republican newspapers in the state.[20]

Clarke County, Kentucky, led the way on July 24 with a series of resolutions approved, "without a voice dissenting," at an outdoor meeting of nearly one thousand people.[21] On August 1, George Nicholas published his "Political Creed," an effort to draw a charge of sedition upon himself.[22] From mid-August to late September, meetings in Kentucky condemning the martial acts of the Federalists in Congress became general. Woodford, Fayette, Franklin, Bourbon, and Mason counties rapidly produced, copied, and celebrated each other's resolutions at meetings attended by thousands of participants. At the meeting held in Lexington, characterized at the time as "one of the largest meetings ever held in the state of Kentucky," over four thousand people flooded the center of town to pass their own set of resolutions.[23]

By mid-September, Kentucky's popular resistance had become generally known to the Atlantic states. William Cobbet, writing in *Porcupine's Gazette,* ridiculed and condemned the Kentuckian petitioners as country bumpkins, illiterates, "savages," and less sober than "the wild Irish."[24] But for Republican-leaning newspapers, the Kentucky remonstrances proved that the "principles of '76" had not been abandoned in America. In a widely published letter, an anonymous Virginian noted with approval the activities of the emerging opposition in Kentucky, referring to the different county resolutions collectively as the "Kentucky Resolutions." While these resolutions were thought by "the government party as factious and violent," the real "friends to liberty, view them in a different light." "Kentucky," the writer asserted, "is now contemplated by many, as the only asylum from foreign and domestic troubles, and from state persecutions."[25] Another supporter hoped the rest of the states, "from New Hampshire to Georgia," would "be roused before it is too late."[26]

Virginia counties soon followed with their own resolutions against the Alien and Sedition Acts. These types of local remonstrances had long been an important part of Virginian civic life, and by the late 1790s attendees at county court days, militia musters, and ad hoc committees were regularly complaining about the encroachments of the federal government. During the pro-war frenzy of the spring of 1798, a number of local resolutions attacked supporters of war with France.[27] Beginning in July with Albemarle County—which encouraged speculation that "a certain Oracle" was involved in the drafting—specific resolutions and remonstrances against the Alien and Sedition Acts, standing armies, and the new borrowing powers of the president soon poured in from Amelia, Buckingham, Caroline, Dinwiddie, Essex, Goochland, Hanover, James City, Louisa, Orange, Powhatan, Prince Edward, and Spotsylvania counties.[28] Some, like the remonstrance of the "Democratic-Republican freeholders of Prince Edward County," mimicked the laudatory petitions of the Federalists and were sent directly to John Adams.[29] Others called for a nationwide petitioning of the next congressional session for the repeal of the acts.[30] Most, however, like the Albemarle resolves, called upon the state's representatives to "use their utmost excursions to obtain a repeal."[31]

The local resolutions of Virginia and Kentucky emerged from political practices that reflected the shared political traditions of the two states. In both states the local resolutions were approved at pre-announced "meetings," usually set for court days and militia musters. In each case, orations would precede resolutions, which would either be produced on the spot, in a committee created for the purpose while the speeches continued, or drafted beforehand, by elected officials, local notables, or others closely tied to the Republican Party.

In Virginia, in 1798, the vast majority of conflicts in local politics reflected a contest among elites over who represented the true voice of the county. By the late eighteenth century, numerous families could claim "natural" leadership through deep and overlapping ties of kin, so these protests of the Alien and Sedition Acts, which were always presented as "unanimous" declarations of the voice of the people, were often challenged by other local elites—"the friends of the government"—who supported the administration. Outwardly, the forms of local authority essentially mimicked colonial deferential political behavior—great men still ruled. But the experience of the Revolutionary War in Virginia had shattered the placidity and unanimity of colonial Virginia politics, which had led to an increasing "move away from deferential politics," toward a politics based more in "conflict between legislative factions over public policy, and issues oriented appeals to constituents."[32] In the late 1790s, this competitive politics manifested itself, not by direct challenges from below or by the claims of traditionally marginalized communities, but by more visible and public conflict at the top. So a veneer of deference hid an increasingly organized, loud, and participatory politics.[33]

One telling example of how such factions failed to function within older modes of consensual expression can be seen in the drama surrounding the Albemarle County resolutions of May 1798. Those resolutions, attacking the "pro-British" policy of the Adams administration, had been passed during May's court session with "only one dissenting voice." At the June court, Colonel John Nicholas and Justice of the Peace Benjamin Brown attempted to pass a *pro-Adams* address. Opposing Nicholas was Wilson Cary Nicholas, his cousin, and Thomas Mann Randolph, Thomas Jefferson's son-in-law, each of whom spent the majority of the day "consumed in haranguing the people." Finally, as recriminations turned personal, the question was called, and in the vote "the people" were divided, with a large number but not a majority, standing with the Federalist John Nicholas. Nicholas had not been present at the May court, where Wilson Cary and Randolph had been able to stage a "unanimous" popular condemnation of the Adams administration and thereby present the fiction of both deferential authority and community unanimity, ideas that reinforced one another. But with two equal claimants to authority at the June court, the day was spent in faction and recrimination, with the divisions of the people open for the world to see.[34]

In Kentucky, the meetings against the Alien and Sedition Acts usually involved many more participants and were more raucous, enthusiastic, and spontaneous affairs. No Virginia elites were ever literally "carried away" by the crowd. At least four Kentucky meetings claimed participants in the thousands, while no Virginia local resolutions claimed the participation of more than a few hundred. Kentucky's politics at the end of the 1790s reflected a much more direct and open socioeconomic conflict than Virginia's, with certain Kentucky elites (connected to great Virginia political families) competing with ambitious newcomers over the direction of state politics. In the spring of 1798, for example, Kentuckians were deeply divided over a movement to call a new state constitutional convention, with slaveholding large planters, led by George Nicholas and John Breckinridge, competing for ascendancy with small farmers and non-slaveholders, increasingly led by Henry Clay, who often assailed "aristocrats" in the name of the yeomanry.[35]

Yet the Kentucky opposition to the Alien and Sedition Acts did represent more real unanimity among the citizenry as a whole than the Virginia remonstrances. As the meeting in Lexington where Clay spoke after Nicholas shows, the Alien and Sedition Acts provided a common enemy for both political interests in the state, since both shared fundamental beliefs about the unconstitutional nature of those acts and of the danger inherent in gross abuse of federal power. Federalists certainly existed in Kentucky, but compared to Virginia, their influence at the end of the decade was almost completely spent. The letter by a Virginian "to his friend in Kentucky," extolling the local resolutions, recognized this fact explicitly: "Your unanimity is a most happy thing for your country. There is nothing here but the most violent altercations, bickerings and heart burnings; friends against friends, brethren against brethren."[36]

Following the lead of the local mobilizations in Kentucky and Virginia over the course of the summer, Jefferson, John Taylor of Caroline, and Madison agreed that the battle against the Alien and Sedition Acts could be fought in the state legislatures. They would try to focus the widespread outrage. To assure Virginia's role, Madison agreed to stand for a seat in that state's House of Delegates, and he drafted a set of resolutions to be presented there. Jefferson, for his part, used the relative seclusion of Monticello to draft another set of resolutions he intended for the North Carolina legislature, so that Virginia would not stand alone. By October, however, Jefferson's political allies in Albemarle, including Wilson Cary Nicholas—the brother of George Nicholas of Kentucky—assured him that Kentucky would prove a surer ally for his resolutions. In an auspicious coincidence, leading Republican John Breckinridge of Kentucky had traveled to Virginia to take the cure at Warm Springs while he actively sought someone who would be willing to prepare resolutions for the Kentucky legislature.[37] At a meeting there in late September, Breckinridge was given Jefferson's draft resolutions by Wilson Cary Nicholas, and all agreed that Breckinridge would use them as the basis for Kentucky's remonstrance in the upcoming November meeting of the Kentucky legislature.[38] Meanwhile, Madison's resolutions were put into the hands of John Taylor, to be introduced in the Virginia legislature when it convened in December. The result was the "Virginia and Kentucky Resolutions," a watershed moment in the debate over the meaning of the U.S. Constitution vis-ã-vis the rights of individuals and states.

Outside of Kentucky and Virginia, the first significant remonstrances emerged in the backcountry of Pennsylvania. Heavily populated by recent immigrants and ethnic enclaves, both Irish and German, western Pennsylvania provided a sustained and defiant opposition voice to the

Federalist war measures. Although the Federalist laws would help excite a small rebellion in the spring of 1799, in the summer of 1798 numerous Pennsylvanians sought the traditional redress of petitions to voice their opposition. Two different strains of political behavior shaped the character of resistance in Pennsylvania.

First, Pennsylvania was being aggressively organized by Republican Party editors and elected officials, so many of the earliest formal resolutions emerged in the context of federal, state, and local elections, as local party committees met to declare and publicize their candidates.[39] Albert Gallatin, the leader of the Republicans in the U.S. House of Representatives, received numerous laudatory addresses from his constituency, not only defending him for being a naturalized American citizen and supporting his reelection to the House, but assuring him that his supporters did not support war with France and thought the Alien and Sedition Bills were "impolitic, unjust, and unconstitutional."[40]

But a broader type of political agitation in Pennsylvania, which would be seen in its most radical form in the tax rebellion of John Fries in the spring of 1799, grew not out of party politics but directly out of a tradition, dating back to Independence, of local resistance to taxes, pro-speculation land laws, and pro-creditor monetary policies. The petitioning that emerged in these regions, particularly in the counties of York, Lancaster, and Northampton, often reflected a deep antagonism to iniquitous taxation as well as to the alien and sedition laws.[41] Many of these petitioners would have claimed to be Federalists, identifying themselves with Washington—if they claimed any party at all. Petitioners from York County passed four resolutions, only one of which dealt with the Alien and Sedition Acts, while the remaining three worried about the creation and funding of a standing army. The petitioners complained that the new taxes would fall unfairly on Pennsylvania householders and less on the great speculators. As they argued, "It is well known, that the owners of houses in Pennsylvania will pay much more in proportion to the value of their property, than the holders of uncultivated lands."[42] In Lancaster, Pennsylvania, at the beginning of March, petitioners worried over the Alien and Sedition Acts, but also over the creation of the "unequal tax on the people of the United States as that called the direct tax is looked upon." The direct tax, together with the stamp tax, "is sowing the seed of discontentment among the people."[43]

One way to evidence this resistance is in the appearance throughout Pennsylvania of "liberty poles," which marked a community's opposition to the government. The poles were a potent symbol of revolution, and they would soon spread throughout the Mid-Atlantic and even into Federalist New England. They had been widely erected during the era of the Whiskey Rebellion in Pennsylvania, New Jersey, and Maryland, and they remained a prominent symbol for protest.[44] Alexander Graydon remembered the summer of 1798 and the winter and spring of 1799, in the run-up to Fries's Rebellion, in vivid terms: "The sedition which began in the county of Northampton, ran in a vein through the counties of Berks and Dauphin, spreading the infection by the means of liberty poles, successively rising in grand colonnade, from the banks of the Delaware to those of the Susquehanna."[45] In fact, the "colonnade" of poles did not end at the banks of the Delaware, for resisters to the Federalist drive for war erected numerous poles in northern New Jersey as well.[46] The poles were so thick in eastern Pennsylvania by early 1799 that, months before the open conflicts that became known as Fries's Rebellion, the Federalists began organizing associations to "destroy the sedition poles."[47]

Similar contests emerged throughout the country. In Dedham, Massachusetts, the "ringleader" of a group that erected a liberty pole was brought to Boston, where he was held in jail for interrogation and eventually tried for sedition.[48] In Mendham, New Jersey, on August 11, twenty-three young men wearing "black cockades" (a Federalist badge) and armed with pistols, swords, and clubs, rode into town in the middle of the day, cut down the liberty pole that had been erected on July 4, and stole the liberty cap. The town put up another pole and cap that weekend.[49]

Numerous other poles elicited the scorn of Federalist newspapers and often the attacks of armed gangs who attempted to cut down the poles or steal the caps that topped them. "On the road to Providence," several poles could be seen with "the American cockade and tar and feathers below." The editors of the *Columbian Centinel* believed that men who would erect such poles were "born to be slaves or to be hanged."[50] In Vermont, at Wallingford, Republicans erected a liberty pole at which they burned copies of the Alien and Sedition Acts. In response, "the pole was cut down, burnt to ashes and scattered to the wind" by a group of "true republican federalists," otherwise known as a Federalist mob.[51] The same paper reported that "a spirit of insurgency" similar to the one exhibited by the Wallingford Republicans "was rising in the back part of New York State."[52] Another Federalist paper celebrated a similar destruction of a pole at Vassalboro, Maine.[53] In Hackensack Village, New Jersey, a liberty pole that had stood in the town since the heady days of 1793 was shorn of its liberty cap, and an eagle was placed on top.[54] In Newark, a running battle between Federalists and Republicans over the liberty cap atop the town liberty pole saw at least three different caps placed atop the pole and subsequently stolen.[55] The political climate of 1798 began to resemble that of 1775: "a spirit of insurgency."

In December, as the Virginia House of Delegates approved their resolutions and as the Kentucky legislature's resolutions were being circulated in the East, Republican congressmen in Philadelphia made clear their intention to challenge the constitutionality of the Alien and Sedition Acts and move for a repeal of all the war measures. These pronouncements, together with the example of Kentucky and Virginia, precipitated another massive petitioning drive, so that throughout January and early February 1799 Republican congressmen received hundreds of petitions "praying for a repeal of the alien and sedition acts."[56] With multiple petitions from Philadelphia and its immediate suburbs, and with numerous remonstrances from Washington, Cumberland, Montgomery, Lancaster, York, Dauphin, Franklin, Mifflin, Chester, Berks, and Northampton counties, over eighteen thousand signatures were collected from Pennsylvania alone.[57] By late February 1799, Congress had received petitions not only from Kentucky, Virginia, Pennsylvania, and New Jersey, but from New York and Vermont as well.

In northern New Jersey, opposition to the Alien and Sedition Acts had spread along with the liberty poles, but it was increasingly organized by local party operatives. The most important operatives were associated with Daniel Dodge and Aaron Pennington, the publishers of Newark's *Centinel of Freedom.* In 1798, this weekly paper was only two years old, but it served an important readership in the region around Newark, which was producing the first signs of an organized resistance to the traditionally Federalist-controlled state.[58] Aaron Pennington's brother William served as a leader of the Republican faction in the New Jersey legislature. For his constant newspaper attacks on the governor of New Jersey, Aaron Pennington was beaten in August of 1798, and both editors were charged with seditious libel.[59] By 1798, the paper was part of a growing network of papers aligned with the Republicans throughout the country—including the *Philadelphia Aurora,* the Pennsylvania *Herald of Liberty,* the Kentucky *Guardian of Freedom,* the New York *Time Piece,* the *Virginia Argus,* and others. These newspapers were increasingly partisan in their operation and closely tied to politics, both on the ground and in the legislatures.[60]

By December of 1798, the editors of the *Centinel of Freedom* were clearly attempting to instigate the type of local remonstrances that had characterized Kentucky, Virginia, and Pennsylvania. They celebrated the spirit of resistance that they "with pleasure" saw emerging "in the different counties of the states of Virginia, Kentucky and the back counties of Pennsylvania." They enthusiastically supported both the ideas and the example of the resolutions of the Kentucky legislature, and they encouraged the "real republicans" of New Jersey to act in the same fashion, "by convening together in either township or county meetings, as convenience may dictate, and there request your public agents by way of remonstrance to repeal the Alien and Sedition Laws, which have been enacted in open violation of the Constitution."[61] In January 1799, nearly six hundred people met in front of the courthouse in Newark, where they resolved that the Alien and Sedition Acts were unconstitutional and petitioned both their state and federal legislators to move for a repeal of the acts.[62]

As part of their efforts to mobilize supporters, Pennington and Dodge also produced and published political songs. Songs were common in the newspapers of the early republic; often, a particular space—the "Muse's Corner"—was reserved for new poetry and songs. These could be innocuous, ribald, or banal; or they could be great art or base doggerel; but often, as in the case of the songs of Pennington and Dodge, they could be *overtly* political. Political songs were crucial to the culture of American, and indeed Atlantic, politics at the end of the eighteenth century, and political songs played a significant role in the agitations of 1798.[63] As tangible as cockades for marking affiliations in 1798, political songs were often also crucial as polemics for the transmission of political ideas and prejudices, and in some cases they became significant instruments of mobilization.

With the success of "Hail Columbia" in Federalist circles, a series of other popular Federalist songs were rapidly produced and circulated in newspapers and pamphlets throughout the summer of 1798, which served to continue the effusive patriotism of the previous spring by urging continuing support for the president and the war with France, and an ideal of national unity.[64] But Republicans quickly challenged these efforts to control the music of the country with their own protest songs. Often these songs simply lampooned the Federalists. In the *Herald of Liberty,* a mocking "New Federal Song" satirized Adams and his cabinet as would-be kings and nobility.[65] Often the anti-administration songs invoked defiance and resistance. One untitled song by "A DEMOCRAT," published in the (now extremely rare) Nashville newspaper *The Rights of Man,* called for a rejection of the Constitution and a new "Revolution." As it lamented, "Freedom was our former glory / All devoted to her cause / Now—Constitution is the story / And Obedience to the laws." The remedy was clear: "Raise the Bill of feign'd sedition" and "Send us Lord, a Revolution!"

Raise the Bill of feign'd sedition,
All its evils do away;
Send the makers to perdition,
So let every patriot pray.
Build a hell of fierce Damnation,
For our Demi-British clan—
Send, to the rest O God! Salvation,
Bless them with the *Rights of Man!*[66]

With such emotions possible in verse, singing occasionally gave way to confrontation and violence, as partisans literally fought over the proper music for Americans. In New York City in late July 1798, a small riot erupted from this politics of singing. At ten thirty at night, a group of five young men excited by the visit of the president to New York, were walking near the Battery singing "Hail Columbia." Soon a "much larger" group of "boatmen and low fellows from the wharves and docks" confronted the Federalist chorus, encircled them, and began singing the "Carmagnole," the French Republican song. A brawl ensued, with the near death of one of the Federalist singers. The following day, nearly four hundred men wearing black cockades assembled near the Battery, arranging themselves "in a military manner." This time, the "Democrats," by their lack of numbers, were "forced to observe a profound silence" as the young Federalists marched "round and round them repeatedly, singing Hail Columbia."[67]

In the same issue of the *Centinel of Freedom* in which they published the Kentucky Resolutions, Pennington and Dodge also published a "new song" that specifically called for a petitioning drive against the Alien and Sedition Acts. The song's lyrics reveal to us the character of one constituent group the newspaper's editors were attempting to mobilize.[68] They are written in the first person, in the voice of the song's composer, self-identified only as "a needy war-worn soldier," which immediately distinguishes him from "the well-born":

I grub all the day so the well-born can feast
Tho' they can afford the enjoyment
Our rulers can feast on six dollars per day
the poor must be taxed their extortion to pay
And if we do against them any thing say
They will trump a bill of sedition.

From this powerful beginning, the soldier recounts his experience of the Revolutionary War and its aftermath. For him, the war had begun as a rich man's fight, but it became his own through his sacrifice and service in the cause of "freedom and right." With peace, the soldier relates a familiar tale: that he received no cash for his service but "worthless paper"; and that he must sell "at two pence per shilling" in order to feed his sick children and distressed wife. Shocked by the funding of the national debt at par, or what he describes as "robbing the soldiers," he laments his fate and decides, "What a fool was the poor man for fighting."

At this point, the song quickly changes tone. It attacks the alien and sedition laws, the naval expenditures, the standing army, and "federal extravagance," noting that the laws are "aimed at the vitals of freedom." Finally, the song calls for direct action:

> Then free men assemble at liberty's call.
> Resolve—and to Congress petition;
> That the Alien law to nothing may fall,
> And also the bill of sedition.

Whether it was sung or not,[69] the song represented an attempt to move public feeling and to frame the conflict for a mass of people who had been marginalized in the triumphant message of the Federalist regime. And indeed, the call for petitioning in the song certainly did not go unheeded. Emphasizing the lot of the poor veteran presented a powerful counternarrative of the independence movement at a time when the Federalist-oriented newspapers were filled with laudatory celebrations of Adams and calling for a formal declaration of war with France.

Such an appeal had strength in the Mid-Atlantic.[70] Since the 1780s, financial laws that favored creditors and speculators, which at once diminished the money supply and increased taxation, had bred resistance—in the form of court closings, road closings, and petitioning—and even open rebellion in this region. The additional taxes of the Federalist program of 1798 once again promised real economic dislocation for people who depended on stable debt relationships merely to survive as farmers, large and small.[71] The soldier of the tune, who ridiculed the pretensions of "the well born," would have been one of this "lower sort"—a common laborer, debtor farmer, or lesser artisan. In Newark, at least one such individual angered by the Sedition Act was Luther Baldwin, the operator of a garbage scow. In perhaps the most venal application of the law, Baldwin, a friend of his named Brown Clark, and a person known only as "Lespenard," were indicted, fined, and eventually jailed for drunken comments they made in and around John Burnet's dram shop. They had apparently expressed the hope, in fine colloquial language, for a certain celebratory cannonade to come to rest in Adams's "arse."[72]

North of New Jersey, New York Republicans had been outspoken opponents of the Alien and Sedition Acts from the moment of their passage. New York congressman Edward Livingston had given a strident condemnation of the Alien Act before the third reading of the bill, in a speech that circulated widely as a leading opposition pamphlet in the summer of 1798.[73] Although local Federalist newspapers thought "Virginia would be disappointed" in any hope of finding a kindred spirit of resistance among New Yorkers, by December the New York Republicans were rapidly mobilizing and petitioning against the Alien and Sedition Acts.[74] By February of 1799, the leading Federalist paper could only beg New Yorkers to "reflect before they sign the petitions which are now circulated by the Jacobins of this city against the Alien and Sedition laws."[75] In New York City, nine hundred protestors mobilized in a large public meeting against the Alien and Sedition Acts, and within two days their petition for Congress had twenty-six hundred signatures.[76] In upstate New York, Jedidiah Peck, a member of the New York House, was charged under the Sedition Act for circulating a petition against the Alien and Sedition Acts.[77] Peck's problems reflected a political contest developing in Otsego County between himself and William Cooper, which mingled both socioeconomic and generational divisions. Cooper demanded and received deference, and ruled the county as a large land speculator, developer, and judge. By April of 1799, Cooper publicly threatened anyone circulating a petition against the Alien and Sedition Acts with two years in federal prison and a $2,000 fine. Peck had turned against the Federalists because of their pro-war stance, and was beginning to emerge, because of his martyrdom during the petitioning movement, as the chief representative of the tenants, smallholders, and independent yeoman of upstate New York. He presented himself as a new man and a democrat, a true inheritor of the American Revolution attacking the pretensions of Cooper to rule the county like the patriarchs of old.[78]

Among petitions circulating in New York City was one representing "Natives of Ireland" living in America. This petition, like similar petitions sent from Irish aliens in Philadelphia, represented an awkward (or bold, depending on your point of view) assertion by non-citizens of an authority to interpret the U.S. Constitution, decrying what they believed was the "unconstitutional" nature of the Alien Act and asking for its repeal. The quickness with which the petitions were organized also reveals the maturity of ethnic political mobilization in some of the urban centers of the young republic. The Irish petition in Philadelphia came from the nexus of civil society and partisan politics. The petition was organized by the editor of the *Aurora,* William Duane, with the assistance of the printers James and Mathew Carey, Dr. James Reynolds (a recent radical émigré and an elected official of the Hibernian Society), and a few "Irish gentlemen" within days of a call for petitions against the Alien and Sedition Acts. By the late 1790s, the Hibernian Society, whose president was the chief justice of the Pennsylvania Supreme Court, Thomas McKean, had emerged as an important bulwark of an increasingly organized political party that connected recent immigrants to Philadelphia and Irish radical political emigrants with local and national Republican elites.[79] The Federalist majority in Congress at first refused to accept the petitions, arguing that aliens had no right to petition, before finally sending them to committee.[80]

Of the New England states, only Vermont presented much organized petitioning against the Alien and Sedition Acts, and this was done without any necessary inspiration of the Kentucky and Virginia agitations. In fact, most of the Republican reaction to the acts related directly to the extraordinary imprisonment of Vermont congressman Matthew Lyon under the Sedition Act, in the summer of 1798. Lyon, who had been a particularly hated member of the Republican Party for his Irish descent, his extreme republicanism, and his outspoken insolence toward New England elites, had finally earned the eternal contempt of the Federalists in 1797 for spitting on the Connecticut congressman, Roger Griswold. The resulting and well-known brawl—set in the not yet hallowed halls of Congress and featuring Griswold brandishing a hickory cane while Lyon defended himself with a nearby set of fire tongs—almost resulted in their expulsion from the House.[81] With the Sedition Act, Federalists succeeded where formal censure had failed, and Lyon was convicted of sedition, imprisoned, and heavily fined. Throughout the summer and fall of 1798, Lyon became a symbolic martyr for the Republican cause, and while in jail, was overwhelmingly reelected to his seat in Congress.[82]

With their congressman in jail, Vermonters sent numerous petitions to Adams and Congress complaining of their lack of representation and the "unconstitutional" nature of the Sedition Act. The majority of Vermont's petitions were brought to Philadelphia by the Connecticut agitator and itinerant preacher John Cosens Ogden, who began in January 1799 to write for the *Aurora*. While the petitions to Adams were summarily rejected, the petitions to Congress were presented by New York's Edward Livingston, and they took their place alongside the numerous other petitions against the Alien and Sedition Acts.[83]

In other states, the evidence of sustained and organized petitioning and remonstrance against the Alien and Sedition laws is more difficult to find. Here we see a dynamic that reflects both the importance of local politics and the importance of newspapers—as organizers of dissent and as some of the only extant evidence for the historian seeking to re-create a moment. In New England, we can find some liberty poles, an occasional burning effigy, many charges of sedition, and a few newspapers, but no petitioning. Tennessee and North Carolina present small examples of a formal critique of the Alien and Sedition laws. The lower house of the General Assembly of North Carolina passed an abrupt resolution declaring the Alien and Sedition laws "unconstitutional," which then failed to pass the Federalist-dominated senate.[84] But North Carolina lacked a Republican-leaning newspaper in 1798, and therefore had a correspondingly weak ability to organize a popular movement or compete with the version of events being described by the Federalists.[85]

In Tennessee, antagonism to the East and to John Adams characterized nearly the entire political world of the new state, and on superficial reflection one would expect to find attacks on the Alien and Sedition laws similar to those from Kentucky. Indeed, as we have seen, one of the most radical newspapers in the country, *The Rights of Man,* had published a song in 1799 calling for a new "Revolution." The evidence of such resistance in Tennessee is thin, but not inconsequential, however.[86] The grand jury of the Hamilton District in Tennessee (one of two districts), representing the most populous eastern region of the state, passed a series of resolutions which declared the Alien and Sedition laws "unconstitutional, oppressive, and derogatory to our general compact," and called upon the state legislature to "draw up a memorial" and seek a repeal of the Federalist legislation.[87] No evidence exists to suggest that the Tennessee legislature acted on these suggestions. Tennessee was notorious for extremely short sessions of the legislature, and the emergency session of December 1798 was no doubt dominated by the impending need to find a replacement for Senator William Blount, who was in the process of being impeached for implication in the so-called Spanish Conspiracy.[88] In addition, the governor of the state was the infamous Indian fighter John Sevier, and in the summer of 1798 he was striving hard to get a commission as a brigadier general in the new national army and therefore desired to downplay the local anger over the Federalist legislation. Any attempt at resolutions in the legislature against the Alien and Sedition Acts was no doubt squashed by Sevier's faction.[89] The population of Tennessee was still small enough in the 1790s for a handful of political elites and land speculators like Sevier, Blount, and Andrew Jackson to control political processes within the state, and at that moment Sevier had a clear ascendancy in state politics.[90] Nevertheless, by early 1799, rumors circulated that the Alien and

Sedition laws had "met with the same fate in Tennessee" as they had in Kentucky and Virginia.[91]

The resolutions, petitions, songs, and liberty poles emerging from the different areas of the country were products of extremely different types of local politics, diverse local political cultures, and often quite different polities. Some were more "grassroots" than others. Some emerged from a rough-and-ready democratic, urban, ethnic political milieu. Some mimicked the consensual local politics of an idealized colonial rural past. Some mingled an uneasy coalition of frontier democracy with established forms of public debate. Some emerged from a spirit of resistance still directly connected to the conflicts of the 1760s and 1770s. Others resulted from pure mature party politicking—producing agendas of support for election campaigns, written by party activists. But all the petitions were interpreted and eventually lumped into the same rigid polarization by both Federalist and Republican observers watching, hearing, and imagining the mobilization unfold. This politics in motion was captured in the newspapers and made into a coherent narrative. For Federalists the opponents were "Jacobins" and dupes of a faction, while for Republicans all those against the acts, no matter who or where, were "the real republicans."

At the top, Thomas Jefferson elided differences reflexively as he watched petitions pour into Congress. Reporting to Aaron Burr in New York, Jefferson, in Pennsylvania, noted with pleasure that "the public opinion in this state is rapidly coming round" and even "the German counties of Lancaster and York are changing sides."[92] Here the assumption of a two-sided contest both limited and framed the meaning of the opposition for Jefferson. Were the "Germans" literally "changing sides"? Not really. It is doubtful that they would have considered their protests in that fashion, but the effect of their petitions would be the same, both in the mind of Jefferson and in the statehouse, and it would be eventually felt in their votes. Jefferson always assumed there was one thing that drove the success of either side: the amorphous yet palpable "public mind." As he noted in a letter to Madison, the "public sentiment" was now "on the creen," and the coming year would allow Republicans to capitalize on the presumption of a changed public mind.[93] In fact, Jefferson and his correspondents were obsessed with "the progress of public opinion,"[94] and even as they saw the petitions as markers of the movement of the public mind, they eagerly tried to influence that movement with the organization of a new polemics, and even a new newspaper. At his most enthusiastic, Jefferson imagined a complete transformation of the political situation of the country, as he saw "the materials now bearing on the public mind will infallibly restore it to its republican soundness in the course of the present summer, if the knolege of facts can only be disseminated among the people." With these sentiments, he enclosed a series of pamphlets to be distributed "to such as have been misled."[95]

In essence, we see the mobilization of many different types of *publics* in the opposition to the Alien and Sedition Acts, each emerging out of traditions of resistance and political action that reflected the diversity of American politics and experience. But together they were amalgamated into the "public mind" by the Republicans, just as the Federalists had attempted to lump the many pro-Adams addresses into a national unanimity that never existed. In Congress, all the petitions were lumped into a group and dealt with as a whole; even the petitions from the "Natives of Ireland" were essentially undifferentiated from the hundreds of other petitions from citizens against the Alien and Sedition Acts.

But this was not all invention. While the differences among the petitioners—ethnic, socioeconomic, regional, and local—were real, the opponents of the Alien and Sedition Acts nevertheless shared some common concerns and a willingness to see their complaints as widely held and representative of popular objections—indeed, as fundamental. Thus, the Albemarle County petitioners connected themselves to the popular resistance being recorded throughout the United States with special toasts to Pennsylvania's Albert Gallatin, New York's Edward Livingston, and the militia companies in New Jersey that voiced their opposition to the rush to war. The diversity of the movement against the Alien and Sedition Acts shared the practical benefit of being an opposition movement. They were criticizing, not building anything, so the differences within their perspectives and immediate interests were easily subsumed within the common perspective of their complaints and the common language of their anger.

In addition, by celebrating the French and the rebelling Irish, the remonstrances connected themselves to an international and universalist revolutionary transformation of the world. As they toasted, "The spirit of SEVENTY SIX; May it prevail all over the world."[96] When Samuel Brown of Kentucky first described the local remonstrances of Kentucky to Thomas Jefferson, he emphasized the international context of their fight against the Federalist legislation. He hoped that the state legislatures would give "solemnity to the voice of the people," but whatever happened, "Republicans ought not to despair," for "the Irish are fighting for us" and "the French will never be conquered."[97] The "voice of the people" that Brown invoked was speaking in the language of revolution: the Irish were in the field, and the French were still engaged in what Brown clearly considered to be the same cause as America's in 1776. The popular politics surrounding the opposition to the Alien and Sedition Acts, "a spirit of insurgency," speaks to this point well. The localities and states that resolved and petitioned to various authorities resembled the mobilizations of the 1760s and 1770s.[98] The liberty poles that sprung up in Pennsylvania hearkened to a moment of revolution, and against a Federalist policy of centralization and celebration of national character, they invoked the universal ideals of the Revolution. The Tennessee newspaper, *The Rights of Man,* and the New Jersey *Centinel of Freedom,* whose masthead was embellished with a cartouche representing "The Rights of Man" draped across the globe, spoke to an active belief among many Americans that their Revolutionary Age was still open and their activities as crucial as any of 1776 to the creation of a world distinct from the ancien régime that they believed their Independence should have destroyed.

States' Rights and the Rights of Man: The Language of Opposition

Aside from rhetoric of revolution, what were the shared concerns for this opposition to the Alien and Sedition Acts? How do these common complaints help us understand the potential for defeat of the Federalists that so excited Jefferson in February of 1799, and that certainly assured that the Federalists would not easily maintain their control of power? What do the shared ideas of the many resolutions clarify about popular perceptions of the meaning of rights and federalism at the end of the 1790s? What, in effect, was at stake for these opponents of the Alien and Sedition Acts?

The invocation of the "rights of man" played an important role in the articulation of the grievances of the petitioners. Here the petitioners are not referring to any one of the French Declarations of the Rights of Man and of the Citizen, or to Paine's defense of the French Revolution, but to inalienable natural rights, broadly considered, that they believed existed before and without government. The vast majority of the petitioners began their complaints by asserting their natural right to assemble. Typical are the petitioners from Buckingham County, Virginia, who asserted "that the people have an inherent right, peaceably, to assemble together" and "express their approbation or disapprobation of all and a very measure or measures, regulation or regulations, whether civil, commercial, political or military."[99] So their whole resistance was framed by first principles.

In the specific attacks against the Alien and Sedition Acts, the employment of the notion of absolute rights attached to individuals promised radical pressure on traditional understandings of particular privileges in American society. The people who supported, drafted, and

FIGURE 3. Masthead of the *New Jersey Centinel* celebrates the universalist orientation of the Republican Party. (Courtesy of the American Antiquarian Society)

signed the many petitions, resolutions, memorials, and remonstrances in 1798–99 advocated a potent reinterpretation of the meaning of a "free press" and the right of jury trial that was absolute, radical, and Revolutionary. When they attacked the "constitutionality" and validity of the Alien and Sedition Acts, it was never *simply* a question of constitutional rights or so-called civil liberties, but represented a secular concern for universal human rights, in this case, understood to be the Revolutionary principles of the rights of man. The rights were the rights of nature; constitutions protected those rights but did not create them. It is important to note and emphasize that these arguments did not look to "constitutional rights," as they are often understood today, as something *granted* by the Constitution, but rather understood the U.S. Constitution, and the many state declarations of rights, as definitions and limitations of the powers of government to interfere with the essential and natural rights of man.[100]

The petitioners did not need positive expressions of statute or constitution to define rights that they preferred to understand as natural and inalienable. Indeed, the voices of resistance often emphasized the lack of a need of an explicit constitutional guarantee of what they considered a basic "right of man." As the petitioners in Mason County, Kentucky, resolved, it was "unnecessary to resort to written documents" to prove "the existence of a natural right so essential to our happiness," such as the ability to enjoy "freedom of press and of speech."[101] Or, as the Montgomery County remonstrances noted, "The free communications of thoughts and opinions is one of the invaluable rights of man, and can never be restrained, but by despotic governments."[102] This sentiment mimicked language of the Virginia Declaration of Rights of 1776. Such assertions raised the freedom of the press well beyond the limits of eighteenth-century jurisprudence, which understood a free press to be a press free from prior restraint, not one that could publish any sentiment against the government without fear of consequence. Their belief—that a man had a right to criticize, censure, and opine on any subject relating to the operation of the government without fear of governmental reprisal—was novel, absolute, and Revolutionary.[103]

This concern for the "rights of man" was extended easily to complaints leveled against the Alien Act. From the earliest petitioners in Kentucky, to the polemicists in the opposition newspapers, to the final remonstrances to Congress—the Alien Act seemed a crass and gross abuse of federal power and the rights of man. At stake was the right of trial by jury, presumably a sacred right protected by the amended Constitution—at least for citizens—but which the petitioners also argued was an inalienable right of man applicable to aliens. The Alien law was considered by all Republican petitioners, as the Woodford County remonstrance asserted, "*an infringement on the rights of humanity.*"[104] The dissenting minority of the Pennsylvania legislature argued that the Alien law greatly expanded the power of the presidency "at the expense of the powers of Courts and Juries, and the rights of man."[105] The remonstrators made arguments about the rights of aliens that Federalists would never make and considered patently absurd. As Federalists repeated again and again, aliens were not parties to the Constitution and therefore had no rights but those granted as a "matter of favor," favors that could be rescinded at any time. One noted, "The Constitution was made for CITIZENS, not for ALIENS, who of consequence have no RIGHTS under it." While they "remain in the country, and enjoy the benefit of the laws," they do so "not as a matter of right, but merely as a matter of favor."[106]

Like their absolute construction of the liberty of the press, the complaints against the Alien Act extended the normal protections of charters and constitutions to inalienable rights attached to individuals as human rights, which extended beyond mere civil jurisdictions. It was, again, a radical formulation of the rights of individuals in society, one that attempted to assure that the principles of Revolution—that people have natural rights inalienable—were fundamentally grafted onto the institutions of the state. The Federalist "Juricola" chided the petitioners for their utopian notions of rights. He was surprised that so many people did not know "how to distinguish the constitutional rights of citizens from the privileges of aliens, which are always derived from the gratuitous indulgence of municipal regulations." Fortunately, however, Federalist "minds had not then been corrupted by the delusive and visionary doctrines of universal citizenship."[107]

But while petitioners against the Alien and Sedition Acts presented a notion of citizenship that prized the universal principles of the age, their critique of the acts was never *purely* "libertarian" or a simple assertion of individualism against the power of the government, as too many scholars have suggested. For while the petitioners emphasized the importance of individual rights, they understood themselves to be part of important collectivities with specific interests and often specific identities—solidarities as important as their national affiliation—namely, they considered themselves as part of truly "sovereign" states. The rights of the states were as important as the rights of individuals for the maintenance of republican government in America. In fact, the rights of the states in the Union protected natural rights—not surprising, since the rights and duties of all individuals were defined by the republicanized common (natural) law of the individual states. The *Union* guaranteed republican citizenship.

To point out the dangers to the Union implied by the Alien and Sedition Acts, the petitioners looked to the Tenth Amendment: "The powers not delegated to the United States by the Constitution, nor prohibited by it to the States, are reserved to the States respectively, or to the people." There was no national common law. They lived in a confederation of states, not a consolidated government. So the petitioners from Spotsylvania County, Virginia, asserted that "the constitution of the United States contains a limitation of power, to be exercised in the form and manner therein specified." It did not, and could not, "authorize the use of any powers but what are expressly enumerated in it," because "the people of America in framing their own constitution intended to establish a confederation, and not a consolidated government."[108] The petitioners from Suffolk County, New York, agreed that the general government had only "defined and limited powers," and it was not "consistent with their political happiness, and the preservation of their liberties, that this general government should legislate in every possible cause."[109] Local resolutions in Essex County, New Jersey, declared that "any assumption of power or authority that transcends" the delegated authority of the Constitution "is an invasion of the rights and sovereignty of the states, and can produce no law of any binding force."[110]

Specifically, the Alien and Sedition Acts assumed powers that the central government could never possess. The petitioners from Dinwiddie County, Virginia, asserted, "*The power of punishing libels is not expressly given*" to the Congress.[111] The Alien Act, in this regard, was considered a dangerous expansion of national power to control persons under the municipal jurisdiction of the states. The petitioners from Cumberland County, Pennsylvania, for instance, in addition to their concern that the Alien law would diminish immigration and the movement of wealth into Pennsylvania, worried that the law was specifically interfering with state policy by "curbing the freedom of migration to the different states, which their respective legislatures have thought proper to admit."[112] The petitioners referred to Article I, Section 9, of the Constitution, the provision typically associated with the protection of the slave trade until 1808.[113] As the Suffolk County, New York, petitioners also argued, the passage in question provided that Congress should make no law affecting the "migration or importation of such *persons* as any states now existing shall think proper to admit." As they noted, "aliens are *persons*," and "by the practice and laws of several states their migration into this country is now admitted."[114]

These assertions reveal an important aspect of early republican political culture. The Constitution could be read and interpreted by any citizen equally, and when the non-judges looked into the text, they tended to read the document literally: aliens were in fact "persons," Congress was in fact limited to specific enumerated powers, the Tenth Amendment did in fact reserve all unmentioned powers to the people and the states. So the shared vision of Union articulated by the petitions, memorials, and remonstrances against the Alien and Sedition Acts represented a widely held understanding of the proper relationship between national power, the natural rights of individuals, and the states. Rights were not something granted by the Constitution, but protected by it; the rights themselves were the rights of nature. States reserved the power to regulate the municipal relations of their own citizens, and any attempt by the federal government to encroach upon the power of the states would inevitably work against the distinct interests of the sovereign people of the states. A strict construction therefore was essential for the maintenance of the fruits of the Revolution—the natural rights of man and republican government.

So, in the end, it was all related. Federalist attacks upon the rights of man and general Revolutionary principles were considered numerous and dangerous. Federalists were not only showing a blatant disregard for the rights of man, protected in both state and federal constitutions and given life by each state's common law, but they seemed to be attempting to consolidate the states into one giant sovereignty which would be run by an executive with unchecked powers for the interest of the Eastern commercial and mercantile classes against agricultural interests. They would use the Alien and Sedition laws to crush dissent at the same moment they used the new army and navy to create an unnatural war, expand the national government with placeholders and pensioners, and overawe the states. It is also clear that although the opposition was made up of numerous constituencies with often different sectional and class interests—differences that could theoretically weaken their ability to operate as a cohesive challenge to the Federalists—the Alien and Sedition Acts offended *fundamental sensibilities* over the nature of rights and the Union that were widely shared by a broad opposition movement against the acts.

Taken together, the resistance presented by the county remonstrances and petitioners from around the Union presented a nice foil to the Federalist nationalism. While the Federalists asserted the need to solidify and glorify a homogeneous national citizenry—a national community defined by an energetic national government and protected from the excesses of "foreign" ideas by the power of law, armies, and taxes—the Republicans countered with a vision that raised state citizenship and individual rights to an equally exulted height. It was in essence a model of nationhood which eschewed "national character." Since individual rights—which were defined by *universal* principles and not national charters—must be protected, and since the states most closely represented the interests of their citizens, the opposition effectively challenged the national vision of the Federalists. America was not an organic national people, but a collection of contracting peoples. The local affiliation of every citizen to a sovereign people of a state was as important to the maintenance of the freedoms of an "American" as any homogeneous sense of national character.

If Federalists would not relent, the future was bleak. John Taylor concluded his introduction to the Virginia Resolutions by threatening civil war. After rejecting the Alien and Sedition Acts for being destructive of "human rights," he saw the moment itself as auspicious for the survival of the Union. He believed the Adams administration was moving toward "the system of Divine right," and that the small states of New England were colluding to "govern America." This "*oppression,*" he believed, "was the road to civil war." Any attempt to give the president more power "would establish executive influence, and executive influence would produce a revolution." To those who worried over the impact of such pronouncements, and to those who claimed "We must not disunite," Taylor answered, "Remove oppression, and union would take place."[115]

Null and Void: The Remedy

But short of a civil war, which no one wanted, what did the opposition wish to do about these supposedly unconstitutional, unnecessary, and "impolitic" laws? What, in effect, was the remedy they sought? George Nicholas had a plan of opposition in mind. It was similar to the plan he laid bare to the thousands of Kentuckians massing in Lexington. There were two types of laws, he noted, that the Congress had passed in the spring session. One type, like the Naturalization Act or the Naval Establishment Act, however ridiculous such acts, "however we differ in opinion, from those who passed them," and however much "we will exercise our undoubted right of remonstrating against such laws," they are "binding on us." As to "the second class, or the unconstitutional laws," which the Federalists had passed so eagerly and which included the Alien and Sedition laws, "we consider them as dead letters."[116] Although Nicholas believed that Kentuckians could lawfully "use force" to oppose these unconstitutional laws, he looked to the federal courts to disallow them before such extremes were needed. If the courts failed to act—and in all likelihood they would, considering that the bench was made up of rabid Federalists[117]—then, God knows, the right of resistance to oppression "is a natural right."[118]

The idea that the unconstitutional laws should be resisted and would be considered "as dead letters" was an oft-repeated sentiment in the numerous county resolutions of both Kentucky and Virginia. This speaks to the widespread belief—not that *any* law could be declared unconstitutional, but that the federal government simply did not have the power to make such a law and so therefore it did not exist. This is a language drawing on common law constitutionalism. At a meeting in Paris, Kentucky, after asserting that the right to criticize public measures was "one dictated by the laws of nature," the group noted "that all laws made to impair or abridge it, are void."[119] The Lexington resolutions used similar language, noting that the right of speech was "inestimable" and that "all laws made to impair or destroy it are void."[120] In Essex County, Virginia, Republicans noted that any laws which "encroach on the sovereignty of the people [are] in their nature void," and in Richmond, petitioners noted that the laws had "no binding force, and are not entitled to the respect and obedience of the people."[121] Some county resolutions ominously combined their critique of the Federalist legislation with an implied threat of future violent resistance. The remonstrance from Bourbon County resolved: "That standing armies are dangerous to liberty, and ought not to be exercised in free governments—that a well organized militia are the most proper, and the only safe defenders of our country—that for that purpose the general and state governments ought to provide them with arms and ammunition—that as they have neglected to do this, every free man ought to consider it his duty to provide both for himself."[122] Other resolutions in Kentucky and Virginia called upon citizens to use all their energies to ensure that such laws would not operate. As the petitioners from Amelia County, Virginia, resolved: "Any 'Act' violating the Constitution, is, we conceive, a nullity, and ought not to be carried into effect by any person acting in a civil or military capacity; but on the contrary, we think it to be the duty of every citizen to oppose [every] attempt to violate the Constitution, whether such attempt be made by private individuals, or by those clothed with public offices or acting as public functionaries."[123] That the laws should be "a nullity" was apparently self-evident.

Northern petitioners also used similar language, and as the editors of the New Jersey *Centinel of Freedom* noted, any law which violated the Constitution "of course becomes a nullity."[124] The resolutions of Essex County, New Jersey, said the acts possessed no "binding force."[125] In Mifflin County, Pennsylvania, their condemnation of the Sedition Act went as far as any in their appeal to natural rights and their rejection of the laws when they resolved: "That the free communication of thought and opinions is one of the most valuable rights of man, and cannot be abridged or restrained without an infraction on the liberties of the people and the law of nature; therefore all laws restraining the freedom of speech and of the press, are nugatory and void."[126] Since Congress did not have the power to pass such laws, they were "nugatory and void."

Americans in many different forums had been declaring laws "null, void, and of no force" for a generation, so it should be no surprise that numerous groups were eager to do so in this case. *Everyone* agreed that courts could declare laws "unconstitutional" and therefore void; where Federalists and Republicans disagreed was on whether the courts were the *only* places which could decide upon the legality of law. In the late 1790s, no such genre as "constitutional law" existed. Federalists were moving toward such a special designation, by which cases could be decided only by qualified judges in particular courts, but this success would not come until the 1830s and beyond.

The Virginia and Kentucky Resolutions therefore broke very little new ground in resolving that the laws should be deemed unconstitutional, or "null and void." From the numerous county resolutions, many groups of citizens had already made such declarations, and the arguments against the legitimacy of the laws made in the Kentucky and Virginia Resolutions mirrored the arguments made in the popular resolutions. The main contribution of the Kentucky and Virginia Resolutions to the opposition to the Alien and Sedition Acts lay in their assertion that the sovereign states possessed both a right and a duty to adjudge the constitutionality of federal laws and, if need be, to declare federal laws void. Both of the sets of resolutions elaborated this remedy by presenting a "compact theory" of the relationship of the states to the federal government, of which Jefferson, John Taylor of Caroline,[127] and John Breckinridge of Kentucky were particularly enamored.

Historians have tended to argue that John Breckinridge weakened the argument of Jefferson's original resolutions considerably by taking out the word "nullification," which figured prominently in Jefferson's eighth resolution.[128] But in fact, one must not be unsettled by the hindsight that the word "nullification" would become important in the infamous controversies in the nineteenth century. There are other ways to say what "nullification" implies, and the Kentucky Resolutions, even as amended, offer all the necessary language to assert a state's right to defeat the operation of a federal law by simply declaring it "void"—"voidification," if you will. The changes that Breckinridge made to Jefferson's original resolutions were largely cosmetic. In fact, one need only look at the first resolution to find the clear argument that a state may adjudge the constitutionality of any given federal law. As the Kentucky legislators resolved, the "several states composing the United States of America" are not joined in absolute submission to their "general government," but rather by a "compact" to which each state "is an integral party, its co-states forming as to itself, the other party," in the form of the amended "Constitution of the United States."[129] And so, like any party to a contract where there is no authority higher than the parties themselves, each state may judge "as to the mode or measure of redress" whenever the government created by that compact "assumes undelegated powers." If the federal government created laws deemed by the states to violate the Constitution by one of the parties to the Constitution, those laws are "unauthoritative, void, and of no force."[130]

Upon this foundation, the Kentucky Resolutions argue and "prove" that the Alien and Sedition laws are unconstitutional, and that they are therefore "void and of no force."[131] There is no need, then, for an explicit invocation of the term "nullification," and to all who read the resolutions at the time, the declarations were unambiguous. As the most prominent Federalist newspaper in Virginia noted succinctly, "The resolutions of the Kentucky legislature have been received and read in the house, declaring the alien and sedition laws unconstitutional, null and void."[132] At the same time, the resolutions did call upon support from the other states, asking "for an expression of their sentiments" on the constitutionality of the acts, but they had little doubt that "the co-states, recurring to their natural right in cases not made federal" would "concur in declaring these acts void and of no force."[133]

Virginia, of course, concurred in the sentiments of the Kentuckians, although their own resolutions as amended are in fact slightly more cautious. In their final form, the Virginia Resolutions did not include explicit language declaring the laws "null" or "void." The resolutions merely declared them "unconstitutional," and implied that they would be resisted. That the Virginians did not express such extreme sentiments as the Kentuckians is not because the leading Republicans of

Virginia disagreed with the arguments of the Kentucky Resolutions, but because of the strength of the Federalist minority in Virginia. The original draft of the resolutions, largely written by Madison, but edited in the final version by Jefferson, and possibly by their sponsor, John Taylor, concurred almost perfectly with the sentiments of the Kentucky Resolutions. The difference in their final appearance from the resolutions passed in Kentucky falls entirely on the difference in style between Madison, Jefferson, and Taylor—and on the difference in composition of the Virginia House of Representatives, which possessed a number of moderate, independent-minded delegates and a large and well-spoken Federalist minority led (in the absence of Patrick Henry) by George Keith Taylor and Henry "Light-Horse Harry" Lee, who succeeded in stripping the resolutions of more sweeping implications.[134]

Lee, with an opening salvo that reportedly left the chamber in silence "for some time," should be credited with expunging the explosive potential of the original seventh resolution. Initially the resolution declared that the Alien and Sedition laws were "unconstitutional, and not law, but utterly null, void, and of no force or effect." Lee convincingly argued that such language would lead to popular resistance, resistance to contempt of government, and "insurrection would be the consequence."[135] Ultimately, the Virginia Resolutions declared the laws simply "unconstitutional," and whether or not they were considered to be therefore "utterly null and void" would remain for later generations to ponder.

Federalist George Keith Taylor, the brother-in-law of John Marshall, also succeeded in substantially weakening the states' rights implications contained in the resolutions by successfully arguing for the deletion of one word, with two long speeches defending the Alien and Sedition Acts. Originally, the crucial third clause of the Virginia Resolutions asserted—in a similar fashion to the Kentucky Resolutions—that the powers of the federal government resulted "from compact, to which the states alone are parties."[136] Noting that the resolutions had gradually struck him with "complete aversion and entire disgust," Taylor attacked the belief that the states *alone* were parties to the Constitution; pointing to the Preamble, he argued that the Constitution was "a creature of the *people* of United America."[137] Although the Republicans in Virginia would not concede George Taylor's national interpretation of the Constitution, they were persuaded to drop the word "alone" from the third article, a change which implied a more complex relationship of the states to the Union than originally proposed.[138]

Nonetheless, and despite the skills of the Federalist minority in the House of Delegates, it was clear that the laws were to be deemed unconstitutional and would be resisted in the states of Virginia and Kentucky. This position, ratified by the resolutions themselves, was given powerful consequence by the numerous popular speeches, essays, and petitions that circulated throughout the two states urging resistance to the "tyranny" of the Federalist program. In addition—and this must be remembered in the discussion of the broader reaction to the Virginia Resolutions presented below—when the resolutions were circulated in the newspapers, the *unamended* version was the only version printed outside of Virginia.[139]

Finally, the Virginia legislature did not stop with the resolutions, but printed an incendiary "Address to the People," which was presented as a warning to the people of Virginia of the dangers inherent in the Federalist legislation, and as a justification of the Virginia Resolutions.[140] Theodore Sedgwick, Federalist senator from Massachusetts at the time of the publication of the address, considered its circulation as "little short of a declaration of war."[141]

Like Sedgwick, Federalists responded to the Virginia and Kentucky Resolutions with equal parts disgust and horror. In Federalist northern Virginia, newspaper writers argued that John Taylor of Caroline was inciting civil war.[142] In Maryland, Federalist newspaper essayists saw the Kentucky and Virginia Resolutions as "part of a concerted plan, to embarrass the measures of government, and dismember the union."[143] Similar sentiments were expressed throughout the Northern papers, and in New England whispered rumors of the desire of Virginia to "separate from the General Union" were commonplace.[144] One observer noted that Taylor's speeches and resolutions were "fraught with the most direful sentiments to the government of the United States." He considered the times "alarming," with "civil dissentions, if not actual civil war" inescapable.[145] Federalist polemicists in New York asserted that "ALL the candidates for public offices in Virginia, who style themselves pure Republicans," speak "the language of their very souls; for—Revolution—Revolution is their darling wish."[146] In New Jersey, Federalist papers insisted that the government must support "its violated authority by an appeal to arms." In private, Alexander Hamilton expressed his willingness to use the new professional army to "subdue a *refractory and powerful state.*"[147]

The state legislatures that responded to the Kentucky and Virginia Resolutions were all dominated by Federalists, and they universally rejected the arguments made within them. Some, like the lower house of New Jersey, refused to even discuss the resolutions, to keep "such treasonable correspondence" from their journal.[148] The General Assembly of Maryland voted to "highly disapprove of the sentiments and opinions contained in the resolutions of the legislature of Virginia," noting particularly that any implication that a state government had a competency to "declare an act of the federal government null and void" was utterly "unwarrantable," as it presented "an improper interference with that jurisdiction which is exclusively vested in the courts of the United States." For effect, they added that they considered the Alien and Sedition Acts to be both "wise and politic."[149] Notably, the Federalist legislature of Pennsylvania considered the Kentucky Resolutions as "a revolutionary measure, destructive of the purest principles of our state and national compacts." They considered the resistance of Kentucky as tending to "overwhelm with dismay the lovers of peace, liberty and order," and asserted that only "the Supreme judiciary of the nation" possessed "the high authority, of ultimately and conclusively deciding on the constitutionality of legislative acts."[150] Delaware considered the Virginia and Kentucky Resolutions to be "a very unjustifiable interference with the General Government," having "dangerous tendencies" and therefore "not a fit subject for the further consideration of this General Assembly."[151] The New York legislature argued that the right to decide on the constitutionality of all federal laws was a right "appertaining to the judiciary department," and any "assumption of that right" by a state had "a direct tendency to destroy the independence of the General Government." They therefore resolved to "disclaim the power" assumed in the Virginia and Kentucky Resolutions.[152] Other states, including Rhode Island, Vermont, and Massachusetts, also dismissed the Virginia and Kentucky Resolutions, asserting a belief in judicial review as the *only* judge of the constitutionality of federal legislation.

Sympathetic Republicans in the Northern and Middle Atlantic states, however, heartily celebrated the Kentucky and Virginia Resolutions for their condemnation of the Alien and Sedition Acts, and often concurred with the constitutional arguments advanced by the resolutions—specifically, the right of states to adjudge the legitimacy of federal acts that encroached upon state power and the rights of the citizenry.[153] In Pennsylvania, for instance, the Republican minority in the House had few qualms about declaring a federal act unconstitutional and seeking its repeal.[154] Local papers would go even further in their evidence of support of the arguments of the Virginia and Kentucky Resolutions. As one queried, "Is not the Constitution a contract between the different states? Are they not to judge whether this contract can be broken or violated?"[155]

While the Federalist majority in the legislature of New Jersey succeeded in dismissing the resolutions without much discussion, the Republicans in New Jersey continued to draw inspiration from them. A leading Republican newspaper not only encouraged local emulation of the defiant petitions of the Kentucky and Virginia counties, but argued, in sympathy with the resolutions, that "the constitution is a solemn compact, made between the individual states, as sovereignties, and the U. States collectively."[156] As such, the essayist noted that if the doctrine of judicial review was the only remedy for unconstitutional federal acts, and if "the states, individually, have no right to judge when the Constitution is violated by Congress," then "there is an end to all state sovereignty" and "we are at once consolidated."[157] In a remarkable move, which was only narrowly defeated in the state legislature, New Jersey Republicans called for another nationwide constitutional convention, "to accurately define the powers" given to the federal government and specifically enumerate the prerogatives and privileges retained by the state governments.[158] The Republican legislators dismissed the idea of judicial review, arguing that confusion had arisen because there existed "no common judge to fix the precise boundary" between the powers of the federal government and the powers of the sovereign states.[159]

In New York, the Republicans in the House worked hard to support some of the arguments of the Virginia and Kentucky Resolutions, despite the proclivity of the Federalist majority to dismiss them. In four attempts, the Republicans tried to amend the majority assertion of the doctrine of judicial review, tried to get support for a claim that the Alien and Sedition Acts were unconstitutional, and also attempted to assert the right of the legislature to judge the constitutionality of federal law.[160] In the final motion, mentioned above, in which the Republicans of the legislature asserted that Congress did not have the explicitly enumerated power to punish libels, only four votes kept the New York House of Representatives from approving an extremely limited sphere for the federal government.[161] And yet they did not describe a remedy, such as state nullification, if the federal government overreached.

In Massachusetts, there was very little organized Republican power available for a strong movement in favor of the Virginia and Kentucky Resolutions—or resistance to the Alien and Sedition Acts in general—but sympathetic Republicans, such as they were, tended to support the arguments expounded in the resolutions. In the senate of the Massachusetts General Court, the lone Republican, John Bacon, of Berkshire County, used his little influence to condemn the dismissal of the Virginia and Kentucky Resolutions in a very sympathetic speech. In the House, the handful of Republicans similarly worried about the adamant Federalist belief in judicial review as the sole remedy for questionable federal legislation. As Dr. Aaron Hill, Republican from Cambridge, argued, "While the individual States retain any portion of their sovereignty, they must have the right to judge of any infringement made on their Constitutions." If such a right was "transferred exclusively to Congress, or to any department of the federal government, no vestige of sovereignty can remain to the individual states." If federal judicial review was the sole remedy for unconstitutional laws, the government of the United States would "become a consolidated rather than a Federal Government."[162] This concern was taken up by the Republican press in Massachusetts. One anonymous correspondent declared that in May of 1798 Massachusetts was a "free, sovereign and independent state," but that with the answer to the Virginia and Kentucky Resolutions the General Court had done what the British had failed to do in 1776: destroy the sovereignty of the people of Massachusetts. For what sovereign people, the writer asked, "*shall have no right to decide on any invasion of his constitutional powers?*"[163] For this boldness, Thomas and Abijah Adams, the two editors who published these sentiments, were indicted by the grand jury of the Supreme Court of Judicature, which was holding a timely session in Boston. Although Thomas Adams died before he could be tried, his younger brother Abijah was sentenced to thirty days in jail and fined $500 for this seditious libel on the General Court of Massachusetts.[164] In fact, the strength of the Federalist machine in Massachusetts can be seen in their quick and definitive repression of any semblance of dissent.

In Vermont, the only New England state with a substantial number of Republicans in the legislature, the move by the Federalist majority to dismiss the arguments of the Virginia and Kentucky Resolutions met with strong resistance. Ultimately, the Federalist majority succeeded in passing resolutions that succinctly denied the legitimacy of the Virginia Resolutions and attacked the logic of each of the Kentucky Resolutions. But the Republican minority of the state, representing a third of the House, signed an extensive protest to the majority report, which confirmed the doctrines contained within the Kentucky and Virginia Resolutions. Arguing that "the states individually, compose one of the parties to the federal compact or constitution, it does of course follow, that each state must have an interest in that constitution being pure and inviolate." States therefore could stop the execution of laws deemed to encroach on their reserved powers.[165]

The Meaning of a Clamor

So what can we make of this extraordinary movement against the Alien and Sedition Acts, which has gone so understudied? At the very least, historians must recognize that the Virginia and Kentucky Resolutions are part of a widespread movement of resolving, petitioning, and remonstrating against the Alien and Sedition Acts that helps frame the constitutional, legal, and political meaning of the resolutions. The overwhelming focus on Jefferson and Madison as both the originators of ideas and the organizers of any and all formal protest against the Alien and Sedition Bills has hopefully been decisively overturned.

The petitions to Congress failed in their purpose: the immediate repeal of the acts. These petitions, which flooded Congress in January and February of 1799, were referred to a select committee that would make a recommendation to the House.[166] At the end of February, as the committee was about to report, petitions were still being submitted. The Federalist-stacked committee responded with a lengthy polemic and three resolutions which argued that neither the Alien nor Sedition Act, nor any of the other acts passed to defend the country, including the taxes and the provisional army bills, should be repealed.[167] The committee's report answered the numerous grievances of the petitioners in meticulous detail. In their rejections of the petitioners' complaints, we can clearly perceive fundamental differences between Federalist and Republican notions of citizenship, rights, and national power in this crucial moment.

On the question of whether the Alien Act was unconstitutional, because it violated an alien's right to trial by jury, the committee asserted the common Federalist response. First, as the practice and law of nations assured, asylum for aliens "is a mere matter of favor, resumable at the public will." Aliens had no right to jury trial, because "the Constitution was made for citizens, not for aliens, who of consequence have no rights under it." Aliens "remain in the country and enjoy the benefit of the laws, not as a matter of right, but merely as a matter of favor and permission, which favor and permission may be withdrawn whenever the Government charged with the general welfare shall judge their further continuance dangerous."[168]

As for the petitioners' claims that the Alien law was unconstitutional because the Constitution did not specifically enumerate a power to remove aliens, the committee argued that Congress possessed the power, by the "necessary and proper clause," to make any law proper to protect the county. Any law designed to prevent an invasion of the country, therefore, was "of course a measure that Congress is empowered to adopt."[169] As for the contention of many of the petitioners that the Alien law was additionally unconstitutional because Article I, Section 9, specifically forbade Congress from prohibiting the migration and immigration of "persons" thought to be necessary until 1808, the Federalists tersely noted that the article in question was meant to apply to the slave trade.[170]

Federalists rejected the novel assertion of an absolute right to free speech articulated by the petitioners. As they argued, "The liberty of the press consists not in a license for every man to publish what he pleases without being liable to punishment." Thus, the Federalists asserted the common law notion of the liberty of the press, which, they averred, "has always been understood in this manner, and no other."[171] Federalists pointed out that they had actually improved the common law, by allowing "truth" to be a defense in trials of sedition. On the question as to whether Congress had the power to punish seditious libels, despite the fact that it was not explicitly enumerated as a power of Congress, the Federalists maintained that the power to legislate necessarily implied the power to ensure the execution of law, and it also claimed that the federal government could avail itself of the national common law—which the Republicans denied existed, since it had not been explicitly listed in the Constitution. Since seditious libel served primarily to frustrate the operation of government, the federal government possessed an implied power to punish seditious libel.[172]

Finally, in addition to reaffirming the necessity of the numerous bills relating to the establishment of the army and navy, and the taxes to pay for them, the committee added a final flourish by emphasizing that the very language and reasoning of the petitions threatened the foundations of all society, by an all-too-eager celebration of Revolutionary conceptions of rights. The committee noted that the "vehement and acrimonious remonstrance" of the petitioners was made of "principles of that exotic system which convulses the civilized world," a system that for too long had been "the bane of public as well as private tranquility and order." As citizens and representatives, the committee could not therefore "be justified in yielding any established principles of law or government to the suggestions of modern theory." Instead, they would revel in their national heritage and "transmit to posterity the civil and religious privileges which are the birthright of our country."[173] Here again the Federalists would challenge "modern theory" with nationalism and the "established principles of law and government." Once again it was understood as a contest between law and order, tradition and precedent—against the visionary Rights of Man.

In the elections of 1799, the Federalists generally succeeded in sending more of their own to Congress. But significantly, the most extensive victories for the Federalists came from areas that show little evidence of having engaged in this mobilization against the Alien and Sedition Acts. North Carolina, Georgia, and South Carolina sent Federalists, or people assumed to be Federalists, to Congress. North Carolina had no Republican newspaper until 1799. Republicans achieved solid victories in Kentucky and Vermont, won overwhelming victories in Pennsylvania, and made slight advances in northern New Jersey and New York State.[174] Virginia is the one clear exception to this generalization, where the pro-administration candidates gained some ground. But Virginia is a case that must be qualified. Like most of the states, Virginia stood at this moment between a politics still dominated by local great personalities and one verging on democratic ideological and interest politics. John Marshall, Henry Lee, Bushrod Washington, George Washington, and Patrick Henry were "great men" and extremely active Federalists in the elections of 1798.[175] Crucially, unlike most non-Virginian pro-administration candidates, both John Marshall and Patrick Henry had made a point of publicly denouncing the Alien and Sedition Acts.[176] In the final analysis, Washington was upset by the *closeness* of some of the elections, as he noted: "The Elections of Generals Lee and Marshall are grateful to my feelings. I wish however both of them had been elected by greater majorities: but they *are Elected,* and that alone is pleasing."[177]

Besides the immediate effects of the petitioning and resolutions, the opposition to the Alien and Sedition Acts helps reveal how politics worked in the early republic, as Americans struggled to match their ideals and traditions with their burgeoning, albeit limited, democracy. From the perspective of the *Centinel of Freedom* of December 18, 1798, we have an excellent vantage to survey the tumultuous scene of American national politics in action. This one edition connects the disparate agitations against the Alien and Sedition Acts into one movement. The local remonstrances of Kentucky, where the first widespread meetings began, are tied to the sympathetic local meetings in Virginia and Pennsylvania, which are directly connected to the arguments of the Kentucky Resolutions, which are in turn connected to a call for direct local action. In the issue we can see the easy combination of elite action (Jefferson's authorship of the Kentucky Resolutions) with local agitation inflated and sustained by an invocation of popular outrage in song—like the many songs and symbols awakening and moving public opinion—and creating, as it were, "an alarm" in the "public mind." The song served both to tell a story of the moment and encourage ongoing protest, resistance that the editors also directly and successfully invoked to organize a Newark petition within a month. The masthead placed the whole moment into an international revolutionary contest that would hopefully lead to the "rights of man" being extended across the globe.

The mobilization of this opposition cannot be seen as either some rarified "bottom-up" or "top-down" story, but a process of politics in motion in the early republic—representative politics before the institutionalization of a party system. The editors of the newspapers are key actors, but so are the elites, and none of them could function or gain influence without the participation of hundreds of common citizens giving voice to their complaints in formal petitions. We have seen that politics is local, even personal, but ideas matter, and can be the glue that holds national politics together. The shared ideas of the petitioners against the Alien and Sedition Acts, about the nature of rights and the Constitution, about the importance of the states in the meaning of nationhood and the Union, masked their diverse interests and subsumed their peculiar grievances within a fictional unanimity, a unanimity that was invoked successfully in political campaigns leading to the wide defeat of the Federalists in 1800 and 1801.

Jefferson understood his election in 1800 to be the effect of a "mighty wave of public opinion"; and in this moment of national opposition to the Alien and Sedition Acts we can glimpse the first swelling of the tide.[178] We can begin to think about American democratic politics, even at this early date, as a fight to control, captivate, understand, and influence "the public mind." Public opinion—variously called "the voice of the people," "the public sentiment," "the public mind"—has a crucial and fundamental power in the perceived legitimacy of the American state. The Age of Revolutions destroyed notions of legitimacy that rested upon the assumptions of the ancien régime—or, at best, on tradition, precedent, and rigid law—and raised popular sovereignty to the level of active participation. Thus, the public, and their collective mind, have been a crucial, if foggy agent in the affairs of American governance; "public opinion" has provided legitimacy and ensured consent. Since the Revolution, the public mind has been subjected to many attempts to quantify, measure, poll, and understand it, but it is still an imaginary construct—it doesn't really exist, yet it has tremendous power in the functioning of American democracy.[179]

Finally, from the ideas and concerns of this large mobilization against the Alien and Sedition Acts, we can begin to make some broader arguments about the contested meaning of American citizenship and nationhood at the end of the first decade of life under the U.S. Constitution. The arguments the petitioners made about the rights of free speech and the rights of aliens were as modern and as revolutionary at the time as they remain today.[180] The Federalists were correct to recognize that the opposition to the Alien and Sedition Acts confronting them was indulging in Revolutionary tactics, language, and arguments to challenge their legitimacy. Federalist-dominated assemblies dismissed the Virginia and Kentucky Resolutions as dangerous and ridiculous; the Pennsylvania assembly noted that the arguments advanced in the resolutions were "a revolutionary measure, destructive of the purest principles of our state and national compacts."[181] The popular nullification called for by many of the remonstrators evoked a revolutionary practice, or often at least a threat of revolution. The petitioners to Congress were dismissed by a Federalist-dominated committee that could not fathom the arguments against the bills—arguments derived from "principles of that exotic system which convulses the civilized world."

Understanding that the politics of citizenship and nationhood in the 1790s still reflected the fundamental problems of America's Revolutionary birth is essential to a comprehension of the stakes at play in the Federalist and Republican fight for power at the end of the 1790s. It is not in the politics of style that the parties are to be distinguished, although there are differences, but in their different understanding of the importance and meaning of the American Revolution as it touched the fundamental aspects of American life. By emphasizing that the institutions of the national state—the Constitution, the law, and the political order in the United States—were still unsettled, fluid, and open to contestation, we can begin to grasp the larger significance of this broad moment of opposition. As Abraham Baldwin noted in 1799, "causes peculiar" to American independence still haunted the political landscape. When would conflicts tainted with Revolution finally end? Before we explore that question, we need to more closely examine some of the limits—and possibilities—of American citizenship in these founding years.

6

"Hordes of Foreigners"

THE IMMIGRANT MOMENT AND THE POTENTIAL OF THE HYPHENATED CITIZEN

Emigrants, discontented with their native country, bring with them minds prepossessed against any government at all; and, fattened by the unnatural children of our country, take advantage of licenses dictated by a genuine freedom, and pervert it to the expression of sentiments the most ungrateful, into schemes the most treasonable and base. Would to God, that they could be collected, and re-transported to the climes from whence they came; *there* to take their chance of seditious measures. —"Centinal," 1798

Led hither by the pursuit of ordinary business, or driven from our homes, like your venerable forefathers, by civil and religious oppressions, our views only extended to personal safety, peace and freedom. . . . Suffer *us* then to enjoy among you, the peace, liberty and safety, which our gallant countrymen have helped to establish, till gracious Heaven, by dispensing to Ireland, the same blessings, shall grant the remainder of our mutual prayers.—"Natives of Ireland," 1799

On February 9, 1799, newspaper editor William Duane visited St. Mary's Catholic Church in midtown Philadelphia to collect signatures. Born of Irish parents in New York before the Revolution, Duane and three recent arrivals from Ireland—Dr. James Reynolds, Robert Moore, and Samuel Cuming—were preparing "a memorial for the repeal of the Alien Bill," and they specifically sought support from those "natives of Ireland" who worshipped at St. Mary's. They spread out their petition in the church graveyard after Mass, and as numerous celebrants congregated to sign the memorial, other Catholics—some Irish—approached using abusive language and threats. In the next confusing moments, in the midst of curses, shouts of "Turn him out," pushing, and kicking, Reynolds pulled a pistol, and a general melee ensued. Only the timely arrival of the local constables saved the riot from spreading beyond the brick enclosure of the churchyard. Once hauled in front of the mayor, the four men were charged with disturbing the peace, or as the mayor put it, for being "evilly disposed persons who willfully and maliciously stirred up a riot on an holy day and in an holy place."[1]

The trial was held in the Philadelphia County Court of Oyer and Terminer, with a prosecution team led by the arch-Federalist Joseph Hopkinson. A recent appointee of President John Adams, we have already encountered Joseph Hopkinson enjoying fame as the composer of the unofficial national anthem "Hail Columbia!"—and as the author of the most celebrated pamphlet of the Federalist spring of 1798, calling for new laws regulating immigrants and dissent.[2] For Hopkinson, the trouble at the churchyard had a clear and lamentable provenance. "I will say that the greatest evils this country has ever endured," Hopkinson told the jury, "have arisen from the ready admission to foreigners to a participation in the government and internal arrangements of the country." It was to be regretted that with "the frank and generous failings of youth," the country had "commenced its career as an independent nation" by "becoming an asylum for the unfortunate and oppressed of all countries." Foreigners, "with those dangerous habits and propensities they too often bring with them," had been "the bane of the country." "We have even seen," he reminded the jury, "persons come among us who could not speak our language, enjoy the same benefits and do the same things, as our citizens!" The "intrigue and delusion" sponsored by "these designing demagogues" had corrupted "many honest and true Americans." If Americans had been left alone, he continued, "we should not this day have been divided and rent into parties," and certainly "it would not have been necessary that one party should carry pistols and dirks for defense." The Federalist government, Hopkinson noted approvingly, had recently passed a naturalization act that extended the residence requirement for citizenship from five to fourteen years. The change was necessary "to accommodate these people to our manners and customes," and "if aliens do not like the laws of this country, God knows there are ways and wishes enough for them to go back again."[3]

Standing against Hopkinson was Alexander J. Dallas, the secretary of the State of Pennsylvania and a founding member of the Democratic Society of Pennsylvania. We have also met Dallas before, as an aggressive advocate of the natural right of expatriation, during the trial of William Talbot—and as one of the most articulate voices of the need to interpret law to suit a "modern system of citizenship." With his fellow members of the Democratic Society, Dallas often toasted American immigrants, with the hope that "those who have sought an asylum in this country, find in every American a brother and a Friend."[4] He was himself an immigrant, and a leading member of the St. George's Society, an immigrant-aid society founded to help English immigrants in distress. In this trial, Dallas not only disputed the facts of the case, but he decried what he considered "a party case, a party question altogether." The mayor had committed a grave injustice by insinuating that these natives of Ireland were part of "a dark conspiracy" formed to destroy the Constitution and overthrow "the very principles of our government." Certainly the defendants were recent immigrants, but "have aliens no rights, no claims to freedom or justice?" These men had fled tyranny "by the most flattering views of freedom," and with "their arrival, after bringing with them their affections, and those dear ties of family which secure affections," had found "all their travail fruitless." As for their presence in a churchyard on Sunday, "they are [justified] by the habits of the people whom they particularly addressed, the natives of Ireland, where it is the universal custom to transact business after service." Indeed, laws must make "allowance for the inoffensive customs of those [whom] they implicate." In summary, then, "these men—tortured and persecuted, engaging in a respectful address (certainly a lawful pursuit) determined to do here what they had been accustomed to do in other places; and to take the opportunity when the people were collected in the neighborhood of the church"—should be considered not guilty.[5] A sympathetic jury agreed.

In the most basic analysis, the petitioning of the Irish at St. Mary's and the men's subsequent trial can be understood as a typical moment of confrontation in the bitter party conflicts of the late 1790s. The defendant's petitioning against the Alien Bill was but a single piece of the massive opposition that greeted the alien and sedition laws in the year after passage. This particular petition had been organized quickly, in the few weeks following the return of Congress, as part of the effort, described in the preceding chapter, by the Republican opposition to flood Congress with protests, and in that context the political significance of the petition, riot, and trial is easily surmised. This is the way most histories have dealt with the riot. In brief, the petitioners were challenging the government of the Federalists and were arrested and prosecuted by partisans of John Adams and his Federalist agenda; or, as Alexander Dallas had averred, it looked like "a party case." William Duane, the often offensive publisher of the notorious Philadelphia newspaper, the *Aurora,* by now the leading Republican paper in the country, was continually targeted by the administration, and was eventually prosecuted (though not convicted) under the Sedition Act.[6]

But the petitioning, riot, and trial should also be understood as an exceptional example of the growing maturity of self-aware ethnic political mobilization in the new republic—a phenomenon of American representative politics that has significantly influenced the character and meaning of citizenship in the United States. By mobilizing their political protest on the basis of shared nationality, the Irish petitioners at St. Mary's emphasized the legitimacy of distinct ethnic political participation within America. Their argument was not simply that aliens should have the rights of man, but it also included a specific defense of the Irish as a particularly worthy national people. In the face of criticism that immigrants needed to assimilate to the "manners and custumes" of native-born Americans before they could participate in the governance of America, these Republican Irish argued that laws "must make allowance for the inoffensive customs" of aliens. Their vision of citizenship was radical and revolutionary. Merging the idealism of the French and American revolutions with the realities of American representative politics, ethnic groups throughout the republic succeeded in creating a pluralist vision of American citizenship and in legitimating self-aware ethnic political organization: they revealed the potential for the "hyphenated" ethnic-American.

To grasp the broader meaning of this moment of riot, we need to reconstruct the place of immigrants in the politics of the 1790s. How and why did these particular men arrive with their petition when they did, advocating a radical notion of citizenship and exciting enough distrust to spark a brawl in the cemetery at St. Mary's Church? What place did these immigrants hold in the political and social world of post-Independence America? How did their arguments relate to other arguments about the place of ethnic groups in the body politic of the young country?

All immigrant groups certainly did not exhibit the political and ideological persuasion of these Irish petitioners, but by the end of the 1790s immigrant groups and ethnic societies were well placed and equipped with powerful ideas to challenge any view that denied different ethnicities a place in the American body politic. Historians and history have too often missed the significance of immigrant political activity in the early republic, and specifically in the 1790s as immigrant groups seized an important moment in a crisis of American national citizenship to assert their own legitimate place in the politics of the United States. Their successful opposition to restrictive national legislation against aliens and their dissent secured their position in party politics and American citizenship for the next generation, helping to establish the potential of a self-aware ethnic politics in the American representative system that has yet to lose momentum in American local and national politics. While the specifics of this particular moment would be lost to later generations of immigrants and ethnic groups, the logic of the Irish challenge of 1798 would be remade repeatedly in American history as immigrant groups called upon universal rights and their own particular ethnic solidarity to seize access to representation and political citizenship in an American society that found it hard to deny the legitimacy of their arguments.

The Politics of Ethnic Association

Immigrants in the early republic have been understudied. Problems associated with ethnic difference are largely assumed to be a nineteenth-century phenomenon, attendant to such structural transformations as "urbanization" and "industrialization," and accompanying the relatively high numbers of immigrants to the United States after 1840.[7] Scholars of national identity and citizenship in the early republic have been slow to incorporate ethnicity (if not race) into their interpretations, and the lack of attention to immigration and ethnicity in the early republic is exacerbated by a continuing misconception that only an insignificant number of the foreign-born characterized the early republic.[8] As we have noted, however, between 1783 and 1810 an estimated 275,000 Europeans and Euro-Caribbeans migrated to the United States.[9] Although this migration represented a decline from the high levels of the 1760s and early 1770s, immigrants were highly visible in the 1790s. At least three circumstances helped assure that the postwar migrants had an immediate and disproportionate impact on newly independent America.

First, unlike the earlier European migrations to colonial British America, the vast majority of European migrants after American independence—with the dwindling exception of some German immigrants—arrived without the burden of an indenture: they arrived as free aliens, not servants.[10] The immediate consequence of this change in the status type of immigrants is not readily apparent, but it is clear that immigrants in post-Independence America were setting up their own independent households much more quickly after their initial arrival than typical immigrants during the colonial period. While servant immigrants lived by necessity under the rule and household of a master for numerous years, post-Independence immigrants lived on their own authority almost immediately.[11] For the male heads of households, this had a direct impact on their status in common law, and on their potential to be publicly active. For women, it gave them the power to choose the household they would join. At least one contemporary suggested that post-Revolutionary trends would encourage the growth of immigrant communities, as "the present emigrants will now settle in the midst of friends, speaking their own language, and following their own customes."[12] Living together as part of immigrant communities provided stability and protection—and political activism and participation in the civic life of the community were both more available and more immediately beneficial for a free head of household than an indentured servant. Immigrants were still very much immigrants when they joined active political society after American independence.

Second, the stream of immigrants, especially after 1789, included a significant number of political refugees, many of whom became highly and immediately influential in the party politics and ideological debates of the early republic.[13] Refugees from the plots and uprisings in Ireland, political exiles from Scotland, England, and Wales, and the numerous temporary migrants to the United States from the French Revolution and the rebellion in St. Domingue landed, in the midst of international revolution, with unprecedented power—and often the deep desire—to influence American politics. The extraordinary growth in newspapers in the 1790s was only possible because of the large number of immigrant printers and polemicists who quickly spread out across the United States establishing party papers. While a few emigrants, like William Cobbett, lent their voices to the Federalists, the vast majority of the printers followed the politics of Thomas Paine and added their significant energy to the presses and point of view of the Republicans.[14]

Finally, the migration fell with particular impact upon the urban centers of the Mid-Atlantic, with both Philadelphia and New York experiencing rapid growth in the decade from the effects of migration, both local and international. New York City doubled in size, from 33,151 to 60,489 inhabitants, with an estimated two-thirds of this growth attributed to transnational migration.[15] Philadelphia grew at a similar pace, from an estimated 42,000 to nearly 70,000, during a decade when high mortality rates assured that births represented only a marginal surplus over deaths. Billy Smith has argued that internal and European migration alone "was sufficient to account for the rapid population expansion" of Philadelphia in the 1790s.[16] While cities were very much the exception in the American social order, Philadelphia and New York were the two national capitals in the 1790s, and they played a disproportionate role in the political order of the early republic. The visibility, prominence, and significance of immigrant groups in the leading cities of the United States, combined with the contested legitimacy of American representative governance in an age of international revolution, magnified both the real and perceived power of immigrants to effect the character of American citizenship in the early republic.

When these immigrants arrived with such weight onto America's shores, they encountered a society with decided attitudes and institutions already vying to control and characterize the immigrant populations. In the colonial world, the realities of servitude, not unfamiliar, had often directed the flow of migration and the incorporation of immigrants into society. In the cities, for those immigrants who had no immediate household, a few institutions existed to find the unlucky (if not always "the undeserving") a place. Churches helped to connect fellow nationals, but the most important institutions for the formation of American ethnic sensibilities within the British Empire were the ethnic immigrant-aid societies. These societies were an important part of the mosaic of civil society in the early republic, and they generated the foundations for the wide acceptance of ethnic difference in American national citizenship.

The immigrant-aid societies had deep roots in North America. As early as the 1650s, the Scot's Charitable Society of Boston was formed to assist Scots immigrants to the New World.[17] By the eve of the American Revolution, numerous immigrant and ethnic benevolent societies existed in the largest cities of the North American British colonies. Charleston had an active St. Andrew's Club, a German Society, and a society of descendents of French Huguenots; New York had a St. Andrew's Society, a St. George's society, a Society of the Friendly Sons of St. Patrick, and a St. David's Society; Philadelphia possessed versions of Scots, German, Welsh, Irish, and English immigrant-aid societies and social clubs. From Savannah to Boston, ethnic social and benevolent clubs were common and prominent ornaments of colonial society.[18]

The benevolent societies represented a unique opportunity for association among fellow nationals because they accommodated all religious persuasions. Religious requirements, which had existed for some of the clubs in the seventeenth and early eighteenth centuries, had been repealed by the mid-eighteenth century.[19] This aspect of the immigrant-aid societies helped diminish the role of churches as the sole sites of ethnic belonging in the urban centers, and it accelerated the emergence of nonsectarian ethnic solidarity. Baltimore, for instance, is typical of the Middle Atlantic cities in possessing a strong German immigrant community by the time of the American Revolution—albeit a German interest divided across congregations. Before Independence, the Germans in Baltimore maintained a large Reformed congregation, two Lutheran congregations, a Calvinist congregation, and a Dunkard congregation—all with services in German, all with their own parish schools. But the German Society of Maryland, formed to protect poor German immigrants and redemptioners, united elite Germans from across the city and across religious lines into a single, powerful ethnic lobby.[20] The Society of the Friendly Sons of St. Patrick, in pluralist Philadelphia, reflected a similar trend. By uniting Irish Quakers, Presbyterians, Anglicans, and Catholics, the elite Irish society created a powerful elite ethnic interest across religious lines.

Voluntary associations, like the benevolent organizations, were readily recognizable in eighteenth-century Anglo-American society. Masonic lodges, debate societies, social clubs, religious groups, political clubs, reading societies, hunting clubs, voluntary fire companies, and drinking societies were normal aspects of male public life across the British Atlantic.[21] From the frivolous to the political, associating was common in British America, especially in the growing seaports.[22] In fact, chapters of the first "voluntary" associations of the American resistance to Britain, the Sons of Liberty, often emerged out of existing political and social clubs like the Charleston Fire Company and the Boston Caucus.[23]

These societies were never completely apolitical, since they fortified and reinforced notions of the social and fraternal function of the leading figures of colonial and imperial society—men in positions of public power. As leaders of their communities—in law, business, and government—such men existed at the top of colonial hierarchy, and their benevolence to their "poor countrymen" reflected as much noblesse oblige as social reform. The societies also reflected public norms by excluding women from active membership. Just as colonial notions of representation reflected hierarchical understandings of the place of great men in society, the members of these organizations sought a consensual understanding of their own eminence among immigrant communities. Thus, when founding members of the German Society in Baltimore protected redemptioners, they spoke in the name of all Germans in the colonies, presuming an ability to speak for their entire community—women and men, rich and poor, Dunker and Lutheran.[24] Members of the St. Andrew's Society of New York, probably the most elite organization of its kind in British America, included numerous sons of the Scottish aristocracy, high-ranking colonial administrators, and other scions of New York society. Their notion of the importance of rank in social organizations is reflected in their behavior. When the Scotsman John Murray, fourth Earl of Dunmore, was appointed royal governor of New York in 1771, upon his arrival he was immediately given the presidency of the St. Andrew's Society, of which he became an avid supporter.[25]

In Philadelphia and New York, the Irish societies did not attain the level of social prominence of the Scots benevolent societies before Independence, but they did conform to this pattern. Most members were leading men of their communities. At the time of the war, the Philadelphia Society of the Friendly Sons of St. Patrick included some of the most wealthy members of Philadelphia society. When the Philadelphia elite organized the Bank of Pennsylvania in 1780 to help Congress fund the war, members of the St. Patrick's Society pledged one-third of the original capital.[26] Many of the wives of members participated in committees to raise money for destitute soldiers, including one committee dominated by the wives of members that raised $300,000 for shirts for the army.[27] In the turmoil of Revolutionary Philadelphia, members of the society were much more likely to be inside the houses being assaulted—as they were during the mob action against James Wilson's house—as with the people "out of doors."[28]

But the members of the St. Patrick's Society were nearly unanimous supporters of the Patriot cause. Only one member is known to have supported Great Britain in the war, and he, an Irish half-pay captain, was promptly and unanimously expelled.[29] In their aggressive support of Independence, the Irish benevolent societies were exceptional. Most of the other societies, reflecting the country and the immigrant groups themselves, were split by politics, ideology, and interest. At the eve of hostilities, the St. George's Society in Philadelphia represented the most prominent Tories of the city, and numerous Quaker neutrals, but one-third of the members, in the words of John Adams, were "staunch Americans." On April 23, 1776, St. George's Day, members of the society split into three equal parts—American, Briton, and "Trimmer"—and held their annual dinner in three different taverns.[30] In New York, the St. Andrew's Society simply disintegrated during the war years, with many of its leading members actively fighting for the Loyalist cause.

With the proliferation of voluntary societies after Independence, the political activities of these essential public institutions both reflected and accelerated the polarization of American politics in the early republic. In New York City, for example, the abundance of clubs, fraternal organizations, mutual aid societies, and benevolent associations orbited around the political dynamics of the urban polity, with some societies clearly visible in the politics of the city, while others remained apart and only indirectly related. There were fraternal organizations, like the Society of St. Tammany, various Masonic lodges, and the Black Friars, each group with its distinct paraphernalia, rituals, and rich symbolism. Tammany, of course, used an Indian motif, with officers of the society designated "sachems," its meeting hall being the "wigwam," and its members parading in feathers and buckskins.[31] The most famous example of the politicization of these societies is the capture of the Society of St. Tammany for the Republican Party in New York City. The Society of St. Tammany, like many other fraternal organizations, existed before the Revolution, but it apparently played little role in politics, being merely a fraternal and mutual-benefit association. By the early 1790s, however, the society had become large, and "weighted heavily with tradesmen and artisans."[32] Over the course of the decade, Tammany remained nominally nonpartisan, but the tenor of its politics increasingly revealed a Republican sympathy, and in 1795 the Federalist members of the society left over a "dispute."[33] In time, the Society of St. Tammany actually supplanted the Democratic club as the premier political organization of the city, and it would, with a few other societies, help coordinate Democratic politics in New York into the nineteenth century.[34]

Like the other voluntary associations, the great ethnic benevolent associations of the elite of colonial North America could not escape the push and pull of American politics in the early republic. For some of them, the façade of elite consensus simply could not hold together. In Baltimore, for instance, the powerful German Society simply fell apart from political differences in the 1790s. It did not reappear as a society until the 1810s.[35] For others, the demands of ideological and interest politics proved decisive, and Federalist and Republican members of the societies parted ways.

In New York City, the extremely elite St. Andrew's Society was reconstituted after the war and resumed its place at the forefront of New York society, albeit with fewer titled members. In 1792, Robert Livingston was forced out of the presidency of the St. Andrew's Society, which he had held since the society was re-formed after American independence. Livingston was a prominent man of a prominent New York family, a strong and personal opponent of John Jay, whom Benjamin Franklin called the "Cicero of America." He had been active in the Continental Congress during the war years and had served as the chancellor of the State of New York since Independence. In the early 1790s, he became, with Aaron Burr, one of the important elite leaders of the Republican interest whom Madison and Jefferson courted in their thrust against Hamiltonianism.[36] In his place, the St. Andrew's presidency was given to Walter Rutherford, a Tory during the American Revolution and a Federalist in politics and sympathy. Rutherford traced his ancestry back to James Rutherford, of Roxboroughshire, Scotland, whose manorial patrimony had been granted by King James IV of Scotland in 1492.[37] Walter Rutherford had been president of the St. Andrew's Society before Independence, and his return to leadership and the ouster of Livingston signaled the takeover of the society by the

Federalists and old Tories. In 1794, with Walter Rutherford as president and Hamilton's friend and confidant, Robert Troup, as first vice president, the Federalist takeover of the St. Andrew's Society was complete. It would remain a Federalist stronghold into the nineteenth century.[38]

With the St. Andrew's Society in the hands of the Federalists, many Scottish immigrants in the 1790s found themselves ignored, and even despised, by the elite organization. This is not surprising, since many of the Scots immigrants to New York were implicated in the radical disturbances of the Scottish Society of Friends, the Scottish National Convention, and the failed Watt Conspiracy of 1794—movements that expressed sympathy for the Republican French and the radicalism of Thomas Paine. One of these emigrants of the early 1790s noted that his compatriots, largely comprised of weavers from southwest Scotland and artisans and minor professionals from Edinburgh, were a group of "hot characters . . . which all the waters of the Atlantic could not cool."[39] They were "hot" in their admiration of the principles of political confrontation, explained in both parts of Paine's *The Rights of Man,* and they maintained these politics in America. In late 1794, a group of these radical émigrés in New York established their own benevolent society, the Caledonian Society, to assist "Scotch patriots forced from their native country." Their president was Donald Fraser, an officer in the Democratic Society and the treasurer of the first union for teachers in America, the Society of Associated Teachers.[40]

The story of the St. Patrick's Society in Philadelphia is distinct, but the trajectory is similar. After the war, the society emerged as one of the leading social clubs in the country, hosting impressive galas for America's new national heroes.[41] But by the end of the 1780s, some recent migrants to the city considered the society as merely a social club, and they formed the Hibernian Society for the Relief of Emigrants from Ireland to answer the philanthropic impulses of many leading Irishmen and the growing needs of Philadelphia's immigrant Irish.[42] Established in 1790 and incorporated in 1792, the Hibernian Society originally attracted nearly all of the members of the St. Patrick's Society, and numerous others. These included members of various political persuasions: both supporters and opponents of the Pennsylvania Constitution of 1776, as well as anti-federalists and federalists from the 1787–88 period.[43]

Gradually, the Hibernian Society came to be associated with the emerging Republican Party, and the already weakened St. Patrick's Society began to diminish into insignificance. In this case, it was not the rise of opposition to Alexander Hamilton that eventually killed the St. Patrick's Society, but the course of revolution in France and the Irish rebellion of 1793. With the beheading of the French king and the creation of the French Republic, the St. Patrick's Society and the Hibernian Society severed their connection. At its annual dinner, on March 22, 1793, the Hibernian Society toasted the French Republic and celebrated "the volunteers of Ireland, and all who arm in the cause of the *Rights of Man*."[44] By 1794, numerous Federalist members of the Hibernian Society had ceased their attendance and interest in the society, and the offices of the Hibernian Society were dominated by Republicans.[45] The schism in the Irish community in Philadelphia did not reflect confessional lines. The benevolent societies, fire companies, and militia included Catholic and Presbyterian Irish, as well as a number of Deists and non-Trinitarians, while the Society of the Friendly Sons of St. Patrick were Anglican, Catholic, and Presbyterian. The St. Patrick's Society ultimately dwindled to the size of a small social club, while the Hibernian Society became an important institutional support and bulwark of the Republican Party.[46] At the last recorded meeting of the St. Patrick Society in Philadelphia, fewer than twenty members attended, all of them rich Federalists.[47]

There were other clubs, of course, that attempted to combine an active ethnic interest without any connection to the contentious politics of the decade. Profoundly aware of the polarization that had split the benevolent societies in the 1790s, the Welsh Society forbade any discussion of the "religious and political opinions" of prospective members, and mandated that "no controversies on these subjects could be introduced whilst the President was in his chair, under the penalty of five dollars."[48] All of these ethnic societies, however, whether engaged in direct electoral politics or not, played a part in fashioning notions of ethnic citizenship in the young United States.

The State, Civil Society, and the Language of Ethnic Citizenship

Theorists and historians often emphasize the gulf between the institutions of civil society and those of the state, as if the two are necessarily defined in opposition to one another.[49] The very name "voluntary association" implies a high standard of liberal self-fashioning. But the voluntary nature of the societies is only one aspect of their relationship to both the public and the state. Indeed, the efficacy of civic institutions to serve as guarantors of specific privileges and rights against the authority of the state (or to "contest" the "hegemony" of absolutist culture) could often be severely limited without a legal charter of incorporation—the legal arm of the state that supported the goals of the voluntary association. Specifically, incorporation provided substance and weight in society. In the United States, an incorporated voluntary association typically received the power to hold and alienate property, to defend that property in the courts of the country, to protect that property from most taxes of the municipality and the state, and to claim the priceless legitimacy of public sanction.

Incorporation created a new body in law, empowered with rights and responsibilities, and therefore an institution dependent upon the extended legal lattice of the state, to be defined and defended in legislatures and courts. In many cases, the very power, prestige, and legal authority of voluntary organizations could implicate their private functions into the public governance of the community.[50] The problem of incorporation involved directly a problem of citizenship. As Madison noted, a charter of incorporation created "an artificial person not existing in law," and by doing so conferred "important civil rights and attributes, which could otherwise not be claimed."[51] Incorporation of a voluntary society impacted not simply the "voluntary" associators, but the status of every unassociated citizen as well. The unassociated citizen would be inherently less powerful (in general) to influence public opinion, set social regulations, and organize a political agenda. Incorporation gave power to a select group of citizens. Thus, the ability of voluntary associations to dispute the authority of the government and to serve as a check on the authority of state institutions can be (and often is) limited without the tacit recognition of their right to exist by the state.[52]

This inherently public facet of voluntary associations, and the place of such societies in relationship to the state, assumed a keen relevance in early republican society. After the Revolution, the common understanding of the state as being controlled and representative of the will of the citizenry could encourage serious resistance to associations perceived to unite *specific* interests antagonistic to the common good of the "people"—even when incorporation was not sought. What was and was not antagonistic to the common good, of course, varied with the origin of the complaint.

At its broadest level, the notion of associating in *any* form elicited protest. In New England, where a burst of associating immediately followed the successful end of the war, many people resented the notion that citizens could escape the theoretically tidy and closed local jurisdiction of the town in favor of associations that extended across traditional boundaries of authority and influence. With the proliferation of dissenting associations, some people complained that Revolutionary ideas and "new religion" had destroyed the unitary purpose of state and society that they remembered from before Independence.[53] One famous series of assaults on voluntary associations after Independence attacked the members of the Society of the Cincinnati for ostensibly attempting to make former officers of the Continental Army into an

American hereditary aristocracy.[54] George Washington (and many others) attacked the notion of voluntary societies with an *overtly* political mission when he blamed the Whiskey Rebellion on the meddling and misinformation of the "self-created" Democratic-Republican Societies. Local political fights often accompanied attempts at incorporation, as seen in the controversies over the Mechanics Association's efforts to receive a charter of incorporation in post-Revolution Boston.[55]

For ethnic benevolent societies, the legitimacy to organize in voluntary associations could seem particularly suspect. In the mid-1780s, leading members of the German community of New York City attempted to incorporate a society "for encouraging emigration from Germany; relieving the distresses of emigrants, and promoting useful knowledge among their countrymen." After being approved in the legislature, the charter of incorporation was vetoed by the Council of Revision repeatedly, which argued that such an empowerment would be "productive of the most fatal evils to the state." It was a question of policy and power. The council argued that the incorporation of an ethnic society would provide a precedent for the establishment of innumerable societies to encourage emigration, thus flooding the country with aliens "ignorant of our Constitution, and totally unacquainted with the principles of civil liberty." Although similar incorporations quickly became common throughout America, the Germans in New York were not able to formally incorporate their society until 1804.[56]

Despite occasional complaints and concern over the place of voluntary associations in the early republic, the momentum of association proved overwhelming. Nonetheless, voluntary associations often sought to justify their legitimate relationship to public purposes in their founding compacts. Embedded in bylaws, constitutions, and acts of incorporation of these early benevolent societies are statements of their missions that highlight the extent to which notions of voluntary organization always reflected an awareness of the demands of the public. These sentiments of the ethnic benevolent societies reveal an important justification and framework for ethnic citizenship in the United States.

The earliest statement of this kind is in the preamble to the "Rules and Orders" of the Scots Society of New York City, which circulated as a broadside in the city in 1744. The founding members—"Gentlemen, Merchants and others of the Scots Nation, residing in New York"—announced their intention to create a charitable society, "from a compassionate Concern and Affection to their indigent Countrymen in these Parts." Encouraged by the earlier societies of Boston and London, formed in the seventeenth century, these New York Scots admitted that their situation in the eighteenth century had changed—they were now integrated fully into Great Britain by the Act of Union—but they considered themselves justified in forming this private organization. So, notwithstanding "the late more intimate Union of North and South Britain," they believed "it not inconsistent or improper to continue this our private Charity to our quondam Townsmen and Neighbors." Such private interest, they noted, could only be justified because they had no "desire or Expectation of being excused from contributing towards the public Provision for the Town Poor in general." They felt compelled to acknowledge their public duty even as they celebrated their distinct connection to fellow Scots in trouble.[57]

After Independence these societies continued to offer similar apologetics, particularly now that their members were no longer constituent peoples of a multinational empire, with an allegiance tied personally to the Crown as subjects, but citizens of a new national people. Scots could be Britons, for obvious reasons, but could they be "Americans"? The St. Andrew's Society in New York noted that people who "fall into Misfortune and Distress" in the far parts of the world, "remote from the Place of their Nativity," often look to fellows of their same nationality, "on the Supposition that they may possibly have Connections by Blood with Some of them."[58] So men of Scots "parentage" associated to answer the needs of distressed Scots, but the society also emphasized that their particular interest in the fate of Scots would not "in the least prevent our acting up to the Principles of universal Charity on other Occasions."[59] At the end of the century, the Welsh Society in Philadelphia clearly stated the implications of these attitudes. The Welsh Society was reasserting the bond of an ethnic heritage it presumed was disappearing. The members noted that "the spirit of migration from Wales, till of late years, has partly subsided," and "the friendship and fraternization which usually existed between the ancient Britons in this country" has become "less fervent." The Society therefore hoped to "revive and increase social intercourses and mutual attachments." Most important, the Welsh Society argued that its members could be *both* Welsh and American: "To be good citizens of the World and the Nation we live in, yet to have especial fellowship with the descendants of our ancestors, is perfectly consistent with true patriotism and universal philanthropy."[60] This "especial fellowship with the descendants of our ancestors" had characterized the desire of immigrants to the Americas from the beginning, and with the continued existence and proliferation of ethnic benevolent societies in the United States, this rational assertion of the legitimacy of ethnic solidarity within an American nation would continue to be an important affirmation of the United States as a nation of immigrants.

These societies presented a notion of national belonging that relied upon the tolerant precepts of eighteenth-century enlightenment. That is to say, they recognized the existence of national difference, lamented notions of prejudice and intolerance among people of different nationalities, and yet affirmed the responsibility of fellow nationals to help their own kind. It was a humanistic tolerance expected of gentlemen of liberal education and a commitment to reason in the eighteenth century.[61] This notion was expressed most clearly in the constitution of the Society of the Sons of St. George in Philadelphia, which advanced a theory of ethnicity and race that began at the beginning: "Were we to trace their origin to that primordial past, with whom the author of nature completed the grand work of creating, we should find all mankind related to each other." While "national attachments and prejudices are for the most part idle and unnecessary," and when such prejudices "operate so far as to make us injure or despise persons born in a different country from ourselves, they are indeed very reprehensible." Yet, although "national distinction should on most occasions be avoided," on "some occasions it may answer the best purposes." Recently, "numbers of Englishmen have arrived in this city, and being disappointed in their expectations, have been reduced to the lowest ebb of distress." These recent trends, and not a wish to revive "invidious national distinction," which "ought particularly to be avoided between the different nations which compose the United States of America," had encouraged the creation of their Society. In the United States, "all the freemen (from wherever they originally migrated) are *brethren, friends, and countrymen.*"[62] Here the point is clear: "ethnic" organization in America was sometimes necessary for practical purposes, and people needed the help and encouragement of national fraternity. Such sentiments of tolerance for national difference held broad appeal across party in eighteenth-century American society.

Such pleasing hopes of toleration were enlarged and politicized by the Republican turn of many of the societies in the 1790s. Not only was "keeping alive any invidious national distinction" something to be avoided, ethnic societies allied with Revolutionary thought looked forward to the day when national distinctions completely disappeared. Here is the difference between "Enlightenment" and "Revolutionary" thought. The German Republican Society of Philadelphia, the very first "Democratic-Republican" society formed in celebration of the French Revolution, set the tone in 1792 by designing their ethnic association to the eventual extinction of German difference with an aggressive agenda of spreading the English language to German enclaves. Because of the inability of vast numbers of Germans to speak English, the society would provide their lessons in citizenship in the German language, but "it is more the distinction of language than of nation," and the society intended to cease its existence as soon as "the English language shall become the mother tongue of every citizen of the state."[63] Their efforts were part of a larger vision of global revolution that many of the popular Republican associations celebrated. Members of the Democratic Society of Pennsylvania, at a civic festival held jointly with the German Republican Society of Pennsylvania, toasted themselves and their fellow societies by hoping that all such societies would "preserve and disseminate their principles" until "the Rights of Man shall become the Supreme Law of every land, and their separate Fraternities be absorbed, in One Great Democratic Society, comprehending the Human Race."[64] In addition, they toasted "the Great Family of Mankind," with the hope that the "distinction of language and of nation, be lost in the association of Freedom and of Friendship, till the inhabitants of the various sections of the Globe shall be distinguished only by their virtues and their Talents."[65] For the Caledonian Society in New York, their motto—"The Rights of man we will defend / And objects of Distress befriend"—served the same future hope.[66] Similarly, at a meeting of the Hibernian Society in Philadelphia, in March of 1793, toasts were extended to the "political and Religious Freedom to all the nations of the earth," and to the hope that the "*Universe* be formed into one *Republican Society,* and every honest man enjoy the blessings thereof."[67]

This happy vision could lead some of the more idealistic to see a millennial future born of the leveling principles of the Revolutionary Age. Consider the raptures of Tunis Wortman, whose "Oration on the Influence of Social Institutions upon Human Nature and Happiness" (1796), given at a meeting of the St. Tammany Society in New York, offered the optimistic prophecy of a future based upon the purest principles of the American Revolution. He looked to "that happy aera" in which "no distinctions will be known but those which are derived from a happy combination of virtue with talents." Art, commerce, agriculture, and manufactures would flourish, while "philosophy, the sciences, and the liberal arts will advance in a continued and accelerated progression." And in this future paradise, "persecution and superstition, vice, prejudice and cruelty will take their eternal departure from the earth," and "national animosities and distinctions will be buried in eternal oblivion."[68]

At its best, this type of secular millennialism—of believing in the eventual realization of a liberal brotherhood of man, beyond the constraints of national institutions, when "national animosities and distinctions" would be "buried in eternal oblivion"—inspired the utopian hopes of Republican stalwarts. The language employed had decidedly political overtones, and many Federalists simply considered such ruminations as what they were: the naive, utopian, ridiculous fruit of the "wild, visionary" philosophies of the Age of Revolution. But for Republicans, recognizing the universal brotherhood of man reinforced their commitment to the principle of natural rights of individuals in society that transcended national allegiance, constitutional charter, or statutory promise. These very sentiments formed the ideological context for the broad defense of the rights of aliens against the Alien Friends Act that followed the Federalist passage of these acts.

But the ethnic communities, when faced with the challenge of the Alien Act and the Naturalization Act of 1798 as a concrete assault upon their enjoyment of American citizenship, were not willing merely to rest their hopes on a utopian future, or even on the numerous defenses of their common human rights. After all, many of the Federalists had based their support for the Alien Act on a vision of national unity that had inspired the new naturalization act, intended, as Hopkinson put it, "to accommodate these people to our manners and customes."[69] Building upon the tradition of tolerating specifically ethnic difference in the American body politic, immigrant groups and ethnic coalitions rejected the implication of Hopkinson's statement. They rejected the belief that America needed to represent a homogenous national culture, and they asserted their own legitimacy—not simply as fellow rights-bearing humans, which the Federalists also denied, but as specific and coherent ethnic cultures—to participate equally in American public life. They politicized the benevolent justification of the "friendly" societies. The remainder of the chapter will follow one of the strongest and most articulate advocates of this vision, the Republican Irish community in Philadelphia.

The Irish Moment and the Invention of the Hyphenated Citizen

The most powerful spur to Irish political mobilization in the early republic was the spread of active rebellion in Ireland. During the American War for Independence, reform pressure from militias created to defend Ireland (the Volunteers) and political pressures within the Anglican Ascendancy, encouraged England to offer legislative independence for the Irish Parliament and the elimination of numerous trade restrictions. But these small reforms still left much of the Irish population on the outside of effective participation in their own governance, and agitation for drastic imperial reform, and even self-rule, grew within both the majority Catholic population and the dissenting Protestants, most of whom resided in Ulster. The combined influence of American independence and the outbreak of the French Revolution helped mobilize the unsatisfied Irish in a renewed Volunteer movement, which led to the founding of the Society of the United Irishmen in 1791, signaling an increasingly organized political resistance to the status quo. As the French Revolution turned bloody, Irish politics became fraught with danger: initial reforms in favor of Catholics ceased, and England employed strong tactics to ensure order as it fought the widening war against the French Republic. These efforts alienated many of the United Irishmen, and by the middle of the 1790s the movement had become a massive secret society intent upon republican revolution in Ireland. Of course, large secret societies are rarely secret, and the British authorities began to infiltrate the movement. With the successful machinations of the United Irish leader Wolfe Tone and the attempted invasion of fifteen thousand French troops in 1796, the United Irish movement became increasingly militaristic, and the British began arresting, deporting, and harassing the leaders. Nevertheless, in late May of 1798, the United Irishmen were able to coordinate a massive uprising, a "Great Rebellion," which would eventually lead to tens of thousands of casualties and a flood of radical émigrés to the United States.[70] Although the rebellion was crushed by July, throughout 1798—during the opposition to the Alien and Sedition Act—many Americans still considered the rebellion successful. In New York, for example, as late as mid-November, John Beckley reported after conversing with eight Irish emigrants from Cork, that "Ireland appears to be irrecoverably lost to the British Empire for every future and useful purpose."[71]

In the 1790s, Irish-Americans and Irish immigrants in the United States received an abundance of information on this "home cause." Many of the Irish émigré printers in the United States had been actively involved in rebellion in Ireland, and they continued to follow Irish politics attentively. Mathew Carey, James Carey, and William Duane in Philadelphia, and John Daly Burk in New York City, set the Irish rebellion into an American context. In 1796, the Irish émigré printers—all members of the Hibernian Society—published *Paddy's Resource: Being a Select Collection of Original and Modern Patriotic Songs, Toasts and Sentiments.* The poem dedicating the book noted that it intended "To fan the Patriotic flame / To bid the Irish Youth aspire / [to] vindicate his native land." Songs inside the book included "Irishmen now United," "Hibernians' Harp Strung by Liberty," and "The Exiled Patriot."[72] A second edition soon came out in New York, "at the request of a number of Hibernians in this country," which included the "Address to the free electors of the county of Antrim," written by United Irishman Arthur O'Connor.[73] Such nationalistic encouragement would serve to unify the collective identities of the Irish throughout Philadelphia, and the country more generally.

Irish émigré and New York writer and printer John Daly Burk's widely distributed *History of the late war in Ireland, with an Account of the United Irish* argued that the Irish rebellion was a direct inheritance of the American legacy: "The United Irishmen [walked] in the footsteps of the Americans of '74." Burk also argued that the collective action of the Irish in remonstrating against the British government had made them into "A PEOPLE"—a process he believed to be identical to that of the American national awakening in the American Revolution. The book also played a role in distributing Irish songs and poems intended to help émigrés remember the "accumulations of centuries" of British tyranny. Burk linked the American and Irish experiences in his career as well as his history, writing the fantastically successful play, *Bunker-Hill,* as well as an ambitious *History of Virginia* that was used into the twentieth century.[74]

Part of the "republicanization" of the Hibernian Society related directly to the increasing numbers of Irish revolutionaries in the city. These émigrés provided a tangible connection to the international politics of revolution, and all of them saw their actions against Britain as a natural extension of the American War for Independence. The leading spirit of the society, Mathew Carey, had been the editor of the *Volunteer Journal* in Ireland in the early 1780s, and he explicitly connected the rebellions of the 1790s to his own efforts to "free" Ireland and fight against Federalism in America. Notably, he was more moderate in his political views than many of the Irish émigrés of the 1790s. Many of these new Irish émigrés became members of the Hibernian Society—and some became involved in the leadership. William Duane, after emigrating in 1796, immediately became a member, and he eventually became a leader of the society in the early 1800s. He also became captain of a Republican militia group, composed of Irish immigrants, known as the "Greens." Dr. James Reynolds, the man who pulled a pistol at the St. Mary's churchyard riot, was an extremely active United Irishman, and he became one of the physicians of the Hibernian Society (an elected office) within a year of his arrival. At a meeting to denounce the Jay Treaty that was organized by the Democratic-Republican Society and led by a committee containing numerous members of the Hibernian Society, toasts were made to "Archibald Rowan Hamilton, the Irish patriot, who had arrived in the city a few days before."[75]

While the radical émigrés certainly had their impact, it was the local elite leaders of the Republican interest in Philadelphia who assured the importance of the Hibernian Society as a political institution, and its integration into a web of voluntary societies controlled by the nascent Republican Party. Thomas McKean, chief justice of Pennsylvania and the president of the Hibernian Society throughout the 1790s, possessed an impeccable record as a leader of the American independence movement and was a prominent figure of independent Pennsylvania. The president of the Democratic Society was Blair McClenachan, an active member of the Hibernian Society and the Hibernian Fire Company, a leader of the Pennsylvania anti-federalist movement, and a Republican congressman in 1797–99. After Jefferson's election, he was appointed to the profitable position of commissioner of loans.[76] The Hibernian Society played an essential part in the reconciliation of the political interest of McClenachan and the many anti-federalists in the state with the supporters of McKean, who had been a leader in the movement to ratify the Constitution.

The Hibernian Society connected the poor immigrant Irish and the radical Irish émigrés to the local and national Republican elite, helping to consolidate the power of the Irish to mobilize an ethnic solidarity across class and religious lines. The society had two active standing committees, both of which played a role in uniting urban ethnic societies with political organizations. The Governing Committee, or "Acting Committee," was responsible for receiving and distributing funds for Irish emigrants and inspecting all vessels arriving from Ireland. The other committee, a "Committee of Correspondence," raised money, sent information to Irish ports, encouraged the establishment of other Hibernian Societies, and shared information with other immigrant-aid societies. Members of the Hibernian Society greeted every ship that arrived from Ireland, checked the conditions of the passage, and helped Irish men and women to housing, work, legal advice, medical care, and transportation.[77] Mathew Carey, McClenachan, McKean, and the other leadership used the charitable auspices of the society to establish a strong relationship with the rapidly growing frontiers and suburbs of Philadelphia—the Northern Liberties and Southwark districts—where most of the immigrant Irish were settling. By the middle of the decade, the Hibernian Society was being used to great effect in the Irish immigrant community by pro-Jefferson forces in the presidential election. These areas became the stronghold of William Duane's political power in the late 1790s and early 1800s.[78]

Finally, by the late 1790s, a group of the Philadelphia Irishmen, including Dr. James Reynolds and Duane, created a "United Irish Society" of their own, to "promote the emancipation of Ireland, and the establishment of a republican form of government there." The evidence about the nature and extent of this organization is conflicting. Opponents of the Republicans considered the organization dangerous and formidable. William Cobbett, who personally led the assault on this semi-secret society, estimated the membership at fifteen hundred.[79] But Cobbett was inflating numbers to inflame the fantasies of his readership. More likely, the group was never more than a small collection of extremely radical Republicans, but they were active, and their political efforts often overlapped with other efforts to mobilize the Republican Party. Mathew Carey and his brother James adamantly denied that they were involved in the organization, but a leading student of Carey's political activities believes he was a leader in the group.[80] In line with the ideology of world revolution, the society was not restricted to men of Irish descent, but it retains importance as part of the ethnic political mobilization in the city because of its members' connection to the cause of Ireland.[81]

The importance of these cross-connections between the Irish and the Republican Party in Philadelphia can be seen in the prelude and aftermath of the St. Mary's Church riot in February 1799. The Irish community had already been stirred by a rising nativism that characterized the colorful Federalist press in Philadelphia. And from July 1798 to February 1799 Mathew Carey was engaged in a highly public newspaper, broadside, and pamphlet contest with William Cobbett and John Fenno and his son, John Ward Fenno, one that often took on the explicit purpose of defending the Irish from prejudicial attacks. In a typically strong defense of the Irish in America and the failed rebellion of 1798 in Ireland, Mathew Carey attacked the efforts of Federalists to debase the Irish. Noting that Pennsylvania held "at least 30,000 natives of Ireland, and as many more children of Irishmen," Carey chastised any author who exhibited the "baseness of condemning nations by wholesale." For John Ward Fenno he had nothing but contempt: "This Editor, a lad just from College, embraces every opportunity of railing against Irish out casts—Irish vagabonds—Irish vagrants—Irish cutthroats—Irish bloodhounds—wild Irish—and in fact employs against the nation every opprobrious epithet that the language can furnish."[82] Mathew Carey defended the Irish rebellion as a liberation movement akin to the American Revolution. He argued that the "revolution of 1688, that of 1775, and the rebellion in Ireland in 1798, all depend for their condemnation and justification, on the same grand and sublime principle, that man has the true right of self-government."[83] While the Fennos could stigmatize the Irish as mere rebels, "a different issue of affairs" would have made these men great "revolutionists." Indeed, "had general Howe possessed more energy in the early stage of [the War for Independence], especially after the battle of Long Island, it is not improbable that many of those who now vilify the Irish outcasts, would be to this day out casts and fugitives themselves."[84]

The Irish community responded strongly to these defenses, and it was highly mobilized by the Republican Party when the Republicans in Congress announced that they would attempt to repeal the Alien and Sedition Acts in the new session of 1798–99. After learning that the House of Representatives would be considering the sundry petitions it had received for the repeal of the Alien Act, a "meeting of gentlemen," most of them of Irish descent, convened at a local tavern on Friday, February 7, 1799, to draw up a petition from "natives of Ireland, residing within the United States of America," to repeal the Alien Act. Who exactly was at the meeting is difficult to discern. William Duane was there, and the two Careys were implicated. Together, they drafted a petition and put in place a plan to get Irish signatures to it. At the meeting, it was noted that St. Mary's Church would be a perfect venue, because "*three forths*" of the congregants were Irish aliens. According to the testimony of an Irishman who went to church solely to sign the petition, "great numbers" of the Irish had learned of the memorial by Friday night.[85]

On Sunday, however, as we have seen, the petition drive turned into a brawl. This is not surprising, since we know that the Irish community in Philadelphia had strong Federalists among its ranks, and that the St. Patrick's Society—which counted a number of Catholics as members—had opposed the Republican turn of the Hibernian Society. In fact, many Irish Federalists had been particularly antagonistic to any attempt by Irish Republicans to connect the Irish rebellion to the American Revolution or the interest of the Republican Party. The rumors of the activities of a United Irish Society in Philadelphia had been attacked eagerly by an unknown "Loyal Irishman" writing for the Federalist papers.[86] Another complaint against the leaders of the petition drive at St. Mary's was their non-Catholic status; Duane himself was an avowed Deist. So the presence of these particular petitioners excited at least two fonts of animosity.[87] At the same time, however, as related in the testimony of a man who had attempted to sign the petition at the churchyard, it was widely understood that the vast majority of the congregation wished "for the petition to be brought there that day to obtain signatures."[88]

When the constables arrived at the church, Duane, Reynolds, Samuel Cumings, and Robert Moore were detained and taken into custody by the Federalist mayor, Hillary Baker. Within an hour or so, Thomas McKean (the aforementioned chief justice of Pennsylvania and president of the Hibernian Society) arrived at the mayor's office and "banged on the door," calling for the immediate release of the petitioners. After an angry confrontation between McKean and the mayor, McKean paid the bail money for the men, an extremely high $4,000 each.[89]

Despite the riot and trial, the petitions went forward.[90] Similar petitions emerged from across the United States, and many Federalists in Congress wondered whether the non-citizen natives of Ireland could petition at all. Samuel Sewell complained that petitions from aliens did not represent any true feelings of the citizenry, but merely "evidences of the seditions feelings and seditious principles" that generally animated aliens.[91] The petitions were ultimately accepted by a close vote and stashed in the committee set to rule on all the petitions against the Alien and Sedition Acts.

But although the petitions were lumped with hundreds of petitions that the citizenry had sent against the Alien and Sedition Acts, the Irish petitions represented a unique voice in the cacophony of complaints. First and foremost, the Irish chastised their attackers: "The republican citizens of the United States are often affected and indeed, sometimes greatly disgusted, by the abuse, which is cast by all the anglo-federal, and by some of the federal prints, on *the people of Ireland.*" Indeed, the Irish were willing to believe that the Americans who passed the laws were misled by some "malignant souls," but "the representations incessantly propagated concerning us and our countrymen" had created "unjust impressions concerning the Irish residents in the United States, and Irish in general." Because this manufactured prejudice "may have contributed to the adoption of this law," the petitions attempted to correct the record and assert the cultural compatibility of the Irish and the Americans.

The petitioners emphasized the common Irish and American experience of the British yoke. Indeed, they argued, "the Irish nation groaned under much greater political evils from the same power that sought to oppress you." The rebellions of the Irishmen since the American Revolution sprang from "*the American principle*" that "all men are created equal." Irishmen belonged to a particular immigrant group "whose native country [had] been engaged, by a pursuit of your conspicuous and influential example, in an effort for liberty," a fact which made them feel "much more sensible than any other class of aliens" to the problems with the Alien law.[92]

To emphasize the cultural compatibility of the Irish and their native American brethren, the Irish would toast "that the Irish harp play

Yankee Doodle."[93] They had also much in common with the ancestors of Americans, for they had been "lead hither by the pursuit of ordinary business, or driven from our homes, like your venerable forefathers, by civil and religious oppressions." The petitioners recognized that Irish immigrants had "pledged lives [and] fortunes with American companies, as stockholders," and even held shares in "the National Bank." The Irish reminded the Americans that the Continental Congress of 1775 had invited them to flee British tyranny to "the fertile regions of America," where they could find that "*safe asylum* from poverty and, in *time*, from *oppression also*."[94]

A common argument made by the Irish to prove their compatibility with American citizenship was a reference to their service in the Revolutionary War. Matthew Lyon is a typical example. Lyon was an Irish-born congressman from Vermont who refused to join his fellow legislators in a ceremonial trip to the President's House. When Federalists mocked that there would be "American blood enough" at the procession, Lyon defiantly attacked the New Englanders who had been forward in their abuse of the Irish. He declared that he did not claim ancestry

> from the bastards of Oliver Cromwell, or his courtiers, or from the Puritans who punished their horses for breaking the Sabbath, of from those who persecuted the Quakers, or hanged the witches. He could however, say that this was his country, because he had no other; and he owned a share of it, which he had bought by the means of honest industry; he had fought for his country. In every day of trouble he had repaired to her standard, and had conquered under it. Conquest had led this country to independence, and being independent, he called no man's blood in question.[95]

He believed his service in the war, not any opinion about the true nature of American "blood," justified and legitimated his citizenship. The Federalists were not impressed. As we have seen, Lyon was eventually broken by the Sedition Act, and expelled from the House of Representatives in the summer of 1798.[96]

But the Irish petitioners would go even further in their claims to inherit American freedoms, for "the blood of the Irish flowed in your service here." They claimed the legacy of the Revolution, not because they *themselves* had fought in the war, but because their "countrymen" and ancestors had fought for American independence. "We glory in the belief," they asserted, "that of the Irish residents in the United States, a *greater proportion* partook of the hazards of the field and of the duties of your independent republican councils, than of the native American." When the war finally ended, "every uninfluenced Irishman, felt a true brotherhood for the United States." "Suffer *us*," they pleaded, "to enjoy among you, the peace liberty and safety which our gallant countrymen have helped to establish."[97]

The petitions of the Irish were essentially ignored, but the arguments made within them, and the belief among Irish Republicans that their continued celebration of their Irishness was not an impediment to their full status as "Americans," catalyzed their political activism in the winter and spring of 1799. The conflict between the Irish and the federal government immediately bled into the gubernatorial election of 1799, which began with serious organization by the end of February, mere weeks after the riot at St. Mary's. Judge Thomas McKean was running for the Republicans, and his Irishness was very much a campaign issue. McKean ran a strident race against Federalist James Ross that focused, as one scholar has noted, not on "local issues," but on the belief "that the very existence of the nation depended on the selection of the Pennsylvania Governor." In the course of the campaign, Federalist committees charged that McKean planned to send "an army of 50,000 United Irishmen" in a pillaging raid across the state. One broadside clearly doubted McKean's legitimacy to govern, arguing that "the ensuing election for a governor of the State of Pennsylvania, is one of our most important crisis that this State has ever experienced: It is to determine whether we are to govern ourselves or be governed by foreignors." McKean was no American, he was "a Jacobin, a Foreigner." Of course, Republicans gave as good as they got.[98]

With the election of McKean, the first victory in the Republican "Revolution of 1800" had been achieved. The success of McKean at the polls also secured a Republican lower house, and a small one-seat majority for the Federalists in the state senate, which although it would nearly tie up the electoral votes of Pennsylvania, assured that a majority of them would go to the Republican candidate. McKean's candidacy had presented a complete rejection of the Federalist vision of the national state and national citizenship. As president of the Hibernian Society of Philadelphia and ardent advocate for states' rights in constitutional interpretation, McKean reflected everything the Federalists despised. As chief justice of the Pennsylvania Supreme Court, McKean had argued in 1798 that the Constitution was a mere "league or treaty made by the individual States as one party and all the States as another"—a logic identical to the theory justifying the state nullification power asserted in the Kentucky Resolutions and in numerous popular resolutions of the same year.[99] McKean's election helped add a new phenomenon to the local politics of American life: the self-conscious ethnic-American constituent group and the idea of the hyphenated citizen. Rejecting the logic of Federalist notions of the need for a homogeneous American citizenry, immigrant groups argued for their particular legitimacy, not only to share in the benefits of citizenship in the United States, but to do so without completely rejecting the peculiarities of their ethnic distinctiveness. As their coalition noted, laws must make "allowance for the inoffensive customs of those [whom] they implicate."[100] McKean's election (and eventually Jefferson's) took advantage of the self-conscious ethnic mobilization of numerous Irish and Germans making this argument in 1799.[101]

By the end of the 1790s, the Irish in Philadelphia were able to mobilize based on their immigrant experience and a collective sense of their Irish heritage—a heritage which they glorified in part to legitimate and explain their place in American culture and society in the face a competing nationalism. They thus "invented" an ethnic identity. The idea that American citizens could be both Irish and American, and that law needed to take account of the peculiar cultures that would be influenced by it, were Revolutionary concepts. The significance of their argument must be emphasized. By fusing their interest in Irish revolution with their belief that the American Constitution embodied universal rights of man in its principles, these immigrants invented the notion of the hyphenated citizen. It was made as the counter to a clearly nationalist and sometimes nativist argument being put forth by the Federalist government, both in rhetoric and in law. Ethnic politics in America would become an important part of the immigrant experience in the United States, and as immigrants could gain power by solidarities based upon their ethnic heritage, they gained legitimacy in American politics by referencing their adherence to the principles of the American Revolution. Such a process of ethnic politicization became almost formulaic in nineteenth-century urban polities throughout the United States.

The Irish-American Beyond 1800

The Irish community and political organization in Philadelphia continued its success after the election of McKean. Combined in an alliance with the Germans in Philadelphia and statewide, William Duane built an Irish political machine that exerted influence well into the nineteenth century. In 1802, they helped the Republican Party to repeal the restrictive naturalization law of 1798.

But like many important political factions, the Irish in Philadelphia never reached the level of unanimity they achieved as part of the opposition to Federalist Pennsylvania and the presidency of John Adams.

The Philadelphia Irish were split by ideological and class differences between William Duane and Thomas McKean, as well as by differing personalities vying for control of the Irish interest. Duane contended with another United Irish radical émigré, John Binns, who often fought with Duane over the future direction of the Republican Party and the Hibernian Society. Each of them authored attacks and rebuttals challenging the other's "Irishness" and Americanism. The Irish would only see broad unanimity in politics briefly, during the War of 1812, when Britain once again served as the common enemy.[102]

In some respects, the unification of the Irish in the politics of the late 1790s reflected the attempt by the United Irishmen in Ireland to create an Irish nation based upon principles of Revolutionary equality and not upon sectarian difference. In Ireland, the United Irish movement and the subsequent rebellion failed miserably to achieve any of the broadest intentions of the revolt. The dream of a united, free, and republican Ireland, where the distinctions between Protestants and Catholics disappeared into insignificance, represented the exact opposite of the fallout of the 1798 rising. In 1801, the British incorporated Ireland into the United Kingdom, and the tensions between Protestants and Catholics in Ireland became increasingly exacerbated.[103] The English represented the rising of 1798 as a largely Catholic affair, keeping the evidence of Presbyterian rebellion in Antrim and Down from general circulation. Within a generation, the association of Irish Protestantism with the British, and Irish Catholicism with rebellion, characterized all Anglo-Irish politics.[104]

In time, American Irish politics would reflect a similar sectarianism, and the early story of Irish organization would be largely obscured and forgotten. For in American society and in American scholarship, many of the individuals associated with Irish politics in the early republic would be given the moniker of "Scotch-Irish"—a rather peculiar ethnic term that is not used in Ireland (North or South) to designate Ulster Presbyterian Irishmen, but that in the United States, by the end of the nineteenth century, had become a unique category, a unique race. Judge Thomas McKean, for instance, is still described in the literature as "Scotch-Irish," even though he never called himself such and always was considered a leader of the Irish in Philadelphia. The problem relates directly to the way that immigrant groups have invented and reinvented their ethnic identities based upon the politics of their own era, and it is perhaps telling that the notion of a hyphenated citizen could have led directly to the invention of a hyphenated ethnicity, the Scotch-Irish "race."

In the late nineteenth century, Irish nationalist scholars argued that the notion of a Scotch-Irish ethnicity substantially elided the history of Irish-Americans, in the service of late-nineteenth-century notions of ethnography. As one such text noted, in recognizing the myth of the Scotch-Irish: "Take the history of the Friendly Sons of St. Patrick, the leading Irish organization prior to and during the Revolution. Most of them were what would now be considered as 'Scotch-Irish,' and yet they organized an Irish Society, not a Scotch one; they met on St. Patrick's Day not on St. Andrew's Day."[105] The Irish nationalist historians have a point. The Irish in Philadelphia in the 1790s, although many are today considered "Scotch-Irish," mobilized around a notion of shared Irishness, encouraged by a nationalist nonsectarian rebellion in Ireland, and they emphasized their Irish identity as a defense against American nativism. There was no "Scotch-Irish" Society in the United States until the latter half of the nineteenth century, when very different notions about the racial characteristics of ethnic groups dominated scientific and cultural perceptions of difference. Here is a case where notions of the constructed nature of ethnicity can be deconstructed, and dressed in original clothes. Irish ethnicity mattered in the 1790s because certain immigrants depended upon a shared identity in their battles for power. American citizenship has often reflected the optimism of the Irish Republicans of 1798–99. When the Irish émigré John Binns confronted the rise of the Know-Nothing Party in the 1840s, he reacted with disgust—but also with a certain confidence. Such bitter nativism, he recognized, was doomed, because it was un-American.[106]

{ 7 }

White Citizen, Black Denizen

THE RACIAL RANKS OF AMERICAN CITIZENSHIP

I am one of that unfortunate race of men, who are distinguished from the rest of the human species, by a black skin and wooly hair. . . . Can it be contended that a difference of colour alone can constitute a difference of species? . . . Are we not entitled to all the same rights, as other men?—A FREE NEGRO, 1789

The mass of mankind in this country may be divided into two classes—free people and slaves; but the class of free people includes many who are not citizens. The same mass may be divided into three classes—citizens, aliens, and denizens; the latter description of persons being those who are admitted to some portion of the rights and privileges of citizens, but not all those rights and privileges. Such of the free negroes in our country, as are not aliens, may be denizens, but none of them, it is apprehended, are citizens. . . . The free negro who would claim all the privileges and immunities of a citizen in another State, must show a right to all those privileges and immunities in his own. —CONGRESSMAN ALEXANDER SMYTH, VIRGINIA, 1820

ON JUNE 22, 1807, THE LONGEST DAY OF THE YEAR, AN incident three leagues west of the mouth of the Chesapeake Bay nearly precipitated a war between Britain and the United States. The HMS *Leopard* attacked the unprepared U.S. frigate *Chesapeake,* the captain of the *Chesapeake* having refused to allow the British to search his ship for deserters from the Royal Navy. After a warning shot, the *Leopard* systematically disabled the *Chesapeake* in less than twenty minutes—before the Americans could even load and run out their guns. Once the *Chesapeake* had struck her colors, the British seized four sailors, three of whom were American citizens. The *Chesapeake* was left to limp ingloriously back to Hampton Roads, in full view of the British fleet, which was anchored in American waters at Lynnhaven Bay. Its rigging and sails in tatters, with eighteen wounded sailors and three corpses, the ship arrived in port with three and a half feet of the bay in the hold.[1]

The anger of the American citizenry spread along with the news of the British audacity, from Norfolk to the Mississippi, as the country was roused at the insult to American sovereignty, honor, and independence. Of particular concern was the fate of the three dead sailors and the four men seized by the British ship. Their loss represented a symbolic slap at every American citizen, and the cry of vengeance animated the hundreds of public resolutions passed in the days and weeks following the "British outrage." The writers of one such remonstrance characterized the British seizure of the "four American citizens" as an "unprovoked cold-blooded, and dastardly attack" in which "a series of unprincipled depredation and robbery is crowned by inhuman murder, riotous devastation, and atrocious insult." Their anguish, enlivened by a deep sense of sympathy "with our suffering fellow-citizens," demanded immediate "retaliation."[2] It did not, apparently, matter that two of the sailors were black.

If nations are partially "imagined communities," the American people at that moment of crisis—even the slaveholding president Thomas Jefferson—were able to imagine the black sailors as representative citizens of the American nation. And even if imagination failed, law dictated the passionate reaction, for in international law all black Americans, whether slave or free, were considered to be citizens of the United States. If the seizure of the men was another British impressment of American citizens, of any color,[3] the act was a clear violation of international law and American sovereignty.[4]

But, in domestic law, the status of non-enslaved black Americans was strikingly distinct from that of white citizens; in fact, these men would probably not have been considered citizens at all. Consider the options of the two black sailors, William Ware and Daniel Martin, if they had chosen to make a life in the Virginia Chesapeake instead of enlisting on the frigate *Chesapeake.* What rights and privileges would these martyrs of American honor have possessed as free men in the Virginia of 1807?

First, as "mulattoes," they were considered in Virginia law as "free Negroes"; they were not white—a distinction with considerable implications. Free blacks, in the Virginia state codes, were closely regulated in their property and their persons, unlike any similar laws relating to all whites. As such, the men could not have owned firearms without a proper license, they could not have traveled without proof of their identity and their status as free, and they could not have lived anywhere without registering with the state.[5] If either Ware or Martin chose to enter retail business, he would have to be particularly wary of dealing with white customers on credit—the common practice in a cash-poor economy—since he could not testify against any white person, or in any case involving a white plaintiff or defendant. Being successful in retail also would have meant participating in an "un-free market," because blacks in trade, whether enslaved or free, were required to pay extra duties on every good sold.[6] If either man were accused of violating the law, he would be subject to evidence from slaves without oath. Neither of the men would be allowed to vote. Of course, all of these possibilities would depend on whether these two men could even migrate legally into the Commonwealth of Virginia, which explicitly forbade the immigration of "free negroes and mulattoes" in 1793.[7] If Ware or Martin were able to take up residence in the state, their employment opportunities would have been limited. They could have eked out a living as watermen, working ferries and tobacco barges up and down the swamps and waterways of Tidewater Virginia, but they would never be able to become a captain of an American merchant vessel—as one free black in Norfolk learned, once he reached that position—because only citizens of the United States could command, and as U.S. Attorney General William Wirt (a Virginian) pointed out in 1821, "Free colored persons in Virginia are not citizens of the United States."[8]

But if the "free colored persons" of Virginia were not citizens of the United States in the early republic, what were they? What about free blacks in other states?[9] For the most part, the vast majority of non-enslaved blacks across the United States lived within the bounds of the law, but not as accepted citizens of the United States of America. At best, they could attain an approximation of citizenship within a particular state, as specified by the individual state legislatures. The status of free black men or women in law in Pennsylvania was quite different from free blacks' legal status in Virginia, which again was different from their legal status in Massachusetts. And their status was liable to change with the whims of politics; they had no sacred rights. The diversity of status reflected much more than differing laws regulating the franchise, or the generally federal nature of American citizenship in the early republic, which affected whites as well as blacks. The status of free blacks throughout the country suggested a state intrusion and interest over the bodies, property, and movement of black Americans, simply because they were black, which was never considered acceptable for white citizens. American blacks were not aliens, as the episode of the *Leopold* and *Chesapeake* shows, but white aliens often possessed more protections of the courts than free black Americans. How can we conceptually understand the status of free blacks in the laws of citizenship and the fictions of belonging in the early republic?

The most comparable status in eighteenth-century British law is that of "denizen"; under British law, denization occurred under one of two processes that provided rights and privileges to aliens. The first was naturalization, which fictively created "natural-born" subjects from aliens. Naturalized aliens were considered to be "natural-born" citizens, their status equivalent to that of native-born citizens (except that in the United States after Independence they could not serve as president or vice president). The other process was denization, which extended only *some* of the rights and privileges of citizens—plus, specific grants of denization were often quite different among different denizens. A denizen was not considered part of the body politic and was not governed by the laws related to aliens, but was allowed to have certain privileges by fiat. One denizen might perhaps be given only the right to hold property, while another might hold all the rights and protections of English law, except the right to alienate a specific piece of real property. Denization also remained conditional, and privileges once extended could be revoked. Naturalization was permanent. In the United States after Independence, the states used a similar power to subscribe privileges and rights to blacks as a group. Free blacks throughout the Union were placed in a legal status between slave and unfettered citizen, and were thus excluded from cultural inclusion in the imagination of the white American body politic. They were not considered to be Americans, but neither were they aliens. In a few states, free blacks possessed nearly all the rights of white citizens, but their citizenship was never truly national.[10]

In a dramatic debate over the admission of Missouri into the Union as a slave state in 1820, Virginia Congressman Alexander Smyth argued this point. Attempting to make sense of the status of free blacks in a country which he considered a white republic, Smyth asserted that the body of free people in the United States could be divided into "citizens, aliens, and denizens," with free negroes being denizens.[11] Upon hearing Smyth's contention that free blacks were mere denizens of the United States, James Strong, of New York, reacted with disgust. In "some of the states," he pointed out, the fathers of free blacks "fought the battles of the Revolution." In many of the states, "they are recognized as citizens" and are "eligible to hold office, entitled to hold real estate, to vote, to sue and be sued." How can it be, then, that "free negroes" lost their national citizenship?[12] This chapter answers Strong's question.

Since the publication of Edmund Morgan's *American Slavery,*

American Freedom, developments that unfolded long before the Revolution have been burdened with the responsibility for giving birth to the "American paradox": the existence of slavery and racial discrimination in a nation founded upon ideals of freedom. Morgan placed the fatal choice in the seventeenth century, when, as a consequence of Bacon's Rebellion, the Virginia planter elite opted to solve the problem of persistent internal conflict by adopting African slavery, thereby creating a veneer of white liberty on the backs of enslaved blacks. But recent scholarship suggests the limits of Morgan's chronology, and of his ultimate analysis. Enslaved labor had been the choice of Virginia's elites long before Bacon's Rebellion—as it had been throughout the Atlantic World—and as the institution evolved in the eighteenth century, it was deeply associated with the growth of neo-feudal, not liberal, attitudes toward land, inheritance, and property.[13]

Choices about the relationship of race and citizenship, slavery and freedom, needed to be remade in the era of the American Revolution—the only era that could have given birth to a paradox relating to a notion of equality of rights. The Revolutionary era represented the first moment of emancipation in the United States, and like other emancipatory moments in the Atlantic World, emancipation helped define the meaning of modern "freedom."[14] In the United States, freedom and citizenship were intimately connected. During the War for Independence, free blacks actually made some gains toward full and equal inclusion into American citizenship, but the problem of creating a national community out of the separate states necessitated a closer scrutiny of the racial composition of the nation. The denization of free blacks in the United States was not a one-time decree, but a process of exclusion that occurred gradually, everywhere, in the decades after Independence. The inherently political nature of this process reveals the choices and bargains made by the Revolutionary generation as they defined the racial limits of American citizenship. Denization did not simply happen; it was a status imposed upon a new and growing free black population by whites, with eyes wide open, confronting the challenge of making a nation. The exclusion of blacks was only complete when white Americans *openly* abandoned the promise of Revolutionary equality for all men, constructing a Union which provided no legal *national* remedy for free blacks chafing at the limits of their political belonging.

Understanding the scale of manumission, and the Revolutionary potential of the rising free black communities after 1783, is crucial to properly historicizing how and why white Americans turned away from the Revolutionary promise of freedom for black Americans in the face of black claims for rights and equal status. The fundamental problem was not slavery, but citizenship. As more and more free blacks clamored for access to power, more and more restrictions were placed upon their citizenship. Ultimately, even those liberal whites who wished to end slavery and *did not* argue that blacks were inherently inferior to whites could not imagine a republic in which blacks and whites could live together as equal citizens. Unlike subjecthood, citizenship demanded equality—and equality was out of the question. In time, free blacks became mere denizens among a white citizenry. Even in the face of growing and insistent black protest, the American republic became a white nation in the generation following Independence. By the early 1800s, no political or legal remedy that kept the Union intact could have achieved an equal citizenship for free blacks. Before examining how they became denizens, we must recognize how they became free, for there were no substantial numbers of non-enslaved blacks living in North America until after the War for Independence.

The Revolutionary Birth of the American Free Black Communities

From the beginning of the Revolution through the first decade of the nineteenth century, the free black population of the United States grew at a rate faster than that of the enslaved population. This was a window of time characterized by revolution in the status of people throughout the United States, and a time of historic opportunity for black Americans. The War of Independence weakened slavery in the United States and encouraged the growth in the number of free blacks in America in three crucial ways.[15]

First, the chaos of war created innumerable opportunities for slaves to escape from their bondage as armies moved and authority shifted throughout the American colonies. The British army, in particular, encouraged blacks to leave slavery and often freed or forcibly impressed slaves from American farms and plantations. American slaveholders tended to accuse the British of "carrying off" their property, but this fiction was designed to satisfy lawyers' and planters' egos, for the truth remains that thousands of slaves aggressively escaped from their masters at the earliest opportunity during the war. In one notable case, a dozen black refugees murdered a slave owner who tried to recover his runaway slaves, under British protection in New York City, in 1782.[16] In fact, the extent of the slave resistance to slavery during the Revolution has only recently become a mainstay of American historiography. The best recent estimates place the number of fugitive slaves during the war at between ten thousand and twenty thousand.[17]

In addition to those slaves who found an opportunity to flee and escape slavery during the war, male slaves could gain their freedom by fighting. Slaves seized an unprecedented opportunity to free themselves by participating in the war, either by enlisting with the British or by fighting as substitutes for white recruits. The first opportunity emerged with the fateful declaration of Virginia's royal governor, Lord Dunmore, who offered freedom to slaves who would fight for King George in 1775. Later opportunities for slaves included joining with the Black Pioneers, a collection of spies, couriers, guards, pilots, guides, and Indian translators; or with the Black Corps, an auxiliary force of irregulars—as well as service in the British navy or merchant marine.[18] On the Patriot side, fewer blacks participated, but many slaves who took their master's place in numerous state militias during the War for Independence were freed by the state legislatures after the war, and these freed men stayed in the country.[19]

Finally, and most importantly, the logic that allowed Independence enabled slaves, free blacks, and anti-slavery whites to place enormous philosophical pressure on the moral legitimacy of slavery. With the sentiments of "All men are created equal" and the numerous declarations of the natural rights of individuals, the obvious contradictions of slavery loomed large. The notion of men with natural rights gave slaves and former slaves a powerful rhetoric with which to assault the legitimacy of slavery. As early as 1773, a group of blacks in Boston led a precocious attack on slavery based upon the language of rights and liberty that had sounded loudly in Boston for a decade. This represents one of the first times in Western history that slaves challenged the institution of slavery in the abstract, rather than simply asking for their own freedom or the redress of grievances.[20] As we have seen, by 1774 the former slave Caesar Sarter directly connected the American struggle against the British to the slave's struggle against bondage, noting that "the *natural rights and privileges of freeborn men*" seemed particularly applicable to "a poor, though freeborn African, who, in his youth, was trepanned into Slavery."[21] Such sentiments were common, and although whites could never speak with such authority "from experience," the powerful logic that permitted a declaration of independence—that all men have inherent natural rights that they never cede to any authority—dramatically weakened the institution of slavery.

Colonial and Revolutionary governments did not always hear the pleas of blacks and others, but in many states after the war, the belief in the natural rights of man transformed slavery in North America.[22] Slavery in Massachusetts and New Hampshire, although maintained in the first legislatures of those states, was swept away by the judiciary in legal arguments that declared slave status incompatible with the natural rights of individuals.[23] Over ten thousand free men and women were instantly created from mere chattel. The Republic of Vermont, carved from New York and New Hampshire during the war, was created without original sin, for its first constitution specifically forbade slavery, justifying the policy in familiar terms: "that all men are born equally free and independent, and have certain natural, inherent, and unalienable rights."[24]

In other states reflecting a budding belief that slavery was unjust and against the principles of the Revolution, so-called free-womb laws and gradual abolition bills were passed, intended to end slavery in a generation. These laws created a mixed legacy. While gradual abolition bills exalted the principles of the rights of man, they established careful, rather than revolutionary, transformation. By assuring that the children of slaves would labor for masters until their late twenties, the laws essentially compensated masters for their loss of capital. Pennsylvania passed the first such bill in 1780, intended to gradually abolish slavery in twenty-eight years, a system that the state believed had robbed blacks "of the common blessings that they were by nature entitled to."[25] Thomas Paine drafted the preamble. In 1784, declaring that "all men are entitled to life, liberty, and the pursuit of happiness," a Rhode Island law allowed freedom for all the children of slaves after a term of service.[26] But even as these bills weakened slavery by decreasing the numbers of slaves and increasing the numbers of free blacks, under them it would be still be decades before slavery would be completely extinguished. Piecemeal abolition allowed time for masters to migrate with their slaves, or sell their slaves in states with fewer scruples about the rights of man. In Connecticut, a free-womb law was passed in 1784, then another law was needed in 1797, until slavery was finally made illegal in 1848—another revolutionary year.[27]

For states with enslaved populations that represented a significant economic interest of a large minority of the white population, emancipation came gradually and in the face of strong political opposition. New York and New Jersey, states that passed gradual abolition bills in 1799 and 1804, respectively, were the slowest to accept complete emancipation. Both possessed substantial rural planter interests who clung to slavery well into the 1840s, even as urban slavery largely disappeared by the 1810s. These states also experimented with a limited compensation scheme for slave owners who "abandoned" and then maintained black children for a year after their birth. The cost of the program became prohibitive in New York, but it remained in place in New Jersey. Indeed, New Jersey did not officially make slavery illegal until 1865, when it ratified the Thirteenth Amendment.[28]

In states where slavery represented the dominant social system and sustained the state elite, the powerful ideal of the equality of all men could not simply sweep away property interests and prejudice. Nevertheless, in the Chesapeake, where fully one-half of all blacks in America lived in 1776, the principles of the natural rights of man encouraged the slaveholding leadership to hold out the promise of voluntary manumission for slaves. As St. George Tucker remembered, when describing the motives of those who passed the first bill allowing the individual manumission of slaves in Virginia since 1723: "That act was passed at the close of the revolutionary war, when our councils were guided by some of our best and wisest men; men who looked upon the existence of slavery among us not as a blessing but as a national misfortune, and whose benevolence taught them to consider the slave not only as property, but as men."[29] The Virginians called this a "partial emancipation of slavery."[30] Under that law and the encouragement of conscience, the free black population of Virginia grew, from fewer than three thousand to nearly thirty thousand, between 1782 and 1810.[31] More blacks were freed by personal manumission in Virginia than were freed by state abolition in all of the New England states combined. In Maryland and Delaware, similar laws expanded the free black population, with equal speed. The free black population in Maryland grew more than tenfold, to 29,656, from 1776 to 1810, which represented fully 25 percent of all blacks in the state.[32] In Delaware, the free black percentage of the overall black population in the state grew from 30 percent in 1790, to 76 percent in 1810.[33] Nearly one-third of the free blacks in the United States lived in Virginia, Maryland, and Delaware in 1810. The rapid growth of the free black communities in the Upper South was not simply a matter of white benevolence. Freed blacks tended to *free* blacks, as freedmen and women could finally purchase and free their family members once they could earn money outside of slavery.[34] At the same time, the promise or possibility of individual manumission could weaken the ability of slave communities to collectively resist, as they had during the chaos and opportunity of the war.[35]

For many middling and large towns in the Upper South, and for many cities in the Middle States and New England, distinguishable free black communities first emerged in the last decades of the eighteenth century, as manumitted slaves sought employment and protection in communities of their own. By 1810, many towns throughout the country that had never possessed appreciable numbers of free blacks exhibited visible black communities. In Boston, for instance, a black community consisting of nearly eight hundred slaves and a handful of free blacks before the Revolution, grew from natural increase and migration into a free black community of almost fifteen hundred by

1810.[36] Similar trends occurred in New York, Newport, Norfolk, and Baltimore. In Baltimore, in 1800, the free black population reached 10 percent of the total population.[37] In Philadelphia, the free black community grew from two hundred in 1776, to over six thousand at the turn of the eighteenth century.[38] In New York, a free black community of one thousand in 1790 reached nearly thirty-five hundred in 1800, and over seven thousand by 1810.[39]

The growth in the number of free blacks throughout the country corresponded with a growing "Americanization" of the black population of the United States, both enslaved and free. Slave populations in the early eighteenth century were comprised of large numbers of African-born adults, representing many distinct tribal, ethnic, and language groups. By the end of the century, the black populations were dominated by American-born blacks in populations that were more evenly spread throughout coastal regions and into the backcountry of the slaveholding states.[40] The proportion of Africans in South Carolina's adult slave population, for instance, fell dramatically, from 45 percent in 1760, to 9 percent by 1800. This trend was greatly increased by the Revolution, which not only effectively ended the importation of "unseasoned" African slaves but also moved black populations throughout the states, thereby increasing the mingling of blacks who might otherwise have remained more widely separated and more distinct populations.[41] The spread of evangelical Christian religion among enslaved blacks contributed to making black cultural and spiritual life less alien to white society, even as Christianity provided a common spiritual touchstone for American blacks.[42] As one scholar has effectively shown, by the 1790s black Americans "increasingly viewed one another as sharing a racial identity" based upon skin color and African descent.[43]

Among free black communities, the trends are even more easily perceived. In the late eighteenth century, free blacks throughout the country organized themselves consciously as "African-American" communities and participated in the civic life of the cities as eagerly as any immigrant group.[44] Free blacks found solidarity in secular voluntary societies, including the Brown Fellowship Society of Charleston; the Friendly Society of St. Thomas and the Free African Society in Philadelphia; the African Societies of Boston and Providence; and the African Union Society of Newport, Rhode Island, founded during the war in 1780.[45] The famous Prince Hall, a free black veteran of the American Revolution, founded a Masonic lodge in Boston that was chartered by British authorities, after continually being denied a charter by local whites, and he eventually established satellite lodges in Providence and Philadelphia.[46] Even more substantial than the secular organizations of American blacks were the independent black churches, which rapidly provided the major institutional gravity for free black communities throughout the country.[47]

The Promise of Black Citizenship

With the growth of distinct free black communities and new ideological pressure on the institution of slavery, the years immediately following American independence presented a unique opportunity for free blacks eager to claim legitimacy in the new country. Blacks were widely known to have participated in the Revolutionary War effort with honor, and as a people, free blacks could be seen to represent the ideal of the free American—once enslaved, now independent. Free blacks in Boston certainly seized the moment, with a series of petitions to the General Court, first attacking slavery and then attempting to achieve equal citizenship based upon war service, natural rights, and Christian principles of justice.[48]

In the debates over the adoption of a state constitution for Massachusetts Bay, we can espy the early potential for free blacks to be willingly accepted as equal members of the American polity (at least in Massachusetts). Article V of the 1778 draft constitution excluded "negroes, Indians, and mulattoes" from the right to vote. Numerous towns protested this limitation on citizenship, considering it a direct violation of the principles of natural equality. The town of Westminster, in its suggestions for revisions to the proposed constitution, complained that "Article the 5th," which "deprives a part of the humane Race of their Natural Rights, mearly on account of their Couler—Which in our opinion no power on Earth has a Just Right to Doe: therefore ought to be Expunged the Constitution."[49] Upton similarly believed that "every freeman twenty one years of age possessed of suitable property ought to enjoy full right of electing officers of State with other freemen," since "all Nations are made of one blood." Citizenship needed to be equal and "without regard to Nation or Colour."[50] Georgetown ridiculed the notion of restricting the privileges of citizenship to whites, and wished to reject the constitution "because in the Fifth a Man being born in Africa, India or ancient American or even being much Sun burnt deprived him of having a vote for Representative."[51] The 1778 constitution was rejected by a majority of the towns for many reasons, but this exclusionary fifth article was an important one, and it was not included in the 1780 constitution, which Massachusetts adopted.

The possibility of a trend toward a racially inclusive body politic in the newly independent United States was also reflected in the debates over citizenship requirements in the Articles of Confederation.

In the summer of 1778, as the Articles were being debated, a delegate from South Carolina moved to amend the fourth fundamental article, which read: "The free inhabitants of each of these States, paupers, vagabond, and fugitives from justice, excepted, shall be entitled to all the privileges and immunities of free citizens in the several States." He attempted to insert the word "white" before "inhabitants," to effectively assure that America would be a white nation from its first organization. With only two states supporting the amendment, one state divided, and eight states voting against the amendment, the Articles of Confederation provided U.S. citizenship to free blacks in numerous states. In the midst of war, free black Americans who pledged allegiance to the cause were more fully citizens of the United States than they would be by 1800.[52]

The potential of equal citizenship for black Americans in a nation of newly independent states diminished as the necessities of the war movement merged into the problems of nation-building and, ironically, as slavery became less of a national fact and more of a "peculiar institution." The first evidence that the dual problems of slavery and race would continue to bedevil the new republic emerged as the Confederation government dealt with the prospect of eventual expansion. In 1784, as the Congress devised a system of settlement and governance of the Western territories, a committee headed by Thomas Jefferson presented a plan to divide the West into states, each of which would be equally accepted into the Confederation as their populations increased. One added provision restricted slavery in *any* of the new Western states after 1800, but this provision failed to pass because one of the delegates from New Jersey was at home sick in bed. The vote reflected a clearly sectional character, with Jefferson and only one other Southern delegate voting for the provision. When a similar attempt was made in 1785 to exclude slavery from all the Western territories, the slaveholding interest had taken precautions to assure such a provision would not be supported. North Carolina, when ceding its Western territory to the United States, attached a proviso forbidding Congress to regulate slavery in the new territory. The attempt in 1785 received only limited support.[53] With slaveholders interested in protecting the institution of slavery in part of the West, the U.S. Congress, in the Northwest Ordinance of 1787, finally only excluded slavery from the Western lands north of the Ohio River, and in doing so, they also assured that fugitive slaves escaping into the Northwest Territory could be regained by slaveholders. By 1787, the political logic of national unity already necessitated the use of federal power to support the principles of slavery.[54]

Nevertheless, the passage of the Northwest Ordinance was not the final word on the place of slavery and race in the United States, as black Americans struggled for equality and white Americans struggled with the problems presented by their principles, politics, and prejudice. In fact, the trends among the literate elite in the Upper South, Middle States, and New England was shifting strongly toward principled anti-slavery, as evidenced by a rapid growth of secular anti-slavery societies, which grew from two in 1785, to twenty by 1792, with organizations as far south as Virginia. The 1780s also saw the birth of a number of literary and political magazines intended to provide a distinctly American voice in the popular world of eighteenth-century magazines. These new publications, including Noah Webster's *American Magazine,* the *Columbian Magazine,* and the *New-York Magazine,* published by the brothers James and Thomas Stone, were filled with essays, anecdotes, polemics, and poems opposed to slavery and the slave trade.[55] In Philadelphia, Mathew Carey alone almost single-handedly created a national forum for the discussion of slavery with the publication of the *American Museum.* The November 1789 issue included a character sketch of the Creoles of St. Domingue by Moreau de St. Mery; an essay on the education of black children; a "Plan for improving the condition of free blacks" by Benjamin Franklin; a statement on the slave trade in Kingston, Jamaica; and an illustration of a muzzle designed as a punishment for recalcitrant slaves.[56]

For publications with a broadly anti-slavery message intended for a purely American audience, the most common theme emphasized the gulf between American principles and the continued existence of slavery in the United States. In the late 1780s and early 1790s, it was common for American essayists and orators to blame the cruelty and injustice of the Old World for the presence of slavery in the New World. With Independence and the principles that justified the destruction of the colonial system, polemicists of the new country saw a spectacular opportunity to complete the exorcism of tyrannical institutions from American life. As the Union was refashioned in the late 1780s, an emerging anxiety to eradicate this blight on American character fueled the energies of numerous American anti-slavery writers in this early period. Slavery was simply un-American.[57] A free black writing as "Othello" from Baltimore struck the common theme. Othello called the continued existence of slavery in America "the most abandoned apostasy that ever took place" since God created the world.[58] Noting that America was born of the principle "that all men are by nature and of right ought to be free," he maintained that the continued example of slavery in the United States violated the cause of humanity, wounded justice, and polluted "national honor deeply and lastingly."[59]

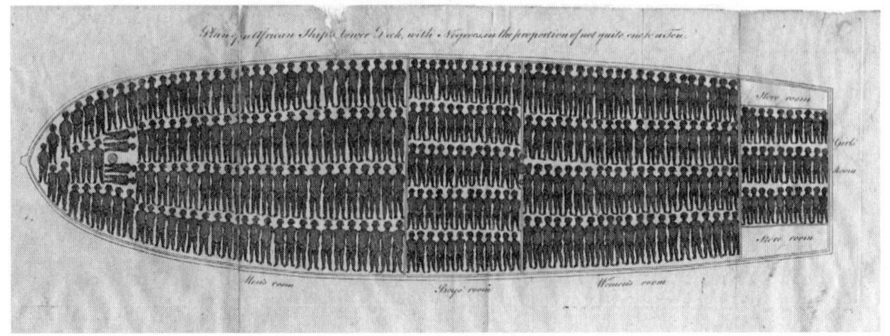

FIGURE 4. This broadside, published as a supplement for Mathew Carey's *American Magazine,* was the first dramatic engraving of a slave ship published in America—an enduring image of men and women, boys and girls, stacked row upon row that is still used to teach the horrors of the Middle Passage. (Courtesy of the American Antiquarian Society)

The Politics of Slavery and the Problem of Union

Within weeks of the first meeting of Congress in 1789, the Virginian Josiah Parker made the first attempt to encourage the new Congress to take steps to end the slave trade, with an eye toward ending slavery forever in the United States. Parker moved to insert a provision for a tax of $10 on every slave imported to the United States into a general revenue bill that established duties on numerous imports, from mirrors to "crockery-ware." Parker made his intentions clear. He was not really interested in revenue, but in ending the expansion of slavery, using all congressional influence to weaken slavery itself in an effort "to restore to human nature its inherent privileges, and if possible wipe off the stigma that America labored under."[60] He spoke very much in the spirit of the public debate that preceded and enveloped his moment: slavery was *un-American.* He was "sorry the Constitution allowed importation at all," as he had concluded that slavery was "contrary to the revolution principles."[61] Americans, he argued, "are justly charged" with "inconsistency in our principles," and the stain on the national reputation would only be removed when "we may show by our actions the pure beneficence of the doctrine we held out to the world in our declaration of independence."[62] His motion was delayed for later discussion.

Later discussion did occur; as a subject for debate, slavery came before Congress numerous times—in bills relating to commerce, naturalization, the slave trade, fugitive slaves, and foreign affairs. These debates in the Congresses of the 1790s reflected the striking fact that an overwhelming majority of senators and representatives claimed to hate both the theory and reality of slavery in the American republic. Fisher Ames often emphasized that "no one could suppose him favorable to slavery, he detested it from his soul."[63] Connecticut's Roger Sherman assured congressmen that his opposition to slavery sprang from "principles of humanity and policy."[64] Pennsylvanian Thomas Scott noted that "if there was neither God nor devil," he would oppose slavery "on principles of humanity, and the law of nature."[65] James Madison called slavery an "evil."[66] Virginian and slave owner Theodorick Bland "had made up his mind upon" slavery, and "wished slaves had never been introduced into America." He noted that "if it was impossible at this time to cure the evil, he was very willing to join in any measures that would prevent its extending further."[67] There were plenty of good intentions to go around.

But Congress settled the problem decisively in 1790, when a number of petitions attacking slavery and the slave trade were presented from Mid-Atlantic Quakers and the Abolition Society of Pennsylvania, whose president was Benjamin Franklin. After much debate, and a referral of the petitions to committee, Congress eventually passed two resolutions which stated that Congress had no power to affect slavery where it existed and no power to end or seriously restrict the slave trade until the constitutionally mandated date of 1808. In addition, Congress entered a large portion of the debate, including the committee report and other resolutions supporting the spirit of the petitions that were never voted down, into the journals, to help clarify any future questions by providing a thicker meaning and context for the sentiments of the House in regard to slavery. Unfortunately, their prudence has not clarified their intentions, for many historians continue to misread this fundamental debate.

With the vast majority of representatives expressing a disdain for slavery both within the halls of Congress and "out of doors," why were so many so willing to let these matters disappear with such dispatch? Some historians have suggested hidden deals and secret compromises, with Northern legislators receiving the concession of assumption in exchange for pledges not to make slavery an issue of national legislation. One historian sees Madison moving like a magician behind the scenes in a sinister plot to bury the problem neatly away.[68] But the truth, although less spectacular, demands considerable attention—namely, that the vast majority of representatives simply did not believe the federal government possessed the constitutional power to affect slavery where it existed: slavery had become a municipal concern. If all the congressmen had wanted to end slavery, perhaps something could be devised, but because some delegates defended slavery, even the most ardent abolitionist could not have successfully made slavery an issue for national legislation, unless the Constitution was amended. There were no secret deals; in fact, there was a common understanding that the general government created by the Constitution possessed *no power* over slavery without the direct cooperation of the slaveholders.

David Brion Davis, among others, misses this fundamental truth by lamenting the decision of 1790 as "a clear victory for the South."[69] But this would only be true with hindsight. In 1790, slavery still flourished in New York and New Jersey, and not a single slave had been freed by the gradual emancipation bill of Pennsylvania. In fact, the delegates from the two most southern states, Georgia and South Carolina, who decried the tone and implications of the committee report, had failed at each step of the debate: in February, they had failed to stop the memorials of the Quakers from being sent to committee; in March, they had failed in their efforts to amend the committee report in all the particulars they desired; and finally, they had also failed in their efforts to stop the hated committee report from being entered in the journals.

The debate was never about whether Congress had power to affect the institution of slavery. *Everyone* agreed—with the possible exception of the petitioners—that it did not, especially without the cooperation of American slaveholders. In fact, most delegates, including James Madison, Josiah Parker, and Elias Boudinot, could not understand the root of the fears expressed by the delegates from Georgia and South Carolina. As Boudinot emphasized, "There certainly is no foundation for the apprehension which seems to prevail in gentlemen's minds."[70] Massachusetts congressman Theodore Sedgwick showed his belief in the limits of the Constitution and tried to calm Southern fears. He did "not apprehend that any state, or any considerable number of individuals in any state," could be "seriously alarmed at the commitment of the petition, from a fear that congress intend to exercise an unconstitutional authority, in order to violate their rights; I believe there is not a wish of the kind entertained by any member of this body."[71] There is no reason, or evidence, to doubt the sincerity of Sedgwick's assertion.

Even the most forward anti-slavery voices in the House admitted that Congress had *no power* to interfere with local property. Elbridge Gerry offered the most aggressive suggestion of congressional authority to meddle with slavery by arguing that Congress could offer to buy all the slaves of the South, and pay for them with the proceeds of Western land sales. But even he did not believe the Congress could *force* slaveholders to sell their slaves to the government, suggesting rather that the government could "make a proposal to the Southern States."[72] Another adamant anti-slavery voice who wished Congress to do all that was constitutionally possible to stop the slave trade admitted that he "was sorry that the framers of the constitution did not go farther, and enable us to interdict it for good and all." This legislator recognized that "in our legislative capacity, we can go no further than to impose a duty of ten dollars [on imported slaves]."[73]

Because scholars have been tempted to believe that numerous representatives in 1790 thought the national government *could* do something about slavery, they have made the wrong conclusions about the failure of Congress to move against the institution and agree to a positive assertion of the limits of congressional power in regard to slavery. As with the passage of the Eleventh Amendment by overwhelming numbers in 1793, the vast majority of congressmen and the American people were highly suspicious of the power of the federal government to meddle in the internal affairs of the American citizenry.

The limits of federal power to affect slavery crystallized during the debate, as slave owners successfully positioned slavery as a purely *local,* municipal issue. Early in the debate, Roger Sherman of Connecticut attempted to emphasize the national scope of the problem of slavery in America by calling for a committee with a member from each state, because, as he noted, "several states had already made some regulations on this subject."[74] But his suggestion was resoundingly rejected, as Southern speakers underlined the local aspect of slave property. James Jackson asked the House to "respect the members who represent that part of the Union which is principally to be affected."[75] Michael Jenifer Stone of Maryland similarly rejected the righteousness of the Quakers and others who lived to meddle "with concerns in which they had nothing to do."[76] Aedanus Burke represented slavery as a problem of local property, and warned that "the rights of the southern states ought not to be threatened, and their property endangered, to please people who are unaffected by the consequences."[77] William Loughton Smith, a defender of Hamiltonian nationalism in issues of finance, rejected congressional interference and queried incredulously, "Will Congress and those states not concerned in the event, undertake to decide for those states who are?" Such an arrogant assumption of federal power would be "an interference with their local politics, which congress" is "prevented by the Constitution."[78]

But the Deep Southerners most successfully defined slavery as a purely local issue by their *unique* pro-slavery voice. The representatives of Georgia and South Carolina exhibited the only overtly pro-slavery arguments, and they permeated their speeches with a deeply racist feeling. In the 1789 debate over a proposed tariff on imported slaves, Congressman James Jackson of Georgia exhibited typical contempt for anti-slavery voices. He began rather innocently, acknowledging the latest fashion in the House for "the enchanting sound of liberty" and recognizing that polite people tended to "favor the liberty of slaves." Such idealism was perhaps to be expected in this Revolutionary Age, he argued, but there existed "a great distinction between the *subjects* of liberty." When a white man enjoyed liberty, it was a great blessing—but what would happen if a slave was freed? Would a black freed person "work for a living"? No, he answered. The experiment had been made in Maryland, and the freed blacks there were no more than "common pickpockets." He thought that "the sound of liberty would lose its charms" when white men lived among free blacks.[79]

The commitment to slavery was the distinguishing feature of the delegates from South Carolina and Georgia. No legislator from either state could appear in Congress if his support for slavery was doubtful. When the Northern-born and outspoken critic of slavery, David Ramsay, ran in the Charleston District in the mid-1790s, he only received the support of the great families after giving "unequivocal assurances" during numerous interviews that he would never support the introduction of federal emancipation legislation.[80] The maintenance and extension of slavery quickly became the most important issue for legislators from these two states. In 1800, when a number of free blacks in Pennsylvania petitioned Congress for a repeal of the Fugitive Slave Act of 1793, complaining of the kidnapping of free blacks and praying to Congress to take steps to "prepare the way for the oppressed to go free," Georgia congressman James Jones declared that he "did not think [slavery] is any evil," and in respect to those members who wanted to table the petition, he wanted the petition "thrown under the table."[81] South Carolina's John Rutledge Jr. mocked "the black *gentlemen*" who complained that "these people are in slavery—I thank God they are!"[82] In 1803, before the slave trade was nationally ended in 1808, South Carolina reopened its slave trade and became the only slave-importing state in the United States, a sign of the state's early alienation from the trends of the Union.[83]

Many congressmen were struck dumb that Americans would readily *defend* slavery. Pennsylvania's Thomas Scott called one diatribe "*a Phenomenon in Politics.*"[84] Certainly men were expected to be cautious, but aggressively pro-slavery voices were rarely heard in the great national discussion of slavery until these Southern politicians arrived on the national stage. Some similar sentiments had been expressed at the Constitutional Convention, but the happenings of the convention were not public. The pro-slavery speeches made in the Congress exposed the gulf between the attitudes of some of that body's members.[85] Since much of the national debate had begun with the understanding that slavery was against the principles of the Revolution—that slavery was un-American—the defiance of the legislators from Georgia and South Carolina revealed a challenge that many anti-slavery voices had never imagined until the congressional debates over slavery. More distasteful than the attacks on the Quakers were the positive assertions by South Carolina's William Loughton Smith that "slavery was so ingrafted into the policy of the Southern States, that it could not be eradicated without tearing up the roots of their happiness, tranquility and prosperity."[86] Slavery, it seems, was not so un-American after all. Anti-slavery congressmen needed to choose between American Union and slavery. As far as William Smith was concerned, the choice had already been made. As he noted, "The Northern states adopted us with our slaves, and we adopted them with their Quakers."[87] It was obvious: the American Union existed because slavery was allowed to exist.

After 1794, a growing majority of the representatives supported motions that would make the issue go away as quickly as possible. Once Congress agreed that slavery largely existed as a problem of the states, legislators began to simply dismiss petitions from abolition societies, free blacks, or Quakers out of hand. Most of the men may have been against slavery, but they were not abolitionists; they tended to be content to call slavery unnatural and leave the problem to the slaveholders.

A good example can be seen in the attempt by the state of Delaware to obtain federal help in defeating the "mischievous practice" of the kidnapping of free blacks. Delaware possessed strong state laws discouraging the kidnapping of free blacks by unscrupulous slave traders—a convicted kidnapper would have his ears pinned and cut off—but the proximity of the Delaware River and the Chesapeake Bay made enforcement extremely difficult.[88] The petition of Delaware was originally referred to the Committee of Commerce and Manufactures, whose anti-slavery chair, John Swanwick, developed a policy—apparently without organizing a full committee meeting—requiring all ship captains to carry documentation listing the exact number and condition of all blacks on board their ships. He hoped "the measure would not at all be opposed," because "our unfortunate negroes and mulattoes are exposed by their color to much insult." He noted that "if these people were black or white" did not matter, if they were free "they ought to be protected in their enjoyment of their freedom, not only by the State legislatures but by the General Government."[89] Here was another chance for the national government to assure that free blacks were to be protected by the national government, as any American citizen.

Immediately, however, some representatives began to complain.

Joshua Coit, from Connecticut, "wished to know whether it was necessary for the United States to intermeddle with this," since he believed the state laws were adequate to address the problem. Coit was supported by the usual suspects. South Carolina's William Loughton Smith announced that he thought the representatives should adjourn and "get rid of the business altogether."[90] Any issue relating to free blacks and slavery "was altogether a municipal regulation" and "therefore ought to be left to the State legislatures to settle."[91] Others, including William Vans Murray of Maryland and North Carolina's Nathaniel Macon, agreed with Coit and Smith, and they took action to assure that the issue would vanish. First, they orchestrated a postponement. When Swanwick brought the issue to the floor again, it was resubmitted to committee, and this time Smith and Coit attended the committee meeting. The next report out of committee presented a short resolution to the House which simply asserted that it was "not expedient for this House to interfere with any existing law of the States on this subject."[92] The issue disappeared.

By the end of the decade, congressional dismissals of the problem of slavery and the status of free blacks in the states had become reflexive. In 1800, when the leaders of the free black community in Philadelphia introduced their petition calling for the repeal of the Fugitive Slave Act of 1793, the end of kidnapping abuses, and the gradual emancipation of all slaves, the petition was dismissed with prejudice. Only George Thatcher, from Massachusetts, voted against the resolution to condemn the petition.[93] Thatcher based his opposition on a belief that the national government possessed jurisdiction over this matter, and he noted defiantly that his vote against dismissing the petition signified his belief that "the House had a right to take up the subject, and give it a full, free, and deliberate discussion." With great understatement, he concluded, "This did not appear to be the general opinion."[94] It was not, and never had been.

By the middle of the 1790s, any mention of slavery brought excited complaints about the dangers of even discussing the issue, and events in the West Indies precipitated a quick end to the national debate. The revolution in St. Domingue spooked white Southerners and Northerners alike, and the reformers in Congress lost the chamber even as a place to debate the problems attendant to slavery. In the first years of the Congress, James Madison and many others were quite willing to discuss the problem of slavery in the United States. In the debate over a proposed tariff on slaves in 1789, Madison even highlighted the importance of debating the issue in the House, saying that he welcomed "an opportunity of evidencing their sentiments, on the policy and humanity of" the slave trade, and that, in fact, he believed "the dictates of humanity, the principles of the people, the national safety and happiness, and prudent policy requires it of us."[95] As we have seen, however, by 1794, when the subject of slavery was introduced during the debate over the naturalization bill, Madison was imploring the Congress to cease frivolous discussion of the issue. Arguing that "the operation of reducing the number of slaves was going on as quickly as possible" in Virginia, Madison declared that any talk of congressional interest in weakening slavery "had a very bad effect" on the slaves themselves.[96] Not only did Congress have no power to deal with slavery, by the middle of the decade they had no stomach for a discussion of slavery.

So it quickly became clear, after Congress affirmed in 1790 that it possessed no jurisdiction over the institution of slavery, that the nation's legislators would do little more than wring their hands and count the days until they could outlaw the importation of slaves into America. The most active effort the Congress undertook in regard to slavery was to strengthen the national presence of the institution by passing the Fugitive Slave Act of 1793. The act had risen out of a controversy over the alleged kidnapping of a free black man, his re-enslavement in Virginia, and the inability of the states of Pennsylvania and Virginia to resolve the matter.[97] Pro-slavery interests crafted a fairly strong bill, but the nature of the Union provided little enforcement, and the same demands for local autonomy that assured slavery would remain a local issue limited the ability of the national government to force state courts to take cognizance of cases relating to fugitive slaves. Yet the lack of a clear federal arm essentially gave slaveholders and bounty hunters a license to kidnap free blacks, who were presented to local magistrates or federal judges without the benefit of habeas corpus.[98]

The legislative power of the federal government was not the only national power that could do little to alter slavery and protect free blacks in the states. After the passage of the Eleventh Amendment—which affirmed states' immunity from suit by individual citizens in federal court, and which, as we have seen, was supported by an overwhelming majority of the American citizenry—free blacks were unable to force states to lift local restrictive policies toward them. With states establishing a growing number of limitations on the privileges of free blacks, the inability created by the Eleventh Amendment greatly weakened black options in the face of state power. Free blacks were therefore unable to appeal for the protections of the federal Bill of Rights, and without any way to assure that the states treated all free blacks equally with white citizens, free black national citizenship was placed in constitutional limbo. The U.S. Constitution makes very few direct statements illuminating the precise nature of American citizenship, but Article IV, Section 2 (the Comity Clause), states: "The citizens of each state shall be entitled to all privileges and immunities of citizens in the several states." If free black citizens had been allowed to sue states in federal court, this "privileges and immunities clause" could have potentially served as federal justification to force states to repeal laws that restricted free blacks within their own state.

But without an ability to enforce this clause, free black claims to *national* citizenship were weakened in the nineteenth century. A number of justices in the nineteenth century, reflecting upon the various laws that controlled free blacks throughout the Union, were often quick to conclude that free blacks were not citizens, because, as one justice noted, "Free Negroes, by whatever appellation we may call them, were never in any of the States entitled to all the 'privileges and immunities of citizens,'" as guaranteed to citizens in Article IV, Section 2, of the Constitution.[99] This became more and more evident as the status of white men became gradually more regularized in the nineteenth century. In the 1822 Kentucky case *Amy (a woman of colour) v. Smith*, the claims of "Amy" were denied because "free negroes and mulattoes are, almost everywhere, considered and treated as a degraded race of people; insomuch so, that, under the constitution and laws of the United States, they cannot become citizens of the United States."[100] In the *Dred Scott* case, Justice Taney used the many different laws regulating the lives of free blacks in the different states, and therefore the failure of black citizenship to resemble the promises of the privileges and immunities clause, as important evidence in his denial of U.S. citizenship to American free blacks.[101]

But the persistence of slavery, as well as the status of blacks throughout the country, was never defined only by the power of "states' rights." There was another, equally important truth which guaranteed that the cause of enslaved and free blacks in the United States would not become a subject of national legislation in the early republic. This was the widely held assumption that "Americans" were white.

Imagining a White Community

Even if we dismiss the opinions of those whites who believed blacks to be naturally inferior, as white Americans confronted the problem of emancipation, it became increasingly clear that blacks were not thought to be part of the "American" community in all of its imagined manifestations—past, present, and future. The problem was citizenship—in its broadest, republican sense. Being an American meant being part of the sovereign people, sharing in the governing of the state, and having an equal protection of the laws—and blacks were not considered to be part of the sovereign people.

In the 1780s and 1790s, whether or not blacks were inferior to whites was a red herring which spoke more to problems of slavery than citizenship. Benjamin Banneker's talents were more interesting to Jefferson as a curiosity among scientists than as a fact that would change the status of blacks in the United States. Jefferson's comments about black inferiority were widely read, and perhaps even influential, but his opinions about the institution of slavery were considered *as* important, if not more so.[102] When John Adams first perused Jefferson's *Notes on the State of Virginia,* reading them aloud with his daughter and Abigail in a carriage en route to Calais, he noted that "the Passages upon slavery, are worth Diamonds, they will have more effect than Volumes written by mere Philosophers."[103] Edward Long *had* been republished, but not approvingly; his work was presented specifically to be rebutted. Anti-slavery writers could ridicule the notion that blacks were inferior to whites as a way to challenge slavery, but such barbs did little to ease the real problem, as understood by Southern slaveholders: what to do with the freed slaves.

Even among those liberal-minded planters who decried the institution of slavery, the notion of free blacks living as equal citizens among whites seemed dangerous and deadly. It was not black *freedom,* but black *citizenship,* that was the fundamental sticking point. No serious plan for the emancipation of slaves could be contemplated in the United States if the freed blacks were to remain in the midst of white society as equal American citizens. Even if blacks could be shown to be equal to whites, Jefferson believed blacks could not live as equal citizens among whites—he had equally important "political" reasons to accompany his "physical and moral reasons," that touched upon the inferiority of blacks.[104] Like Locke, Jefferson could imagine absolute slavery to be nothing more than "a state of war" between enemies, but Jefferson worried whether emancipation could be equated with a general armistice.[105] Jefferson's *Notes* explained the problem as one of mutual animosity. The differences between the whites and blacks would divide Virginia into parties and "produce convulsions which will probably never end but in the extermination of either one or the other race."[106]

Ferdinando Fairfax, another earnest, enlightened member of the Virginia planter class, published the first complete (although short) plan for the emancipation of slaves in the *American Museum* in 1790. His work, which agreed with Jefferson on the "political" problem of incorporating blacks as equal citizens, helps delineate the general tenor of the times and the white problem with equal black citizenship. He began his essay by noting, "This subject, has afforded, in conversation, a wide field for argument, or rather, speculation, both to the friends and opposers of emancipation." He perceived two distinct sides in the debate, with those in favor pleading "natural right and justice, which are considered as paramount to every other consideration," while those opposed urge "respect both to the community and to those who are the objects proposed to be benefited." He believed that by appealing to "the cool and deliberate judgment" of his fellow citizens, he could help navigate between both positions.[107]

Any emancipation, he declared, would need to be gradual and must compensate the slaveholders. No government could pay the cost of a full compensation of the slaves, so emancipation would also have to be voluntary—and freed blacks could not be allowed to remain in white society. "It is equally agreed," Fairfax emphasized, stressing the accepted nature of his comments, "that if emancipated, it would never do to allow them *all* the privileges of citizens." If the government took such a rash act, free blacks would quickly form "a separate interest from the rest of the community." But that was not the only problem. Fairfax admitted with unusual candor the limitations of white benevolence in the 1780s and 1790s. Whites simply could not live among blacks. As he noted, "There is something very repugnant to the general feelings, even the thought of their being allowed that free intercourse, and the privileges of intermarriage with the white inhabitants, which the other freemen of our country enjoy, and which only *can* form one common interest." Many things, including "the remembrance of their former situation, and a variety of other considerations, forbid this privilege." "And as a proof," Fairfax continued, "where is the man of all those who have liberated their slaves, who would marry a son or daughter to one of them? And if he would not, who would?" Ultimately, it was "these prejudices, sentiments, or whatever they may be called" that "would be found to operate so powerfully as to be insurmountable."[108]

So the blacks would have to go—but where? Fairfax hoped that America would establish a colony somewhere in Africa, "their native climate," that would be settled under the "auspices and protection of congress." To ensure that the black colonists could govern themselves, Fairfax called for proper education of selected leaders, and the establishment of seminaries "for a like purpose" in the colony itself. He even envisioned a day when the little colony would become "an independent nation."[109]

For St. George Tucker, who developed his plan of emancipation in the years of hopeful opportunity before St. Domingue (in lectures at William and Mary and in an interesting correspondence with Jeremy

Belknap and James Sullivan, ultimately published and presented to the Virginia House of Delegates in 1796), the problem was never the inferiority of blacks, which he doubted, but the evident prejudice of the whites and the seething resentment of the former slaves. Tucker prefaced his plan for gradual emancipation with a familiar complaint, foregrounding the hypocrisy of American idealism. He could not reconcile the fact that "a nation ardent in the cause of liberty," which declared all men equal and independent as "the first article of the foundation of their government," could tolerate the continued existence of slavery.[110]

Tucker attempted to craft a plan most "expedient" for the peculiar habits, manners, and prejudices of the white Virginians. Slaves would be freed gradually, with the children of freed slaves serving until the age of twenty-eight. All freed blacks would be severely restricted in their civil rights, in ways not unlike the ways free blacks would eventually become restricted: no rights to vote or hold office, no property rights, no leases longer than twenty-one years, or rights to marriage, nor right of bearing arms, nor right to be an attorney, or juror, or a witness in court against any white, etc.[111] Lest Tucker's restrictions be seen as base prejudice, he was quick to acknowledge the basic fact of white society in the early republic: "Whoever proposes any plan for the abolition of slavery, will find that he must either encounter, or accommodate himself to prejudice." Tucker chose, as he noted, "the latter." He did not believe blacks and whites could live in peace and equality, so he hoped that "by denying them the most valuable privileges which civil government affords," the freed blacks would be convinced "to seek those privileges in some other climate."[112] They would leave the country of their own free will. Tucker believed the plan would achieve its goal in a little over a century.

Among other broad-minded planters, James Madison also never argued that blacks were inferior to whites, and he believed emancipation of the slaves necessitated "a compleat incorporation" of freedmen into society as citizens. Republican principles demanded no less. But this principle of citizenship was also the problem. The bare fact of racial difference and racial prejudice made any scheme that did not include deportation to some extremely distant land utterly unworkable. In familiar terms, he noted that emancipation and then citizenship for freed blacks in Virginia was "rendered impossible by the prejudice of the whites, prejudices which proceeding principally from the difference in colour must be considered as permanent and insuperable."[113] Madison maintained this position throughout his life. The real problem of equal black citizenship in the United States is reflected by the unwillingness of the leading white Americans of the early republic, even when they did not think blacks to be inherently inferior to whites, to even consider the possibility that blacks and whites could live together as equal citizens.[114] But it was also limited by their extreme vision of citizenship in the United States. These "prejudices, sentiments, or whatever they may be called," limited the imagination of the white nation at a crucial moment in the history of slavery.

The limits of white imagination were not only found south of Mason and Dixon's line. Consider the thoughts of Oliver Wolcott Sr. when he learned of the long debates that accompanied the Quaker/Franklin petitions against slavery and the slave trade in 1790: "I wish myself that Congress would prefer the white people of this country to the blacks. After they have taken care of the former, they may amuse themselves with the other people. The African trade is a scandalous one; but let us take care of *ourselves* first."[115] Here what is implied is as significant as what is explicit. The black people of the country were not the crucial interest of the American Congress. Congress should deal with white people: "let us take care of *ourselves* first." Here Wolcott does not eagerly wish anybody harm, but blacks were simply not imagined to be Americans: it was a white nation.

Similar assumptions about the whiteness of the American people abound in the early republic. The Naturalization Law of 1790, for instance, shows the common bias of the times. This law, already recognized as one the most advanced and progressive invitations to citizenship the world had seen at the time of its drafting, came with a very large caveat: it applied only to "free white persons"—a limitation that was not debated or discussed (at least no evidence of controversy exists), or seen to give offense to any member of Congress. At one level, the fact that it needed to be stated represented an awareness of the type of citizens the act expected to create, but the fact that it elicited no interrogation, among a group of legislators who meticulously debated the precise language of every act, speaks volumes about the basic assumptions of the leadership of the United States. If the defense of slavery reflected an overt racism and commitment to slavery, this lack of interest reflected a racist indifference to the status of blacks in the new American nation. The Naturalization Bill of 1790 also reflected the legislators' concerns about what kind of nation America would become, and a policy of only naturalizing white persons guaranteed that Indians and blacks would not be welcomed as future equal citizens. This vision was effectively ratified in the Militia Act of 1792, which prohibited blacks from participating in American militias, one of the most potent symbols of male citizenship in the new American republic.

Another example of the common indifference with the status of free blacks in the United States can be found in Jedidiah Morse's school geography texts. Morse placed great hope in the power of national geographies to create proper "citizens of a free and independent nation," and he used his books to encourage American youth with a sense of their national identity.[116] Morse himself was deeply committed to anti-slavery principles, and included lengthy attacks on the slave system in his geography texts. In his early school texts, he inserted a large section on Hector St. John de Crèveceour's *Letters of an American Farmer* (1778), which described a punished slave being eaten alive by crows and ravens while dangling in a cage.[117] His little school geographies dominated the American geography textbook market for fifty years and probably represent one of the most widely circulated anti-slavery texts before *Uncle Tom's Cabin.*

But even as he offered a scathing critique of slavery, Morse emphasized the whiteness of the American citizenry. As he wrote, the American nation "is composed of almost all nations, languages, characters and religions, which *Europe* can furnish."[118] In another place, he explained that the majority of Americans were "Anglo-Americans," but "intermingled with the Anglo-Americans are the Dutch, Scotch, Irish, French, Germans, Swedes and Jews"—no mention of either Africans or Indians as being part of the American people, even though both were ever present in the early republic—even in Charlestown, Massachusetts, where Morse wrote.[119] In fact, Morse celebrated the liberality of Boston's public schools, at which, he noted with his emphasis, "the children of *every* class of citizens freely associate."[120] But Boston public schools were not accessible to the city's free blacks, despite the taxes paid by blacks to maintain them.[121] Even worse, Morse consistently highlighted the degraded natures of American Indians and Africans, and reinforced common prejudices about the superiority of white beauty.[122] The American people remained something quite distinct from the people of color in their midst. For Morse, and for most white Americans, only whites were wanted for the great republican experiment.[123]

It was this soft racism of elision and indifference, along with the overt racism of retrenchment offered by the slaveholding class, that helped sustain the denization of free blacks throughout the United States, and that assured that black rights would not, and could not, become an issue for national legislation. The flurry of debates concerning slavery and the status of the American blacks that arose in the years surrounding the creation, ratification, and first implementation of the U.S. Constitution opened the possibility that Americans could solve the dilemma of slavery as they joined in a new national compact, but the sectional politics that necessitated a persistence of the very Union the Constitution created relegated the issue of slavery to the "municipal concerns" of the states. Many Americans considered slavery to be against the fundamental character of their republican principles, even un-American, but very few imagined blacks to be Americans. Without a national policy intended to ameliorate the condition of blacks, either enslaved or free, the states were left to follow the paths of interest and prejudice, in a country increasingly aware that "Americans" meant "white persons." The same impulses that led to the celebration of reason and scientific inquiry, the same humanism that extolled individual rights and human decency, could just as easily serve the interests of oppression and domination when wielded by a master class eager to retain their privileged status in the face of an indifferent or defeated citizenry. Men possessed not only a natural right to liberty, but also a natural right to property, and the American slaveholding class had the will and the power to assure that *their* rights were not endangered.

As the states began constructing racial ranks within the American citizenry, the abolition societies that had spread so rapidly from 1785 to 1792 began to lose their focus. In 1794, a national meeting of the American abolition societies—a meeting that represents the culmination of the great national discussion over slavery—helped pass a national bill that banned American citizens from participating in the international slave trade. But by 1798 the national convention of these societies found them mired and sinking. Slavery was no longer a national issue, and where it was a local concern, slaveholders were reasserting their controls. No New England societies participated in the national convention after 1798, and the societies of Maryland and Virginia disappeared in the face of local restrictions and insults.[124] By 1800, the first *national* American abolition movement was in its death throes.[125]

The Denization of Black Americans

From 1783 to 1820 and beyond, states and municipalities throughout the Union continued to restrict the privileges of free blacks; gradually, black citizens were reduced to mere denizens. As the necessity for slave labor increased with Eli Whitney's invention of the cotton gin, many states began reconstructing the slave societies they had partially dismantled in the 1780s. In states where a slaveholding class held political power, free blacks were seen as an increasing threat to planter dominance and the slave-labor system. In states less resigned to slavery, free blacks still felt the effect of living in a country that depended upon slavery, and they were also subject to increasingly intrusive regulation by the state, as white laborers defended their prerogatives against a growing and ambitious free black population. The new states that opened in the West over the first few decades of the nineteenth century similarly restricted the lives and property of free blacks.

Among slaveholding states, a typical action in this era was the clarification of opportunities for the rapidly growing free black communities of the early republic. In 1787, for instance, Delaware moved to stop enslaved blacks in their state from being sold—a practice that had been abused to include the kidnapping of free blacks. But they also ensured that the blacks remaining in the state would be denizens, not citizens. As "An act to prevent the exportation of slaves and for other purposes" noted: "Manumitted slaves shall not vote, nor hold office, nor give evidence against whites, nor enjoy any other rights of a freeman other than hold property and to obtain redress in law and equity for any injury to his or her person or property."[126] One of the "other purposes" noted in the title of the bill included a provision for transporting any free black convicted of stealing a horse to the West Indies.[127]

None of the slaveholding states allowed blacks to testify against whites, in either criminal or civil trials, and many allowed slaves, without oath, to testify against free blacks. In 1799, in an apparent fit of benevolence, Delaware allowed free blacks to give evidence at court "in certain cases," as long as "no white was present."[128] Tennessee passed a law forbidding free blacks from testifying against whites as early as 1794, even before it was organized as a state.[129] The lack of ability to defend oneself in court presented serious problems for free blacks in Virginia, Maryland, Georgia, South Carolina, and North Carolina, because in each of these states free blacks could be sold into slavery as punishment for certain crimes.[130] The color line moved west with the country, as new states quickly reinforced the denization of free blacks that characterized the East. Laws prohibiting the testimony of free blacks in cases involving whites were eventually passed in Ohio, Indiana, Illinois, Louisiana, Iowa, Nebraska, Texas, California, and Oregon.[131]

In white Kentucky society, which emphasized personal honor and reputation among the male citizenry, free blacks were denied access to the personal code. A law of 1793 declared that any free colored person who lifted "his or her hand in opposition to any person not being a Negro" could be held and punished by a justice of the peace, without trial, with thirty lashes.[132] Similarly, blacks were forbidden to bear arms and buy guns without a license in numerous states. In 1840, the North Carolina legislature passed a statute forbidding free blacks to own bowie knives without a permit from the state.[133]

Hundreds of municipalities forbade blacks from attending public schools, and many restricted the organization of private free black schools. In 1833, Connecticut forbade the establishment of schools for blacks, noting that such institutions would "tend to the great increase of the colored population of the State, and thereby to the injury of the people."[134]

Numerous states enacted laws against miscegenation, promising to void any marriages between people of different races. Massachusetts passed such a law in 1786 and imposed a penalty of fifty pounds on any minister found joining a "white person with any negro, Indian or mulatto."[135] After being organized as a state in 1820, Maine passed a similar statute in 1821.[136] North Carolina, Kentucky, Tennessee, and eventually Indiana, Michigan, Illinois, Iowa, Kansas, Florida, Texas, and the Washington Territory, passed similar laws.[137] In 1807, Delaware also forbade the marriage of blacks and whites, and instituted a penalty against any white woman who gave birth to a mixed-race child. Of course, the legislature also enacted a fine for white men who fornicated with black women, but with a flourish born of utter mendacity, it added a proviso to the bill which declared that "no negro's evidence be received on such cases."[138] A rape of a white woman by a black man was a capital offense in many states, and again, in many of them, black testimony was not allowed. In the early republic, New Englanders exhibited a lurid fascination with the raping of white women by black men, publishing a series of gallows accounts of the final moments of convicted black rapists.[139]

The general lack of black suffrage amplified the effect of special restrictions on the rights of free blacks. After the ratification of the U.S. Constitution, free blacks could vote in North Carolina, New York, New Jersey, Pennsylvania, Massachusetts, Rhode Island, New Hampshire, Delaware, Maryland, and Vermont.[140] In the face of a growing free black community, Delaware restricted the franchise to white men in 1792, Maryland similarly clarified its regulations in 1809, and North Carolina corrected the "oversight" in its constitution of 1835. In 1807, New Jersey closed the gaping loopholes in its original constitution that permitted blacks, aliens, and women to vote.[141] The extent of black voting in Pennsylvania is unclear: a judge in 1835 declared that free blacks were not allowed to vote because of a decision of 1795.[142] In the 1838 Pennsylvania constitution, the vote was limited to free white men. One exception to the general lack of black power at the polls is New York State, in which a black voting bloc in New York City became an important arm of the remaining Federalist Party. After 1800, the blacks of New York voted consistently with the Federalists against a Republican organization in deep national alliance with Southern slaveholders. Beginning in 1808, with additional attempts in 1811 and 1816, the Republican/Democratic Party in New York City, led by the mechanic interest and Tammany Hall, attempted to restrict the black vote by creating increasingly complex registration procedures for free blacks. In 1821, in convention to design a new state constitution, following the Tammany argument that blacks were "degraded, dependant and unfit to exercise" the vote, New York extended the franchise to all white male citizens, but placed a $250 freehold requirement on free blacks, destroying the black voting bloc in New York.[143]

But in spite of the increasing marginalization of free blacks in American society, black Americans, enslaved and free, continued to resist the trend by appealing to the natural rights of individuals. Free blacks claimed an inheritance of the principles of the American Revolution eagerly, and they rejected white attempts to limit the promises of natural rights to themselves. The consolidation and organization of free black communities in churches and voluntary societies in the North continued apace, and these organizations provided a critique of white assumptions. The free black community of Philadelphia, united by Absalom Jones of the African Methodist Episcopal Church and Richard Allen of Bethel Church, began to take on the rudiments of a national leadership of free blacks in the United States as they combined their influence in voluntary and humane societies and Masonic lodges.[144] Jones and Allen defended the black community of Philadelphia against spurious attacks on their character during the yellow fever epidemic in the city in 1793, and included in their pamphlet an attack on slavery.[145] They combined their influence with the cause of abolition societies, fugitive slaves, and the free black communities of New York, Boston, Newport, and Baltimore, and petitioned Congress in 1797 and 1800 to overturn the Fugitive Slave Act of 1793 and end national slavery.[146] Although these efforts failed, Philadelphia's black community would continue to hold a national appeal and presence in the minds of American blacks.[147]

But deep in a resurgent slave society, the only redress for free black communities was supplication, and the tone of petitions in the Lower South reflected a deep awareness of the racial hierarchy that characterized slave society. As one group of Charleston free black petitioners in the early 1790s admitted:

> Your Memorialists do not presume to hope that they shall be put on an equal footing with the Free white citizens of the State in general they only humbly solicit such indulgence as the Wisdom and Humanity of this Honorable House shall dictate in their favor by repealing the clauses the act aforementioned, and substituting such a clause as will effectually Redress the grievances

> which your Memorialists humbly submit in this their Memorial but under such restrictions as to your Humble House shall seem proper.[148]

The petitioners had much to complain about. The Negro Act of 1740 denied free blacks in South Carolina the protections of the courts granted to white citizens. Blacks could not give testimony in the courts for recovery of debts, were denied the protection of the courts in cases of fraud and perjury, and could not give testimony for the state in criminal prosecutions. Free blacks did not receive jury trials and were subject to testimony against them by slaves without oath, an obviously prejudicial position. But even this polite petition, which did not ask for free blacks to "be put on an equal footing with the Free white citizens of the State," was rejected without comment in the Carolina legislature.[149]

In many states, as laws restricting the rights of free blacks were imposed and old laws strengthening the slave regime were reimposed with sinister efficiency, the options for peaceful black resistance nearly disappeared. The desperate status of many free blacks in the United States could be eluded only by escaping from the status of Negro altogether, a prospect often available to mulattoes and light-skinned blacks, but only if their parentage remained hidden. It is unknown, and probably unknowable, exactly how many individuals escaped from their status by simply "blending in" to the often heavily mixed populations of the cities and frontier of the republic—and the increasing anonymity of American life in the early republic certainly offered such a route to some Americans of color. But as a form of individual resistance (although such disappearance gave the lie to the racial justifications of difference, and therefore undermined the philosophies of the white supremacists), blending in did little for the status of blacks as a distinct group, and certainly did not present a public challenge to the accepted denigration of black Americans.[150]

Alternatively, enslaved and free blacks could appeal to Revolutionary principles and outright war to hope for an end to slavery and for equality with the whites. White citizens certainly feared such a possibility. Slave rebellion had long haunted the minds of slaveholders in North America, but the thought of slaves shouting "liberty and equality" while slitting the necks of the planter class excited new and all too familiar dangers. The rebellion in St. Domingue, which produced thousands of white refugees with lurid tales of slave revolt, helped encourage the denization of free blacks and the renewed restrictions of the slave regime. The white nightmare was nearly realized in 1800 in Virginia, when the enslaved artisan Gabriel conspired to overthrow the Virginia slave regime with pikes and the principles of the rights of man.[151]

Gabriel's Conspiracy was perhaps the most ambitious slave uprising contemplated in American history. Gabriel envisioned not only the freeing of the slaves, but a grand revolt that would include the assistance of poor whites and a few mysterious French veterans of the American Revolution.[152] On the eve of the rebellion, Gabriel had hundreds of slaves ready to revolt, and "he expected the poor white people would also join him."[153] Once the revolution began, Gabriel intended to carry a silk banner proclaiming "death or Liberty"—a nice inversion of Patrick Henry's famous speech, perhaps a recognition of the odds of success—and to kill all the whites in Richmond, except presumably the poor whites helping him, and the "Quakers, Methodists, and French people."[154] Once Richmond fell, with the wharfs burned and the city refortified with armed freedmen, Gabriel's hope was that the white merchants of the town would agree to free the slaves and they would all "dine and drink" together on the day of emancipation.[155]

George Tucker understood the implications of Gabriel's Rebellion in the context of the American and international revolution. Comparing Gabriel and his conspirators to the slaves who fought with Lord Dunmore in 1775, Tucker noted that Dunmore's blacks had fought for "freedom merely as a good," while the current conspirators "also claim it as a right."[156] Indeed, Gabriel and his companions were behaving as Virginians under "slavery" were supposed to behave. They were using the language of revolution that had excited the hemisphere; they wanted their "natural rights" and freedom from slavery. The slave Charles—who carried as much ammunition "as two persons could carry"—explained to a gathering of the rebels, "We have as much right to fight for our liberty as any men."[157] When Gabriel went with quiet dignity to the gallows, on October 7, 1800, he did what the leaders of Virginia had promised to do on July 4, 1776: he gave his life in a struggle for freedom. Twenty-six other slaves soon joined him.[158] By early 1801, things had quieted down a bit, and the only slaves being hanged were the ones caught stealing tobacco.[159] All was back to normal.

Although historians differ as to the relationship between Gabriel's Conspiracy and the free black community of Richmond, slave owners clearly believed that free blacks encouraged slave resistance by example—and often by direct instigation.[160] For the free blacks throughout the country, Gabriel's Rebellion accelerated trends that had begun in the early 1790s: they were not wanted.[161] Virginia continued to systematically strengthen the slave regime and restrict the rights of free blacks. In 1800, the state made slave evidence without oath admissible against free blacks in court and required all free blacks to register with their municipalities.[162] In 1801 the Virginia House forbade trade with any slave on a vessel, and in 1803 it provided for the punishment of any slaves found assembling after dark "at meeting houses and places of religious worship."[163] In 1804, the state banned the Overseers of the Poor from teaching any of the black orphans in their care the three R's—"reading writing or arithmetic."[164] And in the 1805–6 legislative session, the state prohibited free blacks from owning or carrying firearms without a license from the Commonwealth.[165]

Virginian planter abandonment of the Revolutionary principles of the natural rights of man, at least for blacks, became complete with the elimination of voluntary manumission in 1806. The change in policy had been hinted at for a few years, but finally became essential in late 1805, as most delegates believed the country to be on the verge of war with Great Britain.[166] In the 1805–6 session of the Virginia legislature, an active movement within the House attempted to end the possibility of manumission outright, with a bill "To prevent the PARTIAL emancipation of slaves."[167] Despite being supported by all the Richmond newspapers, the bill failed in the House of Delegates by two votes. The state senate circumvented the problem by proposing an act that reinstated a pre-Revolutionary regulation to the bill governing the manumission of slaves. Once slaves were manumitted, they were required to immediately leave the state. If freed blacks failed to leave within a year, they would be seized, re-enslaved, and sold for the benefit of the Overseers of the Poor. The bill barely passed. In the senate, it passed by two votes; and in the House of Delegates the bill was deadlocked, with the Speaker casting the deciding vote in favor. State senator William Mumford helpfully noted, in a letter to his constituents, that "this important provision" would prevent "an increase of the mischiefs of partial emancipation."[168]

Mumford was right; the provision effectively ended the opportunities of gradual manumission. Even for those slaves who were manumitted, numerous bordering states barred their entry. Maryland forbade the immigration of free blacks in 1806, Delaware in 1807.[169] Kentucky barred free blacks from entry in 1808, upon penalty of being sold into slavery.[171] No free black from Virginia, by a law of 1788, could "tarry within" the Commonwealth of Massachusetts for more than two months.[171] During the 1806–7 term, the Ohio legislature passed a bill requiring all migrating blacks to give a bond that they would not become a charge on the state.[172] In those states adjacent to Virginia, only into Pennsylvania could a freed slave travel without restriction, in part because of the successful protest of Philadelphia's free black community.[173]

As the remaining American slaveholding states rejected earlier policies that had loosened state control of slavery, and began renewing laws intended to reinforce their slave societies, they made a fateful choice about the meaning and limits of Revolutionary principles that emphasized natural rights. The slim margin of passage of Virginia's bill reflected the conflicted mind of the planter class. The delegates opposed to the new bill argued that ending the option of manumission approximated an effective rejection of the great principles of the Revolution. As John Minor declared, "In past days these halls have rung with eulogies to liberty," and he warned that any comparison between themselves and the Virginians of '76 "would be degrading to us." But the proponents of the bill understood the consequences of their support. As Thomas Roberson complained, "I advocate it from policy; and not because I am less friendly to the rights of men than those who oppose the bill." "Tell us not of principles," he urged, for "those principles have been annihilated by the existence of slavery among us." It was time Virginians admitted their hypocrisy.[174]

But the delegates who passed the bill *were* "less friendly to the rights of men." They chose to explicitly link their own freedom to the subjugation of black Americans, both free and enslaved. Their own liberty could not be protected if the free black population was to be continually augmented by emancipated slaves. One delegate encouraged his fellows not to worry about the added cost required by the extra police measures against free blacks, because he was assured "that this house will always regard our liberties more than riches."[175] By finally ending the possibility of even an extremely gradual emancipation, the Virginians committed themselves to the benefits that slavery afforded whites and resigned themselves to the costs, both to blacks and to their own posterity. One newspaper, celebrating the end of the experiment of "partial emancipation," argued that the end of manumission was not evidence of "a want of sympathy from the sufferings of the blacks." On the contrary, "the imperious law of self-preservation must put to silence the suggestions of compassion." Slaveholders needed to "adopt all the necessary means of defense, unless we would become the victims of an evil that is silently but surely gathering upon us"—the growing free black communities:

> If the aera of a complete abolition of slavery should ever arrive, the soldiers at the barracks, and the restrictions of the statute book, would be a needless precaution. But that aera has not ar-

> rived. We are as yet only in the *iron age,* with crimes to punish and calamities to prevent. What then is to be done, but to employ a *strict* but philanthropic police? And since the evil of slavery is not yet to be remedied, to secure our own tranquility by imposing restrictions on those who may disturb it? It was written in golden characters on the front of the prison of Genoa: *Libertas.*[176]

Virginian liberty would be assured by the protection of the slave regime and the harsh restrictions on freed blacks. This position, which undoubtedly represented the opinion of the majority of white Virginians in 1806, exposes the bargain they were willing to make. The promise of American liberty for white citizens existed only at the expense of the freedom and liberty of American blacks, and that relationship would persist into an indefinite future. The defense of that arrangement became the driving ambition of Southern slaveholders. The potential of Revolutionary politics, which had inspired the manumission bill of 1782, was utterly rejected.

One scholar has recently described the compromises of slavery and race in the early national period as a problem best characterized by "silence." In this version of the story, the Founding Fathers failed to deal with slavery and race at a crucial moment in the National Congress, condemning future slaves born and unborn to a loathsome state, while passing the antagonisms of racial difference to future generations of Americans.[177] But there was no silence at all about the status of blacks in the early republic; there was a growing noise. It was a noise that caused even the most optimistic of revolutionaries to make choices that left little room for compromise, and a noise that often heralded the vilest extremism. But for even the most sanguine of white Americans, the immediate trouble with slavery was the noise coming from the direction of the slave quarters and black churches. It was an all too familiar echo, the same sounds of "equal rights and liberty" that had been heard throughout the Atlantic at the end of the eighteenth century, and this noise, perhaps, proved the most convincing sound of all.

Late in life, despairing of a solution to slavery in his time, Thomas Jefferson could not imagine a world where free blacks and whites lived together as equal citizens:

> On the subject of emancipation I have ceased to think because [it is] not to be a work of my day. The plan of converting the blacks into Serfs would certainly be better than keeping them in their present condition, but I consider that of expatriation to the

> governments of the W[est] I[ndies] of their own colour as entirely practicable, and greatly preferable to the mixture of colour here, to this I have great aversion; but I repeat my abandonment of the subject.[178]

Ultimately, the failure of imagination and the deeply held prejudice of the white citizens of the United States assured both the continuation of slavery and the denization of black Americans.

By Jefferson's second term as president, political equality for blacks in the United States was psychologically impossible for the vast majority of whites to imagine, politically impossible in a federal system that insisted upon local control over the municipal arrangements of the citizenry, and legally impossible after the passage of the Eleventh Amendment. While individual free blacks may have wholly separated themselves from any connection to slavery, no black American could escape the truth of racial slavery throughout the Union. Black people throughout the country were marked by the color of their skin and the prejudice of their fellow Americans. By 1810, no amount of claims of natural right would change this fact.

Blacks often approximated free citizens in the years after Independence, but the United States remained a white republic. Even in the most free of New England states (Vermont), where free blacks possessed nearly all of the privileges of white citizens, black men and women needed to travel carefully, with proper documentation, and not overstay their welcome in any particular town, or they could be warned out and even kidnapped as fugitive slaves. Free blacks throughout the country were like American sailors at sea, constantly under threat of being seized if they could not prove their identity as free Americans.

By the middle of the nineteenth century, some of the laws that had restricted the civil and personal rights of blacks in the United States were being repealed, but as one author noted dispassionately in the 1860s, "Social discriminations maintain the spirit of former legal distinction."[179] Free blacks could ameliorate their condition in separate communities, but they would not be able to achieve equal citizenship in the United States without a dramatic revolution of their own. They may have remained defiant, but they nevertheless remained denizens in a white republic.

8

The Aristotelian Moment

ENDING THE AMERICAN REVOLUTION

The best is often unattainable, and therefore the true lawmaker or statesman ought to be acquainted not only with that which is best in the abstract but also that which is best considering the circumstances. —Aristotle, *The Politics*

I am sensible how far I should fall short of effecting all the reformation which reason would suggest and experience approve, were I free to do whatever I thought best. But when we reflect how difficult it is to move or inflect the great machine of society, how impossible to advance the notions of a whole people suddenly to ideal right, we see the wisdom of Solon's remark that no more good must be attempted than the nation can bear.—Thomas Jefferson, 1801

At the conclusion of the first part of *The Rights of Man,* Thomas Paine describes the late eighteenth century as "an age of revolutions in which everything may be looked for."[1] Paine expressed a sentiment that reached far beyond the immediate boundaries of France to a moment of change throughout the Atlantic World. His comment still applied to the United States and many other countries in the 1790s—it was an age of possibilities. But all ages come to an end eventually, and as the eighteenth century turned into the nineteenth, many of the possibilities of transformation for American national citizenship, possibilities that had been opened by Independence, hung in the balance of national politics.

Thomas Jefferson famously remembered his ascent to the presidency in 1800 as a revolution—in fact, "as real a revolution in the principles of our government as that of 1776 was in its form." Jefferson could make such a judgment with the benefit of nineteen years hindsight, at a time when the Federalist vision that he helped destroy remained possible only in his nightmares and conspiracy theories. Most people in the moment itself, in 1799, 1800, and 1801, saw the time with much less clarity.

They understood Jefferson's rise and the defeat of Federalists across the country, even in their strongholds, as actors within revolutionary moments often do—as a time of great possibility and great danger. Some understood murkily, as Congressman Abraham Baldwin noted in 1799, that the United States had "still not got beyond the reach and influence" of the "causes peculiar" to their revolutionary birth. He thought great revolutions necessarily infect "the whole age," and he did not think the citizens of the United States had yet emerged from their Revolutionary Age.[2] Continuing revolution is precisely what the Federalists feared most vividly, and they worried that Jefferson's election created the possibility for those fears to be realized, as they had been in France, in rivers of blood and stolen property. Fisher Ames could think only in terms of revolution as he watched the transitions of 1800, noting, "We are now in the Roland and Condorcet act of our Comedy—Whether we go on to the Danton and Robespierre acts depends on time and accident."[3]

By 1804, however, when Jefferson was reelected to the presidency with an electoral majority that clarified the permanent defeat of the Federalists, certain possibilities for American national citizenship were no longer achievable in the United States: one vision of the American nation had been decisively overthrown, and the boundaries of American citizenship were placed into a track that would define and limit the meaning of American citizenship for the next sixty years. Some of those possibilities had been quenched in the Republican destruction of the legislation that Federalists hoped would secure American national citizenship; some of the revolutionary potentials of the age disappeared in the changing economic and demographic realities of the day; and some had died with the demise of international revolution itself. But it soon became clear to everyone, with a decisiveness that did not exist in 1783, 1787, or 1799: the politics of revolution was over.

Causes Peculiar and the Revolution of 1800

The possibilities feared and anticipated in 1800 descended directly from problems created when the British colonial resisters began reshaping themselves into American revolutionaries in the last years of the imperial conflict—from the meeting of the Continental Congress in 1774 to the Declaration of Independence in 1776. Assertions of rights and popular sovereignty in the midst of war and state creation had created citizens from subjects, while necessity and desire had crafted a Union from a collection of colonies. But who ultimately controlled the meaning of "American citizenship"? Where did state power end and national power begin? What rights did citizens have to resist their own government? When did opposition become rebellion? No consensus existed on these fundamentals of the political order. By 1800, these problems of citizenship and nationhood had evolved through a number of different political contests; had been polarized, sharpened, and transformed in international revolution; and had become defined in the logic of national party politics. But they had not yet been solved, for the elections of 1800 promised to destroy the solutions offered by the Federalists of 1798–1801 and to reopen the problems of American citizenship that had emerged in Independence.

Driven by popular encouragement and political leadership, Federalists had attempted to settle once and for all the true character of America by restricting access to the rights of citizenship only to "true Americans." Responding to the petitions in favor of the Adams administration in the spring of 1798, which they believed represented the spirit of the whole country, Federalists used their narrow majority in Congress and their control of the national executive and judiciary to create in law the vision of the American nation and citizenship their constituents imagined in the streets. In addition to laws directly related to the defense of the country—including the creation of the Department of the Navy, an act authorizing the president to borrow millions of dollars to raise armies and pay for war, and a new battery of taxes—Federalists also created a series of laws meant to exorcise all foreign elements from the American citizenry. The Naturalization Act of 1798, the Alien Friends and Enemies Acts, and the Sedition Act broke with past efforts to deal with immigrants and political dissidents in the United States. No longer sure that American character could remain inviolate against the perceived dangers of foreign influence, the Federalists in Congress strove to regulate immigrants and aliens and legally deny all legitimacy to any opposition to the Federalist government. More broadly, the Federalists used the moment to ratify in law a national vision of the American citizenry protected and defined by a national common law. To defend against the dangers of international revolution, the citizenry were encouraged to revel in their national distinctiveness. The United States could stand against French expansionism and enthusiasm only as a true nation-state with a homogeneous citizenry united against foreign ideas, disaffected immigrants, and sectional ambition.

The Federalist legislation and push for war against France set the stage for a dramatic contestation of the direction of the American state and the meaning of American citizenship. The vision of the national state and of a national common law establishing the boundaries of American citizenship was immediately resisted by a broad mobilization of hundreds of popular remonstrances, memorials, resolutions, and petitions which provided the ideological and organizational momentum that ultimately destroyed the Federalists as a national political force. These voices were not simply to be found in the agrarian planters who drafted the Kentucky and Virginian Resolutions, but among small farmers from Tennessee to Vermont, among urban ethnic groups along the coast, and among the many representatives of the artisan and commercial classes of the Middle States. The opposition to the Federalists rejected the legitimacy of federal power to regulate the domestic interests of the American citizenry and emphasized instead the importance of local sovereignties to define the active meaning of universal principles—"states' rights" and the "rights of man."

Upon the back of this popular agitation, the Republican Party won a series of political triumphs that included the defeat of John Adams and the election of Thomas Jefferson to the presidency, the decisive overthrow of the Federalist majority in Congress in 1800, and the Republican sweep of local offices in numerous states, including formerly Federalist New Jersey, Pennsylvania, New York, and South Carolina. In Massachusetts, one of the strongest Federalist states in 1798, the delegation elected to Congress was evenly split between Republicans and Federalists in the elections of 1800, and the Republican candidate for governor lost by only two hundred votes, of nearly thirty-five thousand cast.[4]

These elections, which signaled the political "Revolution of 1800" that Jefferson remembered with such fondness, had begun with the capture of the Pennsylvania governorship and Pennsylvania House of Representatives by Thomas McKean and his Republican allies in the elections of 1799, in a direct refutation of the Federalist vision for national Union. As president of the Hibernian Society of Philadelphia—the Irish immigrant-aid society—and as an ardent advocate for states' rights in constitutional interpretation, McKean embodied the rejection of the Federalist model of national character protected by a centralizing, dominant, national state. McKean's election helped legitimate the self-conscious, ethnic-American constituent group and the idea of the hyphenated citizen. When McKean came to office, he immediately fired twenty-four state employees and informed them not to reapply for their office.[5] The spirit of revolution was in the air.

So when Jefferson's party swept the country in 1800, the body politic waited anxiously to see the changes the new regime would bring to the character of the American state and the meaning of American citizenship. The rhetoric of the campaigns had been extreme, and with the Republicans chanting about the rights of man, singing French Republican songs, raising liberty poles, and fighting in the streets, Federalists imagined the worst. One Federalist newspaper heard the rhetoric of the opponents of the administration and complained that all the candidates attempting to unseat the Federalists, "who style themselves pure Republicans," were "in the habit of addressing the people in the canting language: 'I am a patriot of '76—I still hold to the principles of '76.' We believe them for once—we believe they speak the language of their very souls; for—Revolution—Revolution is their darling wish." To "Revolution" the Republicans would "sacrifice all their neighbours property—the sweets of social enjoyment—the authority of the law—the venerable institutions of religion—and the multiplied and incalculable blessings of an equal and stable government."[6] In many ways, the possibilities that the Republicans brought to office in 1801 could easily seem boundless. Their rhetoric mimicked language used by the Americans who had revolutionized the problem of citizenship in 1776, and because their success derived from an opposition movement, they provided a powerful critique of Federalist intentions without having to create anything of their own. Indeed, if taken to extremes, the logic of their arguments could imply disunion and the leveling of differences.

By the time the Republicans seized power, they were not able to enjoy destroying the *entire* Federalist regime of 1798, because the outgoing Federalists had already dismantled some of the more objectionable elements of their design before they lost all power. The first aspects of their triumphant national vision of 1798 to fall were the military establishments, no longer necessary after Adams moved to conclude a peace with the French. This move caused a deep rift among the leadership of the Federalist Party, a rift assured by Hamilton's desire to maintain a permanent army, and sealed by one of the most marvelous acts of political suicide—matched only perhaps by his acceptance of a duel with Aaron Burr—ever seen in politics, let alone American presidential politics: Hamilton's attack on the competency of John Adams.[7] Further enlistments in the army were discontinued in February of 1800,[8] and after firing Hamilton's eyes and ears in the cabinet, Secretary of State Timothy Pickering and Secretary of the Treasury Oliver Wolcott Jr., Adams moved quickly to disband the American army and put the growing fleet in mothballs. When the second session of the Sixth Congress ended, in the spring of 1800, the Alien Act—the administrative portions of which were the only aspects of the bill ever executed[9]—was allowed to silently expire, unheralded and unwanted.[10]

But even with the rift within their party over war and peace, the Federalists in the government continued to buttress national citizenship and national power, even to the last moments of their superiority in a lame-duck Congress. In the second session, the Federalist Congress succeeded in passing a highly controversial bankruptcy bill, which provided protection for merchants and traders who lost their capital and stipulated that bankruptcy cases would be tried in federal courts—a massive expansion of jurisdiction and another opportunity to enlarge the possibility of a national common law. The bill alone created over 250 more federal offices, and by making the cases federal, it ensured the support of the lower federal courts from fines and fees—not unlike the way many states and localities funded their own courts. Republicans saw the bill as an attack on agriculture, an attempt to sustain a national common law, and a continued effort to augment the power of the executive branch and the central government.[11] The Federalists also continued to strengthen and augment their revenue program, not only keeping the new taxes, but creating a new office for a national collector of stamp revenue. But their most substantial attempts to "save the nation" were made in the judiciary.[12]

When Adams finally learned (in the middle of December 1800) that he had lost the presidential election and that a substantial Republican majority would control the Seventh Congress, he also received notice that the chief justice of the Supreme Court, Oliver Ellsworth, had resigned his post—a result of the combined effects of age and ill health. Adams immediately planned to use his appointment to the Supreme Court to save the nation from continuing revolution, from "visionary schemes or fluctuating theories," as he wrote to John Jay, offering him the post.[13] After Jay declined the appointment, Adams tapped John Marshall, who died, still chief justice, in 1835.[14]

With the Republican takeover effective on March 4, Federalists in the last session of the Sixth Congress moved with extreme alacrity in the winter of 1800–1801 to place the judiciary department on a broad and sound national foundation. They had long been dissatisfied with the function of the judiciary in the country and deeply regretted the continued importance of the state courts in the operation of federal law, which they believed included a national common law that would eventually be used to establish a national jurisprudence of membership, citizenship, and belonging. The *Williams* case of 1799, in which Oliver Ellsworth denied the right of expatriation absolutely, and the Federalist justifications of the Sedition Act, relied upon the belief of a national common law. As Ellsworth noted, "The common law of this country remains the same as it was before the Revolution."[15] But without an active and able federal judiciary with an expansive jurisdiction in numerous types of criminal and civil actions, the states had remained in control of the legal meaning of membership in the Union. As one Federalist essay noted, the federal judiciary only appeared to the citizenry "now and then as a phenomenon which the people gaze at" and "which they consider as a foreign intruder." The vast majority of citizens had very little relationship to the federal courts. As the author "Consistent Federalist" explained, it was "necessary to strengthen the Government in the affections of the people by multiplying Federal Courts; the State Courts are more or less infected with Anti-Federalism."[16] In 1799, Hamilton had urged a reformation of the federal judiciary in such a manner as to "extend the influence and promote the popularity" of the national government.[17] Federalist essayists agreed that the judiciary needed to be made truly national. The institutions of the court had to be made "firm, independent, and extensive," so they would more effectively serve as a true national judiciary that could carry "the authority of the law home to the fireside of every individual" in the nation.[18] In the winter and spring of 1799–1800, the Federalists had crafted an extremely ambitious bill to greatly increase the size of the judiciary branch to accompany and enforce the bankruptcy bill, but they overreached and lost a major portion of their plan.

But a broken bill, or even the fact that many of the Federalists had been voted out of office, would not deter them in the last session of the Sixth Congress. They would, as John Rutledge assured Hamilton, "profit of our short-lived majority."[19] Thus, less than a month before Jefferson's inauguration, the Federalist Congress passed a new bill, which although weaker than the one they had left dead the year before, represented a major reorganization of the national judiciary. The Judiciary Act of 1801 decreased the number of Supreme Court justices from six to five, to take effect after the next vacancy, thus assuring that Jefferson would not have an appointee to the Court. The act increased the number of federal districts from seventeen to twenty-two and completely redesigned the circuit court system. Supreme Court justices and district court justices were no longer expected to sit as circuit judges. Three new circuits were created, to accommodate the growth of the country, as well as sixteen new federal circuit court judges, with additional clerks, marshals, and administrators to service them.[20] These structural changes immediately gave the Federalists a chance to extend their patronage. But more important for the future of the country, the act also greatly expanded the *jurisdiction* of the lower courts.

If it had simply been a matter of more judges, the new judiciary act would have been an annoying innovation and an important increase of Federalist lame-duck patronage, but it would only have represented a temporary delay of eventual Republican dominance. But the act expanded both the extent and jurisdiction of the new federal courts, and therefore promised to bring the power of federal law directly to the citizenry—"to the fireside of every individual"—with an impressive augmentation of the visibility and will of the national state. By the original design of the Judiciary Act of 1789, the federal system depended heavily on the state courts. Federal courts possessed original jurisdiction only on federal crimes and cases in admiralty, and possessed concurrent jurisdiction with the state courts on a very few, carefully proscribed, matters. Original jurisdiction in civil cases arising under the Constitution, treaties, and federal laws was only given to the federal courts if the value of the dispute exceeded $500, and where the United States was a party or those cases were between citizens of different states.[21] Any conflict between citizens of the same state, even if arising under federal law, of any amount, was left to the state courts. Thus, the act had been structured in such a way that the federal courts did not even have original jurisdiction on all the cases arising under the Constitution of the United States, federal laws, and treaties—the jurisdiction allowed to the courts in the Constitution.

The Judiciary Bill of 1801, however, restructured the relationship of the federal courts and the national citizenry, and it began by giving the new circuit courts complete jurisdiction over all cases arising under the laws, treaties, and Constitution of the United States. Any such cases begun in state courts were removable to federal court on petition, without regard to the citizenship of the party or the value of the complaint. The circuit courts were also granted jurisdiction in civil cases in which the judicial power of the United States applied and where the matter in dispute amounted to over $400.[22] In *all* cases involving the "title, or bounds" of land, however, the jurisdiction of the new circuit courts was absolute, regardless of the dollar value of the claim. In addition, jurisdiction over all the fines and forfeitures under laws of the United States and occurring within fifty miles of a circuit court were entirely *exclusive* of the state courts, creating little federal judicial spheres in the most populous areas of the country. Criminal jurisdiction was also clarified and extended to crimes committed on the high seas.[23]

Another crucial change in the way federal law would operate in the United States was the grant of an expansive jurisdiction in cases of "diverse" citizenship—meaning if the defendants were aliens, or a citizen or group of citizens of a state other than the state of the origin of the complaint. Under this provision, defendants were allowed to remove their case from state courts to the next circuit court at *any time* in the proceedings if they had not appeared.[24] This option applied in all civil cases where the judgment exceeded $400, and in all land title or boundary cases regardless of the value of the land.[25] It also applied to all cases between citizens of the same state in contests over land ownership and boundaries if one of the parties claimed a title to the land based upon the grant of a different state.[26] In real terms, this meant that individuals could take their case to federal court even after a state court had passed judgment, thus separating themselves from a state judiciary system controlled by local interests and local common law. They could force the case to be held in a federal court which met hundreds of miles from the neighborhood of the species of property at issue—in a court with officers whose political alliances stemmed from interests even further afield. The juries themselves were under the control of the federal marshals, another patronage appointment. Juries could be, and were, regularly packed. Everyone understood the power of the marshals. Federalists saw such a system as essential to guarantee capital and property against the capriciousness of local democracy (or, as they saw it, the power of arbitrary local oligarchy), while Republicans envisioned "an army of judges" controlling the lives and will of the populace, not to mention the rapacious encouragement of land speculation at the expense of the local farmer.[27] Federalists wished to popularize the power of the national government by providing efficient organs of federal judicial power, while Republicans feared federal encroachment on local government and particularly worried about freedom of local polities to govern their own lives and property without the interference of distant capital.

With these changes, the federal courts could rule directly on issues that the states had controlled exclusively—issues the state legislatures considered the purview of local policy. To rule effectively, the new court system would use the notion of a national common law, as Federalists had done to justify the Sedition Act and to deny the right of expatriation. What exactly was or was not in this new national common law would ultimately be up to the judges of the courts and what cases they would consider matters of national common law. The problem with assuming such a system is that, unlike the common laws of the many states, which had been cleaned and republicanized by the state constitutions and statutes, a national common law could be drawn upon at the whim of judges who could import many anti-Republican principles. As St. George Tucker worried, "If the common law of England has been adopted by the United States in their national, or federal capacity," the jurisdiction of "the federal courts must be co-extensive with it." Or in other words, "*unlimited*"—which would also assure that the powers of the federal government "must be likewise, *unlimited.*" Such an extension of jurisdiction would be "unbounded in its operation," and ultimately destructive of those principles "which the states had deemed inseparable from their constitutions, and therefore sacred, and inviolable."[28] Responding to the increasing calls by Federalists for the existence of a national common law, the legislature of Virginia instructed their representatives to oppose any measure sanctioning such a jurisdiction, that would be "novel in its principle, and tremendous in its consequences."[29]

Thus, the new judiciary system promised an important strengthening of the national government and a transformation in the fundamental relationship of the national state to the American citizenry. The Federalists had worked to their last moments to sustain their vision of the national state. With Jefferson about to take power, who could blame them? Reflecting on the coming handover in power, Gouverneur Morris noted that the Federalists "are about to experience a heavy gale of an adverse wind; can they be blamed for casting many anchors to hold their ship through the storm?"[30]

President Adams signed the judiciary bill on February 13, 1801; filled all the empty posts; and finished endorsing the final commissions on March 3—his final day in office and the day the Sedition Act expired.[31] It was his last official act in the Revolutionary political crisis in which he had been engaged since 1776: the attempt to restrain claims of natural rights with law and ordered liberty.

The Aristotelian Strain of American Politics

As Jefferson and his Republican allies took office in the spring of 1801, their eyes were fixed upon dismantling the Federalist system in service of their own vision of the American national state—a highly decentralized, loosely connected union of states where citizenship remained the problem and responsibility of the individual states. The federal government would retain its powers, but these were limited and defined in the Constitution to those objects reflecting international and "mutual" relations. Jefferson set the terms of this policy in his first message to the House and Senate, on December 8, 1801:

> When we consider that this Government is charged with the external and mutual relations only of these States"; "that the States themselves have principal care of our persons, our property, and our reputation, constituting the great field of human concerns, we may well doubt whether our organization is not too complicated, too expensive; whether offices or officers have not been multiplied unnecessarily, and sometimes injuriously to the service they were meant to promote.[32]

Here it was then. The Jeffersonian tendency would be to dismantle, to repeal, to restrict the power of the national government. Before this address, Jefferson had already swept away the inspectors of the internal revenue and decimated the diplomatic corps. Only three permanent diplomatic missions, to Spain, Britain, and France, were retained. He had begun reducing the naval establishment and planned to arm only three frigates out of the thirteen that existed in the final year of the Adams administration.[33] But the most pressing problems of the national state had been "established by law, and therefore by law alone can they be abolished."[34] Encouraged to revoke and repeal, the new Republican Congress set about their work eagerly.

The Seventh and Eight Congresses (1801–5) achieved an extraordinary restructuring of the national government and loosened the bonds connecting the central government to the individual citizen—bonds Federalists had considered necessary to assure the survival of a distinct national culture and a lasting national state. The Congress succeeded because its support stemmed from a national opposition movement that, although not united entirely by interest, region, ethnicity, or even vision of political economy, knew what they did not want: the Federalist vision of a powerful national state and a homogeneous national citizenry. As an opposition movement, the Republicans' talents initially stemmed from their ability to tear down, and the Republican Seventh Congress—in close alliance with Jefferson's executive branch—finally destroyed the Federalist national vision. Alexander Hamilton remarked in a polemical essay that the new leaders of the country were "far more partial to the state governments; than to our national government," and that they were more inclined "to pull down rather than to build up our Federal edifice."[35] Republicans considered these comments as a badge of honor, not as a chastisement. Hamilton was out of touch and increasingly irrelevant; by the time Jefferson was overwhelming reelected to the presidency in 1804, he was dead.

Although they had many complaints, the Republicans saw the destruction of the Judiciary Act of 1801 as essential for the rearticulation of the American national state, and one of the first laws that they absolutely needed to destroy to achieve anything of significance. As William Branch Giles, the leader of the Republicans in Congress, noted, "It is constantly asserted that the revolution is incomplete, as long as that strong fortress is in possession of the enemy; and it is surely a most singular circumstance that the public sentiment should have forced itself into the Legislative and Executive Department, and that the Judiciary should not only not acknowledge its influence, but should pride itself, in resisting its will, under the misapplied idea of 'independence.'"[36] Giles wanted a complete repeal of the federal judiciary, but he was satisfied with the repeal of the Judiciary Act of 1801. In the Senate, Stephen

Bradley of Vermont admitted that the repeal of the judiciary act would be just the beginning—of the overthrow of the Federalist national vision and of the creation of a new, Jeffersonian Union. As he declared during the debate over the repeal of the judiciary act, he saw it "as one part of a great system," a "system recommended by our worthy President." It was a system "to be completed by lessoning all our expenses; by reducing our Military Establishment; by disciplining our militia; by repealing our internal taxes." As soon as the country paid "our debts, and with a great population of free citizens, we shall make all the tyrants of Europe tremble on their thrones, and in the middle of their armies." It was "a glorious system."[37] You can almost hear the Federalists groan.

In the Senate, the movement to repeal the judiciary act was initiated by John Breckinridge, the man who had introduced the Kentucky Resolutions to the Kentucky legislature in the fall of 1798. In both cases, he was encouraged behind the scenes by Jefferson. The Senate was essential, because the Republicans enjoyed only a slim margin, and with Aaron Burr casting the deciding vote in the case of ties, anything might occur. Breckinridge's position on the bill was clear. The courts were expensive and an unnecessary expansion of national power into the states. As Breckinridge argued, "The judicial powers given to the federal courts were never intended by the Constitution to embrace, exclusively, subjects of litigation, which could, with propriety, be left to the State courts." The jurisdiction of the federal courts, he noted, "was intended principally to extend to great national and foreign concerns," not every private consideration of the citizenry and certainly not to land title cases.[38] The debate quickly broke down between the two sides, with no room in between: the judiciary act was to be repealed or kept, not amended.[39]

With the overwhelming Republican majority in the House, the act's repeal was a foregone conclusion, and the "debate" became even uglier. While the problems presented by repealing the law touched on a number of facets of American constitutional thought, including the problems of judicial review and the independence of the judiciary, the congressional debate ultimately degenerated into ad hominem attacks and ridiculous distortions of opponents' arguments. Much of the time was spent attacking the personal character of the judges that Adams had appointed to these offices and the expense of a court system that had not yet been used.[40] Ugly or not, the debate lasted for all of February and March, and was accompanied by a substantial pamphlet and newspaper battle, before the votes were finally taken. The "debate" had done little to sway anyone's position: it was a strict party vote, 59 to 32 in favor of repeal.

The repeal of the Judiciary Act of 1801 stuck many Federalists as completely unconstitutional, a threat to the Constitution and the permanence of the Union, and a final overthrow of the national aspects of the American state. The opening speech of New York senator Gouverneur Morris set the parameters of the Federalist arguments in both the House and Senate. Morris argued that the independence of the judiciary meant that the life-term contracts made between the judges and the nation could not simply be revoked by the legislature. The notion that a legislature "may rightfully repeal every law made by a preceding Legislature" was "untrue." "What!" he exclaimed. "Can a man destroy his own children!" But more to the point, Federalists saw the debate over the judiciary act clearly as a problem of America citizenship—namely, who would define the nature of American citizenship in the Union. As Morris lamented, "We are told that [the states] are the legitimate sources from which the citizen is to derive protection." State judges "are, I suppose, to enforce our laws." These judges are "supported by State authority, supported by State salary, and looking for promotion to State influence, or dependent upon State party." The nation had already been weakened by the passage of the Eleventh Amendment: "One Great provision of the Constitution—a provision that exhibited the sublime spectacle of a great State bowing before the tribunal of justice is gone!" Now, "another great bulwark is . . . to be removed." The people "are told you must look to the States to protection; your internal revenues are to be swept away; your sole reliance must depend upon commercial duties." But "what is the effect of all these changes?" He was "afraid to say; I will leave it to the feelings and consciences of gentlemen. But remember, the moment this Union is dissolved, we shall no longer be governed by votes." Morris continued, "We are now about to violate the Constitution. Once touch it with unhallowed hands" and "we are gone."[41] The survival of the nation itself, as always for the Federalists, was at stake.

Jedidiah Morse lamented the destruction of the judiciary act as one of the great tragedies of world history. In his school geographies he maintained a running chronology of "Remarkable Events, Discoveries, and Inventions," which included such references as 46 A.D.: "Christianity carried into Spain," or 1579: "The Dutch shake off the Spanish yoke." Under the year 1802, Morse noted as a remarkable event: "The famous bill for the repeal of the judiciary act passed." This repeal, he observed succinctly, "the Federalists consider as a direct infraction of the constitution."[42]

Thus, the weakness of the federal judiciary was accentuated over the years by a Congress unwilling and uninterested in funding, supporting, or expanding the lower federal courts. The federal courts became an overburdened system, extremely weak, generally insignificant, and ultimately unable to enforce the federal government's will. Despite the Federalist attempt to secure a national common law, which a real federal court system could have made into a true regulator of national belonging and citizenship, such a development could not occur without an extensive federal court system with expansive jurisdiction. In this situation, state courts were increasingly expected to enforce and defend the interest of the federal government, a structural weakness that merely reinforced the local nature of citizenship in antebellum America as the population and size of the country grew. Not until the Judiciary Acts of 1869 and 1872 would the federal court system begin to look and act like the system imagined in the Judiciary Act of 1801.[43]

With the federal judiciary once again placed at the service of the states, the Republicans in Congress and Jefferson in the executive branch moved quickly to reject all the important legislation that Federalists had passed since the height of their power in 1798. The internal taxes the Federalists had established on stills, whiskey, refined sugars, licenses to retailers, sales at auction, carriages, and stamped paper were systematically repealed, along with the new office of Superintendent of Stamps that the Federalists had created in Philadelphia.[44] Congress also rejected the notion of a permanent funded debt, the alpha and omega of Hamilton's plans, and took measures to place the debt on a course of redemption by appropriating $7,300,000 annually to pay down the principal and interest.[45] In the fall of 1803, the Republicans repealed the bankruptcy act. Republicans also continued to reduce the military establishment, repealing all the Federalist legislation still outstanding since 1798 and designing a stripped-down navy.[46]

Finally, the Federalist Naturalization Act of 1798 was rejected, for a bill that essentially re-placed the provisions of naturalization of the compromise Naturalization Act of 1795. Jefferson called for a new bill in his first message to Congress. "Considering the ordinary chances of human life," he noted, "a denial of citizenship under a residence of fourteen years is a denial to a great portion of those who ask it." He argued that the Federalist policy of 1798 was against the stated wishes and policies of many of the states and an affront to the great universal principles of American liberty. As he wondered (apparently without irony), "Shall we refuse to the unhappy fugitives from distress that hospitality which the savages of the wilderness extended to our fathers in this land!" Would "oppressed humanity find no asylum on this globe"? And should "not the general character and capabilities of a citizen be safely communicated to every one manifesting a *bona fide* purpose of embarking life and fortunes permanently with us?"[47] The House immediately formed a committee to consider a new policy. Over the course of the session, the House received petitions from Irish and German immigrants in New York and Pennsylvania asking for a repeal of the 1798 bill.[48] Alexander Hamilton was enraged by these sentiments. Any change in the naturalization policy which opened citizenship to the easy access of aliens, he considered "an attempt to break down every pale which has been erected for the preservation of a national spirit and a national character; and to let in the most powerful means of perverting and corrupting both the one and the other."[49] The leading Federalist thinkers still hoped the nation could be protected from "hordes of foreigners," but they were no longer in power.

In the new bill, the fourteen-year residency requirement for aliens to become citizens was replaced by one of five years, all citizens were required to renounce any titles they held under a foreign government, and aliens were required to announce their intention to become citizens at least three years before their intended naturalization in any court in the country. In 1804, Republicans expanded the act to allow the immediate naturalization of aliens who had arrived in the United States between the time of passage of the Federalist bill, in June of 1798, and the passage of the new naturalization bill, on April 14, 1802, and who had therefore not declared an intention to become citizens, because at the time they would have had to wait fourteen years to do so.[50] Jefferson's wish was the Republican Congress's command, and the notion of citizenship imagined in the legislation of 1798—of a restrictive policy of naturalization to protect American national character—would not again become the policy of the nation in the nineteenth century. With slight federal regulation, the character of American citizenship was ultimately restored to the states. The rights and duties of aliens would be adjudicated in state common law courts, having been perfected and clarified by state legislation.

That was as far as the Republicans in national government would go: rejecting in principle and dismantling in essence the national centralizing state constructed by the Federalists. For the most ardent of the supporters of the government, it was perhaps not far enough, but for the Federalists, it seemed not only like disaster, but the beginning of the end. Hamilton again set the tone by painting the accomplishments of the administration as revolution. The transfer of power to Jefferson and his friends had achieved "more than the moderate opponents of Mr. Jefferson's elevation ever feared from his administration; much more than the most wrongheaded of his own sect dared to hope; it is infinitely more than any one who had read the fair professions in his

Inaugural Speech could have suspected." All "reflecting men must be dismayed at the prospect before us." For if "such rapid strides have been hazarded in the very gristle of his administration; what may be expected when it shall arrive to manhood?" "In vain," Hamilton argued, "was the collected wisdom of America convened at Philadelphia." The "anxious labours of a Washington," and the works of his administration, "are regarded as nothing better than empty bubbles destined to be blown away from the mere breathe of a disciple of *Turgot;* a pupil of *Condorcet.*"[51]

But Jefferson was following the lessons of Aristotle, not Condorcet. At his inauguration as president, he had revealed the tendency of his thought: "All differences of opinion are not differences in principle"; "we are all federalists, we are all republicans." What did this mean for the country? Would anything change? Shortly after his inauguration, Jefferson wrote to an old college friend and elaborated on the state of his mind, as well as the state of the Union. Jefferson admitted that he would "fall short of effecting all the reformation which reason would suggest and experience approve," because he was not simply "free to do whatever I thought best." Considering "how difficult it is to move or inflect the great machine of society, how impossible to advance the notions of a whole people suddenly to ideal right," he saw again "the wisdom of Solon's remark that no more good must be attempted than the nation can bear." Solon was a good choice for Jefferson, considering his options in 1801. Aristotle describes Solon as not only a theorist of constitutions, but one of those few theorists who "became legislators, engaging in politics themselves." Solon, unlike so many of those who "had something to say about a constitution" but "took no part in political actions," had been forced to establish "both laws and constitutions." Aristotle argued that "the true legislator and statesman" needed to understand "not only that which is best in the abstract" but also "that which is best relative to circumstances."[52] And Jefferson agreed. As he wrote to John Randolph of Roanoke at the end of 1803, "I see too many proofs of the imperfection of human reason, to entertain wonder or intolerance at any difference of opinion on any subject, experience having taught me the reasonableness of mutual sacrifices of opinion among those who are to act together for any common object, and the expediency of *doing what we can when we cannot do all we wish.*" This ability to make mutual sacrifices of opinion in the face of a flawed and complicated world is the soul of Aristotelian politics, and Jefferson the politician embraced it as a limit to revolution.[53]

So despite the fears of the Federalists, the Republicans had gone as far as they would go as a party of revolution. They believed in the need for a Union; they simply did not wish to see a central government ascendant in the lives of the citizenry. The Republican vision of a highly decentralized federal government with the states controlling the municipal arrangements of the citizenry—protecting the natural rights and duties of everyone within their boundaries on their own terms—created a natural boundary to how far the national government could or would interfere in any continuing attempts to make American citizenship more (or less) equal. The consequences for American citizenship were clear, and should be emphasized.

American citizenship in antebellum America, like American democracy, was a largely local affair, not because of any inevitability but because the Federalist vision was defeated, rejected, and overthrown. The Federalists looked toward uniformity of national citizenship and the eventual disappearance of all regional and ethnic differences. They were not backward-looking reactionaries, as they have often been portrayed, but the eager supporters of a modern national state with a coherent national legal system. The Federalist system demanded and hoped for a homogeneous citizenry sharing a national pride of character with a powerful national government operating for a clear national good. Yet, as a whole, the United States embodied diversity, as local groups controlled the parameters of their local economies, educational systems, and municipal arrangements. States' rights, local diversity, and urban ethnic politics became the standard fare of American political organization. As Hamilton worried, the United States represented "a vast variety of humours, prepossessions and localities" in the midst of the "much diversified composition of these states," which could not be contained in one Union unless they were bound by their own interest and the power of a strong national state with a national regulation of belonging and citizenship.[54] But the Republican system accommodated and was built upon the assumption of local difference. As Jefferson noted, the diverse states were responsible for the "principal care of our persons, our property, and our reputation, constituting the great field of human concerns" through their own control over a refined, republican, common law of nature and state declarations of rights, which ultimately defined a jurisprudence of American citizenship.[55] It was precisely because the United States exhibited divergent local interests and local characters that the central government could not dictate the nature of American citizenship in a way compatible with reason and right. This is not some utopian notion of American pluralism, but a recognition that the lack of an overarching and intrusive national state, or even a winning political coalition that could enforce such a vision, assured that local political alliances and the variations of local common law principles would alone define and limit the regulation and legal boundaries—if not always the imagined boundaries—of American citizenship for much of the nineteenth century.

The extended federal republic of the United States, in which the local governments possessed the ultimate control of the municipal arrangements of the citizenry, was not a strange peculiarity or a unique organization of an avowedly national people standing out of time against some mythic vision of the centralizing model European nation-state which must alone represent modernity.[56] The Dutch Republic, Mexico, Argentina, the British Empire of the nineteenth century, Spain between 1839 and 1879, and numerous other states and polities possessed national peoples with highly autonomous local governments. And yet the American Union *was* a modern system, one that advanced the science of federalism well beyond the early modern examples from which it drew freely: the Holy Roman Empire, the Dutch Republic, Switzerland. "Perfected" by Revolutionary understandings of citizenship and the nature of constitutions, some Americans believed, the United States could serve as a model for the government of Europe, and eventually the world. Immediately after the Constitutional Convention ended in 1787, Benjamin Franklin wrote to a friend in Europe that he did not see why Europe could not create "a Federal Union and one Grand Republick of all its different States & Kingdoms," in imitation of the achievement of the United States. Joel Barlow, living in Europe from 1788 to 1808, encouraged the French Republic in 1801 to abandon attempts at centralized control. Barlow acknowledged that "most the philosophers in Europe" thought the federal nature of the American Union to be a great misfortune and that the people in America should be collected into "one state" and not several. Barlow enjoined them to reconsider their "false reasoning on this subject." Massive nations, as republics, could not properly represent the diversity of interests within their borders. The French Republic, "for the purposes of internal regulation and police," should be shaped into "twenty subordinate republics," with all national concerns "concentrated in one great union." Such a union would have a "national legislative and executive, restricted in their powers to the simple objects of great national interest," with specifics "defined with the utmost precision in their general constitution." Barlow believed that the client republics being created on France's borders, instead of being mere pawns of France, should be "made part of the general confederation," a confederation that could eventually include all the various European peoples, "as fast as they become free." This would "presume a great union of republics, which might assume the name of the United States of Europe," and would "guarantee a perpetual harmony among its members." Considering the present (2009) state of Europe, one should immediately recognize that the American Union, born in the American Revolution, should not be considered any less "modern" than the ideal nation-state.[57]

More to the point, Jefferson's election and the implementation of the Republican legislative plan of 1801–3 overturned a very real trend, instituted by Federalists in the 1790s and most forcefully realized in the legislation of 1798 and the Judiciary Act of 1801, which would have placed the national state upon an extremely different trajectory than the one that unfolded after the Republicans took control. What exactly would have happened is difficult to prove or imagine with any great assurance. There may have been twenty civil wars, or none. There may have been a continentwide national state, or a handful of separate republics mirroring the experience of Central and South America. But what can be said with certainty is that the Federalist vision of the national state was rejected in 1801–3, and the meaning and problem of American citizenship in the antebellum United States was the direct consequence of the Republican overthrow of the Federalist vision.

The extended American Union is neither inherently backward-looking nor inherently progressive, for the deeply local nature of American national citizenship was a mixed blessing. The limited nature of the central government assured the persistence of slavery in Virginia, just as it guaranteed free blacks the right to vote in Vermont. Change within this scheme necessarily depended upon local democratic agitation, not top-down mandates from any national executive, legislature, or judiciary. But still, democracy unchecked can be capricious. Even though supporters of the decentralized nature of American citizenship considered the arrangement a fulfillment of the promises of the Revolution of '76, this vision of Union, once it achieved overwhelming consensual support in the years after 1800, helped limit the potential for Revolutionary change by assuring the persistence of local distinctions in the fundamental character of citizenship in the states. We have already seen the limited options for free blacks in their attempts to use national institutions to pry open the privileges of citizenship, but the jurisdictional limitations of the judiciary, legislature, and executive extended without racial bias to all citizens.

Take the question of the religious establishments in Massachusetts and Connecticut. Baptists and other dissenters were restricted in their access to political power in both states. Although Jefferson was a well-known Deist, to the dissenting New Englanders he represented a strong ally for religious toleration and freedom. Upon congratulating him for achieving the presidency, Baptists from Danbury, Connecticut, complained of their lack of religious freedom in terms highly familiar. The petitioners noted that the few privileges they did enjoy in Connecticut were "as favors granted, and not as inalienable rights."[58] But while Jefferson answered them favorably, and believed as strongly as anyone that religious freedom was an inalienable natural right, his understanding of the Union, in which the federal government had no power to affect the local municipal conditions of American citizenship, assured that only the citizens of Connecticut would decide when and if their established church lost its privileges. Jefferson would never send the national guard to assure the rights of Baptists in Connecticut. No federal court could protect the rights of Baptists. There would be no national civil rights legislation in antebellum America, and there *could not* be any such legislation until a new national state with different justifications of its purpose and power existed. Claiming natural rights was still a powerful way to challenge traditional inequalities in government and society, but revolutionary changes in the status of persons, under a Republican vision of the Union, were not possible on a national scale.

The history of the concept of "states' rights" and state sovereignty in the 1790s is often told as the birth of the regressive philosophy that it would become—as an interpretation of the Constitution by interests hoping to hold the line against assaults on slavery and restrictive civil rights laws. From the Nullifiers, to the Civil War, to Jim Crow, to the stubborn resistance of the states to the New Deal, to the local resistance to the racial integration of education—the insistence on the "sovereignty" of the states has often been seen as a negative force in American national history, as a rearguard action against the progressive promises of the Enlightenment. But the states' rights arguments articulated in opposition to the Alien and Sedition Acts, and understood to be a critique of the Federalist national plan of 1798, are better comprehended by their intellectual origins than from the hindsight of nullification and secession. However later proponents of states' rights might change their concerns, the original proponents of the idea of the sovereign rights of states grounded their arguments in the principles of popular constitutionalism, popular sovereignty, equality, and natural rights embodied in the most revolutionary sentiments of American independence.[59]

The right of the states to govern their own people was for many Americans the first cause and most immediate consequence of the War of Independence. It is no surprise that the first committee organized by the Continental Congress in 1774 to draft a set of colonial grievances was called the committee on "States Rights, Grievances and Means of Redress." The claim that the Alien and Sedition Acts were "void, and of no force"—language taken from common law constitutionalism—is more easily related to the resistance to the British Parliament in the

1760s and 1770s than to the Nullifiers in the 1830s. In fact, it was precisely on the grounds of natural rights, and their own interpretation of the imperial British Constitution, that the numerous colonial assemblies of 1765 rejected and effectively nullified the Stamp Acts. By an extraordinary but telling coincidence, just like the Virginia Resolutions of 1798, the famous Virginia Resolves of 1765 that actually passed the House of Burgesses were different from the more radical version that circulated in the newspapers.[60] The late 1790s were still part of an age where no one place provided the sole authority for the interpretation of "constitutional law," and of a time when politics and law were still inseparable. A new order was in the offing, but in the late 1790s it was still over the horizon.[61]

After the Republican ascendancy, change in the fundamental nature of American citizenship happened at the pace of state and local politics, and in some states, in the first years of the nineteenth century, the pace was quite brisk. As the states struggled with the local politics of interest, the *national* consensus of the Republican ascendancy revealed its fragility. American political parties are always collections of diverse interests, and while they could all agree that they could not abide a Federalist vision of the national state, at the state level, the Republican coalition quickly began to fracture and fight. The wits at the time dubbed this process "Quidism," in reference to the so-called *tertium quid* (the "third thing"), referring to the Quid Parties of Pennsylvania and New York, who positioned themselves between the most ardent members of the Republican Party and the old Federalist Party stalwarts. In many ways, the Republican infighting and the third-party Quid movements were the natural progression of politics as Republicans moved from an opposition party to a governing party.

Pennsylvania represented one of the starkest examples of such Republican infighting, as William Duane turned upon his old champion and fellow proud Irish-American Thomas McKean. Duane led a movement to continue to revolutionize Pennsylvanian citizenship, calling for a new state constitution that would provide for elected judges; bring to an end any use of the vestiges of English common law in the state courts; institute universal manhood suffrage; and create a unicameral legislature. McKean, however, wanted none of these innovations. McKean himself had been a judge; he believed that the common law as it had been refined and applied in Pennsylvania protected all the rights of nature, and he saw no need for some drastic whimsical new code. While Duane had used all his influence to help McKean secure the governorship of Pennsylvania in 1798 and 1802, in 1805 he led the movement against McKean's election, and by 1807 he was attempting to have McKean impeached. He was also battling with John Binns in Philadelphia over control of the Irish interest there. So local politics revealed the deep divisions among the citizenry, and with deep division, the vital center set a careful pace.[62]

The final moment in the Revolutionary politics of citizenship, the final battle over the character and direction of the national state, was played out in the drafting of the Twelfth Amendment to the Constitution, the last revision to the fundamental charter of the Union until 1865. Most historians have seen the amendment as little more than a technical revision to fix the problems of the original process of presidential election that had resulted in the tie between Aaron Burr and Jefferson in the election of 1800 and almost resulted in a Burr presidency. The amendment was necessary to fix the problems to be sure, but the choice of amendment ensured that the states would control the process of electing the president. Allowing the states to design how the electors would be chosen, and how the electoral votes would be distributed, assured that the large states would have a preponderant influence. The amendment also separated the election of the president and vice president, which assured that the person receiving the second-highest number of votes would not become vice president. Both of these changes were victories for the Republicans.

But while the amendment was a victory for the Republicans, the debate over the amendment also revealed a grudging recognition that two large national parties would be the norm, not the exception, in American politics. This was the first amendment to the Constitution that was a clear *party* issue. Everyone in the debate recognized this fact. The original Constitution had been the product of "much deliberation and solemn compromise," Connecticut's James Hillhouse noted, but the design of that deliberation "is now attacked by party." He did not find this to be particularly surprising, and insisted that the Senate needed to *assume* the existence of party in their design of the amendment. Hillhouse argued that "the time may not be remote when party will adopt new designations." The old "federal and republican parties have had their day—and their designations will not last long." The "ground of difference between parties will not be the same that it has been," and new "names and new views will be taken as it has been the course in all nations." He thought the amendment should retain the possibility of a vice president of an opposing party, as "they will be checks upon each other."[63] By the end of the debate, similar assumptions about the character of American politics had become commonplace. As Samuel White of Delaware blandly asserted, the "united States are now divided, and will probably continue so, into two great political parties."[64]

The debate behind the Twelfth Amendment—its design and, ultimately, the implicit recognition of the existence of party politics in America—set the parameters for Republican dominance of the executive branch for the next twenty years. The amendment reflected the experience of the decade, and it ultimately helped transform the country's understanding of its political system, from one that denied the usefulness and feared the danger of parties, into a system of national politics that expected organized parties. This was an assumption that helped regularize and stabilize American political life, but one that also limited the transformative power of the vote, as well as the Revolutionary potential of American mainstream political movements. The parties would set the rules of the game. The Twelfth Amendment, and the acceptance that national elections would spawn national parties, marked the end of Revolutionary politics.

A recent historian of the French Revolution has described its ending as the triumph of Hobbes over Rousseau.[65] The Americans ended their own Revolution by abandoning Thomas Paine and embracing Aristotle. By 1807, Thomas Paine was dead in New Rochelle, New York, and Aristotle had been born again in Washington, D.C. Paine had argued in 1792 that "everything could be looked for" in the Age of Revolutions. By 1806, all things imaginable were no longer possible. America would settle, not for what was best in an abstract sense, but the best that could be gotten. It wasn't hypocrisy, it was politics.

Many people consider the ratification of the U.S. Constitution as the end of the American Revolution. Some have included the first ten amendments as well (but never the eleventh) as part of that moment. This reflects a nice symmetry—useful for pedagogy—and it represents the arguments of many of the advocates for ratification, as well as the history told by the Federalist Party that dominated the general government at the end of the 1790s. Both James Wilson and John Jay argued that the Constitution represented the culmination of the national independence movement. They based their belief, expressed in *Chisholm,* in the authority of the national Supreme Court over the states, and in the ultimate equality of citizenship under the justice of the Supreme Court upon that logic. But the country overwhelmingly rejected the Court's decision in *Chisholm,* and with it most of the logic that lay behind it.

It was not the ratification of the Constitution that ended the American Revolution, but the emergence of a consensus about how to interpret the Constitution—about how far the national organs of the state could meddle with municipal regulations of the citizenry. It was this consensus, about the nature of citizenship and Union, that finally ended the continued possibility for a radical change in the rules that governed the federated, sectional, and local character of American nationhood. The first *twelve* amendments were necessary before the country felt comfortable with its fundamental law and with its political system. At the end of Jefferson's first term in office, such a consensus existed; and with consensus, the Revolutionary politics of citizenship ended. Change would continue to occur to American institutions and citizenship, but those changes would occur within largely consensual understandings of the boundaries of transformation—in states and organized party politics. Revolutionary changes to the meaning of American citizenship, especially American *national* citizenship, would have to wait for another revolution.

Conclusion

THE FALL OF UNION, AND THE RISE OF NATION

Mr. Jefferson was an enthusiastic speculative philosopher; Franklin was wise, cunning and judicious; he made no objection to the Declaration, as prepared by Mr. Jefferson, because, probably, he saw it would suit the occasion and supposed it would be harmless for the future. But even Franklin was too much of a physical philosopher, too utilitarian and material in his doctrines, to be relied on in matters of morals or government. We may fairly conclude, that liberty is alienable, that there is a natural right to alien it, first, because the laws and institutions of all countries have recognized and regulated its alienation; and secondly, because we cannot conceive of a civilized society, in which there were no wives, no wards, no apprentices, no sailors and no soldiers; and none of these could there be in a country that practically carried out the doctrine, that liberty is inalienable.—GEORGE FITZHUGH, 1854

All honor to Jefferson—to the man who, in the concrete pressure of a struggle for national independence by a single people, had the coolness, forecast, and capacity to introduce into a merely revolutionary document, an abstract truth, and so embalm it there, that to-day, and in all coming days, it shall be a rebuke and a stumbling block to the very harbingers of re-appearing tyranny and oppression.—ABRAHAM LINCOLN, 1859

IF THE COUNTRY HAD REMAINED STATIC—WITH THE SAME jurisdictional limits, population, and distribution of wealth that existed in 1800—we could construct theoretical scenarios in which the Federalists come again to national power and overthrow the Republican ascendancy, thus continuing a type of national politics that still fought over the final settlement of the Revolution in the institutions of the national government. John Adams thought that the splintering of the Republican coalition that brought Jefferson to power would effect such a transformation and that the country would seesaw back and forth eternally between the Federalists and Republicans. But most good Federalists knew better by 1804.

The accession of Louisiana put the coup de grâce on the Federalist chances of ever attaining national power again. America would be a sprawling agricultural empire, and the period 1800–1820 is one of the few times in American history when the percentage of the American population engaged as a non-farm labor force diminished in proportion to the numbers employed in agricultural pursuits.[1] Federalists recognized the trend explicitly, noting that opening the Louisiana Territory, an "unbounded region," to immediate immigration assured "all the injuries of too widely dispersed population, but by adding to the great weight of the Western part of our territory, must hasten the dismemberment of a large portion of our country, or dissolution of the Government."[2] In 1804, Timothy Pickering had led a brief and halting move to separate the New England states from the Union, a movement that Alexander Hamilton—to his immortal credit—martyred himself to stop.[3] Within a decade of the purchase, the State of Louisiana was incorporated into the Union as an equal state, one with representative institutions but maintaining its *own* distinct domestic legal order—its own civil law, similar to the Napoleonic Code—thus fulfilling the vision of a Union in which the lives of individual citizens would be governed and defined by local institutions. Arch-Federalists despised the admission of Louisiana on these terms, and complained of the acceptance of Louisiana as one of their chief grievances at the Hartford Convention.[4]

But for the Republicans, the acquisition of Louisiana promised the fulfillment of their vision of an ever-expanding American "empire of liberty" that could at once protect against consolidation and regeneration. Land enough for generations of farmers could assure the continued equality and independence of the American citizenry. Republican civilization could move west compactly, and republics of citizen farmers could be incorporated as equal members of the Union as their circumstances permitted. "Enlarging the empire of liberty," Jefferson noted in a letter to the governor of the Territory of Indiana, will "multiply its auxilaries and provide new sources of renovation, should its principles, at any time degenerate, in those portions of our country which gave them birth."[5] It was a vision that doomed the traditional Native American societies, just as it doomed the prospects for the Federalists. Interestingly, Jefferson did not, as later Jacksonians would, necessarily consider this expansion of republicanism as an extension of the power of the United States—as a nationalist crusade ("We are the nation of human progress, and who will, what can, set limits on our onward march?")[6]—but as the continued Revolutionary spread of universal principles. As he wrote in

1804, "Whether we remain in one confederacy, or form into Atlantic and Mississippi confederacies, I believe not very important to the happiness of either part." The people "of the western confederacy will be our children and descendants as those of the eastern, and I feel myself as much identified with that country, in future time, as with this."[7] But by 1804, such sentiments, tainted as they were with Revolutionary utopianism, were on the wane.[8]

To understand nationality within this structure of equal states, Jefferson's allies extended the logic of his obsession with choice and expatriation to construct an unlikely notion of national belonging based upon a dual choice: a choice to become (and remain) a citizen, and to reject all others. We can see some of the full implications of this emphasis on the volitional nature of Jeffersonian citizenship—grounded in a strong understanding of the individual's right to expatriate—in a debate over expatriation in the 1810s. In the midst of the War of 1812, as Americans debated the Madisonian policy of retaliation to the aggressive British impressments of naturalized American citizens—whom they refused to recognize as "Americans," insisting instead on their perpetual allegiance as British "subjects"—Jefferson's ideological and party allies used every breath to castigate the "slavish doctrine" of feudal allegiance enforced by the British Admiralty. Representative John Jackson, born a year after the Declaration of Independence in far western Buckhanon, Virginia, expressed the Republican sentiment well: "He did not expect to hear such a slavish doctrine as that of perpetual allegiance urged in this place."[9]

Yet the Federalists, rump party that they were, continued to deny expatriation and defend the British practice, as they had throughout the 1790s. As William Gaston urged, "The permission of British subjects to leave that country" could not be and was not the same as an ability "to shake off all allegiance to it." "Nature's first great bond" could not be severed, even by naturalization. He could not himself abide by this "modern jargon" of expatriation, and believed that all independent and sovereign states always retained the ability to decide when and where their citizens could relinquish their responsibilities.[10]

But it was Thomas Bolling Robertson, originally of "Bellefield," in Dinwiddie County, Virginia, who delivered the most complete Jeffersonian articulation of the point. Robertson had learned his law at the new law school at William and Mary, a law program that had been built and designed by Thomas Jefferson's "friend and mentor," George Wythe. At William and Mary, Robertson studied with St. George Tucker, who had edited Blackstone's *Commentaries on the Laws of England* for use in America. Following Jefferson, and relying heavily on Jefferson's bill of citizenship, Tucker devoted an extended appendix to ridiculing Blackstone's notions of perpetual allegiance.[11] Jefferson was the great political patron of Robertson, appointing him as secretary of the Territory of Louisiana in 1807. After Louisiana became a state, Robertson was one of the freshmen legislators sent to Congress. He would go on to become attorney general and governor of Louisiana, before returning to Virginia at the end of his life.

Robertson led two failed attempts to pass a federal law of expatriation, in 1813 and 1818. While numerous reasons were given by his opponents for why he was so interested in such a law—he seemed eager to allow Louisiana's citizens to act as privateers against Spain—Robertson argued that legislation was necessary to clarify the right of expatriation, since federal judges, most notably in the *Williams* case, denied this natural right. During the debate over retaliation in 1814, Robertson noted that the "right of expatriation or emigration belongs to man." "It is," he noted succinctly, "derived from the God of nature." In the face of such self-evident truths,

> he could not but express his astonishment that emigration should be a theme of reprobation in the United States. Are we not . . . a community of emigrants? Are we not, remotely or immediately, all of us emigrants? One would really suppose, that, like the Welsh, we had our genealogical trees, and that we could, without difficulty, point to our antediluvian American ancestors. What can be more ludicrous than to find individuals denouncing the principle of emigration, from whose tongue a foreign dialect has not yet worn away.[12]

Robertson's arresting notion of a nation of emigrants who all share some common story of migration and who ultimately share the active choice to participate in a community made up of a collection of individuals reflecting evident ethnic and cultural diversity—one still speaking in a variety of "foreign" dialects—reflects the liberal promise of inclusion implicit in the volitional nature of Republican citizenship and nationhood. The notion of emigration, as opposed to the more common modern usage of "immigration," focuses on the process of leaving a former allegiance, rather than moving into anything already formed. The emigrant flees from tyranny, and that process of rejection reenacts the rebellious choices of the American Revolution, providing the common experience for the ultimate inclusion in a community supposedly based upon choice and not chance. It is a vision of the distinctiveness of the American people, yet it celebrates the universal rights out of which this peculiar "community of emigrants" is legitimately fashioned.

But this vision of a "community of emigrants"—with citizens debating in a cacophony of accents, formed by a shared history of migration—is also inherently exclusionary. It elides, forgets, and distorts the experience not only of numerous white immigrants but of Indians and African-Americans. Native Americans and African-Americans were increasingly imagined in law as permanent children, unable to reason and therefore rationally consent. Such a vision also tended to be gendered masculine. Women did not have the "will" or capacity to choose, a fact clarified in the early nineteenth century in the decision *Martin v. Massachusetts.*[13] The propertied women in New Jersey, who had been voting since the 1780s, lost the vote in 1807. At once expansive and exclusionary, universal and particular, grounded in history but optimistically prophetic, American notions of volitional citizenship as interpreted through the fiction of a "community of emigrants" created a high emphasis on public expressions of patriotism, and even chauvinism, which helps to illuminate numerous persistent American attitudes toward nationhood, patriotism, and allegiance.[14]

International changes assured that revolution would not remain as important a touchstone of American political ideology in the early nineteenth century, as it had in the 1790s. With Napoleon crowned emperor, the possibilities for continuing revolution and the utopian hopes of a future brotherhood of man, which had been an important theme of the Republican Societies and the most radical portions of the Jeffersonian coalition in the 1790s, disappeared rapidly from American mainstream political rhetoric. Haitian independence, guaranteed by 1804, also caused many white Americans to think that revolution was not always a good thing. The United States began to look more and more like an incomparable case, and the cosmopolitanism of the Revolutionary Age dissipated in the Romantic exceptionalism of the nineteenth century. With the opening of the boundaries of the United States into the vast space beyond the Mississippi, the country turned its mind away from Europe and began a century of precocious aggression and expansion within its own hemisphere.

A final demographic circumstance also assured the closing of the Revolutionary Age in the United States and an invigoration in the expansionist tendencies of the populace. Namely, the early nineteenth century saw the rise of a new generation of political leaders who had never been revolutionists, had never been anything *but* American citizens, a generation who had never been British subjects or subjects of any foreign potentates, and who, without that sense of rupture, could not share the sense of revolutionary potential. In fact, the rise of this first generation of Americans would do more for the sense of a growing

American nationality than any of the ambitious hopes of the nationalists of the 1790s. But the closest this generation could come to revolution was reenactment,[15] and the War of 1812, although propagandized as a second War of Independence, would be little more than the sloppy coming-of-age of a new generation of political leadership.

Historian Kendrick Babcock, one of the first serious students of American nationality, recognized the character of this new generation in fitting terms:

> They were the first ripened product of the generation which had grown up since the Revolutionary War. They were patriotic by inheritance, optimistic and self-reliant by force of their surroundings; they had seen the nation grow at a marvelous rate, and they had the most uncompromising faith in the republic's strength and future. Their patriotism was untroubled by the fear of war and its horrors, and untrammeled by any traditional obligations or sentiments regarding foreign relations, unless it was a chronic suspicion of England, bordering on unreason.[16]

These men were "not revolutionaries, but chauvinists," and they would lead the country into its first imperial war in 1812. They exhibited a characteristic that John Quincy Adams assured a German correspondent characterized all citizens that grew up in the United States, namely, "that feeling of superiority over other nations which you have observed." Adams linked that feeling to the belief of the citizenry in their equality, and their sense that the "governments are the servants of the people."[17]

But this American self-importance thrived in a highly decentralized Union of states, and attendant to demands of such a vision of the American national state, the imperial war of this new generation of Americans was a triumphant mess. "ARE WE ONE NATION OR 18?" John Adams asked in the midst of the debacle.[18] Adams was right to be concerned, for the Federalists had built an impressive army and navy, and had legislated the taxes to pay for them, without the nuisance of a declaration of war with France in 1798. For these efforts, Adams had gained a rebellion in Pennsylvania and had lost the presidency. But for Madison, the War of 1812 had been fought without the normal problems of centralization, and without the need for Alien and Sedition Acts. At the Hartford Convention, Federalists had hinted at secession; but with the end of war, the "empire of liberty" remained intact. Adams had to admit, grudgingly, that despite "a thousand Faults and blunders, his Administration has acquired more glory, and established more Union, than all his three Predecessors, Washington Adams and Jefferson, put together."[19]

The sense of the American uniqueness felt by the new political leadership that prosecuted the War of 1812, assured that the independence struggles of Latin America would seem unrelated to the destiny of the citizenry of the United States. The country had extremely different international priorities than the republic that confronted international revolution in the 1790s. The United States had been one of the first nations in the world to officially recognize the French Republic, and a large and vocal part of the country welcomed that country's first minister, "Citizen Genet," as a fellow revolutionary in a continuing struggle against feudal tyranny. But by the second decade of the nineteenth century, as the United States debated the possibilities of recognizing the emerging South American republics, the majority considered the question as a problem of U.S. interest alone, and very few Americans were willing to acknowledge the South Americans as being engaged in a similar revolutionary struggle. In fact, two of the few voices who continued to believe that the South American independence movements shared a common revolutionary mission with the citizens of the United States were the old international Irish revolutionaries, Mathew Carey and William Duane. As William Duane noted, the cause of Spanish America was the cause of the rights of man: "the Cause of Mankind versus the Cause of Despotism."[20] Mathew Carey, for his part, published more Spanish-language translations of American political tracts, pamphlets, and constitutions than all other American publishers combined.[21] But most Americans thought of the South Americans as a degenerate people, separated from their North American cousins by impassable divides of race, culture, and experience. As one of their supporters noted, "The character which we bestow upon our brethren of the South would do injustice to the most uncivilized of our Indians."[22]

The lack of interest in international revolution exhibited by the vast majority of the leading political classes did not necessarily mean that Americans abandoned their own beliefs in the principles of the Declaration of Independence, in natural equality, and in the importance of natural rights in the active meaning of American citizenship; but these ideas increasingly became confined within the boundaries of regularized legal practice. On the surface of political culture the notion of Americans with rights that stemmed from nature remained a potent part of the reflexive American creed. The Declaration of Independence came to be seen as the great philosophy of American rights, much more than the amendments to the Constitution, which were not binding on the states.[23] Even a sophisticate like John Quincy Adams had to admit that rights in America not granted, but assumed: "This is a land, not of *privileges* but of *equal rights*."[24]

But with time American legal practice became more standardized, and the precedents of American jurisprudence and constitutionalism dampened the ability of the citizenry to indulge in claims of natural right. Part of this transition reflected the weakening of the power of the jury to decide upon the meaning of law, and some of this phenomenon reflected a transformation in American law books and legal training, which became more and more specialized, scholastic, and rarified. Law and politics started to become separate realms.[25] Jefferson had learned his legal principles from the first volume of the *Institutes* of Lord Coke—"Coke upon Littleton"—in which he could read of a conception of common law that stood as a barrier to prerogative power. Actions of power could be "void" if they conflicted with "reason." But most Americans of the nineteenth century learned their law from the works of William Blackstone, who carefully limited access to the rights of nature in high notions of parliamentary supremacy. In Blackstone's vision, a subject had little appeal against the sovereign command of King-in-Parliament. When Jefferson looked around for a Republican justice to fill an open position on the Supreme Court, he lamented the trend of American lawyers weaned on Blackstone. Young American lawyers, he noted, "seduced by the honeyed Mansfieldism of Blackstone, began to slide into Toryism."[26] It was on these terms that he lamented the appointment of Joseph Story to the bench, who, although nominally a Republican, was likely only a "psuedo-Republican," and probably a "tory" in legal thinking. Story's *Commentaries on the Constitution* (1833), which "became the standard authority for the nationalist school of interpretation," was lauded by one contemporary as standing in relation to the U.S. Constitution "as Blackstone's great work bore to the British."[27] Story's *Commentaries* also included an aggressive assault upon the legal principles that could be found in Jefferson's letters, published for the first time in 1829.[28]

Yet most Federalists and their intellectual heirs worked within, and not against, the Union—in law schools, lectureships, and learned treatises—to craft a stabilizing understanding of common law principles. James Kent's four volumes of *Commentaries on American Law* (1826–30) served precisely this purpose: to provide a notion of a uniform American law and a standard American jurisprudence that would spread to the multifarious local jurisdictions. Kent was also known as "the American Blackstone." The new American constitutional law, built on Federalist principles, had the potential to defeat Republicanism with a gradual transformation of legal culture, even if high notions of individual rights remained dominant in American democratic political culture. At the very least, it might help hold the country together as it expanded west.[29]

Even so, for groups within the country who wanted to continue to advance the cause of natural rights against the traditional hierarchical arrangements of power and the presumed authority of scholastic constitutionalism, the example of appealing to universal principles, to abstract natural rights as a revolutionary political choice, remained an inspiration and guiding example. Within a generation after Independence, the notion of women with rights had become a powerful resource for antebellum women to celebrate as they asserted their own *equal* place in the American body politic. At Seneca Falls in 1848, a year of international revolution, a nascent women's movement reenacted the Declaration of Independence with a revolutionary assertion of the rights of women, and the right of women to resist governments that did not grant them equality: "We hold these truths to be self-evident: that all men and women are created equal; that they are endowed by their Creator with certain inalienable rights; that among these are life, liberty, and the pursuit of happiness; that to secure these rights governments are instituted, deriving their just powers from the consent of the governed."[30] The women's rights movement identified itself with revolutionary change, and its adherents bundled their energies into the abolition and temperance movements with radical fervor. Notably, American women had very little political use for the national government, which could do nothing to affect their relative status without a constitutional amendment. Although they mobilized support on a national scale, their most effective form of advocacy was as an important pressure group in local democratic politics among the states.

But the local nature of the boundaries of American citizenship, which the Union demanded, could never assure that local autonomy would not ultimately result in counter-revolutionary reaction, an abandonment of the principles the Union had been designed to protect, and eventually secession. With the passage of the Eleventh Amendment and the lack of a federal court system of any vigor, there was no legal or constitutional check on the abuse of power within the states, and no restraint on the rise of a haughty oligarchy inimical to the philosophy and interests of the American Union. The character of American democracy ultimately reflected local political reality, which could include a rejection of democracy itself. The Union was really only held together by compromise and a mutual commitment to the principles and heritage of '76. As the slave states retreated behind slavery, the commitment to the notion of the natural rights of man diminished among the great planters with the disappearance of the Revolutionary generation.

In Virginia, the rejection of Revolutionary principles initiated in the abandonment of voluntary manumission in 1806—done with much hand-wringing in a close vote—eventually culminated in the rejection of the state's Revolutionary heritage entirely, displayed publicly for the first time at the Virginian Constitutional Convention of 1828. The Virginia convention foreshadowed the direction of Southern thought when the representatives of the largest slaveholders and the old Tidewater elite rejected the philosophy of Jefferson, George Mason, and George Wythe, and clung to a fear of change to defend their once prominent, now declining regime. One by one, the representatives of eastern Virginia flaunted their hardened opinions and condemned the wild ideas that had stemmed from Jefferson's enthusiasms for the "rights of man." Benjamin Leigh, of Chesterfield, doubted whether the "natural rights" described in the Virginia Declaration of Rights were little more than "wild and visionary," as they presented "abstractions and substitutes" not to be relied on for the practical considerations of government. The old state constitution, he noted, reflected the traditions and balance of the British Constitution, while the new reforms sprung from an enthusiastic appeal to "the rights of man as held in the French school."[31] Abel P. Upshur concurred. "In truth," he noted, "there are no original principles of Government at all." The governments of Turkey, England, and the United States were all legitimate, because "power" was the only true source of authority.[32] Another delegate feared expanding the franchise, and noted, "To change your Constitution by such a majority, is nothing more than to sound the tocsin for a civil war."[33] An intrepid western Virginia delegate could scarcely believe the direction of his opponents' debate, remarking, "In the opinion of some gentlemen, Government has no principles":

> There was a time when this would not have been endured, when such language would have been offensive to republican ears. In the whole progress of this debate, the name of Thomas Jefferson, the great Apostle of liberty, has never once been invoked, nor has one appeal been made to the author of the Rights of Man, whose immortal work, in the darkest days of our revolution, served as a political decalogue and operated as a talisman to lead our armies to victory. . . . Then, the authority of the sage of Monticello would have stood against the world. . . . Then, was Burke regarded as the enemy of human rights and the firmest defender of aristocracy and monarchy—but now, Burke, Filmer,

> and Hobbes, judging from their arguments, have become the text books of our statesmen.[34]

He was right, but the representatives of the old elite were not impressed. John Randolph of Roanoke, whose evolution from ardent revolutionary to reactionary planter was now complete, assured the convention: "We are not to be struck down by the authority of Mr. Jefferson, if there be any point in which the authority of Mr. Jefferson might be considered as valid, it is the mechanism of the plough."[35] The Tidwater planters had, in fact, developed a deeply suspicious conservatism, characterized by antipathy to any change that could challenge their dominance. Virulently pro-slavery, pro–states' rights, anti-tariff, anti-Northern, and anti-democracy, the reality of the weakened plantation economy underpinned their fears. Benjamin Leigh attributed the decline of Virginia to all the "plagues" that had originated in the North, including natural rights, banks, tariffs, and "the Hessian fly."[36]

These Virginian planters foreshadowed a type of pro-slavery ideology that would come to full bloom in a generation, and would characterize an important perspective of Southern secessionist thinking. Karl Marx understood the movement for secession by the slaveholding South to be a rejection of the great principles of the American Revolution, specifically those abstract principles exposed in the Declaration of Independence—what he termed "the first Declaration of the Rights of Man." He had at least that much in common with George Fitzhugh, the somewhat extravagant Virginian pro-slavery thinker, who happily celebrated Southern secession as a "solemn protest against the doctrines of natural liberty, human equality and the social contract as taught by Locke and the American sages of 1776."[37] They were both right. Secession and Civil War were not born in the minds of those emphasizing natural rights and states' rights in the 1770s, 1780s, and 1790s, but in the heads of those who rejected majority rule and equality in favor of neo-feudal principles of inherited status and absolutism perfected by scientific racism.

So the first American Union ultimately could not sustain the extreme autonomy allowed to its constituent and equal members. With no check on the states, Madison's extended sphere could not last. The Civil War—which began when a Southern "nation," in defense of slavery and its way of life, initiated war against the United States while Lincoln attempted to "preserve the Union" of equal states—precipitated a second revolution in the relationship between the government and the governed in the United States, and another potential national birth of the American people. Near the end of that war, as the non-rebelling members of the Union began to reexamine the relationship of the American citizenry to the national state, the Constitution was amended for the first time since the first term of Jefferson, in amendments that could never have been attempted in the 1790s, and which created the potential for a transformation in the scope and reach of the national state just as they promised a redefinition of the American nation. The Thirteenth, Fourteenth, and Fifteenth Amendments finally promised to make American citizenship a national status of rights-bearing individuals, protected and defended by a national Congress and national courts.

Yet the transformative potential of these amendments still remained at the mercy of political will. Promises made in the 1860s were not kept in the 1870s. The limits of that second American Revolution shaped the future contours of the citizenship revolution—a continuing struggle to reconcile the promise of Revolutionary equality with the pressing demands of law, order, and the pursuit of happiness.

NOTES

ABBREVIATIONS

AA	Abigail Adams
AH	Alexander Hamilton
Annals of Congress	*The Debates and Proceedings in the Congress of the United States with an Appendix, Containing Important State Papers and Public Documents, and All the Laws of a Public Nature*
APW	*American Political Writing during the Founding Era, 1760–1805*
BAJ	*Book of Abigail and John*
CPPJJ	*Correspondence and Public Papers of John Jay*
CRNC	*Colonial Records of North Carolina*
CVSP	*Calendar of Virginia State Papers*
Debates	*Debates in the House of Representatives*
GW	George Washington
JA	John Adams
JCC	*Journals of the Continental Congress, 1774–1789*
JHDCV	*Journal of the House of Delegates of the Commonwealth of Virginia*
JJ	John Jay
JM	James Madison
LCK	*Life and Correspondence of Rufus King*
LDC	*Letters of Delegates to Congress, 1774–1789*
PAH	*Papers of Alexander Hamilton*
PGM	*Papers of George Mason*
PGW	*Papers of George Washington*
PJM	*Papers of James Madison*
PTJ	*Papers of Thomas Jefferson*
ROL	*Republic of Letters*
TJ	Thomas Jefferson
WTJ	*Writings of Thomas Jefferson*
WTP	*Complete Writings of Thomas Paine*

INTRODUCTION

1. Grain exports to British armies in Spain and Portugal rose from 835,000 bushels in 1811 to a peak of nearly 1,000,000 bushels in 1813 (Galpin, "American Grain Trade").

2. Martell, "Side Light on Federalist Strategy."

3. JA to Benjamin Rush, February 23, 1813, in Adams, *Spur of Fame,* 276.

4. *Niles' Weekly Register,* June 27, 1815.

5. TJ, "President's Message," *Annals of Congress,* 7th Cong., 1st sess., Senate, 14–15.

6. Hertzog, *Defining Nations,* 1–6; Tilly, "Primer on Citizenship," 599–602. For an introduction to the extensive literature, see Kymlicka and Norman, *Citizenship in Diverse Societies;* Shafir, *Citizenship Debates.*

7. The historical origins of nationalism and "national identity" continue to be a subject of debate among scholars, but it is clear that the idea of the nation-state—of a unitary government representative of a culturally, linguistically, ethnically, or historically distinct national people—is of only relatively recent vintage, gradually emerging in Europe over the seventeenth and eighteenth centuries and becoming a dominant model in the West during the transformations of the Age of Revolution. For an introduction to the literature, see Hutchinson and Smith, *Nationalism.* The French Revolution provided the apotheosis of the transformative model of the great nation-state. For a recent restatement, see Sewell, "French Revolution."

8. James Otis, "Rights of the British Colonies, Asserted and Proved," *Connecticut Courant,* September 9, 1765. For British nationalism, see Colley, *Britons;* Colley, "Radical Patriotism"; Brewer, *Sinews of Power;* Brewer, "Eighteenth Century British State"; Wilson, *Sense of the People;* Armitage, *Ideological Origins of the British Empire.* For American variants, see Breen, "Revisions in Need of Revising"; Greene, "Search for Identity." This point was also made by Varg in "Advent of Nationalism." A good starting point is still Savelle, "Nationalism and Other Loyalties."

9. See Ward, *Politics of Liberty;* Greene, *Peripheries and Center;* Reid, *Constitutional History;* McIlwain, *American Revolution.*

10. See Maier, *From Resistance to Revolution,* chap. 2.

11. Samuel Adams relied heavily on John Locke; see Locke, *Two Treatises of Government,* 352–58.

12. Inglis, *True Interest of America,* 7, 1.

13. See Greene, "Alienation of Benjamin Franklin"; see also Breen, "Revisions in Need of Revising."

14. For the variety of "constitutional" thinking, see Hulsebosch, *Constituting Empire.*

15. *Boston Evening Post,* October 8, 1759.

16. Anderson, *Crucible of War,* 286–93.

17. *PAH,* 1:101.

18. As quoted in Jensen, "Sovereign States," 226–27.

19. JA to Hezekiah Niles, February 13, 1818, in Morse, *Annals of the American Revolution,* 28, 29.

20. *LDC,* 1:288.

21. Waldstreicher, *Perpetual Fetes,* chap. 1; Parkinson, "Enemies of the People."

22. Hillard, *Last Men of the Revolution,* 3445.

23. "The Crisis, No. XIII, 1783," *WTP,* 1:234.

24. Benjamin Franklin to President of Congress, December 25, 1783, in Giunt, *Emerging Nation,* 1:959–60; Hendrickson, *Peace Pact,* 198–99.

25. Charles Thomson to Hannah Thomson, October 14, 1783, *LDC,* 21:57.

26. "Agrippa," quoted in Kramnick, "Great National Discussion," 10.

27. Edward Thornton to James Bland Burges, in Jackman, "Young Englishman Reports," 112.

28. For a broader discussion of "citizen" in the Western tradition, see Pocock, "Ideal of Citizenship," 29–52.

29. Ramsay, *Dissertation.*

30. Ibid.

31. Alexander Dallas, in *Talbot v. Janson,* 3 U.S. (3 Dall.) 133, 141 (1795). See also chapter 4.

32. Oath taken in Albany County, N.Y., in Palsits, *New York State Commission,* 2:747.

33. Wood, *Radicalism of the American Republic,* 11–92.

34. Keyssar, *Right to Vote;* Williamson, *American Suffrage.*

35. For the rearticulation of women's place in society after the Revolution, see Kerber, *Women of the Republic;* Norton, *Liberty's Daughters.* For the problematic relationship of women to American citizenship, see Kerber, *No Constitutional Right to Be Ladies;* Salmon, *Women and the Law of Property.* See also chapter 2. Americans would also begin to articulate more precisely the "natural" and "inherent" differences between blacks and whites as a justification of slavery and unequal citizenship for free blacks. See chapter 8.

36. Abraham Baldwin, January 11, 1799, *Annals of Congress,* 5th Cong., 3rd sess., House of Representatives, 2629.

37. Kettner, *Development of American Citizenship;* Smith, *Civic Ideals;* Kerber, *No Constitutional Right to Be Ladies.* Although highly compatible in many ways with this argument, all of these works discuss a longer span of time and therefore have a different focus, which flattens the political dimension of the Revolutionary creation of American citizenship. The present volume helps to reveal the sharp political milieu in which Revolutionary notions of citizenship were tested and shaped.

38. Wood, *Creation of the American Republic;* Bailyn, *Ideological Origins of the American Revolution.* See also Pole, *Political Representation in England.*

39. Seminal constitutional studies include Greene, *Peripheries and Center;* Reid, *Constitutional History;* and McIlwain, *American Revolution.*

40. Waldstreicher, *Perpetual Fetes;* Newman, *Parades;* Travers, *Celebrating the Fourth.* I have generally eschewed the term "nationalism" in this book because it has come to be too easily confused with any expression of national consciousness, or national identity—that is, as synonymous with any "patriotic" expression. Nationalism is not only an expression of identity or a sense of consciousness of national commonality, but it is also, as Eric Hobsbawm notes, a program that seeks to make the structures of the state responsive and representative of the nation (see Hobsbawm, *Nations and Nationalism*). As such, "nationalism" as only a vague marker of consciousness serves to confuse matters in the founding of the American Union, because we find competing visions of American nationhood that have extremely distinct understandings of the place of a national state in the lives of the individual members of the nation. These differences are not merely academic, but crucial (as will become evident) to the meaning of American identity and citizenship in the early republic.

41. Onuf and Onuf, *Federal Union;* Hendrickson, *Peace Pact.* See also Edling, *Revolution in Favor of Government;* Hulsebosch, *Constituting Empire.* Onuf and Onuf and Hendrickson are more significant to the arguments of this book; Hulse-

bosch is highly compatible, although his New York–centric view overly emphasizes the Federalists; Edling's focus on military/fiscal issues in the ratification is excellent, but his analysis of the 1790s elides differences among the "federalists" who supported the Constitution. This book uses capital letters to refer to the party of "Federalists" of the 1790s and lowercase "federalists" to describe those who supported ratification of the Constitution, against "anti-federalists."

42. JA to Benjamin Rush, June 12, 1812, in Schutz and Adair, *Dialogues,* 225.

43. Bailyn, *Ideological Origins of the American Revolution;* Wood, *Radicalism of the American Republic,* passim.

44. See, for example, Nash, *Unknown American Revolution.*

45. A new literature on the meaning of "the political" in the era can be found in Pasley et al., *Beyond the Founders.* For a broader discussion of the trend, see idem, "Introduction"; Shade, "Commentary." Thus, in recent years we have seen, with a fullness that had often only been hinted at earlier, the importance of public festivals, symbols, and rituals in the rich cultural "politics of the street" in early America (Waldstreicher *Perpetual Fetes;* Newman, *Parades;* Travers, *Celebrating the Fourth;* Branson, *These Fiery Frenchified Dames*), and the importance of thinking creatively about the numerous meanings and function of law in society (Tomlins and Mann, *Many Legalities of Early America*).

46. Much of the historiography of politics in the Revolutionary Era too easily divides scholars into consensus historians (who study ideas) and conflict historians (who tend to study internal state politics); in fact, these authors disagree less than they often believe, for the consensus of the enthusiasm for abstract ideals—things like "rights," "popular sovereignty," or "equality"—leads to conflicts over how those ideals will become actuated in society. Citizenship bridges the ideal and real worlds of the Founding Era. Bill Novak suggests the usefulness of "citizenship" as a model for a resurgent interest in American political history, but demurs from the importance of citizenship in the antebellum United States and worries over the possible anachronism that an emphasis on citizenship might create (see Novak, "Legal Transformation of Citizenship"). The present study explains why citizenship is crucial to understanding the politics of the era, and also why the states remain the most important arbiters of status membership in nineteenth-century America.

47. Some recent scholars of popular politics too often artificially separate the "popular" from the elite, or easily assume that the only truly "popular" ideas are antiestablishment ideas and thus beyond the ken of politics associated with the elite Founders; see Pasley et al., *Beyond the Founders,* 1–9. This critique has attacked all interest in the Founders as "Founders' chic," and lumps histories that are clearly derivative of current (and old) scholarship intended for popular readers with the work of imaginative historians still opening important new avenues to help find the meaning of crucial personalities and ideas in the founding of the American nation. The Founders are the elite of the elite, but they are crucial to any proper telling of how politics worked in the early republic. Among others, important recent works include Banning, *Sacred Fire of Liberty;* Rakove, *Original Meanings;* Onuf, *Jefferson's Empire;* Freeman, *Affairs of Honor;* and Hendrickson, *Peace Pact.*

48. Gordon Wood, "Launching the Extended Republic: The Federalist Era," in Hoffman and Albert, *Launching the "Extended Republic,"* 1–24.

49. The vast majority of historians follow Gordon Wood in *Creation of the American Republic,* and Jack Greene in *Peripheries and Center,* in suggesting that Americans achieved some consensus in 1788 that "the people" as a whole were ultimately sovereign under the Constitution, but the reality is much more murky; see chapter 3.

1 The Revolutionary Moment

1. "James Duane's Notes of Debates," *LDC,* 1:28–30.

2. On the petitions and remonstrances of 1774, see Marston, *King and Congress,* appendix, 69–75, 313–17; Rakove, *Beginnings of National Politics,* 27–34. On the mobilization in New England, see Maier, *From Resistance to Revolution;* Brown, *Revolutionary Politics;* Ammerman, *Common Cause.* On the Continental Congress, see Henderson, *Party Politics.*

3. "James Duane's Notes of Debates," *LDC,* 1:29.

4. Wood, *Radicalism of the American Republic,* 169–71.

5. "James Duane's Notes of Debates," *LDC,* 1:46.

6. Ibid., 1:47. See also the extensive notes of his "Propositions before the Committee on Rights," in ibid., 1:38.

7. Ibid., 1:48.

8. Ibid.

9. Ibid., 1:46.

10. Adams, *Diary and Autobiography of John Adams,* 3:309.

11. "Samuel Ward Diary," September 9, 1774, *LDC,* 1:59.

12. JA to James Sullivan, May 26, 1776, in Adams, *Works of John Adams,* 9:375–76.

13. Maier, *From Resistance to Revolution;* Young, *Shoemaker.*

14. "That it be recommended to the Provincial Convention of New Hampshire, to call a full and free representation of the People, and that the representatives, if they think it necessary, establish such a form of government, as, in their judgment, will best produce the happiness of the people, and most effectively secure peace and good order in the province, during the continuance of the present dispute between Great Britain and her colonies" (*JCC,* 3:317–19).

15. Marston, *King and Congress,* 251–96.

16. Force, *Tracts,* 5:1025–32.

17. J. P. Reid, "The Irrelevance of the Declaration," in Hartog, *Law in the American Revolution,* 48; see also Reid, *Constitutional History,* passim.

18. von Gentz, *Origin and Principles of the American Revolution,* passim, 5.

19. Bentham, *Works of Bentham,* 2:501.

20. McIlwain, *American Revolution.*

21. Bailyn, *Ideological Origins of the American Revolution;* Lutz, "Relative Influence of European Writers." For a specific example of the eclectic sources of an American polemic, which draws willy-nilly from Cesare Beccaria, Montesquieu, Blackstone, Trenchard and Gordon, Puffendorf, Virgil, and Cicero to craft an essay on the importance of natural rights and law in society, see Anonymous, "Rudiments of Law and Government Deduced from the Law of Nature," *APW,* 1:565–605.

22. Tucker, *Blackstone's Commentaries,* 2:129.

23. *PAH,* 1:122. Compare this to Thomas Paine in 1792: "But men who can consign over the rights of posterity forever on the authority of a mouldy parchment, like Mr.

Burke, are not qualified to judge of this revolution" (*The Rights of Man,* in Paine, *Political Writings,* 1:61).

24. Most of these authors are cited throughout this chapter.

25. Appleby, *Republicanism and Liberalism;* Kloppenberg, *Virtues of Liberalism.*

26. TJ to JM, August 30, 1826, *WTJ,* 10:267–68.

27. Breen, *Lockean Moment,* passim; Maier, *American Scripture,* 87; Becker, *Declaration of Independence;* White, *Philosophy of the American Revolution;* Rodgers, *Contested Truths,* 20–55; Kramnick, *Republicanism and Bourgeois Radicalism,* 160–200.

28. JA to AA, June [July?] 10, 1776, *BAJ,* 143.

29. "First Draft of the Virginia Declaration of Rights," *PGM,* 1:276–87.

30. Brendon McConville's recent *The King's Three Faces* helps show just how shocking the rejection of kings could be.

31. Pocock, "States, Republics, Empires," 61–62.

32. JA to AA, June [July?] 10, 1776, *BAJ,* 143.

33. Ryerson, "Political Mobilization"; Ryerson, "Republican Theory," 99. See also Rosswurm, *Arms, Country, Class.*

34. Ryerson, "Republican Theory"; Rosswurm, *Arms, Country, Class.*

35. *Pennsylvania Packet* (Philadelphia), May 27, 1776.

36. State of Pennsylvania, "The Proceedings Relative to the Calling the Conventions of 1776 and 1790 the Minutes of the Convention that Formed the Present Constitution of Pennsylvania" (Harrisburg, 1825). "A petition from the German associators of the city and liberties of Philadelphia, was read, praying that all associators, who are taxables, may be entitled to vote" (ibid., 38). On the attempts of the German Reformed communities to gain access to political power before 1776, see Rothermund, *Layman's Progress;* Hanna, *Benjamin Franklin;* Hutson, *Pennsylvania Politics,* 1–20, 40–75.

37. *Pennsylvania Packet* (Philadelphia), March 4, 1776; Rosswurm, *Arms, Country, Class,* 66–72.

38. *Lee Papers,* 3:431.

39. Constitution of Pennsylvania (1776).

40. For an alternative reading, see Gaynard, "Radicals and Conservatives."

41. "Creed of a Rioter," in Iredell, *Papers of James Iredell,* 1:420.

42. "To his Majesty George the Third, King of Great Britain, &ct.," February 1777, in ibid., 1:424.

43. Ibid.

44. William Hooper to Samuel Johnston, September 26, 1776, *CRNC,* 10:819.

45. William Hooper to the Congress at Halifax, October 26, 1776, *CRNC,* 10:867.

46. Gilpatrick, *Jeffersonian Democracy,* 1–16; Gaynard, *Emergence of North Carolina's Revolutionary State Government.*

47. Kruman, *Between Authority and Liberty,* 96; *CRNC,* 10:932–33.

48. Gilpatrick, *Jeffersonian Democracy,* 26–28.

49. For the extremely high turnover of the elections to the Revolutionary Virginia legislatures, see McDonnell, *Politics of War,* 32, 200–204, 551.

50. The draft Declaration of Rights of Virginia was the only version published outside of the state in the Revolutionary Age. The Frenchman Jacques-Pierre Bris-

sot de Warville celebrated "*l'immortelle declaraction de l'Etat de Virginie sur la liberte des cultes*" (an immortal declaration of the State of Virginia on freedom of religion). Jean-Antoine-Nicolas Caritat, marquis de Condorcet, noted that the "author of the Virginia Declaration earned the eternal gratitude of mankind" ("First Draft of the Virginia Declaration of Rights," *PGM,* 1:276–87).

51. Ibid., 1:276.

52. "The Petition of a Baptist Church at Occagon, Pr. William County," June 20, 1776, Religious Petitions, 1774–1802, Library of Virginia. The Library of Virginia has the petition cataloged under June 20, 1776, but the petition was "signed on behalf of the Church, on this 19th day of May 1776."

53. There were eleven thousand signatures, based upon rough estimates of the adult white male population of Virginia, taken from McKusker and Menard, *Economy of British America.*

54. Miscellaneous Petition ("Ten-Thousand Name"), October 16, 1776, Religious Petitions, Library of Virginia.

55. Miscellaneous Petition, October 24, 1776, Religious Petitions, Library of Virginia. The most tepid petition of 1776, a long argument from a German Lutheran congregation of Culpeper County, did not attempt to break from the established church. Instead, members of the congregation merely wanted to have their own ministers incorporated into the establishment, so that they could practice their religion as "taught by their Parents in Europe." Such an accommodation was necessary, considering that they were "fellow Citizens in common" who were "obliged to bleed for Freedom" (German Lutheran Congregation, October 22, 1776, Religious Petitions, Library of Virginia).

56. Albemarle, Amherst, Buckingham, October 22, 1776, Religious Petitions, Library of Virginia.

57. Draft of the "Act for Establishing Religious Freedom," section 3, *PTJ,* 2:546–47. Very much has been written about the process of disestablishment in Virginia. See the long note by Julian Boyd for guidance (*PTJ,* 2:547–53). The most concise study is Buckley, *Church and State in Revolutionary Virginia.* For two different takes on the political process of disestablishment, see Isaac, *Transformation of Virginia,* 275–95; and Butler, *Awash in a Sea of Faith,* 261–64.

58. Brown, *Middle Class Democracy;* Taylor, *Western Massachusetts in the Revolution.*

59. As quoted in Taylor, *Western Massachusetts in the Revolution,* 64.

60. Ibid., 78–80; Hoerder, *Crowd Action in Revolutionary Massachusetts.*

61. Nobles, *Divisions throughout the Whole,* table 7, 196.

62. "The Petition Remonstrance and Address of the Town of Pittsfield to the Honourable Board of Councellors and House of Representatives of the Province of Massachusetts Bay in General Assembly now setting in Watertown," in Handlin and Handlin, *Popular Sources,* 62.

63. Ibid.

64. "Petitions," May 29, 1776, in ibid., 92.

65. "Statement of the Berkshire County representatives, Nov. 17, 1778," in ibid., 374.

66. Ibid., 374, 376–78.

67. Ibid., 254.

68. Hall, *Politics without Parties.*

69. There were seventeen conventions and closings in Hampshire County and seven in Worcester from 1781 to 1787 (see Brooke, "To the Quiet of the People," 433–34).

70. Quoted in Minot, *History of the insurrection in Massachusetts,* 86.

71. "Berkshire, February 15, 1787," in ibid., 146–47.

72. Bellesiles, "Establishment of Legal Structures."

73. Of course, in the midst of war and revolution, it was not even clear that Vermonters would be Americans, let alone independent. Pressed on all sides by Yorkers, Yankees, and Britons, Ethan Allen promised only to keep fighting, if need be "into the Desolate Caverns of the mountains," to wage war "against human nature at large" (Ethan Allen to Samuel Huntington, March 9, 1781, in Allen, *Ethan Allen,* 1:110).

74. These fights over the character of the new American republics have sometimes been interpreted too easily as "class" conflicts. There were groups with distinct socioeconomic grievances, to be sure, like many of the New England farmers who closed the courts, or the Pennsylvania privates who fought over the relative compensation of officers, or the small landowners of Virginia who relished their upstart leader Patrick Henry, but in general, "classes," in the Marxian sense of the word—interests defined by their relationship to the means of production—did not exist and were not being formed in the Revolution, in part because all of these groups were attempting to access equal admission into the great Revolutionary class: "the people." This also should not be read to suggest that *all* traditionally marginalized groups or individuals were enthusiastic for American independence, or responded in predictable ways based on an outsider status. In fact, numerous groups hoped to challenge their traditional exclusion from power by aligning themselves with the Crown against their landlords and masters. On the importance of popular royalism, see McConville, *King's Three Faces,* 170–91.

75. *LDC,* 1:139

76. Brewer, *By Birth or Consent,* 174–77.

77. Alexander Addison, *APW,* 2:1078.

78. Ibid., 2:1082. In a society where over 90 percent of the people lived in rural areas and engaged in farming and the related trades, there should be little surprise that the basic regulations of crime, the household, and property looked as much natural as contrived.

79. JM to GW, November 6, 1786, *LDC,* 24:486.

80. Tucker, *Blackstone's Commentaries,* vol. 1, note E, "Of the Unwritten, or Common Law of England; and its Introduction Into, and Authority Within the United American States." On the importance of the language of "repugnancy" to American constitutionalism, see Bilder, *Transatlantic Constitution,* 2–7, 40–46, 186–90.

81. North Carolina Constitution (1776); Maryland Constitution (1776), Article XIV.

82. Maryland Constitution (1776), Article IV.

83. Levy, *Palladium of Justice;* John Murrin, "Magistrates, Sinners and a Precarious Liberty: Trial by Jury in Seventeenth-Century New England," in Hall et al., *Saints and Revolutionaries,* 207–46.

84. Pennsylvania Constitution (1776), Article XI.

85. Lois Schwoerer, "Law, Liberty, and Jury Ideology: English Transatlantic Revolutionary Traditions," in Morrison and Zook, *Revolutionary Currents,* 35–64.

86. Brewer, *By Birth or Consent,* 173–80.

87. Tucker, *Blackstone's Commentaries,* vol. 1, note E, "Of the Unwritten, or Common Law of England; and its Introduction Into, and Authority Within the United American States."

88. Kent, "Introductory Lecture," 940, 948.

89. Smith, *Comparative View of the Constitutions of the Several States;* Channing, *History of the United States,* 3:459–62; Nevins, *American States;* Main, "Government by the People."

90. Historians differ about the exact timing of some of these changes. Bernard Bailyn, in *Ideological Origins of the American Revolution,* sees new ideas about rights, representation, and sovereignty as evolving out of a great polemical whirlwind during the 1760s; as American pamphleteers thought through the problems of their resistance to Parliament, these ideas become manifest in the changes of the 1770s. Gordon Wood, in *Creation of the American Republic,* would date some of these changes to a later period, while Marc Kruman, in *Between Authority and Liberty,* argues effectively against such later dating. Jackson Turner Main, in "Government by the People," asserts that many of these changes came from the interplay of "Whig" and "democratic" ideas in the period of state constitution writing.

91. Ramsay, *Dissertation,* 3, 4, 5.

92. Ibid., 4. David Ramsay wrote from South Carolina, where the assumption that free blacks were not citizens was nearly unanimously held (among whites) from the very beginning. But in other states, and in other political movements, the relationship of free blacks to citizenship had not been entirely settled by 1789, and much evidence exists of the strong antagonism to excluding men from citizenship based solely upon skin color; see chapter 8.

93. For a brilliant running engagement of "ascriptive" aspects of citizenship in America, see Smith, *Civic Ideals,* passim.

94. Caeser Sarter, "Essay on Slavery," in Nash, *Race and Revolution,* 167–70.

95. Force, *Tracts,* 4:334.

96. Randolph, *History of Virginia,* 253.

97. Schmidt and Wilhelm, "Early Virginian Pro-Slavery Petitions"; Kukla, "Irrelevance and Relevance of Saints George and Thomas."

98. Randolph, *History of Virginia,* 329. See also chapter 8.

99. The quote is taken from Novak, "Legal Transformation of Citizenship," 105, but the argument is intended to answer some of his suspicions about the importance of citizenship in the founding era.

100. AA to JA, March 31, 1776, *BAJ,* 121.

101. Richard Henry Lee to Hannah Corbin, March 17, 1778, in Lee, *Letters,* 1:392–94.

102. *New York Journal,* March 7, 1776.

103. Klinghoffer and Elkis, "Petticoat Electors," 159–94; McCormick, *History of Voting in New Jersey;* Turner, "Women's Suffrage in New Jersey"; Philbrook, "Woman's Suffrage in New Jersey"; Pole, "Suffrage in New Jersey." For a stunning reassess-

ment of the dynamic problem of women's rights and the Revolution, as well as the important lasting legacy of female voting in New Jersey, see Zagarri, *Revolutionary Backlash.*

104. Joan Hoff Wilson, "The Illusion of Change: Women and the America Revolution," in Young, *America Revolution,* 385–445; Linda Kerber, "'History Can Do It No Justice': Women and the Reinterpretation of the America Revolution," in Hoffman and Albert, *Women in the Age of the America Revolution,* 3–42; Elaine F. Crane, "Dependence in the Era of Independence: The Role of Women in a Republican Society," in Greene, *American Revolution,* 253–75.

105. Extended essays on the ways women were imagined as a significant part of the national community—in ways never allowed to blacks, for instance—can be found in the now classic works: Kerber, *Women of the Republic;* Norton, *Liberty's Daughters,* 155–94, 225–27; Gunderson, "Independence, Citizenship, and the American Revolution." For women in the "public sphere," see Brown, *Knowledge Is Power;* Kelley, "Reading Women."

106. Newman, *Parades,* chap. 5; Branson, *These Fiery Frenchified Dames,* chap. 2; Newman and Branson, "American Women and the French Revolution"; Zagarri "Rights of Man and Woman."

107. Warren, *History,* 1:83. For a more inclusive overview and excellent bibliography, see Gunderson, *To Be Useful to the World.*

108. Recollections of Benjamin Harrison, *LDC,* 2:381.

109. Thomas Burke to Richard Caswell, April 29, 1777, *LDC,* 4:673.

110. JA to AA, August 14, 1776, *BAJ,* 154.

111. Dunbar, *Paxton Papers,* 193–94.

112. His arguments came too late for me to incorporate them into this analysis, but see Griffin, *American Leviathan.*

113. See chapter 8.

114. Laws and a comparison of the laws can be found in Van Tyne, *Loyalists in the American Revolution,* appendixes B, C.

115. William Peirce to St. George Tucker, July 20, 1781, *Magazine of American History* 7 (1881): 434.

116. Kettner, *Development of American Citizenship,* 174–83.

117. Some leading works on general "loyalism" include Calhoon, *Loyalists in Revolutionary America;* Moore: *Revolution, Exile, Settlement;* Van Tyne, *Loyalists in the American Revolution;* Brown, *Good Americans;* Smith, "American Loyalists"; and Kim, "Limits of Politicization."

118. Norton, "Eighteenth Century American Women."

119. Ramsay, *Dissertation,* 5, 6.

120. "A Bill Declaring Who Shall be Deemed Citizens of this Commonwealth," *PTJ,* 2:476–77.

121. "A few Solitary Hints, Pointing out the Policy and Consequences of admitting British Subjects to Engross our trade and Become our citizens. Addressed to those who either risqued or lost their all in bringing about the revolution" (Charleston and New York, 1786), 4, 7.

122. Francis Kinloch to Thomas Boone, September 1, 1783, in Kinloch, "Letters of Francis Kinloch."

123. Zeichner, "Loyalist Problem in New York"; Fox, *Decline of Aristocracy.*

124. On the changes in politics in Pennsylvania, see Brunhouse, *Counter-Revolution in Pennsylvania.*

125. See chapter 8.

2 } STATE VS. NATION

1. There was no "majority opinion" in the case, as each justice read a distinct opinion from the bench.

2. Elliot, *Debates,* 1:75–76.

3. *LDC,* 6:672–73.

4. Elliot, *Debates,* 1:77–78.

5. "Vices of the Political System," *PJM,* 9:348–58, 353.

6. The best general volume on the problems leading to the Constitutional Convention for my thinking is Fiske, *Critical Period of American History,* 139–248; for an answer to Fiske, see Jensen, *New Nation;* Wood, *Creation of the American Republic;* Main, *Political Parties;* Onuf, *Origins of the Federal Republic;* Onuf, *Statehood and Union;* Hoffman and Albert, *Sovereign States in an Age of Uncertainty.*

7. Henry Knox to Rufus King, July 15, 1787, *LCK,* 1:228.

8. GW to JJ August 15, 1786, *PGW,* Confederation Series, 4:213.

9. TJ to JM, December 16, 1786, *PTJ,* 11:679. See Madison in the Virginia ratifying convention: "The powers in the general government are those which will be exercised mostly in time of war" (Elliot, *Debates,* 4:283–84). See also TJ to Edward Carrington, August 4, 1787, *PTJ,* 11:679, "My general plan would be, to make the states one as to every thing connected with foreign nations, & several as to everything purely domestic."

10. JM to TJ, *ROL,* 498–500. Note the difference between this letter to Jefferson and Federalist No. 10, in which Madison takes out all the references to the national veto, which he desired.

11. Federalist No. 45, 292–93.

12. Farrand, *Records,* 1:285.

13. Ibid., 1:297.

14. Ibid., 1:287, 298.

15. Ibid., 2:645–46.

16. AH to Gouverneur Morris, February 27, 1802, as quoted in Stourzh, *Alexander Hamilton,* 39.

17. Federalist No. 72, 435–36.

18. Farrand, *Records,* Supplement: 83.

19. Sharp, *American Politics,* 32–33; Miller, *Alexander Hamilton,* 225.

20. Alexander Hamilton, "Further Provision for the Public Credit," *PAH,* 7:235.

21. Civil List, year ending October 1, 1792, United States, *Documents Legislative and Executive,* 57–68.

22. See AH to Charles Cotesworth Pinckney, August 3, 1791, *PAH,* 10:280.

23. More patronage was available for the Hamiltonians in South Carolina, as compared with the merely moderate and often anti-Hamilton Federalists (Rogers, *Evolution of a Federalist,* 191–92, 227–30). Compared to the other executive departments, Hamilton's patronage machine was overwhelming. Thomas Jefferson, sec-

retary of the Department of State, possessed direct control over the appointment of only seven clerks, with annual salaries worth a paltry $4,100 in 1792. Outside of his immediate office, Jefferson also controlled the Mint, which had four employees in 1792, with salaries worth $5,012 (Civil List, year ending October 1, 1792, United States, *American State Papers,* 57).

24. Rogers, *Evolution of a Federalist,* 230. On the importance of George Cabot to Federalism, see Fischer, *Revolution of American Conservatism,* 2–6.

25. "Defense of the Funding System, July 1795," *PAH,* 19:4. See also McDonald, *Alexander Hamilton,* 392n18 and 285–307.

26. George Lee Turberville to JM, April 7, 1790, *PJM,* 13:143. The idea that Virginians did not understand Hamilton's plans is without merit.

27. Channing, *History,* 4:93–94; American Historical Association, *Report of the American Historical Association,* 1:838.

28. Beverly Randolph to JM, July 12, 1790, *PJM,* 13:277.

29. *JHDCV* (1790), 38.

30. Commonwealth of Virginia, *Statutes at Large,* 8:237–39.

31. Oliver Wolcott Jr. to Oliver Wolcott Sr., November 24, 1790, in Gibbs, *Memoirs,* 1:59.

32. TJ to GW, September 9, 1792, *PTJ,* 24:352. Jefferson's memory of the occasion for the dinner table compromise also reflects the fact that he felt completely unable to speak on the relative merits of Hamilton's funding plan; he arrived in Philadelphia in the midst of the debate over assumption, as he noted, "a stranger to it. But a stranger to the ground, a stranger to the actors on it, so long absent as to have lost all familiarity with the subject, and as yet unaware of its object, I took no concern in it." In Jefferson's version of it, Hamilton took him aside and pleaded for help, for a solution to the stalemate that had met the bills in the House of Representatives—thus, Jefferson created the occasion for the dinner table agreement, "to form a compromise which was to save the Union" (Jefferson, *Complete Ana of Thomas Jefferson,* 32–34).

33. Jefferson later noted, "That when we reflected that [Hamilton] had endeavored in the Convention to make an English constitution of it, and when failing in that we saw all his measures tending to bring it to the same thing it was natural for us to be jealous" (October 1, 1792, Conversation with Washington, *PTJ,* 24:435).

34. In this belief, Jefferson and Madison shared much with opposition voices that stemmed from many different sectional and socioeconomic backgrounds across the Union, but they epitomized particularly the concerns of the enlightened agrarians of Virginia's slaveholding planter elite, including such important former Virginian anti-federalists as George Mason and John Taylor of Caroline. Of the many books that have looked carefully at Jeffersonian commitment to agrarian political economy in the context of republican thought, Drew R. McCoy's *The Elusive Republic* is perhaps the most important. But McCoy tends to overemphasize the natural pessimism about America's future entailed in the vision of an agrarian political economy always under threat of degeneration, which distorts the vision of the Revolutionary republicanism of these Virginian agrarians by largely ignoring their outspoken and optimistic commitment to the transformative power of natural rights.

35. JM to Henry Lee, April 13, 1790, *PJM,* 13:147. See also Madison speech to the House of Representatives, April 22, 1790, *PJM,* 13:167.

36. Thomas Jefferson, "Note on the National Debt," *PTJ,* 24:810. The funding scheme failed to provide an avenue for a rapid remittance of the debt, and by his own calculations in 1792, Jefferson considered the United States as "tho the youngest nation in the world we are the most indebted nation also" (TJ to JM, June 21, 1792, *PTJ,* 24:106). He based this notion not on the relation of gross national product to debt, as most modern economists would, but public debt to annual revenue. As such, he estimated the British to have a debt-to-revenue ratio of 16 to 1 in 1786, the French in 1785 of 8 to 1, and the United States, roughly 20 to 1. For his figures on European debt, he used von Zimmermann, *Political Survey of the Present State of Europe.*

37. TJ to GW, September 9, 1792, *PTJ,* 24:355.

38. TJ to JM, July 10, 1791, *PJM,* 14:43.

39. Conversation with Benjamin Rush, *PJM,* 14:272n1.

40. "Memoranda of Conversations with the President," *PTJ,* 23:184.

41. With Hamilton playing the part of Walpole, it's not surprising that the Virginians would draw heavily on an important language of eighteenth-century English opposition thought, both Tory and Whig. These authors, like the Tory Henry St. John Viscount Bolingbroke and the Whigs John Trenchard and Thomas Gordon, worried over the excesses of speculation and the role of the debt and the patronage system in the corruption and ultimate destruction of the beautifully balanced British Constitution. Where Jefferson and Madison differed from these political theorists related to their remedy—not a patriot king, or suffrage reform, but an emphasis on the limits imposed by a strict reading of the U.S. Constitution.

42. AH to Edward Carrington, May 26, 1792, *PAH,* 11:443.

43. TJ to JM, October 1, 1792, *ROL,* 2:741.

44. Duer, *Adams Federalists.* William Manning's *The Key of Liberty* represents a populist critique of Hamilton's system and style of administration, which resonated widely in rural America. It was a critique in many ways compatible with the Virginian agrarianism, but which could potentially be used to attack the slaveholding oligarchy of Virginia as well. Other groups and interests, particularly in the artisan and mechanic communities of the Northern ports, wanted the Hamiltonian system to more strongly protect American manufactures with punitive tariffs on British imports, and disliked the close Hamiltonian relationship with the British (see Manning, *Key of Liberty*). For more on the language of dissent in the early 1790s, see Cornell, *Other Founders,* 147–213.

45. He had been felled in the winter of 1787 by "rheumatism," and later by an inexplicable pain in his left side. And in April of 1788, with the Federalist series almost complete, Jay was incapacitated by the blow of a cobblestone to the head from a mob attempting to break into the jail to assault doctors who had been experimenting on cadavers.

46. [John Jay,] "An Address to the People of the State of New York, on the Subject of the Constitution" (New York, 1788), *CPPJJ,* 3:294–319

47. As quoted in Monaghan, *John Jay,* 311.

48. AH to JJ, November 13, 1790, *PAH,* 7:149.

49. JJ to AH, November 28, 1790, *PAH,* 7:166–67.

50. JJ to GW, January 7, 1787, *CPPJJ,* 3:227.

51. As quoted in Warren, *History,* 1:70.

52. The best source for a summary and explanation of the trial is Mathis, "*Chisholm v. Georgia*," which I have used and which corrected many of the problems in Warren, *Supreme Court in United States History,* the version which many constitutional law books still follow. The best contemporary records of the case are in the newspapers, particularly a summary of the trial in *Dunlap's American Daily Advertiser,* February 21, 1793.

53. *Farquhar v. Georgia,* as quoted in Mathis, "*Chisholm v. Georgia,*" 22.

54. Mathis, "*Chisholm v. Georgia,*" 22–23.

55. 2 U.S. (2 Dall.) 419 (1793). Mathis, "*Chisholm v. Georgia,*" 19–29, argues that the petition of Georgia was never read in the court. He bases this assertion upon the claim of Alexander Dallas in the newspapers, to the effect that "Nor did any Counsel argue upon this occasion, in opposition to the Attorney General." This contemporary note, he believes, contradicts the report of the case, and he notes that Dallas "wrote report of the case long after the events," implying that Dallas had somehow become confused and inserted the petitioning episode as a mistake. But there is no contradiction between the newspaper and the report. While the report states that Dallas presented the remonstrance for Georgia, it is clear that he did not act as "Counsel" for the state of Georgia, and in fact was forbidden by "positive instructions" to make any argument in the case. In his newspaper note, Dallas was simply correcting the popular notion that he was the counsel for the defense, when in fact he had simply been retained to present their remonstrance and do no more. The evidence from Randolph's speech shows that the petition was presented, since Randolph referred directly to it, and also to a petition circulated by Virginia.

56. 2 U.S. (2 Dall.) 419, 421 (1793).

57. *Dunlap's American Daily Advertiser,* February 21, 1793.

58. *Chisholm v. Georgia,* 2 U.S. (2 Dall.) 419, 467 (1793).

59. Ibid., at 452–53.

60. Ibid., at 448–49.

61. Ibid., at 453.

62. Ibid., at 453–66.

63. Ibid., at 459.

64. Irdell, *Life and Correspondence,* 2:394.

65. *Chisholm v. Georgia,* at 465–66.

66. Ibid., at 470.

67. Ibid., at 470–71.

68. Ibid., at 471–72.

69. Ibid., at 472.

70. Ibid., at 471–72.

71. Ibid., at 472–73.

72. See Newmeyer, *John Marshall,* passim.

73. Federalist No. 2, 40–41.

74. *CPPJJ,* 3:143.

75. *Dunlap's American Daily Advertiser,* February 21, 1793; *Aurora General Advertiser,* February 22, 1793; *Gazette of the United States,* February 23, 1793.

76. See the complaints of the *National Gazette,* August 10, 1793.

77. *Connecticut Courant,* February 25, 1795.

78. *Dunlap's American Daily Advertiser,* February 21, 1793.

79. *Salem Gazette,* July 23, 1793; Jay's decision printed in the *Salem Gazette* on July 23 and 30, 1793.

80. "Crito," in *Salem Gazette,* July 30, 1793.

81. *Columbian Centinel,* July 31, August, 3, 7, 10, 1793.

82. "Crito," in *Salem Gazette,* August 27, 1793.

83. As a newspaper in New England declared, "When the persons in opposition to the acceptance of the new Constitution" complained that the "extensive and alarming" scope of the judiciary would call a "State itself as a party to an action of debt, this was denied peremptorily by the federalists as an absurdity in terms." But in the decision of the Court, apparently, "the eloquent and profound reasoning of the Chief Justice has made that to be a right which was, at first, doubtful and improper." It represented an extraordinary "stride of authority" (*Independent Chronicle,* April 4, 1793).

84. Monaghan, *John Jay,* 302; *PGM,* 3:1053–54.

85. Federalist No. 81, 488.

86. *Boston Gazette,* August 5, 1793.

87. *National Gazette,* June 1, 1793.

88. *Independent Chronicle,* July 18, 1793.

89. *Boston Gazette,* August 5, 1793.

90. *Salem Gazette,* January 14, 1794.

91. Ibid.

92. *Columbian Centinel,* March 23, 1793.

93. Ibid.

94. *Independent Chronicle,* July 25, 1793.

95. *Salem Gazette,* September 16, 1793.

96. Ibid., October 29, 1793.

97. Ibid., September 24, 1794.

98. Ibid.

99. Ibid., October 15, 1793.

100. Ibid., October 29, 1793.

101. Ibid., October 1, 1793.

102. *Columbian Centinel,* September 27, 1793.

103. *Salem Gazette,* October 1, 1793.

104. Virginia, South Carolina, and New York also set up rival state banks to challenge the supremacy of the National Bank branches.

105. *Salem Gazette,* February 18, 1794.

106. Ibid.

107. One exception is Artemas Ward.

108. Madison's notes of Ellsworth's speech, June 25, 1787, Farrand, *Records,* 1:406.

109. Madison's notes of Ellsworth's speech, June 30, 1787, ibid., 1:492.

110. Oliver Wolcott Jr. to Noah Webster, May 20, 1793, in Gibbs, *Memoirs,* 1:99.

111. Young, *Shoemaker,* 123.

112. Oliver Wolcott Jr. to Oliver Wolcott Sr., February 8, 1793, in Gibbs, *Memoirs,* 1:86.

113. Chauncey Goodrich to Oliver Wolcott Jr., in ibid., 1:88

114. Chauncey Goodrich to Oliver Wolcott Jr., March 24, 1793, in ibid., 1:91.

115. Lemuel Hopkins to Oliver Wolcott Jr., August 21, 1793, in ibid., 1:105.

116. Oliver Wolcott Jr. to Noah Webster, August 10, 1793, in ibid., 1:104.

117. For the Connecticut case, see Warren, *Supreme Court in United States History,* 66. For Georgia, *Samuel Braisford v. James Spalding;* South Carolina, *Higgenson v. Greenwood;* Rhode Island, *Champion v. Casey,* see ibid., 66–67. For additional evidence of the success of British creditors in the federal courts, see the letter of Thomas Pinckney to TJ, May 9, 1793, *PTJ,* 23:489, viz, "the foederal Courts are in the exercise of their powers."

118. *LCK,* 1:424–25.

119. *JHDCV* (1793), 125.

120. *JHDCV* (1793), 90. For a list of the proposed amendments and bill of rights, see Kaminski and Saladino, *Documentary History of the Ratification of the Constitution,* 6:200–206.

121. Salary bills in the Senate to only go into effect after new elections (Kaminski and Saladino, *Documentary History of the Ratification of the Constitution,* 6:202–3).

122. The debate became so heated that people almost came to blows, as it was reported in the journals: "Francis Corbin, a delegate from the county of Middlesex, in his speech, expressed himself to the following effect, and nearly in the following words, to wit: 'It is a notorious fact, that the two gentlemen representing this State in the Senate of the united States were originally opposed to the federal constitution, they were violently opposed to it, they were opposed to it tooth and nail, and advice coming from them on the subject of amendments, appear to me to come in questionable shape—I suspect they mean to destroy the constitution—I dislike the advice—I dislike the advisors.'" He was confronted by Monroe's friends in the lobby (*JHDCV* [1793], 121–22).

123. *JHDCV* (1793), 125. Passed in the Senate on December 11 (ibid., 127–28).

124. Introduced on January 14, 1794—the same day the Eleventh Amendment passed the Senate—the bill originally called for a prohibition against serving in Congress for any person holding stock or any office in *any* bank that traded in public securities, and also provided for an inclusion of a prohibition against the creation of "any charter of incorporation, or any commercial or other monopoly" by the federal government. As John Taylor and James Monroe worked to make the amendment more acceptable, it eventually only asked for a prohibition against anyone holding an office in the Bank of the United States holding a seat in Congress (see *Annals of Congress,* 3rd Cong., 1st sess., Senate, 31–32). At least two directors of the bank in the Senate, George Cabot and Rufus King, and one man closely connected to the interest of the bank in Charleston, Ralph Izard, voted against the amendment. The vote was a microcosm of precisely the problem Virginians had with Hamilton's stockholders. Theoretically, the amendment would have passed if it had not been defeated by the votes of a private interest, votes that therefore were seen to distort the "real" interest of the country.

125. The Indiana Company, like many other land companies in Virginia before and during the war, such as the Ohio, Virginia Loyal, Henderson, Mississippi, and Vandalia companies, attempted to lay claim to lands in the West that Virginia was

not ready to support. Virginia denied the claims of the Indiana Company and asserted the state's absolute sovereignty over all claims by negotiating a deal with Congress (Onuf, *Origins of the Federal Republic,* 86–89).

126. *JHDCV* (1793), 125.

127. Anonymous, *House of Delegates.*

128. *JHDCV* (1793), 125.

129. *Annals of Congress,* 3rd Cong., 1st sess., Senate, 30, 31.

130. On the same day, Peter Trezevant presented the following petition: "Peter Trezevant, of the city of Charleston, in the State of South Carolina, in behalf of his wife Eliza, the only child and sole legatee and devisee of Robert Farquhar, was presented to the House, and read, praying the liquidation and settlement of a claim for supplies furnished by the deceased, for the use of the Army and Navy of the United States, pursuant to an order of the Governor and Executive Council of the State of Georgia, during the late war." Trevezant and the other executors actually settled their lawsuit with the state of Georgia for a fraction of what they had requested in trial. Most likely, as this petition represents, Trezevant believed he could get more from the U.S. government, although the original debt had been ostensibly settled (*House Journal,* 3rd Cong., 1 sess., March 4, 1794, 2:78). No record of action on this petition could be found. On the continuing problems of Trezevant with Georgia, see Mathis, "*Chisholm v. Georgia,*" 28–29.

131. *House Journal,* 3rd Cong., 1 sess., March 4, 1794, 2:78, 79, 80; *Annals of Congress,* 3rd Cong., 1st sess., House of Representatives, 475–78.

132. *Annals of Congress,* 3rd Cong., 1st sess., Senate, 66.

133. *Salem Gazette,* January 28, 1794.

134. U.S. National Archives, *Ratified Amendments,* reel 1.

135. *Senate Journal,* 4th Cong., 2nd sess., January 31, 1797, 315–16.

136. *Senate Journal,* 5th Cong., 2nd sess., January 8, 1798, 420. Warren mistakenly claims that "South Carolina failed to take any action" (*History,* 4:101). South Carolina approved the amendment on December 1, 1797. On January 23, 1798, Timothy Pickering wrote to Governor Charles Pinckney that the act enclosed from Pinckney lacked the state seal. "An authenticated copy of the act, as here suggested, I request your Excellency to cause to be made out & sent to my office, to be deposited with the constitution." He continued, "You will probably have noticed in the newspapers that the ratification of this act by Kentucky has been received and communicated to Congress. This made the twelfth ratification; & consequently the amendment has become a part of the constitution. The ratification by South Carolina makes the 13th" (Timothy Pickering to Charles Pinckney, January 23, 1798, U.S. National Archives, *Ratified Amendments,* reel 1). Warren also believed that "the records of the office of the Secretary of State show only six States as having ratified the Eleventh Amendment." In fact, however, the evidence is clear.

137. *Hollingsworth v. State of Virginia,* 3 U.S. (3 Dall.) 398 (1795).

138. Mathis, "*Chisholm v. Georgia,*" 25. Charles Warren writes, "The real source of the attack on the *Chisholm Case* was the very concrete fear of extensive prosecution by former loyalists." Warren also assumes the long delay between 1798 and 1794 reflects a lack of concern about the principles of state sovereignty that were put forward in favor of the amendment (*Supreme Court in United States History,* 1:99).

139. *Independent Chronicle,* July 18, 1793.

140. *House Journal,* 3rd Cong., 1st sess., March 4, 1794, 2:78, 79, 80; *Annals of Congress,* 3rd Cong., 1st sess., House of Representatives, 475–78; *Annals of Congress,* 3rd Cong., 1st sess., Senate, 30, 31.

141. "First Draft of the report of the Committee of Detail" (Philadelphia, 1787), accessible at Library of Congress Web site.

142. The comma does not exist on the manuscript version of the original Constitution but showed up immediately in the printed versions. For three examples out of many: United States, *Proceedings of the Federal Convention* (Boston, 1787); United States, *The foederal Constitution, being the result of the important deliberations of the Foederal Convention, who completed their business on the 17th September, 1787, at Philadelphia* (New York, 1787); or, in German, "Wir, das Volk," *Verfahren der vereinigten Convention, gehalten zu Philadelphia, in dem Jahr 1787, und dem zwölften Jahr der americanischen Unabhängigkeit. Auf Verordnung der General Assembly von Pennsylvanien aus dem Englischen übersetzt* (Frederick Town, Md., 1787).

143. Hendrickson, *Peace Pact,* 13.

144. Addison, *On the Alien Act.* Judges continued to use the preamble in cases stressing national authority; see John Marshall in *McCulloch v. Maryland,* 17 U.S. 316 (1819).

145. JJ to JA, January 2, 1802, *CPPJJ,* 4:285–86.

146. AH to Gouverneur Morris, February 29, 1802, *PAH,* 25:544.

3 ⁑ The Politics of Citizenship

1. *United States v. Gideon Henfield,* in Wharton, *State Trials,* 44–97, 95 (hereafter cited as Henfield's Case).

2. George Hammond to TJ, May 8, 1793, *PTJ,* 25:685–86.

3. Henfield's Case, 73–74.

4. Ibid.

5. See Franklin, *Legislative History of Naturalization.*

6. Tucker, *Blackstone's Commentaries,* 1:2, 369.

7. Since no British subjects could alienate themselves from their responsibilities to king and country, and since the British recognized as "American citizens" only those who had moved to America before 1783 or were born in the United States, their heavy-handed seizure of seamen remained a point of contention. Lord Grenville noted to Secretary of State Timothy Pickering that the British government "cannot accede" to "the principles" behind American notions of naturalization. "No British subject," he declared, "can, by such a form of renunciation as that which is prescribed in the American law of naturalization, divest himself of his allegiance to his sovereign. Such a declaration of renunciation, made by any of the King's subjects, would, instead of operating as a protection to them; be considered as an act highly criminal on their part" (Lord Grenville to Rufus King, March 27, 1797, *Annals of Congress,* 5th Cong., appendix, 3319–20). The Federalist Timothy Pickering, when secretary of state, refused to challenge the British policy toward naturalized Americans (see, for example, Clarfield, "Postscript to the Jay Treaty," 111; Kettner, *Development of American Citizenship,* 44–61).

8. Commonwealth of Virginia, *Statutes at Large,* 9:1775–78, 10:129–30.

9. TJ to Albert Gallatin, June 26, 1806, in Jefferson, *Writings of Thomas Jefferson,* edited by Lipscomb and Bergh, 8:454.

10. Constitution of Pennsylvania (Philadelphia, 1776); Constitution of Vermont (1777).

11. There are interesting conversations about emigration in this context by the delegates to the Continental Congress in 1774, as they tried to decide what English authorities they were beholden to and fought over which language to use to protest the Parliamentary actions against Boston after the Tea Party (see *LDC,* 1:28–46).

12. "British subjects became aliens, and being at war, they were alien enemies" (Jefferson, *Notes on the State of Virginia,* 155).

13. Hamilton, *Works of Alexander Hamilton,* 4:256.

14. [Alexander Hamilton,] A Letter from Phocion to the Considerate Citizens of New York, *PAH,* 3:488.

15. Ammon, *Genet Mission;* Henderson, "Isaac Shelby and the Genet Mission"; Turner, "Origin of Genet's Projected Attack."

16. Sharp, *American Politics,* 70, 87–88.

17. Long considered an important "pressure group," the societies have lately come under attack as a rather unimportant phenomenon. Stanley Elkins and Eric McKitrick, in *The Age of Federalism,* in particular, have characterized the groups as extremely unimportant, filled with desperate men whom no one took seriously. I take a very different view of the societies. While I would admit not *all* societies were of equal significance in their regions, in South Carolina, New York, Maryland, Vermont, Kentucky, and Pennsylvania, especially, the societies played a major role, not only in distributing political literature and articulating opposition ideology but also in organizing an opposition party to the Washington administration. Elkins and McKitrick make the incredible claim that "few members of the Democratic societies ever reach positions of prominence in public office" and that "the leading Republicans in all the states tended to stay well clear of the Democratic Societies" (459, 460). These are great overstatements. I would, rather, point to prominent members, like eventual U.S. Senator and Attorney General John Breckinridge and Senator Robert Todd of Kentucky, Governor Moultrie of South Carolina, Jefferson-appointed U.S. District Attorney Alexander Dallas, David Rittenhouse, Benjamin F. Bache, U.S. Congressman and Senator Michael Lieb, Henry Kammener, Peter Du Ponceau, Governor and later U.S. Senator from Kentucky James Brown, Clerk of New York and Governor Clinton ally Tunis Wortman, numerous members of the Baltimore Democratic Society, and many others.

18. Democratic-Republican Society of Pennsylvania, *Principles, Articles and Regulations,* 1.

19. *General Advertiser,* May 31, 1798.

20. *Columbian Centinel,* July 23, 1794.

21. *American Minerva,* December 16, 1793.

22. He was clashing openly with Secretary of War Knox and Secretary of Treasury Alexander Hamilton in the policy meetings that Washington regularly held. He found Attorney General Edmund Randolph, an erstwhile Virginian ally and friend, unpredictable and often independent in his politics. As Jefferson complained to Madison, Randolph was "the poorest Cameleon I ever saw having no colour of

his own, & reflecting that nearest him" (TJ to JM, August 11, 1793, *PJM,* 15:57–58). Washington tended to go with majority vote, so Jefferson consistently lost policy debates and yet had to publicly support positions he often believed to be against the interest of the country. At the time of the arrival of Genet, Jefferson had already taken great steps to expand the influence of "the republican interest" in America by—with James Madison—setting up Philip Freneau as editor of the opposition paper *National Gazette.* He had given Freneau a job as a translator in the State Department, and even had tried to get Thomas Paine the job as postmaster general, to entice Paine to America.

23. TJ to JM, May 19, 1793, *ROL,* 2:775–76. This was part of the resistance to the whiskey excise which would culminate a year later in the Whiskey Rebellion.

24. Jefferson would later assert that Michaux's trip was little more than an innocent scientific journey. Here Jefferson is not to be believed; Genet himself requested the letter, and Jefferson knew well what Genet was planning in the West (see Miller, *Federalist Era,* 134; De Conde, *Entangling Alliance,* 248–50).

25. *General Advertiser,* May 24–June 5, 1793.

26. Jackson, *Privateers in Charleston.*

27. United States, *State Papers and Publick Documents,* 1:34.

28. Ibid.

29. Ibid., 1:94–96.

30. Ibid.

31. *National Gazette,* November 23, 1793.

32. See Foner, *Sourcebook,* 46n85. See also Wolfe, *Jeffersonian-Democracy in South Carolina,* 77–81.

33. I disagree with many historians that Jefferson's increasing distrust of Genet had to do with a desire to maintain the sovereignty and honor of the United States. In fact, I would link it more to Jefferson's anger at being drawn publicly into a controversy over the "rights of man" on the "aristocratic" side of the question (see Malone, *Jefferson,* 3:121–23). Telling in this regard is the fact that the leaders of the Republican Party throughout the country never abandoned Genet in the terms Jefferson called for, and even the leaders of the Republicans in Virginia—James Madison, James Monroe, and John Taylor of Caroline—refused to really get concerned about the activities of Genet.

34. Rawle, "Memoir."

35. Henfield's Case, 72, 88.

36. Ibid., 77–78.

37. Ibid., 81–82.

38. Ibid.

39. Ibid., 87.

40. *General Advertiser,* August 5, 1793.

41. *Independent Chronicle,* August 15, 1793. Wilson's charge to the jury was printed in the *Chronicle* in full. The version in Wharton's *State Trials* is shorter. I have relied on both.

42. Henfield's Case, 89.

43. Ibid., 90.

44. Ibid., 92.

45. "Circular to the Collectors of Customes," and "Rules adopted by the President of the United States," in *National Gazette,* August 17, 1798. See also TJ to JM, August 18, 1793: "Orders are given to drive out of our ports the privateers which have been armed in them before the 5th. Of June . . . : and we are seising the prizes brought in since August 7. to restore them to their owners. For those between June and August we engage restitution or compensation" (*PJM,* 15:57–58).

46. *Annals of Congress,* 3rd Cong., 1st. sess., House of Representatives, 136–37 (emphasis added).

47. Jefferson tried to downplay the jury's obstinacy by arguing that they had merely believed Henfield did not know the criminal nature of his acts. This was, of course, not how the Republican press interpreted the verdict, seeing it rather as a critique of Washington's policy of neutrality as well as a democratic victory of natural rights over feudal restraints and ancient politics. Jefferson actually used the letter to explain the American right of expatriation, reasserting his own commitment to it but stating that Henfield had not really been expatriated, because he did not intend to shed his citizenship until it became clear that he needed to, to escape punishment. This was *not* the official position of the Washington administration.

48. *National Gazette,* August 7, 1793, 322.

49. Ibid., August 3, 1793, 319.

50. *General Advertiser,* August 6–9, 1793; Henfield's Case, 95. Within days of the acquittal of Henfield, reports that Genet had boasted that he would appeal to the American people over the president's Proclamation of Neutrality began filtering out of Philadelphia. The first such report that reached New York was publicly confirmed by none other than John Jay and Rufus King, in the *New York Diary* for August 12, 1798.

51. French Republic, *They Steer to Liberty's Shores.*

52. *General Advertiser,* August 10, 1793.

53. *National Gazette,* August 17, 1793.

54. "Toasts Drunk to celebrate the French ship 'L'Embuscade's' victory (actually it was an escape) over the British frigate 'Boston,'" August 29, 1798, in Foner, *Sourcebook,* 380. See also *General Advertiser,* August 14, 1798.

55. *Talbot v. Janson.*

56. Ibid.

57. Ibid., at 139.

58. Ibid.

59. Ibid., at 140.

60. Ibid., at 141.

61. Ibid., at 150.

62. Ibid.

63. Ibid., at 151.

64. $1,755.53 for the cost of the ship, $82.00 for court costs; $4,897.58 for nearly three hundred days' interest on the value of the cargo of the ship (ibid., at 170).

65. Patterson is chiefly known as the delegate at the Constitutional Convention who introduced the "small state plan." Politically, Patterson was in close alliance with the most ardent nationalists, and ideologically he was deeply opposed to the prin-

ciples of the French Revolution. In 1800, he was the first choice of the Hamiltonian faction of the Federalist Party for the chief justice's seat that Marshall eventually filled (see Turner, "Appointment of Chief Justice Marshall").

66. Cushing and Rutledge thought that the question of expatriation generally, although crucial, was not the important question of the case. Wilson made no comment, because his decision in the circuit court had been upheld.

67. *Talbot v. Janson,* at 162.

68. Ibid.

69. Ibid., at 71–72.

70. Ibid., at 73.

71. Iredell, *Iredell,* 2:484–85.

72. Williams' Case, Case No. 17,708, Circuit Court, D. Connecticut 29 F. Cas. 1330; 1799 U.S. App. Lexis 39; 2 Cranch 82, 1–3.

73. Ibid., 4–6.

74. "Resolutions Adopted on Jay's Treaty," September 25, 1795, in Foner, *Sourcebook,* 405.

75. "Toasts Drunk at a Meeting," June 24, 1794, ibid., 392.

76. "Citizens of the State of South Carolina to the Citizen Edmond Charles Genet," August 1793, Genet Papers, Library of Congress.

77. For more on this argument, see Bradburn, "Revolutionary Politics," 33–74.

78. In particular states, the local politics of personal and regional interest rapidly began realigning after 1790. In New York, the "federalist" pro-Constitution Party was broken by 1792, when Robert Livingston joined the anti-federalist leader, George Clinton, against his old allies, John Jay and Alexander Hamilton. In many of the other states, the Constitution had passed so quickly that no real organized opposition ever existed. In others which opposed the Constitution the longest, like Rhode Island, their internal politics had little to do with national issues until after 1801, when the "agrarian" party finally realized that they shared more with the Jeffersonians in power than with New England capitalists. On the varieties of anti-federalist thought, see Storing, *What the Anti-Federalists Were For;* Cornell, *Other Founders.*

79. Saul Cornell notes that "the creation of a Democratic-Republican opposition was an amalgam of ideas from various parts of Anti-Federalism and those more closely associated with Jefferson and Madison" (*Other Founders,* 168). But this elides the continuity of Revolutionary principles in the character of American political thought. What the party did share, from its old republican planters, to its proto-liberal commercial radicals, to its backcountry farmer democrats—and what has too often gone unstressed—was consistent enthusiasm for the French Revolution, a continuing willingness to invoke "natural rights" and the "rights of man" to express their particular grievances, and a deep sense of localism.

80. I follow Richard Hofstadter, *The Idea of a Party System;* and Ronald P. Formisano, *The Transformation of Political Culture.* James Roger Sharp, in *American Politics,* calls them "proto-parties" in reasserting that these are parties but not a "party system," largely because each group absolutely denies the legitimacy of the other. The "polarization of political rhetoric" is crucial to the development of these parties, because although there are often discordant strains within the parties themselves,

they do put the other into these broad polarities quite rapidly, and with few pangs of conscience. The best local study on the birth of a party in the 1790s remains Alfred F. Young's *Democratic Republicans of New York,* which shows, in microcosm, the many distinct elements of the Republican Party in New York, but also stresses the tendencies of thought and interest which they shared. Other crucial texts to understand the increasing organization of national party politics are Jeffrey L. Pasley, *"The Tyranny of Printers,"* which reemphasizes the crucial role of printers as party organizers and shows the birth of men who are really "politicians"; and Simon Paul Newman, *Parades,* which shows the way popular celebratory rituals become engrafted into a national party politics, or political culture.

81. See "The Union: Who are its real friends?" *PJM,* 14:274–75; "A Candid State of Parties," *PJM,* 14:370–72.

82. TJ to JA, June 27, 1813, in Adams, *Adams–Jefferson Letters,* 335.

83. On the political philosophy of John Adams, the best is Thompson, *John Adams and the Spirit of Liberty.* Also excellent is Haraszti, *John Adams and the Prophets of Progress.*

84. *WTJ,* 5:354ff.

85. TJ to JM, May 9, 1791, *WTJ,* 5:329.

86. Burke had been a champion for the cause of the American resisters in the years leading up to Independence. He supported American claims to receive "English liberties"—the liberties that all Englishmen shared as their birthright, liberties protected by the British Constitution, the most perfect form of government in the world. He *never* supported the American cause, as one of his astute recent biographers has pointed out, "because they asserted abstract rights like those enumerated in Jefferson's 'Declaration of Independence'" (O'Brien, *Great Melody,* lxxi). It should also be recognized that Jefferson probably never read the Davila essays with great attention (Malone, *Jefferson,* 3:359).

87. The debate between Paine and Burke is in many ways a continuation of the conversations held in the Continental Congress of 1774, where congressmen argued over whether natural rights should be employed over traditional constitutional principles (see chapter 2). By 1791, with the first disturbances of the French Revolution in St. Domingue promising bloody slave revolt, and as the French Revolution itself entered its extreme phase—with the execution of the king in 1792 and the excesses of "the Terror"—the suspicions of some traditionalists seemed proven. Edward Thornton, assistant to the British ambassador in Philadelphia, reflected many elite concerns when news of the arrest of Louis XVI reached America: "The arrival of a ship at New York after a short passage has acquainted us with the horrible transactions which have passed in France during the middle of August. Good God! What will become of that miserable country and the still more unhappy creature whom they mocked with the name of the King of it! . . . What a commentary are those transactions on the works of Burke and Payne! What a complete triumph to the prophetic reasoning of the former! What an overthrow to the pernicious doctrines of the other!" (Edward Thornton to James Bland Burgess, October 3, 1792 in Jackman, "Young Englishman Reports on the New Nation," 117).

88. Menk, "D. M. Erskine," 258. More acquainted with the stable party system of

his home, he wrote to his father: "I really think from what I have seen" that his earlier description "can scarcely come up to the violence which rages equally on both sides . . . the intolerance is greater in this Country by much, upon the subject of Politics, than it is with us." He was shocked that the parties "think nothing of wishing each other destroyed; each Party openly descanting upon the probability of its becoming a matter of necessity to extirpate the opponent one."

89. Adams, *Political Writings,* 1:340n.

90. Gibbs, *Memoirs,* 1:567.

91. *Columbian Centinel,* November 1, 1794.

92. *Columbian Centinel,* October 18, 1794.

93. *PJM,* 17:52.

94. *Aurora,* October 8, 1799; see Smelser "Federalism and the Menace of Liberty"; and Smelser, "Menace of Monarchy."

95. From Jefferson's letter to Mazzie, printed in the Philadelphia newspapers in early May 1797: *Gazette of the United States,* May 4, 1797; *Aurora General Advertiser,* May 5, 1797; *Porcupine's Gazette,* May 4, 1797.

96. See Newman, *Parades;* Waldstreicher, "Rites of Rebellion"; Waldstreicher, *Perpetual Fetes;* Travers, *Celebrating the Fourth.*

97. On the rise of the First Party System, see Charles, *Origins of the American Party System;* Chambers, *Political Parties;* Hofstadter, *Idea of a Party System;* Cunningham, *Jeffersonian Republicans;* Bell, *Party and Faction.*

98. *Columbian Centinel,* January 1, 1794.

99. See chapter 7, note 9.

100. "Emigration to America," *Columbian Centinel,* November 8, 1794.

101. New York Society for the Information and Assistance of Persons Emigrating from Foreign Countries, *Bye Laws.*

102. *Annals of Congress,* 3rd Cong., 1st sess., House of Representatives, 169–73. For a more extensive discussion of the character of this immigration, see chapter 7.

103. Young, *Democratic Republicans,* 411.

104. *American Minerva,* June 14, 1794.

105. See chapter 7.

106. Baseler, *Asylum for Mankind,* 260–65.

107. *American Minerva,* December 11, 1794.

108. *Columbian Centinel,* July 23, 1794.

109. *Philadelphia Gazette and Universal Daily Advertiser,* August 15, 1794.

110. *Andrew's Western Star,* January 13, 1795.

111. *Philadelphia Gazette and Universal Daily Advertiser,* August 15, 1794.

112. *New Hampshire Gazette,* September 2, 1794.

113. *Columbian Centinel,* November 19, 1794. Such complaints were common in the papers surrounding election days, as each party accused the others of cheating. The extent of foreign participation in the elections cannot be established from the partisan nature of the newspapers, but the impression of illicit foreign participation at the polls was a common Federalist complaint.

114. *Annals of Congress,* 3rd Cong., 2nd sess., House of Representatives, 1004

115. *Debates,* 12:146.

116. Ibid.

117. Good discussion of the context of the debate is in Baseler, *Asylum for Mankind,* 247–60. Baseler presents an overly skeptical interpretation of "Republican" attitudes toward immigration in general by focusing a bit too much on Jefferson's theoretical comments in his *Notes on the State of Virginia* in the 1780s, and less on the Republican attitudes toward immigrants in the 1790s. Baseler also suggests that the Naturalization Bill of 1790 was a "compromise" bill, but this really overstates the number of people who thought it "illiberal." From my reading of the debate, only one or two members thought such an easy process was too harsh.

118. *Debates,* 12:162.

119. *Annals of Congress,* 3rd Cong., 2nd sess., House of Representatives, 1004

120. Ibid., 1005.

121. Ibid., 1006.

122. Ibid., 1006–1008.

123. Ibid., 1023.

124. Ibid., 1021.

125. Ibid., 1021, 1034.

126. Ibid., 1034–35.

127. Ibid.

128. Ibid., 1035.

129. Ibid.

130. Ibid., 1039.

131. Ibid., 1048.

132. Ibid., 1040.

133. Ibid., 1054.

134. Ibid., 1039.

135. Ibid., 1040.

136. Ibid., 1054. Only five members voted for the passage of both amendments, and only nine voted against both.

137. The debates are generally scarce, but the impression of fatigue and compromise is evident. See ibid., 1069–70.

138. For an enthusiastic argument about the importance of newspapers for the creation of early national political culture, see Newman, *Parades,* 3 and passim. For Newman, as for Waldstreicher and others, the newspapers played an important role in spreading reports on parades, feasts, fetes, and occasions which helped articulate and reinforce a popular national political culture. Political "festive culture" had both local participants and a national audience through the reporting of the newspapers, and "this sharing of information made possible the emergence of a common national language of ritual activity." I would also argue that the central importance of congressional debates to newspapers, not only in serving as the main content of the newspapers but their role in setting the agenda of the political essays which filled the columns of early national newspapers, and oftentimes created the impetus for spontaneous fetes and parades, reflect a time—perhaps unlike many others—in American national politics where the day-to-day dramas of so-called high politics heavily influenced the politics of the street. See also Pasley, *The Tyranny of Printers,* passim.

139. Henfield's Case, 95. Wharton, commenting on Genet's arrogant offer of French protection to Henfield, reminds us: "Unfortunately, however, for Henfield,

this 'protection' was not very potent, for, elated with the honor of French citizenship, he sallied forth in a new excursion, which resulted in his capture by a British cruiser" (ibid.).

4 "True Americans"

1. *Philadelphia Gazette and Universal Daily Advertiser,* May 7, 1798.

2. Historians have long considered this period as representing the height of Federalist nationalism, but few have given such assertions any context, either historical or theoretical. Many historians of the mid-twentieth century considered the nationalistic ambitions of the Federalists little more than crass political strategy; see John C. Miller's classic *Crisis in Freedom.* David Brion Davis and Richard Hofstadter have emphasized the "paranoid style" of Federalist leaders in this moment, linking the motives of the party in power to later periods of "extremism" in American political life. Both Miller and these other scholars link the Federalists with twentieth-century McCarthyism, as examples of conservative reactions to dangerous ideological challenges. Recent students of nationalism, including Waldstreicher, Newman, Travers, and others, have perhaps too easily accepted "nationalism" as little more than a synonym of "patriotism," or an expression of national identity, and therefore muddle the differences between Federalist and Republican attitudes toward citizenship, the states, and rights.

3. On the modernity of the terms "ethnic" and "ethnicity," see Sollors "Theory of American Ethnicity," 259–61.

4. By the middle of the eighteenth century there was general consensus about the nature of *European* peoples. The English tended to use "national character" to describe the general characteristics of particular nations, while the French used both "national character" and "national spirit" to understand national distinctions. "National character" often referred to a "sentimentality" and feeling that existed among nationals—what we might characterize as "national identity." In *Le Encyclopèdie* (Paris, 1751–65), the philosophes define the "caractères des nations" as consisting "dans une certaine disposition habituelle de l'âme, qui est plus commune chez une nation que chez une autre, quoique cette disposition ne se rencontre pas dans tous les membres qui composent la nation: ainsi le caractère de français est la lègèretè, la gaiete, la sociabilite, l'amour de leurs rois et de la monarchie même, etc." (in a certain habitual provision of the heart, which is more common with one nation than another, though this provision is not met by all the members who make the nation: thus the French character is, cheerfulness, sociability, even the love of their kings and the monarchy, etc.).

5. Montesquieu, *Spirit of the Laws.* See also, "It is important for the one who should govern not to be imbued with foreign maxims . . . men care prodigiously for their laws and their customs; these make the felicity of every nation" (ibid., 516).

6. Hume, "Of National Characters," 198.

7. Berkley, "Querist," Query 91, 430.

8. GW to Henry Laurens, November 14, 1778, in Washington, *Writings of George Washington,* 13:254–55.

9. Vattel, *Law of Nations,* 4. See also Bernard Mandeville's celebration of English "national happiness," wherein the character of the English people is perfectly

reflected by the activities of their national state (Mandeville, "National Happiness," in *Free Thoughts on Religion*).

10. See Knight, "Images of Nations"; Hayman, "Notions on National Characters"; Duffy, *Englishman and the Foreigner;* Dalinoff, "Familiar Stranger."

11. See, for instance, the most popular English-language geography in pre-Revolution America: Guthrie, *New System of Modern Geography,* 452. See also the first American geography, Jedidiah Morse's *Geography Made Easy* (1784), and his later productions, the *American Universal Geography* (1789, 1792, 1800).

12. See any issue of Mathew Carey's *American Museum, or, Universal Magazine, containing essays on agriculture—commerce—manufactures—politics—morals—and manners. Sketches of National Characters—natural and civil history—and biography. Law information—public papers—intelligence. Moral tales—ancient and modern poetry,* vols. 1–12 (Philadelphia), January 1787–December 1792.

13. The papers are filled with this sort of ephemera; *New Hampshire Mercury,* Portsmouth, N.H., December 31, 1794, excerpted from the "London Magazine."

14. In addition to the following discussion of Zimmerman, see Montesquieu, "On the vanity and arrogance of nations," in Montesquieu, *Spirit of the Laws,* 312. See also Guthrie, *New System of Modern Geography:* "The Germans are not fettered with those absurd and contemptible prejudices, through which most nations are so prone to extol themselves, and to disparage and degrade all others. A German does not despise, he rather esteems a man, because he is a foreigner." He goes on to note that the Germans are "so justly famous" for this "liberality of sentiment" which undoubtedly forms one of the traits in their national character" (452). Oliver Goldsmith's *The Citizen of the World* is another example, where he writes from the perspective of a fictitious Chinese observer and mocks European xenophobia; see "Letter XXXIII," in Goldsmith, *Citizen of the World.*

15. Although largely forgotten today, Zimmerman's book remained in print in English, French, and German throughout the eighteenth century and into the early nineteenth century. Originally published in German in 1758, the book went through numerous editions, including a corrupted English duodecimo volume published in 1771, and a 1799 English version translated from the French, which this essay uses (Zimmerman, *Essay on National Pride*).

16. Ibid., 43, 70.

17. Ibid., 69. Zimmerman's favorite targets included the English: "stuffed with beef, pudding and porter, heartily despises every other nation of Europe"; the Greeks: "this vainglorious people adopted the persuasion, that nearly all other nations of the earth were colonies of Greece"; the Italians: "the present squalid inhabitants of Campania speak of Roman consuls, generals and emperors, as their townsmen and relations"; and the French: "in their own estimation . . . the only thinking beings in the universe" (ibid., 70–80).

18. Ibid., 90, 98.

19. *City Gazette & Daily Advertiser,* January 6, 1798. This last statement echoes Montesquieu's confession that "the various characters of the nations are mixtures of virtues and vices, of good and bad qualities" (*Spirit of the Laws,* 313). Some Americans seemed to be generally familiar with Zimmerman's work and quoted him to good effect. As the anonymous polemicist "Marcellus" wrote in March 31, 1798, "It is an

admirable observation of the intelligent and elegant Zimmerman, that 'a nation will never lose its honour as long as its virtue remains unpolluted, and its virtue will never be tainted, as long as patriotism gives a free and lofty flight to every sentiment of the heart'" (*Gazette of the United States,* March 31, 1798).

20. JA to Hezekiah Niles, February 13, 1818, in Morse, *Annals of the American Revolution,* 28, 29.

21. "The Crisis, No. 13, 1783," in Paine, *Life and Works,* 3:79, 243–45.

22. Webster, *Sketches of American Policy,* 34.

23. Webster focused on reforming the English language for an American audience (as he wrote, "A national language . . . is a bond of national union" [*Essays,* 45]), and his series of grammars, spellers, and readers were also designed with an eye to encouraging students to learn the geography of the new nation. Unlike the English spellers that his *American Speller* (1782) replaced, Webster included a large series of American place names. His *American Reader* (1786) included a section on geography, defining the terms, boundaries, peoples, and history of the United States (Webster, *Collection of Essays,* 45, 76). The 1782 edition of his speller was the second part of his *A Grammatical Institute of the English Language,* which was popularly called "The Little Blue Book" and later known as *The American Spelling Book* (Webster, *Grammatical Institute of the English Language,* 70).

24. *PAH,* 2:154.

25. Jay, Federalist No. 2, 38–39.

26. Hamilton, Federalist No. 85, 527.

27. Butterfield et al., eds., *Adams Family Correspondence,* 1:368.

28. Jefferson, *Notes on the State of Virginia,* 84–85.

29. Quoted in Kramnick, "Great National Discussion," 10.

30. "Observations on Faces," *Pennsylvania Magazine; or, American Monthly Museum* 1 (July 1775): 303.

31. "Essay on Smuggling," *American Museum* 6 (July 1789): 61.

32. "Pro Republica," "Thoughts on the present Situation of the Foedral Government of the United States," *Columbian Magazine* 1 (December 1786): 171.

33. "The Governor's Address to both Houses, June 2 1786," *Boston Magazine* 3 (June 1786): 251–54.

34. Crèvecoeur, *Letters from an American Farmer,* letter 3.

35. Ibid.

36. Morse, *American Geography,* 67–68. For Morse, like Crèvecoeur, there is no room in their vision of assimilation for Native Americans, Africans, or people of African descent. See chapter 8.

37. *American Museum* 6 (November 1789): 391–93.

38. Waldstreicher, *Perpetual Fetes;* Newman, *Parades;* Travers, *Celebrating the Fourth.*

39. *Annals of Congress,* 4th Cong., appendix, 2871.

40. Ibid., 2873–74.

41. Ibid.

42. Ibid., 2878.

43. Ibid., 2873.

44. John Jay, October 27, 1797, *CPPJJ,* 4:232.

45. *Philadelphia Monthly Magazine; or, Universal Repository of Knowledge,* 1: 111–21.

46. *Newburyport Herald and Country Gazette,* August 14, 1798.

47. *Philadelphia Gazette and Universal Daily Advertiser,* April 14, 1798.

48. *Philadelphia Gazette and Universal Daily Advertiser,* April 24, 1798.

49. Ibid., May 15, 1798.

50. Rufus King to AH, London, May 12, 1798, *LCK,* 322–23.

51. *Philadelphia Gazette and Universal Daily Advertiser,* April 30, 1798.

52. "Manlius," *Philadelphia Gazette and Universal Daily Advertiser,* April 14, 1798.

53. In appendix A to "Revolutionary Politics," I document the 246 petitions which I have culled to construct this argument. These represent all the petitions I could find published in the chief Federalist newspapers in Pennsylvania, Connecticut, North Carolina, Massachusetts, and New York, and the extant petitions in the Adams Papers (Massachusetts Historical Society) and some others which were collected in Austin, *Selection of the Patriotic Addresses.* This does not presume that "Americans" were united around the Adams administration; on the contrary, as we can see below, and as chapter 6 shows, resistance to the petitioning and the Federalist legislation was immediate and sustained, leading directly to a massive Republican petitioning drive in the Mid-Atlantic, as well as to the Virginia and Kentucky Resolutions.

54. Austin, *Selection of the Patriotic Addresses,* May 15, 1798.

55. Few historians consider this petitioning as little more than generic expressions of loyalty. Simon P. Newman, for instance, sees them from the context of the "Politics of Popular Leadership" and as Adams's only real approximation of the "cult of Washington" which characterized Federalist political culture. But as I argue, the petitions exert an ideology of nationalism and a vision of citizenship which mirrors and justifies the efforts of the Federalists in the Congress (Newman, *Parades,* 76–79).

56. This includes the petition from the State Society of the Cincinnati and the petitions of both houses of the Pennsylvania legislature.

57. Anonymous, *There is a Snake in the Grass!!*

58. See Pincus, "Nationalism"; and, more generally, Pincus, *Protestantism and Patriotism.*

59. "Inhabitants of the towns of Arlington and Sandgate in the county of Bennington in the state of Vermont," in Austin, *Selection of the Patriotic Addresses,* 10.

60. "Inhabitants of Concord in Massachusetts," in ibid., 49.

61. "Inhabitants of Quincy, Massachusetts," in ibid., 73.

62. "Congregational Ministers of the Commonwealth of Massachusetts," in ibid., 85.

63. "Young Men of Richmond," in ibid., 284.

64. Reply to "Inhabitants of Kent County," in ibid., 245.

65. Ibid., 12. Other leading Federalists attached the universalism of French principles to the traditional universal domination achieved by "Papists." As Supreme Court Justice William Cushing pronounced at the opening of the grand jury in Richmond, Virginia: "The Pope, called Antichrist, whose spiritual romantic power over nations has been declining for ages . . . but succeeded by another antichrist, composed of atheism, military despotism, and the prostration of all principles, civil,

moral, and religious" (William Cushing, "A Charge Delivered to the Federal Grand Jury for the District of Virginian, on the 23rd Nov. '98," in *Newburyport Herald and Country Gazette,* January 8, 1799).

66. This is not to say that earlier fears of Louis XIV were not of "ideas" that subverted national rights, but that these new ideas were a product of the French Revolution.

67. "Students of Williams College," in Austin, *Selection of the Patriotic Addresses,* 130.

68. "Students of Harvard University," in ibid., 102–3.

69. "The Grand Jurors of the County of Hampshire," September 25, 1798, Adams Papers, reel 391.

70. "The Inhabitants of the Borough of Harrisburg, Pennsylvania," *Porcupine's Gazette,* May 31, 1798.

71. "Officers of the Guilford Regiment of Militia and the Inhabitants of the County, North Carolina," in Austin, *Selection of the Patriotic Addresses,* 330.

72. Austin, *Selection of the Patriotic Addresses,* 12.

73. "Adams' Response to the Inhabitants of the Borough of Harrisburg, Pa.," in ibid., 223. In his reply to the "Young Citizens of Philadelphia," Adams declaimed, "I will hazard a prediction that after the most industrious and impartial resources, the longest liver of you all, will find no principles, institutions, or systems of education, more fit in general to be transmitted to your posterity, than those you have received from your ancestors" (*Philadelphia Gazette and Universal Daily Advertiser,* May 7, 1798). This particular argument incensed Thomas Jefferson, who viewed it as an abandonment of the best ideals of the Revolutionary Age, and after the Republicans gained power he noted this passage as proof of the Federalists backward-looking "bigotry" (TJ to J. Priestly, March 21, 1801, *WTJ,* 8:21–22).

74. "Mayor, Aldermen, Common Council and Freemen of the city of Vergennes, in the county of Addison and the state of Vermont," in Austin, *Selection of the Patriotic Addresses,* 14.

75. "Address of Citizens at Hunter's Hotel," *Gazette of the United States,* May 16, 1798.

76. *Philadelphia Gazette and Universal Daily Advertiser,* May 2, 28, and June 14, 1798.

77. "Inhabitants of Luzerne County," in Austin, *Selection of the Patriotic Addresses,* 115.

78. "Inhabitants of the County of Otsego, New York," in ibid., 153.

79. "Officers of the Brigade of the City and County of New York and County of Richmond," Adams Papers, reel 388, May 12, 1798.

80. "Youth of Portsmouth," New Hampshire, in Austin, *Selection of the Patriotic Addresses,* 22–23.

81. "Inhabitants of Carlisle and its vicinity," in ibid., 204.

82. "Citizens of the county of Westmoreland, Virginia," in ibid., 306.

83. "Citizens of Caroline County," in ibid., 270.

84. "Mayor, Alderman and Citizens of the City of Philadelphia," *Philadelphia Gazette and Universal Daily Advertiser,* April 23, 1798.

85. "Inhabitants of the County of Otsego, New York" in Austin, *Selection of the Patriotic Addresses,* 154.

86. "The Soldier Citizens of New-Jersey," in ibid., 184.

87. *Philadelphia Gazette and Universal Daily Advertiser,* May 1, 1798.

88. Adams's reply to "Inhabitants of the town of Arundell, Maine," in Austin, *Selection of the Patriotic Addresses,* 118.

89. *Virginia Argus,* August 10, 1798.

90. Ibid., June 25, 1798.

91. TJ to JM, May 10, 1798, *PTJ,* 30:343–45.

92. New York Federalist James Jones was killed in the duel; see *Philadelphia Gazette and Universal Daily Advertiser,* May 11, 1798.

93. The illiteracy of the offending party can be dismissed, because they left a telling little poem next to their handiwork: "Adams the great / In envy'd state / Issu'd a proclamation / That each free state / Abstain from meat / with deep humiliation / Let 'Ristocrats / Those scurvy brats / Keep fast with fear and mourning / But we'll conspire / To build a fire / and put his image burning" (*Philadelphia Gazette and Universal Daily Advertiser,* June 23, 1798).

94. *Philadelphia Gazette and Universal Daily Advertiser,* May 16, 1798.

95. AA to JQA, April 13, 1798, Adams Papers, reel 388.

96. AA to JQA, April 21, 1798, ibid.

97. "Inhabitants of Dedham, and other towns in the vicinity," in Austin, *Selection of the Patriotic Addresses,* 70.

98. "Citizens of Calvert County," Maryland, in ibid., 258.

99. "The State Society of the Cincinnati of Rhode-Island and Providence Plantations," in ibid., 120.

100. *Gazette of the United States,* April 18, 1798.

101. *Porcupine's Gazette,* April 17, 1798.

102. *Philadelphia Gazette and Universal Daily Advertiser,* April 25, 26, 1798.

103. An American [Joseph Hopkinson], *What is our situation?* 7.

104. Ibid., 8, 11.

105. Joseph Hopkinson to GW, May 9, 1798, *PGW,* 3:259.

106. [Hopkinson,] *What is our situation?* 19.

107. Ibid.

108. Ibid., 20.

109. Ibid., 35.

110. AA to JQA, April 3, 1798, Adams Papers, reel 388.

111. William Shaw to AA, May 20, 1798, ibid. William Shaw was made the personal secretary to President Adams in the summer of 1798.

112. *Federal Gazette,* June 28, 1798.

113. Ibid.

114. The committee was composed of five Federalists and two Republicans, namely, Samuel Sewell (F), Mass.; Samuel Dana (F), Conn.; James Imlay (F), N.J.; Samuel Smith (R), Md.; Josiah Parker (R), Va.; David Brooks (F), N.Y.; and John Rutledge Jr. (F), S.C.

115. *Annals of Congress,* 5th Cong., 2nd sess., House of Representatives, 1566.

116. Ibid., 1567.

117. Ibid., 1567–68 (emphasis added).

118. In fact, an amendment to the Constitution that would have denied any

naturalized citizen the right to hold office was introduced by Federalists in July of 1798. It was tabled and never revived, partly because Federalists were so successful in controlling the rights of aliens in the new Naturalization Act and the Alien and Sedition Laws. The amendment was later passed by Massachusetts and numerous New England states in the summer and fall of 1798, but was rejected by a majority of states by early 1799.

119. Sitgreaves opined, "In attaining an object in which all seemed to concur, they might avoid any Constitutional embarrassment; and this it was allowed might be done by extending to time of residence of aliens so far, as to prevent them from ever becoming citizens" (*Annals of Congress,* 5th Cong., 2nd sess., House of Representatives, 1572).

120. "An Act Concerning Aliens," *Annals of Congress,* 5th Cong., 2nd sess., House of Representatives, 3745.

121. Ibid., 3745–46.

122. An act, in addition to the act entitled, "An act for the punishment of certain crimes against the United States" (ibid., 3776–77).

123. *Annals of Congress,* 5th Cong., 2nd sess., House of Representatives, 2098.

124. Ibid., 2095, 2100.

125. Bradburn, "Revolutionary Politics," appendix B.

126. Miller, *Crisis in Freedom,* 43.

127. Bradburn, "Revolutionary Politics," appendix B.

128. Rogers Brubaker, in his excellent analysis of different attitudes toward naturalization in nineteenth-century France and Germany, *Citizenship and Nationhood in France and Germany,* emphasizes the difference in approach between *jus soli* (the right of the soil) and *jus sanguinis* (the right of the race). He considered them distinct "cultural idioms."

5 ⁜ States' Rights and the Rights of Man

1. Reuben Durrett, "Manuscript biography of Colonel George Nicholas," box 1, folder 1, Reuben T. Durrett Collection, George Nicholas Papers, Special Collections, University of Chicago; "Treatis[e] on War," box 1, folder 29, Reuben T. Durrett Collection, George Nicholas Papers. Quotes from resolution in *Palladium,* August 21, 1798.

2. For Clay's presence at the meeting, see McElroy, *Kentucky in the Nation's History,* 223. Henry Clay continued to consider his politics to be consistent with those of the Republican Party that resisted the Alien and Sedition laws; see his speech delivered in Hanover County, Virginia, June 27, 1840: "The whigs of 1840 stand where the republicans of 1798 stood, and where the whigs of the revolution were, battling for liberty, for the people, for free institutions, against power, against corruption, against executive encroachments, against monarchy" (Clay, *Works of Henry Clay,* 1:510).

3. For contemporary accounts of the meeting, see *Palladium,* August 21, 1798; *Kentucky Gazette,* August 15, 1798. See also McElroy, *Kentucky,* 223; Harrison, *John Breckinridge,* 74.

4. *Daily Advertiser,* December 21, 1798.

5. "Calm Reflections on Rash Proceedings," *Daily Advertiser,* February 4, 1799.

6. *Newburyport Herald and County Gazette,* May 15, 1798.

7. The definitive study of the prosecutions under the Sedition Act is Smith, *Freedom's Fetters.*

8. Commonwealth of Massachusetts, *In the House of Representatives.* The amendment was quickly approved by most of the New England states, but, although passing the New York Senate, was defeated by the Middle and Southern states. The newspapers of the country followed the proposed amendment with great interest from September 1798 to February 1799, when it was officially dead. For some debates upon the proposed amendment, see *Kline's Carlisle Weekly Gazette,* January 15, February 6, 1799; *Centinel of Freedom,* December 25, 1798, January 22, February 12, 1799; *Palladium,* September 25, 1798.

9. *Kline's Carlisle Weekly Gazette,* November 28, 1798.

10. *LCK,* 2:482.

11. The *only* sustained modern investigation of the "grassroots" origins of the Kentucky Resolutions is Smith, "Grass Roots Origins of the Kentucky Resolutions." Bits and pieces of the story can be found in some of the literature of state politics cited below.

12. This reflects an understandable lack of interest in the politics of 1798 by historians examining the legacy of "states' rights" ideas from the anti-federalists to the Civil War. See, for instance, the treatment of the Kentucky and Virginia Resolutions in such classics as Carpenter, *South as a Conscious Minority,* 43–44, 140, 201; and Freehling, *Prelude to the Civil War,* 207–10. A recent example is Sinha, *Counterrevolution of Slavery,* 21–29.

13. For example, Cornell, *Other Founders.* In a long discussion of the "oppositional constitutionalism" of Jefferson and Madison, Cornell has one paragraph that mentions the popular local mobilization in Kentucky (see ibid., 230–42, 245, 253–73). The most recent study of the Virginia and Kentucky Resolutions similarly does not investigate the broader context of the resolutions in their own moment, preferring again to study Madison, Jefferson, and a few others (see Watkins, *Reclaiming the American Revolution*). The most useful recent review of the opposition to the Alien and Sedition Acts is Onuf, *Jefferson's Empire,* but the story is understandably limited to a problem of "Jefferson and his political friends" (96).

14. For many recent scholars who have written on the moment, the origins of the Kentucky and Virginia Resolutions are best understood as "the capstone of the Jefferson-Madison collaboration," with nary a mention of the popular resistance to the acts that proceeded and provided legitimacy to the action of the state legislatures (see Ellis, *Founding Brothers,* 199). This is also the tack taken by the notable work by Adrienne Cook and Henry Ammon in "The Virginia and Kentucky Resolutions," a work still heavily relied upon. In James Roger Sharp's *American Politics,* the Kentucky and Virginia Resolutions emerge wholly as the product of the strategic decision of the leading Virginian political figures—Jefferson, Madison, and John Taylor of Caroline—to check "the progress of Federalist domination" in the states (194). In some studies—for example, John C. Miller's *Crisis in Freedom,* the detail of resistance to the acts was restricted to newspaper critics of Federalist uses and abuses of the Sedition Act.

15. Waldstreicher, *Perpetual Fetes,* 152–73; Seth Cotlar, "Cultural Offensive," in Pasley et al., *Beyond the Founders,* 274–99; Robertson, "Look on This Picture"; Hale, "Many Who Wandered in Darkness," 174–75.

16. The most recent article on the Sedition Act notes that "it played some role in bringing on the defeat of the Federalists in the 1800 election" (Lender, "Equally Proper at All Times," 421).

17. Cunningham, *Jeffersonian Republicans,* 129. There is also a strain of work which consistently argues that the Virginia and Kentucky Resolutions are not important in the eventual defeat of the Federalists. Stanley Elkins and Eric McKitrick, in *The Age of Federalism,* describe the resolutions as an "opening shot" in the presidential election of 1800 but ultimately unimportant. Here they closely follow a broad tradition of American political history, dating to Edward Channing, who declared it was impossible to "trace any connection" between the resolutions and the overthrow of the Federalists (*History of the United States*). In fact, Elkins and McKitrick regard discussion of the resolutions as "somewhat of a digression." In their interpretation, the Federalists lost national influence, not because their ideas about the national state, citizenship, and the Constitution were rejected in a broad and popular political movement, but because of the political mistakes of Adams and Hamilton in the spring and summer of 1800, "a sequence of political madness" (*Age of Federalism,* 721, 732).

18. An old argument, important to the work of Noble E. Cunningham and Norman Risjord, recently revived by Waldstreicher (see *Perpetual Fetes,* 177–245) and Pasley (see *The Tyranny of Printers;* and "The Cheese and the Words: Popular Political Culture and Participatory Democracy in the Early American Republic," in Pasley et al., *Beyond the Founders,* 31–56).

19. *Kentucky Gazette,* July 4, 1798.

20. See, for instance, essays by "A Friend to the Peace," *Kentucky Gazette,* July 4, 11, 1799; "Letter from Representative John Fowler, Esq.," *Palladium,* August 7, 1798.

21. *Kentucky Gazette,* August 1, 1798.

22. Ibid. This short statement asserting a right to express his opinion on political matters was circulated widely in the East.

23. *Palladium,* August 21, 1798.

24. *Porcupine's Gazette,* September 21, 1798.

25. "A letter from a Virginian to his friend in Kentucky," [September 12, 1798], *Palladium,* October 9, 1798; this letter was also published in the December 18 issue of the *Centinel of Freedom.*

26. *Alexandria Advertiser,* September 18, 1798.

27. See, for instance, the resolutions of the meeting of "numerous people of Henrico" and the City of Richmond in the *Virginia Argus,* April 6, 1798; and the anti-address of "Captain Bernard Magnien's Company of Grenadiers, at the muster ground on the commons of Portsmouth, VA," *Centinel of Freedom,* May 22, 1798.

28. *Winchester Gazette,* January 9, 1799, lists many of the counties that produced addresses. The "oracle" is obviously meant to be Jefferson, who certainly knew of the Albemarle remonstrance, and perhaps knew who had organized it, but there is no evidence that he wrote the resolutions, which are discussed below. A broadside circulating in Virginia described some *Proceedings in the Different Parts of Virginia,*

on the Subject of the late Conduct of the General Government. For Orange County, see *Aurora,* December 1, 1798; for Louisa County, *Aurora,* February 25, 1799; for Goochland County, *Aurora,* September 3, 1798; for Buckingham County, *Virginia Argus,* November 20, 1798; for Powhatan County, *Virginia Argus,* September 25, 1798; and for Hanover County, see Pope, *A Speech,* 31–37.

29. "Freeholders of Prince Edward County, in the state of Virginia," *Alexandria Advertiser,* September 25, 1798. Adams never received the petition because it was sent to Secretary of State Timothy Pickering, who refused to pass it on, believing it to be an "*insult.*" For Pickering's response to the original petition, see *Aurora,* November 6, 1798. For Edward's response, see *Aurora,* November 22, 1798, under the heading "Manly Reply."

30. See, for instance, the petition of the "Citizens of Richmond" to John Clopton, esq., August 13, 1798, in *Aurora,* August 20, 1798. Below I will consider the attempt by the Republicans to use broad congressional petitioning to help secure a repeal of the acts.

31. *Alexandria Advertiser,* September 18, 1798.

32. McDonnell, "Popular Mobilization," passim.

33. The end of the 1790s represented a period of the highest voter turnout in early Republican Virginia politics, but importantly, this increased participation largely disappeared by the 1810s, speaking to the growth of a new "harmony," or perhaps more correctly, "hegemony," of one-party politics after the destruction of the Federalists in 1800 (see Risjord, *Chesapeake Politics,* 534–72).

34. Details of meeting in the *Virginia Argus,* June 15, 1798.

35. See, for instance, Clay's essay, "To the electors of Fayette County," April 16, 1798, in Clay, *Papers of Henry Clay,* 1:3–8; Harrison, *John Breckinridge,* 93, 113.

36. *Centinel of Freedom,* December 18, 1798.

37. John Breckinridge asked his colleague, Judge Caleb Wallace, to prepare resolutions for the upcoming November session of the Kentucky legislature before he left for Virginia. Wallace declined, claiming a lack of expertise for such an important document (McElroy, *Kentucky in the Nation's History,* 237).

38. There has been much controversy over the sequence of events. The two important letters to discern the most likely narrative of events are Jefferson's letter of approbation of Breckinridge and of sending his resolutions to Kentucky (see TJ to Wilson C. Nicholas, October 5, 1798, *WTJ,* 7:281–82); and a letter from Wilson C. Nicholas to John Breckinridge, October 10, 1798, box VI, Reuben T. Durrett Collection, Miscellaneous Manuscripts, in which Nicholas mentions Jefferson's support for Breckinridge and refers to the resolutions.

39. See, for instance, *Herald of Liberty,* October 8, 1798; *Aurora,* December 19, 1798.

40. Some of the earliest petitions against the Alien and Sedition Acts in Pennsylvania were tributes to Gallatin from his constituents in Greene, Allegheny, and Washington counties (see *Herald of Liberty,* October 1, 1798).

41. Bouton, "No Wonder," 21–38.

42. "The Petition of the Subscribers, Inhabitants of the County of York, in the state of Pennsylvania," *Aurora,* January 22, 1799.

43. "The Memorial of the Subscribers, Inhabitants of the County of Lancaster," *Aurora,* March 6, 1799.

44. On the poles during the Whiskey Rebellion, see Baldwin, *Whiskey Rebels,* 83–85, 91.

45. Graydon, *Memoirs,* 393.

46. See "MORE, *MORE,* SEDITION POLES!" *Centinel of Freedom,* March 12, 1799.

47. *Federal Gazette and Baltimore Advertiser,* February 6, 1799.

48. *Aurora General Advertiser,* November 22, 1798.

49. *Time Piece,* August 28, 1798.

50. *Columbian Centinel,* August 19, 1798.

51. *Federal Gazette and Baltimore Advertiser,* January 31, 1799.

52. Ibid.

53. *Alexandria Advertiser,* December 21, 1798.

54. *New York Gazette and General Advertiser,* July 11, 1798.

55. *Carey's United States Recorder,* July 19, 1798.

56. *Annals of Congress,* 5th Cong., 3rd sess., House of Representatives, 2785–3017.

57. Most of the petitions that are extant were published in the newspapers and the signatures do not exist. The figure is from a debate over the petitions in Congress. These specific petitions are discussed below.

58. For the rise of the Jeffersonian Republicans in northern New Jersey, see Prince, *New Jersey's Jeffersonian Republicans,* 18–40.

59. *Centinel of Freedom,* August 7, 14, 21, 28, 1798; Prince, *New Jersey's Jeffersonian Republicans,* 38.

60. Pasley, *The Tyranny of Printers,* 153–75.

61. *Centinel of Freedom,* December 18, 1798.

62. "Inhabitants and Freeholders of the County of Essex, State of New Jersey," *Centinel of Freedom,* January 22, 1799. The resolutions were passed on January 17, 1799; they were published in the *Centinel of Freedom,* January 22, 1799. Similar resolutions were passed by Republicans throughout the state; see ibid., January 22–February 6, 1799.

63. Songs have not yet received their full due as part of the political culture, but see Newman, *Parades;* Pasley, "The Cheese and the Words: Popular Political Culture and Participatory Democracy in the Early American Republic," in Pasley et al., *Beyond the Founders,* 39.

64. "Support the Constitution," *Newburyport Herald and Country Gazette,* May 4, 1798. In the pro-Republican literary newspaper, the *Time Piece,* angry Republicans assert that "Hail Columbia" could often be heard intermingled with "Rule Britannia" and "God Save the King," as a consequence of nightly street serenades from Federalists and refugees from Nova Scotia (*Time Piece,* June 25, 1798).

65. *Herald of Liberty,* November 12, 1798.

66. *Rights of Man, or The Nashville Intelligencer* (Nashville, Tenn., 1799), n.d. The only copy of this newspaper is held by Special Collections, University of Chicago; song is by "A Democrat."

67. *Daily Advertiser,* July 30–31, 1798.

68. Untitled in the original publication, the song was meant to be sung to the tune of "Multum in Parvo," a popular eighteenth-century ditty that we now recognize as the tune of "How Much Is That Doggie in the Window?"

69. The song obtained some popularity at least, because a slightly different ver-

sion of the tune, now named "The Sedition Act," was published as late as 1811 by a Boston bookseller advertising a collection of popular "Songs (by the Gross, Dozen, or Single)" (see Anonymous, "Sedition Act").

70. See the address of the "Subscribers, Officers, Soldiers and Citizens of NJ," *Centinel of Freedom,* June 12, 1798.

71. Bouton, "No Wonder the Times Were Troublesome"; and, more generally, Bouton, "Road Closed." For the place of a "labor theory of value" in the ideology of the farmers of the Revolution in New Jersey, see McConville, *Daring Disturbers,* passim. Terry Bouton, in *Taming Democracy,* and Woody Holton, in *Unruly Americans and the Origins of the Constitution,* have strongly reestablished the importance of conflicts related to debt finance into the fundamental character of democratic political development in Revolutionary America.

72. Smith, *Freedom's Fetters,* 270–74.

73. Livingston, *Speech of Edward Livingston.* In February of 1799, Livingston was called to account for some of the language of his speech, specifically, "that the States ought to resist the law, the people ought to resist the law, and he hoped to God the people would resist the law" (*Annals of Congress,* 5th Cong., 3rd sess., House of Representatives, 2893).

74. *Daily Advertiser,* February 20, 1799.

75. Ibid.

76. *Daily Advertiser,* February 18, 1799.

77. Smith, *Freedom's Fetters,* 391–93.

78. Young, *Democratic Republicans,* 273–74, 509–14, 567; Taylor, "From Fathers to Friends."

79. Their effort to recruit signatures at the churches of Philadelphia led to a riot at St. Mary's Church, which led to a trial, the publicity of which led to increased circulation of their petitions. See chapter 7.

80. *Annals of Congress,* 5th Cong., 3rd sess., House of Representatives, 2884–2906.

81. They were required to pledge that they would commit "no act of violence" for the remainder of the session (see *Annals of Congress,* 5th Cong., 2nd sess., House of Representatives, 1040–43).

82. Lyon's imprisonment was the subject of numerous Republican attacks on the Sedition Act; one example of many is *Aurora,* December 1, 1798.

83. *Daily Advertiser,* February 16, 1798. On Odgens and the petitions to Adams, see Briceland, "Philadelphia Aurora," 9–11, 16–17.

84. *Stewart's Kentucky Herald,* February 26, 1799. There was no Republican newspaper in North Carolina until 1799 with the organization of the *Raleigh Register.*

85. In places where there was no local anti-administration newspaper, the meaning of events and policies could be considerably contained by a Federalist press; see TJ to JM, February 5, 1799, *PTJ,* 31:10, concerning the New Hampshire legislature: "There has been a general complaint among the members that they could hear but one side of the question, and a great anxiety to obtain a paper or papers which would put them in possession of both sides"; and see Paisley, "The Cheese and the Words: Popular Political Culture and Participatory Democracy in the Early American Republic," in Pasley et al., *Beyond the Founders,* 42.

86. Most of the political leadership of Tennessee considered the Alien and Sedition Acts, as well as the Federalist pro-war measures, to be dangerous. Consider the letter of William Charles Cole Clairborne, who as a representative from Tennessee voted against the legislation, to Andrew Jackson, senator from Tennessee at the time of the passage of the acts (although absent). Writing in 1802 and remembering the "awfully tempestuous" political world of 1798, Clairborne wrote, "The Alien Law had subjected the unhappy fugitives from Tyranny and persecution, to the uncontrolled will of an individual, who was inflated with power, and thirsted for still greater prerogative: The Sedition Act had fettered the freedom of the Press, and awed into Silence, many of the Lovers of Man, and his Rights" (William Charles Cole Clairborne to Andrew Jackson, March 20, 1802, in Jackson, *Papers of Andrew Jackson,* 1:284–85).

87. *Aurora,* November 9, 1798.

88. There is a gap in the journals of the Tennessee legislature.

89. Sevier boasted to Washington that the state was coming around to Federal enthusiasm, noting "A Military ardor and Spirit Warmly diffuses itself throughout the State of Tennessee" (John Sevier to GW, *PGW,* Retirement Series, 3:286). Sevier received a commission, but Washington worried about his qualifications, noting: "As to Severe, the only exploit I ever heard of his performance, was the *murder* of Indians" (GW to James McHenry, September 14, 1798, *PGW,* Retirement Series, 3:598).

90. Ray, "Progress and Popular Democracy," 66–103.

91. *Kline's Carlisle Gazette,* February 7, 1799.

92. TJ to Aaron Burr, February 11, 1799, *PTJ,* 31:22.

93. TJ to JM, February 5, 1799, *PTJ,* 31:10.

94. TJ to Edmund Pendleton, February 14, 1799, *PTJ,* 31:36.

95. TJ to Archibald Stuart, February 13, 1799, *PTJ,* 31:35.

96. *Alexandria Advertiser,* September 12, 1798.

97. Samuel Brown to TJ, *PTJ,* 30:510–11.

98. On the mobilization in the summer of 1774, see Marston, *King and Congress,* appendix, 69–75, 313–17; Rakove, *Beginnings of National Politics,* 27–34.

99. *Virginia Argus,* November 20, 1798.

100. For a contrary view, see, for instance, Bork, *Tempting of America,* 223–27.

101. "Citizens of Mason and the adjacent Counties," *Palladium,* September 4, 1798.

102. "Resolutions of Montgomery County Republicans," *Palladium,* August 21, 1798.

103. Before 1798—save perhaps for a few eccentric examples—the most aggressive libertarian interpretations of the meaning of a "free press" in America asserted that "truth" could be used as a defense during prosecution for seditious libel. This argument, which in the American context had evolved from the famous Zenger case in colonial New York, was an interpretation of a free press that broke from a common law, or "Blackstonian," definition, which defined a free press as one free from prior restraint or censure. Leonard Levy has used a few pamphlets to make this argument, but it was more widely held and more popular than scholarship has recognized. In addition, Levy maintains that the argument was born of "expediency," and so fails to recognize the Revolutionary aspects of the rhetoric, strategies, and ideologies that empowered the opposition to transform the understanding of free speech in this

crucial moment. Levy and other scholars have looked to a few important pamphlets to make a similar argument—namely: Wortman, *Treatise;* Hay, *Essay on the Liberty of the Press;* Tucker, *Blackstone's Commentaries.*

104. "Resolutions of Montgomery County Republicans."

105. "Address of the Dissenters of the Minority of the House of Representatives of Pennsylvania," *Carlisle Gazette,* February 6, 1799.

106. *Winchester Gazette,* March 27, 1799.

107. "Juricola," in *Winchester Gazette,* January 9, 1799.

108. "Inhabitants of the county of Spotsylvania," *Aurora,* November 20, 1798.

109. "Inhabitants of the County of Suffolk, in the State of New York," *Aurora,* January 30, 1799.

110. "Inhabitants and Freeholders of the County of Essex," *Centinel of Freedom,* January 22, 1799.

111. "Freeholders of the County of Dinwiddie," *Aurora,* December 6, 1798.

112. "The petition and remonstrance of the subscribers, inhabitants of the county of Cumberland," *Aurora,* January 10, 1799.

113. "It is an infringement of the federal constitution which declares, 'Congress shall have no such power, previous to the year 1808'" (ibid.).

114. "Inhabitants of the County of Suffolk, in the State of New York."

115. Virginia House of Delegates, "Virginian Report of 1799–1800," 25, 27, 28.

116. Nicholas, "Letter from George Nicholas," 35.

117. See the charges to the grand juries by Judge Alexander Addison and Judge John Faucheraud Grimke, and by Justice William Cushing to the federal grand jury of the District of Virginia on November 23, 1798 (*Newburyport Herald and Country Gazette,* January 8, 1799; Addison, *Liberty of Speech and of the Press*). Addison would write, "Liberty without limit is licentiousness and licentiousness is the worst kind of tyranny, a tyranny of all." See also *Newburyport Herald and Country Gazette,* January 29, 1799.

118. Nicholas, "Letter from George Nicholas," 36–38, quoting, of all people, Blackstone. Again, Americans drew freely from all sources to make their particular points.

119. "Meeting of a large number of citizens of the county of Bourbon, with some of the counties adjacent, at the town of Paris on Monday the 20th," *Palladium,* September 4, 1798.

120. *Palladium,* August 21, 1798.

121. "People of Essex County," *Aurora,* November 19, 1798; "Citizens of Richmond," *Aurora,* August 20, 1798.

122. "Meeting of a large number of citizens of the county of Bourbon, with some of the counties adjacent, at the town of Paris on Monday the 20th," *Palladium,* September 4, 1798.

123. "Light Infantry Company belonging to the Second Battalion of the First Regiment in the County of Amelia, VA," *Alexandria Advertiser,* August 17, 1798.

124. *Centinel of Freedom,* July 17, 1798.

125. "Inhabitants and Freeholders of the County of Essex, State of New Jersey," *Centinel of Freedom,* January 22, 1799. The resolutions were passed on January 17, 1799; they were published in the *Centinel of Freedom,* January 22, 1799.

126. "Meeting of the Citizens of that part of Mifflin County, in the State of Pennsylvania," *Aurora,* January 23, 1798.

127. See John Taylor to TJ, June 25, 1798, in Taylor, "John Taylor Correspondence"; Cornell, *Other Founders,* 238–39.

128. A common, but incorrect, argument. Joseph Ellis writes, "Fortunately for Jefferson, the leadership of the Kentucky legislature decided to delete the sections of his draft endorsing nullification, presumably because such open defiance of federal law seemed excessive and unnecessarily risky" (*Founding Brothers,* 200). There is little evidence that the Kentuckians worried about any "risk" from the federal government, or anyone. And in fact, Breckinridge used the concept of nullification numerous times in his speech presenting the resolutions, and in the 1799 Resolution passed by the Kentucky House in vindication of their earlier resolutions. The resolution in question was probably edited more for length than content. Jefferson's original resolution, a discursive polemic against the motives and character of the Federalist administration that ran to twelve pages in manuscript, was more suitable for a pamphlet than a resolution.

129. Virginia House of Delegates, *Virginia Report of 1799–1800,* "Resolutions of the Kentucky Legislature," 1st Res., 162.

130. Ibid. Breckinridge also explicitly used the word "nullify" throughout the debates over the resolutions. As he noted, "I hesitate not to declare it as my opinion that it is then the right and duty of the several states to nullify those acts, and to protect their citizens from their operations" (Harrison, *John Breckinridge,* 79, 83). And in the Kentucky Resolution of 1799, passed a year later to reassert Kentucky's position in the face of contrary arguments, the Kentucky House repeated their understanding of the compact theory of Union, claimed the right to judge federal laws, and argued for "a nullification" as a remedy of "all unauthorized acts." The answer of the Kentucky legislature can be found in the *Virginia Gazette & General Advertiser,* December, 20, 1799; viz, "That the several states who formed that instrument, being sovereign & independent, have the unquestionable right to judge of its infraction; and that a nullification, by those sovereignties, of all unauthorized acts done under color of that instrument, is the rightful remedy."

131. Virginia House of Delegates, *Virginia Report of 1799–1800,* "Resolutions of the Kentucky Legislature," 3rd Res., 163; 4th Res., 163–64; 5th Res., 164; 6th Res., 164.

132. "The Centinel," *Winchester Gazette,* January 2, 1799.

133. Virginia House of Delegates, *Virginia Report of 1799–1800,* "Resolutions of the Kentucky Legislature," 9th Res., 166–67.

134. Some scholars are too quick to associate the Kentucky and Virginia Resolutions as the voice of Jefferson and Madison, respectively, on constitutional questions, never really acknowledging that the resolutions were amended and passed by the official representatives of the people of two states. It was not, for instance, "Madison's more temperate response" which characterized the Virginia Resolutions' lack of an assertion of an individual state's right to declare an act of Congress void, but rather the effective Federalist opposition in a parliamentary process, that secured the final version. For a typical reading of the resolutions as the product of Madison's mind alone, see Cornell, *Other Founders,* 240–41.

135. Virginia House of Delegates, *Virginia Report of 1799–1800*, "Resolutions of the Kentucky Legislature," 108.

136. Ibid., 149–50.

137. Ibid., 123.

138. The strong Republicans, led by Nicholas, offered to amend the third resolution because of the effect of George Taylor's arguments on the moderates (ibid., 140–47).

139. See, for instance, *Herald of Liberty*, January 21, 1799; *Aurora*, December 22, 1798.

140. "The Address of the General Assembly," *Aurora*, February 5, 1799.

141. Theodore Sedgwick to Rufus King, January 20, 1799, *LCK*, 2:518.

142. *Alexandria Advertiser*, January 24, 1799.

143. *Stewart's Kentucky Herald*, January 30, 1799; *New Jersey State Gazette*, December 11, 1799.

144. See especially the *Connecticut Current*, February 11, 1799.

145. "Extract of a letter from a gentleman of respectability in Richmond, to his friend in this town, dated Jan. 20, 1799," *Newburyport Herald and Country Gazette*, February 8, 1799.

146. *New York Daily Advertiser*, in *Centinel of Freedom*, December 18, 1798.

147. AH to Theodore Sedgwick, February 22, 1799, Sedgwick Papers, Massachusetts Historical Society.

148. *Stewart's Kentucky Herald*, January 19, 1799.

149. *Winchester Gazette*, February 6, 1799.

150. *Carlisle Gazette*, February 20, 1799.

151. *Connecticut Current*, February 18, 1799.

152. *Daily Advertiser*, February 22, 1799.

153. Recent historians have not recognized this fact, or have denied it. But the evidence is clear. See Elkins and McKitrick, *Age of Federalism*, chap. 12; Onuf, *Nationhood*, 72–73; Ellis, *Founding Brothers*, 195–202; Sharp, *Politics*, 200.

154. "Address of the Dissenters," *Carlisle Gazette*, February 6, 1799.

155. As quoted in Anderson, "Alien and Sedition Acts," 50–51.

156. *Genius of Liberty*, March 7, 1799.

157. Ibid.

158. *Centinel of Freedom*, January 29, 1799.

159. Ibid.

160. See Anderson, "Alien and Sedition Acts," 56.

161. See the debates in the legislature of New York, under the heading "Virginia and Kentucky Resolutions Disposed Of," *Daily Advertiser*, February 22, 1799.

162. *Independent Chronicle*, February 25, 1799. For this speech, Hill was rewarded by having the windows of his home broken out by a Federalist mob. As a show of defiance against disorder, however, the Federalist leadership supported his reelection, at "the largest town meeting" ever held in Cambridge (Anderson, "Virginia and Kentucky Resolutions," 229).

163. *Independent Chronicle*, February 18, 1799.

164. The trial became in part another public examination of the Virginia and Kentucky Resolutions, the logic of which the leading Republican lawyers of Boston

agreed with entirely. Adams, however, was not tried under the Sedition Act, but under common law criminal libel. Anderson gives much more extensive detail on the trial (see Anderson, "Alien and Sedition Acts," 58–63; Anderson, "Virginia and Kentucky Resolutions," 225–29).

165. "Protest of the Vermont Minority," in appendix to Anderson, "Virginia and Kentucky Resolutions," 251.

166. For references to the petitions and the debates they occasioned, see *Annals of Congress,* 5th Cong., 3rd sess., House of Representatives, 2785, 2795, 2798, 2802, 2807, 2884, 2906, 2907, 2934, 2955, 2957, 2959, 2985.

167. Each of these resolutions was voted on in the full House in turn, with Republicans attempting at every moment to postpone, delay, and otherwise defeat the approval of the committee report. But Republicans were unable to stop passage of the committee report and were unable to secure a repeal of the Federalist legislation.

168. *Annals of Congress,* 5th Cong., 3rd sess., House of Representatives, 2986, 2987.

169. Ibid., 2986.

170. Ibid.

171. Ibid., 2986, 2988, 2989.

172. Ibid., 2986, 2988.

173. Ibid., 2986, 2992.

174. Cunningham, *Jeffersonian Republicans,* 133–35.

175. Risjord, *Chesapeake Politics,* 546. Even with strong mobilization of Federalist candidates, the Virginia House of Delegates retained a large Republican majority, or in Marshall's words, "The strength of parties is not materially varied" (ibid., 547).

176. "Patrick Henry said in his speech at Charlotte Court House in March 1799 where he was a candidate for the Legislature 'The Alien and Sedition Laws were only the fruit of that Constitution the adoption of which he opposed'" (Scrap Memo, John Henry, Mss2H39633a, Virginia Historical Society). On Marshall, see Marshall, *Papers of John Marshall,* 3:496.

177. GW to Bushrod Washington, May 5, 1799, *PGW,* 4:51.

178. TJ to Joseph Priestly, in Jefferson, *Writings of Thomas Jefferson,* edited by Lipscomb and Bergh, 9:385.

179. For the variety of ways "public opinion" is important in the nineteenth century, see Schmeller, "Imagining Public Opinion."

180. It is still debatable what rights aliens have in America—including trial by jury.

181. *Carlisle Gazette,* February 20, 1799.

6 "Hordes of Foreigners"

1. Wharton, *State Trials,* 348. Duane published a pamphlet, *A Report on the Extraordinary Transactions* (Philadelphia, 1799), which included a partisan description of the events leading to the trial, the transcript of the proceedings, and a copy of the petition.

2. [Hopkinson,] *What is our situation?*

3. Duane, *Extraordinary Transactions,* quotes are from 37 and 38.

4. Foner, *Sourcebook,* 105.

5. Duane, *Extraordinary Transactions,* quotes about "party" from 19, "conspiracy" from 18, all others from 23 and 24.

6. A somewhat extravagant recent book on Duane is Rosenfeld, *American Aurora.*

7. See, for instance, Conzen et al., who argued the following: "Why did Americans start seeing ethnicity [in the 1830s] when they had not done so before ("Invention of Ethnicity," 7).

8. Representative new studies on nationalism also ignore ethnicity (see Waldstreicher, *Perpetual Fetes;* Newman, *Parades;* Travers, *Celebrating the Fourth;* Purcell, *Sealed with Blood*). A typical example of many others is Appleby, *Inheriting the Revolution,* 158–59.

9. This does not include the 110,000 Africa and Afro-Caribbean slaves who were imported during this period (see Fogleman, "Slaves, Convicts, and Servants," 73–76, and tables A.5 and A.6). Fogleman gives a figure of 273,200 for immigrants of European descent, and 110,000 for African slaves; it is unclear where free blacks and mulattoes fit into his figures. See also, for similar figures, Grabbe, "European Immigration," 194, table 2. Gemery estimates total European migration to the United States in the period 1780 to 1820 at 1,004,100, a figure Fogleman considers as "surely much too high." It is in fact more than double the estimates of Fogleman for the same period, and nearly triple the numbers of Grabbe (see Gemery, "Disarray in the Historical Record," 123–27).

10. Fogleman, "Slaves, Convicts, and Servants"; Grubb, "German Immigration."

11. On the decline of the need and importance of indentured servants more generally in the post-Independence United States, see Salinger, "Colonial Labor in Transition"; Salinger, *"To Serve Well and Faithfully";* Grubb, "German Immigration."

12. Richard Champion, "The Situation of the First and Present Settlers in America, Contrasted," *Columbian Magazine* 1 (November 1787): 1753.

13. See Grabbe, "European Immigration," 194; Durey, *Transatlantic Radicals.*

14. Two recent works in particular, Michael Durey's *Transatlantic Radicals and the Early American Republic* and David Wilson's *United Irishmen, United States: Immigrant Radicals in the Early Republic,* have greatly advanced our appreciation of the number and importance of British and Irish radical émigrés to the politics of the early decades of nationhood. I am indebted to their work, which built upon the substantial scholarship of Richard J. Twomey's *Jacobins and Jeffersonians: Anglo-American Radicalism in the United States.* Durey's work, a joint biography of over two hundred radical émigrés from Britain and Ireland from 1780 to 1815, compares the intellectual influence of this diverse group to "the arrival of the Puritan ministers in the seventeenth century and the Jewish exodus from Germany in the 1930s" (*Transatlantic Radicals,* 290). Durey, partly by design and partly by interest, tends to treat these migrants as individuals. Wilson treats his migrants, however, as a group—the "United Irishmen"—which is a political description that includes Irish migrants who had never been a part of the "United Irish" movement in Ireland, and he does make a convincing contribution about the origins of Irish American nationalism in the late eighteenth century.

15. Pomerantz, *New York,* 199–201. Pomerantz (202–3) estimates two thousand to three thousand immigrants per year entered the city from 1790 to 1800. "The boom

resulted from natural growth, migration from New England, and beginning about 1793 immigration from France, the French West Indies, Ireland, Scotland, and England" (see Young, *Democratic Republicans,* 469).

16. Smith, *The "Lower Sort."* For population figures and general demographic information, see appendix B, 204–12; for immigration, see 60–61.

17. Morrison, *Saint Andrew's Society,* 6.

18. Knauff, *History of the Society of the Sons of Saint George;* Cameron and van Dyke Hubbard, *Historical Sketch of the Saint Andrew's Society;* Hennignausen, *History of the German Society of Maryland;* Hartmann, "Welsh Society of Philadelphia"; Risch, "Immigrant Aid Societies"; Gongaware, *History of the German Friendly Society.*

19. For the Irish societies, see Crimmins, *Irish-American Historical Miscellany,* 46. The Scots Charitable Society of Boston, established in 1657, originally refused aid to Catholics, but by the eighteenth century these restrictions had been repealed (Morrison, *Saint Andrew's Society,* 6).

20. Hennignausen, *History of the German Society of Maryland,* 45–47.

21. For the importance of club life in the social order in colonial North America, see Conroy, *In Public Houses;* Salinger, *Taverns and Drinking,* 76–82.

22. John L. Brooke, "Ancient Lodges and Self-Created Societies: Freemasonry and the Public Sphere in the Early Republic," in Hoffman and Albert, *Launching the "Extended Republic,"* 284.

23. Ibid., 289; Walsh, *Charleston's Sons of Liberty;* Maier, *From Resistance to Revolution,* 85–86.

24. See, for instance, John Conrad Zollikoffer to Capt. Claus Kulkens: "The brutal advantage which has been taken by some Masters of Vessels, of their power over their passengers, has induced a number of inhabitants of this place (in imitation of their brethren in Philadelphia) to form themselves into a Society, for the protection of such of their countrymen as may be induced to come into this State, and guard them from the oppression and barbarity of unfeeling men" (in Hennignausen, *History of the German Society of Maryland,* 43–44).

25. Morrison, *Saint Andrew's Society,* 65–68.

26. Robert Morris, the noted financier, was an honorary member of the St. Patrick's Society (Campbell, *History of the Friendly Sons of St. Patrick,* 49–50).

27. Ibid., 48.

28. Ibid.

29. Ibid., 41.

30. JA to AA, April 23, 1776, *LDC,* 3:572.

31. Young, *Democratic Republicans,* 399.

32. Ibid., 398.

33. Ibid., 286, 398–99.

34. Ibid., 399; Myers, *History of Tammany Hall;* Cunningham, *Jeffersonian Republicans,* 181; Fischer, *Revolution of American Conservatism.*

35. Hennignausen, *History of the German Society of Maryland,* 50–53.

36. Young, *Democratic Republicans,* 160–61, 180–82, 194–95, 197–99.

37. For information on Rutherford, see his historical sketch in Morrison, *Saint Andrew's Society,* 59–60.

38. On the leadership and officers of the St. Andrew's Society, and the expulsion

of Republican sympathizers from positions of influence, see the list of officers in St. Andrew's Society, *Historical Sketch of the Saint Andrew's Society,* 37–41. None of the histories of the society tell this story of politicization, but it nevertheless is evident from the course of leadership and the politics of America in the 1790s.

39. Thornburn, *Forty Years Residence in America,* 92. On the character and importance of radical Scottish immigration to the United States in the 1790s, see Durey, *Transatlantic Radicals,* 50–79; Brims, "From Reformers to 'Jacobins'"; Brims, "Scottish Jacobins."

40. Young, *Democratic Republicans,* 400–402; Link, *Democratic-Republican Societies,* 168.

41. At one meeting in 1782, the St. Patrick's Society hosted the complete general staff of the Continental Army, including General Washington, General Benjamin Lincoln, General Stuben, General Howe, General Moultrie, General Knox, General Hand, and General McIntosh. Edward Hand was a member, and George Washington an honorary member of the society (Campbell, *History of the Friendly Sons of St. Patrick,* 81–82).

42. Carey, *Autobiography,* "Letter VI," 29.

43. The original membership list was 219; see the Hibernian Society for the Relief of Emigrants from Ireland, *Constitution and Bye Laws.* The St. Patrick's Society never had more than 101 members (Campbell, *History of the Friendly Sons of St. Patrick,* 93–94).

44. Campbell, *History of the Friendly Sons of St. Patrick,* 166.

45. Mathew Carey remembered the contentiousness between the two societies vaguely and reports on a brawl between members of the two societies (*Autobiography,* "Letter VI, 29"). Campbell downplayed the differences among members in this period and fails therefore to follow his own evidence. His wishful belief that the St. Patrick's Society simply turned into the Hibernian Society is not supported by the facts. It was important to the Hibernian Society of the late nineteenth century—and it continues to be important today—that the society possessed direct and unbroken ties with the great "heroes" of the Revolution. Consider, for instance, the peroration that prefaces Campbell's history of the society: "Rank injustice has been done to Pennsylvania for her share in the Revolution by Bancroft and other American historians. The services of such men as Wayne, Hand, Dickenson, Cadwalader, Moylan and many other distinguished citizens of this State have been slighted or glossed over, and no justice at all has been accorded to Irish-Americans, who formed such a large percentage of the State's population" (*History of the Friendly Sons of St. Patrick,* 3). Yet each of these men left the Hibernian Society after the Irish Rebellion of 1793, and all of them were important Federalists in Philadelphia in the 1790s, alienated from the vast bulk of the Irish population in the city. Thus, ethnic groups continue to reinvent themselves in relation to the needs of their times.

46. The decline of the St. Patrick's Society also related to its failure to properly arrange its affairs. While the Hibernian Society organized around a mission of aiding immigrants, and incorporated for that purpose, the St. Patrick's Society remained largely a social institution with a highly unorganized treasury (see the letter of Samuel Campbell to J. M. Nesbitt, March 6, 1793, in Campbell, *History of the Friendly Sons of St. Patrick,* 91).

47. This list included such prominent men as General Stephen Moylan; Commodore John Barry, "Father of the American Navy"; Thomas Fitzsimons, Federalist congressman; John Leamy, president of Marine Insurance Company; John Barclay, president of the Bank of Pennsylvania and former mayor of Philadelphia; and Federalist printer and publisher John Dunlap. The group included Catholics, Presbyterians, and Episcopalians (Campbell, *History of the Friendly Sons of St. Patrick,* 60–61, 95, 105, 108, 110, 123–24, 131–32).

48. Welsh Society of Pennsylvania, *Constitution and Rules.*

49. See, for instance, the definition of Philip Nord: "civil society" is defined as associations and institutions that are not part of the state (Nord, "Introduction," in Bermeo and Nord, *Civil Society,* xiv).

50. John Adams wrote that the men who associated in Massachusetts, "in academies of arts and sciences, in agricultural societies, in historical societies, in medical societies and in antiquarian societies, in banking institutions and in Washington benevolent societies *govern* the state, at this twenty-sixth of December 1814" ("Letters to John Taylor," in Adams, *Political Writings,* 205 [emphasis added]). Adams was writing on the "natural aristocracy."

51. Speech in Congress, February 2, 1791, *PJM,* 13:378.

52. Students of civil society in absolutist cultures often wonder, in opposition to Habermas and others, whether civil society can be said to exist if it is not permitted to exist (see Bradley, "Subjects into Citizens").

53. See Brooke, *Heart of the Commonwealth,* 184.

54. See Burke, *Considerations on the Society or Order of Cincinnati.*

55. Sharp, "Whiskey Rebellion," 119–33.

56. Pomerantz, *New York,* 206–7.

57. Scots Society, *Rules and Orders.*

58. "Advertisement," St. Andrew's Society, *Rules.*

59. Ibid.

60. Welsh Society of Pennsylvania, *Constitution and Rules.*

61. See, for instance, May, *Enlightenment in America,* 3–55.

62. Society of the Sons of St. George, *Rules and Constitution,* 6, 7, 8.

63. Foner, *Sourcebook,* 54, 55.

64. Ibid., 104.

65. Ibid., 103.

66. Young, *Democratic Republicans,* 402.

67. Campbell, *History of the Friendly Sons of St. Patrick,* 166.

68. Tunis Wortman, "Oration on the Influence of Social Institutions upon Human Nature and Happiness," delivered before Tammany Hall, New York, May 12, 1796, as quoted in Foner, *Sourcebook,* 23.

69. Duane, *Extraordinary Transactions,* 38.

70. Elliot, *Partners in Revolution;* Smyth, *Men of No Property;* Curtin, *United Irishmen;* Whelan, *Tree of Liberty;* McBride, *Scripture Politics.*

71. John Beckley to Tench Coxe, November 12, 1798, in Beckley, *Defending Jefferson,* 154.

72. Anonymous, *Paddy's Resource: Being a Collection of original and modern patriotic songs,* 4, 13.

73. Ibid., frontispiece.

74. Burk, *History of the late war in Ireland,* v, vii. For the many literary endeavors of Burk, see Wilson, *United Irishmen,* 100–111.

75. Campbell, *History of the Friendly Sons of St. Patrick,* 175. While Archibald Rowan Hamilton was courted by the Irish societies, he, like many of the elite leaders of the United Irish movement, some of whom became quite alienated by American society, played little role in American politics (see Durey, *Transatlantic Radicals,* 135, 214–15). Rowan, like many United Irish leaders, eventually returned to Ireland.

76. Campbell, *History of the Friendly Sons of St. Patrick,* 126.

77. Carey, *Autobiography,* "Letter VI," 96–97; Scharf and Wescott, *History of Philadelphia,* 2:1466–67; Durey, *Transatlantic Radicals,* 185.

78. Carter, "Political Activities of Mathew Carey," 194–95.

79. Cobbett, *Detection of a Conspiracy; Porcupine's Gazette,* May 10, 1798.

80. Carter, "Political Activities of Mathew Carey," 260–63.

81. On the importance and size of the United Irish Society in Philadelphia, two recent scholars differ somewhat. For Durey (*Transatlantic Radicals,* 249–51), the society is of negligible importance, while Wilson (*United Irishmen,* 36–57) sees it as much more important and tends, I think incorrectly, to conflate all Irish republicanism in Philadelphia with the activities of this rather small group.

82. Carey, *To the Public,* 8.

83. Ibid.

84. Ibid.

85. Duane, *Extraordinary Transactions,* 5, 18, 17.

86. See the efforts of "A Loyal Irishman" in *Gazette of the United States,* November 21, 22, 1798.

87. Mathew Carey remembered the riot as a religious disruption (Carey, *Autobiography,* "Letter IX," 40).

88. Duane, *Extraordinary Transactions,* 17–18.

89. Samuel Cuming was not released, but McKean did pay his bail (ibid., 4, 6, 7–12, 15–17).

90. Anonymous, *To the Senate and House of Representatives.*

91. *Annals of Congress,* 5th Cong., 3rd sess., House of Representatives, 2886.

92. Anonymous, *Plea of Erin,* 1; Duane, *Extraordinary Transactions,* 4.

93. *Herald of Liberty,* May 1798.

94. Duane, *Extraordinary Transactions,* 6; see also Anonymous, *To the Friends of freedom;* Anonymous, *To the Senate and House of Representatives.*

95. *Annals of Congress,* 4th Cong., 3rd sess., House of Representatives, 235.

96. On Lyon, see Austin, *Matthew Lyon.*

97. Duane, *Extraordinary Transactions,* 5, 6.

98. Tinkom, *Republicans and Federalists in Pennsylvania,* 237–38. These charges were repeated with slight variations in numerous broadsides and Federalist newspapers; see Anonymous, *To the Electors of Pennsylvania;* Anonymous, *Sir, Deeply Interested in the Approaching Election.* Many newspapers carried such arguments; see *Porcupine's Gazette,* September 27, 1799. By Republicans, Ross was described as "an Englishman" and "an enemy to the poor" and "an aristocrat," and so forth.

99. *Respublica v. Cobbett* 3 U.S. (3 Dall.) 467 (1798). On the authority of judicial

review, McKean also struck a Republican attitude: "There was no provision in the Constitution that the Judges of the Supreme Court of the United States shall control and be conclusive" (ibid., 473).

100. Duane, *Extraordinary Transactions,* 23–24.

101. Rowe, *Thomas McKean,* 309–12.

102. For the conflicts between Duane and Binns, see Wilson, *United Irishmen,* 73–74.

103. Ibid., 34.

104. Patterson "Aftermath of the Irish Rebellion."

105. Campbell, *History of the Friendly Sons of St. Patrick,* 28. See also O'Brien, *Hidden Phase of American History,* esp. chap. 16, "The 'Scotch-Irish' Myth," 286–95; Crimmins, *St. Patrick's Day;* Crimmins, *Irish-American Historical Miscellany.*

106. Wilson, *United Irishmen,* 95.

7 White Citizen, Black Denizen

1. Malone, *Jefferson,* 5:415–24.

2. "Resolutions of Citizens of Franklin, Kentucky," in Flournoy, *Calendar of Virginia State Papers,* 9:551–52.

3. I use "if" because the British insisted that they were simply seizing British deserters, which in fact all four men assuredly were (see Malone, *Jefferson,* 5:415–24).

4. For the use of the term "citizen" in the United States in regard to international law, see Westlake, *Treatise on Private International Law,* 26: "A slave or a person of color, whatever his rights at home, is internationally a member of the body called the United States, since that is the government under which he stands in relation to foreigners."

5. Commonwealth of Virginia, *Statutes at Large of Virginia,* 2:300.

6. Ibid., 2:94.

7. Ibid., 1:239.

8. United States, *Official Opinions of the Attorneys General,* 1:506–9; Blogger, *Free Blacks,* 63.

9. No judicial or legislative decision ruled authoritatively on the question until the *Dred Scott* case, sixty-eight years after the ratification of the U.S. Constitution.

10. On denizens in British practice, see Kettner, *Development of American Citizenship,* 30–32. After 1688, Kettner notes that a restriction on the rights of Dutch followers of William "reduced them to the status of denizens." A similar situation confronted German immigrants who followed George I (ibid., 33). Not all contemporary legal authorities defined free blacks as "denizens." Some chose "wards" or "degraded persons," or "not citizens," while some, in the North, did assert that free blacks were citizens. In fact, there was no consensus, so my argument should be qualified to suggest that free blacks were increasingly "like denizens" (ibid., 287–333).

11. *Annals of Congress,* 16th Cong, 2nd sess., House of Representatives, 556.

12. Ibid., 571.

13. For a more historically accurate description of the transition to slavery, see Coombs, "Building 'the Machine.'" For the neo-feudal character of the institution, see Brewer, *By Birth or Consent;* Brewer, "Entailing Aristocracy."

14. Holt, *Problem of Freedom.*

15. "Outlaw" communities of free blacks and others were never a sustained problem in the United States (Aptheker, "Maroons"; Berlin, *Many Thousands Gone,* 67, 121; Philip D. Morgan, "Black Society in the Low Country," in Berlin and Hoffman, *Slavery and Freedom,* 139).

16. Hodges, *Root and Branch,* 155.

17. Pybus, "Jefferson's Faulty Math." Earlier estimates are in Berlin, *Many Thousands Gone,* 217–90.

18. Quarles, *Negro in the American Revolution,* 160–81; Mullin, *Flight and Rebellion,* 124–39; Pullis, *Moving On;* Frey, *Water from the Rock,* chap. 2.

19. Guild, *Black Laws of Virginia,* 191; Berlin, *Many Thousands Gone,* 256–89.

20. David Brion Davis, "American Slavery and the American Revolution," in Berlin and Hoffman, *Slavery and Freedom,* 276; Genovese, *From Rebellion to Revolution.* The original petition can be found in Anonymous, *Appendix.*

21. Sarter, "Essay on Slavery," 167–68.

22. For a narrative of emancipation in the North, see Zilversmit, *First Emancipation.*

23. The *Quock Walker Case,* in Commonwealth of Massachusetts, *Commonwealth v. Nathaniel Jennison.* The judge's charge noted: "I think the idea of slavery is inconsistent with our Conduct and Constitution; and there can be no such thing as perpetual servitude of a rational creature."

24. Constitution of Vermont (1777). Article I continues: ". . . amongst which are the enjoying and defending life and liberty; acquiring, possessing, and protecting property, and pursuing and obtaining happiness and safety. Therefore, no male person, born in this country, or brought from over sea, ought to be holden by law to serve any person, as a servant, slave or apprentice, after he arrives at the age of twenty-one years, nor female, in like manner, after she arrives to the age of eighteen years."

25. *WTP,* 2:21–22.

26. Zilversmit, *First Emancipation,* 200–222.

27. Some people in Connecticut apparently thought slavery had been abolished in the 1780s. In a trespass action in 1788 against a man accused of being a runaway slave, the plaintiff complained about the stated opinions of one juror who declared "that no Negro, by the laws of this state, could be holden a slave" (see *Pettis et al. v. Jack Warren,* in Catterall, *Judicial Cases,* 5:422–23).

28. Zilversmit, *First Emancipation,* 200–222. On other problems with gradual abolition laws, see Davis, *Problem of Slavery,* 86–90.

29. Catterall, *Judicial Cases,* 1:184. The preamble to the act mentions that the delegates were inspired to pass the law by "applications [made] to this present general assembly" (Commonwealth of Virginia, *Statutes at Large,* 9:1775–78, 11:39). These applications always emphasized the natural rights of man; see, for instance, the petitions of the Pleasants family in Virginia, including the letter of Thomas Pleasants to Governor Patrick Henry in 1777, viz., "[The Quakers] have been educed to embrace the present favourable juncture, when the Representatives of the people have nobly declared all men equally free" (see James Kettner, "Persons or Property? The Peasants Slaves in Virginia Courts," in Hoffman and Albert, *Launching the "Extended Republic,"* 141).

30. See *Enquirer,* January 18, 1806.

31. Blogger, *Free Blacks,* 30. A free black community did not exist in Norfolk in 1782. The exact number of 31,570 is higher than the published census number (see Richard S. Dunn, "Black Society in the Chesapeake, 1776–1810," in Berlin and Hoffman, *Slavery and Freedom,* 49–82, 50).

32. Again, this number is different from the published census numbers (see Dunn, "Black Society," 50).

33. Jordan, *White over Black,* 407.

34. Berlin, *Slaves without Masters,* chap. 1, emphasizes the importance of slaves laboring to buy their own freedom at sometimes above-market rates. Blogger notes that 39 percent of manumissions of Norfolk slaves from 1791 to 1820 were the result of blacks saving money to free family members (*Free Blacks,* 14).

35. Slave conspiracies were often betrayed by individual slaves, who could receive manumission as a reward (see Sidbury, *Plowshares in Swords,* 34; Egerton, *Gabriel's Rebellion,* 70–71).

36. Gary Nash, "Forging Freedom: The Emancipation Experience in the Northern Seaport Cities 1775–1820," in Berlin and Hoffman, *Slavery and Freedom,* 5, table I.

37. Curry, *Free Black in Urban America,* table A-8, 251.

38. Nash, "Forging Freedom," 5, table I; Curry, *Free Black in Urban America,* appendixes A-C, 245–69.

39. Hodges, *Root and Branch,* 163–64.

40. Mullin, *Africa in America,* chap. 1.

41. Morgan, "Black Society in the Low Country," 129.

42. Sobel, *World They Made Together;* Sylvia Frey, "'The Year of Jubilee Is Come': Black Christianity in the Plantation South in Post-Revolutionary America," in Hoffman and Albert, *Religion in a Revolutionary Age,* 90–95.

43. Sidbury, *Ploughshares into Swords,* 38. Benjamin Quarles calls the process one of "transculturation," arguing, "Most blacks by 1774 had undergone a transition from Africans to Afro-Americans and were no longer the 'outlandish' blacks slave traders had deposited in the New World" (Quarrels, "The Revolutionary War as a Black Declaration of Independence," in Berlin and Hoffman, *Slavery and Freedom,* 294).

44. See also Pierson, *Black Yankees,* 144–60.

45. Benjamin Quarles, "The Revolutionary War as a Black Declaration of Independence," in Berlin and Hoffman, *Slavery and Freedom,* 297.

46. Wesley, *Prince Hall,* 121–26, 142–45.

47. Still useful is Woodson, *History of the Negro Church,* 23–121. For the role of black churches tying black communities together, see Hodges, *Root and Branch,* 180–86; Nash, *Forging Freedom,* 183–211.

48. For examples of these petitions, see Nash, *Race and Revolution,* 171, 176; Rosavich, "Three Petitions."

49. Handlin and Handlin, *Popular Sources,* 312.

50. Ibid., 263.

51. Ibid., 277.

52. *JCC,* 11:652.

53. The attempt—in this case, by Rufus King—to exclude slavery from the West was published as a pamphlet report in 1785 (United States, *Committee consisting of &c.*).

54. Onuf, *Statehood and Union;* Fehrenbacher, *Slaveholding Republic,* 253–55; Jordan, *White over Black,* 321–22. On some of the speculations about the motives behind the final passage of the exclusion, see Finkelman, "Slavery and the Northwest Ordinance"; Fehrenbacher, *Dred Scott Case,* 80–81; Robinson, *Slavery,* 381–90; Davis, *Problem of Slavery,* 153–54n74; Lynd, "Compromise of 1787."

55. For an example of the place of American magazines in the larger attempt to create a distinctly American literary culture, see Nord, "Republican Literature."

56. Moreau de St. Mery, "Character of the Creoles of St. Domingo," *American Museum* 6 (November 1789): 359–61; J. Murray, "Education of negro children," *American Museum* 6 (November 1789): 383; Benjamin Franklin, "Plan for improving the condition of free blacks," *American Museum* 6 (November 1789): 384; "Statement of the importation into Kingston, Jamaica, from the united states of America, from December 31, 1786, to March 18, 1787, in British built vessels," *American Museum* 6 (November 1789): 401; "A slave's muzzle," *American Museum* 6 (November 1789): 408.

57. It should also be recognized that British anti-slavery voices shared a similar nationalistic tone (see Colley, *Britons,* 321–61).

58. "Othello," "Essay on Negro Slavery, No. 1, "*American Museum* 4 (November 1788): 412.

59. Ibid.

60. *Debates,* 10:645–46.

61. Ibid., 10:633, 644.

62. Ibid., 10:645–46.

63. Ibid., 10:646.

64. Ibid.

65. Ibid., 12:307.

66. Ibid., 12:647.

67. Ibid., 12:650.

68. There are numerous problems with such a thesis, not least of which is that William Smith, one of the strongest defenders of slavery, was also a leading advocate for assumption, and that Madison consistently voted against assumption, which as we know involved a bargain with the North over the place of the capital. For another view, see Wiecek, *Sources of Antislavery Constitutionalism.* Paul Finkelman also has suggested similar quid pro quo arrangements (see Finkelman, "Kidnapping of John Davis"; Paul Finkelman, "Slavery and the Constitutional Convention: Making a Covenant with Death," in Beeman et al., *Beyond Confederation,* 219–24). But Finkelman's view is not supported by the evidence (see a persuasive critique in Fehrenbacher, *Slaveholding Republic,* 40–47). Howard A. Ohline has also suggested this thesis (see Ohline, "Slavery, Economics, and Congressional Politics"; see also Ellis, *Founding Brothers,* 81–119).

69. Davis, *Problem of Slavery,* 90–150. In addition, I strongly disagree with Joseph Ellis's reading of this debate. In similar fashion with Davis, Ellis argues that the goal of the "Deep South, now with the support from Massachusetts and Virginia, was to have the committee report tabled." In fact, two resolutions were to be passed, and the rest were to be inserted into the journals, thus appeasing all those who wanted to see the committee report accepted in its original *and* amended form. The "Deep" Southerners were the only delegates actually *unhappy* with this solution. They wanted a

much more clear dismissal and an explicit statement of support for slavery (see Ellis, *Founding Brothers,* 116). Ellis misreads a quote by William Loughton Smith in the debate, and also misreads the meaning of the original second resolution, which was intended to restrict Congress from any power to deal with slavery where it already existed. As noted below, *no representative,* at any phase of the debate, intimated that Congress possessed a power over slavery where it already existed (cf. Ellis, *Founding Brothers,* 116, with *Debates,* 12:844). It is also clear that Burke, Tucker, and Smith strongly opposed recording any of the rejected resolutions to the journal, which they rightly considered as a highly unorthodox situation (*Debates,* 12:841–44).

70. *Debates,* 12:288. Later, Boudinot noted that he had "never heard any gentleman say we ought to interfere," and that "the Constitution is sacred; it is a rock that ought not to be moved" (ibid., 12:764–65). Madison noted that [the proceedings] "could never be blown up into a decision of the question respecting the discouragement of the African-trade, nor alarm the owners with an apprehension that the general government were about to abolish slavery in all the states; such things are not contemplated by any gentleman" (ibid., 12:289).

71. Ibid., 12:288.

72. Ibid., 12:305.

73. Ibid., 12:307. He did assert a striking opinion, however, that if he were a federal judge he might "go as far as I could" if "those people were to come before me and claim their emancipation" on the principles of natural right (ibid.).

74. Ibid., 12:284.

75. Ibid.

76. Ibid., 12:285.

77. Ibid., 12:286.

78. Ibid., 12:730.

79. Quotes taken from two versions of the same speech (ibid., 10:635, 646 [emphasis added]).

80. Rogers, *Evolution of a Federalist,* 268.

81. *Annals of Congress,* 6th Cong., 1st sess., House of Representatives, 235.

82. Ibid.

83. Fehrenbacher, *Slaveholding Republic.*

84. *Maryland Journal and Baltimore Advertiser,* April 6, 1790.

85. Pro-slavery thought was not hard to come by, however; see Schmidt and Wilhelm, "Early Virginian Pro-Slavery Petitions." Nevertheless, public defenses of slavery were not widely evident in the *published* opinions of Americans in the late eighteenth century.

86. *Annals of Congress,* 1st Cong., 2nd sess., House of Representatives, 1455–1524.

87. Ibid., 1508.

88. *Annals of Congress,* 4th Cong., 2nd sess., House of Representatives, 1731.

89. Ibid., 1730, 1733.

90. Ibid., 1731.

91. Ibid., 1732.

92. Ibid., 1896.

93. *Annals of Congress,* 6th Cong., 1st sess., House of Representatives, 229–45.

94. Ibid., 244.

95. *Debates* 10:647, 648.

96. *Annals of Congress,* 3rd Cong., 2nd sess., House of Representatives, 1040.

97. Finkelman, "Kidnapping of John Davis."

98. Ibid., 417–22; Fehrenbacher, *Dred Scott Case,* 39–42.

99. *State of Tennessee v. Claiborne* (1838), in Meigs, *Digest of All Published Decisions,* 1:331.

100. *Amy v. Smith,* 1 Litt. 326, 335 (1822). In *Crandall v. The State of Connecticut,* Chief Justice Dagget argued: "Yet it is proper to say that sec. 2 of art. 4 of the Federal Constitution presents an obstacle to the political freedom of the Negro which seems to be insuperable. It is to be remembered that citizenship as well as freedom is a constitutional qualification, and how it could be conferred so as to overbear the laws imposing countless disabilities on him in other States is a problem of difficult solution" (*Crandall v. The State of Connecticut,* 10 Conn. 340). See also *Hobbs v. Fogg* (1835), in Watts, *Reports of Cases,* 6:553; and *Pendleton v. The State of Arkansas,* 6 Ark. 509 (1846), also in Watts, *Reports of Cases,* 6:560, in which the opinion states: "Nothing beyond a kind of quasi-citizenship has ever been recognized in the case of colored persons" (511). On the dilemmas imposed by Article IV, Section 2, see Hurd, *Law of Freedom and Bondage,* 2:319–41.

101. "And if persons of the African race are citizens of a State, and of the United States, they would be entitled to all of these privileges and immunities in every State, and the State could not restrict them; for they would hold these privileges and immunities under the paramount authority of the Federal Government, and its courts would be bound to maintain and enforce them, the Constitution and laws of the State to the contrary notwithstanding. And if the States could limit or restrict them, or place the party in an inferior grade, this Clause of the Constitution would be unmeaning, and could have no operation, and would give no rights to the citizen when in another State. He would have none but what the State itself chose to allow him. This is evidently not the construction of the meaning of the clause in question. It guarantees rights to the citizen, and the State cannot withhold them. And these rights are of a character and would lead to consequences which make it absolutely certain that the African race were not included under the name of citizens of a State, and were not in contemplation of the framers of the Constitution, when these privileges and immunities were provided for the protection of the citizen in other States" (Taney's opinion in *Dred Scott,* in Hurd, *Law of Freedom and Bondage,* 2:296).

102. Jefferson, whose racial ideas and attitudes still excite partisan debate in the twenty-first-century United States, was often at the center of American arguments over race and the status of black Americans in the early republic. Contemporaries attacked Jefferson from both sides of the argument. As a way to delegitimize his followers, anti-slavery Northern Federalists emphasized the obvious limits of Jefferson's celebration of universal notions of rights. One author in the *Connecticut Courant* derided the sincerity of Jefferson's liberal ideals and asked why the country should follow the policies of Jefferson, "when the colossus of liberty holds his fellow men in absolute slavery; when the staunch advocate for the rights of man attempts to prove that a part of mankind are an inferior race of beings?" (*Connecticut Courant,* February 11, 1793). But Southern Federalists were equally skeptical about Jefferson's commitment to slavery and attempted to excite racial animosity to garner votes. William

Loughton Smith mocked Jefferson's well-publicized letter to Benjamin Banneker and called up racial demons to garner votes for John Adams (especially ironic, considering Adams's anti-slavery stance): "[Mr. Jefferson] was so influenced by a ridiculous vanity, so tickled by a silly compliment from 'an unsavoury animal of an inferior race.' [What] shall we think of a secretary of state thus fraternizing with Negroes, writing them complimentary epistles, stiling them his black brethren, congratulating them on the evidences of their genius, and assuring them of his good wishes for their speedy emancipation?" (Smith, *Pretensions of Thomas Jefferson,* 8, 10). For similar racially charged attacks on Jefferson by Smith, see Smith, *Politicks and Views.* Jefferson's anti-slavery sentiments were so well publicized by Federalists in the South that Jefferson needed to assure Southerners in the election of 1800 that if elected, he would make no move against slavery. As the author of the Kentucky Resolutions, he knew what language to use to calm Southern fears.

103. JA to TJ, May 22, 1785, *Adams–Jefferson Letters,* 1:21.

104. Jefferson, *Notes on the State of Virginia,* 138.

105. For Locke on slavery, see Locke, *Two Treatises of Government,* 122, 155. Peter Onuf, in *Jefferson's Empire,* makes good use of the notion of slavery as a state of war in his description of Jefferson's belief that blacks were in an enslaved nation, within a white nation.

106. Jefferson, *Notes on the State of Virginia,* 138.

107. Ferdinando Fairfax, "Plan for Librating the Negroes within the United States," in Nash, *Race and Revolution,* 146–50.

108. Ibid., 147.

109. Ibid., 147–49.

110. St. George Tucker, "A Dissertation on Slavery: With a Proposal for the Gradual Abolition of It, in the State of Virginia" (Philadelphia, 1796), in Nash, *Race and Revolution,* 151–58, 153.

111. Ibid., 154.

112. Ibid., 154–55.

113. Hunt, "William Thorton," 51–52; Hunt, "James Madison's Attitude."

114. One exception is Robert Carter III of Nomini Hall. Carter freed as many slaves by personal initiative as the State of New Hampshire did by judicial order. Carter's bold abandonment of the planter class and his rejection of its privileges and power stand in stark contrast to hundreds of elite planters who loathed slavery but kept their slaves (Barden, "Flushed with Notions of Freedom").

115. Oliver Wolcott Sr. to Oliver Wolcott Jr., April 23, 1790, in Gibbs, *Memoirs,* 1:45 (emphasis added).

116. Bruckner, "Lessons in Geography."

117. Morse, *Geography Made Easy,* 70–71. The excerpt is from Crèvecoeur, *Letters from an American Farmer,* letter 9.

118. Morse, *Geography Made Easy,* 96.

119. Morse, *American Geography,* 67–68.

120. Morse, *Geography Made Easy,* 411.

121. See the complaints of Prince Hall, "A Charge Delivered to the Brethren of the African Lodge," in Porter, *Early Negro Writing,* 67.

122. Morse, *Geography Made Easy,* 411.

123. Africans and Indians were almost always ignored when authors attempted to describe the American people or symbolically represent an American. Crèvecoeur famously noted that America's "new man" was a "mixture of English, Scotch, Irish, French, Dutch, Germans, and Swedes" (*Letters from an American Farmer,* 70–71). Or, as Paine's *Common Sense* noted, "Europe, and not England, is the parent country of America," and "this new world hath been the asylum for the persecuted lovers of civil liberty from *every part* of Europe" (Paine, *Political Writings,* 18). One of the first proposals for the Great Seal was a depiction of the "arms of the Several Nations from whence America has been peopled, as English Scotch, Irish, Dutch, German, &c . . ." flanked by Liberty and a Rifleman (*BAJ,* 154).

124. Jordan, *White over Black,* 342–45. Complaining of the meddling of abolition societies, in 1795 Virginia passed a law penalizing any person or voluntary society helping a slave in a freedom suit if the judgment was rendered in favor of the slaveholder (Commonwealth of Virginia, *Statutes at Large,* 1:363). In 1797 Virginia passed a law that forbade members of abolition societies from sitting on the juries of cases involving the status of slaves (see ibid., 2:147).

125. Jordan, *White over Black,* 344–46.

126. Hurd, *Law of Freedom and Bondage,* 2:75.

127. Ibid.

128. Ibid., 2:77.

129. State of Tennessee, *Code of Tennessee,* 3808–9.

130. Hurd, *Law of Freedom and Bondage,* 2:8, 13, 21, 23, 77, 87, 96, 97.

131. Ibid., 2:118, 128, 131, 135, 164, 177, 186, 197, 204, 217.

132. Ibid., 2:14.

133. Ibid., 2:88.

134. Ibid., 2:45.

135. Ibid., 2:29.

136. Ibid., 2:29–35.

137. Ibid.; Mass., 29; Me., 34; N.C., 86; Tenn., 92, Idaho, 128; Ill., 135; Mich., 140; Iowa, 177; Kans., 187; Fla., 193; Tex., 199; Washington Territory, 218.

138. Ibid., 2:7.

139. Joseph Mountain [David Daggett?], *Sketches of the life of Joseph Mountain;* Fortis, *Last words and dying speech;* Powers, *Narrative and confession.* The narrative of Joseph Mountain was published no less than four times in the 1790s: in New Haven, Connecticut, in 1790; in Hudson, New York, in 1790; in Norwich, Connecticut, in 1796; in Walpole, New Hampshire, in 1796. Scholars disagree about the relationship of these crime narratives to early American attitudes toward race, but I tend to find Richard Slotkin, who stressed the deeply embedded racist assumptions behind the fascination with black on white crime in the early republic ("Narratives of Negro Crime") most convincing. For an alternate reading and the currently ascendant revisionist view, see Cohen, "Social Injustice." Arguments that claim whites were not as racist as previously assumed tend to argue from the absence of evidence; I find ample evidence in the denization of blacks in society, not least of which are the miscegenation laws, which Cohen does not acknowledge.

140. Quarles, *American Revolution,* 299–300.

141. Hodges, *Root and Branch,* 192.

142. *Hobbs v. Fogg* (1835), in Watts, *Reports of Cases,* 6:553.

143. The story of the black vote in New York City is still well told in Fox, "Negro Vote in Old New York." See also Hodges, *Root and Branch,* 191–92, 200, 253, 256–57 (Hodges notes that "By 1828 there were only 298 black votes in New York in a total population of 29,701" blacks [192]); McManus, *Black Bondage,* 184–85; Litwack, *North of Slavery,* 75.

144. Nash, *Forging Freedom,* 183–211.

145. Allen et al., *Narrative of the proceedings of the Black people.*

146. Both petitions can be found in Aptheker, *Documentary History of Negro People,* 2:40–42, 44.

147. Nash, *Forging Freedom,* 212–79. New York free blacks also possessed a strong national presence and a strong regional voice, especially with their ability to influence electoral politics in favor of the Federalists. On the significant place of New York free blacks in this period, see Hodges, *Root and Branch,* 163–226, passim.

148. "The Memorial of Thomas Cole Bricklayer P. B. Mathews and Mathew Webb Butchers on behalf of themselves & others Free Men of Colour," in Aptheker, *Documentary History of Negro People,* 2:98–99.

149. Ibid.

150. A recent intriguing study of a family crafting a "white" life for themselves is O'Toole, *Passing for White.*

151. In contemporary records, Gabriel was never referred to as "Gabriel Prosser," but always "Prosser's Gabriel." It seems a historical injustice to inflict a surname on a man who planned his master's murder with such audacity.

152. The best studies of the rebellion are Egerton, *Gabriel's Rebellion;* and Sidbury, *Ploughshares into Swords.*

153. *CVSP,* 9:164.

154. Ibid., 9:165.

155. Ibid.

156. [Tucker,] *Letter to a Member of the General Assembly.*

157. *CVSP,* 9:160.

158. On the controversy over the number of slaves hanged in the rebellion, see Egerton, *Gabriel's Rebellion,* appendix 3, 186–88.

159. *CVSP,* 9:189. A slave named Billy was hanged on January 23, 1801, for breaking into a warehouse and stealing $20 worth of tobacco.

160. Winthrop Jordan, for instance, sees no evidence of any free blacks participating in or inciting the rebellion (*White over Black,* 406, 409–10), while James Sidbury shows some awareness of the larger place the free black community played in aiding slave resistance (*Ploughshares into Swords,* 118–47).

161. Both Winthrop Jordan and Douglas R. Egerton argue that Virginians began restricting the freedom of blacks as a direct result of Gabriel's Rebellion. In fact, the rebellion only accelerated a trend that had begun as early as 1793, when the state forbade the migration of free blacks into the state. By 1807, Virginians were still divided over whether to allow manumission, although, as I note, they were conscious of an abandonment of Revolutionary principles when they finally restricted the ability of planters to free their slaves.

162. Commonwealth of Virginia, *Statutes at Large,* 2:279, 300.

163. Ibid., 2:326, 3:76.

164. Ibid., 3:123–24.

165. Ibid., 3:290.

166. "Call of a Convention" speech of Mr. Ball, *Enquirer,* January 28, 1806; and speech of Mr. Mallory, *Enquirer,* February 4, 1806.

167. *Enquirer,* January 18, 1806.

168. William Mumford, "Mr. William Munford of the Senate letter to his constituents, in the senatorial district of Brunswick, Lunenburg, Mechlenburg, and Greensville," *Enquirer,* February 4, 1806.

169. In 1810 they increased the penalty to being sold for a term of years.

170. Hurd, *Law of Freedom and Bondage,* 2:16.

171. Ibid., 2:31.

172. Ibid., 2:118.

173. James Forten, "Letters from a Man of Colour on a Late Bill before the Senate of Pennsylvania" (1813), in Nash, *Race and Revolution,* 190. Eventually, North Carolina (1826), Tennessee (1831), South Carolina (1822), Georgia (1859), Indiana (1851), Illinois (1853), Mississippi (1842), Alabama (1832), Louisiana (1841–42), Missouri (1843), Arkansas (1843), Iowa (1851), Florida (1832), Texas (1840), and Oregon (1849) passed laws forbidding the immigration of free blacks (Hurd, *Law of Freedom and Bondage,* 2:11, 15, 18, 20, 78, 86, 92, 97, 109, 117, 130, 131, 135, 136, 149, 151, 152, 158, 161, 163, 168, 170, 172, 176, 193, 197, 216).

174. *Enquirer,* January 15, 1806; *Virginia Argus,* January 17, 1806.

175. *Enquirer,* January 18, 1806.

176. Ibid.

177. Ellis, *Founding Brothers,* 81–119.

178. TJ to William Short, January 18, 1826, Jefferson Papers, Library of Congress.

179. Hurd, *Law of Freedom and Bondage,* 2:330.

8 ⁜ The Aristotelian Moment

1. Thomas Paine, *The Rights of Man,* Part I, in Paine, *Political Writings,* 1:143.

2. Abraham Baldwin, Congressman from Georgia, in a speech attacking the Alien and Sedition Bills, January 11, 1799, *Annals of Congress,* 5th Cong., 3rd sess., House of Representatives, 2629.

3. Fisher Ames to Rufus King, May 27, 1801, *LCK,* 3:459. For a recent collection about the problem of the election of 1800, see Horn et al., *Revolution of 1800.*

4. Republicans captured sixty-nine House seats, and the Federalists won only thirty-nine—from numbers nearly the opposite—and the Senate was controlled for the first time by the Republicans. New Jersey, Georgia, Kentucky, and Tennessee sent complete Republican delegations to Congress; Virginia sent only one Federalist; Pennsylvania and New York were majority Republican delegations. Elkins and McKitrick list the number at sixty-five and forty-one (see *Age of Federalism,* 741); Miller says there were "approximately" sixty-five and forty (*Federalist Era,* 274).

5. Rowe, *Thomas McKean,* 309–12.

6. *New York Daily Advertiser,* printed in *Centinel of Freedom,* December 18, 1798.

7. Historians have overemphasized the role of Hamilton's attack on Adams as an

explanation for the complete overthrow of the Federalists in 1800–1803. It certainly did not help matters, but the overwhelming victory of the Republicans in state and local elections spoke to causes much deeper than the personal animosity between Hamilton and Adams. In fact, Adams did relatively better than his party (see Elkins and McKitrick, *Age of Federalism,* 726–43).

8. "An act to suspend, in part, an act, entitled 'An act to augment the army of the United States, and for other purposes,'" (U.S. Congress, *Public and General Statutes,* 1:718).

9. Some historians have assumed that the Alien Act was never enforced because no aliens were deported by executive fiat, but the bill also included an extensive system for registering all immigrants and Timothy Pickering closely followed the reports of the local federal officials (see Timothy Pickering to Philip Moore, esq., November 1, 1798, Domestic Letters of the Department of State, June 30, 1798–June 29, 1799, reel 11, vol. 11, National Archives: "I have received your letter of the 24th inclosing your monthly return of Aliens registered for September last, and in which you refer to me for the several forms of returns. . . . [These returns should include] a suitable description of the name, age, native residence and occupation of the Alien"). More examples of such letters exist; I have not found the originals of these returns. This is a topic that needs more research.

10. Section 6 of the act limited its operation to two years (U.S. Congress, *Public and General Statutes,* 1:516).

11. On the Bankruptcy Act, see McCoy, *Elusive Republic,* 180–85.

12. Recent studies of the Federalists and the Federalist era have completely ignored the existence of the Judiciary Act of 1801, and the importance of the place of the federal courts in the Federalist vision of the national state more generally. Elkins and McKitrick's *The Age of Federalism* has nothing on the Judiciary Act. Thus they have also missed the importance of the repeal of the act and the meaning of that repeal for the decrepit state of the federal judiciary in the antebellum United States.

13. JA to JJ, December 19, 1800, in Adams, *Works of John Adams,* 9:91–92.

14. For a nice review of the reasoning and politics behind Marshall's appointment, see Turner, "Appointment of Chief Justice Marshall."

15. Williams' Case, Case No. 17,708, Circuit Court, D. Connecticut 29 F. Cas. 1330; 1799 U.S. App. Lexis 39, 1–3.

16. "The Consistent Federalist," *Columbian Centinel,* January 14, 1801; see also *Columbian Centinel,* January 31, February 4, 7, 18, 1801.

17. AH to Jonathon Dayton, in Hamilton, *Works of Alexander Hamilton,* 10:329.

18. *Columbian Centinel,* February 4, 1801.

19. John Rutledge to AH, January 10, 1801, in Hamilton, *Works of Hamilton,* 6:510–11.

20. U.S. Congress, *Public and General Statutes,* 1:797–811.

21. This also applied to cases where an alien was a party and the United States was a party, subject to the same monetary limit (ibid., 1:56–57).

22. Federalists had attempted to make the dollar limit $100, but the Republican opposition succeeded in achieving the higher amount (*Annals of Congress,* 6th Cong., 2nd sess., House of Representatives, 897).

23. Places for holding the circuit courts were Providence, and Newport, R.I.;

Boston; Portsmouth and Exeter, N.H.; Portland and Wiscasset, Me.; New Haven and Hartford, Conn.; Windsor and Rutland, Vt.; Albany and New York, N.Y.; Trenton, N.J.; Philadelphia and Bedford, Pa.; Dover, Del.; Baltimore, Md.; Richmond and Lexington, Va.; Raleigh, N.C.; Columbia and Charleston, S.C.; Savannah, Ga.; Knoxville and Nashville, Tenn.; Bairdstown, Ky; and Cincinnati, Ohio (U.S. Congress, *Public and General Statutes,* 1:800–801).

24. Originally, removal only could be done before a trial began, and only in cases of over $500 value.

25. U.S. Congress, *Public and General Statutes,* 1:801.

26. Ibid., 1:802.

27. *Annals of Congress,* 7th Congress, 2nd sess., House of Representatives, 534.

28. Tucker, *Blackstone Commentaries,* 1:360, 427.

29. Ibid., 1:438.

30. Gouverneur Morris to Robert R. Livingston, February 20, 1801, in Sparks, *Life of Gouverneur Morris,* 3:153–54.

31. These became the so-called midnight appointments. The Federalists had attempted to continue the operation of the Sedition Act and had succeeded in the House of Representatives to support the report of a committee that encouraged the continuation of the law (*Annals of Congress,* 6th Cong., 2nd sess., House of Representatives, 976); but the final bill, which would have continued the operation of the act, failed by four votes (ibid., 1050).

32. Ibid., 7th Cong., 1st sess., Senate, 11–16.

33. On Jefferson's naval plans, see Malone, *Jefferson,* 3:102–3.

34. *Annals of Congress,* 7th Cong., 1st sess., Senate, 11–16.

35. Alexander Hamilton, "The Examination, Number IX," January 18, 1802, in Hamilton, *Papers of Alexander Hamilton,* 25:501–2.

36. William Giles to Thomas Jefferson, June 1, 1801, Jefferson Papers.

37. *Annals of Congress,* 6th Cong., 1st sess., Senate, 161.

38. Ibid., 30–31.

39. See the speech of John Breckinridge of February 3, 1802, in which he describes the different debates on the bill (ibid., 158–59).

40. See ibid., 476–81, 510–982.

41. Ibid., 40–41.

42. Morse, *Geography Made Easy,* 432.

43. Presser, *Original Misunderstanding,* 5–6.

44. U.S. Congress, *Public and General Statutes,* 2:845.

45. Ibid., 2:862–63.

46. Ibid., 2:909–10.

47. *Annals of Congress,* 7th Cong., 1st sess., Senate, 16.

48. Ibid., 198, 315, 361, 375, 404, 602.

49. Hamilton, "Examination, Number IX," 500–501.

50. U.S. Congress, *Public and General Statutes,* 2:942–43.

51. Hamilton, "Examination, Number IX," 502.

52. Aristotle, *Politics,* Book IV, chap. 1, 82.

53. TJ to John Randolph Jr., December 1, 1803, Jefferson Papers.

54. Hamilton, "Examination, Number IX," 502–4.

55. *Annals of Congress,* 7th Cong., 1st sess., Senate, 14–15.

56. The theoretical literature on nations and nationalism is obsessed with the notion of the nation-state—even if it is seen as problematic—as the *only* "modern" form. For a recent example of such an argument, see Jack Greene, "State Formation, Resistance, and the Creation of Revolutionary Traditions in the Early Modern Era," in Morrison and Zook, *Revolutionary Currents,* 1–34. For nice corrective, see Onuf and Onuf, *Federal Union.*

57. Joel Barlow, "To His fellow Citizens of the United States," *APW,* 2:1104–6.

58. On the Danbury address and Jefferson's reply, see Malone, *Jefferson,* 5:108–9.

59. It is noteworthy that while Jeffersonians developed a justification for state resistance and nullification based upon Revolutionary principles—that is, as a defense of the "natural rights" of individuals against federal government encroachment—high Federalists developed a theory of the right to secession at the Hartford Convention as a *constitutional check* on majoritarian threats to property. It is not surprising that John C. Calhoun, whose ideas of nullification seemed absurd to James Madison, studied at Yale with Federalist Timothy Dwight (see Wood, *Radicalism of the American Republic,* 268; Banner, *Hartford Convention*). Theodore Dwight, the secretary and a constant defender of the Hartford Convention, explicitly connected and supported the nullification *doctrines* of the conventioneers to South Carolina's nullification convention but denied the legitimacy of South Carolina's fears (see Dwight, *History of the Hartford Convention,* appendix, 423–47). Calhoun rejected the notion of natural rights, considering them "nonsense," like Bentham. No rights existed except for those granted by the states. With no belief in natural rights, there was no need for a federated Union intended to protect those rights. Calhoun's vision of secession could never be the defense of natural rights, but a blatant state right to nullify any law; whereas Jefferson noted that nullification could really only be appropriate as a last measure against a tyrannical central government that made an *unconstitutional* law, which the tariff was certainly not. States had to obey laws that the federal government had been given the power to create, even if they believed them to be unjust. Everyone in antebellum America agreed that states had a right to defend their prerogatives from the federal government; even Hamilton had to admit that states had rights, he just did not let that get in the way of his effort to build a real nation-state on the corpse of a Constitution he called a "vile and worthless fragment."

60. Morgan and Morgan, *Stamp Act Crisis.*

61. See Hulsebosch, *Constituting Empire.*

62. On the Quid movement as a third party between Republicans and Federalists, see Cunningham, "Who Were the Quids?" On the politics of Duane and Binns, see Wilson, *United Irishmen,* 73–74.

63. Duane, *Report of a Debate,* 18–19.

64. Ibid., 90.

65. Brown, *Ending the French Revolution,* ix, 358.

Conclusion

1. Brownlee, *Dynamics,* 125, table 5.

2. See Kastor, *Nation's Crucible.* Kastor shows, in an excellent study, that the taking of Louisiana continued a politics related to American national character, which

also depended upon numerous problems related to incorporation, rights, and the Union.

3. Hamilton accused Burr of an ambition to break the Union and become the president of a new Northern Confederacy at a Federalist meeting in Albany, which spurred Burr's challenge to a duel.

4. The Second Amendment to the Constitution suggested at the Convention would have required a "two-thirds" vote of both houses of Congress to admit a new state to the Union (Dwight, *History of the Hartford Convention,* 377). Another of their proposed amendments was a denial of any naturalized citizen the privilege of serving in any elected office under the United States, or any civil office of the federal government (ibid., 378). Dwight's history began with the French Revolution.

5. As quoted in Onuf, *Jefferson's Empire,* 109–47, and passim, whose understanding of the "empire of liberty" I am indebted to.

6. John O'Sullivan, "The Great Nation of Futurity," *United States Democratic Review* 6 (November 1839): 426–30.

7. TJ to Joseph Priestly, January 29, 1804, in Jefferson, *Writings of Thomas Jefferson,* edited by Lipscomb and Bergh, 7:295.

8. See also Lewis, *American Union.*

9. History of the Proceedings of Congress, Part 5, *Historical Register of the United States* (1812–14), January 1, 1814, chap. 3, 168.

10. Ibid. 168–70.

11. Tucker, *Blackstone's Commentaries.*

12. History of the Proceedings of Congress, Part 5, *Historical Register of the United States* (1812–14), January 1, 1814, chap. 3, 170–72.

13. Kerber, *No Constitutional Right to Be Ladies;* Brewer, *Birth or Consent,* 351–67.

14. For more on the relationship between a "community of emigrants" and American ideas of citizenship and belonging, see Bradburn, "Nation of Emigrants."

15. American party politicians would play at revolution—like the electioneering "liberty poles" of Henry Clay and Andrew Jackson (competing "ash" and "hickory" poles, respectively), but such later party symbolism never attained the threatening meaning of symbolic universalism of the Age of Revolution.

16. Babcock, *Rise of American Nationality,* 17.

17. John Q. Adams, "Emigration to the United States," *Niles' Weekly Register,* April 29, 1820.

18. JA to Benjamin Rush, February 23, 1813, *Dialogues,* 276.

19. JA to TJ, February 2, 1817, *Adams–Jefferson Letters,* 2:508.

20. *Aurora,* November 7, 1817.

21. Bibliography of Publications of Mathew Carey, American Philosophical Society.

22. Anonymous [Henry Marie Brekenridge], *South America,* 15–16. I am indebted to Monica Henry for pointing this pamphlet out to me. See also Langley, *Americas in the Age of Revolution,* 239–240; Whitaker, *United States and the Independence of Latin America,* 333–36.

23. Which John Marshall confirmed in *Barron v. Baltimore,* 7 Pet. 243 (in Warren, *Supreme Court in United States History,* 1:780).

24. Adams, "Emigration to the United States."

25. For the "mansfieldization" of the jury, see Alschuler and Deiss, "Brief History of the Criminal Jury in the United States"; "Changing Role of the Jury in the Nineteenth Century"; Horowitz, *Transformation of American Law;* Nelson, *Americanization of the Common Law.* See also Schmeller, "Twelve Hungry Men."

26. TJ to JM, February 17, 1826, in Jefferson, *Writings of Thomas Jefferson,* edited by Lipscomb and Bergh, 12:456.

27. Newmeyer, "Justice Joseph Story," 481.

28. Peterson, *Jefferson Image,* 32–35.

29. See Hulsebosch, *Constituting Empire,* 274–95.

30. Anthony et al., *History of Women's Suffrage,* 1:70.

31. State of Virginia, *Proceedings and Debates,* 54.

32. Ibid., 69, 70.

33. Ibid., 318.

34. Ibid., 411.

35. Ibid., 533. Randolph went on to note that Jefferson's plow "of least resistance" was an utter failure—a nice touch.

36. Ibid., 172.

37. As quoted in Sinha, *Counterrevolution of Slavery,* 255–56.

BIBLIOGRAPHY

Collections

Adams Papers. Massachusetts Historical Society. Boston.

Broadsides. American Antiquarian Society. Worcester, Mass.

Duane, William J., Papers. American Philosophical Society. Philadelphia.

Durrett, Reuben T., Collection on Kentucky and the Ohio River Valley. Special Collections, University of Chicago.

Genet Papers. Library of Congress. Washington, D.C.

Jefferson Papers. Library of Congress. Washington, D.C.

Religious Petitions. Library of Virginia. Richmond.

Sedgwick Papers. Massachusetts Historical Society. Boston.

Newspapers and Magazines

Alexandria Advertiser (Alexandria, Va.)

The American Minerva, Patroness of Peace, Commerce, and the Liberal Arts (New York)

American Museum (Philadelphia)

Andrew's Western Star (Stockbridge, Mass.)

Aurora General Advertiser (Philadelphia)

Boston Evening Post

Boston Gazette

Carey's United States Recorder (Philadelphia)

The Centinel of Freedom (Newark, N.J.)

City Gazette & Daily Advertiser (Charleston, S.C.)

Columbian Centinel (Boston)

The Columbian Magazine; or Monthly Miscellany (New York)

Connecticut Courant (Hartford)

Dunlap's American Daily Advertiser (Philadelphia)

The Enquirer (Richmond, Va.)

Federal Gazette (Philadelphia)

Federal Gazette and Baltimore Advertiser (Baltimore)

The Gazette of the United States (Philadelphia)

The Genius of Liberty (Morristown, N.J.)

Herald of Liberty (Washington, Pa.)

Independent Chronicle (Boston)

Kentucky Gazette (Lexington)

Kline's Carlisle Weekly Gazette (Carlisle, Pa.)

Maryland Journal and Baltimore Advertiser (Baltimore)

National Gazette (Philadelphia)

Newburyport Herald and Country Gazette (Newburyport, Mass.)
New Hampshire Gazette (Portsmouth)
New Hampshire Mercury (Portsmouth)
New Jersey State Gazette (Trenton)
New York Argus
New York Daily Advertiser
New York Diary
New York Gazette and General Advertiser
New York Journal
New York Magazine; or, Literary Repository
Niles' Weekly Register (Baltimore)
Northern Centinel (Salem, N.Y.)
The Palladium: A Literary and Political Weekly Repository (Frankfort, Ky.)
The Pennsylvania Magazine; or, American Monthly Museum (Philadelphia)
Pennsylvania Packet (Philadelphia)
The Philadelphia Gazette and Universal Daily Advertiser
The Philadelphia Monthly Magazine; or, Universal Repository of Knowledge
Porcupine's Gazette (Philadelphia)
Raleigh Register (Raleigh, N.C.)
Rights of Man, or The Nashville Intelligencer (Nashville, Tenn.)
Salem Gazette (Salem, Mass.)
Stewart's Kentucky Herald (Lexington)
Time Piece (New York)
The Tree of Liberty (Pittsburgh)
The United States Democratic Review (New York)
Virginia Argus (Richmond)
Virginia Gazette & General Advertiser (Richmond)
Winchester Gazette (Winchester, Va.)

Other Sources

Adams, Abigail, and John Adams. *The Book of Abigail and John: Selected Letters of the Adams Family, 1762–1784*. Edited by L. H. Butterfield, Mary-Jo Kline, and Marc Friedlaender. Cambridge, Mass., 1975.

Adams, Henry. *History of the United States: During the Administrations of Jefferson and Madison*. Abridged by George Dangerfield and Otney M. Scruggs. 2 vols. Englewood Cliffs, N.J., 1963.

Adams, John. *Diary and Autobiography of John Adams*. Edited by Lyman H. Butterfield. 4 vols. Cambridge, Mass., 1961.

———. *The Political Writings of John Adams*. Edited by George A. Peek Jr. Indianapolis, Ind., 1954.

———. *The Spur of Fame: Dialogues of John Adams and Benjamin Rush, 1805–1813*. Edited by John A. Schutz and Douglass Adair. San Marino, Calif., 1966.

———. *The Works of John Adams*. Edited by Charles Francis Adams. 10 vols. Boston, 1850–56.

Adams, John, and Thomas Jefferson. *The Adams–Jefferson Letters: The Complete Cor-*

respondence Between Thomas Jefferson and Abigail and John Adams. Edited by Lester Cappon. 2 vols. New York, 1959.

Adams, John Quincy. *The Writings of John Quincy Adams.* Edited by W. C. Ford. New York, 1913.

Addison, Alexander. *Liberty of Speech and of the Press, A charge to the Grand Juries of the Circuit Courts of the Fifth Circuit of the state of Pennsylvania.* Washington, Pa., 1798.

———. *On the Alien Act. A Charge to the Grand Juries of the County Courts of the Fifth Circuit of the State of Pennsylvania.* Washington, Pa., 1799.

Allen, Ethan. *Ethan Allen and His Kin, Correspondence, 1772–1819.* Edited by John J. Duffy. Hanover, N.H., 1998.

Allen, Richard, Matthew Clarkson, Absalom Jones, and Maxwell Whiteman. *A narrative of the proceedings of the Black people, during the late awful calamity in Philadelphia, in the year 1793 and a refutation of some censures, thrown upon them in some late publications.* Philadelphia, 1794.

Alschuler, Albert, and Andrew Deiss. "A Brief History of the Criminal Jury in the United States." *University of Chicago Law Review* 61 (1994): 867–928.

An American. [Joseph Hopkinson.] *What is our situation? And what our prospects? A few pages for Americans, by an American.* Philadelphia, 1798.

American Historical Association. *Report of the American Historical Association for 1896.* Washington, D.C., 1897.

Ammerman, David. *In the Common Cause: American Response to the Coercive Acts of 1774.* Charlottesville, Va., 1974.

Ammon, Henry. *The Genet Mission.* New York, 1973.

Anderson, Benedict. *Imagined Communities: Reflections on the Origin and Spread of Nationalism.* London, 1983.

Anderson, Frank Maloy. "Contemporary Opinion of the Alien and Sedition Acts, I." *American Historical Review* 5 (October 1899): 45–63.

———. "Contemporary Opinion of the Virginia and Kentucky Resolutions, II." *American Historical Review* 5 (1899): 225–52.

Anderson, Fred. *The Crucible of War: The Seven Years' War and the Fate of Empire in British North America, 1754–1766.* New York, 2000.

Anonymous. *The appendix: or, Some observations on the expediency of the petition of the Africans, living in Boston, &c. lately presented to the General Assembly of this province. To which is annexed, the petition referred to. Likewise, thoughts on slavery. With a useful extract from the Massachusetts spy, of January 28, 1773, by way of an address to the members of the assembly. By a lover of constitutional liberty.* Boston, 1773.

Anonymous. *A few Solitary Hints, Pointing out the Policy and Consequences of admitting British Subjects to Engross our trade and Become our citizens. Addressed to those who either risqued or lost their all in bringing about the revolution.* Charleston and New York, 1786.

Anonymous. *The House of Delegates, Tuesday, 28th November, 1793 . . .* Broadside. Richmond, Va., December 3, 1793.

Anonymous. *Paddy's Resource: Being a Collection of original and modern patriotic songs, toasts, and sentiments.* Philadelphia, 1796.

Anonymous. *Paddy's Resource: Being a select collection of original and modern patriotic songs/compiled for the use of the people of Ireland; to which is added, Arthur O'Connor's address.* New York, 1798.

Anonymous. *The Plea of Erin; or the Case of the Natives of Ireland in the United States, fairly displayed, in the fraternal address of the First Congress in the year 1775; and in the respectful memorial of the republican Irish, who had, consequently sought an "asylum" in America, addressed by them to the Congress in the year 1798.* Broadside. Philadelphia, 1798.

Anonymous. "The Sedition Act, A Song." American Antiquarian Society. Broadside. 1811.

Anonymous. *Sir, Deeply Interested in the Approaching Election . . . Recommending James Ross.* Broadside. Philadelphia, 1799.

Anonymous. [Henry Marie Brekenridge.] *South America: A Letter on the Present State of that Country, to James Monroe, President of the United States, by an America.* Washington, D.C., 1817.

Anonymous. *There is a Snake in the Grass!!* Broadside. Lexington, Ky., August 15, 1798.

Anonymous. *To the Electors of Pennsylvania When a Candidate.* Broadside. Philadelphia, 1799.

Anonymous. *To the Friends of freedom and public faith, and to all lovers of their fellow men.* Broadside. Philadelphia, 1799.

Anonymous. *To the Senate and House of Representatives, the respectful memorial of the subscribers, natives of Ireland, residing within the United States of America.* Broadside. Philadelphia, 1799.

Anthony, S. B., E. C. Stanton, and M. J. Gage, eds. *History of Women's Suffrage.* 4 vols. New York, 1887.

Appleby, Joyce. *Inheriting the Revolution: The First Generation of Americans.* Cambridge, Mass., 2000.

———. *Republicanism and Liberalism in Historical Imagination.* Cambridge, Mass., 1992.

Aptheker, Herbert. "Maroons within the Present Limits of the United States." *Journal of Negro History* 24 (1934): 167–84.

———, ed. *A Documentary History of Negro People in the United States.* 2 vols. New York, 1951.

Aristotle. *The Politics.* Edited by Steven Everson. Cambridge, 1995.

Armitage, David. *The Ideological Origins of the British Empire.* New York, 2000.

Austin, Aleine. *Matthew Lyon, "New Man" of the Democratic Revolution, 1749–1822.* University Park, Pa., 1981.

Austin, William, ed. *A Selection of the Patriotic Addresses, To the President of the United States. Together with the President's Answers.* Boston, 1798.

Babcock, Kendrick Charles. *The Rise of American Nationality, 1811–1819.* New York, 1906.

Bailyn, Bernard. *The Ideological Origins of the American Revolution.* Cambridge, Mass., 1967.

———. *Voyagers to the West: A Passage in the Peopling of America on the Eve of the Revolution.* New York, 1986.

Bailyn, Bernard, and Philip D. Morgan, eds. *Strangers within the Realm: Cultural Margins of the First British Empire*. Chapel Hill, N.C., 1991.

Baldwin, Leland D. *Whiskey Rebels: The Story of a Frontier Uprising*. Pittsburgh, 1939.

Balmer, Randall H. *A Perfect Babel of Confusion: Dutch Religion and English Culture in the Middle Colonies*. New York, 1989.

Banneker, Benjamin, and Thomas Jefferson. *Copy of a letter from Benjamin Banneker, to the secretary of state, with his answer*. Philadelphia, 1792.

Banner, James M., Jr. *To the Hartford Convention: The Federalists and the Origins of Part Politics in Massachusetts, 1789–1815*. New York, 1970.

Banning, Lance. *The Sacred Fire of Liberty: James Madison and the Founding of the Federal Republic*. Ithaca, N.Y., 1995.

Barden, John Randolph. "'Flushed with Notions of Freedom': The Growth and Emancipation of a Virginia Slave Community, 1732–1812." Ph.D. diss., Duke University, 1993.

Baseler, Marilyn C. *Asylum for Mankind: America 1607–1800*. Ithaca, N.Y., 1998.

Becker, Carl L. *The Declaration of Independence: A Study in the History of Political Ideas*. New York, 1922.

Beckley, John James. *Defending Jefferson: The Political Writings of John James Beckley*. Edited by Gerard W. Gawalt. Washington, D.C., 1995.

Beeman, Richard, Stephen Botein, and Edward C. Carter, eds. *Beyond Confederation: Origins of the Constitution and American National Identity*. Chapel Hill, N.C., 1987.

Bell, Richard M. *Party and Faction in American Politics*. New York, 1973.

Bellesiles, Michael A. "The Establishment of Legal Structures on the Frontier: The Case of Revolutionary Vermont." *Journal of American History* 73 (March 1987): 895–915.

Bentham, Jeremy. *Works of Bentham*. Edited by John Bowring. 10 vols. Edinburgh, U.K., 1843.

Berkley, George. "The Querist." In *The Works of George Berkley*. Edited by Alexander Campbell Fraser. 4 vols. Bristol, U.K., 1994.

Berlin, Ira. *Many Thousands Gone: The First Two Centuries of Slavery in North America*. Cambridge, Mass., 1998.

———. *Slaves without Masters: The Free Negro in the Antebellum South*. New York, 1974.

Berlin, Ira, and Ronald Hoffman, eds. *Slavery and Freedom in the Age of the American Revolution*. Urbana, Ill., 1983.

Bermeo, Nancy, and Philip Nord, eds. *Civil Society Before Democracy: Lessons from Nineteenth Century Europe*. Lanham, Md., 2000.

Bilder, Mary Sarah. *The Transatlantic Constitution: Colonial Legal Culture and the Empire*. Cambridge, Mass., 2004.

Blackburn, Robin. *The Overthrow of Colonial Slavery, 1776–1848*. London, 1988.

Bland, Richard. *An Inquiry into the Rights of British Colonists*. Williamsburg, Va., 1766.

Blethen, H. Tyler, and Curtis W. Wood, eds. *Ulster and North America: Transatlantic Perspectives on the Scotch-Irish*. Tuscaloosa, Ala., 1997.

Blogger, Tommy. *Free Blacks in Norfolk Virginia, 1790–1860*. Charlottesville, Va., 1997.

Bodle, Wayne. "Themes and Directions in Middle Colonies Historiography." *William and Mary Quarterly*, 3rd ser., 51 (July 1994): 355–88.

Boorstin, Daniel. *The Genius of American Politics*. Chicago, 1953.

Bork, Robert. *The Tempting of America: The Political Seduction of the Law*. New York, 1989.

Bouton, Terry. "'No Wonder the Times Were Troublesome': The Origins of Fries Rebellion, 1783–1799." *Pennsylvania History* 67 (Winter 2000): 21–39.

———. "A Road Closed: Rural Insurgency in Post-Independence Pennsylvania." *Journal of American History* 83, no. 3 (2000): 855–87.

———. *Taming Democracy: "The People," the Founders, and the Troubled Ending of the American Revolution*. Oxford, 2007.

Boyd, Steven R., ed. *The Whiskey Rebellion: Past and Present Perspectives*. Westport, Conn., 1985.

Bradburn, Douglas. "A Clamor in the Public Mind: Opposition to the Alien and Sedition Acts." *William and Mary Quarterly*, 3rd ser., 65 (July 2008): 565–600.

———. "A Nation Made Easy: Geography, Pedagogy, and American Identity." *Mapline* 91 (2000): 6–7.

———. "A Nation of Emigrants: Consent and the Jeffersonian Citizen." In *Jefferson for Today*, edited by Gene Smith. Charlottesville, Va., forthcoming.

———. "Revolutionary Politics, Nationhood, and the Problem of American Citizenship, 1787–1804." Ph.D. diss., University of Chicago, 2003.

———. "'True Americans' and 'Hordes of Foreigners': Nationalism, Ethnicity, and the Problem of Citizenship in the United States, 1789–1800." *Historical Reflections* 28 (Summer 2003): 19–41.

Bradley, Joseph. "Subjects into Citizens: Societies, Civil Society, and Autocracy in Tsarist Russia." *American Historical Review* 107 (October 2002): 1094–123.

Branson, Susan. *These Fiery Frenchified Dames: Women and Political Culture in Early National Philadelphia*. Philadelphia, 2001.

Branson, Susan, and Simon P. Newman. "American Women and the French Revolution." In William Pencak, *Riot and Revelry in Early America*, edited by Matthew Dennis and Simon P. Newman, 229–54. University Park, Pa., 2003.

Breen, Timothy. *Lockean Moment: The Language of Rights on the Eve of the American Revolution*. Oxford, 2001.

———. "Revisions in Need of Revising: Ideology and Nationalism on the Eve of the American Revolution." *Journal of American History* 84 (June 1997): 13–39.

Brewer, Holly. *By Birth or Consent: Children, Law, and the Anglo-American Revolution in Authority*. Chapel Hill, N.C., 2005.

———. "Entailing Aristocracy in Colonial Virginia: 'Ancient Feudal Restraints' and Revolutionary Reform." *William and Mary Quarterly*, 3rd ser., 54 (April 1997): 307–46.

Brewer, John. "The Eighteenth Century British State: Contexts and Issues." In *An Imperial State at War: Britain from 1689–1815*, edited by Lawrence Stone, 52–71. London, 1994.

———. *The Sinews of Power: War, Money, and the English State, 1688–1783*. New York, 1989.

Brewer, John, and J. H. Plumb. *The Birth of Consumer Society: The Commercialization of Eighteenth-Century England*. Bloomington, Ind., 1982.

Briceland, Alan V. "The Philadelphia Aurora, the New England Illuminati, and the Election of 1800." *Pennsylvania Magazine of History and Biography* 100 (1976): 9–17

Bridenbaugh, Carl, and Jessica Bridenbaugh. *Rebels and Gentlemen: Philadelphia in the Age of Franklin*. New York, 1942.

Brims, John. "From Reformers to 'Jacobins': The Scottish Association of the Friends of the People." In *Conflict and Stability in Scottish Society, 1700–1850*, edited by T. M. Devine, 31–50. Edinburgh, 1990.

———. "The Scottish Jacobins, Scottish Nationalism and the British Union." In *Scotland and England, 1286–1815*, edited by Roger A. Mason, 247–65. Edinburgh, 1987.

Bromwell, William J. *History of Immigration to the United States*. New York, 1856.

Brooke, John L. *The Heart of the Commonwealth: Society and Political Culture in Worcester County, Massachusetts, 1713–1861*. Cambridge, Mass., 1989.

———. "To the Quiet of the People: Revolutionary Settlements and Civil Unrest in Western Massachusetts, 1774–1789." *William and Mary Quarterly*, 3rd ser., 46 (July 1989): 425–62.

Brownlee, Elliot. *Dynamics of Ascent: A History of the American Economy*. 2nd ed. Belmont, Calif., 1978.

Brown, Howard G. *Ending the French Revolution: Violence, Justice, and Repression from the Terror to Napoleon*. Charlottesville, Va., 2007.

Brown, Richard D. *Knowledge Is Power: The Diffusion of Information in Early America 1700–1865*. New York, 1989.

———. *Revolutionary Politics in Massachusetts: The Boston Committee of Correspondence and the Towns, 1772–1774*. Cambridge, Mass., 1970.

Brown, Robert E. *Middle Class Democracy and the Revolution in Massachusetts, 1774–1775*. Ithaca, N.Y., 1955.

Brown, Wallace. *The Good Americans: The Loyalists in the American Revolution*. New York, 1969.

Brubaker, Rogers. *Citizenship and Nationhood in France and Germany*. Cambridge, Mass., 1992.

Bruckner, Martin. "Lessons in Geography: Maps, Spellers, and Other Grammars of Nationalism in the Early Republic." *American Quarterly* 55 (June 1999): 311–44.

Brunhouse, Robert. *The Counter-Revolution in Pennsylvania*. Philadelphia, 1942.

Buckley, Thomas J. *Church and State in Revolutionary Virginia*. Charlottesville, Va., 1977.

Bullock, Steven. *Revolutionary Brotherhood: Freemasonry and the Transformation of the American Social Order, 1730–1840*. Chapel Hill, N.C., 1996.

Burk, John. *History of the late war in Ireland, with an account of the United Irish*. Philadelphia, 1799.

Burke, Aedanus. *Considerations on the Society or Order of Cincinnati; lately instituted by the Major-Generals, Brigadier-Generals, and other Officers of the American Army, Proving that it creates a Race of Hereditary Patricians, or Nobility. Interspersed with Remarks on its Consequences to the Freedom and Happiness of the Republic. Blow Ye the trumpet of Zion*. Philadelphia, 1783.

Butler, Jon. *Awash in a Sea of Faith: Christianizing the American People*. Cambridge, Mass., 1990.

———. *The Huguenots in America: A Refugee People in a New World Society*. Cambridge, Mass., 1983.

Butterfield, L. H., et al., eds. *Adams Family Correspondence*. Vols. 1–2. Cambridge, Mass., 1963.

Cain, P. J., and A. G. Hopkins. *British Imperialism: Innovation and Expansion, 1688–1914*. London, 1993.

Calhoon, Robert M. *The Loyalists in Revolutionary America, 1763–1781*. New York, 1983.

Cameron, Robert Moore, and Cortlandt van Dyke Hubbard. *Historical Sketch of the Saint Andrew's Society of Philadelphia and the Relics, Flags, and Insignia of the Society*. Philadelphia, 1983.

Campbell, John Hugh. *History of the Friendly Sons of St. Patrick and of the Hibernian Society for the Relief of emigrants from Ireland*. Philadelphia, 1892.

Carey, Mathew. *Autobiography*. Facsimile. New York, 1942.

———. *To the Public*. Philadelphia, 1799.

Carkson, Thomas. *An essay on the slavery and commerce of the human species, particularly the African, translated from a Latin dissertation which was honoured with the first prize in the University of Cambridge for the year 1785, with additions*. Philadelphia, 1787.

Carpenter, Jesse T. *The South as a Conscious Minority, 1789–1861: A Study in Political Thought*. New York, 1930.

Carter Edward C., II. "The Political Activities of Mathew Carey, Nationalist, 1760–1814." Ph.D. diss., Bryn Mawr College, 1962.

Catterall, Helen Tunnicliff, ed., *Judicial Cases Concerning American Slavery and the Negro*. 5 vols. Washington, D.C., 1936.

Cerami, Charles A. *Benjamin Banneker: Surveyor, Astronomer, Publisher, Patriot*. New York, 2002.

Chambers, William. *Political Parties in a New Nation: The American Experience, 1776–1809*. New York, 1963.

"Changing Role of the Jury in the Nineteenth Century." *Yale Law Journal* 74 (1964): 170–92.

Channing, Edward. *History of the United States*. New York, 1905–25.

Charles, Joseph. *The Origins of the American Party System*. Williamsburg, Va., 1956.

Clarfield, Gerard. "Postscript to the Jay Treaty: Timothy Pickering and Anglo-American Relations, 1795–1797." *William and Mary Quarterly*, 3rd ser., 23 (January 1966): 106–20.

Clark, J. C. D. *Language of Liberty, 1660–1832: Political Discourse and Social Dynamics in the Anglo-American World*. Cambridge, 1994.

Clarkson, Thomas. "A fancied Scene in the African Slave Trade." *New-York Magazine; or, Literary Repository* 1 (1790): 464–67.

Clay, Henry. *The Papers of Henry Clay*. Edited by James Hopkins. 11 vols. Lexington, Ky., 1959–92.

———. *The Works of Henry Clay; Comprising His Life, Correspondence and Speeches*. Edited by Calvin Colton. 10 vols. New York, 1904.

Cobbett, William. *Detection of a Conspiracy, Formed by the United Irishmen, with the Evident Intention of Aiding the Tyrants of France in Subverting the Government of the United States of America.* Philadelphia, 1798.

Cohen, Daniel A. "Social Injustice, Sexual Violence, Spiritual Transcendence: Constructions of Interracial Rape in Early American Crime Literature, 1767–1817." *William and Mary Quarterly,* 3rd ser., 56 (July 1999): 481–526.

Cole, Thomas, and Mathew Webb. "The Memorial of Thomas Cole Bricklayer P. B. Mathews and Mathew Webb Butchers on behalf of themselves & others Free Men of Colour." Edited by Herbert Aptheker. *Journal of Negro History* 31 (January 1946): 98–99.

Colley, Linda. *Britons: Forging the Nation, 1707–1837.* New Haven, Conn., 1992.

———. *In Defense of Oligarchy: The Tory Party, 1714–60.* London, 1982.

———. "Radical Patriotism in Eighteenth Century England." In *Patriotism: The Making and Unmaking of British National Identity,* edited by Ralph Samuel, 1:169–87. London, 1989.

Commonwealth of Massachusetts. "*The Commonwealth v. Nathaniel Jennison.*" *Proceedings of the Massachusetts Historical Society, 1873–1875.* Boston, 1875.

———. *In the House of Representatives, June 28, 1798. Whereas it is highly expedient that every Constitutional Barrier should be opposed to the introduction of foreign influence into our national councils, and that the Constitution of the United States should be so amended as to effect and secure, in the best manner, the great objects for which it was designed.* Broadside. Boston, 1798.

Commonwealth of Virginia. *Proceedings and Debates of the Virginia State Convention of 1829–1830.* Richmond, 1830.

———. *The Statutes at Large, Being a Collection of All the Laws of Virginia.* Edited by W. W. Hening. 13 vols. Richmond, 1809–23.

———. *The Statutes at Large of Virginia, from October Session 1792, to December 1806.* Edited by Samuel Shepard. 3 vols. Richmond, 1835.

Conroy, David W. *In Public Houses: Drink and the Revolution of Authority in Colonial Massachusetts.* Chapel Hill, N.C., 1995.

Convention of Delegates from the Abolition Societies Established in Different Parts of the United States. *Minutes of the Proceedings of a Convention of Delegates from the Abolition Societies Established in Different parts of the United States, Assembled at Philadelphia.* Philadelphia, 1794.

Conzen, Kathleen Neils, David A. Gerber, Ewa Morawska, George E. Pozzetta, and Rudolph J. Vecoli. "The Invention of Ethnicity: A Perspective from the U.S.A." *Journal of American Ethnic History* 12 (Fall 1992): 3–41.

Cook, Adrienne, and Henry Ammon. "The Virginia and Kentucky Resolutions: An Episode in Jefferson and Madison's Defense of Civil Liberties." *William and Mary Quarterly,* 3rd ser., 5 (April 1948): 145–76.

Coombs, John C. "Building 'the Machine': The Development of Slavery and Slave Society in Early Colonial Virginia." Ph.D. diss., College of William and Mary, 2004.

Cornell, Saul. *The Other Founders: Anti-Federalism and the Dissenting Tradition in America, 1788–1828.* Chapel Hill, N.C., 1999.

Crèvecoeur, J. Hector St. John de. *Letters from an American Farmer and Sketches of Eighteenth Century America.* Edited by Albert E. Stone. New York, 1981.

Crimmins, John D. *Irish-American Historical Miscellany*. New York, 1905.

———. *St. Patrick's Day: Its Celebration in New York and Other American Places, 1737–1845*. New York, 1902.

Cunningham, Noble E., Jr. *The Jeffersonian Republicans: The Formation of Parry Organization, 1789–1801*. Chapel Hill, N.C., 1957.

———. "Who Were the Quids?" *Mississippi Valley Historical Review* 50 (1963): 252–63.

Curry, Leonard P. *The Free Black in Urban America, 1800–1850: The Shadow of the Dream*. Chicago, 1981.

Curtin, Nancy J. *The United Irishmen: Popular Politics in Ulster and Dublin, 1791–1798*. Oxford, 1994.

Dalinoff, Donna Isaacs. "A Familiar Stranger: The Outsider of Eighteenth Century Satire." *Neophilologus* 57 (1973): 121–34.

Dallas, Alexander J., ed. *Reports of Cases Ruled and Adjudged in the Courts of Pennsylvania before and since the Revolution*. 3rd ed. 4 vols. Philadelphia, 1830.

Dana, James. *The African slave trade: A discourse delivered in the city of New-Haven, September 9, 1790, before the Connecticut Society for the Promotion of Freedom*. New Haven, Conn., 1791.

Davidson, Cathy, ed. *Reading in America: Literature and Social History*. Baltimore, 1989.

Davis, David Brion. *The Problem of Slavery in the Age of Revolution, 1770–1823*. Ithaca, N.Y., 1975.

Deane, Phyllis. *The First Industrial Revolution*. 2nd ed. Cambridge, 1979.

Debates in the House of Representatives, First Session, April–May 1789. Edited by Charlene Bangs Bickford, Kenneth R. Bowling, and Helen E. Veit. Vol. 10 of *The Documentary History of the First Federal Congress of the United States of America, March 4, 1789–March 3, 1791*. Baltimore, 1992.

Debates in the House of Representatives, Second Session, January–March 1790. Edited by Helen E. Veit et al. Vol. 12 of *The Documentary History of the First Federal Congress of the United States of America, March 4, 1789–March 3, 1791*. Baltimore, 1995.

De Conde, Alexander. *Entangling Alliance*. Durham, N.C., 1958.

Democratic-Republican Society of Pennsylvania. *Principles, Articles and Regulations, Agreed Upon, Drawn and Adopted, May 30, 1793*. Philadelphia, 1793.

Dickson, P. G. M. *The Financial Revolution in England: A Study of the Development of Public Credit, 1688–1756*. London, 1967.

Duane, William. *Report of a Debate, In the Senate of the United States, On A Resolution for Recommending to the Legislatures of the Several States, An Amendment to the Third Paragraph of the First Section of the Second Article of the Constitution of the United States, Relative to the mode of Electing a President and Vice President of the Said States*. Philadelphia, 1804.

———. *A Report on the Extraordinary Transactions*. Philadelphia, 1799.

Duer, Manning J. *The Adams Federalists*. Baltimore, 1953.

Duffy, Michael. *The Englishman and the Foreigner: The English Satiric Print 1600–1832*. Cambridge, 1986.

Dunbar, John R., ed. *The Paxton Papers*. The Hague, 1957.

Durey, Michael. *Transatlantic Radicals and the Early American Republic*. Lawrence, Kans., 1997.

Durrett, Reuben. "Manuscript biography of Colonel George Nicholas." George Nicholas Papers, Box 1, Folder 1, Reuben T. Durrett Collection, Special Collections, University of Chicago.

———. "The Resolutions of 1798 and 1799." *Southern Bivouc* 10 (March 1886): 578–664, 760–70.

Dwight, Theodore. *A History of the Hartford Convention*. New York, 1833.

———. *History of the Hartford Convention; with a review of the policy of the United States Government which led to the War of 1812*. New York, 1833.

Edling, Max. "The Problem of American State Formation: Politics and Taxation and the Creation of the Federal Government." Working Paper No. 01–13, Harvard University, Summer 2001.

———. *A Revolution in Favor of Government*. Oxford, 2003.

Edwards, Jonathan. *The injustice and impolicy of the slave trade, and of the slavery of the Africans illustrated in a sermon preached before the Connecticut Society for the Promotion of Freedom, and for the Relief of Persons Unlawfully Holden in Bondage, at their annual meeting in New Haven, September 1; to which is added, A short sketch of the evidence for the abolition of the slave-trade, delivered before a committee of the British House of Commons*. Providence, R.I., 1792.

Egerton, Douglas. *Gabriel's Rebellion: The Virginia Slave Conspiracies of 1800 and 1802*. Chapel Hill, N.C., 1993.

Elkins, Stanley, and Eric McKitrick. *The Age of Federalism: The Early American Republic, 1787–1800*. New York, 1993.

Elliot, Jonathan, ed. *The Debates in the several State conventions on the adoption of the Federal Constitution as recommended by the General Convention at Philadelphia in 1787*. 2nd ed. 5 vols. Philadelphia, 1836–45. Facsimile ed. Philadelphia, 1941.

Elliot, Marianne. *Partners in Revolution: The United Irishmen and France*. New Haven, Conn., 1982.

Ellis, Joseph. *American Sphinx: The Character of Thomas Jefferson*. New York, 1997.

———. *Founding Brothers: The Revolutionary Generation*. New York, 2000.

Epstein, David F. *The Political Theory of the Federalist*. Chicago, 1984.

Farrand, Max, ed. *The Records of the Federal Convention of 1787*. 4 vols. Rev. ed. New Haven, Conn., 1966.

Fehrenbacher, Don E. *The Dred Scott Case: Its Significance in Law and Politics*. New York, 1978.

———. *The Slaveholding Republic: An Account of the United States Government's Relations to Slavery*. Compiled by Ward M. McAfee. Oxford, 2001.

Ferguson, James E. *The Power of the Purse: A History of American Public Finance, 1776–1790*. Chapel Hill, N.C., 1961.

Finkelman, Paul. "The Kidnapping of John Davis and the Adoption of the Fugitive Slave Law of 1793." *Journal of Southern History* 56 (August 1990): 397–422.

———. "Slavery and the Northwest Ordinance: A Study in Ambiguity." *Journal of the Early Republic* 6 (1986): 351–53.

Fischer, David Hackett. *Albion's Seed: Four British Folkways in America*. New York, 1989.

———. *The Revolution of American Conservatism*. New York, 1965.

Fiske, John. *The Critical Period of American History, 1783–1789*. Boston and New York, 1888, 1898.

Flournoy, H. W., ed. *Calendar of Virginia State Papers, and other manuscripts*. 11 vols. Richmond, Va., 1875–93.

Fogleman, Aaron S. "From Slaves, Convicts, and Servants to Free Passengers: The Transformation of Immigration in the Era of the American Revolution." *Journal of American History* 85 (June 1998): 43–76.

———. *Hopeful Journeys: German Immigration, Settlement, and Political Culture in Colonial America, 1717–1775*. Philadelphia, 1992.

Foner, Philip S., ed. *The Democratic-Republican Societies, 1790–1800: A Documentary Sourcebook of Constitutions, Declarations, Addresses, Resolutions and Toasts*. Westport, Conn., 1976.

Force, Peter. *Tracts and Other Papers Relating Principally to the Origin, Settlement, and Progress of the Colonies of North America: From the Discovery of the Country to the Year 1776*. 5 vols. New York, 1836.

Ford, Worthington C., et al., eds. *Journals of the Continental Congress, 1774–1789*. 34 vols. Washington, D.C., 1904–37.

Formisano, Ronald P. *The Transformation of Political Culture: Massachusetts Parties, 1790s–1840s*. New York, 1983.

Fortis, Edmund. *The last words and dying speech of Edmund Fortis, a Negro man*. Exeter, Mass., 1795.

Fox, Dixon Ryan. *The Decline of Aristocracy in the Politics of New York*. New York, 1919.

———. "The Negro Vote in Old New York." *Political Science Quarterly* 32 (1917): 252–75.

Franklin, Frank George. *The Legislative History of Naturalization in the United States: From the Revolutionary War to 1861*. Chicago, 1906.

Freehling, William W. *Prelude to the Civil War: The Nullification Controversy in South Carolina*. New York, 1966.

Freeman, Joanne. *Affairs of Honor: National Politics in the New Republic*. New Haven, Conn., 2002.

French Republic. *They Steer to Liberty's Shores*. Broadside. Philadelphia, 1793.

Frey, Sylvia R. *Water from the Rock: Black Resistance in a Revolutionary Age*. Princeton, N.J., 1991.

Galpin, W. Freeman. "The American Grain Trade to the Spanish Peninsula, 1810–1814." *American Historical Review* 28 (1922): 39–44.

Gaynard, Robert L. *The Emergence of North Carolina's Revolutionary State Government*. Raleigh, N.C., 1978.

———. "Radicals and Conservatives in Revolutionary North Carolina: A Point at Issue: The October Election, 1776." *William and Mary Quarterly*, 3rd ser., 24 (October 1967): 568–87.

Gemery, Henry A. "Disarray in the Historical Record: Estimates of Immigration to the United States, 1700–1860." In *The Demographic History of the Philadelphia Region, 1600–1860*, edited by Susan E. Klepp, 123–27. Philadelphia, 1989.

Genovese, Eugene. *From Rebellion to Revolution: Afro-American Slave Revolts in the Making of the Modern World*. Baton Rouge, La., 1979.

Gibbs, George, ed. *Memoirs of the Administrations of Washington and John Adams*. 2 vols. New York, 1846.

Gibbs, R. W., ed. *Documentary History of the American Revolution*. New York, 1855.

Gilpatrick, Delbert Harold. *Jeffersonian Democracy in North Carolina*. New York, 1931.

Giunt, Mary A., ed. *The Emerging Nation: A Documentary History of the Foreign Relations of the United States under the Articles of Confederation*. Washington, D.C., 1996.

Gjerde, Jon. "'Here in America there is neither king nor tyrant': European Encounters with Race, 'Freedom,' and Their European Pasts." *Journal of the Early Republic* 19 (Winter 1999): 673–90.

Glazer, Nathan, and Daniel Moynihan. *Beyond the Melting Pot*. Cambridge, Mass., 1963.

Gleason, Philip. "American Identity and Americanization." In *Concepts of Ethnicity*, edited by Stephan Thernstrom, 67–68. Cambridge, Mass., 1982.

Goldsmith, Oliver. *The Citizen of the World*. Edited by Arthur Friedman. In *Collected Works of Oliver Goldsmith*. Oxford, 1966.

Gongaware, George. *History of the German Friendly Society*. Richmond, Va., 1935.

Grabbe, Hans-Jurgen. "European Immigration to the United States in the Early National Period, 1783–1820." *Proceedings of the American Philosophical Society* 133 (1989).

Graydon, Alexander. *Memoirs of his Own Time*. Philadelphia, 1846.

Green, Jack, ed. *Imperatives, Behaviors and Identities: Essays in Early American Cultural History*. Charlottesville, Va., 1992.

Green, John C. "The American Debate on the Negro's Place in Nature, 1780–1815." *Journal of the History of Ideas* 15 (June 1954): 384–96.

Greenberg, Douglas. "The Middle Colonies in Recent American Historiography." *William and Mary Quarterly*, 3rd ser., 36 (July 1979): 396–427.

Greene, Jack P. "The Alienation of Benjamin Franklin, British American." In *Understanding the American Revolution: Issues and Actors*, edited by Jack P. Greene, 247–84. Charlottesville, Va., 1995.

———. *Peripheries and Center: Constitutional Development in the Extended Polities of the British Empire and the United States, 1607–1788*. Athens, Ga., 1986.

———. "Search for Identity: An Interpretation of the Meaning of Selected Patterns of Social Response in Eighteenth Century America." In *Imperatives, Behaviors and Identities: Essays in Early American Cultural History*, 43–173. Charlottesville, Va., 1992.

———, ed. *The American Revolution: Its Character and Limits*. New York, 1987.

Griffin, Patrick. *American Leviathan: Empire, Nation, and Revolutionary Frontier*. New York, 2007.

Grubb, Farley. "German Immigration to Pennsylvania, 1709–1820." *Journal of Interdisciplinary History* 20 (Winter 1990): 417–36.

Guild, June Purcell. *Black Laws of Virginia: A Summary of the Legislative Acts of Virginia Concerning Negroes from Earliest Times to the Present*. New York, 1936.

Gunderson, Joan R. "Independence, Citizenship, and the American Revolution." *Signs* 13 (1987): 59–77.

———. *To Be Useful to the World: Women in Revolutionary America, 1740–1790*. Chapel Hill, N.C., 2006.

Guthrie, William. *A New System of Modern Geography: or, A Geographical, Historical, and Commercial Grammar; and Present State of the Several Nations of the World.* 2 vols. London, 1774.

———. *A New System of Modern Geography: or, A Geographical, Historical, and Commercial Grammar; and Present State of the Several Nations of the World.* Edited by Mathew Carey. 2 vols. Philadelphia, 1794.

Hale, Matthew Rainbow. "Many Who Wandered in Darkness: The Contest over American National Identity, 1795–1798." *Early American Studies: An Interdisciplinary Journal* 1 (Spring 2003): 127–75.

Hall, David D., et al., eds. *Saints and Revolutionaries: Essays on Early American History.* New York, 1984.

Hall, Timothy. *Contested Boundaries: Itinerancy and the Reshaping of the Colonial American Religious World.* Durham, N.C., 1994.

Hall, Van Beck. *Politics without Parties.* Pittsburgh, 1972.

Hamilton, Alexander. *The Papers of Alexander Hamilton.* Edited by Harold C. Syrett et al. 27 vols. New York, 1961–87.

———. *Works of Alexander Hamilton.* Edited by H. C. Lodge. 10 vols. New York, 1904.

———. *The works of Alexander Hamilton: containing his correspondence, and his political and official writings, exclusive of the Federalist, civil and military.* Edited by John C. Hamilton. 7 vols. New York, 1850–51.

Hamilton, Alexander, John Jay, and James Madison. *The Federalist Papers.* Edited by Clinton Rossiter. New York, 1961.

Handlin, Oscar, and Mary Handlin, eds. *The Popular Sources of Political Authority.* Boston, 1966.

Hanna, William. *Benjamin Franklin and Pennsylvania Politics.* Palo Alto, Calif., 1964.

Haraszti, Zoltan. *John Adams and the Prophets of Progress.* Cambridge, Mass., 1952.

Harrison, Lowell H. *John Breckinridge: Jeffersonian Republican.* Louisville, Ky., 1969.

Hartmann, Edward George. "The Welsh Society of Philadelphia, 1729–1979." Unpublished manuscript. Balch Institute.

Hartog, Hendrick, ed. *Law in the American Revolution and the Revolution in the Law.* New York, 1981.

Hay, George. *An Essay on the Liberty of the Press.* Philadelphia, 1798.

Hayman, John. "Notions on National Characters in the Eighteenth Century." *Huntington Literary Quarterly* 35 (1971): 1–17.

Henderson, Archibald. "Isaac Shelby and the Genet Mission." *Mississippi Valley Historical Review* 6 (March 1920): 451–69.

Henderson, H. James. *Party Politics in the Continental Congress.* New York, 1974.

Hendrickson, David. *Peace Pact: The Lost World of the American Founding.* Lawrence, Kans., 2003.

Hennignausen, Louis P. *History of the German Society of Maryland.* Baltimore, 1909.

Herberg, William. *Protestant, Catholic, Jew.* Garden City, N.Y., 1960.

Hertzog, Tamar. *Defining Nations: Immigrants and Citizens in Early Modern Spain and Spanish America.* New Haven, Conn., 2003.

Hibernian Society for the Relief of Emigrants from Ireland. *Constitution and Bye*

Laws of the Hibernian Society for the Relief of Emigrants from Ireland. Philadelphia, 1790.

Higham, John. "Multiculturalism and Universalism: A History and Critique." *American Quarterly* 45 (June 1993): 195–219.

Hill, Christopher. *The Century of Revolution, 1603–1714.* 4th ed. New York, 1979.

Hillard, E. B. *The Last Men of the Revolution.* Edited by Wendell D. Garett. Hartford, Conn., 1864. Reprint, Barre, Mass., 1968.

The Historical Register of the United States. Edited by T. H. Palmer. 4 vols. Washington, D.C., 1814–16.

Hobsbawm, Eric. *Nations and Nationalism since 1780: Programme, Myth, Reality.* Cambridge, 1990.

Hobsbawm, Eric, and Terence Ranger. *The Invention of Tradition.* New York, 1983.

Hobson, Charles F. *The Great Chief Justice: John Marshall and the Rule of Law.* Lawrence, Kans., 1996.

Hodges, Graham Russell. *Root and Branch: African Americans in New York and East Jersey, 1613–1863.* Chapel Hill, N.C., 1999.

Hoerder, Dirk. *Crowd Action in Revolutionary Massachusetts, 1765–1780.* New York, 1977.

Hoffman, Ronald, and Peter J. Albert, eds. *Launching the "Extended Republic": The Federalist Era.* Charlottesville, Va., 1996.

———, eds. *Religion in a Revolutionary Age.* Charlottesville, Va., 1994.

———, eds. *Sovereign States in an Age of Uncertainty.* Charlottesville, Va., 1981.

———, eds. *Women in the Age of the America Revolution.* Charlottesville, Va., 1989.

Hofstadter, Richard. *The Idea of a Party System.* Berkeley, Calif., 1969.

Holt, Thomas. *The Problem of Freedom: Race, Labor, and Politics in Jamaica and Britain, 1832–1938.* Baltimore, 1992.

Holton, Woody. *Forced Founders: Indians, Debtors, Slaves and the Making of the American Revolution in Virginia.* Chapel Hill, N.C., 1999.

———. *Unruly Americans and the Origins of the Constitution.* New York, 2007.

Home, Henry Lord Karnes. *Six sketches on the history of man. Containing, the progress of men as individuals. . . . With an appendix, concerning, the propagation of animals, and the care of their offspring.* Philadelphia, 1776.

Hopkins, Stephen. *The Rights of Colonies Examined.* Providence, R.I., 1764.

Horowitz, Morton. *The Transformation of American Law, 1780–1860.* Cambridge, 1977.

Horn, James P., Jan Lewis, and Peter Onuf. eds. *The Revolution of 1800: Democracy, Race, and the New Republic.* Charlottesville, Va., 2002.

Howe, John R. "Republican Thought and the Political Violence of the 1790s." *American Quarterly* 19 (1967): 147–65.

Hulsebosch, Daniel J. *Constituting Empire: New York and the Transformation of Constitutionalism in the Atlantic World, 1664–1830.* Chapel Hill, N.C., 2005.

Hume, David. "Of National Characters." In *Essays, Moral, Political and Literary.* Edited by Eugene F. Miller, 197–215. London, 1987.

Hunt, Galliard. "James Madison's Attitude toward the Negro." *Journal of Negro History* 6 (1921): 74–102.

———. "William Thorton and Negro Colonization." *American Antiquarian Society Proceedings*, New Series, 30 (1920): 32–61.

Hurd, John Codman, *The Law of Freedom and Bondage*. 2 vols. Boston, 1862.

Hutchinson, John D., and Anthony D. Smith, eds. *Nationalism*. New York, 1994.

Hutson, James H. *Pennsylvania Politics, 1746–1770: The Movement for Royal Government and Its Consequences*. Princeton, N.J., 1972.

Hyneman, Charles S., and Donald S. Lutz, eds. *American Political Writing during the Founding Era, 1760–1805*. 2 vols. Indianapolis, Ind., 1983.

Ignatiev, Noel. *How the Irish Became White*. New York, 1995.

Inglis, Charles. *The True Interest of America, Impartially Stated*. Philadelphia, 1776.

Iredell, James. *Life and Correspondence of James Iredell, One of the Associate Justices of the Supreme Court of the United States*. Edited by G. J. McRee. New York, 1949.

———. *The Papers of James Iredell*. Edited by Don Higgenbotham. Raleigh, N.C., 1976.

Isaac, Rhys. *The Transformation of Virginia, 1740–1790*. New York, 1982.

Jackman, S. W., ed. "A Young Englishman Reports on the New Nation: Edward Thornton to James Bland Borges, 1791–1793." *William and Mary Quarterly*, 3rd ser., 18 (January 1961): 85–121.

Jackson, Andrew. *The Papers of Andrew Jackson*. Edited by Sam B. Smith and Harriet Chapell Owsley. 7 vols. to date. Knoxville, Tenn., 1980–.

Jackson, Melvin. *Privateers in Charleston*. Charleston, S.C., 1963.

Jay, John. *The Correspondence and Public Papers of John Jay*. Edited by Henry P. Johnston. 3 vols. New York, 1890–93.

Jefferson, Thomas. *The Complete Ana of Thomas Jefferson*. Edited by Franklin B. Sawvel. New York, 1903.

———. *Notes on the State of Virginia*. Edited by William Peden. New York, 1954, 1982.

———. *The Papers of Thomas Jefferson*. Edited by John Catanzariti et al. 31 vols to date. Princeton, N.J., 1950–.

———. *Thomas Jefferson's Farm Book*. Edited by Edwin Betts. Charlottesville, Va., 1953, 1976.

———. *Thomas Jefferson's Garden Book*. Edited by Edwin Betts. Philadelphia, 1944.

———. *The Writings of Thomas Jefferson*. Edited by Paul Leister Ford. 10 vols. New York, 1892–99.

———. *The Writings of Thomas Jefferson*. Edited by Andrew A. Lipscomb and Albert Ellery Bergh. 20 vols. Washington, D.C., 1903–4.

Jefferson, Thomas, and James Madison. *The Republic of Letters: The Correspondence between Thomas Jefferson and James Madison, 1776–1826*. Edited by James Morton Smith. 3 vols. New York, 1995.

Jensen, Merrill. *The New Nation: A History of the United States during the Confederation 1781–1789*. New York, 1950.

———. "The Sovereign States: Their Antagonisms and Rivalries and Some Consequences." In *Sovereign States in an Age of Uncertainty*, edited by Ronald Hoffman and Peter J. Albert, 407–21. Charlottesville, Va., 1981.

Johnson, Herbert A. *The Chief Justiceship of John Marshall, 1801–1835*. Columbia, S.C., 1997.

Jones, Absalom, and Richard Allen. *A narrative of the proceedings of the black people, during the late awful calamity in Philadelphia, in the year 1793: and a refutation of some censures, thrown upon them in some late publications*. Philadelphia, 1794.

Jordan, Winthrop D. *White over Black: American Attitudes Towards the Negro, 1550–1812*. Chapel Hill, N.C., 1968.

Kaminski, John P., and Gaspare J. Saladino, eds. *The Documentary History of the Ratification of the Constitution*. 25 vols. Madison, Wis., 1995.

Kammen, Michael, and Stanley Katz, eds. *The Transformation of Early American History: Society, Authority, and Ideology*. New York, 1991.

Kars, Marjoleine. *Breaking Loose Together: The Regulator Rebellion in Pre-Revolutionary North Carolina*. Chapel Hill, N.C., 2002.

Kastor, Peter J. *The Nation's Crucible: The Louisiana Purchase and the Creation of America*. New Haven, Conn., 2004.

Kelley, Mary. "Reading Women/Women Reading: The Making of Learned Women in Antebellum America." *Journal of American History* 83 (1996): 401–24.

Kerber, Linda. *No Constitutional Right to Be Ladies: Women and the Obligations of Citizenship*. New York, 1998.

———. *Women of the Republic: Intellect and Ideology in Revolutionary America*. Chapel Hill, N.C., 1980.

Kettner, James. *The Development of American Citizenship, 1608–1870*. Chapel Hill, N.C., 1978.

Keyssar, Alexander. *The Right to Vote: The Contested History of Democracy in the United States*. New York, 2000.

Kim, Sung Bok. "The Limits of Politicization in the American Revolution: The Experience of Westchester County, New York." *Journal of American History* 80 (1993): 868–89.

King, Rufus. *The Life and Correspondence of Rufus King*. Edited by Charles King. 4 vols. Boston, 1894–1900.

Kinloch, Francis. "Letters of Francis Kinloch to Thomas Boone, 1782–1788." Edited by Felix Gilbert. *Journal of Southern History* 8 (1942): 97–98.

Klein, Rachel N. *Unification of a Slave State: The Rise of the Planter Class in the South Carolina Backcountry, 1760–1808*. Chapel Hill, N.C., 1990.

Klepp, Susan E., ed. *The Demographic History of the Philadelphia Region, 1600–1860*. Philadelphia, 1989.

Klinghoffer, Judith Apter, and Lois Elkis. "'The Petticoat Electors': Women's Suffrage in New Jersey, 1776–1807." *Journal of the Early Republic* 12 (Summer 1992): 159–94.

Kloppenberg, James L. *The Virtues of Liberalism*. New York, 1998.

Knauff, Theodore C. *A History of the Society of the Sons of Saint George*. Philadelphia, 1923.

Knight, Charles A. "The Images of Nations in Eighteenth-Century Satire." *Eighteenth-Century Studies* 22 (Summer 1989): 489–511.

Koch, Adrienne, and Harry Ammon. "The Virginia and Kentucky Resolutions: An Episode in Jefferson and Madison's Defense of Civil Liberties." *William and Mary Quarterly*, 3rd ser., 5 (April 1948): 145–76.

Kramnick, Isaac. "The 'Great National Discussion': The Discourse of Politics in 1787." *William and Mary Quarterly*, 3rd ser., 45 (June 1988): 3–32.

———. *Republicanism and Bourgeois Radicalism: Political Ideology in Late Eighteenth Century England and America*. Ithaca, N.Y., 1990.

Kruman, Marc. *Between Authority and Liberty: State Constitution Making in Revolutionary America*. Chapel Hill, N.C., 1999.

Kukla, John. "The Irrelevance and Relevance of Saints George and Thomas." *Virginia Magazine of History and Biography* 102 (April 1994): 261–70.

Kulikoff, Allan. "The Origins of Afro-American Society in Tidewater Maryland and Virginia, 1700–1790." *William and Mary Quarterly*, 3rd ser., 35 (April 1978): 226–58.

———. "Revolutionary Violence and the Origins of America Democracy." *Journal of the Historical Society* 2 (Spring 2002): 229–60.

———. *Tobacco and Slaves: The Development of Southern Cultures in the Chesapeake, 1680–1800*. Chapel Hill, N.C., 1986.

Kymlicka, Will, and Wayne Norman, eds. *Citizenship in Diverse Societies*. New York, 2000.

Langley, Lester D. *The Americas in the Age of Revolution, 1750–1850*. New Haven, Conn., 1996.

Lavallee, Joseph. *The Negro equalled by few Europeans translated from the French; to which are added, Poems on various subjects, moral and entertaining, by Phillis Wheatley, Negro servant to Mr. John Wheatley, of Boston, in New-England*. 2 vols. Philadelphia, 1801.

Lee, Charles. *The Lee Papers*. New York Historical Society Collections. 4 vols. New York, 1871–74.

Lee, Jean Butenhoff. "The Problem of Slave Community in the Eighteenth Century Chesapeake." *William and Mary Quarterly*, 3rd ser., 43 (April 1986): 331–61.

Lee, Richard Henry. *The Letters of Richard Henry Lee*. 2 vols. Collected and edited by James Curtis Ballagh. New York, 1911–14.

Lender, Mark. "'Equally Proper at All Times and at All Times Necessary': Civility, Bad Taste, and the Sedition Act." *Journal of the Early Republic* 24 (Fall 2004): 419–44.

Levy, Leonard. *Emergence of a Free Press*. New York, 1985.

———. *Legacy of Suppression: Freedom of Speech and Press in Early American History*. Cambridge, Mass., 1960.

———. *The Palladium of Justice: Origins of Trial by Jury*. Chicago, 1999.

Lewis, James E., Jr. *The American Union and the Problem of Neighborhood: The United States and the Collapse of the Spanish Empire, 1783–1829*. Chapel Hill, N.C., 1998.

Lien, Scott. "Liberty Fraternity and Inequality: Legal Foundations of Charity in the United States." Ph.D. diss., University of Chicago, 2004.

Link, Eugene Perry. *Democratic-Republican Societies, 1790–1800*. New York, 1942.

Litwack, Leon F. *North of Slavery: The Negro in the Free States, 1790–1860*. Chicago, 1961.

Livingston, Edward. *Speech of Edward Livingston in the House of Representatives of the United States, on the third reading of the Alien bill, June 21, 1798*. Philadelphia, 1798.

Locke, John. *Two Treatises of Government*. Edited by Peter Laslett. Cambridge, 1960, 1993.

Lubell, Samuel. *Future of American Politics*. New York 1956.

Lutz, Donald S. "The Relative Influence of European Writers on Late Eighteenth

Century American Political Thought." *American Political Science Review* 78 (1984): 189–97.

Lynd, Staughton. "The Compromise of 1787." *Political Science Quarterly* 81 (June 1966): 225–50.

Maclay, William. *Journal of William Maclay: United States Senator from Pennsylvania, 1789–1791*. Edited by Edgar S. Maclay. New York, 1927.

Madison, James. *The Papers of James Madison*. Edited by William T. Hutchinson and William M. E. Rachal et al. Chicago, 1962–77. Charlottesville, Va., 1977–91.

Maier, Pauline. *American Scripture: Making the Declaration of Independence*. New York, 1997.

———. *From Resistance to Revolution: Colonial Radicalism and the Development of American Opposition to Britain, 1763–1776*. New York, 1972.

Main, Jackson Turner. "Government by the People: The American Revolution and the Democratization of the Legislatures." *William and Mary Quarterly*, 3rd ser., 23 (July 1966), 391–407

———. *Political Parties Before the Constitution*. Chapel Hill, N.C., 1973.

Malone, Dumas. *Jefferson and His Times*. 6 vols. Boston, 1948–91.

Mandeville, Bernard. *Free Thoughts on Religion, the Church and National Happiness*. 1720. Facsimile ed. Boston, 1981.

Mann, Michael. *States, War and Capitalism*. Oxford, 1988.

Manning, William. *The Key of Liberty: The Life and Democratic Writings of William Manning. "A Laborer," 1747–1814*. Edited by Michael Merrill and Sean Wilentz. Cambridge, Mass., 1993.

Marshall, John. *Papers of John Marshall*. Edited by Herbert A. Johnson and Charles T. Cullen. 12 vols. Chapel Hill, N.C., 1974–2006.

Marston, Jerrilyn Green. *King and Congress: The Transfer of Political Legitimacy, 1174–1776*. Princeton, N.J., 1987.

Martell, J. S. "A Side Light on Federalist Strategy during the War of 1812." *American Historical Review* 43 (April 1938): 553–66.

Maryland Society for Promoting the Abolition of Slavery, and the Relief of Free Negroes, and Others, Unlawfully Held in Bondage. *Constitution of the Maryland Society, for Promoting the Abolition of Slavery, and the Relief of Free Negroes, and Others, Unlawfully Held in Bondage*. Baltimore, 1789.

Mason, George. *The Papers of George Mason*. Edited by Robert A. Rutland. 3 vols. Chapel Hill, N.C., 1970.

Mathis, Doyle. "*Chisholm v. Georgia*: Background and Settlement." *Journal of American History* 54 (June 1967): 19–29.

May, Henry F. *The Enlightenment in America*. New York, 1976.

McBride, Ian. *Scripture Politics: Ulster Presbyterians and Irish Radicalism in the Late Eighteenth Century*. Oxford, 1998.

McConville, Brendan. *The King's Three Faces: The Rise and Fall of Royal America, 1688–1776*. Chapel Hill, N.C., 2006.

———. *These Daring Disturbers of the Public Peace: The Struggle for Property and Power in Early New Jersey*. Ithaca, N.Y., 1999.

McCormick, Richard P. *The History of Voting in New Jersey: A Study of the Development of Election Machinery, 1664–1911*. New Brunswick, N.J., 1953.

McCoy, Drew. *The Elusive Republic: Political Economy in Jeffersonian America*. Chapel Hill, N.C., 1980.

McDonald, Forrest. *Alexander Hamilton: A Biography*. New York, 1979.

———. *Novus Ordo Seculorum: The Intellectual Origins of the Constitution*. Lawrence, Kans., 1987.

———. *The Presidency of Thomas Jefferson*. Lawrence, Kans., 1976.

McDonnell, Michael. *The Politics of War: Race, Class, and Conflict in Revolutionary Virginia*. Chapel Hill, N.C.: 2007.

———. "Popular Mobilization and Political Culture in Revolutionary Virginia: The Failure of the Minutemen and the Revolution from Below." *Journal of American History* 85 (December 1998): 946–81.

McElroy, Robert McNutt. *Kentucky in the Nation's History*. New York, 1909.

McIlwain, Charles. *The American Revolution: A Constitutional Interpretation*. Ithaca, N.Y., 1923.

McKusker, John, and Russell Menard. *The Economy of British America*. Chapel Hill, N.C., 1986.

McLaughlin, J. Fairfax. *Matthew Lyon: The Hampden of Congress*. New York, 1900.

McManus, Edgar J. *Black Bondage in the North*. New York, 1973.

Meigs, Jonathan Return. *A Digest of All Published Decisions of the State of Tennessee*. St. Louis, 1917.

Memorials presented to the Congress of the United States of America, by the different societies instituted for promoting the abolition of slavery, &c. &c. in the states of Rhode-Island, Connecticut, New-York, Pennsylvania, Maryland, and Virginia. Philadelphia, 1792.

Menk, Patricia Holbert, ed. "D. M. Erskine: Letters from America, 1798–1799." *William and Mary Quarterly*, 3rd ser., 6 (April 1949): 251–84.

Meyer, Duane. *The Highland Scots of North Carolina, 1732–1776*. Durham, N.C., 1961.

Miles, Jack. "The Coming Immigration Debate." *Atlantic Monthly* (April 1995), 130–40.

Miller, John C. *Alexander Hamilton: Portrait in Paradox*. New York, 1959.

———. *Crisis in Freedom: The Alien and Sedition Acts*. Boston, 1951.

———. *The Federalist Era*. New York, 1960.

Minot, George Richards. *The History of the insurrection in Massachusetts*. 2nd ed. Boston, 1810.

Monaghan, Frank. *John Jay: Defender of Liberty*. New York, 1935.

Montesquieu. *The Spirit of the Laws*. Edited and translated by Anne M. Cohler, Basia Carolyn Miller, and Harold Samuel Stone. Cambridge, 1989.

Moore, Christopher. *Revolution, Exile, Settlement*. Toronto, 1984.

Morgan, Edmund S., and Helen M. Morgan, *The Stamp Act Crisis: Prologue to Revolution*. Chapel Hill, N.C., 1995.

Morrison, David Ballie, ed. *Two Hundredth Anniversary of the Saint Andrew's Society of the State of New York*. New York, 1956.

Morrison, George Austin, Jr. *History of the Saint Andrew's Society, 1756–1906*. New York, 1906.

Morrison, Michael A., and Melinda Zook, eds. *Revolutionary Currents: Nation Building in the Transatlantic World*. Madison, Wis., 2004.

Morse, Jedidiah. *The American Geography; Or, A View of the Present Situation of the United States of America*. 2nd ed. Hartford, Conn., 1792.

———. *Geography Made Easy*. Hartford, Conn., 1784.

———. *Geography Made Easy: Being an Abridgement of the American Universal Geography*. Boston, 1806.

———, ed. *Annals of the American Revolution; or, A record of the causes and events which produced, and terminated in the establishment and independence of the American Republic*. Hartford, Conn., 1824.

Mountain, Joseph [David Daggett?]. *Sketches of the life of Joseph Mountain, a Negro who was executed at New-Haven on the 20th day of October, 1790, for a rape committed on the 26th day of May last*. New Haven, Conn., 1790.

Mullin, Gerald W. *Flight and Rebellion: Slave Resistance in Eighteenth-Century Virginia*. New York, 1972.

Mullin, Michael. *Africa in America: Slave Acculturation in the American South and the British Caribbean, 1736–1831*. Urbana, Ill., 1992.

Myers, Gustavus. *The History of Tammany Hall*. 2nd ed. New York, 1917.

Nash, Gary. *Forging Freedom: The Formation of Philadelphia's Black Community, 1720–1840*. Cambridge, Mass., 1988.

———. *Race and Revolution*. Madison, Wis., 1990.

———. *The Unknown American Revolution: The Unruly Birth of Democracy and the Struggle to Create America*. New York, 2005.

Nelson, John R. *Liberty and Property: Political Economy and Policymaking in the New Nation, 1789–1815*. Baltimore, 1987.

Nelson, William. *The Americanization of the Common Law*. Cambridge, 1975.

Nevins, Allan. *The American States during and after the Revolution, 1775–1789*. New York, 1924.

Newman, Simon Paul. *Parades and the Politics of the Street: Festive Culture and the Early American Republic*. Philadelphia, 1997.

Newmeyer, R. Kent. *John Marshall and the Heroic Age of the Supreme Court*. Baton Rouge, La., 2001.

———. "A Note on the Whig Politics of Justice Joseph Story." *Mississippi Valley Historical Review* 48 (December 1961): 480–91.

New York Society for the Information and Assistance of Persons Emigrating from Foreign Countries. *Bye Laws and Constitution of the New York Society for the Information and Assistance of Persons Emigrating from Foreign Countries*. New York, 1794.

Nicholas, George. *A letter from George Nicholas of Kentucky to his Friend, in Virginia. Justifying the conduct of the Citizens of Kentucky, as to some of the late Measures of the General Government; And Correcting Certain False Statements, which have been made in the different States, of the Views and Actions of the People of Kentucky*. Lexington, 1798.

Nobles, Gregory H. *Divisions throughout the Whole: Politics and Society in Hampshire County, Massachusetts, 1740–1775*. New York, 1983.

Nord, Davis Paul. "A Republican Literature: Magazine Reading and Readers in Eighteenth Century New York." In *Reading in America: Literature and Social History*, edited by Cathy Davidson, 114–39. Baltimore, 1989.

Norton, Mary Beth. "Eighteenth Century American Women in Peace and War: The Case of the Loyalists." *William and Mary Quarterly*, 3rd ser., 33 (July 1976): 386–409.

———. *Liberty's Daughters: The Revolutionary Experience of American Women, 1750–1850*. Boston, 1980.

Novak, William J. "The Legal Transformation of Citizenship in Nineteenth Century America." In *The Democratic Experiment: New Directions in American Political History*, edited by Meg Jacobs, William J. Novak, and Julian E. Zelizer, 85–119. Princeton, N.J., 2003.

O'Brien, Conner Cruise. *A Great Melody: A Thematic Biography of Edmund Burke*. Chicago, 1992.

———. *The Long Affair: Thomas Jefferson and the French Revolution, 1785–1800*. Chicago, 1996.

O'Brien, Michael J. *A Hidden Phase of American History: Ireland's Part in America's Struggle for Liberty*. New York, 1919.

Ohline, Howard A. "Slavery, Economics, and Congressional Politics." *Journal of Southern History* 46 (August 1980): 335–60.

Onuf, Peter S. *Jefferson's Empire: The Language of American Nationhood*. Charlottesville, Va., 2000.

———. *The Origins of the Federal Republic: Jurisdictional Controversies in the United States: 1775–1787*. Philadelphia, 1983.

———."Reflections on the Founding: Constitutional Historiography in Bicentennial Perspective." *William and Mary Quarterly*, 3rd ser., 46 (April 1989): 341–75.

———. "The Scholars' Jefferson." *William and Mary Quarterly*, 3rd ser., 50 (October 1993): 671–99.

———. *Statehood and Union: A History of the Northwest Ordinance*. Bloomington, Ind., 1987.

Onuf, Peter, and Nicholas Onuf. *Federal Union, Modern World: The Law of Nations in an Age of Revolutions*. Madison, Wis., 1993.

O'Toole, James. *Passing for White: Race, Religion, and the Healy Family, 1820–1920*. Boston, 2002.

Paine, Thomas. *The Complete Writings of Thomas Paine*. Edited by Philip S. Foner. 2 vols. Binghamton, N.Y., 1945.

———. *Life and Works of Thomas Paine*. Edited by William Van der Weyde. New Rochelle, N.Y., 1925.

———. *Thomas Paine: Political Writings*. Edited by Bruce Kuklick. Cambridge, 1989.

Palsits, Victor, ed. *New York State Commission for Detecting and Defeating Conspiracies 1777–1778*. Vols. 1–3. Albany, N.Y., 1909.

Parkinson, Rob. "Enemies of the People: The Revolutionary War and Race in the New American Nation." Ph.D. diss., University of Virginia, 2005.

Pasley, Jeffrey L. *"The Tyranny of Printers": Newspaper Politics in the Early Republic*. Charlottesville, Va., 2001.

Pasley, Jeffery L., Andrew W. Robertson, and David Waldstreicher, eds. *Beyond the Founders: New Approaches to the Political History of the Early American Republic*. Chapel Hill, N.C., 2004.

Patterson, James G. "The Aftermath of the Irish Rebellion of 1798 in Antrim and

Down." Working Paper No. 01-012. International Seminar on the History of the Atlantic World, Harvard University, 2001.

Pennsylvania Society for Promoting the Abolition of Slavery. *The constitution of the Pennsylvania Society, for Promoting the Abolition of Slavery, and the Relief of Free Negroes, Unlawfully Held in Bondage. Begun in the year 1774, and enlarged on the twenty-third of April, 1787. To which are added, the acts of the General Assembly of Pennsylvania, for the gradual abolition of slavery*. Philadelphia, 1788.

Peterson, Merrill D. *The Jefferson Image in the American Mind*. Oxford, 1960.

Philbrook, Mary. "Woman's Suffrage in New Jersey Prior to 1807." *Proceedings of the New Jersey Historical Society* 57 (1939): 870–98.

Pierce, William, and St. George Tucker. William Pierce to St. George Tucker, July 20, 1781. *Magazine of American History* 7 (1881), 434.

Pierson, William D. *Black Yankees: The Development of an Afro-American Subculture in Eighteenth-Century New England*. Amherst, Mass., 1988.

Pincus, Steven C. "Nationalism, Universal Monarchy and the Glorious Revolution." In *State/Culture: State Formation after the Cultural Turn*, edited by George Steinmetz, 182–210. Ithaca, N.Y., 1999.

———. *Protestantism and Patriotism: Ideologies and the Making of English Foreign Policy, 1650–1688*. Cambridge, 1996.

Pocock, J. G. A. "The Ideal of Citizenship since Classical Times." In *Theorizing Citizenship*, edited by Ronald Beiner, 29–52. Albany, N.Y., 1995.

———. "States, Republics, Empires: The American Founding in Early Modern Perspective." In *Conceptual Change and the Constitution*, edited by Terence Ball and J. G. A. Pocock, 55–78. Lawrence, Kans., 1988.

Pole, J. R. *Political Representation in England and the Origins of the American Republic*. New York, 1966.

———. "Suffrage in New Jersey, 1790–1807." *Proceedings of the New Jersey Historical Society* 71 (1953): 39–61.

Pomerantz, Syndey. *New York, American City, 1783–1803*. New York, 1938.

Pope, Nathaniel. *A Speech, delivered by Nathaniel Pope, Junior, in Support of the Resolutions which he prepared and presented to The People of Hanover, at their meeting the 17th day of October, 1789, with which he has incorporated sundry observations written in December of the same year, and originally intended as an answer to the arguments of a gentleman of Richmond, in favour of THE SEDITION ACT*. Richmond, 1800.

Porter, Bruce D. *War and the Rise of the State*. New York, 1993.

Porter, Dorothy, ed. *Early Negro Writing, 1760–1837*. Boston, 1971.

Powers, Thomas. *The narrative and confession of Thomas Powers, a Negro, formerly of Norwich in Connecticut, who was in the 20th year of his age: he was executed at Haverhill, in the state of New-Hampshire, on the 28th July, 1796, for committing a rape*. Norwich, Conn., 1796.

Presser, Stephen B. *The Original Misunderstanding: The English, the Americans, and the Dialectic of Federalist Jurisprudence*. Durham, N.C., 1991.

Prince, Carl E. *New Jersey's Jeffersonian Republicans: The Genesis of an Early Party Machine, 1789–1817*. Chapel Hill, N.C., 1967.

Proceedings in the Different Parts of Virginia, on the Subject of the late Conduct of the General Government. N.p., 1798.

Proceedings of the Federal Convention. Boston, 1787.

Providence Society for Abolishing the Slave-Trade. *Constitution of a society for abolishing the slave-trade. With several acts of the legislatures of the states of Massachusetts, Connecticut and Rhode-Island, for that purpose*. Providence, R.I., 1789.

Pullis, John, ed. *Moving On: Black Loyalists in the Afro Atlantic World*. New York, 1999.

Purcell, Sarah J. *Sealed with Blood: War, Sacrifice, and Memory in Revolutionary America*. Philadelphia, 2002.

Pybus, Cassandra. "Jefferson's Faulty Math: The Question of Slave Defections in the American Revolution." *William and Mary Quarterly*, 3rd ser., 43 (April 2005): 243–62.

Quarles, Benjamin. *The Negro in the American Revolution*. Chapel Hill, N.C., 1961.

Rakove, Jack. *The Beginnings of National Politics: An Interpretive History of the Continental Congress*. New York, 1979.

———. *Original Meanings: Politics and Ideas in the Making of the Constitution*. New York, 1996.

Ramsay, David. *A Dissertation on the Manner of Acquiring the character and privileges of a citizen of the United States*. Philadelphia, 1789.

Randolph, Edmund. *History of Virginia*. Edited by Arthur Shaffer. Charlottesville, Va., 1970.

Rawle, William. "A Memoir of William Rawle." Edited by T. I. Warton. *Memoirs of the Historical Society of Pennsylvania* 4 (1840): 33–91.

Ray, Kristopher. "Progress and Popular Democracy on the Southwestern Frontier: Middle Tennessee, 1790–1824." Ph.D. diss., University of North Carolina–Chapel Hill, 2003.

Reid, John P. *The Constitutional History of the American Revolution*. 4 vols. Madison, Wis., 1986–93.

Risch, Erna. "Immigrant Aid Societies before 1820." *Pennsylvania Magazine of History and Biography* 60 (1936): 15–36.

Risjord, Norman. *Chesapeake Politics, 1781–1800*. New York, 1978.

Robertson, Andrew W. "'Look on This Picture . . . And on This!': Nationalism, Localism, and Partisan Images of Otherness in the United States, 1787–1820." *American Historical Review* 106 (October 2001): 1263–80.

Robinson, Donald L. *Slavery in the Structure of American Politics, 1765–1820*. New York, 1975.

Rodgers, Daniel T. *Contested Truths: Keywords in American Politics since Independence*. Cambridge, Mass., 1987.

———. "Republicanism: The Career of a Concept." *Journal of American History* 79 (1992): 11–38.

Roeber, A. G. *Palatines, Liberty, and Property: German Lutherans in Colonial British North America*. Baltimore, 1983.

Roediger, David R. *The Wages of Whiteness: Race and the Making of the American Working Class*. London, 1991.

Rogers, Clifford J., ed. *The Military Revolution Debate: Readings on the Military Transformation of Early Modern Europe*. Oxford, 1995.

Rogers, George C. *Evolution of a Federalist: William Loughton Smith of Charleston, 1758–1812*. Columbia, S.C., 1962.

Rosavich, Vincent J., ed. "Three Petitions by Connecticut Negroes for the Abolition of Slavery in Connecticut." 17 *Connecticut Review* (1995): 60–85.

Rosenfeld, Richard. *American Aurora: A Democratic-Republican Returns: The Suppressed History of Our Nation's Beginnings and the Heroic Newspaper That Tried to Report It*. New York, 1997.

Rosswurm, Steven. Arms, *Country, Class: The Philadelphia Militia and the "Lower Sort" during the American Revolution*. New Brunswick, N.J., 1988.

Rothermund, Dietmar. *The Layman's Progress: Religious and Political Experience in Colonial Pennsylvania, 1740–1770*. Philadelphia, 1961.

Rowe, G. S. *Thomas McKean: The Shaping of American Republicanism*. Boulder, Colo., 1978.

Rush, Benjamin. "Observations Intended to Favor a Supposition That the Black Color (As it is Called) of the Negroes is Derived from the LEPROSY." *Transactions American Philosophical Society* 4 (1799): 295–300.

Ryerson, R. A. "Political Mobilization and the American Revolution: The Resistance Movement in Philadelphia, 1765 to 1776." *William and Mary Quarterly*, 3rd ser., 31 (October 1974): 565–88.

———. "Republican Theory and Partisan Reality in Revolutionary Pennsylvania: Toward a New View of the Constitutionalist Party." In *Sovereign States in an Age of Uncertainty*, edited by Ronald Hoffman and Peter J. Albert, 95–133. Charlottesville, Va., 1981.

St. Andrew's Society. *Historical Sketch of the Saint Andrew's Society, of the State of New York*. New York, 1856.

———. *Rules for the St. Andrew's Society, of the State of New York*. New York, 1785.

Salinger, Sharon V. "Colonial Labor in Transition: The Decline of Indentured Servitude in Late Eighteenth Century Philadelphia." *Labor History* 22 (1981): 165–91.

———. *Taverns and Drinking in Early America*. Baltimore, 2002.

———. *"To Serve Well and Faithfully": Labor and Indentured Servants in Pennsylvania, 1682–1800*. Cambridge, 1987.

Salmon, Marylyn. *Women and the Law of Property in Early America*. Chapel Hill, N.C., 1986.

Saunders, William Laurence. *The colonial records of North Carolina: published under the supervision of the trustees of the public libraries, by order of the general assembly*. 26 vols. Raleigh, N.C., 1886–1905.

Savelle, Max. "Nationalism and Other Loyalties in the American Revolution." *American Historical Review* 67 (July 1962): 901–23.

Saxton, Alexander. *The Rise and Fall of the White Republic: Class Politics and Mass Culture in Nineteenth Century America*. New York, 1990.

Schachner, Nathan, ed. "Alexander Hamilton Viewed by His Friends: The Narratives of Robert Troup and Hercules Mulligan." *William and Mary Quarterly*, 3rd ser., 4 (April 1947): 203–25.

Scharf, J. Thomas, and Thompson Wescott. *History of Philadelphia, 1609–1884*. Philadelphia, 1884.

Schmeller, Mark G. "Imagining Public Opinion in Antebellum America: Fear, Credit, Law, and Honor." Ph.D. diss., University of Chicago, 2002.

———. "Twelve Hungry Men: Juror Misconduct in the Early Republic." Society for Historians of the Early American Republic Annual Meeting, Philadelphia, 2005.

Schmidt, Frederika Teute, and Barbara Ripel Wilhelm, eds. "Early Virginian Pro-Slavery Petitions." *William and Mary Quarterly*, 3rd ser., 30 (January 1973): 133–46.

Schudson, Michael. *The Good Citizen: A History of American Civic Life*. New York, 1998.

Scots Society. *Rules and Orders Agreed upon By the Scots Society in New York*. New York, 1744.

Sewell, William H., Jr. "The French Revolution and the Emergence of the Nation Form." In *Revolutionary Currents: Nation Building in the Transatlantic World*, edited by Michael A. Morrison and Melinda Zook, 91–125. Madison, Wis., 2004.

Shade, William G. "Commentary: Déjà vu All Over Again: Is There a New New Political History?" In *Beyond the Founders: New Approaches to the Political History of the Early American Republic*, edited by Jeffrey L. Pasley, Andrew W. Robertson, and David Waldstreicher, 387–412. Chapel Hill, N.C., 2003.

Shafir, Gershon, ed. *The Citizenship Debates: A Reader*. Minneapolis, 1998.

Shankman, Andrew. *Crucible of American Democracy: The Struggle to Fuse Egalitarianism and Capitalism in Jeffersonian Pennsylvania*. Lawrence, Kans., 2004.

Sharp, Granville. *Letter from Granville Sharp, esq. of London to the Maryland Society for Promoting the Abolition of Slavery, and the Relief of Free Negroes and Others, Unlawfully Held in Bondage*. Baltimore, 1793.

Sharp, James Roger. *American Politics in the Early Republic*. New Haven, Conn., 1993.

———. "The Whiskey Rebellion and the Question of Representation." In *The Whiskey Rebellion: Past and Present Perspectives*, edited by Steven R. Boyd, 119–33. Westport, Conn., 1985.

Shkar, Judith N. *American Citizenship: The Quest for Inclusion*. Cambridge, 1991.

Sidbury, James. *Ploughshares into Swords: Race, Rebellion, and Identity in Gabriel's Virginia, 1730–1810*. Cambridge, 1997.

Sinha, Manisha. *The Counterrevolution of Slavery: Politics and Ideology in Antebellum South Carolina*. Chapel Hill, N.C., 2000.

Slotkin, Richard. "Narratives of Negro Crime in New England, 1675–1800." *American Quarterly* 25 (March 1973): 3–31.

Smelser, Marshall. "The Jacobin Phrenzy: Federalism and the Menace of Liberty, Equality and Fraternity." *Review of Politics* 13 (October 1951): 457–82.

———. "The Jacobin Phrenzy: The Menace of Monarchy, Plutocracy, and Anglophilia 1789–1798." *Review of Politics* 21 (January 1959): 239–58.

Smith, Billy G. *The "Lower Sort": Philadelphia's Laboring People, 1750–1800*. Ithaca, N.Y., 1990.

Smith, James Morton. *Freedom's Fetters: The Alien and Sedition Laws and American Civil Liberties*. Ithaca, N.Y., 1965.

———. "Grass Roots Origins of the Kentucky Resolutions." *William and Mary Quarterly*, 3rd ser., 27 (April 1970): 221–45.

Smith, Jean Edward. *John Marshall: Definer of a Nation*. New York, 1996.

Smith, Paul A. "The American Loyalists: Notes on their Organization and Numerical Strength." *William and Mary Quarterly*, 3rd ser., 25 (April 1968): 259–77.

———, ed. *Letters of Delegates to Congress, 1774–1789*. 26 vols. Washington, D.C., 1976–2000.

Smith, Rogers M. *Civic Ideals: Conflicting Visions of Citizenship in U.S. History*. New Haven, Conn., 1999.

Smith, Samuel Stanhope. *An Essay on the Causes of the Variety of Complexion and Figure in the Human Species*. Edited by Winthrop D. Jordan. Cambridge, Mass., 1965.

Smith, Timothy L. "New Approaches to the History of America in Twentieth Century America." *American Historical Review* 71 (July 1966): 1265–79.

Smith, William. *Comparative View of the Constitutions of the Several States with each other, and with that of the United States*. Philadelphia, 1796.

Smith, William Loughton. *The Politicks and Views of a Certain Party, Displayed*. N.p., 1792.

———. *The Pretensions of Thomas Jefferson to the Presidency Examined; and the Charges against John Adams refuted*. N.p., 1796.

Smyth, Jim. *The Men of No Property: Irish Radicals and Popular Politics in the Late Eighteenth Century*. New York, 1992.

Sobel, Mechal. *The World They Made Together: Black and White Values in Eighteenth Century Chesapeake*. Princeton, N.J., 1987.

Society of the Sons of St. George. *Rules and Constitution of the Society of the Sons of St. George, Established at Philadelphia, for the Advice and Assistance of Englishmen in Distress*. Philadelphia, 1797.

Sollors, Werner. "Theory of American Ethnicity, or: '? S Ethnic?/Ti and American/Ti, De or United (W) States S S1 and Theor?'" *American Quarterly* 33 (1981): 257–83.

Sparks, Jared. *The Life of Gouverneur Morris*. 3 vols. Boston, 1832.

State of Pennsylvania. *The Proceedings relative to Calling the Conventions of 1776 and 1790 the Minutes of the Convention that formed the Present Constitution of Pennsylvania*. Harrisburg, Pa., 1825.

State of Tennessee. *The Code of Tennessee. Enacted by the General assembly of 1857–'8*. Edited by Jonathan Return Meigs. Nashville, Tenn., 1858.

Storing, Herbert J. *What the Anti-Federalists Were For*. Chicago, 1981.

Stourzh, Gerald. *Alexander Hamilton and the Idea of Republican Government*. Stanford, Calif., 1970.

Swan, James. *National Arithmetick or, Observations on the Finances of the Commonwealth of Massachusetts*. Boston, n.d.

Swanson, Donald F., and Andrew P. Trout. "Alexander Hamilton, 'The Celebrated Mr. Necker,' and Public Credit." *William and Mary Quarterly*, 3rd ser., 47 (July 1990): 422–30.

Tallet, Frank. *War and Society in Early Modern Europe, 1495–1715*. New York, 1992.

Taylor, Alan. "From Fathers to Friends of the People: Political Personae in the Early Republic." In *Federalists Reconsidered*, edited by Doran Ben-Atar and Barbara B. Oberg, 225–45. Charlottesville, Va., 1998.

Taylor, John. "John Taylor Correspondence." Edited by William Dodd. *John P. Brach Historical Papers of Randolph Macon College* 2 (1908): 271–76.

Taylor, Robert J. *Western Massachusetts in the Revolution*. Providence, R.I., 1954.

Thernstrom, Stephan Ann Orlov, and Oscar Handlin, eds. *Harvard Encyclopedia of American Ethnic Groups*. Cambridge, Mass., 1980.

Thompson, C. Bradley. *John Adams and the Spirit of Liberty*. Lawrence, Kans., 1998.

Thompson, Peter. *Rum Punch and Revolution: Taverngoing and Public Life in Eighteenth-Century Philadelphia*. Chapel Hill, N.C., 1998.

Thornburn, Grant. *Forty Years Residence in America*. Boston, 1834.

Tilly, Charles. "A Primer on Citizenship." *Theory and Society* 26 (1997): 599–602.

Tinkom, Harry Marlin. *The Republicans and Federalists in Pennsylvania, 1790–1801: A Study in National Stimulus and Local Response*. Harrisburg, Pa., 1950.

Tocqueville, Alexis de. *Democracy in America*. Translated by George Lawrence. Garden City, N.Y., 1969.

Tomlins, Christopher, and Bruce Mann, eds. *The Many Legalities of Early America*. Chapel Hill, N.C., 2001.

Travers, Len. *Celebrating the Fourth: Independence Day and the Rites of Nationalism in the Early Republic*. Amherst, Mass., 1997.

Trumball, Jonathon. "The Correspondent No. 8." *Journal of Negro History* 14 (October 1929): 493–95.

[Tucker, George.] *Letter to a Member of the General Assembly of Virginia on the Subject of the Late Conspiracy of the Slaves, with a Proposal for their Colonization*. Richmond, Va., 1801.

Tucker, St. George. *Blackstone's Commentaries: With Notes of Reference, to the Constitution, and Laws of the federal Government of the United States, and of the Commonwealth of Virginia*. 5 vols. Philadelphia, 1803.

———. *A Dissertation on Slavery: With a Proposal for the Gradual Abolition of It, in the State of Virginia*. Philadelphia, 1796.

Turner, Frederick J. "The Origin of Genet's Projected Attack on Louisiana and the Floridas." *American Historical Review* 3 (July 1898): 650–71.

Turner, Kathryn. "The Appointment of Chief Justice Marshall." *William and Mary Quarterly*, 3rd ser., 17 (April 1960): 143–63.

Turner, Raymond E. "Women's Suffrage in New Jersey." *Smith College Studies in History* 1, no. 4 (1916): 165–87.

Twomey, Richard J. *Jacobins and Jeffersonians: Anglo-American Radicalism in the United States*. New York, 1989.

United States. *American State Papers: Documents, Legislative and Executive, of the Congress of the United States*. 38 vols. Washington, D.C., 1832–1961.

———. *The committee consisting of &c. to whom was referred a motion of Mr. King, for the exclusion of involuntary servitude in the states described in the resolve of Congress of the 23d day of April, 1784, submit the following resolve. Resolved, that after the year 1800 of the Christian area, there shall be neither slavery nor involuntary servitude in any of the states described in the resolve of Congress of the 23d day of April, 1784*. New York, 1785.

———. *The Debates and Proceedings in the Congress of the United States*. 15 vols. Washington, D.C., 1851.

———. *Documents Legislative and Executive, of the Congress of the United States*. Edited by Walter Lowrie. Washington, D.C., 1843.

———. *The foederal Constitution, being the result of the important deliberations of the*

Foederal Convention, who completed their business on the 17th September, 1787, at Philadelphia. New York, 1787.

———. *Journal of the Senate of the United States of America*. Washington, D.C., 1820.

———. *Official Opinions of the Attorneys General of the United States*. 13 vols. Washington, D.C., 1875–1900.

———. *State Papers and Publick Documents of the United States, from the Accession of George Washington to the Presidency, Exhibiting of a Complete view of our foreign relations since that time*. Vol. 1. Boston, 1819.

U.S. Congress. *The Public and General Statutes Passed by the Congress of the United States of America From 1789 to 1836 Inclusive*. Edited by George Sharswood. 6 vols. Philadelphia, 1840.

U.S. Constitutional Convention. "First Draft of the report of the Committee of Detail." Philadelphia, 1787.

U.S. House of Representatives. *Journal of the House of Representatives*. Washington, D.C., 1826.

U.S. National Archives. *Domestic Letters of the Department of State*. June 30, 1798–June 29, 1799. Washington, D.C., 1943.

———. *Ratified Amendments XI–XXVI of the U.S. Constitution General Records of the United States Government Record Group 11*. 15 reels. Washington, D.C., 1990.

Van Tyne, Claude Halstead. *The Loyalists in the American Revolution*. New York, 1929.

Varg, Paul A. "The Advent of Nationalism, 1758–1776." *American Quarterly* 16 (1964): 169–81.

Vassa, Gustavas. *The Interesting Narrative of the Life of Olaudah Equiano; or, Gustavas Vassa, the African*. Philadelphia, 1791.

Vattel, Emerich de. *The Law of Nations, or Principles of the Law of Nature, applied to the Conduct and Affairs of Nations and Sovereigns*. London, 1797.

Vecoli, Rudolph J. "Ethnicity: A Neglected Dimension of American History." In *The State of American History*, edited by Herbert J. Bass, 70–88. Chicago, 1970.

———. "The Resurgence of American Immigration History." *American Studies International* 17 (Winter 1979): 46–66.

Virginia House of Delegates. *Journal of the House of Delegates of the Commonwealth of Virginia; Begun and Held at the Capitol, in the City of Richmond; on Monday, the Twenty-First day of October, One Thousand Seven Hundred and Sixty-Three*. Richmond, 1793.

———. *Journal of the House of Delegates of Virginia*. Richmond, 1790.

———. *The Virginia Report of 1799–1800, Touching the Alien and Sedition Laws; Together with the VIRGINIA RESOLUTIONS of December 21, 1798, the Debate and Proceedings Thereon in the House of Delegates of Virginia, and Several Other Documents Illustrative of the Report and Resolutions*. Richmond, 1850.

von Gentz, Friedrich. *The Origin and Principles of the American Revolution, Compared with the Origin and Principles of the French Revolution*. Trans. [John Quincy Adams]. Philadelphia, 1800. Facsimile ed. by Richard Loss. New York, 1977.

von Zimmermann, Eberhard August Wilhelm. *A Political Survey of the Present State of Europe*. London, 1787.

Waldstreicher, David. "Founders' Chic as Cultural War." *Radical History Review* 84 (Fall 2002): 185–94.

———. *In the Midst of Perpetual Fetes: The Making of American Nationalism, 1776–1820*. Chapel Hill, N.C., 1997.

———. "Rites of Rebellion, Rites of Dissent: Celebrations, Print Culture, and the Origins of American Nationalism." *Journal of American History* 82 (1995): 37–61.

Walsh, Richard. *Charleston's Sons of Liberty: A Study of the Artisans*. Columbia, S.C., 1959.

Ward, Lee. *The Politics of Liberty in England and Revolutionary America*. Cambridge, 2004.

Warfield, Ethelbert D. "The Authorship of the Kentucky Resolutions." *Magazine of Western History* 3 (April 1886): 574–86.

———. *The Kentucky Resolutions of 1798 an historical study*. New York, 1894.

Warren, Charles. *The Supreme Court in United States History*. 3 vols. Boston, 1922.

Warren, Mercy Otis. *History of the Rise Progress and Termination of the American Revolution, interspersed with Biographical, Political and Moral Observations, in two volumes. 1805. Forward by Lester Cohen*. Indianapolis, Ind., 1994.

Washington, George. *Papers of George Washington*. Edited by Dorothy Twhig and W. W. Abbott. Charlottesville, N.C., 1995.

———. *Writings of George Washington*. Edited by John C. Fitzpatrick. 39 vols. Washington, D.C., 1931–39.

Watkins, William J., Jr., *Reclaiming the American Revolution: The Kentucky and Virginia Resolutions and Their Legacy*. New York, 2004.

Watts, Frederick, ed. *Reports of Cases Argued and Determined in the Supreme Court of Pennsylvania*. 10 vols. Philadelphia, 1848–52.

Watts, Steven. *The Republic Reborn: War and the Making of Liberal America, 1790–1820*. Baltimore, 1987.

Webster, Noah. *American Reader*. New York, 1786.

———. *American Speller*. New York, 1782.

———. *A Collection of Essays and Fugativ* [sic] *Writings*. New York, 1790.

———. *Effects of Slavery on Morals and Industry*. Hartford, Conn., 1793.

———. *A Grammatical Institute of the English Language, Part III*. Hartford, Conn., 1785.

———. *Sketches of American Policy*. Philadelphia, 1785.

Welsh Society of Pennsylvania. *Constitution and Rules of the Welsh Society of Pennsylvania*. Philadelphia, 1799.

Wesley, Charles H. *Prince Hall: Life and Legacy*. Washington, D.C., 1977.

Westlake, John. *A Treatise on Private International Law, or the conflict of laws, with principal reference to its practice in the English and other cognate systems of jurisprudence*. London, 1858.

Wharton, Francis, ed. *The State Trials of the United States during the Administration of Washington and Adams*. Philadelphia, 1849.

Whelan, Kevin. *The Tree of Liberty: Radicalism, Catholicism and the Construction of Irish Identity*. Cork, Ireland, 1996.

Whitaker, Arthur Preston. *The United States and the Independence of Latin America, 1800–1830*. New York, 1941.

White, G. Edward. *The Marshall Court and Cultural Change, 1815–1835*. New York, 1988.

White, Morton. *The Philosophy of the American Revolution*. New York, 1978.

Wiecek, William M. *The Sources of Antislavery Constitutionalism in America*. Ithaca, N.Y., 1977.

Williamson, Chilton. *American Suffrage: From Property to Democracy, 1760–1860*. Princeton, N.J., 1960.

Wilson, David A. *United Irishmen, United States: Immigrant Radicals in the Early Republic*. Ithaca, N.Y., 1998.

Wilson, Kathleen. *The Sense of the People: Politics, Culture, and Imperialism in England 1715–1785*. Cambridge, 1995.

Wokeck, Marianne S. *Trade in Strangers: The Beginnings of Mass Migration to North America*. University Park, Pa., 1999.

Wolfe, John H. *Jeffersonian-Democracy in South Carolina*. Chapel Hill, N.C., 1940.

Wood, Gordon S. *The Creation of the American Republic, 1776–1787*. London, 1969.

———. *The Radicalism of the American Republic*. New York, 1992.

Woodson, Carter G. *The History of the Negro Church*. 2nd ed. Washington, D.C., 1921.

Wortman, Tunis. *A Treatise, concerning Political Enquiry, and the Liberty of the Press*. New York, 1800.

Young, Alfred. *The America Revolution: Explorations in the History of American Radicalism*. DeKalb, Ill., 1976.

———. *The Democratic Republicans of New York: The Origins, 1763–1797*. Chapel Hill, N.C., 1967.

———. *The Shoemaker and the Tea Party*. Boston, 1999.

Zagarri, Rosemarie. *Revolutionary Backlash: Women and Politics in the Early American Republic*. Philadelphia, 2007.

———. "Rights of Man and Woman in Post-Revolutionary America." *William and Mary Quarterly*, 3rd ser., 55 (April 1998): 203–30.

Zeichner, Oscar. "The Loyalist Problem in New York after the Revolution." *New York History* 21 (1940): 284–302.

Zilversmit, Arthur. *The First Emancipation: The Abolition of Slavery in the North*. Chicago, 1967.

Zimmerman, Johann Georg. *Essay on National Pride*. Translated by Samuel H. Wilcocke. New York, 1799. Originally published in German as *Von dem Nationalstolze* (1758).

Zvesper, John. *Political Philosophy and Rhetoric: A Study in the Origins of American Party Politics*. New York, 1977.

INDEX

Page numbers in italics refer to illustrations.

JEFFERSONIAN AMERICA

Jan Ellen Lewis and Peter S. Onuf, editors
Sally Hemings and Thomas Jefferson: History, Memory, and Civic Culture

Peter S. Onuf
Jefferson's Empire: The Language of American Nationhood

Catherine Allgor
Parlor Politics: In Which the Ladies of Washington Help Build a City and a Government

Jeffrey L. Pasley
"The Tyranny of Printers": Newspaper Politics in the Early American Republic

Herbert E. Sloan
Principle and Interest: Thomas Jefferson and the Problem of Debt (reprint)

James Horn, Jan Ellen Lewis, and Peter S. Onuf, editors
The Revolution of 1800: Democracy, Race, and the New Republic

Phillip Hamilton
The Making and Unmaking of a Revolutionary Family: The Tuckers of Virginia, 1752–1830

Robert M. S. McDonald, editor
Thomas Jefferson's Military Academy: Founding West Point

Martha Tomhave Blauvelt
The Work of the Heart: Young Women and Emotion, 1780–1830

Francis D. Cogliano
Thomas Jefferson: Reputation and Legacy

Albrecht Koschnik
"Let a Common Interest Bind Us Together": Associations, Partisanship, and Culture in Philadelphia, 1775–1840

John Craig Hammond
Slavery, Freedom, and Expansion in the Early American West, 1787–1820

David Andrew Nichols
Red Gentlemen and White Savages: Indians, Federalists, and the Search for Order on the American Frontier

Douglas Bradburn
The Citizenship Revolution: Politics and the Creation of the American Union, 1774–1804